Treasur
of
Hawaiian Words

REVEREND DOCTOR CHARLES McEWEN HYDE
JUNE 8, 1832–AUGUST 18, 1899

Treasury
of
Hawaiian Words

IN
ONE HUNDRED AND ONE
CATEGORIES

by

HAROLD WINFIELD KENT

Published by
the Masonic Public Library of Hawaii

The author is pleased to submit
the names of Foundations which have contributed
to the publication of

TREASURY OF HAWAIIAN WORDS

Atherton Family Foundation

Samuel and Mary Castle Foundation

Cooke Foundation, Limited

*Mary D. and Walter F. Frear
Eleemosynary Trust*

McInerny Foundation

The G. N. Wilcox Trust

*First printing 1986
Second printing 1989
Paperback edition 1993
Second printing 1995*

Library of Congress Cataloging-in-Publication Data

Kent, Harold Winfield.
 Treasury of Hawaiian words in one hundred and one
categories.

 Bibliography: p.
 1. Hawaiian language—Glossaries, vocabularies, etc.
I. Title.
PL6446.K46 1986   499'.4   86–788
ISBN 0–8248–1071–6

ISBN 0-8248-1604-8 (pbk)

Distributed by
University of Hawaii Press:
Order Department
University of Hawaii Press
2840 Kolowalu Street
Honolulu, Hawaii 96822

In Memory of
*Ekela Elema Keneta**

ME KE ALOHA A ME
MAHALO PUMEHANA

*Ethel Elmer Kent
with warmest aloha
and gratitude

Contents

Foreword

Ei neʻi, eia i aneʻi: Here, here it is!

This Treasury presents us with at least two pleasing surprises: proof that the Hawaiian language is not dead; and evidence that even this late in our history, something new can be added to the number of books that have been written about the language of Hawaiʻi's inhabitants.

The language lives, with an astonishing resilience. It graces the conversations of older folk, and not only those who dwell in Kona or Niʻihau; it is heard in the prayers uttered at weddings, funerals, family gatherings, meetings of clubs and societies, and dedications of buildings, offices, restaurants, and highways. It is spoken in fishing villages and cattle ranches. It quickens the songs and chants accompanying dances and rituals, whether solemn or profane. And it wells up daily in our speech and thoughts, almost always in unconscious response to our island heritage. "From Waipiʻo on Hawaiʻi, where the sun rises, to Mana on Kauaʻi, whence the sun departs," the lovely melodious language, the tongue of a noble people, is surviving longer than did the kingdom their chiefs established to sustain the foredoomed race.

Whatever our ancestry may be, useful Hawaiian words enter into our speech for many reasons. Surely *pau* is the first word (and idea) that almost every island infant acquires, almost as soon as it learns to recognize mama. Its multicultural vocabulary of essential terms is soon extended, to add *opu, tutu, pupu, auwē* (usually corrupted to ow-wee), *piko* and *ʻokole*—not to mention those borrowings from other ethnic groups that are invoked as onomatopoeic aids to certain physiological processes.

As the child grows, it absorbs the expression of peers at school and of elders at home. *Da kine* pidgin, the argot of kids in streets and playgrounds, is made of basic words lifted from our several ethnic dialects, especially Hawaiian, all more or less glued together with English of a sort.

This *Treasury* holds all the Hawaiian words we use daily, and it will provide the inquiring reader with many more to enjoy. Think of the fun everyone, young or old, will have in searching out terms for "steenkmout' talk"—sneers and epithets, curses cruel or fancy, insults in every degree to toss at sundry objects of scorn both in and outside family circles. We all know how, for generations, bored singers in Waikiki, smiling toothily, have been crooning such treacheries at us. Now, with this *Treasury*'s help, we can join 'em in the art (not the act) and snicker over their double-meanings even while they sting—somebody else, of course.

Our teen-agers and adults could not manage to communicate without this rich stock of Hawaiian expressions to draw from (supplemented, naturally, by the whole array of signs devised for body talk).

And, now that we're fast running out of knowledgeable *kupuna,* how will new-made parents ever find a *safe* Hawaiian name for their *keiki* without the aid of this *Treasury,* a supplementing dictionary, and a couple of striving consultants?

As every frustrated tourist maintains, "us locals" simply cannot go *holoholo* anywhere without taking routes marked by names that the visitor can neither read nor pronounce. *Auwē nohoʻi e!* Those grand appellations, those rolling mellifluous tributes to our great ones: they are just too beautiful for us to give up, too full of reminders of our romanticists' past . . .

This *Treasury* will help our visitors, and ourselves, to understand why we love that past. Most of the words it holds will evoke memories—sad, or happy, or proud, or bitter. Even ribald ones, such as lurk among the entries that Kent, with a Victorian's indirection, has assembled under the label "Earthy Expressions."

In short, this *Treasury* offers a wealth of information for everybody: for island residents of any age, ancestry, and interest, ranging from the earthy to the spriritual; for visitors fresh off a plane; for those obtuse creatures who mispronounce "Honolulu," mumble "aloʻa," and garble the glottals in *hoʻopiʻopiʻo.* Kia!

This *Treasury* proves that a surprising number of Hawaiian words from our receding past still help us to express ourselves in the maddening present. At first thought we may want to reject this paradox—until, with second thoughts, we recognize it as one more sign of a very interesting game that we of Hawaiʻi long ago learned to play. We happily accept the best ideas and all the good things that have been brought in by every group of immigrants who have settled here, the while we sensibly discard the alien baggage for which we find no use. (The fact that some bad ideas and things have stolen in, too, just means that human error, alas, is unpredictable. . .)

This *Treasury* shows how, in the mixture of cultures that we have created here, out of components Polynesian, Western, and Eastern, the Hawaiians' contributions—in words, concepts, and values—continue to be vital forces in our common heritage.

O. A. BUSHNELL

Honolulu, Hawai'i
22 February 1983

Preface

While preparing this manuscript, I was frequently asked how this particular book came about. The staff of the Bernice Pauahi Bishop Museum had long known of my research activities in connection with a biography of Dr. Charles M. Hyde.* One staffer showed me a recently "discovered" pasteboard box, the size and shape of a shoebox, in an old *koa* wood wall cabinet in a storage room on the third floor of the Museum. Barely discernible on the box's cover was the name C. M. Hyde and a caption "notes on the Hawaiian language." Inside were hundreds of reporter-type note sheets which, as I was to learn eventually, contained a draft of a Hawaiian Grammar amid a bundle of listings of Hawaiian words arranged according to category or subject.

I asked Dr. Roland Wynfield Force, then Director of the Museum, how he felt about my tackling a study of these listings as a possible future project, to yield perhaps a manuscript or even a publication. He stated that it could be a valuable contribution to the cause of Hawaiian culture which at the time (1971) was beginning to give evidence of a renaissance.

Some of Hyde's sheets were either well-worn from handling or indecipherable from the yellowing of the paper, and brittle from the long drying during the storage of about eighty years. In many instances, Dr. Hyde's close, penciled script itself was illegible.

The ensuing years were devoted to research among available sources for correct spellings, diacritical marks, definitions, and new words for possible inclusion.

Some new categories, not covered in the lists Hyde left in his notes, needed to be added; a few were not used, while still others were altered to accommodate scientific names in parts of the definitions. Hyde's materials supply the largest share of categories in

*See bibliography.

this book. I am happy to acknowledge my obligation to him and his "shoebox." But even more significant than his lists is his idea of the arrangement of Hawaiian words by categories.

I tended to identify with him, as disciples frequently do, and I have been ever mindful of his life story, presence, and personality through all the years I've addressed to this project. This respect for him will explain the frontispiece and the biography in the appendix of this book.

Lorrin Andrews, another major source for this book, was a member of the Third Missionary Company from New England, which arrived in Hawaii in 1828. Hiram Bingham, a member of the First Company, had arrived in 1820. These two men, and a few others among their colleagues, were scholars well trained in Hebrew, Greek, and Latin, as well as in general sciences, the humanities, and mathematics. About the time the first Missionary Company sailed from Boston in 1819, a treatise on the science of "creating" a native language structure was published in America, outlining several approaches. The missionary scholars based their outline of a structure for a written Hawaiian language on one of the scientific options presented in that publication, and adopted a system of five vowels, seven consonants, plus a glottal stop which, because it marks the elision of a consonant, might be called "an eighth consonant." Their system also contained rules for the ordering of words in a phrase or a clause. A number of other provisions and terms were applied to the task, and in this way the creation of a written language was achieved.

Helpful natives and earnest missionaries held almost continuous sessions on words and their meanings. The end product of those discussions was a useful written language so easily taught and learned that it was employed immediately in the lives of the natives. The Mission's work with the native people of the islands was marvelously successful and Hawai'i became both Christian and literate within just three decades. Perhaps the more lasting achievement of the missionaries was the education of Hawaiians in their written language, which in impact was second only to the conversions of the native populace to Christianity.

When Andrews published his *Dictionary of the Hawaiian Language* in 1865 he was not entering an unfertile field. There is quite a list of predecessors. The very first must be recognized as Surgeon William Anderson, one of the scientists aboard the *Resolution,* of which Captain James Cook was Master. Cook spoke of him as "his most useful associate on the voyage," and the keeper of the log considered him "the best linguist expert of the voyage." Anderson's list contained only 250 Hawaiian words.

From 1778 to 1865 there were perhaps twelve additional lists of 20 to 400 words each, except for Lorrin Andrews' first attempt in 1836, which contained 4,500 words. His 1865 *Dictionary of the Hawaiian Language* included about 15,000 words. Most of the earlier compilers built their lists on successive compilations that were available to them. Hyde, in his lists, relied on Andrews for an obvious reason: there was no other dictionary in print during his years in Hawai'i (1877–1899). So AND for Andrews appears very frequently among definitions presented in this book. Another set of initials, CMH, stands for Charles M. Hyde. He contributed many words elicited from his scholars in the North Pacific Missionary Institute. There is some vagueness about these contributions, but my advisors have suggested that all of them should be included since some might present different spellings or modified meanings.

The Pukui-Elbert *Hawaiian-English Dictionary* (PE), in its several revisions of recent years, was of course unavailable to Hyde, but has, along with Andrews, formed the basis for this book. The successive editions have been works of profound achievement, each one a solid advance over the earlier versions. We can look forward to a forthcoming revision that will set new standards.

Most of the references to biblical sources originally entered in the Andrews book are retained. Pukui-Elbert, too, included a fair share of these. Most have been checked in the Hawaiian-English Bible. This practice supports the conclusion that, when a Hawaiian word is used in the Bible, the meaning of that word usually refers to only a specific counterpart from the English, rather than to any of several basic Hawaiian definitions that may be given for that word in a dictionary.

At this juncture, one might ask what use this book will serve. The answer is clear. It should be of interest to all people for many purposes because of its scope: its 101 categories have something for everyone. Some readers will discover unanticipated uses as they peruse its pages (see Foreword).

A fair number of the categories are attuned to certain aspects of the ancient Hawaiian culture that prevailed during the ten or more centuries before Captain Cook anchored offshore in 1778 and 1779. The native culture did not start with his arrival, and it certainly did not terminate with his decease. It continued for two centuries following Cook's discovery, and is now entering upon its third century post-Cook. These have been two centuries of transition and of intermingling with other cultures.

Some people will use this book to gain an acquaintance with the Hawaiian culture in all its aspects, but even more will use it to enhance their speaking and writing familiarity with the language. It is a superb instrument in oratory and poetry, prayer and preaching, writing and teaching.

The categories will aid both teacher and student in their assimilation of the written language which became a tool of the government, courts, land departments, Hawaiian churches, and people. Hawaiian language texts have been published on subjects such as geography, health, Latin, algebra, spelling, history, and others, all for use in public and private schools. Like them, this book can be a leavening element in the further study and use of the Hawaiian language.

Finally, what about the author and this book? I cannot hope to rival or imitate the achievements of Dr. Hyde in his technical understanding and wide employment of the language in speech and written form. But indeed it was a privilege for me to study for short periods with the late Rev. Stephen L. Desha and the highly regarded Mary Kawena Pukui. During my term as president of The Kamehameha Schools, a formal three-year sequence of courses in the Hawaiian language was introduced, which received Advance Placement status at the University of Hawaii. Dorothy M. Kahananui was assigned the work of preparing the entire program, including a text sequence for the three years. It was well received.

Moreover, in a number of other ways the Hawaiian language was restored to recognition at The Kamehameha Schools. Pins, medals, insignia, and certificates were created as means of motivation. Members in student government used Hawaiian titles and articles of dress as symbols of office. A Kamehameha medal of honor, *Pi'imua,* was struck in memory of war casualties among alumni. The order of *Ke Ali'i Pauahi* was the highest honor that The Kamehameha Schools could award an outstanding community leader supportive of The Schools and its program. A large medallion, bearing in its design a *kahili* and a feather cloak, was attached to a riband of yellow and red. An appropriate legend describing the recipient's service was imprinted on parchment, and accompanied the award.

All services in The Kamehameha Schools' Bishop Memorial Church, including those of traveling deputation teams, used the language in prayers, blessings, readings, sermons, hymns, and benedictions. Intramural athletic groups went by the names of *Imua, Aliʻi, Eleu,* and *Moʻi.* The school newspaper was called *Ka Moʻi,* the yearbook, *Ka Naʻi Aupuni.*

There was more to these practices than meets the eye. Thus I would aver that I have a deep and abiding interest in the native students and their families, cultivated and set during my sixteen years as president of The Kamehameha Schools, and during all the years (since my retirement in 1962) as consultant to the Trustees of the Bishop Estate. My acquaintance with the language is not superficial. It has deep roots in the history of Hawaiʻi, in its educational processes, in its music and customs, and in its people.

Me ke aloha pumehana,
a me ʻanoʻai.

Biography
of Reverend Doctor
Charles McEwen Hyde

This "doer of the word" was a New England born, bred, and edu-
cated congregational pastor of five successive pastorates. When
the Hawaiian Evangelical Association and Board of Missions
faltered in the 1870s, he was sent to the Hawaiian Islands to reor-
ganize the North Pacific Missionary Institute and to train selected
Hawaiian young men in seminary subjects. These young pastors
filled vacant pulpits in Hawaiian churches as well as mission areas
in the Southwest Pacific.

He was captivated with the Hawaiians, Chinese, and Ameri-
cans who streamed down to the dock in Honolulu after the flags
raised at the Diamond Head ship-arrival warning center bespoke
the sighting of the U.S.S. *Zealandia*. The welcomers were singing
and cheering and loading the scented leis around the shoulders of
family members.

Dr. Hyde was "captured." He was off at daybreak to check on
the condition and survey the facilities of the Institute. He preached
at Kawaiahao Church his first Sunday morning in Honolulu and
at the Seamen's Bethel that evening. The Hawaiian Evangelical
Association was in its fourteenth Annual Session that week. He
was placed on four committees and elected a director of the Evangelical Association. Two weeks later he was elected a trustee of
Punahou School. This pace of church and community activity
never slackened. He took a personal self-training program in the
Hawaiian language. Six months later he preached to a large con-
gregation at Kawaiaha'o, speaking for twenty minutes in Hawaiian. He preached at Central Union Church after it opened. It was
his home church in membership. He also preached at almost every
church throughout the islands depending upon his schedule and
facilities to get there.

Hyde was the principal influence in the formation of The Social
Science Association, a durable group of Honolulu community stal-

warts. It celebrated its Centennial in 1982. He was a main cog in the predecessor libraries of the Library of Hawaii. He organized a teacher's convention, now the Hawaii Educational Association.

He was a participant—with Charles R. Bishop, Frederick Hatch, and William Oleson—in meetings in the Bishop home to plan the future application of Mrs. Bishop's tremendous estate to useful purposes. The outcome was the funding and founding of The Kamehameha Schools.

In literary fields he authored full biographies of two pastorate towns in Massachusetts—Brimfield and Lee. He wrote out his sermons both there and in Hawai'i. He served as secretary in the YMCA, Social Science Association, and a host of other organizations. Among his writings were publications in Hawaiian; Sunday School lessons; a Hawaiian Grammar; and reports of trips and visits to Japan, the mainland United States, and the Hawaiian Islands. His many contributions appeared in "The Friend," a Congregational Church periodical of Hawai'i, and in Thrum's *Hawaiian Almanac and Annual*.

Churches, schools, and hospitals were always a part of his busy routine. He traveled by horseback, buggy, or on foot.

There was only one serious confrontation in his life—a historical incident involving Robert Louis Stevenson and Father Damien, leper priest of Kalawao. His spirit of Christian confidence reflected his nobleness and serenity in the 1896 portrait painted by Frederick Yates, English portrait and landscape artist. This painting now hangs in the Masonic Public Library of Hawaii.

"No saint or sinner he, just a toiler in the vineyards, a Servant of God."

Acknowledgments

Many people in Hawai'i have been associated with the preparation of this *Treasury of Hawaiian Words:* librarians, authors, researchers, field scientists, university professors, instructors in Hawaiian culture, editors, proofreaders, typists, and other friends, all of whom have been warmly supportive of this project.

First, I express my unbounded gratitude to the late Dorothy Mitchell Kahananui and Donald D. Kilolani Mitchell for their months of counsel, copious notes, editings, comments, and supplements during the drafting of this manuscript. Each had an instinctive familiarity with the Hawaiian language and culture. All three of us, as professional educators, have dealt with broad aspects of the language and culture with a deep and continuing interest.

While Mrs. Kahananui and Dr. Mitchell lent their expertise to the entire manuscript, other consultants reviewed categories related to their professional fields. These experts gave their time generously and helpfully. Derral R. Herbst reviewed thirteen plant categories; John Brent Randall advised on fishes; E. Alison Kay, shellfish; Francis Gard-Howarth, insects; Andrew John Berger, birds; Richard Kekuni Blaisdell, medical subjects; Kenneth Pike Emory, fishhooks, fishnets, bones, and *heiau*s.

Other consultants included Isabella Aiona Abbott and Eleanor Horswill Williamson, both 1937 graduates of The Kamehameha School for Girls, who collaborated on a book about *limu*. Russell Anderson Apple assisted with research on cities of refuge and house thatching. Andrew William Kenn, a patriarch in Hawaiian culture and language, gave advice on definitions.

O. A. Bushnell, writer of books on Hawai'i, made two valuable contributions to this book; namely, a neatly expressed preface and, most of all, a sensitive review of the 101 introductions to the categories which comprise this book. *Salute!*

I am indebted to the University of Hawaii Press for permission to use a share of the definitions in the 1965 edition of the Pukui-Elbert *Hawaiian-English Dictionary* and also their revised edition of *Place Names of Hawai'i*. Also important are the approvals of Charles E. Tuttle of Rutland, Vermont and Tokyo, Japan for similar use of Andrew's *Dictionary of the Hawaiian Language* 1865, and Edward Creutz, former Director of the Bernice Pauahi Bishop Museum for materials from Marie C. Neal's *In Gardens of Hawai'i*.

Librarians Sigrid Southworth and Mandy Bowers of the Frank E. Midkiff Learning Center were always ready to assist, as were Cynthia Timberlake, present librarian, and the late Margaret Titcomb, former librarian of the Bernice Pauahi Bishop Museum Library.

Iris Wiley, executive editor of the University of Hawaii Press, gave excellent advice, which helped steer this *Treasury of Hawaiian Words* into book form. Deep thanks are due her. Samuel Hoyt Elbert also supplied valuable advice in the early planning stages. I must also extend a warm *mahalo* for the typing expertise, accuracy, and enthusiasm of Beatrice Valentine, the ever-ready work of Eloise Bruns, and the kind understanding of Gerry Johansen. I thank Kimber Morris Moulton and Grady Wells, former associates in teaching and management at The Kamehameha Schools. Final acknowledgments must include Janet Heavenridge, head of design and production at the University of Hawaii Press, a remarkable person; Pamela Kelley, reader-editor of the original manuscript; and Darlene Kent Baines, final proofreader.

I am pleased that these people have shared my zeal for this project which was solely and simply to prepare and publish a useful listing of Hawaiian words arranged according to categories. A sincere *mahalo* and *aloha* to each and every one of you!

Abbreviations

(All references are listed in the Bibliography)

A   Andrews, Lorrin. *Hawaiian Dictionary,* 1865.

AP   Andrews-Parker. *Dictionary of the Hawaiian Language,* revised 1922.

AW   Abbott, Isabella and Williamson, Eleanor. *Limu: An Ethnobotanical Study of Some Edible Hawaiian Seaweeds,* 1974.

BHK   Krauss, Beatrice H. *Native Plants Used as Medicines in Hawai'i,* 1979.

Cap   capital letter

CMH   Hyde, Charles McEwen. Missionary in Hawai'i, 1877–1899. Author of many periodicals, articles, and books in Hawaiian and English.

DK   Kahananui, Dorothy M. Hawaiian language texts.

EAK   Kay, E. Alison. *Hawaiian Marine Shells, Reef and Shore Fauna of Hawaii,* 1979.

Eng   Hawaiian words of English origin.

Fig   figuratively

FOR   Fornander, Abraham. *Hawaiian Antiquities and Folklore,* 1917–1918.

HP   Handy, E. S. Craighill. *Hawaiian Planter,* 1940.

HWK   Kent, Harold W. *Dr. Hyde and Mr. Stevenson,* 1973.

KEP   Beckwith, Martha. *Kepelino,* 1922.

KILO   Mitchell, Donald Kilolani. *Hawaiian Games,* 1975.

KL   Beckwith, Martha. *Kumulipo,* 1951.

Lit   literally

MALO   Malo, David. *Hawaiian Antiquities,* 1951.

NEAL   Neal, Marie C. *In Gardens of Hawai'i,* 1965.

NP   Handy. *Native Planters in Old Hawaii,* 1972.

Obs   obsolete

PE   Pukui and Elbert. *Hawaiian-English Dictionary,* 1965, and *Hawaiian Grammar,* 1979.

RA	Apple, Russell A. *The Hawaiian Thatched House,* 1971.
RC	Kamakau, Samuel. *Ruling Chiefs,* 1961.
RKB	Blaisdell, Richard Kekuni. Medical papers.
Redup	reduplication of meanings.
sp, spp	species
Trans	translated
Var	variant, variety

Biblical Abbreviations*

Ke Kauoha Kahiko, Old Testament

Genesis	Kinohi	Kin.
Exodus	Pukaana	Puk.
Leviticus	Oihanakahuna	Oihk.
Numbers	Nahelu	Nah.
Deuteronomy	Kanawailua	Kanl.
Joshua	Iosua	Ios.
Judges	Lunakanawai	Lunk.
Ruth	Ruta	Ruta
Samuel 1, 2	Samuela	Sam.
Kings 1, 2	Nalii	Nal.
Chronicles 1, 2	Oihanaalii	Oihn.
Ezra	Ezera	Ezera
Nehemiah	Nehemia	Neh.
Esther	Esetera	Eset.
Job	Ioba	Ioba
Psalms	Halelu	Hal.
Proverbs	Solomona	Sol.
Ecclesiastes	Kekahuna	Kekah.
Songs of Solomon	Mele a Solomona	Mele
Isaiah	Isaia	Isa.
Jeremiah	Ieremia	Ier.
Lamentations	Kanikau	Kan.
Ezekiel	Ezekiela	Ezek.
Daniel	Daniela	Dan.
Hosea	Hosea	Hos.
Joel	Ioela	Ioela
Amos	Amosa	Am.
Obadiah	Obadia	Oba.

(Continued)

*Taken from the 6th edition of Baibala Hemolele, American Bible Society, 1929.

Ke Kauoha Kahiko, Old Testament *(Continued)*

Jonah	Iona	Ion.
Micah	Mika	Mika
Nahum	Nahuma	Nahuma
Habakkuk	Habakuka	Hab.
Zephaniah	Zepania	Zep.
Haggai	Hagai	Hagai
Zechariah	Zekaria	Zek.
Malachi	Malaki	Mal.

Ke Kauoha Hou, New Testament

Matthew	Mataio	Mat.
Mark	Mareko	Mar.
Luke	Luka	Luka
John	Ioane	Ioane
Acts	Oihana	Oih.
Romans	Roma	Roma
Corinthians 1, 2	Korineto	Kor.
Galatians	Galatia	Gal.
Ephesians	Epeso	Epeso
Philippians	Pilipi	Pilipi
Colossians	Kolosa	Kol.
Thessalonians 1, 2	Tesalonike	Tes.
Timothy 1, 2	Timoteo	Tim.
Titus	Tito	Tito
Philemon	Pilemona	Pil.
Hebrews	Hebera	Heb.
James	Iakobo	Iak.
Peter 1, 2	Petero	Pet.
John 1, 2, 3	Ioane	Ioane
Jude	Iuda	Iuda
Revelation	Hoikeana	Hoik.

AGE

This category includes descriptions of all age groups. The words refer, in brief definitions, to babies, children, and youth, and also include some excellent descriptive phrases about the elderly.

This last group, the elderly, recalls Cicero's essay on old age, *De Senectute,* one of the classics of Roman literature, which certainly was familiar to the missionary scholars who created the written language of Hawai'i between 1820 and 1840.

'ā'aua. Woman beginning to advance in age; appearance of wrinkles.

akule. Aged person, male or female. See **'elemakule, makule.**

'alapu'u mo'o. Scamp of a baby grandchild. (PE.)

'āo'o. Middle-aged, elderly. See **'o'o.**

'āpela. Old, aged. *Obs.* (PE.)

'ehu ahiahi. Phrase meaning old age. *Lit.,* twilight, red of the evening.

'elehine. Old woman.

'elekule. Old fellow, old friend.

'elemakule. Old man, aged man. *He 'elemakule loa ua maumaua,* come to old age.

hahai kaulima. No meaning listed. (CMH.)

hakalunu. Extreme old age, as when one is no longer able to walk.

hānau. Baby, child; to be born.

hānau kahi. Older child. (Sol. 4:3.) See **kāma kahi.**

hiapo. First born baby. Also called *makahiapo.*

hō'elemakule. To act or behave like an old man.

ho'oluahine. To dress and act like an old lady.

ho'opēpē. Baby; to act like a baby.

hope loa. Youngest child.

'ili lua. Seventh stage of life, old age. *He pakapaka ka 'ili,* wrinkled skin. (A.)

kaekae. Young, attractive, plump, as a young woman.

kahiko. Old people.

kaikamāhine, kamahine. Girl.

ka'i kōkō. Bedridden; so old one needs to be carried in a net.

kama. Child.

kāma kahi. Single child, only child. See **hānau kahi.**

kamali'i. Children, group of girls.

kāne 'ole. Spinster, without a husband.

kani ko'o. An aged man who needs to carry a cane. *Lit.,* tapping cane.

kani mo'opuna. The state of old age when one has many grandchildren.

kauko'o. To walk with a cane.

kau maka 'iole. Unable to see clearly; old age. When the eyes dim, the steps falter.

keiki. Child, youngster, son, boy.

keiki hānai. Adopted son or child.

kolopupū. Old, lean, withered, bent over, as an aged person; to walk carefully and feebly. *Lit.,* creep bent over.

kolo'u'a. Worn out old hag.

kua. Fourth in descent, a great-grandchild.

kuahā. Six generations removed.

kuapapa. Ancient, oldest.

kūnewa. To age.

kū'olo. Old, as a person with sagging cheeks.

ku'u mo'o lei. My beloved grandchild.

lei. A beloved child.

leu. Fair-haired youngster. (CMH.)

liko. Child; youth, especially of a chief.

luahine, luwahine. Old woman.

makua. Older; a relative of the parents' generation.

makuahine. Any female relative of the parents' generation.

makua lua. Very old. *Lit.,* twice as mature.

makule. Aged person.

mo'o. Grandchild.

mua, hele mua. Older brother or sister.

muli hope. Youngest child, very last one.

muli loa. Youngest child.

niho kāhi. Derisive term for old age. *Lit.,* tooth one.

niho lena. Jeering epithet for old persons. *Lit.,* tooth yellow.

noho male 'ole. Spinsterhood.

ohi. Youth, young maiden.

'olomeka, olomeda. Old maid. *Eng.*

olopala. Old fellow. *Eng.*

omo wā u'i. To suck at a nipple; a suckling child.

o'o. To ripen, as fruit; to mature, as an adult. Applied to full-grown young people. See '**āo'o.**

'ōpio. Youth or juvenile.

'ōpiopio. Young, immature person.

'ōpu'u. Child.

'ouo, 'ouwo. Youth, young person.

pala lau hala. Advanced loss of hair; last stage of life.

pēpē. Baby. *Eng.*

pī'alu. Weak eyes, characteristic of an aged person.

poke'o. Child.

po'o hina. Gray hairs of an aged person. *Oho hina* (gray), as applied to the head. (Kin. 44:29.)

pua. Child.

pua'aneane, puaneane. Extreme old age (thus, eternity).

pupū. Old man or woman who walks feebly and carefully for want of strength.

u'i. The form and strength of youth.

wā'elemakule. Old age.

wahine kāne 'ole. Spinster, single woman.

wā kamali'i. Childhood.

wā li'ili'i. Childhood.

wā luahine. Old age in a woman.

wā'u'uku. Childhood.

AMUSEMENTS AND GAMES

Play was easy and natural in Hawai'i with its mild climate, its abundance of the materials of play, and its people of imagination and joy. There were amusements, games, and contests for both the mind and the body—for all ages. Children's games are frequently familiar ones: a form of jacks, jumping rope, spinning tops, walking on stilts are examples. All materials, including sennit or string, stones, parts of plants, and selected woods, were local and readily available. Young people may have engaged in foot races, wrestling matches, surfing, swimming, and a variety of other activities. Their energies were athletic. Maturity brought different amusements and game interests: sliding on the *papa holua,* hand-to-hand fighting and wrestling, leaping from cliff to sea, tug-of-war matches, guessing games, cock fighting, and gambling. There was mock warfare, too, in preparation for serious combat.

All such amusements and games are listed in this category.

alaia. Small thin surfboard made of breadfruit or *koa* wood. Also called *omo. Obs.* (PE.)

'au. To swim, float on the surface of the water.

ʻauʻau. To swim, bathe in water, as a person.

ʻauwaʻalakī. Little ships made by children from cane and *kī* leaves. (A.)

ʻauwaʻalaukī. *Kī* (ti) leaves folded into a boat for children. Also called *waʻalauki*.

e pehi i ka ʻulu. To roll the *ʻulu maika* stone in the bowling game.

haʻe nalu. To ride a surfboard. *Lit.,* riding wave.

haka moa. Cock fighting. *Lit.,* quarreling fowl.

hākōkō, hākoʻokoʻo. To wrestle in sport and cause an opponent to fall. (Kin. 32:24.)

hākōkō āeʻo. Wrestling on stilts. (KILO.)

hākōkō noho. Wrestling while seated. Each player attempted to cause his opponent to topple over from an unsteady seated position. (KILO.)

hanohano. To honor, excel, triumph.

hau. Lascivious dance accompanied by singing.

hauka. Out! Word used by a winner in gambling. It is a phonetic version of the English word, out.

hauna. Striking of the hands in playing the *kilu,* a gambling game.

haupeʻepeʻe. To play hide and seek.

heʻe hōlua. To slide down a steep grassy hill on a *papa hōlua* (sledge or sled). Each of the words, sport, hill, and sled, bears the name *hōlua.* A sport of chiefs and chiefesses.

hei. Cat's cradle, a game played largely by adults in the earlier years. A string looped on the fingers was manipulated to resemble a small cradle and many other figures. Over a hundred have been recorded in Hawaiʻi, many with accompanying chants.

helu ʻai. Office of a person engaged in play or in games; scorekeeper.

hiu. Pebbles or small stones, polished and flat, used as counters in playing *kōnane* and other games. Also called *ʻiliʻili*.

holoholo. Ancient sport of kicking a ball adorned with feathers.

hōlua. The sled and the downhill course involved in the sliding. See **heʻe hōlua**.

honuhonu. To swim with hands only, feet being interlocked; to crawl like a turtle. Players wrestled while seated, as in *hākōkō noho*.

hoʻoholomoa. Game of sliding downhill, a practice attended by gambling. (CMH.)

hoʻokakaʻa. Racing by rolling cart wheels. (KILO.)

hoʻoleilei. To swing, scatter, juggle; juggling.

hoʻolele lupe. Kite flying.

hoʻopahuʻa. To dance, sail against the wind, move sideways; the spear dance.

houhou. Game in which participants throw the spear or javelin.

hū. A top. *Hū kani,* a humming top.

hukihuki. Tug-of-war. See **pāʻumeʻume.**

hulehulei. To go up and down, as children on a seesaw.

ihe paheʻe. Spear sliding. Players slid five-foot long spears *(ihe)* between two stakes as evidence of their skill, or they showed their strength by sliding the *ihe* a long distance on a closely clipped field. Closely related to *moa paheʻe.*

ʻio. Game of running and racing, a kind of Hawaiian tag.

kāʻekeloi. To drum with fingers on a *pahu* (drum) and sing at the same time. No other data.

kāhau. A play or pastime. (A.) Sport of hurling lightweight spears of *hau* wood.

kāhinu. To grease the runners of the *papa hōlua* (sled).

kahuakōī. Sliding game; a playground *(kahua)* where children dug into the earth or sand with crooked sticks while repeating a jingle. See **koi.**

kahua leʻa. Place where people gathered for play, games, and other pastimes.

kahuamāika. The path made for playing *ʻulu maika.* (DK.)

kahua mokomoko. Place of boxing. *Mokomoko* is rough, hand-to-hand fighting of any kind whether boxing or free-for-all wrestling.

kākaiāpola. Tail of a kite.

kākā lāʻau. Fencing with long spears. Years ago this sport trained young warriors in hand-to-hand fighting.

kākā pahi. To fence; the sword exercise.

kānekupua. Mock battle fought with spears, staged in anticipation of the arrival of a chief.

kaʻōkaʻa. Game of spinning small gourds like tops. (PE.)

kaupua. Diving for half-ripe gourds, an ancient pastime. (MALO 233.)

keʻa. Children throwing darts of sugarcane stalks.

keʻa pua. Throwing darts made of stems of sugarcane tassels; shooting arrows, as from a *pana* (bow).

kilu. Game for grownups attended by gambling and licentiousness; small gourd or coconut shell used as a quoit in *kilu.*

kimo. Game similar to jacks for children and adults, including chiefs. (PE.) To strike, as with a stick in guessing at *pūhenehene.* (A.)

kiniholo. Game, something like baseball or playing catch on the run.

kini pōpō. To play ball; a general term for all games of ball-playing. *Pōpō,* ball for play.

kio. Practicing martial games. The chiefs indulged in mock war games.

kīoe. Small surfboard.

kīpapa. To turn sideways on a surfboard; balance on top of the surfboard.

kōheoheo. A kind of play among children, such as swinging a rope to be jumped over.

kōhikōhi. Throwing dirt. The object is to make one's playmates (and oneself) dirty. (CMH.)

kōhilōhi ku palalā. Guessing game for an object hidden in the earth or sand.

koi. Child's sliding game. See **kahuakōī.**

kōieie. Toy or plaything thrown into a rapid current of water which either the current or the tide may return.

komokomo. Ancient game or play, probably children dressing up. (CMH.) Boxing, striking with the fists. (AP.)

kōnane. Game similar to checkers, with black and white pebbles lined up in even rows on a wood or stone surface *(papa kōnane).* Also called *kunāne.*

kuala, kuwala. Somersault; to somersault.

kūamuamu. Lascivious play or dance.

ku hele mai. Gambling game where an awl-shaped game implement with a needle point is tossed from the hand, the object being to make it stand erect on the point. Each player tosses in turn until he misses.

kuʻi a lua. Ancient sport of *lua,* hand-to-hand fighting.

kuʻikuʻi. Boxing; to box, smite, buffet (a person). (Isa. 58:4.)

kūkini. Runner in a race, messenger. The *kūkini* was formerly a chief's order carrier to different points on the island. The degree of fleetness determined his value.

kukuluāeʻo. Person walking on stilts; stilts.

kulaʻi wāwae. Foot pushing while seated. This game tests the strength of the leg muscles and the ability to "sit tight" and brace the body with hands and arms. (KILO.)

kulakula. Game like ninepins.

kulakulaʻi. To wrestle, scuffle, push out of bounds by chest slapping.

kumuone. Sandstone used for *lulu maika* stones.

kunāne. Game played on a board with pebbles lined up in even rows. See *kōnane.*

kū pololū. Pole vaulting. Formerly warriors practiced the art of pole vaulting as an amusement and as a competitive sport at the chief's court. Long hardwood *pololū* (spears) were ideal vaulting poles. In times of combat warriors used this skill to vault over ravines, streams, and other obstacles. (KILO.)

kuʻukuʻu. Boomerang. (PE.)

lauʻauʻa. To play at games of chance, gambling, lottery.

lele kawa. To jump from a precipice, *pali,* or other elevation into the sea, making the least possible splash.

lele koali. To swing; jump rope. Swinging on the *koali* vine was an ancient pastime.

lele pahū. To jump or plunge feet first from a cliff into the sea making the greatest possible splash.

lele pali. To leap in sport from a cliff or precipice into water.

lele pinau. Game resembling *kōnane.*

loha. Sport of former times like *kilu.*

loulou. Trial of strength by finger holding and pulling.

loulou lima. To hook and pull one's finger, usually the index finger, with the same finger of another person.

lūlū. To shake dice, as in backgammon.

luna. Chief piece in the game of *kōnane.*

lupe. Kite.

māhikihiki. To teeter-totter, seesaw. Also called *mahiki.*

maika. To play the game called *lulu maika.* (MALO 221.) *See* **ihe paheʻe, ʻulu maika.**

makani ʻōahi. Hurling firebrands. Strong winds sweep out to sea from the lofty cliffs at Hāʻena on Kauaʻi. Seasonally, men formerly took dried, light-weight branches of the *papala* tree (genus *Charpentiera*) to the cliffs of Makana, Makua, and Kamaile, lit the wood, and tossed the firebrands into the winds. A core of soft pith caused streams of sparks to explode like rockets. The buoyant branches floated seaward or mountainward. Great crowds would canoe in from around Kauaʻi and even Niʻihau for the spectacle. (KILO.) See **ʻōʻilʻi pulelo ke aki o Ka-maile.**

moa. 1. Piece of wood used in the game *moa paheʻe.* 2. Game in which children interlock twigs of the *moa (Psilotum nudum),* then pull them apart. The one whose twig breaks first loses, and the winner crows like a rooster. (NEAL 1.)

moa paheʻe. Game where a player slides the *moa,* a wooden, torpedo-shaped dart, between a pair of stakes, each about nine inches apart, as a test of skill; or he can slide the same dart down a long playfield as a test of strength. The event involves gambling. Closely related to *ihe pahe'e*. (KILO.)

mokomoko. Boxing match, hand-to-hand fighting, scheduled for the first day of the year. See **kahua mokomoko.**

na'a pahe'e. Game absorbing one's attention. (CMH.)

na hu pa ipu. Gourd. No other data. (CMH.) *Hu* are spinning tops made from *ipu* (gourds). (KILO.)

newenewewe. Exclamation of *maika* players as they cheer an on-rolling stone.

no'a. To play the game *pūhenehene;* the stone used in the game *pūhenehene.*

nu'uanu. card game. (AP.)

'ō'il'i pulelo ke aki o Ka-maile. 1. To send lighted firebrands down from a *pali.* (A.) **2.** *Lit.,* The fire of Ka-maile rises in triumph. (PE.) Formerly a sport of chiefs. See **makani 'ōahi.**

oka. Top made of a small gourd. No other data. (CMH.)

'ōka'a niu. Top made of a dry coconut.

'ōleha. Game in which the eyes remain fixed in a squinting way.

olo. A very thick surfboard made of *wiliwili* wood.

'olohū. Similar to the game *'ulu maika.*

'omua. To tie a string around the fore end of the *pua* (sugarcane top) to make a *pāpua* (arrow) for playing archery.

'ōnini. A kind of surfboard for experts only.

'ōniu. A spinning top made from a coconut.

'ō'ōihe. To hurl spears; the art of spear throwing; hurling spears into banana trunks, not enemy bodies as in former times.

'ōwili. Thick surfboard made of *wiliwili* wood.

pā'ani. Enjoyment of a pastime. The Hawaiians formerly spent much time in *pā'ani* (games) or *le'ale'a* (sensual gratifications).

paha. Long surfboard of *wiliwili* wood.

pāha'o. In a game, to lay down one's own *pū'olo* (bundle) with others and take one up at random in order to get a better one. (A.)

pahe'e. Game that consists of sliding an implement on grass or gravel. See **ihe pahe'e, moa pahe'e.**

pahipahilima. Ancient game in which children get their hands dirty digging for some object. (CMH.)

pāhi'uhi'u, pāhu'ihu'i. Game, of either throwing darts at a ti leaf laid flat on the ground or pushing a stone to a goal with sharp sticks. The winner is the player whose dart is nearest the center of the ti leaf or whose stone stopped closest to the goal.

pahu. To hurl a spear.

pāhuʻihuʻi. *Var.* of **pāhiʻuhiʻu.**

pahukū. Starting place of a race. *Pahu hope, pahu hopu,* final goal. *Lit.,* reaching goal.

paʻi a paʻi. Stalemate; a drawn game.

paʻi umauma. To play by striking the breast; chest-slapping *hula. Lit.,* slapping breast.

paʻi wale. Drawn game with no winner. Also called *paʻi a paʻi.*

pākā. To skip stones. Also called *pākiki, pihipihi.*

pākiki. To skip stones. (CMH.) Also see *pākā, pihipihi.*

palaʻie. To play the game of loop and ball, using a stick with a loop on one end, a string tied to the stick, and a ball tied to its other end. The object is to catch the ball in the loop as it swings to and fro accompanied by a chant. (KILO.)

pana ʻiole. Shooting mice or rats with bow and arrow, an ancient pastime restricted to the chiefs. (KILO.)

pana pana nīʻau. To shoot a coconut-leaf midrib with the midrib *(nīʻau)* bent like a bow and springing away upon release.

pāpua. To shoot an arrow; archery.

pā uma. Standing hand wrestling. Each player clasps the other's hand and attempts to push his back against the other's chest. This tests the player's strength, endurance, and balance. (KILO.)

pāʻumeʻume. Tug-of-war. One of the few team games from the past. Two teams of equal strength and weight lined up along a stout rope, each trying to pull the other across a middle line. (KILO.) Also called *hukihuki.*

pehi. Game of darts.

pihipihi. To skip stones. See *pākā, pākiki.*

pili hihia. To become involved in gambling, even to the extent where a man would wager his wife or his life.

pilipiliwaiwai. Gambling or betting, with transfer of property involved. *Lit.,* to wager property.

piula. A card game.

polepole. Child's play, consisting of putting up one hand above the other and saying, *polepole ka mamalihini, kaʻa mai, kaʻa mai i kou, i kou kauhale, ʻouʻou ke ʻakia nei kuʻu piko e kaulele la e kō la,* ward off the strangeness, roll here, roll here the *kou* wood, for a *kou* house, a high house, there's a nip of my navel to make an effort to accomplish. (A.) Trans. (PE.)

pua kō. Upper part of the sugarcane in blossom. Often used for arrows by children, hence the name pāpua (archery).

pūhenehene. Game of score or forfeit. Teams consisted of from two to ten players, male and female, sitting in two facing rows across a line of five *kapa* bundles (named *kihi moe, pili puka, kau* (center), *kihipuka,* and *pili moe*). One player hid the *no'a,* a smooth stone or pebble or a small block of wood, under one of the *kapa* bundles or on the person of a team member. (The *no'a* was considered sacred because it lifted a *kapu* [restraint] when found.) A long *kapa* sheet kept the other side from seeing the hiding action. A *maile* (wand) was used to touch the opposing player who guessed the hiding place correctly, and his side scored a point. If the guess were incorrect, the other side scored, ten points per game. In ancient times, merriment prevailed and a *hula* was enjoyed by all. For a supplement to this description, see **Time: Watches of the Night.**

pūheoheo. Exclamation in the game *pūhenehene.* When all is in readiness, the leader calls *pūheoheo!* All went into *ho'opāpā* (repartee). The game was on!

pūkaula. Early betting or guessing game. Using a special knot, a trickster tied the ends of the cords together and gave the free ends to two persons to hold. Onlookers wagered whether the knot could be loosened by pulling on the free ends.

puna. Name of an introduced surfboard, *he kio'e kahiki.*

punipeki. Game like the English fox and geese. Little stones are placed in black and white squares, and players move and jump as in checkers. The fox is called *Bonepate,* from Bonaparte.

pu'u. Hand of cards; a knotted string for drawing lots or guessing numbers.

pu'u lepo. Mound of earth designated for target purposes in archery.

'uha'uha. Inclined to endless reveling.

'ūlili. Small gourd used as a top for spinning; bamboo tube used for blowing on a fire being kindled; *hula* step.

'ulu. Stone used in the *lulu maika* game. This stone is called *olohū* on Maui and O'ahu.

'ulu maika. Game of rolling, using a disk-shaped stone to achieve either the greatest accuracy between two stakes or farthest distance on even ground. See **e pehe i ka 'ulu, kahuamāika, kumuone, maika, newenewewe, 'ulu.**

uma. Hand or wrist wrestling, once very popular in Hawai'i. Two players crouch and attempt to overcome each other's arm thrust. *Uma* tests the competitor's strength and stamina in his hands and arms. In the crouch they clasp hands, with elbows on the ground, and push. (KILO.)

wa'alaukī. *Kī,* ti leaves folded ingeniously to make children's play boats. See **'auwa'alaukī.**

BANANAS

The title of this section suggests only different kinds of bananas, but the terms in this listing refer to all parts of the fruit. Hyde has listed seeds, parts of the plants, how they are planted, and their uses.

Any Hawaiian dictionary contains many terms describing different varieties using the prefix *mai'a* (banana). Pukui-Elbert lists sixty-two such terms and Hyde mentions even more, but unfortunately his writings are now all too often indecipherable. This means many terms have been lost, but the importance of the flavorful fruit emerges from this account.

'a'ao. Species of wild, tall banana.

'āhui. Cluster or bunch of bananas, grapes, or *hala* (pandanus).

'āhui mai'a. A bunch of bananas.

'ekā. Upper part or hand of bananas.

haha. Lower part of the banana stump that is cut off.

halane. Large bunch of bananas. (CMH.)

hapāi. Native banana that grows and matures within the tree trunk. The fruit is yellow, sweet, and edible.

hilahila. Same as the banana, *iho-lena,* a species free of *kapau.*

hua'alua. Double bunch of bananas. (CMH.)

iho-lena. Species of banana permitted to be eaten under the *kapu* system. See **hilahila, pōpōhe.**

ka'aka'alina. Tough, stringy, and not soft or pulpy, as of banana trees.

ka lua pou. Hole for planting bananas. (CMH.)

kapua. A banana, yellow when mature. See **mai'a kaua lau.**

kāpule. A banana hanging until its skin turns black in spots, thoroughly ripe.

kaua lau. Hawaiian variety of banana with light, green spots on dark green skin when young. When ripe, it is yellow and waxy with light-yellow flesh. Good only when baked. (PE.) See **kapua, mai'a kaua lau.**

koa'e. A banana striped white and green. (CMH.) Might be named after the *koa'e* bird. (DK.)

kola. Unripe, a word for bananas placed in the ground which do not ripen. (A.)

kū kanaloa. Shriveled, inedible variety of banana.

lahi. A banana like the *pōpō ulu* but with a soft skin. (CMH.)

lele. *Afusa sapientum.* A tall, wild banana formerly placed near the *lele* (altar). It was offered to the gods and used for love magic.

liko. Banana similar to a Tahitian banana in which the fruit stock bears upward.

līlā. Blasted, shriveled, or thin, as a banana.

maiʻa. The banana, a fruit of many varieties, *kapu* to women in ancient times. (A.)

maiʻa kaua lau. Variety of banana native to Hawaiʻi, dark green when young, yellow and waxy when mature. See **kaua lau.**

maiʻa koana. Seed-producing banana. Also called *ʻōpule.*

maiʻakū kanaloa. Shriveled, blasted banana. (A.)

maiʻa ʻoa. Inedible banana. Also called *ʻoa, poni.*

maiʻa pōpō ʻulu. Hawaiian banana with short green trunk, one of two varieties *kapu* to women. Its root is used for medicine and is edible raw.

maiʻa pūhi. Ancient Hawaiian banana with a green and brown trunk and twisted fruit. Edible only when cooked. *Lit.,* insipid water banana. (PE.) Also called *pūhi.*

manai ʻula. Ancient Hawaiian banana, both cultivated and wild. Inedible uncooked. Also called *maiʻa mālei ʻula.*

manila. Banana tree not used for fruit but for fiber for rope, manila hemp. (CMH.)

maoli. Species of banana, the long, dark colored plantain. Edible, cooked or raw.

maui. To wring the stem of a bunch of bananas to cause it to ripen.

moa. A kind of banana or plantain, large and plump, growing in a small bunch. Edible, cooked or raw. (PE.)

niu-hiwa. Species of banana. See **pōpō ʻulau.** (A.)

noʻu. Native banana growing in small bunches of plump, round fruit. Edible, cooked or raw. (PE.)

ʻōkaʻi. The blossom container holding the young bananas before fruiting. (PE.)

ʻōpuʻu maiʻa. Bunch of bananas; root bud and buds of a banana plant enclosed in their sheaths. (PE.)

paʻaʻā. Skin of the banana; fruit and outside covering sheath of a cluster of bananas; fiber of the banana stalk.

pa'i. Bunch or cluster. *He pa'i mai'a,* a bunch of bananas.

palakū. Thoroughly ripe banana.

pola. The hanging down of the blossom or bunch of bananas.

poni. An inedible banana. See mai'a'oa.

pōpōhe. See hilahila, iho-lena.

pōpō 'ulu. Plantain bearing the short round fruit. See niu hiwa,
no'u.

puapua nui. Variety of banana. Big-tailed banana.

pū mai'a. Bunch of bananas. (A.) Banana stalk. (PE.)

BIRDS OF HAWAI'I

There were several early ornithologists in Hawai'i in the late
1800s, men such as Henry B. Palmer and R. C. L. Perkins.
Charles Reed Bishop, founder of the Bernice P. Bishop Museum
and its chief funder, was not an ornithologist, but he aided scientists in their collecting and was associated with the famed Walter
Rothschild of England in forwarding bird skins collected in
Hawai'i. Bishop at one time corresponded with Perkins about the
position of curator at the Bishop Museum.

Words in this category include terms for such small birds as
honeycreepers and honeyeaters, the thrush, and dove. Attention is
given also to many large birds, including the duck, tern, hawk,
turkey, stilt, bos'n bird, heron, and, of course, the well known,
endangered Hawaiian goose, the nēnē. Of all birds in the islands,
however, the honeycreeper leads in number of species.

'ā. 1. Red footed booby *(Sula sula rubripes).* Nests on Kaua'i and
O'ahu and offshore islets. It is mostly white except for its
webbed feet. 2. Brown booby *(Sula leucogaster plotus).* See 'ā ai
anuhe a Kāne. 3. Masked or blue-faced booby *(Sula personata
dactylatra).* All three may also be called *'ā'ā.* Their range is
throughout the tropical Pacific.

'ā'ā. This honeyeater *(Moho braccatus),* also known as *'ō'ō,* was
famed for its far-heard, beautiful call, but is now extinct. This is
also the name of the dwarf *'ō'ō,* an endangered species found
only on Kaua'i.

'ā ai anuhe a Kāne. Brown booby *(Sula leucogaster plotus)* with an
all-white breast. Like all boobies it flies high and dives straight
down for its fish. See 'ā. (PE 4.)

āe'o. Hawaiian stilt *(Himantopus mudseni).* Endemic to Hawai'i, now an endangered species. See **kukuluāe'o.**

'akakane, apapane. Honeycreeper *(Himatione sanguinea)* with crimson body and black wings and tail. Most common of the surviving honeycreepers, and known for its singing. Found on the principal islands of Hawai'i. Also called *'āpane.*

'akē'akē. Hawaiian storm petrel *(Oceanodroma castro cryptoleucura).* Endemic to Hawai'i. Also called *oeoe, oweowe, lupe-'akeke.*

'akēk'aka. Stripsil. No data. (CMH.)

'akeke'e. Honeycreeper *(Loxops coccinea caeruleirostris),* the Kaua'i *'ākepa.* Indigenous to Kaua'i. Also called *'ō'ū holo wai.*

'akekeke. Ruddy turnstone *(Arenaria interpres interpres),* a winter migrant to Hawai'i. Also called *'ukekeke, 'ukeke.*

'ākepa. Small, scarlet or yellow-green honeycreeper *(Loxops coccinea coccinea).* Indigenous to Hawai'i. There are two subspecies, the Maui *'ākepa (L. coccinea ochracea)* and the O'ahu *'ākepa (L. coccinea rufa).* Also called *'akepeu'ie.*

'akepeu'ie. Same as **'ākepa.**

'akihi a loa. Small, yellow honeycreeper *(Hemignathus obscurus).* The name *'akihi a loa* refers to the long curved bill of the bird. It is an endangered species in Hawai'i except on the islands of Hawai'i, Lana'i, and O'ahu where it is extinct. Also called *akialoa, akihiloa.*

akihi pōlena. Small bird with yellow feathers. (CMH.) Small bird with red feathers. (A.) Bird listed by MALO 39. (PE.)

'akōhekohe. Crested honeycreeper *(Palmeria dolei)* that lived on Maui and Moloka'i. Now extinct on Moloka'i.

ala'alai. Redbilled marshhen. (CMH.)

'alae. Mudhen or Hawaiian gallinule *(Gallinula chloropus sandvicensis),* a black wading bird with red frontal plate. This bird's cry was considered a bad omen. Also called *koki.*

'alae kea. Hawaiian coot *(Fulica americana alai),* a bird frequenting ponds and marshes. Formerly it thrived in the rice fields and taro patches. Its frontal knob is ivory-white. Also called *'alae ke'oke'o, 'alae nu kea.*

'alae ke'oke'o. Same as **'alae kea.**

'alae nu kea. Same as **'alae kea.** *Lit.,* white-beaked *'alae.*

'alae 'ula. Hawaiian gallinule or mudhen *(Gallinula chlorops sandvicensis).* Distinguished from the **'alae kea** by its red frontal plate and bill. This is one of the birds said to have stolen fire from heaven, thereby burning its white forehead red. Extant.

'alalā. Hawaiian crow *(Corvus tropicus)* noted for its early morning noise, a caw sounding like the cry of a young animal. Its habitat extends the length of the Kona side of Hawai'i island. Now endangered.

'alauwahio, 'alauahio. Lāna'i honeycreeper *(Paroreomyza montana)* native to Lana'i and now extinct. Its Hawaiian name is often shortened to *'alauwī* or *lauwī*.

'amakihi. Yellow honeycreeper *(Loxops virens).* Each of the honeycreepers of each main island has a different name: Hawai'i, *virens;* Kaua'i, *stenjnegeri;* Lana'i, *chloroides;* Maui, *wilsoni;* Moloka'i, *kala'ana;* O'ahu, *chloris.* Their feathers were used for feather capes in earlier times. Several capes are at the Bishop Museum.

'āmaui. Hawaiian thrush *(Phaeornis obscura obscura).* Several species of this bird were known throughout the islands by the common name *'āmaui,* but were also known by a second Hawaiian name on individual islands. Only O'ahu was limited to the name *'āmaui.* The bird was noted for its fine singing. Some *'āmaui* still live on Hawai'i island, but it is extinct or on the endangered list elsewhere.

'a'o. Newell's shearwater *(Puffinus puffinus newelli).* This bird is in danger of extinction. Also called Newell's puffin.

'āpane. Short for *'āpapane.* Hawaiian honeycreeper *(Himatione sanguinea),* great singer, probably the most common of the surviving honeycreepers.

'āpapane. See **'āpane, 'ākakane.**

auku, 'auku'u. Black-crowned night heron *(Nycticorax hoactli).* A non-migratory bird inhabiting marshes and muddy shorelines. Its voice is a hoarse, croaking quack. It is common to most of the islands of the group. Also called *'auku'u kahili.*

'ewa'ewa iki. The sooty tern *(Sterna fuscata oahuensis).* Its Hawaiian name means to make one uncomfortable, probably from the constant screeching cries it makes. This tern has a wide range over all the world, including the Hawaiian chain. Also called *'ewa'ewa.*

huna kai. Sanderling *(Crocethia alba).* Breeds deep in the Arctic and winters in Hawai'i. It follows closely after *(huna kai)* receding waves on sandy beaches. When disturbed it squeaks as it rises.

'iao. Bird somewhat like the *moho.* (A.) Possibly the spotted Hawaiian rail (Pennula sandwichensis), a wingless bird that "crows" or burrs on the ground. Now extinct. See **moho.**

ʻiʻawi. Scarlet Hawaiian honeycreeper *(Vestiaria coccinea)* with a bright scarlet body, black wings and tail, and a curved bill an inch long. This is a beautiful bird, and its feathers were long prized in featherwork. Once numerous and native to the islands. Also called *ʻiwi, ʻiʻiwi, ʻiʻiwi pōlena, olokele* (on Kauaʻi).

ʻiʻiwi pōpolo. This is the greenish-yellow, black-spotted young of the *ʻiʻawi* or *ʻiʻiwi*.

ʻio. Hawaiian hawk *(Buteo solitarius)* native to the forests of Hawaiʻi island. A useful scavenger of mice, rats, caterpillars, and even tired mynahs.

ʻiwa. Frigate bird or Man oʻ War *(Fregata minor palmerstoni)* with a wing span of about 7 feet and a body from beak to tail averaging 37 inches. It is a soaring, floating creature that can't stand, walk, or even swim. While homing at day's end, it swoops upon other birds such as booby gannets carrying fish intended for their young, dislodges the fish, and dives unerringly on the bruised fish which it takes to its own nest. It can only take flight from a bush or mound of earth. The hurricane of 1982 was fittingly named *ʻIwa*.

ʻiwi mapu. Duck with red feathers. No data. (CMH.)

ʻiwi pōlena. Hawaiian scarlet honeycreeper *(Vestiaria coccinea)*. Native to all islands. Feathers once widely used for featherwork. Same as *ʻiʻiwi pōlena*.

kaiaʻa. Bird that feeds in the ocean and nests at night in the mountains.

kakā. Domesticated duck. Its name adapted from the English "quack."

kākā wahie. Molokaʻi creeper *(Loxops maculata flammea)*. The Hawaiian name translates, "to break up firewood," referring to the chipping call of the bird. On the road to extinction.

kala. The gray-backed tern *(Sterna lunata)*. See **pakalakala**.

kanono. Red fowl; chicken.

kapalulu. California (Valley) quail *(Lophortyx californicus)*, a vegetable eater. It was brought to the islands early and in the 1890s heavily populated Hawaiʻi and Molokaʻi. (CMH.)

kaʻula. Red-tailed boatswain or tropic bird *(Phaethon rubricauda)*. Bos'n bird. Breeds on islands of the Hawaiian chain and elsewhere. It takes off from a flat surface, usually land, by beating vigorously with its wings. Its tail feathers are used in adorning the *kāhili*. Also called *koaʻe ʻula*.

kauma ʻanalaiʻi. Large bird of Hawaiʻi. (CMH.)

kaʻupu. Large black bird, turkey-sized, found largely on Nihoa and Ka'ula. (A.) Perhaps it is the Laysan albatross *(Diomedea immutabilis)*. *Ka'upu hehi 'ale,* a billow treading *ka'upu.* (PE.) See **mōlī.** The bird skins that hung from the crossbar of the banner of Lono-i-ka-makahiki are said to be of the *ka'upu* bird, which was one of the *kinolau* or earthly forms of Lono. Hawaiian culturists, not ornithologists, call these *ka'upu* gannet or booby birds. (KILO.)

kī. Small, yellow honeycreeper *(Chlorodrepanis virens)* native to Hawai'i island. Its feathers were used in making caps. The green feathers were used occasionally for adornment. See **'amakihi.**

kiki. Bird resembling the plover. No data. (CMH.)

kiniheni. Guinea hen, family Numidae. *Eng.*

kioea, kiowea. Bristle-thighed curlew *(Numenius tahitiensis)* that generally breeds in Alaska and the Arctic and migrates to Hawai'i in the winter. This bird, which makes sounds like its Hawaiian name, is a delicious game bird.

koa'e kea. White-tailed boatswain or tropic bird *(Phaethon lepturus dorotheae)* which nests in cliffs and dives for fish, folding them in its gullet before swallowing.

kōlea. Golden plover *(Pluvialis dominica fulvus).* A winter migrant to Hawai'i in August and September. It returns to Alaska in May or June for breeding and rearing its young. The plover arrives thin and departs fat. The word *kōlea* is an uncomplimentary term applied to persons who, like the bird, arrive in Hawai'i without wealth, become prosperous, then return home to carry on. (KILO.)

koloa. Hawaiian duck *(Anas wyvilliana).* Indigenous to all the main Hawaiian islands, inhabiting coastal lagoons, marshes, ponds, and mountain streams. Facing extinction, it has recently been reared in captivity and successfully released on O'ahu and Hawai'i. The native nonmigratory duck is called *koloa maoli.*

kolo hala. Chinese, ringnecked pheasant *(Phasianus colchicus torquatus),* a popular game bird. Its neck and breast feathers are highly prized for feather hatbands.

kuhukukū. Dove, turtledove. (Kin. 15:9; Ier. 8:7.)

kukuluāe'o. Hawaiian stilt *(Himantopus mexicanus knudseni).* Native to the Hawaiian Islands and considered an endangered species. The term is also applied to a person walking on stilts. See **āe'o.**

laka. Perhaps the name of a bird; lark. *Eng. Kani ka laka,* the lark sings.

lale. Legendary, sweet singing bird, famed in song and story.

lauwī. Honeycreeper of Lāna'i, Maui, and O'ahu *(Loxops macu-lata)* whose yellow feathers are used for featherwork. See **'alauwahio.**

lawekeō. Cry of the Moloka'i stilt. See **kioea.**

leleu. Bird named after the *leleu,* a fruit tree. *O ka manu 'ai leleu,* the bird which eats the *leleu.*

li'oli'o. Sound of the *'a'o* (Newell's shearwater, *Puffinus newelli)* which the bird makes when ruffled or disturbed.

luke'akeke. Storm petrel, sea eagle. No data.

mamo. Black honeycreeper *(Drepanis pacifica.)* Bird with a black, slightly glossy body with feathers of a beautiful yellow on the sides, undersides, and thighs. Now extinct. It was native to Hawai'i island and easily caught with lime or noose. It supplied the best feathers for Hawaiian featherwork.

manu aloha. Parrot, love bird.

manukū. Rock pigeon, wild pigeon *(Columba livia)* that took to wild life readily. There were immense flocks on Hawai'i and Moloka'i in the years before and after 1900. *Lit.,* coo.

manu 'u. Crane. *Lit.,* moaning bird. (Ier. 8:7.)

moa. Fowl, native chicken *(Gallus gallus).* Can be considered a hybrid of historical dimension. There were wild jungle fowl here when Captain Cook arrived. Migratory people carried fowl with them, some released to run wild, others domesticated. The Hawaiians kept them for food, sacrifice, and cockfighting. Feathers were used to adorn the *kāhili* and the head of the dance rattle *('uli'uli).*

mōhā. Shoveler duck *(Spatula clypeata),* also known as spoonbill. See **koloa.** (PE.)

moho. Hawaiian rail *(Pennula millsi),* a bird that crows, burrs, or cries in the grass; it does not fly but walks about. Now extinct. See **'iao.**

mōlī. Laysan albatross *(Diomedea immutablis),* also called gooney or white gooney. Breeds on most of the leeward islands of the Hawaiian chain. It cannot avoid unfamiliar trees and buildings, often crashing against such obstacles. The flesh is edible. The Japanese formerly killed these birds for their feathers, but this ended with the Theodore Roosevelt 1909 National Wildlife Act.

mu. Small bird with yellow feathers. (MALO 39.)

nēnē. Hawaiian goose *(Branta sandwicensis)* native to the Hawaiian group on Hawai'i and Maui. It was intensively hunted but now, after a miracle of protective growth, it is achieving a cautious promise of recovery.

noio. Hawaiian tern *(Anous minutus melanogenys)*, a small, black bird that lives on fish. It frequents the coasts of the main islands of the Hawaiian chain. Also called *lae hina*.

nūkea. White billed *'alae kea* or Hawaiian coot *(Fulica americana alai)*. A pond and marsh dweller distinguished by its white frontal knob.

nūnū. Another name for *manukū* (dove) but thought of as a pigeon because of its sound.

'olo. Noddy tern *(Anous stolidus pileatus)*, also called *noio kōhā*. It is larger than the Hawaiian tern and is sometimes called the sperm whale bird.

olokele. Small, scarlet bird, *'i'iwi (Vestiaria coccinea)*. This is the *'i'iwi* but on Kaua'i it is *olokele*, the honeycreeper.

'oma'o. Hawaiian thrush, commonly called *'āmaui* or *'oma'o (Phaeornis obscura)*. Its original name was *'āmaui. Manu o Maui* and the different island names are corruptions. Still encountered on Hawai'i.

'ō'ō. Black honeyeater. There are four species, three of which *(Acrulocercus apicalis, Acrulocercus nobilis,* and *Acrulocercus bishopi,* on the islands of O'ahu, Hawai'i, and Moloka'i, respectively) are extinct. The Kaua'i honeyeater, *'ō'ō'ā'ā* (Acrulocercus braccatus) was thought to be extinct, but in 1978 John Sincock sighted one deep in the Alaka'i Swamp, a drenched jungle in the Wai-'ale'ale mountain area, claimed to be the wettest spot in the world. The black honeyeater is entirely black except for a tuft of yellow feathers under each wing, which were widely used in the illuminations of capes, helmets, and belts for royalty.

'ō'ō. Bishop's *'ō'ō (Acrulocercus bishopi)*, named after Charles Reed Bishop, founder of the Bernice Pauahi Bishop Museum. This *'ō'ō* was native to Moloka'i and is now extinct. It is similar to the *Moho nobilis,* the black honeyeater.

'ō'ōlamau. This is a bird like the *kōloa*. No other data. (CMH.)

'ō'ō pipi. Female of the *'ō'ō*.

'ō'ō ukaka. Female of the *'ō'ō*.

'ōpe'ape'a. Bat *(Lasiurus cinereus semotus)*, so called from the shape of the wings, which are similar to the ancient sails *(pe'a)* of their canoes. (Kanl. 14:18.)

'ōpu'u. Spur of a very young cock.

'ō'ū. Hawaiian honeycreeper *(Psittirostra psittacea)* that resembles the finch. Hawaiian names are *'ō'ō po'olapalapa* for the male, and *'ō'ū laue'o* for the female, the yellow headed and leaf-green *'ō'ū*. It is native to the main group of islands but close to extinction. It is loved because of its plumage and voice. Its green feathers were used in making capes and *leis*.

pakalakala. Gray-backed tern *(Sterna lunata)*, a bird well distributed over the tropical Pacific. Its food are squid and small fish. Also called *kala*.

palahū, pelehū. Turkey *(Meleagris gallopavo)*. Its name means to swell puffed out and it is so called from the gobble of the male.

palila. A gray, yellow, and white honeycreeper *(Psittirostra bailleui)* endemic to Hawai'i island. It was decreed an endangered species by a federal court in Hawai'i, upheld by the 9th Circuit Court of Appeals February 10, 1981. The *palila* nests in and gets its food from the *māmane* tree *(Sophora chrysophylla)* and the *naio*, bastard sandalwood *(Myporum sandwicense)*, both of which grow on the higher slopes of Mauna Kea, Hawai'i. By coincidence these trees also are the source of food most palatable to sheep and goats. The court order requires prompt elimination of those animals from the *palila* birds' living area.

pa'uohi'i aka. Species of bird. No data. (CMH.)

pelehū. Turkey. See *palahū*.

piha ekelo. Myna bird *(Acridotheres tristris)* introduced from India in 1865. Despite its critics it probably does more good than harm. Mynas hold interesting circle-court events. In one of them a large assembly of the birds forms a ring. If there is a lone culprit myna in the center he may receive only a chatty scolding. If a second steps in from the ring there is a fight. If the victim then tries to escape, the ring dissolves upon him and will peck him to death. The "court" adjourns!

pī wai. Kind of wild duck, *manu kolea pī wai*.

pueo. Hawaiian owl *(Asio flammeus sandwichensis)*. The owl was formerly worshiped as an *'aumakua*. It was numerous in open grass areas, feeding on mice. Despite its reputation as a predator, it needs protection.

'ua'u. Dark-rumped petrel *(Pterodroma phaeopygia sandwichensis)*, endemic to the main islands of Hawai'i. Mongooses have joined pigs and hogs in wiping out this bird on several islands. Native Hawaiians also eliminated their share, killing the bird for food. The meat of the young was reserved for the chiefs and was *kapu* to commoners. The petrel is almost extinct. Also called *'uwa'u, wa'u*.

ua'u kēwai. Large bird of turkey size with black back and white breast and wings. It is probably the dark-rumped petrel *(Pterodroma phaeopygia sandwichensis)*, a sea bird.

ula 'ai hāwane. Small, red Hawaiian honeycreeper *(Ciridops anna)* named after Sanford P. Dole's wife, Anna. Its long Hawaiian name means "the red bird that feeds on the hāwane," the native Hawaiian palm. The bird originally was native to Hawai'i island but is now extinct.

'ūlili. Wandering tattler *(Heteroscelus incanus),* a winter visitor from Alaska, the Yukon, and Prince Edward Sound. It inhabits rocky shores where it feeds on crabs, mollusks, etc. It gets its name *ūlili* (a bamboo pipe or whistle) from its whistling call.

BIRDS OF HAWAII: Glossary of Terms

As a category this deserves a more specific name, for it is largely devoted to the ancient methods of bird entrapment. The English words snare, trap, net, noose, bird calls, lime, and gum give some notion of the many operations involved. Of them all, the technique of catching birds by liming was the most sophisticated.

Other processes involving birds are described by a few spare terms: for example, there is only one word used for bird song, but the noises of the owls, gooneys, hawks, crows, and other fowl are identified.

Some attention has been paid to the Hawaiians' love of beautiful feathers, used for making helmets, capes, and other items of adornment.

'ahele, 'alehe. Snare; to snare. Also called *pahele,* a less familiar word.

'alakō. Bird-catching pole. See 'auku'u.

'alehe. Snare, noose; to snare. See 'ahele.

aua. Voice of the *'alalā,* the Hawaiian crow *(Corvus tropicus);* a caw. See Birds of Hawai'i: 'alalā.

'au'au manu, hō'au'au mano. Snare for catching birds. See 'ahele.

'auku'u. Long bamboo pole with two *maile* stalks across the top, gummed with lime to catch birds. See 'alakō.

'ē'ē. Tuft of yellow feathers under each wing of the 'ō'ō, used in featherwork.

'eheheu. General term for wings of flying creatures.

'ēheu, 'ēkeu. Wings, winged creatures. Similar to *'eheheu.* See pēheu, pēkeu.

hāmau lehua, lehua hāmau. Silent *lehua.* In early times skilled bird-catchers silently *(hāmau)* slipped into the foliage of the *lehua* tree, smeared the twigs and branches with a gummy mixture, and waited for the 'ō'ō, *mamo,* and other honeycreepers and honeyeaters to alight and be entrapped. Certain yellow or red feathers were removed from the crest, tail, or wings and the bird released. The feathers were used in making capes, helmets, cloaks, and other apparel for royal wear. Silence was the key in this ancient skill.

hāpapa. Stick limed to catch birds. It was used especially for catching 'io (hawks). The crosspieces were gummed and a live bird was tied next to it as a decoy. (PE.) See **lā'au kia, oha.**

hehei, hei. To snare or entangle in a net. See **kāpili manu.**

hele. Noose, snare.

hīpuka. Snare for the plover. *Obs.*

hō'au'au manu. Snare. See **'au'au manu.**

holo. Noose.

hū lā'au. Gum of the breadfruit; pitch or resin.

hulu. Feather or quill.

kahekahe. Method of bird-catching in which all but a few *lehua* blossoms were taken from the tree, and the remaining flowers were gummed for snaring. (PE.)

kakala. Spur of a cock; to sharpen.

kāpili. To besmear with something sticky, as lime.

kāpili manu. The art of catching birds with birdlime. An extremely adhesive viscid substance, a gum or milky sap, was mixed usually with the ground-up bark of a tree and smeared on the branches or twigs of certain trees, on the crosspole of two supporting posts, or on the blossoms of a flowering tree. In the latter instance the blossoms of the *lehua* were thinned down and the remaining blossoms smeared. The bird-catcher stood silently, *(hāmau)* within the foliage to take the trapped creatures. Milky sap and ground-up bark of the breadfruit *(Artocarpus altilis)* were placed on its branches and twigs, while the gum and bark mixture of the *kukui* tree *(pīlali)* was placed on the branches and twigs of the *kukui (Aleurites moluccana)* itself. Many ingenious devices were used to trap birds—nets, springs, snares, etc.—but bird liming was almost a science.

kāpi'o. Bird snare made by bending a sapling to attach a noose. The bird entered, dislodged a weight, the sapling straightened up, and the noose tightened and caught the bird.

kaukau. To set or fix a snare, as for birds. (Hal. 141:9.)

kaumanu. Catching birds by tying a caterpillar and a stick at one end of a string. When the bird swallows the caterpillar the stick lodges in its throat. (PE.)

kāwili. To snare birds with lime. See **kāpili manu.**

kēpau. Birdlime; gum, as from ripe breadfruit.

ke'u. To croak, hoot, scold, protest; to croak like a mud hen.

kia manu. Bird-catcher; to catch birds by gumming. See **kāpili manu.**

kikokō. To call a cock. (CMH.)

kīpuka. Snare with a sliding noose used to catch owls. A rat was tied to a sharp stick in a net. The owl, pouncing on the rat, was transfixed.

kolokio. Catching birds with lime gummed on the crosspiece. See **kia manu, hāpapa, lā'au kia, oha.**

kono manu. Method of bird-catching where a bird hunter, imitating the bird, lured it into his snare. Gummed *'ie'ie* roots were used in the snare.

ko'u, kouko. To cluck like a hen.

kuapo'i. Full-fledged, as birds. *Kuapo'i nā manu,* the birds are fully fledged.

kuhea manu. Catching birds by imitating bird calls. *Maka 'ala ke kanaka kuhea manu,* watchful, the man ensnared birds.

lā'au kia. Stick for ensnaring birds; using such a sticky substance as birdlime. See **kia manu.**

lawai'a manu. Bird-catcher; bird-catching with a net. *Lit.,* to fish birds.

lawakeō. Cry of the *kioea* (curlew), commonly a Moloka'i resident.

lepe. Comb of the cock; turkey wattles.

mai'ao. Claw or claws of a bird; nail of finger or toe; hoof of an animal.

manu o Kahiki. Migratory birds. *Lit.,* birds from Tahiti.

nonolo, nunulu. Song of singing birds; to warble, chirp, sing; *mele,* song. *"I ka leo o ka manu a-E nunulu mai ana a-E nonolo mai ana."* (A.)

nuku. Beak or bill of a bird.

oeoe. Long, stretched out, as the neck of a goose. *Oeoe ka 'a'i o ka manu nēnē,* long is the neck of the *nēnē,* goose.

oha. Stick for ensnaring birds. (A.) See **hāpapa, lā'au kia, kolokio.**

'ōku'u. Method of catching birds by gumming artificial *lehua* blossoms made of *ie'ie* vines and attaching them to a tree. (PE.)

'ōpiki, ūpiki. Snare or trap for birds.

oua. Unspurred young cocks. (CMH.)

pahele. Snare, noose or trap.

pahelehele. Snare. (FOR 5:85.)

pehea pueo. Snare for catching owls. (A.)

pēheu, pēkeu. Wing or wings of a bird. See **'ēheu, 'ēkeu.**

pīkoikoi. To call or lure birds for snaring. (A.)

pīlali. Gum of the *kukui* tree, a kind of resin. This was the key element of bird-catching. Birds were held in the gum long enough to be caught.

po'au'au manu. Snare for birds. (CMH.)

pokia. Post or pole smeared at the top with gum so that alighting birds could be caught.

puapo'o. Head blossom, i.e., the comb of a cock or a tuft of feathers on its head.

puapua. To project out and up, as the tail feathers of a cock.

puka lou. Noose or loop used as part of the ensnaring process. See **kāpi'o, kīpuka.**

pūkōkō. To crow like a cock, to coo.

pūnua. Featherless; a fledgling.

pu'u. A method of catching plover; a sharpened bone was half buried and anchored on a string tied to a rock. The bone would become lodged in the *pu'u,* throat of a plover attempting to eat it, which was then held by the string. (PE.)

'ūpiki. A trap or snare. See **'ōpiki.**

CANOES: Kinds, Operations

Several types of canoes were made by the Hawaiians for special purposes; today we call these types single-man, two-man, bait-carrying, outrigger, double, war, and transoceanic canoes. The test of a canoe was twofold: first, the religious clearance for seaworthiness; and second, a ride to witness its confrontation with the weather and the sea. A review of the terminology involved will give the reader a sense of being a participant in this ancient art.

Here, too, mental and physical abilities aided the native Hawaiian in understanding and solving the myriad of perplexing problems of construction and operation involved in this stone-age art. It was a remarkable achievement.

'ākī ko oukou pe'a. To lop or double down, as the top of a sail, when there is a strong wind.

auhā. Building or shed for housing canoes for protection from the sun. See **auolo, hālau waʻa.**

auhele. To sail or drift aimlessly.

ʻauiʻia ka waʻa e kaʻale. The canoe was turned aside by a wave.

ʻaukai. Sailor, seafarer.

aukū. Rise and pitch of a vessel; to stand up, as a canoe, its bow in the wind.

aukū ka ihu i ka makani. To stand up, as the bow of a vessel in the wind. Derived from the resemblance to a man's position in swimming upright in a rough sea. (A.)

ʻaumoana. Sailor; to travel the open sea.

ʻau moku. Fleet of ships.

auolo. Shed for shelter of canoes. See **auhā, hālau waʻa.**

ʻau waʻa. Fleet of canoes.

ʻāwala. To pull steadily and carefully, as a fisherman concerned about his lines.

ʻāweawe. Curling of the water in a ship's wake.

ʻeke. Nice, excellent. Words used in describing a canoe.

halakau. To stand on the edge of one's canoe looking for squid, to lean over.

hālau waʻa. Canoe house, a long thatched structure for sheltering canoes. (KILO.)

haulani. To plunge, as a canoe.

heihei waʻa. Canoe race.

hekau. Strong rope for fastening a canoe; to anchor.

he pea oeoe. Long, high sail; sprit of a sail.

hoʻāpipi. Two canoes joined but not in the fashion of a double canoe.

hoe. To paddle a canoe; a paddle. The words oar and row were not used by the early Hawaiians. They were amused to see Captain Cook's men rowing a boat and laughed at the rowers, seated backwards, who could not see where they were going. (KILO.)

hoe uli. Paddle used for steering, a rudder.

hoe waʻa. Canoe paddle; paddler.

holoholo wale. To sail aimlessly.

holokahiki. Sailor; to sail to other lands.

holomoku. Sailor, canoe passenger, anyone who rides.

holopuni. To sail about, around, anywhere.

hoʻokelekele waʻa. To steer a canoe.

hoʻokele waʻa. Steersman, helmsman.

hoʻokū. To hold water with the paddle when sailing a canoe.

hoʻolala. To change course in sailing; to tack. See **pūnini.**

hoʻopae. To go ashore from a canoe, boat, or vessel; to beach a canoe.

hoʻopāhuʻa. To sail in a zigzag manner; to beat against the wind.

hoʻopīnana. To pitch and toss, as a vessel in a storm. (A.)

īkā. Inclined to fall off before the wind; to drift, be driven by the wind.

ili. To be wrecked; to strike or run aground; the stranding of a ship.

ʻīlio ʻaukai. Experienced sailor, sea dog (nickname).

kaʻalalo. To sail to leeward.

kaʻalelewa. To stand off and on; to drift or be driven by the wind.

kā i ka liu. To bail water.

kākelekele. Boating for pleasure.

Kama-i-huli-pū, Kama-i-huli-waʻa, Kama-i-kahuli-waʻa-pū. God who aided in floating upset canoes, variant spellings.

kamapuʻu. Setting the jib. (CMH.)

kaukāhi. Single canoe.

kaulua. Double canoe, two canoes tied together. See **waʻa kaulua.**

kawele. To row slowly, paddle a canoe slowly.

kela. Sailor. Also called *kelamoku.*

kele. To sail a canoe far out to sea; to steer; a steersman.

kialoa. Long, light canoe used by one man in racing contests.

kiapā. Swift sailing canoe.

kikihi. Going about in a canoe with a sail.

kīpū. To back water with a paddle in turning a canoe. Also called *kīpupū.*

kolo. To row swiftly, as a boat of a warship. (A.)

komo. To sink, as a heavily loaded canoe. The load could have consisted of fish, which can shift in uneasy waters.

koʻo. To struggle, as in paddling against the wind; to push off, as with a pole; to pole a canoe.

koʻolua, kōkoʻolua. Canoe with only two persons.

koukou. Heavy, as an overloaded canoe that sinks instead of floating lightly.

kūpe. To man or direct a canoe, as the one holding the steering paddle.

kūpele. To scoop or dig out the inside of a log for a canoe.

kupeʻulu. Old, broken, worn-out canoe, without sail and other essentials; a canoe with a large bowsprit or *ihu,* nose or fore part. (A.) Short, wide canoe.

lauhoe. To paddle a canoe, as several persons paddling together in unison with great strength and resolution, or similarly and simultaneously in several canoes.

lele. To land or go ashore from a canoe.

leleaoa. Act of sailing quickly in a canoe or in a fleet of canoes for another place.

limilimi. To be turned over and over in the surf. See **lumi.**

liu. Water in the bottom of a canoe; bilge water; to leak, as a canoe.

lolia. To turn on one side, then on the other, like a sleepy person. Canoes, too, will turn from one side to the other when being drawn down from the mountain.

lolo. Hog sacrificed on the finishing of the canoe. The hog's brain was eaten at this time.

luikia. Tying up or binding the outrigger of a canoe expertly and firmly. (A.)

luina. Sailor.

lumaiʻa. To be entangled in the surf; to be turned over and over.

lumi. To be pounded or crushed by the surf, overwhelmed by it. See **limilimi.**

malau. Bait carrier canoe used in *bonito* and *aku* fishing.

manuihu. Nose, snout, or bowsprit of a canoe likened to the beak of a bird.

mea waʻa. Canoe owner or canoe-man.

miomio. Beautiful, like a well-shaped canoe; anything that is trim or neat.

mouo. Buoy or float for a net.

mukumuku. Canoe cut short or in the middle.

newa. Wallow, as vessels at sea.

nianiau. To sail straight ahead, as one's course is changing.

niau. To sail easily, smoothly, peacefully, swiftly.

ō. Sprit of a sail.

ʻōhaikau. Not a canoe but a sea-borne raft. This is the name of a sledge obtained from Captian Cook and worshiped thereafter. (A.)

ʻōkuʻoku. To rise up, as the bow of a canoe on waves in a storm; to pitch.

ʻōlepe. To turn one way or another, as the course of a ship.

oloi. To strike against a rock, run aground, as a canoe.

ʻōlulo. Shipwrecked; castaway.

paʻē. To flap or shake, as a sail.

pahi. Canoe, in Tahitian. (A.)

pākā. To slide a surfboard or canoe on a wave.

pākākā. To glide with a canoe on a wave, on the surf; to skim, as a surfing canoe.

pakīpakī. To spatter and splash the water in paddling a canoe; to divide the water, as the keel of a ship.

pānānā. To paddle a canoe irregularly; a pilot; mariner's compass.

paneʻe. To shove off a canoe into the sea; to shove a canoe along the sand.

pāpā kai. Narrow escape of a canoe landing in the surf. (A.) Shoved, pounded by the sea. (PE.)

paukū. To curve, as the curve of a canoe. (A.)

pāuma. To rock a canoe back and forth, so as to empty it of water. (PE.)

peleleu. Large double canoe used in war; fishing canoe of the largest size, made shorter than customary in proportion to the width.

pihō. To be swamped but not sunk; to be almost filled with water and swamped.

pihōpihō. Heavily loaded canoe, low in the water.

pōʻalaʻala. Going toward land, then out again to sea, as in sailing a canoe along a coast.

poholua. To set the sails to the wind, so as to go neither forward nor backward; to lie to, as a ship.

pōlena. All the sails drawn tightly.

pūkolu. Triple canoe, i.e., three canoes rigged up abreast.

pūlua. Two men in a canoe, both assisting.

pūnini. To change course, to tack.

ʻuili. To steer, as a canoe.

uli. To steer, as a canoe; special servant of the king, his canoe steersman.

ʻuʻu. To hoist a sail.

waʻa. Canoe. *Waʻa kome nona,* canoe, ark of bulrushes. (Puk. 2:3.)

waʻa kaulua. Double canoe.

waʻa kialoa. Long, narrow, trim canoe intended for one-man use.

waʻapa. Canoe made of boards; a boat or skiff shorter or wider than a canoe. (2 Sam. 19:18.)

waʻa peleleu. Very large canoe, perhaps a double canoe.

CANOES: Construction, Parts

The life history of a canoe began with the ceremony of approval of the selected tree in the mountains. The finished product required sacred clearance for seaworthiness and readiness.

Canoe building was an important vocation among the Hawaiians. A great deal of religious effort was applied to assure a busy, successful, and safe future for the canoes.

'aki. Stools on shore on which canoes were placed for care. See **lona.**

ama. Longitudinal stick of the outrigger of a canoe made of *wiliwili* wood. See **kanaka.**

aukāhi. Smooth without knots or rough spots, as a canoe.

'ēkū. Back projection of a *manu ihu* (canoe bow section) on which the *kua po'i* (weatherboard) rested. (PE.)

hae. Flag, banner, ensign. In early times a torn piece of *kapa,* called *hae,* was used as a banner.

hakakauluna. Canoe rest.

hākaokao. Hole in a canoe for inserting the mast.

hālau. Long house with the end in front—beach side—used for storing canoes.

hale lanalana. House on a double-canoe platform.

he'e. Stay rope that supported a mast.

hekau. Large, strong rope for fastening boats, canoes; to anchor.

helēuma. Anchor of stone formerly used to hold a canoe fast and safe. (Heb. 6:19.)

hoana. Stone for polishing canoes; whetstone, grindstone.

hoa wa'a. Tackling or rigging for a canoe; tying on the *'iako* (outrigger boom). (A.)

hoe. Paddle for a canoe, oar for a boat; to paddle, row.

honua. Middle section of a canoe.

ho'okupa. To cut, dig, and hew when routing the hollow of a log into canoe shape.

ho'ola'a wa'a. Ceremony of consecration of a canoe.

hope. Stern of a canoe.

hua. Swelling at the broadest section of the canoe paddle.

hulilau. Large calabash for carrying clothes in a canoe; a receptacle for such.

'iako. Arched sticks connecting an outrigger to a canoe; boom. Usually made of *hau* wood.

ihu. Prow, bowsprit, forepart of a canoe.

ihu nui. Canoe with a large bow hollowed from the large end of a log.

ipu wai. Rollers used for moving a finished canoe safely and unscratched down the rough mountainside to the site of the launching ceremony. (KILO.)

kā. Dish used to bail water from a canoe; a half gourd or wooden bailer.

ka'aoki. To finish off, as a canoe.

kaekae. Canoe, smooth without knots or imperfections.

ka'ele wa'a. Unfinished canoe, bottom of the canoe. (A.)

kahuna kalai wa'a. Master canoe builder.

kalai wa'a. Canoe builder.

kanaka. Aft end of a canoe outrigger.

kaula ka'ili'ili. Line from the forward outrigger boom to the prow for strengthening canoe in stormy weather.

kaula likini. Rigging.

kaula luahine. A rope for fastening the protective mat along a canoe's one side against high seas. *Lit.,* old woman rope.

kaumoli. A short stick with holes down the middle, used to hold gunwales in place while being sewed with sennit.

kauō, kauwō wa'a. To drag canoes down from the mountains when partly finished.

kau po'i. Median canoe-bow cover. (PE.)

kāwelewele. Name of certain short ropes used about a canoe, particularly those attached to the outrigger to assist in righting a capsized canoe. (PE.)

ke'a. Connecting beams of double canoes.

kia. Mast.

kiapopo. Canoe with a deep, curving hull.

kikihi. Going about in a canoe with a sail.

kikoni. To finish out a canoe using a small adze.

kimokimo. To hew, shave, and smooth the inside of a canoe, with most of the operation handled by an adze.

kowa'a. Rope for towing a canoe, usually for dragging an unfinished hull down from a mountain.

kuamo'o. Canoe keel. *Lit.,* back lizard.

kuānuenue. Boom connecting canoe hulls of a double outrigger. (PE.)

kuapo'i. Weatherboard on top, fore, and aft of a canoe.

kupe. Canoe rims or end pieces fore and aft.

ku pou kia. Small hole in the bottom of a canoe for a mast. *Lit.,* stand mast pole.

lā. Name of sail on ancient canoes.

lā'au. General term for end pieces.

lā'au lalo. Boom of a vessel. *Lit.,* stick down.

Laka. Canoe god. Also called Kū ōhi'a Laka.

lanalana. Lashings of sennit binding the *ama* (float) to the *'iako* (outrigger booms).

lauoha. Sail above the spanker on a vessel.

Lea. Goddess of canoe builders. She took the form of an *elepaio* to help canoe makers select the proper *koa* logs.

leuwi. Forepoint of a canoe where the two weatherboards were joined.

likini. Rigging. *Eng.*

liu. Bilge water of a canoe.

lolo. Hog sacrificed upon finishing or launching a canoe, or starting a journey.

lona. Blocks of wood on which canoes rested while out of the water. See **'aki.**

lupe. Flattened end of the fore outrigger float, outside the tied joint of the outrigger float and the boom.

maha. Lower portion of carved ornament on a canoe bow or stern.

maka ihu. Sharp point at the prow of a canoe. *Lit.,* point bow.

maku'u. Crease around each end of a canoe log to hold a rope for dragging and restraining the log down the mountain.

malau. Canoe bait carrier.

manono. Block set across a canoe to which the *'iako* (outrigger booms) were lashed.

manu. Ornamental carvings fitted onto the end pieces of a canoe.

manuihu. Beak carved as the bow-piece, likened to the *ihu* (beak) of a fowl.

miomio. Anything neat and trim like a well-shaped canoe.

moamoa. Sharp point at the stern of a canoe.

Mokuhali'i. God of canoe builders.

momoa. That section of a canoe below the rear cover.

mo'owa'a. Planks fitted on each side of a canoe, extending continuously fore to aft and strengthening the gunwales.

muku. Short, starboard ends of the *'iako* (crosssticks or outrigger booms); starboard side of the canoe.

muli. Stern of the canoe.

niao. Edge or rim of a canoe.

nohona wa'a. Canoe seat; thwart.

oeoe. Sprit of a sail.

'o'io. Name of a kind of stone used in polishing canoes.

'ōkumu. Canoe end pieces.

ōla'i. A pumice; light, porous stone used in polishing canoes.

'ōpea. Small boom holding up the outer and upper ends of a sail.

'ōpe'ape'a. Canoe sails.

pale. Gunwale strakes.

pale hope. Bearers of a canoe enroute from the forest to the beach. This group protected the aft part of the canoe.

pale mua. Bearers of the fore part of the canoe.

pale wa'a. Names of all the bearers "protecting" the new canoe from the forest on the way to the beach.

papa uhi wa'a. Board used to cover the space forward of the front outrigger boom.

pā'ū o Lu'ukia. Ornamental lashing of sennit from the canoe float to the outrigger boom. Named for the chastity belt of Lu'ukia.

pe'a. Canoe sail.

pepeiao. Blocks inside the canoe to which the *'iako* (booms) were fastened; cleats to which canoe seats were affixed.

peu. Point of a canoe bow.

pōhākau. Stone used for an anchor in fastening a ship's cable.

pōhākioloa. Stone used by fishermen as an anchor for a canoe; also used as a weight for deep-sea fishing.

pōhuehue. A kind of stone used in polishing canoes.

pola. High seat or platform between the canoes of a double canoe.

pōlena. Sails drawn tightly, furled, and made fast.

po'o. To press down upon the *ama* of a canoe.

po'o pao'o. Highest tip of the canoe end piece.

pou. Mast of a canoe.

pū. End pieces, fore and aft.

pū'ā. To cut off or hew obliquely, as in shaping the sharp ends of a canoe. (A.)

pueo. Shroud of a canoe or ship.

Pu i ka wa'a. God of the canoe builders.

puwalu. Ancient flag of the Hawaiians placed on the triangular sail of a canoe. (A.)

wae. Knees or side timbers in a canoe, boat, or ship. (A.) The u-shaped canoe spreader. (PE.)

waewa'a. Knees of a canoe; u-shaped canoe spreader.

CLOUDS

Ancient Hawaiians—while not familiar with English names of cloud formations like cumulus, cirrus, stratus, and nimbus*—did have their own words for most standard formations and also for many left undistinguished by Westerners.

To early Hawaiians clouds threatened rains and storms and portended evil as well. They appeared in clusters, banks, and layers, assumed long and short formations, and created majestic pillars and images above the horizon and in masses aloft. They reflected colors, including those of the rainbows.

Hawai'i enjoys the great variety and beauty of its clouds.

'āla'apapa. Long cloud formation.

'ālewalewa. Cloud or smoke floating on the air.

ānuenue. Rainbow. (Kin. 9:13; Ezek. 1:28.)

ao. General term for clouds.

ao akua. Godly cloud. *Fig.,* rainbow. (PE.)

ao 'ele'ele. Black cloud.

ao ho'opehupehu. Billowy, as a cloud.

ao kāhe'a. A kind of cloud as it appears on the horizon. No other data. (A.)

aokū. Cloud of rain or mist.

ao loa. Long cloud, high or distant; a stratus cloud. *O Kū ke aoloa, o Kū ke aopoko,* Kū is the long cloud, Kū is the short cloud.

aonuiho'olahalaha. Broad mass of clouds extending over a great space. (A.)

ao 'ōpiopio. White cloud. (PE.)

ao 'ōpua. Sharp-pointed clouds as they appear in the sky. *Me he mau ao 'ōpua la e kau ana, pela ke kau o ka make māluna o na kanāka,* as sharp-pointed clouds hang in the sky, so death hangs over men. See **'ōpua.**

ao panopano. Dark, thick cloud.

ao poko. Short cloud.

ao pōpolohua. Dark, bluish cloud. See **pōpolohua.**

ao pua'a. Fog or cloud banks assembling over mountains, frequently a sign of rain.

ao uli. Blue cloud, i.e., a blue sky, the firmament.

---

*There is no word for nimbus in Hawaiian.

ʻawaʻawa. Fog, mist, spray.

ʻeʻaʻeʻa. Cloudy; to cloud up.

ʻena. Opening in the clouds, said to be like the jaw of an *aʻu* (swordfish) and a sign of rain. (PE.)

hākuma. Thick cloud threatening rain.

hea. Cloudy, misty.

he ao newenewe. Thick, billowy cloud near the sea.

He ao hoʻomākōmakō. A thick black cloud.

He ao ʻōnohi ʻulaʻula. Expression signifying a rain or storm is near. A cloud with a rainbow is an example.

he oho paʻapū. Thickly or solidly covered over with fog or clouds.

hoʻokokohi. Threatening, as a cloud. *He ao hoʻokokohi,* threatening, as a thick, black cloud.

hoʻonākolo. A rolling of thunder, roaring of the surf.

ʻilio. Cloud with a threat or omen.

kaʻalelewa. Clouds that are driven swiftly or just float through the air (1 Tes. 4:17.)

kaʻapeha. An impressive, large mass of clouds.

kahaʻea. Cumulus or cirrocumulus cloud; a cloud reaching over the heavens, of several colors—variegated black, blue, white, and others—a frequent sign of rain.

kākai. Cloud that hovers near the ground. (A.) See **pali loa.**

ka ʻōpua haʻaheo i ka lewa, the cloud billow stands proudly in the high air.

kaula ʻelaʻe. Cloudless sky where details in the distance are plain.

kaupua. Elevated cloud of singular appearance; banks of clouds. *He kaupua maila nā ao,* the clouds are gathering in banks.

Keaonui. Farmers prayed to this god, Big Cloud, to protect their fields.

Kelaʻaonui. Farmers prayed to this god, Big Black Cloud, to protect the beginnings of their food plantings.

kia ao. Cloud pillar. (Nah. 12:5.)

kiaweʻula. Cloud, reddish or streaked with red.

kiʻikau. Clouds patterned in strips as alternating black and white; variegated.

kilo lani. Predictor who can "read" the clouds.

kiʻo wao. Mist or cloud that almost always settles on the hills of Oʻahu.

koʻiʻula. Rising, floating cloud of rainbow or reddish hue. See **uakoko.**

kōkōliʻi. Thick, black cloud.

Kona kai ʻopua i ka laʻi; ka hawanawana, Kona seas with cloud billows that promise peace.

kūoa. Cloud standing in an upright position. *Lit.*, standing cloud.

lalahiwa. Black, as a cloud.

liki. Rainbow; the bending of an arch upward, as a rainbow.

mākahakaha. The ceasing and clearing of rain; the slow dropping of rain.

māla'e. Cloudless sky.

manino. Calm and quiet after a storm.

māuli. Obscure cloud seen from a distance.

mōla'ela'e. Clear, bright, unobstructed.

nānā ao. Interpreter of clouds for signs and omens.

nulu. To rise and float off, as clouds or smoke. See **pōnulu.**

'ohu. Light cloud on a mountain.

'ōkupu. To rise and cover with dark-colored clouds, especially applied to clouds out on the ocean.

'ōnohi. Segment of a rainbow.

'ōpua. Cumulus cloud; narrow-pointed clouds hanging on the horizon; clouds of a singular shape seeming to rise out of the sea. *'O Kona kai 'ōpua i ka la'i, 'ōpua hīnano kau i ka mālie,* Kona with its billowy clouds and sea in the calm with puffy clouds like *hīnano* blossoms resting in the calm. See **ao 'ōpua.**

'ōpua ki'i. Clouds in the morning or evening taking shape as images.

ōpū ao. Cluster of clouds.

'ōwa'awa'a. Thick clouds portending a storm.

'owela. Land and vegetables scorched in the sun; cloudless drought.

pa'apū i na ao. Cloudy and thick.

paeki'i. Row of clouds on the horizon. *Lit.*, row of images.

pa'ihi. Cloudless.

pālāmoa. Bluish cloud. When seen in the east in the morning, it is considered a sign of rain.

pali kaulu 'ole ka lani. Serene sky without clouds.

pali loa. Cloud that lies low near the shore. See **kākai.**

pāpalaōa. Smooth kind of cloud indicating rain or wind. The name is derived from its resemblance to the fish *palaoa,* a whale or sea-elephant.

paulihiwa. Great thickness of dark, heavy clouds. (A.)

pōhai 'ula. Red cloud, as of dust.

po'ipū. Sky covered over with clouds.

polohiwa. Shining, black cloud.

poluluhi. Thick and heavy, as watery clouds hanging in the atmosphere.

pōnulu. To rise like a thick column of smoke. See **nulu.**

pōpolohua. Blue, as the sky on a clear day; cloudless. (A.)

pōpuaki'i. Place where pointed cloud clusters rise out of the sea.

pūlawa. To cover the sky with thick clouds or fog, rendering land and mountains invisible.

Pulelehua kea. Greater Magellanic Cloud. *Lit.,* white butterfly. (PE.)

Pulelehua uli. Lesser Magellanic Cloud. *Lit.,* dark butterfly. (PE.)

pululuhi. Hazy, foggy, cloudy.

pūnohu. Ascend as smoke, mist, or cloud.

pūnuhu. Cloud standing apparently erect, reflecting rainbow colors.

pu'unohu. Foot of a cloud hanging on a mountain; a thick cloud.

uakoko. Reflection of rainbow colors in an oncoming, erect, raincloud. *Lit.,* rain blood.

ua lanipili. Long-lasting, heavy rain; cloudburst. *He ua lanipili,* a shower touching the heavens. Clouds as they appear to touch the horizon. *Lit.,* sky to adhere.

COLORS

The native Hawaiians were alert to coining words about things in their environment such as clouds, sky, ocean, stones, flowers, birds and fishes. Qualifying adjectives were fashioned for concepts like color: streaked, very light, very dark, spotted, variegated, glossy, glistening, and striped. See the categories "Plants: Shrubs" and *"Kapa"* for other uses of colors.

'a'ai. Bright, as with contrasting colors.

a'ea'e. Dark, obscure, as a vision; to assume a softer, darker shade; to mix a dark or glistening color with a lighter one.

'āhina. Gray, as the head of an older man, *he'e po'o 'āhina;* white haired.

'āhinahina. Very light blue, gray, slate gray.

'ainakini. Navy blue, cotton cloth. (PE.) Blue, drab. (CMH.)

'ākala. Pink.

'ākulu. Species of color or a combination of colors. (CMH.)

'ano. Color.

'ele'ele. Black, dark colored; darkly. *Ke hele 'ele'ele nei au,* I walk in darkness. (Ioba. 30:28.) See **hiwa, polohiwa.**

hā 'ehu'ehu. Reddish brown or sandy, as hair.

hailepo. Ash gray pallor.

hāʻulaʻula. To be a little red.

hāuli. Dark, swarthy; dark clouds; the deep blue sky.

hāwena. Hoariness; the whitishness of gray hair.

helo. Reddish brown.

helohelo. Red, as the *ʻōhelo* berry.

hina. Gray, hoary, applied to the head.

hinahina. Gray, grayish.

hiwa. Clear black, applied mostly to sacrifices to the gods; a black *kapa.* See **polohiwa.**

hōʻaliʻali. Clear; to whiten.

hoʻoluʻu. Dye, color; to dip into coloring matter; to dye. (Puk. 25:5.) To dye, as a garment in a liquid. (Hoik. 19:13.) See **waihoʻoluʻu.**

hūʻali. Bright, clean, as polished metal; pure whiteness.

kaʻaōna. Reddish brown, red, the color of smoked fish.

kala keʻokeʻo. Variety of sweet potato, mainly white in color. See **keʻokeʻo.**

kala poni. Variety of sweet potato, purplish in color.

keʻo. White, clear, glistening white.

keʻokeʻo. White, as cloth or paper; white, as fruit that is white. See **kala keʻokeʻo**

keʻokeʻo ʻōlinolino. Glistening white.

kikokiko. Spotted, speckled in different colors, as a pig; striped.

kolekole. Reddish, as meat half-cooked.

kualiali. White, as lime or white paper; glistening, shining.

kuhe. A change of color in the skin—purple, blue, brown, etc.—a consequence of being long in the water.

lālawahi. Intense blackness. (CMH.)

lelolelo. Reddish, reddened.

lena. Yellow. See **melemele, ōlenalena.**

lipolipo. Deep blue, black.

loke. Rose, rosy. *Eng.*

lolohumea. Appearance of the verge of the ocean to one in a canoe. It seems green or just dark colored.

māʻaweʻawe. Spotted, variegated colors.

mākuʻe. Dark brown, any dark color. See **makuʻo.**

makuʻo. Brown. (A.)

maʻo. Green, greenness. See **ʻōmaʻomaʻo.**

maʻoha. Grayish, when contrasted with black, as gray hair.

māʻokiʻoki. Spotted, having different colors. Kona is noted for its streaked sea or currents in the ocean.

melemele. Yellow.

muimuia. Inharmonious colors compacted, as on a sheet of *kapa*.

nōkea, nākea. White; spotted, as the fish *nōkea*.

'ōhelohelo. Pink, rosy; to color pink.

ohiohi. To have substances of several colors or shades of colors united, as mahogany timber, curl-maple, curly *koa*, etc. (A.)

'ōlenalena. Yellow.

'ōma'oma'o. To be green or appear green, as vegetation.

'ōni'o, 'ōni'oni'o. Spotted, streaked with various colors; to spot or print with colors, as *kapa*.

'ōnohi 'ula. Deep red. (CMH.)

'ōpulepule. Spotted; light and shade.

pa'a. Solid or fast, as colors.

pala'ā. Almost any dark color, brown, purple, etc.

papala. Blue, green, black. *Redup.* of *pala* (yellow). *Ho'opala*, to turn yellow. See **uli, uliuli.**

pāni'oni'o. Variegated, of different colors; to print a *kapa* in gaudy colors. (A.)

pano. Deep blue-black, as ocean depths; black, as a fathomless abyss; deep, dark colored, as heavy clouds.

panopano. Black, glossy black. Intensive of *pano*. (Puk. 19:9.)

pano pa'u. Glistening black. Black streaks in grains of wood.

pāuli. Dark colored. *Pāuli ke kai*, Blue, as the sea.

pāuliuli. Dark blue, as the sky in the evening near the horizon. One of the signs of a *kaiko'o* or high surf. (A.)

pikapika, pikopiko. Variegated, spotted, usually applied to the smooth surface of the ocean in a calm. A meaning close to *mā'oki'oki*.

pō'ele, pō'ele'ele. Dark blue, black of the middle of the night. *Aloha pō'ele'ele!* Good night!

polihiwa. Bright, shiny, as applied to clouds. (A.)

polina. Shiny, black, deep blue. *Obs.*

polohiwa. Shiny black; dark, as a black cloud or *kapa*. (Puk. 19:16.) See **hiwa.**

pōlolohuamea. Deep green of the sea from afar.

polouhiwa. Dark brown, deep blue. Similar to *māku'e*. (A.)

poni. Mixture of colors; light, indistinct shades of color in cloth; a variety of sweet potato, purplish in color. A beautiful red dye can be made from *kalo*, a variety of taro. The stem is stripped off and squeezed in water; then lemon juice and *poi* are added for stiffening. (A.)

po'ohina. Gray haired, ash colored.

popolohua. Blue, as the sky above on a clear day. (A.) Purplish-blue, as the sea; dark, as a bruise.

pouli. To be or become dark, as night.

pulepule. Spotted, speckled, of different colors.

'ula. Red, even scarlet.

'ula hiwa. Purple, red, reddish-brown.

'ula'ula. Red, reddish; blood; a red *kapa*.

'ula'ula 'ahiahia. Faded red, i.e., purple.

uli. Blue or black.

uliuli. Cerulean blue, vegetation green, or dark-cloud black.

wai. Color, dye; general word for anything liquid.

waiho'olu'u. To dye, color; to immerse for coloring; a color or dye.

we'a. Red dye, red coloring matter.

we'awe'a. Red, reddish; spotted with red.

wehi. Blackness; a deep dark color.

wehiwehi. To be deep blue or black; to have black stripes.

wenawena. Red, of a reddish color; glow, as a fire or sunrise.

weo. Redness or rose color; to blush.

weoweo. Reddish, like fresh meat just killed.

CONUNDRUMS OF EARLY HAWAI'I

Hawaiians were fond of riddles. The list that follows was compiled by Dr. Charles M. Hyde and published in *Thrum's Almanac and Annual,* 1886 (68–69). It has been reproduced by other authors, some of whom added other riddles of their own. This is Hyde's original list.

The introductory Hawaiian phrase in each entry is the *nane,* riddle or conundrum; it is followed by the *ha'ina,* the explanation or answer, also in Hawaiian. An English translation of the riddle follows and finally its answer, in somewhat more detail than the simple Hawaiian.

Nane. Riddle, parable; to speak in parables. (Mar. 4:2)

1. *Ku'u punawai kau i ka lewa.*
   Niu.
   My spring of water high up in the clouds.
   Answer: a coconut.

2. *Ku'u wahi manu maka momona.*
   'O'o.
   My little bird with big eyes.
   Answer: the 'o'o, the bird that furnished the yellow and black feathers used in making a chief's cloak.
3. *Ku'u la'au, kokolo ke a'a'moe ka lau: mohala ka lau, moku ke a'a.*
   Wa'a.
   My tree; when the root holds, no leaf will grow: when the leaf grows, the root is broken.
   Answer: a canoe, with its anchor (root) and its sail or paddles (leaves).
4. *Ku'u kua kani loa, 'a'ole kau e pio ai.*
   Nalu.
   My *kapa kua*, log or block used for felting or pounding bark of the paper mulberry, that makes such a sound, *kani,* and I can't stop it.
   Answer: The surf.
5. *Ku'u wahi pu ko'ula i ka moana.*
   Anuenue.
   My bundles of red sugar cane in the ocean.
   Answer: the rainbow.
6. *Ku'u wahi hale iluna ka waha.*
   Wa'a.
   My little house with its door on top.
   Answer: a canoe.
7. *Ku'u wahi kuahiwi, lā'au li'ili'i.*
   Po'o.
   My mountain with little tress.
   Answer: the head with its hair.
8. *Ku'u manu, 'elua nuku.*
   Wa'a.
   My bird with two beaks.
   Answer: a canoe.
9. *Ku'u mau wa'a, he umi ihu.*
   Wāwae.
   My ten-beaked canoes.
   Answer: the feet.
10. *Ku'u moku, maluna ka iwi ka'ele.*
    Hale.
    My ship with my keel on top.
    Answer: a house with its ridgepole.

11. *Ku'u manu, ho'okāhi 'ēheu.*
    Wa'a.
    My bird with one wing.
    Answer: a canoe with one paddle.
12. *Ku'u ipu pākākā po'i pākākā, koko helele'i wale iho.*
    Honua, lani, ua.
    My big dish, with a big cover, dropping in pieces.
    Answer: the earth, the sky, the rain.
13. *Ku'u wahi hale, 'ewalu o'a, ho'okāhi pou.*
    Māmalu.
    My house with eight rafters and one post.
    Answer: an umbrella.
14. *Ku'u manu, e mahi'ai i ka 'ai, a waele i ka nāhelehele.*
    'Ō'ō.
    My bird that cultivates the ground and clears out the weeds.
    Answer: the '*ō'ō*, a digging stick; Hawaiian for spade or spud
    as well as the '*ō'ō* bird.
15. *Ku'u imu kālua loa a lō'ik'i.*
    Hē.
    My long underground oven.
    Answer: a grave.
16. *Ku'u manu noho pu me na kanaka.*
    Pueo.
    My bird, always in my house.
    Answer: the owl, *pueo,* which is the Hawaiian name both for
    that bird and for the strings that tied together the frame of a
    Hawaiian grass house.

CRIME AND PUNISHMENT

Justice in ancient times in Hawai'i was well abreast of the crime
rate. In those days penalties were assessed promptly and were usually directly imposed.

Note the many words for strangling, murder, forcible entry,
snatch and run, and theft and robbery. Also see the category called
"Kapu."

'a'ama. To steal, pilfer.
'aihue. To steal, rob; theft.
'aihue kanaka. To kidnap; one who kidnaps.

'aki. To slander, spread false reports.

'āpuka. To swindle, cheat, defraud, embezzle; forgery. See **kālā 'āpuka, palapala 'āpuka.**

e kaili wale. To seize, snatch, or plunder on the spur of the moment; extortion by force.

hana make. Instrument of destruction; murder; to kill or destroy.

hao. Robber; to take another's property by force.

hewa. Guilty. *Hana i ka hewa,* to do wrong, i.e., to commit adultery.

ho'āhewa. To find guilty. Also called *hoana e hō'eha kakakā.*

ho'āpono. Found not guilty.

ho'okānāwai. To impose a law. *Ho'okānāwai akula ia i kona wahi i hele ai, 'a'ole e hele hou; ho'okānāwai akula i na makamaka,* he made a vow not to go again to that place; he made a rule not to associate with those friends. (PE.)

ho'omake. To kill, cause death.

ho'opa'ahao. To imprison, jail.

ho'opa'i. To punish according to law.

ho'opuhi. To blow, cause to blow. *Fig.,* to steal. (PE.)

ho'opupu'e. To lie in wait; to watch for someone in order to injure him; to seize upon an intended victim suddenly.

huhuhue. To steal often; to filch secretly many times.

ka'ane. Strangling cord.

kā'awe'awe. Strangling, choking sensation.

kā'ili kū. To rob or plunder on the spur of the moment. Also called *kā'ili wale.*

kālā 'āpuka. Embezzlement.

kalaima, karaima. Crime, criminal. *Eng.*

ka lawe ola. Manslaughter, murder.

kānāwai. Law; to obey a law.

kānāwai ho'opa'i kalaima. Penal code.

kawa. To assassinate, kill in the dark.

kīmopō. To kill in the dark, rob in the dark, assassinate.

kinai. To kill by strangling, striking, piercing; to poison with medicine. (A.)

kolohe. To cheat, defraud; mischief maker or rascal.

kona make. Suicide.

ku'i pē. To beat to a pulp.

lawelawe lima. To assault, beat.

lawe malū. To steal.

lawe wale. Extortion; to seize property without the owner's knowledge.

lele. To come upon, as an officer upon a criminal. (A.)

lele kawa. To commit suicide by leaping from a precipice. Can also be a leap into the sea, as a pastime.

lī. To hang by the neck. (A.)

lima ʻāpā. Thief.

lima ikaika. To handle roughly, strongarm.

lima kolo. Murderer, assassin.

lima nui. To attack forcibly, beat.

lua. To kill by breaking the bones; the art of noosing men in order to murder them.

make. Killed, dead.

mio. To make off with quickly, steal.

mōkio. To steal something and dash away.

molulo. Thief; to steal.

moluna. Thief; to rob and plunder.

ʻōlelo a na hoʻike. Evidence, as presented in court.

ʻōlelo hoʻohola. Verdict of a jury.

ʻōlelo hoʻopaʻi. Penalty expressed as a sentence.

pākaha. Seizing another's property; robbery, plundering.

palapala ʻāpuka. Forged document.

paniki. Punishment; to punish. *Eng.*

peloni. Felony. *Eng.*

pepehi a make. To beat to death.

pepehi kanaka. To murder; a murderer.

pili i ka hewa. Found guilty.

poʻi pō. Attack by night.

pōpō ʻauhuhu. Venomous attack; to poison.

pōwā. Robber; to plunder. *E pōwā wale ka hele aku a ko haʻi, ʻāina—make,* like a robber to go on the land of others—death. (PE.)

puʻe. To attack, ravish, rape.

puheʻemiki. To steal and flee.

puʻua. To strangle.

ukuhala. Penalty for wrongdoing.

ʻumi, ʻuʻumi. To strangle.

ʻūpā. *Fig.,* an onslaught, furious attack. (PE.)

waiwai pio. Property taken in a robbery.

wāwāhi hale ʻaihue. Burglary; to break and enter. (PE.)

DIMENSION: Form and Measure

Without a written language and a corresponding ability to record information, the Hawaiians were unable to converse readily in terms of roundness, thickness, and length, unless they illustrated what they were talking about with gestures, using a pointing finger, hands, and even arms and elbows. Obviously, they succeeded well in such conversations, for their word-gestures, created to describe all types of known measures, were easily transferred to written form when the missionaries established the Hawaiian alphabet.

Notice the rather long series of words using *ana* (measure) in connection with the thing being measured. Hyde listed seven of these *ana* pairings and Pukui-Elbert added perhaps again as many; for example, *ana hola* (hourglass), *ana kaumaha* (to weigh), and *ana piwa* (thermometer).

Telling directions of the compass was a natural and necessary thing to do, and such items are covered in this category.

'aha. To stretch the *'aha* cord for the outline of a house so the posts may be properly placed; measure of a side.

'ahakū. Cord used for measuring, as in laying out a garden or a house.

'ahalualike. Figure of four right-angled corners with parallel opposing sides; right angled parallelogram.

'ākau. North, as indicated by a person facing the west, and extending his hand to his right. See **hema, hīkina.**

'aloaloa. Far, at a distance.

'ana. A measure, as cloth; measure of any kind.

'ana 'āina. To survey or measure land.

'ana'anapu'u. Out of a straight line; bent or crooked. (A.)

ana hola. Hourglass.

ana honua. Surveying; to measure the land surface of the earth. (PE.)

ana kaumaha. To weigh.

analipo. Distance; beyond and therefore below the horizon.

ana loa. Measure of length.

anana. Distance between the tips of a man's fingers with the arms extended on each side; a fathom.

anapa'a. Cubic measure.

ana paona. Balance or scales to measure weight. *Lit.,* pound measure. *Eng.*

ana piha. Measure of capacity.

ana pīwa. Thermometer for fever temperature. *Lit.,* measure fever.

anapuni. Circumference. *Lit.,* measure around; to encircle.

ʻanapuʻu. Corner formed by two lines meeting. (A.)

ana ua. Rain gauge; to measure rainfall.

anawaena. Diameter. *Lit.,* measure middle.

anawaena loa. Transverse diameter of an elipse.

ana waina. Liquid measure.

ana wela. Thermometer for measuring heat and cold in a dwelling.

ʻaoʻao kūpono. Perpendicular, of a triangle. (PE.)

ʻaoʻao loa. Hypotenuse. (PE.)

ʻaoʻao moe. Base of a triangle. (PE.)

apo. Circle, as in geometry.

ʻēlau. Pointed end of an object; tip. See **wēlau.**

haʻilima. Distance measured from the elbow to the end of the fingers; half a yard, a cubit.

hālau. To be long, to stretch out. (A.)

hānai. Radius. (CMH.) Also called *kahahānai.*

hema. South, as indicated by a person facing west who extends his left arm.

hīkina. East, the direction to the back of a person facing to the west.

hīkina ʻākau. Northeast.

hikina hema. Southeast.

hoʻana. To measure. See **ana.**

hoʻowiliwili. Circle.

huina. Right angle; corner where two roads meet; corner of a house.

huinahā. Quadrilateral or four-sided figure.

huinahā hiō. Four-sided figure, with equal sides but oblique angles; rhomboid.

huinahā hiō lōʻihi. Oblique parallelogram.

huinahā kaulike. Square.

huinahā like ʻole. Figure with four unequal sides.

huinahā loa. Rectangle.

huinahā lua like. Four-sided figure two of which are parallel.

huinakolu. Triangle.

huinakolu ʻelua ʻaoʻao like. Isosceles triangle.

huinakolu like. Equilateral triangle.

huinakolu peleleu. Obtuse triangle.

huina kūpono. Right triangle.

huinalima. Pentagon.

huina ʻoi. Acute angle.

huinaono. Hexagon.

huina peleleu. Obtuse angle.

huinawalu. Octagon.

iā. A yard, used as a unit of measurement. See **paʻaʻili ono,** a cubic yard.

iwilei. Measure from the collarbone to the end of the longest finger, arm extended; 1 yard.

kaʻawale. Distance between two places.

kaha. A line in mathematics.

kahahānai. Radius of a circle.

kahahiō. Line; multiplication symbol; slanting lines.

kahakū. Unit of measure, probably 8 feet. Fornander calls it 15 feet. (PE.)

kako, kado. Liquid measure of about 42 pints. (PE.) See **mekeleka, metereta.**

kālani. Gallon.

kānoa. Round, outside rim of the *ʻawa* bowl. (A.)

kapuaʻi kuea. Square foot.

kāwā. Distance between two points.

kīkoʻo. Span; measurement made between the thumb and forefinger; a line across the arc of a circle.

komohana. The west, place where the sun enters the sea.

kuaka. Quart.

kuea. Square.

kukuna. Radius of a circle.

lāʻau ana. Yardstick, rod stick, measuring stick. *Lit.,* stick measure.

laina. Line.

lalahū. Convex.

māka. Marker; to mark a line.

makahiʻa. To measure.

mana. Line projecting from another line.

mānoa. Thickness, as of a plank.

mekeleka, metereta. *Eng.* Liquid measure said to hold 42 pints. See **kako, kado.**

muku. Distance from the fingers of one hand to the elbow of the opposite arm when both arms are extended; a yard and a half. (DK.) See **paukū.**

nīao. Edge, groove, projection.

nui. Dimension, in the sense of magnitude, fullness, greatness.

'owa. Measurement equal to half the width of a finger, as applied to the mesh of a fishnet.

pa'a'ili ono. Solid with six sides; a cubic yard. See iā.

paina. Pint.

paukū. Distance from the ends of the fingers of one hand to the elbow of the opposite arm when both are extended. In geometry, a cylinder. See **muku.**

pe'ekue. Thick, as a plank.

pī 'ā. Measure of one's hand span. *Obs.* (PE.)

pio. A measure of cloth, ususally set at 3 feet. (PE.) This would be half a fathom.

pipi'o. Arch; bending line.

piu. A common but indefinite measure once used; the length of the arms extended from the sides of the body, fingertips to fingertips. This was called a fathom and was spoken of as 3 yards; $1\frac{1}{2}$ fathoms.

po'ai. Circle.

poe. Round; circular.

poepoe. Globe, sphere.

poho. Unit of measure equal to half a span. See **kīko'o.**

pūkele. Bushel.

waenakonu, waenakolu. Center of a circle.

wēlau, wēlelau. Tip, top, extremity. *Mai ke kumu, a ka wēlau,* from base to tip. See **'ēlau.**

DRESS

The usual mode of dress was based on the material *kapa.* A climax in ornamentation was achieved with certain kinds of feathers, largely from the '*ō'ō* and *mamo,* both of which were, in a sense, cultivated in their wild state. Apparel of this feathered magnificence was reserved for chiefly persons of the highest rank.

For a detailed consideration of the *kapa*-making process, see all categories under the heading **Kapa.**

This category also lists words for modern dress.

'a'a. Girdle, belt.

'a'ahu. Clothing in general.

'a'ahu ali'i. Royal robe made of colored *kapa;* regal attire reserved for those of high rank. (PE.)

'a'ahu 'olu'olu. Casual attire, *aloha* shirt. Also called *palaka aloha.*

'a'ahu pāwehe. Garment made from the soft *makaloa* mats typical of Ni'ihau. The design on the mat is *pāwehe,* geometric figures plaited in red-brown colors. (KILO.)

'a'ahu'ula, 'ahu'ula. Cloak or royal dress adorned with feathers. Originally such cloaks were red, *ula,* but now all cloaks are *'ahu'ula.*

a'a lole. Clothlike material that grows at the base of the coconut fronds. Other palms produce the *'a'a loulu,* a name applied later to woven foreign cloth. Kaua'i natives first gave this name to cloth. Also called *'a'a niu.*

aha laoa. Hair part of the ivory or whale *lei palaoa.* (CMH.)

'ahu. Fine mat used as a covering for the upper body, arms, and shoulders. See **ahuhīnana.**

ahuhīnana, ahuhīnalo. Garment plaited from fine strands of dried bracts from male flowers of the pandanus tree *(Pandanus odoratissimus).* The term *hīnano* means a fine, soft mat used for clothing. See **'ahu.**

'ahu moena. Fine, figured mat of different colors, usually red-brown or pale brown, used as a body covering in earlier times.

akea ka hua o ka lole. Full skirt. (PE.)

'āki. Locks of hair left behind the head after the hair above is shorn off. Also, long switches of hair added to the wearer's own locks.

'alaneo. Royal cloak or robe made of the feathers of the *mamo* or from those of another single kind of bird. An *'alaneo* garment is of one color only.

ala niho. Long strips of tattoo made on the skin by a tattooing instrument resembling rows of teeth. Points on the tattooing needles were made from bird bone, usually albatross. Shark teeth were not used but were part of the design in some patterns. (KILO.)

ālaulau. To clothe; clothes.

āmū. Shearing or shaving, as the hair from the head. *Kahi'umi-'umi,* to shave off the beard using a *pahi āmū* (razor).

'āne'ene'e. Old clothing.

apo pāpale. Hatband.

'eheu. Hat rim.

'ekeke'i. Short dress. *Lole wāwae 'ekeke'i,* shorts.

hanina. Woman's garment worn in early times, colored with *'ōlena* or turmeric; a *pā'ū,* wrap-around skirt.

hao a pa'ihi. To dress up in one's finery.

haukali. Dressed up in one's best clothes.

hāwele. To tie thongs on sandals or shoes.

hiki'i. To tie on, as a sandal.

ho'a'ahu. To clothe, to wear or put on clothing.

hoakalakala. Bracelet made of tusks or teeth from a boar or dog.

holokū. Loose, seamed dress with a train and usually a yoke, pattered after the Mother Hubbards of the missionaries.

komo lole. To dress.

ho'okomo. To dress another person.

ho'okomo lole. To dress, put on clothes; any garment.

ho'olu'elu'e. Loose, flowing gown.

hui kāhi. Short *malo;* girded in *malo* or *pā'ū* fastened with a single hitch.

hulu'i'i 'iwi. Feather cloak made or adorned with feathers of the *'iwi*. Now spelled *'i'iwi*.

hulu manu. Highly valued bird feathers used for royal dress.

hume. To bind around the loins, as a *malo*.

kā'awe. Cravat.

kā'ei. Hatband.

kāhai, kā'ai. Girdle or belt. (PE.)

kāhiko. To wear finery, dress up, adorn with royal robes of the early kings.

kākini. Sock or stocking.

kāma'a. Sandals or shoes.

kāma'a hakahaka. Openwork sandals or shoes.

kāma'a 'ili. Leather shoes.

kapa komo. Clothing in general. *Lit., kapa* enter (wear).

kepukapuka. Woman's *kapa* put over the head through a hole. (CMH.)

kīhei. Garment formerly worn by men and women. A loose garment of *kapa* thrown over one shoulder and tied in a knot. It was thrown off at work and during the warm part of the day.

kīki. To paint face or hair white with *pālolo* (clay).

kilo, kilo pōhaku. Kind of looking glass; close-grained black lava stone placed in water to give a reflection.

kōheoheo. Frock coat (not a jacket or dress coat); coattail.

komo. To wear or put on any garment, formerly only for the lower part of the body.

kuka. Coat. *Eng.*

kūpe'e. Bracelet or ornament; generally a string of shells *(pūpū-hoāka)*.

lakeke. Blouse, jacket. *Eng.*

laulau. Hat rim.

lei. String of beads, necklace; wreath of green leaves, flowers, or feathers.

lei hala. *Lei* made of *hala* fruit or keys.

lei pāpale. Hatband.

linohau. Beautifully dressed.

lole. Clothes, dress; to wear clothes.

lolehana. Working dress or garment.

lole holoi. Clothes ready for laundry.

lole i ka paʻa mua. Readymade clothes.

lole kahiko. Dress, well ornamented.

lole komo. Clothes, in general.

lole moe pō. Night dress.

lole wāwae. Clothes for the legs; trousers, slacks, panties.

lole wāwae ʻekekeʻi. Shorts.

lole wāwae ʻepane. Overalls.

lole wāwae loloa. Long underwear, long dress.

lole wāwae palemaʻi. Drawers, undershirt.

luʻeluʻe. Long, loose robe, as used by Biblical characters. (Eset. 8:15.)

lulu aliʻi. Garment of bird feathers; robe of royalty.

mahiole. Feathered headdress or helmet worn by chiefs in gala or warlike attire.

malo. Strip of *kapa* worn by men around the loins; loincloth worn when at work.

muku. Short garment, as if the bottom were cut off.

muʻumuʻu. Slip or undergarment worn by females; today usually applied to a long, full, and casual-wear dress.

ʻōkakala. Rough kind of cloth.

ʻōkolepuʻu. Bustle-style dress. *Lit.,* buttocks bumped. (PE.)

ʻōmau. To tuck in the *pāʻū.*

ʻōpū palaoa. Ornament made of a whale tooth. (A.)

pā. Flat-topped hat.

paʻa. Suit of clothes.

paʻa kāmaʻa. Pair of shoes.

paʻa lole. Suit of clothes.

paʻihi. Dressed in one's best clothes.

paikini. Dressed in tight-fitting clothes, a fashion of an earlier time.

pākana. Shirtwaist, blouse.

palaka. Shirt made from block-print cloth; a short shirt.

palaka aloha. An *aloha* shirt.

palaoa. Ornament made from a whale tooth suspended as a necklace by braids of human hair.

pālaulau. Mat of *kapa* used as a wraparound.

palekoki. Skirt, petticoat. *Eng.*

palekoki lōʻihi. Long or lengthened skirt or petticoat.

palemaʻi. Undershirt. *Lolo wāwae palamaʻi,* drawers.

pale maka. Veil for the face.

pālule. Loose undergarment for men; a shirt.

palūpalū. *Pāʻū* colored yellow; a kind of yellow *kapa.*

pāpale. Hat, head covering.

pāpale kapu. Cap.

pāpale kua. Hat made of sugarcane stem. Also called *pāpale kua pō.*

pāpale manila. Manila hat.

pāpale muomuo. Poke bonnet. *Lit.,* hat blunt. (PE.)

pāpale ʻoʻoma. Bonnet, sunbonnet. *Lit.,* bonnet flared.

pāpale pīwa. Beaver hat.

pāpale waiokila. Panama hat.

pāpalu. Dress worn when employed in dirty work that would damage a common dress; an apron, a covering. *Kui ihola lāua i no lau piku a paʻa, i mau pāpalu no lāua,* they sewed fig leaves together and made themselves aprons. (Kin. 3:7; A.)

pāʻū. Principal garment of Hawaiian females, consisting of a number of *kapa,* generally five, wound around the waist and reaching the knees. (A.) Skirt worn by women horseback riders. (PE.)

pāʻū heihei. *Pāʻū* festooned with leaves or ferns; a sarong made of leaves.

pāʻū hula. Dancing skirt. (PE.)

pāʻū laʻi. Ti-leaf skirt.

piko. Hat crown.

pine, pina. Pin or article for fastening the hair on the sides of the head.

pōhaka. Printed or painted *kapa;* girdle or belt.

pōholoholo. Ill-fitting clothes; loose-fitting.

pōhuehue. Poetic name for a fisherwoman's skirt. (PE.)

pola. End of a *kapa* thrown over the back. (A.) Flap or trailing part of loincloth or sarong. (PE.)

pūʻali. *Malo.* Because of its use as a warrior's loin cloth, it needed to be tightly secured around the waist.

pue. Feather *lei* made from short, firm feathers not as soft as *ʻēʻē* feathers.

pūkae. Wash used in dyeing hair.

pūkikī. Term used in describing tight-waisted dresses for females.

pūliki. Vest; any garment girded around the body.

pūloʻu. Veil, covering for the head.

pūlunaluna. Clothes thrown carelessly together.

pūnono. To be dressed gorgeously; to make attractive, as with the red of a *kapa* or other colors.

pūpūhoaka. Bracelet of shells.

wahi. Wrapper, sheath; to bundle up.

waikaua. Robe used in war. (A.) War temple. (PE.)

wāwae olonā. Linen breeches.

DYES: Plant Sources

The first Polynesians from the Marquesas Islands may have arrived in Hawaiʻi about 750 A.D. Whenever it was, they probably brought to this new land their knowledge of dye plants, dye making, and its various techniques. And it is likely that a most significant plant involved was the turmeric, *ʻōlena (Curcuma domestica),* which produces a yellow dye. An important craft was developed around the raising of dye plants, the obtainment of materials and manufacture of dyes, and the creation of designs to be applied to *kapa,* the only "cloth" available.

Many listings of dye plants, colors, and uses include those of William T. Brigham, Samuel M. Kamakau, David Malo, and, in 1978, a new approach by Van Frieling Krohn.

ʻakala, ʻakalakala. Two endemic species of raspberries, *Rubus hawaiiensis* and *R. macraei,* growing mainly above 4,000 feet. Both are called *ʻākala* or *ʻakalakala.* The juice of their berries provides an ingredient for lavender and pink dyes. Attempts at crossing the *ʻākala* with the thimbleberry *(R. rosaefolius)* and the common blackberry have resulted in improving the flavor of the fruit. (NEAL 391.)

ʻalaea. Lipstick plant *(Bixa orellana),* the arnatto dye plant, is called *ʻalaea* because it resembles yellow or red earth. The scarlet covering of the nearly globose seed capsule yields a bright yellow, almost tasteless, dye used to color butter, margarine, and cheese. The common name, lipstick plant, attests another wide and popular use of the red seed covering. Fiber from its bark is used for cordage, and its stems for an Arabic, gum-like substance in South America, etc. (NEAL 589.) A post-Cook introduction.

alahe‘e haole. Mock orange *(Murraya paniculata; M. exotica),* a tree or shrub which is ornamental and its berries inedible. Its leaves are used in dyes. Introduced.

aloalo. Red or Chinese hibiscus *(Hibiscus rosa-sinensis),* now a cosmopolitan hedge bush. When crushed, its red flowers turn black yielding dark, purplish dyes. The leaves are also used for dyes. (NEAL 556.) Introduced.

aloalo pupupu. Double flowering hibiscus. The blossoms from this plant supply dye ingredients. (NEAL 556.) Introduced.

‘awapuhi ke‘oke‘o. White ginger, butterfly lily, ginger lily *(Hedychium coronarium).* A source of pure white flowers very popular for *leis* and also a source of perfume. Its leaves are used for dyes. (NEAL 252.) Introduced.

‘awapuhi ‘ula‘ula. Red ginger *(Alpinia purpurata),* a common ornamental in Hawai‘i. Its leaves supply dye materials. (NEAL 260.) Introduced.

hau-kea kea. Sea hibiscus *(Hibiscus tiliaceus).* Leaves are used for dyes. (NEAL 559.)

hili. General name for the ground-up bark of *kukui, koa, kōlea,* or *noni* trees mixed with gums, saps, etc., and used for dye purposes. All native.

hili koa. Bark of the *koa* tree, used in dyes. See **koa.**

hili kōlea. Bark of the *kōlea* tree, used to dye *kapa* black. See **kōlea.**

hili kukui. Bark of the *kukui* tree, used in dyes. See **kukui.**

hili noni. Bark of the *noni* tree, used in dyes. See **noni.**

kamani haole. False *kamani* or tropical almond *(Terminalia cattapa),* a tree from the West Indies. It grows best on sandy shores. The leaves and fruit supply ingredients for dyes. (NEAL 627.) Introduced.

ki. Shrubby ti plant *(Cordyline terminalis).* For a comprehensive list of uses, see **Plants: Uses.** Leaves of the *ki* are called by such names as *la‘i, laki, lau‘i* and are used for their red and green colorings. (NEAL 203.)

kiele. Gardenia *(Gardenia* sp.), a small shrub. Its scented flowers are used for leis, its leaves for dye. (NEAL 799.) The species called *nānū* is native.

koa. Mimosa *(Acacia koa),* the monarch of trees in Hawai‘i. For its many applications, see **Plants: Uses.** Wood shavings from this tree are processed for obtaining dye materials. (NEAL 410.)

kōlea. Small native tree *(Myrsine* spp.) growing in bogs and wet summit forests. Charcoal from the wood and its red sap are used to dye *kapa,* the wood to make houses, and the logs to beat *kapa.* (NEAL 664.)

kukui. *Kukui* tree *(Aleurities moluccana).* For its many uses, see **Plants: Uses.** It supplies a brown dye from its inner bark, and a black dye is made from the burnt soot of the ripe nuts. (NEAL 506.) Native.

liliko'i. Yellow passion fruit *(Passiflora edulis),* named after a gulch in Maui. The fruit is berrylike and often called granadilla or water lemon. Its leaves are used for a dye. (NEAL 597.) Introduced.

mai'a. Bananas *(Musa* spp.). Classified as large herbs but tree-like in form. Leaves supply a dye, as does the sap. (NEAL 245.) Native and introduced varieties.

manakō. Mango *(Mangifera indica).* Sometimes called the "king of fruits" for it is one of the finest and best known of tropical tress. It grows to about 70 feet and its luxuriant, heavy foliage makes it a good shade tree. The common mango tree bark and Hayden mango leaves supply two dyes. (NEAL 521.) Introduced.

ma'o. Hawaiian cotton *(Gossypium tomentosum),* also called *huluhulu.* A good, green dye can be made from the leaves. (NEAL 566.)

nani o Hilo. Christmas-berry tree *(Schinus terebinthifolius),* also called *wililaiki* (Willie Rice). Highly ornamental because of its gnarled, furrowed trunk, dark-green foliage, and the abundant fruit of the female tree. Both leaves and berries are used for dyes. (NEAL 525.) Introduced.

n'āū, nānū. Two species of the genus Gardenia: **1.** *Gardenia brighami,* a tree with fragrant, white blossoms. The yellow pulp of the fruit is used to dye *kapa* yellow. **2.** *G. remyi,* a tall tree attaining a height of 40 feet. Leaf buds are used as a glue. The pulp of this fruit is used to dye *kapa* yellow. (NEAL 800.)

naupaka kahakai. Beach *naupaka (Scaevola sericea; S. frutescens).* For its many uses, see **Plant: Uses.** The leaves supply materials for dyes. (NEAL 820.)

noni. Indian mulberry *(Morinda citrifolia).* Small evergreen tree or shrub. For uses, see **Plants: Uses.** The root bark is used for red and yellow dyes. (NEAL 804.)

nukolani. Eucalyptus (genus *Eucalyptus).* The Hawaiian name is a combination of New Holland and *palēiwa,* meaning to ward off fever. Some species of these trees supply timber and tannin, others a gum or oil for medicine. Rust-red dyes come from the leaves. (NEAL 640.) Introduced.

ōhai. Monkeypod, rain tree *(Samanea saman)*. See **Plants: Uses.** Leaves of the *'ōhai* are used for dye. (NEAL 401.) Introduced.

'ōhai 'ula. Royal poinciana *(Delonix regia)*. A leguminous tree from Madagascar, one of the most showy ornamentals in Hawai'i. Lavender and purple dyes come from this tree. Introduced.

'ōhi'a'ai. Mountain apple *(Eugenia malaccensis)*, a handsome native tree of India and Malaya. In Hawai'i it grows in most wet and shady valleys. Dyes are extracted from its leaves (NEAL 636.) Introduced.

'ōhi'a kea. White mountain apple *(E. malaccensis)*. Inner bark used for dye. (NEAL 636.)

'ōlena. Turmeric *(Curcuma domestica)*. See **Plants: Uses.** Dyes for *kapa* are derived from the steamed roots, a deep orange; and from the raw roots, a light yellow. (NEAL 256.)

pā nini. Prickly pear *(Opuntia megacantha)*. Fruits, when peeled and treated according to a recipe, may furnish a brown, light green, or red dye, depending on the color of mordanting. (NEAL 607.) Introduced.

pā nini 'awa'awa. Star cactus *(Aloe barbadensis; A. vera)*. A well-known plant in Hawai'i. With their stiffness and radial symmetry they fit well into rock gardens, enjoying direct sunlight. A few species yield the commercial "aloes," a resinous purgative. Aloine is the coloring agent of the dye. (NEAL 196.) Introduced.

piku. Fig *(Ficus carica)*. Perhaps a native of Asia Minor. It is an ancient and valuable fruit tree. All parts of the fruit are edible. Its leaves are a source of dye. (NEAL 309.) Introduced.

pōpō lehua. Ixora *(Ixora casei)*, a common ornamental in Hawai'i. Many small, deep red, odorless flowers develop in clusters up to eight inches in diameter. The handsome leaves provide a source of dye materials. (NEAL 802.) Introduced.

pōpolo. Black nightshade *(Solanum nigrum)*. Small cosmopolitan herb. Its juicy, black berries are edible. An unusual green dye comes from the leaves and berries.

'uki'uki. Native Hawaiian lily (genus *Dianella*), with a short stem and long narrow leaves among which arises a cluster of small blue flowers. The berries supply a choice blue dye. (NEAL 191.)

'ulu. Breadfruit *(Artocarpus altitis)*. An attractive tropical tree that ranges to 60 feet in height. The leaves and inner bark are used for dyes. (NEAL 302.) See **Plants: Uses.**

waiawī ‘ula‘ula. Purple strawberry guava *(Psidium cattleianum;* P. *Littorale).* A shrubby tree, growing up to 20 feet in height, fruit which is edible, is purplish and about an inch in diameter. A dye is made from its leaves. (NEAL 633.) Introduced.

wauke. Paper mulberry *(Broussonetia papyrifera).* A small tree or shrub, also called *po‘a‘aha.* The inner bark is used in making dye. (NEAL 301.)

EARTHY EXPRESSIONS

The expressions in this category are open and frank regarding the relations of men and women. There was a great deal of sexual freedom and permissiveness among the Hawaiian natives, who readily coined words describing all aspects of intimacy. Since such words and expressions were created for use in speech alone, many may have been lost; others are found today in dictionaries of the Hawaiian language.

‘aikāne. Intimate friend or companion of the same sex.

‘ako. Veneral disease.

‘alu‘alu. Fetus, foetus; young in the later stages of development in the womb.

‘eku. Motion of the fetus in the uterus.

hā‘ae. Saliva when worked into foam in the mouth.

ha‘akōhi. Labor pains in childbirth.

ha‘akokōhi. Suffering from strong labor pains. (Hal. 48:6.)

hailepo. To evacuate the bowels.

hāko‘i. Paraphimosis, a physical restriction encountered in male children.

hanawai. Menstruation. (A.)

hawa. To be daubed with excreta; to be defiled.

hēleu, hāleu. *Welu,* a piece of torn *kapa* used to clean the buttocks.

hena. Buttocks. *Mons pubis;* hollow of the thigh; nakedness. See *pu‘ukole.*

he wa‘awa‘a ka lae. Expression of blackguardism, scoundrelism. (A.)

hilo. Running sore, issuance; *waikī* (gonorrhea). (Oihk. 15:3.)

holouka. To break wind. *Makani uka,* wind from behind.

honihoni. To kiss or smell repeatedly, sniff. (PE.)

honowā. Polite term for human excrement, but an insulting epithet for the commoners. See **kūkae.**

hoʻoipo. To woo, court. *Ipomanuahi,* mistress.

hoʻoipoipo. To court or woo romantically.

hoʻokāne. Platonic relationship initiated by the woman.

hoʻokūʻamiʻami. To make the motions of a hinge; to make motions, perhaps indelicate ones, like a hinge. (A.)

hoʻopalani. To cause a strong offensive smell, as that of tar, sulphur, etc.

hoʻopāpā. The condition of a female having a board tied to her abdomen, a taboo to sexual relations. (MALO 138.)

hoʻopiʻopiʻo. Licentious revel. (CMH.)

hoʻoʻulaulauʻaka. To enjoy, as the union of the sexes. (A.)

ʻihaʻiha. Discomfort in restraining oneself from a call to nature.

ʻīloli. Unpleasant sensations of pregnancy.

ʻinaʻina. Reddish evacuation that precedes labor pains.

ipo. Sweetheart, paramour, lover. (Ier. 4:30.)

ipoipo. To make love.

kahaule, kaheule. To circumcise; to slit the foreskin horizontally in the Hawaiian fashion.

kake. Kind of secret, artificial language used in speaking and writing as a means of covert communication among chiefs. *Hula kake,* a *hula* done in a chant using this language. Used mostly for licentious purposes.

kāmehai. Frankly mischievous, as a young boy.

kaomi. To press down, squeeze with downward pressure; to massage firmly with the back of the hand.

kapakapa. Human crotch.

kauhua. State of pregnancy; *ua kauhua, ua kō, ua hāpai.*

kekē. Word of caution to children to cover their nakedness. (A.) Admonition to a female to sit properly. (PE.)

kikiʻo. To void stool, discharge feces.

kiʻo. To break wind, void an excrement.

kiʻona. Dung-hill, privy, backhouse.

koaka. To act the debauchee; a dissolute.

koʻala. Uterus; placenta of the female.

kohe. Vagina.

kohoko. Disease of the uterus. (A.) Probably syphilis. (PE.)

koholua. Hard, polished bone used to induce abortion.

kohopuna. First menstruation.

kokohī. Travail in birth, labor pains.

kola. Term of derision for an oversexed person. (PE.)

kuakoko. Pains of childbirth; to travail. (Isa. 23:4.)

kūkae. Excreta. See **honowā.**

kū'oha. Venereal desease.

lā'aupā. Ancient medicine used to produce an abortion. *Lit.,* medicine barren.

māhū. Homosexual.

māhu'i. Shy conduct in a female by which she hopes to express to a member of the opposite sex her desire for him. (A.)

ma'i. The private parts of either men or women. (A.) Ill, sick, menstruating. (PE.)

ma'i wili. Venereal disease. *Lit.,* writhing sickness.

mau. To terminate, as the menstruation period.

mimi. To urinate. Less commonly called *mī.*

moe'aikāne. Sodomy. *Lit.,* friend mating. (1 Kor. 6:9.)

moekolohe. To commit adultery.

nahu kuakoko. Suffering, pain, as a woman in travail. (Mika. 4:9.)

nahunahu. Throes of birth pains.

nehiwa. Lascivious talk. The word *nehiwa* means *wahine* in secret language (transposed).

neko. Offensive smell, stench. Also called *niku, nikuniku.*

'ō'iliwale. Untimely birth; prematurely unfolded. (Kekah. 6:3.)

'ōkole. Anus, buttocks.

'okolekē. Kind of unintelligible play or foreign language created for unsavory purposes.

'ōlohe. Sick, as a woman in childbirth.

'olomua. Foreskin. (Ier. 4:4.) Called '*ōmaka* in 1884 ed.

'ōpe'a. Testicle, scrotum.

pā. Barren, as a female.

pākiāi. To forsake wife or husband and live in adultery; barren.

pala. Syphilis.

pale. When a midwife delivers a baby.

panipani. To commit adultery. An unsavory word, said to be of Chinese origin by Chamisso, author of the first Hawaiian grammar. (A.)

pānoa. Easily persuaded, as a woman at the call of any man. *Lit.,* touch freely. (PE.)

pela. To be unclean and smelly.

piha. To be pregnant.

pihi. Venereal disease.

pilau. Dirty, filthy, especially having a bad smell.

pi'opi'o. Whoremonger. (Heb. 13:4.)

pipine. Promiscuous person.

poholo. To miscarry by premature birth.

pūʻao. *Os tincae* or orifice of the womb.

puʻe. To solicit strongly; to seduce, as a virgin; to ravish, rape, compel. (Puk. 22:16.)

pūhene. To tempt to different kinds of wickedness.

puhikaokao. To burst open or burst the skin; a venereal sore.

pūhiʻohiʻo, pūhihio. To break wind noiselessly (PE), audibly. (A.)

pūhiʻu. To break wind, audibly. (PE.) To break wind. (A.)

punalua. To have in common several wives or husbands.

puʻukole. *Mons veneris.* See **hena,** hollow of the thigh. (Kin. 32:25.)

puʻupaʻa. In a virgin state, freedom from impurity.

ueueko. Stench; unpleasant to smell.

ūhā. To belch up wind, to hawk up phlegm *(pūhā);* thigh or lap.

uhaua. Testicles. (Ioba 40:17.)

ʻūhene. To play a merry tune; to converse quietly and romantically; to tease coquettishly. (PE.)

ule. Penis.

ule hilo. Gonorrhea. Also called *waikī.*

ule hole. To practice onanism (masturbation).

weka. First dark excreta of an infant; meconium.

wewe. After-birth *(ʻiʻewe);* the connecting of the navel string.

EATING AND FOOD

Great dependence was placed on earth ovens of various types, and the food cooked within them required wrappings or coverings of certain leaves to insulate foodstuffs from the heat and flames.

The high value placed on *poi* is evidenced by its common recurrence in the definitions. In addition to *poi,* a staple food, products of the ocean played an important part in the diet of the native Hawaiians. Fishing was a big business and certainly one of the most important kinds of work.

Eating habits are aptly described, and due notice must be taken of the number of words addressed to the pleasantness or fullness of the stomach after finishing a meal.

ʻaʻaho. To put up *pia* in small packages. See **pia.**

ʻahaʻaina. Feast or large dinner party. For names and kinds of meals and feasts, see entries under *ʻahaʻainu* in Pukui-Elbert.

ahuʻai. Place for storing food. (CMH.)

ahuliʻu. Hot stones heated in an oven; white hot, as stones in an *imu*.

ʻai. Food, vegetable food as distinguished from meat *(iʻa)*; to eat, taste.

ʻai a hewa ka waha. To eat to satiety.

ʻai ahulu. Food baked a long time in the oven; overcooked food.

ʻai ʻakaʻakai. To eat bulrushes (fresh *poi*, which was not liked). (PE.)

ʻai ʻakakai. New, fresh, sweet *poi* just pounded from taro. Such food is also called *polokē*. (A.)

ʻai a māʻona. To eat as much as one likes.

ʻai hāhā. Taro tops, a food of poor people. (A.)

ʻaihue. To steal food; to steal, generally. *Lit.,* food steal.

ʻai ia. Eaten.

ʻai iho. To eat.

ʻai kapu. To eat in accordance with the restrictions of the *kapu;* e.g., the separation of the sexes during meals.

ʻai kau. Method of feeding children or persons of high birth, as dropping a morsel of *poi* into an open mouth. This was looked upon as a game among children. (PE.)

ʻai kohana. To eat alone.

ʻai lau. To eat a great quantity of food.

ʻaina. Meal.

ʻaina ahiahi. Supper, dinner.

ʻaina awakeo. Lunch.

ʻaina kakahiaka. Breakfast.

ʻai noa. To eat, as out from under the restraint of the *kapu.*

ʻai nui. To eat too much.

ʻai pala maunu. To eat a dab of bait. *Fig.,* to eat the leavings of others.

ʻai pilau. To eat filth, rotten food. A word fittingly applied to a sorcerer who prays others to death. (PE.)

ʻai pūepuehu. Partially cooked *taro.* In pounding, its parts are easily scattered.

ʻaiʻuhaʻuha. To eat riotously; a lower class of chiefs eating wastefully.

akaʻai. To eat slowly, carefully.

akepaʻa. Liver. *Lit.,* liver firm. (Oihk 3:4.)

ake pipi. Beef liver.

ālaʻalae. Hard or half cooked, as *taro.*

ʻalaʻalaheʻe. Spawn or black substance in squid eaten with *kukui* nuts as a relish. (A.)

alaō. To swallow small fish, including *'o'opu,* whole.

ala'oma. To swallow greedily, as a fish swallows bait. A variant of *alaō, ala'ume.*

alapoho. To gulp down, swallow whole.

ali. To swallow whole.

'amu. To eat voraciously.

ana poluea kēhu. To be so full that one is nauseated and the abdomen distended.

'ānuhenuhe. Not sufficiently cooked; the eating of food, fish or meat, that is spoiled. (A.)

'ao. Dried *taro* or sweet potatoes. Also applied to hardtack.

aumiki. Water kept in a calabash. The chief drinks *'awa,* which is very bitter, then drinks this water which he thinks is very bitter.

'eho. Red-hot stones placed inside a carcass in cooking, especially in cooking underground. The *'eho* stones in the Bishop Museum are the size for chickens and wild birds.

hā'ae. Beer made from fermented sugarcane. (A.) Beer made from a variety of sweet potato. (PE.)

hala 'ai. Edible pineapple *(hala).*

hala 'aina. Eating house for women in early times.

hala-kahiki. Foreign pineapple.

hala-kea. White pineapple.

halalē. To eat noisily; to slurp, as soup. (PE.)

hala 'ula. Red-tinged pineapple.

hamu. To eat voraciously; to scrape up and eat what is left.

hanaiahuku. To feed well; filled out and plump.

hanai 'ai. Provider of food.

haona. Certain calabashes used for food when first cooked.

hapu'u. Edible fern.

haupa. To eat heartily.

hāupia. Pudding made from a mixture of arrowroot *(pia)* and coconut.

hāwai. To throw water on an earth oven to make steam.

hiala 'ai. To eat hungrily.

hō'ā. To kindle a fire.

hoa 'ai. Eating companion. (1 Nal. 1:41.)

hō'ai. To thin with water to make a good consistency of *poi.*

ho'ina. Parting gift after a feast.

holo 'ai. Food package, especially a ti-leaf bundle of hard *poi.* (PE.) See **kīholo.**

ho'ohiala. To eat greedily, cram food.

ho'ohiala'ai. To encourage stuffing with food.

ho'okukū. To eat to uncomfortable fullness, eat voraciously.

hoʻolua. To cook over again, bake twice.

hoʻomahu. To eat sparingly.

hoʻomāʻona. To fill oneself with food.

hoʻonapele. To digest food.

hoʻonuʻu. To stuff to fullness, eat greedily.

hoʻopāiki. To eat sparingly.

hoʻopiha. To eat heartily.

hoʻowale. To digest food.

hopilole. To eat slowly and carefully, as a sick person.

huaʻi. To open the oven. Also called *huaʻai*. Also an egg for eating; grain, as fruit for food.

iʻa lāwalu. Fish cooked in ti leaves or broiled over coals.

imu. Earth oven, a place for baking made by heating stones underground. See **umu.**

ʻīnai. Food eaten with *poi*.

ʻinamona. Meat of the *kukui* nut roasted and pounded with salt, as a relish. See **kukui.**

ʻio. Bundle or package of food.

ʻioliu. Tenderloin. The outside flesh is called *uhao*.

ipu. Watermelon *(Citrullus vulgaris)*. Also called *ipu haole, ipu ʻai maka,* words for gourds in general. (NEAL 810.)

kaʻa. Chewed food.

kaea. Loss of appetite. A phonetic Hawaiian term for tired.

kaʻele. Partly-filled calabash, with some empty space remaining at the top. (A.) Empty hollowness. (PE.)

kāʻeo. Full, as a calabash with food.

kaheaʻai. Summons to dine.

kāhela. One who has eaten much. Generally said of one who has finished a good meal.

kahukahu. To offer food and prayers.

kaielo. Water of the coconut, mixed with other ingredients such as shrimp and served as sauce.

kai helo. Shrimps pounded with water and other ingredients. Same as *kaielo. Lit.,* sauce red.

kaikea. Fat of hogs or other animals.

kalo. Taro *(Colocasia esculenta)*. It has many uses, but *poi* is the most important. A staple food in Hawaiʻi.

kā palu. Deprecatory word for food.

kelekele. Fat, grease; fat meat generally.

kēpā. Fruit of the almond tree used in seasoning food.

kī. Ti, tea. *Eng.*

kiʻai ʻai. Food guardian.

kīhamu. To eat daintily and proudly; to eat fragments.

kīhau. To eat sparingly.

kīholo. Package of food. See **holoʻai.**

kinanape. Crammed, stuffed with food.

kiʻo poi. *Poi* calabash. (A.)

kō. Sugarcane. See **Plants: Uses.**

kōʻalaʻala. Food scraps.

kōʻelepālau. Pudding made of sweet potatoes and coconut.

kohi. Fat piece of pork.

kōkaʻa. Lean meat.

kolekole. Meat that is not well cooked.

kope. *Eng.* Coffee, coffee beans. (NEAL 800.)

kopole. Cooking fish by wrapping it in leaves and roasting. (A.)

kuaina. Twine, string.

kualakai. Kind of raw fish mashed finely with other foods in preparation for hand-feeding in pulp form by the *kau* method. (PE.) *Mālolo* fish were frequently served in this way. (A.)

kuawa. Guava. *Eng.*

kuenenuʻu. Completely stuffed.

kuhinia. Unpleasant feeling from eating rich foods.

kukui. The *kukui* nut cooked as a relish. See **ʻinamona.**

kukuli. Unpleasant feeling in the stomach, as produced by food. (A.)

kūlepe. To split a fish open from head to tail for salting and drying.

kūlolo. Pudding made of grated taro mixed with grated coconut and baked in an earth oven.

kūpalu. To stuff with food, fatten.

kupo ʻakai. To eat *poi* with salt or relish, *ʻinamona,* and sweet potatoes, without greens or meat. (PE.)

kūpuʻu. Taro or sweet potatoes eaten with no other preparation than scraping or baking. (PE.)

laiki. Rice.

lau ʻai ia. Salad.

laulau. Food package wrapped in ti or banana leaves, containing foods baked in an underground oven.

laulau puaʻa. Entrails of a pig cooked in an underground oven.

lāwalu. Fish wrapped in ti leaves and roasted on coals.

lelo. Hung up in the smoke; smoked red. This term refers to well-cooked meat, particularly pork, because old-time Hawaiians did not use much meat. (DK.)

lilio. Plump, full, well fed. (A.)

lūʻau. Young taro leaves, gathered and cooked for food; a Hawaiian feast.

lumi ʻaina. Dining room.

lumi kuke. Kitchen.

luna ʻai. Food inspector.

mahaha. Soft and mealy, as potatoes.

maia. Bananas. See **Plants: Uses; Bananas.**

maka. Raw, in contrast to cooked, as with any raw, uncooked flesh.

mama. To chew without swallowing.

mana ʻai. Food chewed by an adult for a child to eat.

manakō. Mango.

māʻona. Fullness of food; to satisfy oneself with food.

māʻona ʻai. To eat sparingly.

māʻona loa. Completely full.

māʻona ʻoe? "Have you eaten?"

mea ʻai. Food.

mea ʻai no ke kakahiaka. Breakfast.

mea hoʻonoʻono ʻai. Salad dressing.

meainu hoʻohuihui. Cool punch.

miki. To eat *poi* with fingers.

miki pālua. To eat *poi* with two fingers.

miko. Seasoned with salt.

mikoi. To nibble, eat in small pinches, as salt or relish (ʻinamona) with *poi.*

mikole. To eat slowly or fastidiously.

mikomiko. Relishable, seasoned, as food.

moa. Chicken.

moa ʻalae. Completely black chicken, so called because the mudhen *(ʻalae)* was black.

moa hiwa. Black chicken.

moa nahea. White chicken.

momomoni. To swallow.

momoni. To swallow, gulp down.

moni. To swallow, consume.

mūkā. Smacking sound from the lips indicating the food is tasty. *ʻAi mūkā,* to smack the lips and eat with enjoyment.

mulemule. Pungent, bitter to the taste.

nakinaki. Overindulged with food. (A.)

namu. To chew with the mouth closed.

nau. To chew, masticate, munch.

nau kamu. To chew gum.

nehu. Dried fish. (CMH.) A small bait used live; anchovy, used for food and to chum bonito. (PE.)

niole. To eat slowly without appetite.

nome. To munch along.

no'u. To eat in large mouthfuls, eat greedily.

nu'u. To eat with relish and good appetite.

ō. Readying provisions for a journey.

'ōhia. Fruit somewhat like the apple or tomato. *'Ōhia ai,* mountain apple.

'ōhinu. To roast, as meat. (Isa. 44:16.) The stick used as a spit to turn the roast over a fire. Basting, using meat juices or cooking oil, while roasting.

'ō'io lomi. Kind of prepared fish. *'Ō'io,* a hard boned fish, was shredded or mashed and worked with the fingers in a mix with *limu* and *'inamona.* It was eaten uncooked because of the fine bones.

'omo'omo palaoa. Loaf of bread.

'ona'ona. Faint from want of food; unpalatable food; stagnant water.

'oninini. To pick at food, as a sick child; to eat fastidiously and slowly.

o'opulu'ūa. Liver served with other things, as a sauce.

'ōpū palula. Sweet potato leaves.

pai. One who has eaten much.

pai 'ai. Bundle of pounded taro packed in ti leaves. Water would be added later to make *poi.*

pā'ina. Meal, dinner; small group eating together.

pā'ina ahiahi. Supper.

pā'ina 'ai poi. *Poi* supper.

pā'ina poi. *Poi* lunch.

paipaie'e. Breadfruit pudding.

pake'ai. To eat to excess.

pākela 'ai. To overeat; glutton.

pala niho. Scraps of food.

palaoa. Bread from English flour.

palaoa papa'a. Toast.

palula. Food dish made by roasting sweet potato leaves among hot stones. It may also be cooked like spinach, not necessarily with hot stones. (DK.)

papa 'aina. Dining table.

papa'a palaoa. Slice of bread for toast. See **palaoa.**

papao. To cram wood into an oven; stoke a stove.

papa wili 'ai. Food trough.

pehu. Longing to eat; hungry.

pelena, berena. Bread.

pelena hū 'ole. Unleavened bread.

pelena pa'a. Hardtack.

penu. To dip a piece of fish in gravy.

pepeie'e. Overripe breadfruit blended with coconut cream, wrapped in ti leaves, and placed in the oven. It could be preserved for a season. (PE.)

pia. Any white starchy substance, such as flour or arrowroot, eaten by Hawaiians in time of scarcity only.

pī'ai. Fruit of the *kukui* tree. Any berry-like fruit.

piele. Grated taro, cooked in a pudding of other ingredients.

piele kalo. Same as *piele* except the taro is finely grated.

piha loa. Stuffed, as a stomach.

pīholoholo. Thin *poi* made of potatoes or taro, given to the sick.

pikala. Pickle.

poi. Paste or pudding of taro pounded and thinned with water. It was a chief food of the Hawaiians.

poi palaoa. *Poi* made from flour and water. Sometimes taro *poi* is added.

poi palau. Mixture of potatoes and coconut used for food.

poi ulu. *Poi* made of breadfruit.

poke'ina. Calabash made from the *'ina,* a species of sea egg. (A.) Sea urchin.

polokē. Fresh food, as *poi* just pounded up from taro. See **pololei, 'ai 'akakai, 'ai 'aka'akai.**

pololei. Fresh poi.

pōpō pelena. Loaf of bread.

pū. To eat little and without relish.

pū'ā. Bundle of sticks for lighting a fire; to pass food from mouth to mouth in order to feed infants and the aged.

pūhā'a-ā. Having large light spots, as taro or potatoes when partially roasted (the uncooked part whiter than the rest).

pūholo. To steam fish with hot rocks in a sealed calabash.

pūholoholo. Food made of tender shoots of the *'āheahea, lau lele, pakai,* and *popolo.* It is cooked by placing hot stones around and among the shoots in a covered gourd.

pu'ipu'i. Bitter, pungent to the taste. (A.)

pūlehu. To roast on coals or embers.

punapuna. Dry and mealy or hard, as a cooked potato.

puni 'ai. Longing to eat.

pūpū. The meat of a snail, as eaten by the Hawaiians; a relish.

pūpū ʻai. To eat only a little.

puʻuwai. Food made of different vegetables tied in bundles and placed in an oven.

ʻuala. Sweet potato. See **Sweet Potato: Glossary.**

ʻuina ka puʻu. Sound of swallowing.

ʻūkaʻe. Person without teeth; difficult to eat neatly.

ula. Lobster *(Panulirus japonicus),* a Hawaiian lobster.

ulu. To poke out hot stones from the hole in which food was to be baked; to spread oven stones with a stick.

ʻulu. Cooked, unpounded breadfruit.

umu. Earth oven. (Ezek. 22:20.)

unoʻo. Uncooked vegetables; not well cooked, as food.

unuunu. To pull, scrape off, or roll over hot stones the hair of dog or hog.

wahie. Wood for burning, firewood, fuel.

wai huaʻai. Fruit punch.

wai kī. Tea.

waiu. Milk.

waiūpaka. Butter. Also called *paka.*

ENGLISH LOAN WORDS

The origination of any Hawaiian equivalent is due to lack of a native term for an English word. Sometimes it is easier to coin a word in Hawaiian that sounds like the English word. In all such cases, the Hawaiian word is a phonetic equivalent. Spellings and soundings are generally recognizable.

Andrews (515–519) presents a number of introduced words culled from English, Latin, Greek, and Hebrew. English words are in the majority, and only those taken from the English are included here. Pukui-Elbert is an excellent reference for loan words; see the references at the end of appropriate letters of the alphabet.

The words contained in this category are Hawaiian followed by English meanings. If there are several words in the definition, the equivalent word is italicized for convenience. Readers will doubtless know of other loan words that could have been included; this list is considered representative.

ʻaha! Aha!

ʻahamaka, makʻaha. *Hammock; Kapa* fastened between two posts and swung in between; swinging bed of sennit mesh.

'**aiana.** *Iron,* flat iron; to iron or press, as articles of clothing, etc.
'**ailana.** Island.
'**akake.** Agate. Also called *agata, akaki, agati.*
'**akama, adama.** Adamant.
'**akena.** Agent.
'**akoleana.** Accordion.
'**akolika.** Ostrich.
'**akukane.** Adjutant.
'**alabata.** Alabaster.
'**Ālaka.** Alaska.
'**alapaka.** *Alpaca;* alabaster; ointment vase of alabaster. (PE; Luka 7:37.) Also called *alabata.*
'**alea, area.** Area.
'**aleko, aleto.** Alto.
'**alemanaka.** *Almanac,* calendar.
'**alemone, alemona.** Almond.
'**alepapeka, alepabeta.** Alphabet.
'**āmala, amara.** *Armorer;* blacksmith. The first ships to the Islands carried blacksmiths who were called armorers.
'**ameki, amete.** Amethyst.
'**āmene.** Amen.
'**anaka.** Anchor.
'**anakala.** Uncle.
'**anakē, anate.** Aunt.
'**ana paona.** Balance or scale for weight. *Lit.,* measure pound. See **paona.**
ana piwa. Thermometer for checking fever.
'**anekaio.** Angle.
Aneke, Aneda. Andes (mountains).
'**ānela.** Angel.
'**anini.** Awning. Also called *pale lā.*
'**apokaka.** Apostate.
'**apokekolo, aposetole.** Apostle.
'**auka.** Out, as in baseball.
aunaki, aunake, auneki. Ounce.
biwa, piwa. Beaver.
boe. Boy.
dia. Deer.
'**eka.** Acre, of land.
'**enamela.** Enamel.
'**enemi.** Enemy.
'**enikini.** Engine.

eukalitia. Eucalyptus tree.

Eulopa, Europa. Europe, European.

gasa. Gas.

hai. To hire.

hai kalima. Ice cream. *Lit.,* creamed ice.

hainakā, hainikā. *Handkerchief,* napkin.

haleoneka. Clarinet.

halo. Harrow.

hamale, hamare. Hammer. (Lunk. 4:21.)

hame. Ham.

hapa. Harp half.

Hapenuia. Happy New Year.

helekika, heretina. Heretic.

helele, herela. Herald.

hila. Heel.

hipa. Sheep.

Hipahipa. Hip, hip, hurrah!

hō. Hoe; to hoe; colter of a hoe.

hoka. *Hoax;* frustrated; to be ashamed because of failure. (Roma 9:33.)

hōkele, hotele. Hotel, motel.

hoki. In early times the word was applied to *horses* (from which it derives), later to donkeys, and still later to mules. A horse is now called *lio.*

holina! Haul in!

home. *Home.* Place of one's family and residence.

hone. *Honey.* This word may have been coined in 1857 when bees were first brought successfully to Hawai'i.

honi. To kiss; a kiss.

huelopoki, hueloboti. Whaleboat.

huipa. Whip.

huka. Hook.

hupa. Hoop.

hūpō keliko, hūpō karito. *Hypocrite,* used as such by the translators of the New Testament. Later, *ho'okamani* has been used in its stead. (Hal. 32:2.)

iaka. Yak.

iakala. Jackal.

Iapana. Japan.

Iehowa, Iehova. Jehovah.

ikamu. *Item,* as a news item.

Ilikini, Inikini. Indian of Southwest Asia or America.

ilikiuma, iridium. Iridium.

Ilinoe. Illinois.

Ilio pulu. Bull dog. *Lit.*, dog bull.

Inia. East Indian; India.

Inidiana, Inikiana. Indiana.

iniha. Inch.

inika. Ink.

inikō. Indigo.

inipakete. Pocketed, in the pocket.

Iowa. Iowa.

Iulai. July.

Iune. June.

Iunipela, iunipera. Juniper. (1 Nal. 10:4.)

Iupika, Iupita. *Jupiter,* the planet.

iupile, iubile. Jubilee.

kaimana, daimana. Diamond.

Kaimana-Hila. Diamond Head. *Lit.*, diamond hill.

kaina. Kind.

kaka. Quack, used to mean a domesticated duck.

Kākana, Satana. Satan.

kake. Cartridge.

kākela. Castle; gazelle.

kālā. Dollar, money, silver.

kalaima, karaima. Crime, criminal.

kalakoa. *Calico,* spotted, streaked or variegated in colors; to spot or print on *kapa* or calico cloth with colors.

kalaleka, kalareta. Claret.

kalamela, karamela. Caramel.

kalamo. Calamus. (Mele 4:14.)

kalana, kānana. To sift, as flour; to strain, as poi; sieve, strainer, *colander.*

kalanakula, taranatula. Tarantula.

kalanomeka, karanometa. Chronometer.

kalapa, sarapa. Sulphur.

kalaunu, karauna. Crown, corona.

kalaunu bīhopa. Bishop's mitre.

kalaweka. Cultivator.

Kalawina. Calvinistic, Congregational.

kalena, talena. Talent. (Mat. 25:15.)

kalenekalio, calenedario. Calendar.

kālepa. Scraper.

kalepona, carebona. Carbon.

Kaleponi. California.
Kalewali, Kalevari. Calvary.
kalika, galika. Garlic. (Nah. 11:5.)
Kalikiano, Kristiano. Christian.
Kalikimaka, Kalikamaka. Christmas.
kalikone, karitone. Cretonne.
Kalilaia, Galilaia. Galilee.
kalima. Cream.
kalina. Sardine.
kalioneke, kalionete. Clarinet.
kaloke. Carrot.
kaloline, kalorine. Chlorine.
kalomela. Calomel.
Kālona. Sharon.
kāmaki. Garment.
kamanā, kamenā. Carpenter. (Zek. 1:20.)
kāmano. Salmon.
kame. Chamois.
kameki. Cement.
kāmelo. Camel.
kamipulu. Damn fool.
kamu. *Gum. Nau kamu,* to chew gum.
kana, kana. Ton.
Kanada. Canada.
Kanahai. Shanghai.
Kanakaloka. Santa Claus.
kanakalū, kanagaru. Kangaroo.
kanakē. Candy.
kanapapiki. Son of a bitch.
kanapi. To snap.
kanapī. Centipede.
kaneka, ganeta. Garnet.
kanela. Canal.
kanikela, kanipele. Consul.
kao. Scow.
kaolo. *Jowls,* double chin, sagging chin.
kaona. Town.
kapaea, sapaea. Sapphire. See **kapeilo, sapeiro.**
kā paka. Container for *tobacco,* pipe, or matches.
kapaki, sabati. Sabbath.
kapeilo, sapeiro. Sapphire.
kāpena. *Captain* or master of a ship.

kapenekine, tapenetine. Turpentine.

kāpiki. Cabbage.

kapikola. Capital; capitol.

kapioka. Tapioka.

kapolena. Tarpaulin, canvas.

kapu. Cap; tub.

kauka. *Doctor,* physician.

kaʻukama. Cucumber *(Cucumis sativas).* (Nah. 11:5.)

kaukani, kausani. Thousand.

kaukini, kausini. Cousin.

Kauliki. Southeast.

Kauna. Count (title).

kaunakeke, kaunatese. Countess (title).

Kaweke. Southwest.

kāwele. Towel, napkin; to wipe cloth.

kea. Share, as of stock.

keaka. Jack, in a deck of cards.

keka, seka. Sex, gender.

kēkake. Jackass, donkey.

Kēkēmapa, Deremaha. December.

kekimala, dekimala. Decimal.

keko. *Sago,* a powdered starch used in puddings; sago palm; silvertree fern.

kekona, sakona. Second (unit of time). (Hal. 30:5.)

kela, kela lole. Tailor; dressmaker.

kela, sela. Sailor.

kelaki, keraki. Celery *(Apium graveolens).*

kelakona, daragona. Dragon. (Hoik. 12:3.)

kelama, derama. Dram (weight).

kelawini. Gale. *Lit.,* gale wind.

kele. To sail; jelly, jam.

kelekalama, teregerama. Telegram.

kelekalapa, telegrapa. Telegraph.

Kelemania. Germany.

kelemomeka, teremometa. Thermometer.

kelepona, telepona. Telephone.

kelikoli. Territory.

keliluma kelemana. Delirium tremens.

Kēlō! Sail Ho!

kelokokile, kerokerodile. Crocodile.

kenali, denari. Penny.

keneka. Cent.

kenekile, genetile. Gentile.
kenekulia, keneturia. Century.
kenele. Canary.
keni. Small change, money.
kenika, denisa. Tennis.
keonimana. Gentleman.
Kepanī. Japanese.
Kepania, Sepania. Spain; Spanish.
kepela, sepela. Spelling.
kepemineka, sepemineta. Spearmint.
kī. Key, lock; trigger; to set a clock.
kia. To steer.
kiakona. Deacon.
kiapolō, diabolo. The devil, tempter. (Mat. 4:5, 3:5.)
ki'ikena. Painting.
kīkā. Guitar.
kike. Kitty.
kikelona. Citron.
kikina. Season.
kila. *Steel;* steel flint for striking fire; general name for chisels.
kilape. Giraffe.
kilika. Silk. (Sol. 31:22.)
kīnā. Sin, blemish, error. *Cap.,* China.
kinamona. Cinnamon. (Hoik. 18:13.)
kini, tini. Tin, can or pail.
kinihame. Gingham.
kinihene. Guinea hen.
kīpō. Depot.
kipo koma. Semicolon. *Lit.,* dot comma.
kipuwe. To keep away.
Kiu. Jew; Jewish.
kiule, kiure. Jury.
kiulela, kiurela. Squirrel.
koaka. *Quarter,* of a dollar.
kō'ala. To roast over *coals;* to broil in the coals. (Luk. 24:42.)
kō'eko'e aku. Go away.
ko'ele. Equality in numbers or strength. *Kaulike,* equitable, just.
kōkō. Cocoa.
kole. Story; to tell stories.
kolona, korona. Colon; crown; solon.
kolone. Column; colon.
kolopā. Crowbar.

kolopoma. Chloroform. (PE.)

kolowaka. Soda water. (PE.)

koma. Comma.

komako. Tomato.

koma luna. Apostrophe.

komike. Committee.

kona, kana. Ton.

kone. Cony, species of hare. (Kanl. 14:7.) Perhaps the gooney, *Kone.*

koneka. Cornet.

koneko. Doughnut.

konelā. Colonel; tunnel.

kopa, sopa. Soap.

kopalā. Shovel.

kope. *Coffee;* shovel.

kopela, kopera. Camphor.

kope lehu. Rake or shovel for ashes.

kopiana. Scorpion.

kopola, cobora. Cobra.

kopolano, soperano. Soprano.

korona. Crown; rosary.

koukā, kouga. Cougar.

kua. Sewer.

kuaina. Twine or string.

kuawa. Guava.

kuba. Cube. *Cap.,* Cuba.

kueka. Sweater. *Cap.,* Quaker.

kuhi. Cookie.

kuila. *Twill,* twilled cloth; foreign cloth.

kuka. Coat.

kuke. Cook; to cook; cookie; customs duty.

kūkū. Cuckoo. (Oihk. 11:16.)

kulima, kalima. Cream.

kūmeka. Shoemaker.

kupa. Soup, stew; cooper.

kupau, kupai. Good-bye; to say good-bye.

laiki, raisi. Rice.

laikini. License.

laina. Line.

laipila. Libel; to libel.

laka. Lark; lock; to lock.

lakaheke. Loghead. *Colloq.*

lakana. Lantern. *Ladana,* London.

Lā Kāpaki. Sabbath Day.

lakeke. *Jacket,* blouse.

laki. Lucky. Also called *pōmaikaʻi.*

lakika, radika. Radix.

lakike, latike. Lettuce. Also called *lekuke.*

lakikū, latitu. Latitude.

Lākina, Latina. Latin.

lakio, ratio. Ratio.

lakuna, rakuna. Raccoon.

lamie, lamia. Ramie. A strong fiber used for rope.

Lanaho! Land ho!

lede. Lady.

Leiko! Let go!

leka. Leek; an herb. (Nah. 11:5.)

leki. Lace; tape for dress trimming.

lekuke. Lettuce.

lenekila, lenetila. Lentils. (Ezek. 4:9.)

lēpela, lēpelo, lepero. Leper.

likini. Rigging; rope for the mast.

Liko anela! Let go the anchor. (CMH.)

lilina. Linen.

liona. Lion.

lipaki, libati. Liberty.

lipina, ribina. Ribbon. Also called *lipine, ribine.*

loio. Lawyer.

loke. Rose, rosy.

lokeli, loteri. Lottery. *Loki,* horse of a roan color.

lope, lopi. *Rope;* thread, sewing thread. This word was most commonly used for thread. (Lunk. 16:12.) Also called *rope, ropi.*

lopine. Robin.

luka, luti. Lute.

luka, ruda. *Rood,* as in surveying.

lukau. To look out, be careful.

lukini. Russian.

lukipa, lucifa. Lucifer.

lula, rula. Ruler.

lumakika, rumatika. Rheumatism.

lupepa. Rhubarb.

mākā. To mark; marker.

mākē. Masthead.

mākeke. Market.

makela, maseba. Muscles.

makelia. Material.

makemakika. Mathematics.

māki. To march.

makika. Mosquito.

Makona, Masona. *Mason. Hui makona,* Masonic Lodge.

maline. Marine.

manakō. Mango tree, mango fruit.

manomano. *Many,* manifold.

mapala. Marble.

mauna. Mountain. In the Islands land masses rise from the sea to a central area, the top. This is the *mauna.*

mekala, medala. Metal, medal.

mekele, metere. Meter; metric.

mekia. Major, in the military service.

Mekokiko, Metodito. Methodist.

melanikia. Melanesia, Melanesian.

Mele Kalīkimaka! Merry Christmas!

melekiana, merediana. Meridian.

melekule. Marigold.

melokia, melodia. Melody.

melokiana. Melodeon.

metala. Metal.

mikelio, meterio. Mystery.

mikiona, misiona. Mission.

mikionale, mikanele, misionari. Missionary.

miliona. Million.

minao. Minnow.

mine. Mine, as for minerals.

mineka, mineta. Mint.

minelala, minerala. Mineral.

minuke, minute. Minute.

miula. Mule. (Kin. 36:24.)

mole. Mole. (Oihk. 11:29.)

molaki, moraki. Mortgage. (PE.)

molala, morala. *Moral. Pono,* goodness.

mōneka. Monk.

Moneke, Monede. Monday.

monekekili, moneseteri. Monastary.

moni. *Money,* price of a thing sold. (Kin. 44:12.)

monika, monita. Monitor.

monokune, monosune. Monsoon.

nau. To gnaw.

nika. Nigger, vulgar term for a negro; black.

noliki. Northeast.

Nowa Kekokia. Nova Scotia.

noweke. Northwest.

Nuhōlani. New Holland.

nūhou. News.

nūpepa. Newspaper.

ofa. Oat.

'oka. Oak tree. Also called *ofa, ota.*

'okana. Organ.

'oliwa, oliva. Olive tree.

'Olohana. *All hands,* the name given to John Young. His other name was Keoniana. It was also the name of a trusted lieutenant of Kamehameha I.

'ololaiki. All right.

'olomeka, olomeda. Old maid.

'olomene. Old man.

'olopala. Old fellow.

'ona. Owner. (PE.)

'opiuma. Opium; also the name of a tree.

Ota. Oat. Also called *ofa.*

padi. Paddy.

pahu meli. Beehive.

pai. Pie, tart.

paika. To fight; a fight.

paila, baila. Pile, heap; to boil.

paina. *Pint; pine* or fir tree.

pakalaki. Unlucky; bad luck. (PE.)

pakapaka. Heavy rain shower; *patter of heavy drops,* as on dry surfaces.

pake, pate. Putty, softness.

pākeke. Variety of sweet potato. *Baketa,* bucket or pail. *Pakete,* pocket; *packet,* ship.

pakī. Barge.

pakika, kapika. To *slip,* to slide when walking; slippery.

pakō, baso. *Base* or support.

pala, bala. Barley.

palai, parai, farai. To cook or fry in a pan. (Oihk. 7:12.)

palalā, palela. Barrel.

palama. Plum; plumber. *Pālama,* palm, sacred enclosure.

palau. Plow.

paleki. Brake.

palekoke. Petticoat.

palelona, farelona. Furlong.

palima. Primer.

paloke. Broken.

palū. *Flu,* influenza.

pāma. *Palm* tree; *balm.* (Kanl. 34:3.)

pāna, bana. Band.

panakalupa. Bankrupt. *Panakō, banako,* bank.

pani. *Pan. Pa kini,* tin pan.

pāniki. To pinch, punish. (PE.)

paoka, paoda. Powder.

paona. Pound; measure, scales, balances. See **ana paona.**

Papa. Pope.

papaia. Papaya.

pauka, pauda. Powder.

pehemo, behemo. Behemoth. (Ioba 40:5.)

pekana, begana. Pagan.

pekula. Picul, the weight of a sandalwood unit in the China trade, 133½ lbs.

pekunia. Petunia *(Petunia hybrida).* A flowering garden plant or herb of many colors. (NEAL 739.)

pelamika, pelamida. Pyramid.

pela uwea. Bedspring. *Lit.,* balewire.

peloni. Felony. (PE.)

pena. Paint; to paint.

pepa. Paper, card.

pēpē. Baby.

piano. Piano.

pī'āpā. Name of the first primer or spelling book in Hawaiian. Like the word alphabet, the word is formed from the first two letters of the Greek, and was similar to the expression "ABCs," meaning the rudiments of all letters. The missionary said to his pupil "b a ba." The pupil using a "p" for the "b" would say "pī ā pa."

pihi. Fish.

pīkāke. Peacock. (1 Nal. 10:22.)

pika wai. Water pitcher. *Pika pua,* flower pitcher.

piku, figu. Fig.

pila. Fiddle.

pine, pina. Pin used as a hair fastener; pin, needle, peg, bolt.

pinika. Vinegar.

pīwa, fiwa. Fever. *Biwa,* beaver.

pōkē. Bouquet.

pola, bola. *Bowl. Ke bola,* cup.

polū. Blue, as clothes, not the sky or sea.

popoki. Cat. Hawaiian word for "poor pussy," a missionary term commonly used in speaking of cats.

pouka. Powder.

puhele. Bushel.

puki. Boot.

pulekina, buletina. Bulletin.

pulikana, pulitaro. Puritan.

puluka. Flute.

pūlumi. Broom.

punana meli. Beehive.

rai. Rye.

sia. Dear.

sila. *Seal;* deed; patent.

topido. Torpedo.

'uiki, 'uwiki. Wick of a lamp or candle. (Mat. 12:20.)

'uwaki, uaki, waki. Watch, clock.

uwea, uea. Wire.

waina. Wine; grapevine.

waiolina. Violin.

walanuka, walanuta. Walnut.

wale, walea. Welshman.

waniki. Varnish.

wanila. Vanilla.

wele weka. Velvet.

wīneka. Vinegar.

wini. Wind.

Wo! Whoa!

FISHES: Kinds

The sheer size of this category makes obvious the importance of the fishing industry in the cultural and social lives of Hawaiians, and the ever-present challenge of the sea. On the other hand, this list is also long because of the presence of seemingly endless varieties of small reef fishes.

There were many uses for fishes and their products besides their principal use as human food. They provided fertilizer and a source of bones for fishhooks, they were used as offerings in sacrifices and worship, and they were objects of ornamentation.

The alphabet and written language created by the missionaries opened a new world to Hawaiians. Setting to paper their descriptions of fishes remains a great achievement. In few of the categories in this book do we find such splendid descriptive words and phrases.

One thing should be noted: Hawaiian names were applied to all known fishes up to about 1890. After that point, Ichthyologists continued to enlarge their lists, but gave little attention to perpetuating the colorful Hawaiian names. Palmer and Perkins' work in the 1890s, along with successors, provided the first full listings in the complete scientific style: family, genus, species, date of capture, and Latin name. Interest in relating Hawaiian names to the scientific ones did not keep pace. In the early 1900s, however, much thought was given this point. This modern emphasis on ancient Hawaiian culture was a welcome beginning.

It is obvious, however, that there is a large void in the cultural biology of the post-Cook years, covering perhaps 1780 to 1890, that even now is crying out for careful and complete research and publication.

ā. Young of the Hawaiian dascyllus, a demoiselle *(Dascyllus albisella)*. Also called *'a'ā*. For the adult fish, see **'alo'ilo'i.**

'a'akimakau. Andrews identifies this hook-biting fish with *ā*.

'a'ala'ihi. Young of the white-spotted squirrelfish *(Adioryx lacteoguttatus)*. For the adult fish, see **'ala'ihi.**

'a'ala'ihimaoli. Same as the 'a'ala'ihi. The suffix *maoli* tends to emphasize the indigenous or local quality of this fish.

'a'awa. Hawaiian hogfish or black-spot wrasse *(Bodianus bilunulatus)*. A reef fish, which grows to 24 inches. It adjusts its coloration with age, the older fishes changing from largely white to bluish black. Once called a sandfish. See **pō'ou.**

'a'awa lelo. Wrasse, reddish with white stripes and common in Hilo Bay.

'aha. Several species of the needlefish family (Belonidae) go by this name and are found in Hawaiian waters. These are voracious surface fishes, some growing to 40 inches in length. Its young are called *heahaaha*. See **keke'e.**

'ahi. Albacore *(Thunnus alalunga)* has a tunalike body and a very

long pectoral fin. It weighs 40 pounds or more and has a blackish blue topside and silvery sides. Its flesh is highly prized for
eating.

'āhole. Hawaiian flag-tail fish *(Kuhlia sandvicensis)*, both a salt-
and freshwater fish. It attains a length of 9 inches. The young,
āholehole, live close to the shore line.

'āhuluhulu. Middle stage of the goatfish *(Parupeneus porphyreus).* Reddish when small. Reaches at least 12 inches in length.
See **kūmū.**

aki lolo. Bird wrasse *(Gomphosus varius).* A long-nose species of
hīnālea. The *kahuna lapaʻau* used this fish as a *pani,* or closure,
for diseases or illnesses of the head.

aku. Bonito or skipjack tuna *(Euthynnus pelamis).* Also called
striped tuna and little tunny. It is perhaps the most important
fish in Hawaiʻi. According to tradition, Pili, a king in Tahiti,
was persuaded to come to Hawaiʻi to strengthen the kingly line.
On his trip he was accompanied by two schools of fish: one of
aku, which took care of the paddling, and the other of *ʻōpelu,*
which calmed the winds. (MALO 6–7.)

akule. Big-eye scad *(Selar crumenophthalmus).* Schooling fish in
Hawaiian coastal waters. It reaches about 15 inches and is a
valuable food fish. The young, *hahalalū,* grow to about 7 inches
and are herded in schools by the *ulua* or *kawakawa.*

'akupa. Hawaiian sleeper *(Eleotris sandwicensis).* Found largely
in Hawaiian waters, chiefly around Kauaʻi. It rests motionless
on the bottom for long periods. The young develop in the sea,
but adults do not enter salt water unless in estuaries. Grows to 9
inches. See **nuʻu kole, ʻoau** (Oʻahu, Maui), **ʻoʻopu, ʻoʻopuʻoau,
ʻowau.** Also called *ʻōkuhe.*

'alaʻihi. Squirrelfish *(Adioryx lacteoguttatus).* More of a deep-
water fish. Young are called *ʻaʻalaʻihi.*

'āloʻiloʻi. Adult of the Hawaiian dascyllus, a demoiselle *(Dascyllus
albisella).* An oval-shaped fish, usually black, growing to 6
inches in length. Lives in large heads of finger coral. Young are
called *ā, ʻāʻā.* See **paʻapaʻa, ula paʻapaʻa.**

'amaʻama. Striped mullet *(Mugil cephalus).* Occurs along open
coasts, usually cached in fish ponds. It dredges its food, diato
and other organic matter, from the bottom. Grows to more than
12 inches. This was and is a highly prized fish. It was cared for
as a vocation in the fish ponds of ancient Hawaiʻi.

'āmoʻomoʻo. Middle stage of the bonefish *(Albula* spp.*).* For the
adult fish, see **'ōʻio.**

'anae. Largest of the striped mullet *(Mugil cephalus)*. Grows to 12 inches. *'Anae* is the adult stage; *ama'ama,* the middle stage; *'olola,* the young stage.

'ānuhenuhe. Pilot or rudderfish *(Kyphosus* spp.) A variant of *nenue.* Feeds on plant food, herbivorous, which makes a less palatable flesh for eating. Attains 24 inches.

'ao'ao nui. Young of the blackspot sergeant *(Abudefduf sordidus).* For the adult fish, see **kūpīpī.**

'ao'ao wela. Fish, green in color. No data. (A.)

'api. Sailfin tang or sailfin surgeonfish *(Zebrasoma veliferum).* It has a zebra-striped body and grows to 16 inches. It may be seen as individuals or in small schools.

a'u. Blue marlin *(Makaira nigricans).* A member of the billfish family, which is pelagic. It attains a weight of 1,400 pounds and a length of 11 feet and is the most common marlin in Hawaiian waters. It has a deep metallic-blue color when swimming that turns leaden-gray at death.

'au lepe. Sailfish *(Istiophorus platypterus).* A pelagic fish reaching 12 feet in size and weighing up to 200 pounds. Its body is purple-blue on top and yellow-gray below. Fishermen like it for sport as it leaps and dives when hooked. All giant marlin are female. Males do not exceed 300 pounds. The world's record with hook and line is 221 pounds.

awa. Milkfish *(Chanos chanos).* Young are called *puawa;* the medium size fish, *awa 'aua;* commercial size, *awa;* very large, *awa kalamoho.*

awa kalamoho. Very large *awa,* milkfish *(Chanos chanos).* An important fish raised by aquaculture in ponds in Asia. See **kalamoho, kalamoku.**

'āwela. Christmas wrasse *(Thalassoma fuscum).* Has a distinctive side marking of erect oblong boxes in two rows alongside most of the body. It grows to 12 inches. Its young are called *'ōhua pa'awela.*

'āweoweo. *(Priacanthus cruentatus.)* This fish is called big-eye among English-speaking peoples. Its young are known as *'ala-lauwā* (redfish), a name applied when spectacular schools of them would appear in Honolulu harbor. Such schools were taken as an omen of sickness or death in the royal family. See **pāeaea.**

ehe ula. Mature stage of the *hapu'u (Epinephelus quernus).* A deep-water grouper, dark purple-brown in color with pearly white spots on the sides. It is edible and grows to 3 feet. Its young are called *hāpu'upu'u.*

hāhālua. Manta ray *(Manta alfredi).* This creature is reported to attain a spread of 30 feet in Hawaiian waters. In spite of its enormous size it is not a threat to man. The species was named after Prince Albert, son of Britain's Queen Victoria.

hai'e'a. Wrasse, similar to the *'a'awa lelo.* No other data.

hailepo. Spotted eagle ray *(Aetobatus narinari).* Also called *hīhī-manu.* Among the early Hawaiians it was forbidden as food for women.

hā nui. Demoiselle, the chocolate-dip chromis *(Chromis hā nui).* A species known only in Hawai'i. Similar to *mokumoku hā nui.*

hāpue'e. Species of fish. No data. (A.)

hāuliuli, hauliuli pūhi. The "snake" mackerel *(Gempylus serpens).* Body color is a uniform dark-blue slate. It is occasionally caught in the open sea of Hawai'i. It reaches up to 3 feet in length and inhabits the surface regions down to several hundred feet. See **weleku.**

heahaaha. Young of the needlefish (family Belonidae). For the adult fish, see **aha.**

hou. Surge wrasse *(Thalassoma purpureum).* A shallow-water fish many of whose young have Hawaiian names: *kanaloa, 'ōlale, 'ōlani, pakaiele, pā'ou'ou, pūhi 'āwela.* Grows to 18 inches.

huhu. Perhaps the *uhu.* No data.

hukīki. Perhaps the *'ūkīkīkī.*

humuhumu. The triggerfish (family Balistidae), with many species. See **'uī'uī, 'uwī'uwī.**

humuhumu hi'u kole, humuhumu uli. Pinktail triggerfish or durgon *(Melichthys vidua).* Lives outside the reef, reaching a length of 15 inches. *Lit.,* red-tailed *humuhumu.*

humuhumu nukunuku a pua'a. This name applies to both *Rhinecanthus aculeatus* and *R. rectangulus.* These two fishes reach about 9 inches. Nevertheless, their Hawaiian name is probably the longest with twenty-one letters. It was well known in the 1800s but became famous in song in the 1900s. It was believed to be one of the forms of the pig god Kamapua'a.

'iao, i'iao. Silversides *(Atheninomorus insularum).* A small schooling fish second only to the *nehu* as *aku* or tuna bait. It has a broad silver stripe along the sides from which it gets its name and is phosphorescent. It grows to 4 inches.

'ilioehe. Species of fish. No data. (A.) May be some relation to *'oeha* shrimp.

kākū. Barracuda. See **kawele'a.**

kala. Unicornfish *(Naso unicornis),* a member of the surgeonfish family (Acenthuridae). So called because in its adult stage it grows a horn on the snout. An inshore fish, it attains 18 inches in length. Young are called *pākala*. The tough scaleless skin is used for the tympanum on the *puniu* drum.

kalalea. Eel found on the mountain Kalalea, site of the fishing shrine Ka Lae.

kalamoe. Fish of the sand diver family (Trichonotidae). Its habitat is the sandy bottom in shallow water, where it burrows and lives. (A.)

kalamoho, kalamoku. The largest *awa (Chanos chanos),* or milkfish. See **awa kalamoho.**

kamano, kamanu. Rainbow runner or Hawaiian salmon *(Elagatis bipinnulatus).* A pelagic fish that grows to 4 feet. It is highly prized as food. (MT.)

kapuhili. Butterfly fishes (*Chaetodon* spp.). Their bodies are usually yellow or white with distinctive dark markings and grow to 6 inches in length. Three species are known only in Hawai'i. See **lauhau, kīkākapu.**

kau-maka-nui. Ocean sunfish *(Mola mola).* This fish looks as if its tail has been bitten off. It reaches 11 feet in length and up to two tons in weight.

kawakawa. Bonito, little tuna, black skipjack *(Euthynnus yaito).* Rarely exceeds 30 inches in length. Its young are called *kawakawa kīna'u, 'oeo'e.* See **pua 'akuhinu.**

kaweke, weke. Goatfish (family Mullidae). Also known as surmullets.

kawele'a. Barracuda *(Sphyraena helleri).* Much smaller than the *kākū,* 2 feet in length. See **kākū.**

kawelo. No data.

keiki a ka manō. Shark sucker or remora *(Echeneis naucrates).* Attains 36 inches in length. It uses the larger sharks as host.

keke'e, 'aha. Needlefish of the (family Belonidae), a fish that swims crookedly near the surface. See **'aha.**

kī'ahamanu. Common goby *(Chonophorus stamineus).* A stout, short, and heavy fish that can attain 12 inches. It has a dark, olive-brown upper body and lighter lower regions. Its habitats are fresh-water streams and river mouths. See **nākea, nōkea, 'o'opu lehe.**

kīkākapu. Ornate butterfly fish *(Chaetodon ornatissimus).* Grows to 7 inches. Similar to *kapuhili, lau hau.*

koa'e. Snapper *(Etelis marshi).* Has a reddish body and grows to 24 inches. This is a food fish which lives beyond the reef.

koholā. Humpback whale, so called from its spouting, forcing up the water like waves hitting a reef. Its flesh is *kapu* to women. This is a mammal, not a fish.

kōkala. *Porcupine fish (Diodon hystrix);* spiny puffer *(D. holocanthus).* Their bodies inflate like the balloon fish, and the flesh may be poisonous. Also called *hoana.* See **'o'opu hue.**

kole, ukole. Yellow-eyed surgeonfish *(Ctenochaetus strigosus).* Has a yellow ring around the eye and a brown body. It lives in shallow water on the reef and reaches a length of 7 inches. Also called *'o'opu mākole.*

kolekolea. Goatfish *(Parupeneus multifasciatus).* Red and black colored fish. Attains about 1 foot in length. Found only in Hawaii. See **moano.**

kūkāpalani. Name of a fish to which a chief may be likened. No data. (A.)

kule. Variant of *'ulae,* lizardfish of the family Synodontidae. Certain species burrow in the sand. They reach a length of up to a foot. *'Ulae* is a common name for lizardfishes in Hawai'i.

kūmū, kūmu'u. Goatfish *(Parupeneus porphyreus).* The adult stage is called *kūmū;* the middle stage, *'āhuluhulu.;* the young stage, *'ōkūkū.*

kūnehi. Ocean sunfish, *Ranzania laevis.* Also called *'āpaku, mākua.*

kūpala. Barracuda. Also called *kākū.* See **kawele'a.**

kūpīpī. Blackspot sergeant, a demoiselle *(Abudefduf sordidus).* It grows in length to 9 inches and is found in shallow waters of the reef. Its young are called *'ao'ao nui.* See **'ō'ōnui.**

kūpoupou. One of the wrasses *(Cheilio inermis).* Its habitat is not only on both the reef and shore but also among rocks and seaweed. It grows to 18 inches and is a good food fish, raw or cooked.

lae nihi, le'enihi. High-headed razorfish *(Xyrichthys umbrilatus),* one of the wrasses. Attains about a foot in length. The fish enjoys quiet, sandy bottoms outside the reef.

lai. Runner, skin fish *(Scombroides lysan),* St. Peter's leather (S. *sanctipetri)* of older literature. It is a bright slate-blue, tapering to a silver-white on the belly. Lives in shallow water along the coasts, growing to 25 inches.

lā'ī pala, lauī pala. Yellow tang or surgeonfish *(Zebrasoma flavescens).* A brilliant yellow reef fish which grows to 8 inches. *Lit.,* yellow ti leaf. A favorite in the aquarium fish trade. See **lau kī pala.**

lālākea. Hawaiian shark or spiny dogfish *(Squalus fernandinus)*. A deep-water shark. It is largely gray and attains a length of four feet. *Lit., fins white.*

lā'ō. Ornate wrasse *(Halichoeres ornatissimus)*. A multicolored reef fish that matures at about 7 inches.

lau hau. Threadfin butterfly fishes *(Chaetodon auriga)* and other species of *Chaetodon,* growing to about nine inches. See **kīkā-kapu.**

lauhua. Balloonfish *(Arothron hispidus)*. A short-bodied fish displaying a mixture of colors, gray, brown, and yellow. It reaches about 20 inches in length and can inflate its body. Its flesh is poisonous. See **'o'opu hue.**

lauia. Hawaiian parrotfish *(Scarus dubius)*. The male form is called *lauia.* Its body is multicolored and attains 12 inches. It is a good food fish.

lau ka hi'u. Thresher shark *(Alopias vulpinus),* long tailed with its tail as long as its body and growing to 20 feet. Also called *manō hi'u kā.*

laukī. Species of fish. No data. (CMH.)

lau kī pala. Same as *lā'ī pala.*

lau milo. Eel with coloring like a yellow *milo* leaf. See **pūhilau milo.**

le'enihi. Variant of *lae nihi.*

lele pō. Flying fish *(Parexocoetus brachypterus)*. Also known as *mālolo.* This is likely the most common species. It grows to nine inches. The young are called *pūhiki'i.*

loloa'u. Flying gurnard *(Dactyloptena orientalis)*. Described as a family containing "some of the most bizarre of fishes." This is the only Hawaiian species. The gurnards move largely on the bottom by walking on their pelvic fins. They do not approach the surface, much less fly. Also called *lolo oau, pinao.*

lupe. See **hailepo,** sting ray.

mahae. See **lā'ī pala.**

mahaha. Large unicornfish *(Naso unicornis)*. Member of surgeonfish family (Acanthuridae). In its adult stage it grows a horn on the snout. It feeds on sargassum and sea plants generally, growing to 24 inches. See **kala.**

mahimahi. Common dolphin *(Coryphaena hippurus)*. A game fish prized for its flesh. Reaches 6 feet and 70 pounds. Also known as dorado.

maiko. Blueline surgeonfish *(Acanthurus nigroris)*. A dark brown, shallow water fish that matures at about 10 inches.

makā ā. One of the sand filefishes or blanquillos *(Malacanthus brevirostris)*. It is a benthic fish that reaches 12 inches and is edible. It is light green except for a white ventral region.

makali'i 'ōhua. Tiny *'ōhua* spawn.

makimaki. Balloonfish *(Arothron hispidus)*. This fish, inhabiting the shoreline and moderate depths, may grow to 20 inches. It has an inflatable body and is poisonous—not for eating. See **'o'opu hue.**

mākolu. General term for wrasses of the genus *Coris:* the *lamalama (Coris ballieui)*, the lined coris; and the *hilu (Coris flavovitatta)*, the yellowstripe coris. They grow to be 14 and 18 inches respectively.

male. Young of the parrotfish *(Scarus perspicillatus)*, also called *'ōmale, 'ōmalemale*. For the adult fish, see **uhu.**

mālolo. General term for all flying fish *(Cypselurus* spp., family Exocoetidae).

mama'o. Hawaiian sergeant *(Abudefduf abdominalis)*. A demoiselle (family Pomacentridae). It grows to 9 inches, living in tide pools and quiet shoreline waters. Also called *mamamo, mamo, ma'oma'o*. See **palapala.**

manini. Convict tang or surgeonfish *(Acanthurus triostegus sandvicensis)*. Body light gray above and white below with black bars. It inhabits the reef shallows where it grows to 9 inches. This is the adult stage. Other stages are called *makali'i 'ōhua maninini, 'ōhua, 'ohua liko, 'ōhua līpoa*.

maninini. Middle stage of the *manini* young.

manō. General term for sharks.

manō ihu-wa'a. Shark believed to have rested its head on the outrigger of a canoe, where it was welcomed and fed by fishermen.

manō kanaka. Shark believed to have been born of a human mother and a shark god. An *'aumakua*.

manō kihikihi. The scalloped hammerhead shark *(Sphyrna lewini)*. This shark reaches 15 feet in length and is seen along shorelines and out to sea. It has often been seen in Kaneohe Bay. Its flesh is used for food.

me'eme'e. Tropical halfbeak *(Hemiramphus depauperatus)*. This elongate silvery fish grows to 16 inches and moves in schools. Also called *iheihe*.

moa. Trunkfish *(Ostracion meleagris)*. Reaches 9 inches in length. See **pahu.**

moano. Red and black banded goatfish *(Parupeneus multifasciatus)*. Found only in Hawai'i. See **kolekolea.**

moi. Pacific threadfin *(Polydactylus sexfilis).* Reaches 3 feet in length. Its stages of growth are: *moi,* the adult stage; *palamoi* (Kaua'i) and *manamoi* (Hawai'i), the middle stage, about 5 inches; and little *moi,* the youngest stage, about 2 or 3 inches long. The adult is often trapped in the net at a *hukilau.*

mokule'ia. Amberjack *(Seriola dumerili).* A silvery gray fish with a yellow stripe that attains a length of 6 feet. Its young are called *halahala.*

momoni. Blue jack *(Caranx melampygus).* An *ulua* that reaches 36 inches. See **nuku mone'u, 'ōmilumilu.**

na'ena'e. Orange-banded surgeonfish *(Acanthurus olivaceus).* Its body is a grayish brown with an orange band on the shoulder area and grows to about 12 inches. It inhabits the outer side of the reef where there is wave action and a sandy beach. Also called *mahamea.*

nai'a. Species of blackfish or porpoise *(Pocaena* spp.) that is *kapu* to women. A mammal, not a fish. See **nua'o.**

nehu. Hawaiian anchovy *(Stolephorus purpureus).* Grows to four inches. Lives in the quiet waters of bays and estuaries, such as the waters around Kona, Ewa Beach, Kaneohe Bay, etc. It is a most important bait fish in Hawai'i, especially popular for catching bonito.

nenue, nenuwe. Rudderfish *(Kyphosus* spp.). Found off Kahuku and along the Hilo coast. It grows to 24 inches and has an ash-colored body. It is herbivorous, which makes a less palatable fish for eating. See **'ānuhenuhe.**

niuki. The great white shark *(Carcharodon carcharias).* Man-eating shark. The male is gray on top, soiled white on the bottom, and grows to at least 21 feet. The most feared of all sharks, it eats almost anything. It inhabits the open sea but occasionally comes into shallow waters.

nohu. Term used for two scorpionfishes, the titan *(Scorpaenopsis cacopsis)* and the devil *(S. diabolus).* They are similar, one growing to 20 inches, the other to 12 inches. Both inhabit the outer edge of the reef and the shallow waters of the shoreline. Also called *nohu 'omakaha.*

nōkea, nākea. Common goby *(Chonophorus stamineus).* This is a stout, heavy goby, with a dark, olive-brown upper body, and lighter lower regions. It can attain 12 inches in length. It feeds in fresh water—stream, river mouth, etc. See **o'opu lehe, kī'aha-manu.**

nua'o. Porpoise. *Kapu* to women. See **nai'a.**

nuku mone'u. Blue jack *(Caranx melampygus)*. More slender than the white *ulua*, it is an active predator, often swimming in small schools. It can attain up to 2.5 feet. See **momoni, 'ōmilumilu.**

nūnū. This name is applied to two fish. **1.** Two-barred goatfish *(Parupeneus bifasciatus)*. Grows to 11 inches. Also called *moano*. **2.** Trumpetfish *(Aulostomus chinensis)*. A brown, green, or orangish fish. Occasionally one sees a yellow phase. It attains over 3 feet in length. Also known as *nuhu*.

nu'u kole. Hawaiian sleeper *(Eleotris sandwicensis)*. This fish rests motionless on the bottom for long periods. It grows to about one foot. Also known as *'o'opu, 'ōkuhe, 'oau, hi'u kole.*

'oama, 'owama. Young of the yellow-striped goatfish *(Mulloidos flavolineatus)*. The body is whitish with a lateral yellow stripe and can show a mottled red pattern. It is a common shoreline fish and attains 15 inches. Also called *weke, weke'ā, weke'o'a.*

'oau, 'owau. Hawaiian sleeper, *Eleotris sandwicensis,* a fresh and brackish water fish with a growth to nine inches. Same as *'o'opu, hi'u kole.*

'oeo'e. Young of the wavy-back skipjack *(Euthynnus yaito)*. Also called little tunny, bonito. See **kawakawa.**

'ōhi'uhi'u. Parrotfish *(Scarus perspicillatus)*. Also called blue *uhu*. This is a beautiful species with brilliant green and blue hues and salmon markings. Grows to 2 feet.

'ōhua. Youngest stage of the *manini*, convict tang or surgeonfish *(Acanthurus triostegus sandvicensis)*. See **makali'i.**

'ōhua kūkae pua'a. Name for young of the triggerfish, *humuhumu (Rhinecanthus rectangulus* and *R. aculeatus)*. In another place it is called the young of the *hou*, one of the several Hawaiian words including *'āwela* listed as the optional names of the wrasse *Thalassoma purpureum.*

'ōhua liko. Earliest stage of growth of the *manini (Acanthurus triostegus sandvicensis)*. This stage is transparent.

'ōhua limu kala. A species of small fish. No data. (A.)

'ōhua līpoa. Young of the *manini (Acanthurus triostegus sandvicensis)*. They feed on the *līpoa*, seaweed.

'ōhua pa'awela. Young stage of the *'āwela (Thalassoma fuscum)*.

'ōhua palemo. Young of the *uhu*, a parrotfish *(Calotomus carolinus)*.

'ōhua unahi nui. Same as *'ohua palemo*. Lit., very scaly.

'ōhuna, 'ōhune. Brown goby *(Bathygobius fuscus)*. Flourishes in tide pools, growing to 5 inches.

'ō'ili. 1. Fantail filefish *(Pervagor spilosoma)*. Grows to 5 inches.

Also called *'ō'ili lepo*, *'ō'ili 'uwi'uwī*. **2.** Barred filefish *(Cantherhines dumerili)*. Body color varies from gray to brown. Grows to one foot.

'ō'ili lepa, 'ō'ili lapa. Filefish *(Alutera scripta)*. Resembles the *'uwī'uwī*.

'ōilo. Young of the *'ōio*, bonefish *(Albula* spp.).

'ō'io. Bonefish *(Albula* spp.). A long fish like the *awa* (milkfish) that grows up to 3 feet. It is a popular food fish.

'ōkuhekuhe, 'ōluheluhe. Young *'ōkuhe*, sleeper (family Eleotridae) after the *hinana* stage. For the adult fish, see **'akupa.**

'ōkūkū. Young stage of the goatfish *(Parupeneus porphyreus)*. For the adult fish, see **kumu.**

'ōlale, 'ōlali. Young stage of the *hou (Thalassoma purpureum)*; other names for the young stage; *pākaueloa*, *'āwela*, *kanaloa*, etc. These are all shallow water fishes.

'ololā, 'o'ololā. Young stage of the mullet *(Mugil cephalus)*. For the adult fish, see **'anae.**

'ōmaka. Belted wrasse *(Stethojulis balteata)*. This fish makes spawning visits in small groups in Puako Bay, Hilo, Hawai'i. Called *makiawa* in Hilo.

'ōmalemale. Young stage of the *uhu*. See **male.**

'ōmilumilu. *Ulua (Caranx melampygus)*. One of the most frequently caught of the *ulua*. See **momoni, nuku mone'u.**

'ōnihoniho. Term used for several lizardfishes, *ulae* (family Synodontidae). Maximum size of any is 16 inches. They burrow in sand for protection. Some prefer deeper waters.

ono. Wahoo *(Acanthocybium solandri)*. Attains 6 feet in length. Usually taken by trolling, it is a popular food fish.

'o'onui. Black sergeant or demoiselle *(Abudefduf sordidus)*. See **'ao'ao nui, kūpīpī.**

'o'opu. Hawaiian sleeper or goby of the families Eleotridae and Gobiidae, a small bottom-dwelling fish. Young are called *hinana*.

'o'opu hapu'u. A grouper *(Epinephelus quernus)* that lives in deep water. Its young stage is called *hāpu'upu'u*.

'o'opu hue. Several fishes carry this Hawaiian name: **1.** Puffer *(Arothron hispidus)*. Has a rough skin and is ugly. Well known for its poison. Also known as *makimaki, lauhua*. **2.** Spiny puffer *(Diodon holocanthus)*. It can puff up its body. It grows to a length of 20 inches, feeding on a great variety of benthic life in quiet waters. See **kōkala, makimaki. 3.** Porcupine fish *(Diodon hystrix)*. Has an astonishing appearance, featuring erectable spines, large cow-like eyes, strong jaws, and fused teeth. Attains 20 inches in length. Lives in quiet shoreline waters. Also called *hoana, kōkala.*

ʻoʻopu kāhaʻihaʻi. Two hawkfishes: **1.** *Cirrhitops fasciatus.* This one grows to 6 inches. Also called *ʻoʻopu kai, pili koʻa.* **2.** *Paracirrhites fosteri.* This hawkfish has an oblong shape, brown body above and white below with a blackish band on the upper side. It grows to 10 inches. See **pili koʻa.**

ʻoʻopu kai. Two fishes bear this Hawaiian name: **1.** Stocky hawkfish *(Cirrhitus pinnulatus).* Has an oblong shape and an edible flesh. Reaches 9 inches in length. Also called *poʻopaʻa.* **2.** Redbar hawkfish *(Cirrhitops fasciatus).* Grows to a length of 5 inches. See **ʻoʻopu kāhaʻihaʻi, pili koʻa.**

ʻoʻopu lehe. Goby, male of the *nākea (Chonophorus stamineus).* Reaches more than 6 inches in length. Also called *nōkea.*

ʻoʻopu nākea. Goby *(Chonophorus guamensis).* A small, white-spotted goby, the largest in the islands. It is a popular food fish.

ʻoʻopu nāpili. Goby *(Sicydium stimsoni).* A small-scaled, freshwater species, reaching 7 inches in length.

ʻoʻopu oau. Hawaiian sleeper *(Eleotris sandwicensis)* called *ʻoau* on Oʻahu and Maui. Grows to 9 inches. Also called *ʻŌkūhe, ʻapohā.*

ʻoʻopu ōkuhekuhe. See **ʻōkuhekuhe.**

ʻōpelu. Mackerel scad *(Decapterus pinnulatus).* This fish along with the *aku,* is believed to have accompanied Pili to the islands. It reaches 20 inches in length and is bluish in color on its upper third and white below. Also called *ʻōpelumama.* See **palahū.**

ʻōpule, ʻōpulepule. Pearl wrasse *(Anampses cuvier).* Grows to 15 inches. Also called *hilu (Coris flavovittata).* Its young are called *ʻālinalina.* See **mākolu.**

ʻōpule laliʻi. Group of several kinds of *ʻōpule,* wrasse *(Anampses cuvier).*

ʻōpule lā uli. *Anampses cuvier.* No other data.

ʻōpule mākole. Surgeonfishes (family Acanthuridae).

ʻōpulepule. Pearl wrasse *(Anampses cuvier),* attains about 15 inches in length.

ʻōpuʻupuʻu. Shore fish. No data. (Malo 46).

ʻowau, ʻoau. A variety of *ʻōʻōpu (Eleotris fusca)* Cf. *ʻoau, ʻowau.* Also called *ʻōkuhe, ʻapohā.* See **ʻakupa.**

paʻapaʻa. Hawaiian dascyllus, a demoiselle *(Dascyllus albisella).* Lives in large heads of finger coral. Reaches 5 inches in length. See **ʻaloʻiloʻi, ula paʻapaʻa.**

pāeaea. Redfish or big-eye. See **ʻaweoweo.**

pahaha. Young stage of the mullet *'ama'ama*. Also called *kahaha*, hand-length size.

pāhenehene. No data. (CMH.) Might refer to *paheuheu*. No data. (PE.)

pahu. Trunkfish *(Ostracion meleagris)*. A very common species, growing to 9 inches. It lives in quiet waters along the shore line, and if disturbed it emits a poison from the skin. The fish is *kapu* to women. See **moa.**

pahuhu. Young of the *uhu*, parrotfish (family Scaridae).

pakaiele. Young of the surge wrasse, *hou* fish *(Thalassoma purpureum)*. Other young-stage names are *'āwela, 'ōlali, 'ōlani, pākanaloa, pakueloa, pā'ou'ou*.

pākala, pākalakala. Young of the unicornfish *(Naso unicornis, N. brevirostris)*. For the adult fish, see **kala.**

pakiī. Common flounder *(Bothus mancus)*. Grows to 18 inches. Lives in shallow waters on sandy bottoms.

palahoana. Many-whiskered brotulid fish *(Brotula multibarbata)*. Grows to 24 inches. Secretive and shy, it lives in the crevices of the reef. Also called *pūhi palahoana*.

palahū. Mackerel scad *(Decapterus pinnulatus)*. It is bluish in color on its upper third and white below. Grows to 20 inches. See **'ōpelu.**

palani. Surgeonfish *(Acanthurus dussumieri)*. The body of this fish is pale yellowish-brown with fine blue longitudinal lines and a yellow band through the eye. It lives in deeper waters outside the reef, growing to 18 inches. It is one of the most important species caught by trap fishermen. Its skin and flesh have a strong odor.

palapala. Hawaiian sergeant, a demoiselle *(Abudefduf abdominalis)*. See **mama'o.**

palemo. Young of parrotfish, *uhu (Scarus perspicillatus)*.

palu. Cardinalfish *(Apogon taeniopterus)*. Grows to 9 inches in length.

pālukaluka. Parrotfish, *uhu* (family Scaridae). Similar to *pāuhuhu*.

pā niho loa. Wrasse *(Thalassoma purpureum)*. Has a red body with green markings. Grows to 18 inches.

pānukunuku, pōnukunuku. Parrotfish *(Scarus perspicillatus)*. Second stage growth of the *uhu*.

pāo'o. Rockskipper, zebra blenny *(Istiblennius zebra)*. The first name comes from its accuracy in leaping from pool to pool along a shoreline as a means of escape. It inhabits tide pools.

pāoʻo kauila. Short-bodied blenny *(Exallias brevis)*. Grows to 6 inches. Lives on coral reefs. Also called *ʻoʻopu pāoʻo.*

pāoʻo lehei, pāoʻo lekei. A rockskipper that can hop and leap, like a goat over a wall.

pāoʻo pūhi. Freshwater eel that inhabits Hilo's coastal waters.

paʻopaʻo. Yellow jack, *ulua (Gnathanodon speciosus)*. The adults are whitish with faint dark bars; the young are yellow with distinct black bars. Grows to 3 feet. Popular for eating raw. Also called *ulua paʻopaʻo.* See **momoni, nuku moneʻu.**

pāʻouʻou. Young of the wrasse, *hou (Thalassoma purpureum)*. See **pakaiele.**

papaʻohe. Young of the big-eyed scad *(Selar crumenophthalmus)*. For the adult fish, see **akule.**

pāuhuhu, pāuhuuhu. Parrotfish, *uhu (Scarus perspicillatus)*. Also known as *uhu ʻuliʻuli.*

paʻūʻū. Middle growth stage of the crevalle or jack *(Caranx ignobilis)*. A game and food fish. Adult attains a length of three feet.

pīhā. Round herring *(Spratelloides delicatulus)*. Grows to a length of 4 inches.

pili koʻa. Redbar hawkfish *(Cirrhitops fasciatus)*. See **ʻoʻopu kāhaʻihai, ʻoʻopu kai.**

pipiʻo. Fish. No data. (CMH.)

poʻopaʻa. Stocky hawkfish *(Cirrhitus pinnulatus)*. See **ʻoʻopu kai.**

pōʻou. Two wrasses: **1.** Hawaiian hogfish *(Bodianus bilunulatus)*. Colors vary with growth. Attains a length of 2 feet. See **ʻaʻawa.** **2.** Ringtail wrasse *(Cheilinus unifasciatus)*. Similar to *ʻeʻa, hilu.*

pua ʻāholehole. Young of *ʻāhole (Kuhlia sandvicensis)*. See **ʻāhole.**

pua ʻakuhinu. Smooth bonito, tuna fish *(Euthynnus yaito)*. Also called *pohopoho.* See **kawakawa.**

pua ʻamaʻama. Striped mullet *(Mugil cephalus)*. See **ʻamaʻama.**

pua ʻamamaha. Young of the mullet, *ʻamaʻama (M. cephalus)*.

pua ʻanae. Adult of the mullet *(M. cephalus)*.

pua kāhala. Young of the amberjack *(Seriola dumerili)*. See **halahala,** also young of the *kāhala.*

pua lele. No data. (CMH.)

pualu, puwalu. Two surgeonfishes: **1.** Yellowfin *(Acanthurus xanthopterus)*. Grows to slightly more than 2 feet. **2.** Ringtail *(A. mata)*. It is difficult to distinguish between the two species.

pua nanalu. No data. (CMH.)

pua ʻoama. Young of the *weke,* goatfish (family Mullidae). Both red and light colored *weke* were sought as offerings to the gods.

pūhi. General name for eels.

pūhi ʻaha. No data. (CMH.)

pūhi ʻāwela. Young stage of the *hou,* surge wrasse *(Thalassoma purpureum).* See ʻāwela.

pūhi kaʻawili. No data. (CMH.)

pūhi kāpā. Voracious, fighting eel.

pūhikiʻi. Young of all flyingfish (family Exocoetidae). Attains a length of up to 7 inches. Also called *kaʻawili.*

pūhi kīnaʻu. Small, white eel, mentioned in chants as eating "pandanus keys falling from heaven." (PE.)

pūhi kowali, pūhi koali. A variety of white eel. *Lit.,* eel morningglory.

pūhi lau milo. Moray eel *(Lycodontis undulatus).* An appetizing variety, often classified as *Gymnothorax. Lit.,* milo leaf eel.

pūhi lei hala. Eel. Its colors resemble a *lei* of pandanus keys.

pūhi lele. Eel. No data. (CMH.)

pūhi loʻulu. Eel whose coloration resembles the greenish-white of the *loʻulu,* palm.

pūhi moemoe. Eel awaiting its food in ambush.

pūhi nauʼai. Eel. *Lit.,* eel food chewer.

pūhi nukuʼula. Eel. *Lit.,* eel red-mouth.

pūhi ʻōilo kapa. Eel that creates havoc among many fishes.

pūhi ʻōmole. Smooth, white eel. *Lit.,* eel smooth.

pūhi ʻōpakapaka. Eel with a crinkled, rough exterior.

pūhi paka. Ferocious eel with sharp teeth that attacks even humans.

pūhi poʻolāʻau. Eel. No data (CMH.)

pūhi wela. Eel. *Lit.,* eel warm.

pū kaʻi. No data. (A.)

pūkiʻi. See *puhikiʻi.*

pūloa. Octopus. A night creature with a long body and tentacles. Very popular as bait.

uhu. Blue parrotfish *(Scarus perspicillatus).* Called *ʻōhiʻuhiʻu* at Kawaihae. Its young are called *male, ʻōmalemale.* Its second stage is called *pānahu.*

ʻuīʻuī, ʻuwīʻuwī. Triggerfish (family Balistidae). The name comes from a squeaky sound made by the fish. It lives in deeper waters outside the reef. See **humuhumu.**

ʻūkīki, ʻūkīkīkī. Small-scaled snapper, *ʻōpakapaka (Pristipomoides microlepis).* A very marketable fish that grows to 3 feet. It lives in deep waters offshore. Also called *ʻakiki, kiki, koʻi.*

uku. Blue-green snapper *(Aprion virescens).* Grows to 40 inches. Lives along the shoreline. A good food fish.

ʻulae. Two lizard fishes: **1.** *Saurida gracilis.* A slender fish living over sandy areas that grows to 12 inches. **2.** *Synodus variegatus.* A common lizardfish that grows to 16 inches.

ula pa'apa'a. Hawaiian dascyllus, a demoiselle *(Dascyllus albisella).* See **pa'apa'a.**

'ula'ula. Two snappers: **1.** *Etelis carbunculus.* Red in color above, pale yellowish below. Lives in deep water and grows to 36 inches. **2.** Marsh's snapper *(Etelis marshi).* A reddish body above, silvery below. Lives in deep waters outside the reef.

'ula'ula koa'e. Red snapper (sub-family Etelinae). Lives beyond the reef in deep water. Named for the tropic bird *koa'e* because of the long streamer on its tail.

ulua. Six-banded jack *(Caranx sexfasciatus).*Has a blue-green body with lighter hues below. Attains 60 inches. Its young are called *pā'ū'ū,* second stage, and pāpio, the youngest stage.

umaumalei. Surgeonfish *(Naso lituratus).* Has a dark brown body with orange on its caudal spine. Inhabits inshore reefs.

'upāpalu. Two cardinalfishes: **1.** spotted cardinalfish *(Apogon maculiferus).* A mostly reddish body, growing to 6 inches. **2.** Iridescent cardinalfish *(Apogon kallopterus).* A pale-reddish or brownish body, marked with dark spots. Grows to 9 inches. Both of these fishes are also known as *'ūpalupalu, 'upapalu maka nui.*

'uwī'uwī. Triggerfish (family Balistidae). See **'uī'uī.**

waleā, weleā. Snakefish *(Trachinocephalus myops).*This most distinctive member of the lizardfish family (Synodontidae), attains a length of 12 inches. It inhabits the deeper waters beyond the reef.

walu, wolu. Oilfish *(Ruvettus pretiosus).* Can grow up to 6 feet and weigh over 100 pounds. Lives in the 500 to 2,500 foot depth and is caught by hook and line. Edible but unsettling.

weke 'ula. Two goatfish: **1.** Golden banded goatfish *(Mulloides vanicolensis).* Its body is light yellow, with fins a deeper yellow. Grows to 16 inches. It is a bottom dweller. **2.** Pfluger's goatfish *(M. pflugeri).* Has a large red body, grows to 24 inches.

weleku. Snake mackerel *(Gempylus serpens).* Body color is a uniform, dark-blue slate. Grows to five feet. It inhabits the surface regions down to several hundred feet. Also known as *hāuli, hāuliuli, hāuliuli pūhi.*

weuweu. Small, round herring *(Sprattelloides delicatulus).* Slate colored above, silvery below. Reaches four inches in length. It is said that it can only be caught at night, hence its figurative meaning "success in night iniquity." See **pīhā.**

wolu, walu. Oilfish. See **walu.** Once called a mackerel.

FISHES: Fishing Glossary

The words in this category refer to the miscellany of materials that made fishing successful: bait, lines, snares, nets, baskets, sinkers, and so on. Methods are also listed: deep sea, long-line and shallow-water operations, intoxicating or stupefying the fish, diving, gathering into baskets, or driving into nets. The long list of fishes in the preceding category makes it obvious that fishing was the leading industry of the islands. With no other materials than bits of bone, lava, shells, lines of coconut fiber, parts of certain trees, and shrubs and roots, Hawaiian fishermen achieved an astonishing technology, developed and capitalized upon their powers of observation, refined their manual skills, and followed the fish with strength, persistence, and success. Theirs was a problem of survival, and indeed they solved it out of sheer necessity.

'aea. Rope or cord connecting two fishing nets. See **kūka'i.**

'ahele. Snare or trap for fish. Same as *pāhele,* but used more often. See **'alehe.**

aho. Line or cord, as a fish line.

aho kākele. Trolling line.

aho kālewa. To cast with hook and line, as for *ulua.*

'ā'ili. To pull up a line. See **kā'ili.**

'ākia. Bark of a poisonous shrub (*Wikstroemia* spp.) used in fresh water to stupefy fish. The fish may be eaten.

'aki'aki. To nibble, snap, attack, as a fish. (CMH.)

'āku'iku'i. To strike regularly upon the water with a stick to drive fish into a net. *Pāku'iku'i* has the same meaning but with greater force.

'ala'ala. Soft substance (the liver) in squid used for bait in fishing. See **wekaweka.**

'ala'alahe'e. Spawn or black substance found in the squid, used for bait. (A.)

ala'oma. To swallow bait, as the *'o'opu* and *āholehole,* whole; greedily.

'alehe. Snare, trap, noose. See **'ahele, pāhele.**

'alihi. Cords or light ropes used for fastening sinkers and floats to a net.

'alihi kepau. Lower cord for holding sinkers to the net.

'alihi pīkoi. Upper cord for holding floats to the net.

'āpua. Shell or cup for scooping up *'o'opu;* a fish trap; shank knob of a fishhook. See **pai, pai 'o'opu.**

apuapu. Beard or barb of a fishhook; rasp, file, or polishing tool for finishing a fishhook.

'apu 'auhuhu. Cup holding the poison of the *'auhuhu* shrub used to poison or stupefy fish.

'auhola. To drug fish with *'auhuhu.* See **pāholahola, hola.**

'auhuhu. Poisonous shrub *(Tephrosia purpurea)* used to stupefy fish in salt water, as *'ākia* is used in fresh water. Its pods supply the poison.

aulau. Bundle of cane or other leaves bound together, used to drive fish into a net.

aumaiewa. Many persons engaging in catching fish, using the *lau hala 'ākia.* There is no data on *lau hala'ākia,* which may refer to a group of wanderers tarrying in a fresh water area to catch fish by intoxicating them with the bark of a shrub.

'aupula. To catch fish by driving them into a net using a leafy branch called *pula* or *pūlale.*

'āwala. To pull steadily on a fishing line. A line in Andrews, " *'Āwala a'e ia me ka huki a'e i kāna he'e iluna o ka wa'a,"* can be translated, "He leaned back pulling his squid into the canoe." (A.)

'ea'ea. To cover the eyebrows, as a fisherman, to shade the eyes while looking into deep water for fish. *"Ka lawai'a nui i 'ea'ea na ku'emaka, i 'ehu'ehu no lihilihi."* (A.) "The great fisherman whose brows are sprayed with sea and whose lashes are reddened." (Translation, PE.)

'eke. Bag-shaped part of a net; bottom of the net.

hā'ali'ali. To catch fish by the gills.

hā'awa pūhi. Stick for catching eels. (CMH.)

hakakau. To stand with precarious footing, as on the edge of a canoe looking for squid.

hakakauluna. Stools on which canoes are rested. Also called *lona.* "The only relation to fish here is that this is a canoe roost." (DK.)

hakakū. Frame or platform for drying fish.

hala pia. Native pandanus, the head of which was used in exorcising evil spirits that might otherwise obstruct success in fishing.

hale ho'ahulaina. Storehouse for lines.

hanona. Deep sea fishing lure; to drag a long line toward the shore. (A.) Fishing net for *mālolo* or *'iao;* a bagnet. (PE.)

haoa pūhi. Object of *hā'awa* wood, tied at the midpoint of a fish line, easy to swallow but difficult to eject. Used in catching eels.

heau. Place where fishermen set the basket for catching fish.

hehei. To entangle, as fish in a net.

helea. To place a noose around the head of a shark.

hī aku. Place in the sea for casting for *aku, bonito.* 'Umi, an early chief, was famous as a farmer and fisherman. He was specifically remembered as one who cast for bonito.

hīna'i. Basket fish trap, braided out of the *'ie* vine using principally its aerial rootlets. See **nao maka lua.**

hi'u. Tail section of a fish.

hōkeo. Elongated gourd used as a container for fishing gear including lines.

hola. To poison or intoxicate fish, preferably in the daytime. See **'auhuhu, 'ākia, 'auhola.**

ho'olu'ulu'u. Catching fish in a basket while diving. (A.)

huakukui. Schools of fish that show their heads above water, the *'ama'ama* or *'anae* (mullets).

hui. Flippers of the sea turtle.

hului. To draw together a bag fish net when full of fish. Also called *huli, papa hului.*

ikāmū. Gathering of fish about a hook with none biting. See **kīkāmū.**

'īloli. Strong odor emanating from shark.

'inalua. Vines widely used in making baskets for catching fish. Other such vines included *pōniu, huehue, lā'au hihi, 'ie'ie.*

ipu lē'ī. Container for fishhooks.

ka'ā. Thread or line, as *olonā* fiber, to fasten hook to line; snell of a fishing line; snood.

ka'au. The number forty, used in counting fish.

ka'awili. School of fish. Also called *i'a ku, kauhulu, kahe.*

ka'i. Snood of a fishhook.

kā'ili. To take away. This word can be applied to a fishing net for that is its use. *'Ā'ili,* to take fish with a hook.

kākele. To cast with hook and line, as for *ulua.*

Kāne makua. God of the fishermen who caught *mālolo* in nets.

kapau'u. To rustle or drive fish into a waiting net by swishing, splashing, or striking the water with a leafy branch. See **kāpēike'i.**

kāpēike'i. To drive, as fish into a net by splattering water. Also called *kāpeku, kāpekupeku.* See **kapau'u.**

kaukau ulua. Catching or snaring of the *ulua.*

kāwa'a. Method of deep-sea fishing with nets.

ke aho lawai'a. Fish line. (A.)

kī. To blow chewed, oily *kukui* nut from the mouth into the sea to quiet the surface so a fisherman can look down in the water.

kialoa. Long fishing line. (A.)

kīkākala. To draw up with a hook in fishing for squid.

kīkāmū. Gathering of fish about a hook which they hesitate to bite, *īkāmū.*

kīkī'alo. To scoop fish out with a net.

kikokiko. To nibble, as fish at bait.

kīkomo. To fish with a pole in shallow water.

kilo. To look for fish on the bottom.

kilo i'a. To look for schools of fish from a high place *(pali)* and signal the fishermen.

kīlou. To catch fish with a hook.

kilu makau. Wooden vessel for fish hooks.

kīmōkīmō. To pound up fish for bait.

kini lau. Multitude of fish. *Kini a lau me ke one o kaila,* numberless as the sands of the seashore. (DK.)

kiwi. A pulling here and there, as a fish caught on a hook.

kohe. Inside barb of a fishhook.

kōheoheo. Float for a fishhook, as a stick or buoy.

kōhikōhi. To separate good fish from bad after a large haul. (A.)

koi. Fishing pole for use in the *nao maka lua* (fish-basket trap) made of *'inalua* vines. See **mākoi, mōkoi.**

konohiki. Fishing rights, named after the manager of such rights, the *konohiki.* See **pono kai lawai'a.**

ko'olau loa. Long *ulua* fishline, 15 fathoms or more.

kowali. Stick or buoy for floating a fishhook; the morning glory vine.

kuakua. Section or piece of a fishing net.

kualā. Fore-fin on the back of a fish, dorsal fin.

kū'au. Shank limb of a fishhook.

kūhinu manō. Shark hunting. (CMH.)

kūka'i. Rope fastening two fishnets together.

kuku. Stick standing perpendicular at the edge of a fishing area supporting and distending a net. (CMH.)

kūpali. To stand on a rock or cliff and fish with a pole.

kūpalu. To fish by distributing bait among fishes; chumming; to attract fish by chumming, as with decayed pork.

ku'u. To let down a net for fish.

lā'au melomelo. Herbs used to oil pieces of smooth wood, a club or stick, which, so treated was lowered into the water to attract fish. Such a stick may be smeared with bait to achieve the same effect. See **melomelo.**

lamalama. Fishing on the reef by torchlight.

lawaiʻa. Business or efficiency in one's fishing; a fisherman.

loʻe. End of fishhook opposite the point.

lona. Canoe rest, a block of wood to support a canoe out of water. See ʻaki, hakakauluna.

lualua, luelue. Round net or basket used in fishing.

lūheʻe. To pull up and down on the line, as in catching squid; octopus lure.

mahamaha. Gills or fins of a fish; fore-fins of a fish. (A.)

mākāhā. Outlet or inlet of a man-made fishpond where the sea flows in and out; a sluice gate.

makali. To bait a hook; to angle for fish. (A.)

mākoi, mōkoi. The art of deceiving fish and capturing them; fishing rod. (A.)

malau. Place where bait for *aku* is found. *Paʻimalau,* calm place in the ocean favored for *aku* fishing. (A.) Canoe bait carrier, two or three fathoms in length, with holes pierced in the sides and bottom to admit water, as used for bonito fishing. (PE.)

mali. String used in tying bait to a hook, a hook to a line, or around the end of a rope to keep it from unraveling.

maunu. General name for bait. Certain crabs and most worms are common.

melomelo. Piece of wood or a club or stick, which, smeared with bait, was let down in the water, *lāʻau melomelo.*

mikimiki. To nibble, as a fish at a hook. Also called *konikoni.* See namunamu.

moaha. White substance connected with a fish line in taking fish. (A.)

moka. Something connected with the hole of the squid; refuse matter, offal.

mōuouo. Float or buoy for a fishing net.

nae. Fishing net with very small meshes.

namunamu. To nibble, as a fish at bait. Also called *konikoni.* See ʻakiʻaki.

nao maka lua. Fish trap for small fish made from the *iʻe* vine braided into basket form. The trap was used for eels, shrimps, and wrasses. *ʻInalua* vines were used for the same purpose. See hīnaʻi.

nukuāʻula. Frame of a fishing net. (A.) Fishing net with mesh so fine that only the very tip of a finger *(nuku)* could be inserted.

ʻōlapu. Catching *ʻoʻopu* by feeling around in the water.

ona. Waiting for fish to come around the bait. (CMH.)

onaona. To come around, as fishes when a baited hook is let down. *Ho'onaona i ka i'a,* to attract fish, as with the *melomelo* (baited stick).

'ōnini. Stupefied state of fish after swallowing some *'auhuhu.* (CMH.)

paeāea. To fish with a rod or light pole offshore; pole-fishing.

pāhoe. Fleet of canoes fishing for *mālolo* (flyingfish). (A.) To drive fish into a net by beating rhythmically against the canoe with paddles. (PE.)

pāholahola. To poison or stupefy fish with the *'auhuhu,* a shrubby, slender legume *(Tephrosia purpurea).* Its pods supply the poison.

pai. Fish trap, a closely woven, funnel-shaped wicker basket for catching small fish, shrimps, etc. *Pai,* meaning to lift up or raise, gives the basket its name. See **'āpua, pai 'o'opu.**

pai 'o'opu. Shell or cup for scooping up the *'o'opu,* small fish; a basket trap for small fish. See **'āpua, pai.**

paka. Stone used as a sinker on a fishing line in deep waters; to fish with a hook and line not using a pole, as with *ulua.*

pākali. To distribute bait slowly, bit by bit, to lure fish to the hooks; chumming.

pakelo. To slip out, as a fish from one's hands.

pāku'iku'i. Net laid in a coral reef into which fish were driven by beating the water; stick used to drive the fish. See **āku'iku'i.**

palu. Entrails of fish used in taming or chumming fish.

pāno'ono'o. To be bare of fish, as the beach at very low tide.

papa'u, papau'u. Shallowness, no depth, as at low tide.

papa waha nui. Taking fish with a long net. (A.) Large baglike net used for *akule.* (PE.)

pau heoheo. A person returning from fishing without any fish is *pau heoheo.* (A.)

peleleu. Fishing canoe of the largest size, made proportionally shorter than usual. This was also a canoe made by Kamehameha's builders to use in visiting the islands.

pepekeu. No data. (CMH.)

pihi. Fish. *Eng. Ua loa'a mai ka pihi nui,* got the big fish. (from a song, PE.)

pīkoi. Any substance, such as wood, that will cause a fishing net to float; small buoy.

pīkoni. Cords connected with buoys and sinkers of a fishing net; a float attached to a net; a buoy.

pikopiko, pikapika. Ink of the squid emitted from under its tails. The water assumes different colors depending on how much ink is released into the water. Also, the suction cups on octopus tentacles.

pōhākialoa. Sinker used as a weight on a deep sea line.

poho. Deep basket or container made of the *'ie* vine and used to hold fish as they are caught.

poho aho. Container for fishing lines.

pono kai lawai'a. Fishing rights.

pū'ā. School of fish; to cut or hew off obliquely, as in shaping the ends of a canoe; fishhook used in catching the *'ea* (turtle).

puhipuhi. To blow any substance that has been chewed in the mouth into the sea to decoy or intoxicate fish.

puka'aki. To divide fish among the families of the fishermen.

puka nui. Basket used in catching fish; *hīna'i puka nui,* widemouthed basket. (A.) Basket made of the *'ie'ie* vine aerial roots for carrying fishing gear. (PE.)

pula, pūlale. Leafy branch of coconut, pandanus, or *ilima,* used as a broom to drive fish into a net or to flush them out of rock crevices. (PE.)

punihei. Ensnared, entangled, caught, as in a fish trap; surrounded, as in a net.

pu'u i'a. Heap of fish; string of fish, as on a ti leaf.

uhina. Throw or cast net.

uhu pākali. An *uhu* used as a decoy for other fish. The purpose is to deceive and catch fish.

ulawai'a. To fish.

unahi. To scale, as a fish; the scales of a fish.

'upena hola. Net used with *'auhuhu* to spread the poison among the fish.

'ūpiki. To trap, snare.

wai'ele. To poison or intoxicate fish with *'auhuhu;* to catch fish by benumbing them.

wailuku. Fishing line for *ulua.*

wekaweka. Soft substance in squid used for bait. It is mixed with *'auhuhu* and used as bait. See **'ala'ala.**

FISHES: Fishhooks

Researchers among the islands of Polynesia have determined that fishhooks can serve as a major clue in determining the migrations of people. The examination and comparison of fishhooks found in new excavations are a relatively reliable means of establishing authentic migration routes. Morever, by subjecting their finds to C14 analysis, anthropologists are setting actual dates for the migrations among the many groups of Pacific islands.

Kenneth Emory, the distinguished anthropologist, has charted specific migration periods from islands south of the equator to the Hawaiian islands, and his projections have been generally accepted.

In all the Hawaiian islands, fishhooks were fashioned from the bones of humans, dogs, and hogs. Mollusk and tortoise shells, too, were used in making smaller hooks. Fishermen were skilled craftsmen, despite the limitations of their materials and tools. Their ability to adapt materials to their needs and to design exactly the right fishhook for catching a certain kind of fish was clearly an exceptional trait.

ahi. Hook for catching the bonito, yellow-fin tuna.

auaue'a. No data. (CMH.)

'auku'u. Fishhook with a long slender shaft, shaped like a heron's neck.

hi'ikala. Fishhook used for the *kala* (surgeonfish) with *kala,* a seaweed, for bait. It had inside and outside barbs.

hiohio. Whistling lure used in trolling.

ho'olaoa. Hook for catching eels.

ho'onoho. Bone hooks lashed together; two points on one shank. (MALO 79.)

hulu. Hawaiian hackle, made of pig bristles lashed crosswise to the long axis of the shank making the lure ride on its back with the point up when trolling.

kaianoa. Bonito lure made of shell or a fishhook of bone, using two small barbless hooks. (MALO 79.)

kakaka. Deep sea fishing with a weighted line. (PE.)

kakala. Squid lure. See **kakalahe'e.**

kakalahe'e. Squid hook used with a stone weight and a cowry shell. (PE.) Art of making fishhooks. (CMH.) See **kakala.**

ke'aawaileia. Fishhook with many barbs.

kīholo. Large wooden hooks used for sharks and other large fish. See **makau.**

kīkalake'e. Fishhook. No data.

kīki'i. Fishhook with a bend that followed a spiral close to the shank. (MALO 79).

kiu. Fishhook. No data.

koehonua. Two-pronged fishhook.

kue. Fishhook, its point curved backward almost to the shaft, for catching large fish; rotating hooks.

lawa. A hook for catching sharks.

lea. Barb. *Cap.*, goddess of fishermen and of canoe makers.

leho he'e. Cowry-shell lure, used at 80 to 120 fathoms, with the fisherman shaking *(lu he'e)* the lure. Called the octopus lure.

lihi. Pearl-shell lure, used for bonito.

lou. To come up on a hook, as a fish; fishhook. (Puk. 27:3.)

lu'aloa. Large fishhook used for large fish.

maka pūhi. Hook with opposing barbs, used for eels. *Lit.*, point eel.

makau. General term for fishhook; shark hook. See **kīholo.**

makau 'ea. Turtle-shell hooks.

makau hanona. Hook for use with the *hanona* (long fishing line).

makau iwi kanaka. Fishhook made of human bone.

makau manō. Shark hooks made of hard wood. The hook was made of a bone point held in a wooden hole and lashed with *olonā* strips and thread. Also called *'aweoaweo, koai'e, uhiuhi, walehe'e.*

makau palaoa. Fishhook made of ivory from a whale.

makau pāpaua. Fishhook of pearl shell.

mana. Fishhook for catching eels.

manamana ho'i hope. Barb. (CMH.)

mūhe'e. Mother-of-pearl lure, which has colors suggesting the pattern of the *mūhe'e* (cuttlefish).

nuku. Series of hooks attached to a longline.

'ōhi'uhi'u. Hook for the *uhu.*

'ōmau. Barbless hook.

pā. Term for bonito hooks made of pearl shell used throughout Polynesia. The word refers to the shank, a surfboard shaped segment of pearl shell, to which the point or hook is tied. (KILO.)

pā ānuenue. Pearl-shell lure of rainbow colors.

pā hau. White pearl-shell lure.

pā hi aku. Bonito hook.

pāhoehoepele. Hook for catching sea turtles.

pākau ulua. Hook of wood for *ulua.*

pā mae. Pearl shell with variegated colors.

pāuihi. Mother-of-pearl bonito lure used when the sun is bright overhead.

pua. Hook used for catching turtle.

uhi. Hooks made of pearl shell.

uhi pa'a. Mother-of-pearl hook that can be used in any light during the day.

FISHES: Fishing Nets

This category, together with the preceding one on hooks, makes a valuable supplement to the major listing of fishes. The specialization of nets for different purposes was as comprehensive as that of hooks.

There are shallow water nets, scare nets, "drive-ins," and seines; there are nets with various sizes of mesh, and nets designed for catching only a single species of fish. Some are baskets, bags, or traps; others are draw or drag nets.

The making of nets demanded good powers of observation, skills in the craft of making strong cords from *olonā* or sennit, and boundless energy.

'a'ai, 'a'ei. The fine meshed net used to catch *'ōpelu* and *maomao*.

'ahu'ula. Net with small meshes. Others with fine mesh; *nae, puni, naepuni* and *'upena 'ōhua palemo*.

'aki'iki'i. Round dip-net for the *pahuhu,* young of the *uhu.* Also called *'upena pāki'iki'i, 'upena āki'iki'i.*

'alihilele. Dragnet used for catching the *'anae* (mullet).

'apai. Deep, long net for catching *'ōpae;* a fish trap.

'āpi. Decoy stick-basket with a large mouth, replaced later by a trap of very small mesh.

'apo'apo. Kind of net suspended in a canoe in deep-sea fishing *(ho'olewalewa).* (CMH.)

'eke. Bag net; properly, the bottom or the bag part of the net.

hano. Bag net used to catch flying fish *(mālolo)* and *'iao* (silversides).

holahola. Small surround-net used in shallow water with a drug from the *'auhuhu* plant.

holowa'a. Fishnet. No data.

ho'olewalewa. Two-and-a-half-inch-mesh gill net suspended from the side of a canoe in deep sea fishing. (DK.)

ho'olu'ulu'u. To dive and take fish in a basket *(hīnalea).*

kae'epāo'o. Species of net for catching the *pāo'o;* net hung on an ellipsoidal frame.

kae'epo'o. No data. (CMH.)

ka'i. Snare type of net.

ka'i'i. Small-meshed net.

kā'iki. Net of fine meshes.

kā'ili. To snatch or take away, as with a net or line; might be called a snatching net; a net for mackerel.

kāwa'a. Net used in deep-sea fishing; a deep water surround-net.

kūe'e'ōhua. Species of fishnet. No data. (A.)

kūpō. Scoop net; long net stretched across the path of fish, one end in deep water, the other in shallow. (MALO 210).

ku'u. To let a net down for fish.

lau kapalili. Trembling or vibrating net; leaves tied to a net to frighten the fish into the net, as in the *hukilau.*

lualua. Round net for catching fish, *he 'upena poepoe.* See **luelue.**

luelue. Long flexible net, *he 'upena luelue;* bag net with finger width meshes, lowered by four cords. See **lualua.**

māhā, maka. Net of four-finger-size mesh. (PE.)

mākāhi. Net of one-finger-size mesh. (PE.)

mākini. Species of fishnet. No data. (A.)

mālua. Net of two-finger-size mesh. (PE.)

mākolu. Net of three-finger-size mesh. (PE.)

nae. Net of quarter-inch-fine mesh.

nukunukuwā'ula. Smallest mesh of the long nets, only the finger tips can gain entrance. See **pāloa.**

pahu. Gill net for shrimp, *'ōpae.*

pāki'iki'i. Small net for fishing in the shallows.

pāku'ipai. Net for shrimp, *'ōpae.* See **pāloa.**

pāloa. Same as *pāku'ipai.*

papa. Middle section of a net.

papa hului. A bag net; to draw together, as a net when full of fish.

puka nui. A basket used in catching fish.

puni. Fishnet with small meshes. See **nae.**

uhina. Net for taking fish; throw or cast net.

'uī'uī. Shallow basket for the *'uī'uī,* triggerfish family. (CMH.)

uluulu. Species of fishnet; diving or scoop net.

'upena. Cord of which fishnets are made; sennit; a net, trap.

'upena 'āki'iki'i. Dip net. See **'āki'iki'i, 'upena pāki'iki'i.**

'upena ani. Drag net. (CMH.)

'upena 'iao. Net for bait, for such fish as *aku* and bonito.

'upena kaka. No data. (CMH.)

'upena kāwa'a. Deep-sea fishing net about 40 fathoms long. Used with canoes to spread *(kāwa'a)* the nets.

'upena kolo. Seine; a deep bay; large net.

'upena ku'u. Species of net; gill net.

'upena nehu. No data. (CMH.)

'upena 'ōhua palemo. Net used for the young of the *palemo,* parrotfish.

'upena 'ōio. Fishnet with three- to four-inch mesh for *'ōio, nenui, 'awa,* two to three fathoms.

'upena 'ōpule. Special net for wrasse fishes. (CMH.) See **'ōpule** in **Fishes: Kinds.**

'upena pahu. Gill net used in shallow waters. (MALO 213.)

'upena pāki'iki'i. Dip net. See **'āki'iki'i.**

'upena pāku'ipai. Fine meshed net into which *opae,* shrimp were "splashed," as a way of catching them.

'upena papa. Combination three-net bag with each scaled from a wide opening, *pūhi nui* through a smaller mesh-middle net, *pūhi iki* into the smallest, *mole* or *pūpū. Lit.,* layer net.

'upena pili. Nets attached to the sides of the opening of the *pāku'iku'i. Lit.,* net joining.

'upena poepoe. Round net for taking fish.

'upena pōuouo. Net supported by buoys, floats or lighters. *Mouo, mōuouo* is the float or buoy itself.

'upena pua. Float or buoy for a net. (CMH.)

'upena uhu. Net for the *uhu,* parrotfish.

GODS AND GODDESSES

There was an infinite variety of deities in the Hawaiian pantheon —for individuals, classes, or families. One prolific source of such divinities grew out of the founding generation of a population. Each member of that generation was given a personality and a power as, in a similar fashion, human characteristics were given to the gods of ancient Greece.

Hawaiians utilized their imaginations, clothing in supernatural guise fishes, animals, and birds, wind and rains, sky and clouds, oceans, mountains, and plains. There were gods of waters, husbandry, dances, fishermen, speech, and inspiration—in short, every area conceived of by the minds of men.

While some of the names of the gods and goddesses were simple, of perhaps one to three syllables, others could be long, imaginative compounds: for example, Leleho'oha'aha'a, with eight syllables, and Mahikipo'oki'eki'e-ukewa, with twelve.

This category is filled with rich images ranging from qualities ascribed to the universe and the awesome zodiacal calendar, to those imbued with the earthliness of humans. Just as they sang their genealogies, so they recited the sagas of the gods.

'Ā'āhuali'i. Dwarf of great strength said to have come from the center of the earth. Progenitor of all dwarfs.

'Aholoa. God of the fisherman. See **Kū'ula.**

Āi 'a'a kū'ula. God of the fishermen of Hawai'i, son of Kū'ula, father, and Hinahele, mother. *Lit.,* red Kū.

Ākea, Wākea. Ancestor of all Hawaiians who founded the island kingdom of Papahaunaumoku.

akua. General name for god; night when the moon was perfectly full.

Akua-'aumakua. God of persons who died long ago and are now gods. (A.)

Akua-haiamio. God of silence. (CMH.)

Akua-hānai. God of poison; poison itself. (A.)

akua ho'ounauna. Class of gods sent on errands like the Greek Mercury; god given a mission of destruction.

akua lā'au. God figure of wood.

akua lapu. Ghost, specter, evil spirit.

Akualele. Flying god, meteor. When the Hawaiians first saw pictures of angels they called them *akualele.*

Akua-mo'o. God of the lizard and of all reptiles.

akua noho. Class of gods considered to be the spirits of men deceased. (MALO 15–17). The practice of *ho'onohonoho akua* (obsession) was of hoary antiquity and a source of influence on the natives. According to Malo, the whole thing was nonsense.

Akua-ulu. God of inspiration.

'Āla'amaomao, La'amaomao. God of the winds. "Eolus" of the Hawaiian Islands. (A.) *Ka ipu makani o La'amaomao* is an elongated calabash in the Bishop Museum that may have held the bones of the god or goddess of the winds. (KILO.)

'alae ke'oke'o. Bird, a coot, worshiped as a god or *'aumakua.* A black bird with a white frontal knob above the beak.

'alaneo. Class of gods, males only; hermaphrodite healers from Kahiki (Tahiti).

'Āma'uma'u. God growing among the ferns on the mountains.

'Anahua. God of husband-men, second son of *Lua ho'omoe,* a star. (A.)

Apukohai. Evil god infesting the waters of Kaua'i. (CMH.)

'aumakua. Class of ancient, ancestral family gods, trusted by living descendants. Each was a spirit deified and worshiped. Emerson said that in a popular sense each may be considered a cross between a mascot and a guardian.

eho. Stone idol: *he akua o Lono-ka-'eho.*

'Ewa. Name of a god. (CMH.)

'Ewa'amahiki. Name of a god. (CMH.)

Ha'i. God of the *po'e kuku kapa.* (CMH.)

hakuakea. Phrase in praise of Lono; a lord of extensive power.

Ha'u-lili. God of speech on Kaua'i. (CMH.)

Haumea. Mother of the war god Kekauakahi. She was associated with Papa as the "earth-mother" goddess.

heiau. Enclosure of 1 to 5 acres, with walls 10 feet thick and 20 feet high, capped perhaps with slabs tapered up. Inside the enclosure is a wood or stone temple *(luakini)*, house of sacrifice. Within is the *anu'u* of wicker work. (CMH.) See **Heiaus.**

Heka. Godlings of Hamakua. (CMH.)

hiaka. Company of gods belonging to Pele; among the *akua noho* class. (A.)

Hi'i-aka. General name for the gods and goddesses of volcanoes. Also the prefix name of Pele's twelve sisters. Each had power over one of nature's forces such as volcanoes, waves, or disease. Haumea was the mother of these thirteen sisters.

Hinahele. Goddess of fishes, often called Hina. She was mother of 'Āi'ai-a ku'ula, god of fishermen.

Hinakuluiua. Goddess of rain who had two sisters, Hinakeali'i and Ho'oku'ipa'ēle.

Ihumāka'imaka'i. Evil god infesting or inhabiting the waters of Kaua'i.

Kā'anahua. God of husbandmen, second son of high priest Luaho'omoe.

Kaeha'akeakua. No data. (CMH.)

Kaekae. Name of a star.

Kaha'ea. A god. No data. (CMH.)

kahiko o ke akua. Poetic phrase speaking of the adornment of the gods.

Kahuila-o-ka-lani. One of the names of Kālai-pāhoa, said to be a god from a foreign country.

kai a pōkea, kai o poke'o. Long prayer used after the *kauila* celebration at a *heiau* dedication. The sea water used for the ceremony was poured into a bleached skull. (MALO 181).

Kā'ili. Great feather god of Kamehameha the Great and the line of chiefs from which he came. Also called *Kūka'ili.* See **Kūkā'ili-moku.**

Kakaka. God of fishermen. (CMH.)

Kālai-pāhoa. Tree forms of three gods: Kahuila-o-ka-lani, Kāne-i kaulana-'ula, and Kapo. The wood of these trees was believed to be poisonous. The trees grew at Mauna-loa, Moloka'i.

Kalehuokēakua. Name of a god. No data. (CMH.)

Kalo. One of the class of gods called *akua noho.* Kiha-wahine, the lizard goddess of Maui, was also of that class. Both were presumed to possess the spirits of departed mortals.

Kaluanu'unohoni'oni'o. One of the gods in the *luakini.* (A.)

Kama. Powerful tutelary god of all the islands. (CMH.)

Kama-i-huli pū, Kama-i-kāhuli wa'a. Names of gods who aided in floating upset canoes.

Kamakalei'oku. God made of the *koa lau lani* tree, a species of *koa.* One of Kahekili's sons was named Koa-lau-kani.

Kamanoakeakua. No data. (CMH.)

Kama-pua'a. Son of the fabled hog, *kupua* or wizard. He was the husband of Pele and their son was 'Ōpeluho'oli'i, or 'Ōpelu-nuikauha'alilo. *Lit.,* son of a hog. Kama-pua'a could take the form of a handsome man, a hog, or a fish. (KILO.)

Kamilohae. A god. No data. (CMH.)

Kamokoali'i. Pele's older and favorite brother. (DK.) He was called King of the Sharks.

Kanaloa. Fallen Hawaiian angel, prince of darkness and chief of the infernal world, who was placed in the pantheon of gods with Kū, Lono, and Kāne. He was called the god of mischief and of healing. (DK.) Also called the god of the sea and, with Kāne, a digger of springs of water.

Kāne. Architect and builder, one of the four great gods. God of creation, sunlight, fresh water, and forests. There were no human sacrifices in his *heiau.* Prayers were offered to some seventy forms of *Kāne.* (KILO.)

Kāne'āpua. Younger shark brother of Kāne and Kanaloa; perhaps a brother of Pele. He was a trickster *(kupua).*

Kānekaula. A god. No data. (CMH.)

Kāne lā'au uliuli. God who died because he swore by the law.

Kāne milohai. Relative of Pele who came from Kahiki, Tahiti, to visit Hawai'i. Called Kāne, accepter of sacrifice.

Kāne nui'akea. General name for the class of thirteen gods connected with the larger *heiaus*: Kāne-hakia; Kāne-holepali, god of precipices; Kāne'ika'alei; Kāne-ikamakaukau; Kāne-ikapuahakea; Kāne-ikapualena, god of Kawelo, son of Māhunaliʻi and Malai; Kāne-ikokea; Kāne-kiʻi; Kāne-kohala; Kāne-ielo; Kāne-makua, a god of the fisherman; Kāne-paina, a living thing like a fish, worshiped as a god; Kāne-pōhākaʻa, god of thunder, rolling stones.

Kāne-ōpua. God worshiped by Lanaʻi fishermen.

Kāne-popolo hiwa. God who had charge of the black clouds and the deep black and red clouds.

Kāne-popolo hua. God who took care of the sea.

Kāne-puaʻa. God of husbandry.

Kāne-ʻuala. God of the fishermen who netted small fish.

Kāne-ulala. God of the insane.

Kapoʻohaʻakea. A god. No data.

Kaualoku. A god. No data. (CMH.)

Keakua-manō. Shark god.

Kealoewa. Wooden image in the Bishop Museum labeled goddess of rain.

keawakoʻo. Name of a stone idol near the top of Mount Waiʻale-ʻale on Kauaʻi. (A.)

Keawenuikauohilo. One of the class of gods called *akua noho.*

Keoloewa. One of the class of gods called *akua noho,* worshiped in the *heiau*s of Maui.

Kihanuilulumoku. A god of Maui; father of Liloa, *aliʻi nui kapu,* sacred high chief. *Lit.,* lizard shaking island.

Kiha-wahine. Lizard goddess classed among the *poe akua noho.*

Kīnaʻu. A god. No data. (A.)

Kineokeakua. No data. (CMH.)

kōleamoku. *Heiau* named after the first man to learn the use of herbs in healing, who was deified after his death. The chief who built the *heiau* recovered from a serious illness through the herb treatment.

Kū. One of the four great gods, god of war, male generating power, and medicine. There are thirty forms of *Kū.*

Kuahana. God who killed men wantonly.

Kuahuia. No data. (CMH.)

Kuakai. Gods of the seashore. See **Kuaʻuka.**

Kualanawao. God who was given the use of the mountainside for food.

Kuamū. Goddess for whom all have deference.

Kuaʻuka. Gods of the mountains as opposed to the gods of the shore. (A.) See **Kuakai.**

Kūkāʻilimoku. The feather war god. See **Kāʻili.**

Kū Kanaloa. God prayed to, as on the *kāloa* days of the month. These were the 24th, 25th, and 26th days of the lunar month.

Kū kanalu. Priests of Kū who served at the *luakini*. They were of *ali'i* ancestry.

Kūka'ōhi'akaka. God of husbandmen and Kū of the *'ōhia lehua* tree.

Kūkao'o. God of husbandmen.

Kūkeolowalu. God who makes things grow.

Kūmokuhāli'i. God who, "watching over the spreading of the land," added land for food thus "giving the mountain." Kamakau adds, "spreading forests on the land."

Kupa-'ai-ke'e. God of the canoe makers, his tongue helped eat out the hollow logs. *Lit.,* adze eating crookedness. Kamakau adds, "*Kū* the smoother of rough places."

Kūpulupulu. A god "brooding over" favorable growth of forest plants. Kamakau also adds, "*Kū,* giver of verdure."

Kū'ula. God of fishermen. If he did not give them the fish they prayed for, they sought the intercession of his wife Hina, the goddess of fishermen. See **'Aholoa.**

La'a-maomao. Goddess of winds and mother of Pāka'a. (DK.)

Lā'auli. Ancient god whose laws were not to be broken. Also called Kāne la'a uli. (A)

Lae'apua. God worshiped by fishermen of Lana'i. See **Kāne apua.** (A.)

Lakakāne. God of dances. (A.)

Lākuakea. Name for Lono, lord of great progress. (CMH.)

Lananu'u-mamao. One of the gods whose image stood outside the *heiau.* (A.)

lananu'u mamao. Oracle tower of a *heiau*. The high priest stood at the top to conduct services. (PE.)

Lanu'u. One of the gods whose image stood outside the *heiau.*

Lauhuki. God who was worshiped by *kapa* makers and *poi* pounder shapers.

Laukāhi. Son of Kuhaimoana. Now associated with Kuamo'o and Kapo, sister of Kālaipāhoa. (CMH.)

Laukahia. A god. No data. (CMH.)

Leleaioio. God who inflicted bodily pain such as *mūke'e* (twisting the face) and *'o'opa* (crippling the legs). (A.)

Leleho'oha'aha'a. Goddess, female counterpart of Leleaioio. (A.)

Li'e. Goddess of the mountain who braided leis; *ke ano o (Li'e) Lei wahine.*

Lono. One of the four great gods. He was the god of agriculture, fertility, wind, and clouds.

Lonoakiki. Eel god. (A.)

Lono-'i-ka-'auali'i. God worshiped in the *heiaus* of O'ahu. (CMH.)

Lono-i-ka-makahiki. God of the annual harvest *makahiki* trip for collecting taxes around the island. Patron of sports.

Lono-i-ka-ou-ali'i. Lono in the chiefly signs of the heavens.

Luanu'u. Name of two gods in the house of Lono. (A.)

Mahiki-po'o-ki'eki'e uke-'wa. Name of a god. No data. (CMH.)

Mahulu. Name common to three gods in the house of Lono. (A.)

Makauoa. Lono's gods. (CMH.)

Maliu. Chief, deified, who entered the ranks of *'aumakua.* (A.)

Manu. Name of two gods at the gate of Lono's yard. (A.)

Milu. Successor of 'Ākea. He is the "Pluto" of the Hawaiian underworld. (A.)

Moa'ali'i. Great shark god of Moloka'i and O'ahu. (CMH.)

Mō'ī. One of the gods in the *luakini.*

Mokuali'i, Mokuhāli'i. Canoe makers' god.

Moloka'i-a-Hina. Moloka'i and the following four major islands each had its own god or goddess: Kaua'i-a-manokalanipō, he of double royal lineage; Hawai'i-a-Keawe, son of Keakealani of Hilo; Maui-a-Kama, Kamalālāwalu with eight descendants, often used in Maui songs; O'ahu-a-Kā-kuhihewa, object of attention in songs. Once Lono-i-ka-makahiki was an incognito guest of Kākuhihewa of O'ahu. His identity was discovered when his wife, coming in search of him, recited his genealogy.

Mo'o'ale'o. Gnome of Lana'i conquered by Kaululā'au, prince of Maui. (CMH.)

Mo'o Kū. Worship of Kū by the priests of his lineage.

mo'o Lono. Priests of Lono lineage, devoted to his worship. The other great gods were Kāne and Kanaloa, who had their own priestly followings.

'ōhi'a. Class of gods under the general name of *akua noho.*

'Olopue. This god belonged to a god-class, *papa kahui,* that led spirits to or back from the spirit land.

'ōpua. Class of gods among the *po'e akua noho;* cloud gods.

'Ōuli. God of those who prayed people to death.

Pahulu. Ancient god who lived in the hole of a certain rock on Lana'i. The word means nightmare. Pahulu was killed by Kaululā'au, a Maui chief. The goddess Ho'okokukalani, the daughter of Wākea and Papa, conceived and the result was Lana'i. She was known as the sorcery goddess of that island.

pai-kauhale. Once a vagabond but formerly a god. (CMH.) Name of a star.

Papa. Wife of Ākea (var. Wākea), fabled mother of the islands and the men on them; planet Saturn.

Pele. Volcano goddess.

Pikuku. Powerful god of Hawai'i. (CMH.)

Piopio. No data. (CMH.)

Pō. One of the gods among the *po'e akua noho.*

Pohā ka'a. God supposedly living in ravines or precipitous places from whence stones were often rolled down. Kāne-i-kapōha-ka'a, or Kāne of the rolling stone *(pōhaku ka'a).*

Pohākau. A god. No data. (CMH.)

po'opua'a. One of the wooden gods in a *heiau,* the head of which resembled that of a hog; image of a hog, used as a boundary marker of the land division *ahupua'a.*

Pua. Goddess, sister of Kālai-pāhoa and Kapo, who came from a foreign country and entered certain trees, sources of poison. Also the goddess of mercy.

pueo. Owl, formerly worshiped as a god-in-darkness; one of the *po'e akua mana.* Also a family *'aumakua.*

pūku'i. Assembly of gods at the luakini.

Ukanipō. Shark god of Hawai'i. (CMH.)

'Ula'ulakeahi. The god who presided over distillation. (A.)

Uli. Name of a god to which a prayer was addressed in the *pule 'anāanā.* (A.) Goddess of sorcery, said to have come from Kahiki. (PE.)

'Ulopo. A god. No data. (CMH.)

'Unihipili. One of a class of gods called *akua noho.* *'Aumakua* was another. They were the departed spirits of deceased persons.

Wahieloa. God of a canoe-builder.

GREETINGS AND SALUTATIONS

Here are familiar good-byes, sailing terms, exclamations, commands, and salutations—some ancient, others modern. The word *aloha* means many things, as is confirmed by the *aloha* listings in this category.

aī. Exclamation of sudden surprise.

aikola. Ejaculation of scorn or derision.

'ala! Get up!

aloha. Affections, greetings, salutations, sympathies.

aloha ahiahi. Good evening.

aloha; a hui hou aku. Good-by, until we meet again.

aloha akua. God's blessing.

aloha auwinalā, auinalā. Good afternoon. *Lit.,* declining sun.

aloha 'ino! What a pity! Alas!

aloha kakahiaka. Good morning.

aloha kakahiaka aku. Late morning greeting.

aloha kakahiaka nui. Early morning greeting.

aloha kākou. Friendship and love to more than one person.

aloha kāua. May there be love and kindness between us (said to one person).

aloha mai. My great love to you.

aloha no. My deep love to you.

aloha no ia mau lā o na makahiki ke kanalima i kūnewa akula! Affectionate (memories) of those days of fifty years past! (PE.)

aloha nui. Great love to you.

aloha 'oe. Much love to you.

aloha paina. Grace at a meal.

aloha pō'ele'ele. Good night! A farewell *aloha* during a starless, overcast, black night.

'ano'ai. Ancient word meaning *aloha;* a warm salutation, still used.

auwē. Oh dear! Alas! Too bad!

auwī! Ouch!

e 'āwiki mai'oe! Hurry up!

ei ne'i, eia i ane'i! Here, here it is!

e maealani. Get up.

e ola au i ke *Akua*. So help me God (conclusion of an oath or obligation).

hapenūīa, hauoli makahiki hou. Happy New Year.

hauka! Out!, as used by a winner in gambling.

hauoli makahiki hou. Happy New Year.

hele aku! Go away!

hipahipa! Hip, hip, hurrah!

holina! Haul in!, as applied to fish or sails.

honi. To press noses.

ho'omaika'i. To render thanks, to praise, to congratulate.

ho'ōho. To exclaim, shout, halloo; exclamation. (Puk. 24:3.)

'i. Interjection of scorn, used idiomatically.

'ike, i ka ike. What does he know?

i le'a ia'oe. If you please, if it pleases you.

kā. Exclamation of mild disapproval or surprise.

kāhāhā. Exclamation of surprise or displeasure.

kāhihi. Cry of disapproval or disbelief.

kāhōhō, kāhūhū. An interjection of surprise or anger.

kai. How great! How terrific! How beautiful!

kala mai ia'u. Excuse me.

kapu moe. Moe! To kneel prostrate and cry before the chiefs.

ke aloha no. Love and affection.

kelo! Sail ho!

keonimana. Gentlemen!

kūkālā. Calls of the auctioneer.

kulikuli. Be quiet! Shut up! Quiet!

laki. Lucky.

lanaho. Land ho!

leikō anakā. Let go the anchor!

lukau. Look out; Be careful!

maikai. Fine. (A reply to "How are you? *Pehea'oe?*")

maika'i fine. Feeling very good.

maika'i no. Very good indeed.

me ke aloha pumehana. With the warmest affection.

Mele Kalīkimaka. Merry Christmas.

newenewe. Exclamation of players as they cheer on a rolling *maika* stone.

'ō. To whoop, hail.

oha. To greet, show great affection.

oho. To call, cry out.

pehea 'oe? How are you?

'ui. To ask, appeal to, turn to for counsel.

weli, welina. A greeting similar to *aloha* but more anciently used.

welina me ke aloha. Used as a salutation in a letter.

HAWAIIAN WORDS FOR SOUNDS

The following category is unlike any other in this book with the exception of one devoted to the making of *kapa* ("Kapa: A Woman's World"). It is a roundup of words relating to the subject, presented in the form of an essay instead of an alphabetical list.

This category appeared in Thrum's *Hawaiian Almanac and Annual* for 1888, as prepared by Dr. Charles M. Hyde.

The general term for sound in Hawaiian is *leo*, although properly speaking this is the word for "voice." It is related to *'ōlelo* (speech or language), and *alelo* (tongue). The term conversation has a more exact equivalent in *kama'ilio* or, if dialogue, *kikē*. If this last should be the saucy rejoinder of a child to a parent, or servant to mistress, it would be *pākīkē*.

Pule is the word for prayer. Since the uttering of incantations constituted the prevalent form of worship in ancient times, it is not surprising that lunatic is *pupule* in Hawaiian. The old priests knew something of ventriloquism *(ho'olele leo)* and could make the *akua* speak from under the altar, to the dismay of frightened worshipers. The group of which the Hawaiians were most aware was the *ni'ani'a* (accusers, gossipers, slanderers). News is *nūhou,* the first syllable indicating a mixture of Hawaiian and English notions in these days of newspapers. *Lono* is the word for tidings or a message of special importance. Rumor, or common fame in Virgil's apt description, is *wawā;* the confused talk of a multitude is *walā'au.* The sound of the *kapa* mallet *(ko'eko'ele)*—once universal throughout the islands, from early morning to darkening night—can also be applied to the not infrequent sounds of matrimonial squabbling (Hawaiians often compared wedlock to the tying together of cat and dog). Faultfinding, with its angry undertones *(huhū),* finds fitting designation in the word *'ōhumu.* The accompanying feeling of dissatisfaction and displeasure is, with equal forcefulness, called *kunukunu,* and chiding or nagging is *nukunuku.* Sullenness is *nunuha.* Backbiting speech has its equivalent in the epithet *'aki'aki,* similar in meaning to our English word (1 Kor. 6:10).

Hawaiians were (and are) fond of oratory or "talkee-talkee," as Chinese would call it. To *pa'ipa'i* is to tell another what he ought to do (Kanl. 11:2), while instruction, the other element of preaching, is *ha'ia'o;* the common word for sermon, as opposed to address, which is *ha'i'ōlelo.* English palaver, talking and not doing anything, is *palauolelo.* The braggart is not unknown in Hawai'i *nei* and his style of talk is termed *kaena;* if delivered with abundant gesticulation, it is *liki.*

Hawaiians were adept also in speaking a peculiar lingo known as *kake;* it was not exactly like the thieves' talk in the London slums, but was often used for secret purposes. To stammer or stutter is *'u'u'u,* while to be dumb is *'ā'ā.* To sit silent is *mumule,* while babbling is *namunamu,* a word applied to the speaking of a foreign language not understood by the listener, as well as to rapid, indistinct articulation. There is no term for mincing words, since it is not often that one finds even affected modesty in Hawaiians. As there are no sibilants, there is no kissing or lisping. But whispering has a very appropriate Hawaiian designation: *hawanawana.* The clicking sound heard in Hawaiian speech, owing to an occasional dropping of an obsolete k sound, is called *kaiʻi.*

There are also many words referring to suppressed speech. The word *kuʲikuli* is often heard in bidding children or grown people to keep still. The word for rapt attention, the solemn hush of a listening assembly, is *ʻeʻehia.* Some of the old words with which prayers were closed—like *ʻeliʻeli, kapu* or *ʻāmama, ua noa*—probably have a significance similar to the amen which is used in closing Christian prayers. Hawaiians are averse, usually, to loud noises and to obstreperous, rude talk. Gentleness in speech and manners is popularly expressed by *waipahē,* smooth as water when undisturbed. Wailing for the dead or tearful crying about lesser troubles is *uwē* or, if protracted, *kaniʻuhū* or *kūmākena,* the mourning one often hears in passing a house where the deceased lies awaiting burial.

All musical sounds come under the general designation *kani,* which may be compared with the Latin *cantus* (chant). Cantillation, specifically, in Hawaiian style is *olioli,* as distinct from *mele,* which has more melody than the simple recitative. In singing, different qualities of voice are recognized. Thus, we have *ikuwā,* full and strong, and *nahenahe,* with silvery clearness or mellifluous sweetness. The zephyr that blows softly is *ahe,* while the common blowing of the wind is *puhi,* perhaps like the English puff. The strong blast that strikes like a blow is *pā.* Other qualities of voice are *hanapilo* (hoarse); *oi* (sharp, shrill); *oeoe* (steam whistle); *henehene* (screech, scream). The *hula,* is *kuolokani;* the drum, *pahu kani;* its booming sound, *kaʻeleloi;* the whistling of the nose flute, *hoʻokio;* any flutelike sound, *palali;* while trilling sounds, quick vibrations are *kapalili.* On the *ʻūkēkē,* the Hawaiian musical bow (see *"Music: Instruments"*), the Hawaiian maestro can produce cries and calls that the listener comprehends as distinctly as a letter received from a friend.

Non-musical sounds, with various irregular vibrations, have their own names. *Halulu* is thundering; its vibrating peal is *nakulu;* the long reverberation, *hākuʻi. Kāpinaʻi* is an echo. Snap *(pana)* has almost the identical letters of the English word, but reversed. This denotes also the regular beat of the pulse. The reduplicated form, *pūpanapana,* distinguishes the pistol with its pop from the musket *(pūpoʻohiwi)* carried on the shoulder. A crackling sound in rapid succession is *nakeke; paʻapaʻaʻina,* the crackling of oily wood on fire, is also applied to the snapping noise of the firecracker, *paupauhu*. Boots once commanded higher prices if they had plenty of squeak (*'ui'ui*) so that the proud wearer could not but be noticed as he stalked late into a meeting house, or up to the front rows of worshipers. The Hawaiians have a word, too, to distinguish the peculiar sound a man makes when he walks with his boots full of water—*'upī'upī*.

Kūkālā (stand and call), the old Hawaiian word for proclamation, is now applied to the auctioneer's cries as he offers up his wares. *Kīkēkē* is to knock, while a tolling of the bell, a modern sound, has its specific Hawaiian equivalent, *kanikē*. The old conch shell (*pū*), which in early missionary days hung at chapel doors to summon the neighborhood to worship, is seldom heard now. *'Ōlē* means speaking through a horn or trumpet. What we call halloo is *ho'ōho* in Hawaiian. *Kihe* means to sneeze; *nonō* to snore (often confused by foreigners with *no'ono'o*, to meditate or consider). To scratch is *neke*; *nau* is the English word gnaw; to smack the lips, *mūkī*; to suck, *omo*; to swallow, *moni*. *'Olā'olā* is gargling, or the gurgling sound of swallowing; *hawewe* is a rattling or clattering sound; *kunu* is to cough; *mauli'awa* is to hiccough, but this is confused with heartburn.

Water plays a very important part in human life; but while ocean waves constantly wash Hawaiian shores, there are few babbling brooks or purling rivulets. The mountain torrent or cataract (*kahawai*) rushes down hillsides; but we seldom find a river (*muliwai*) that remains a constant flowing stream. To squirt water is *kī*; to pour it, *ninini*; to sprinkle it, *kapīpī*. The pattering of raindrops is *paka* or *lokuloku*; their gentle dripping would be called *nākulukulu*. The dashing of waves against seacliffs is *'ūhā*; the rippling of waves, *nē*; the murmuring, *kamumu*.

The fauna of the Hawaiian islands is even now very limited. Of quadrupeds there were in early times the hog (*pua'a*); the dog (*'īlio*); the rat (*'iole*); and the lizard (*mo'o*), which figures in Hawaiian legends much as does the dragon in China's fables. Horses—called *lio* because of their staring eyes when thrown overboard from ships to swim to shore—were introduced. Through a strange confusion of the English names, *hoki* means mule, and *miula* is the word for jackass (which sometimes receives its proper title, *kēkake*). But Hawaiians have words of their own for the horse's neigh (*ihiihi*) and snort (*ha'u*). The first cows were brought to the islands in 1793. Their lowing is *umō*, their bellowing, *uwō*. The cat is called *'owau*—anyone who has ever heard a caterwaul knows why; both mewing and purring are called *nino*. Rats abounded in old Hawaii, but the squeal *(wīwī)* of the native rodent is no longer heard, it having been supplanted by the more formidable Norway rat. The Malay fowl was here when Captain Cook arrived and crowed his *'o'o'o* then as now; the hens did their cackling *(pukakā)* and clucking *(pūkōkō)*. The native Hawaiian geese, however, do not know what it is to hiss, and their name, *nēnē,* is utterly unlike our idea of what hissing is. The duck *(kakā)* does as much quacking here as elsewhere. The dog's bark *(o'aoa)* is Hawaiian for bow-wow; his yelp is called *nā,* and his growl, *nunulu.* The grunt of the hog is *hū* (hoggish men are called *'ukā*). *'Alalā* is the word for the bleating of sheep and for the cries of the young of all animals. The chirp or twitter of birds is *'io;* their peep, *pio.* The owl *(pueo)* has his hoot *(ke'u);* the turkey gobbles *(kolokolo),* and the dove coos *(nūnū)* as he woos his mate. The names of many Hawaiian birds come from their peculiar cries: *alani, 'a'o, 'ālala, 'elepaio, nau, 'ūlili, kioea,* and *kōlea* among others.

Like many other peoples, Hawaiians heard mysterious sounds coming out of the darkness after nightfall. These were believed to be made by the *'ūhini* or the *'unihipili,* ghosts inhabiting the shades of night. Other night noises, such as the stridulent squeaking of crickets, are attributed by older Hawaiians to certain tree-snails *(pūpū kani oe).*

HEIAUS

This category is related to several others: "Gods and Goddesses" and "The Supernatural: Meanings and Applications."

The *heiau*s (temples) were the boldest and most common among the more massive structures in old Hawai'i. In 1910, Thrum's *Hawaiian Annual and Almanac* printed statistics of the number of *heiau* foundations that could be found on the main islands of the Hawaiian chain: Hawai'i 138, Maui 39, Moloka'i 24, Kaua'i and Ni'ihau 124, O'ahu 96, a total of 421. Most of these *heiau*s are in ruins or have been denuded of rock for various projects.

*Heiau*s were erected for many purposes; but all had a basic, common function as a place of worship. Some—at least two on each island—were places of refuge for people endangered in time of war. Others were for treating the ill, or insuring good fishing or rain. Religious ceremonies of dedication or consecration, with appropriate sacrifices of humans, animals, or certain material offerings, were conducted. Most of those ceremonies had some connection with practices of war. Some of the smaller *heiau*s also served as meeting places for the *kahuna*.

A *heiau* was extensive and well planned, constructed with one or more parallel walls. Larger *heiau*s had at least four walls and a central enclosure. Within the outermost walls were several other structures such as raised platforms, terraces, thatched huts, oracle towers, sacrificial pits and altars, and carved images.

In the Hawaiian Bible, *heiau* is translated to mean a place of Christian worship (Isa. 15:2).

Ahuʻena. *Heiau* at Kailua, Kona, built or restored by Kamehameha I and considered to be his. It was next to Kamakahonu, the residence of Kamehameha I, who died there in 1819. The site was the welcoming beach for the Christian missionaries in 1820. It is now part of the site of the King Kamehameha Hotel.

Aʻiaʻi kamahina. *Heiau* toward the sea of Kukuipoliʻu, Kohala.

alaō. A class of *heiau;* temple without a *lele* (altar).

ʻĀleʻaleʻa. *Heiau* near Hale-o-keawe, Hōnaunau, South Kona, Hawaiʻi. This was a *heiau* of sports and games, but was within the famous city of Refuge.

ʻĀpuakehau. *Heiau* near Waikīkī, Oʻahu, where *Kauhi a kama* was sacrificed with unusual indignities. Site unknown.

Hālulu koakoa. *Heiau* at Lahaina, Maui. Site unknown.

Hauʻole. *Heiau* in Hoʻea gulch, Kauaʻi, built to commemorate the recognition of Ola as a prince of the royal house.

heiau. There were many kinds of *heiau;* some had special purposes: one for treating the ill, *hoʻola;* for good fishing, *hoʻoūlu iʻa;* for rain, *hoʻoūlu;* human sacrifices, *poʻo kanaka;* temple of war, *waikaua;* city of refuge, puʻuhonua.

Helehelekelani. Small *heiau* near Kalemo, Kealakekua, Hawaiʻi. ʻŌpū-kāha-iʻa, who inspired the American Board of Commissioners for Foreign Missions to send the first Christian Missionaries to Hawaiʻi, was trained as a native priest here by his uncle Lepeamea. Site unknown.

Hikiʻau. *Heiau* at Kealekekua, Hawaiʻi. This is the *heiau* illustrated by Captain Cook's artist, Ellis. Cook was received as the god Lono on this spot.

Hōnaunau. Puʻuhonua, City of Refuge, Kona, Hawaiʻi, an enclosure 715 feet by 404 feet with walls 12 feet thick. Idols were mounted on the walls at 40 rod intervals. Four *heiau* foundations, one a platform of solid stone 126 feet by 60 feet and 10 feet high, were placed within the enclosed walls. The only *heiau* functioning in 1800 was Hale-o-Keawe. Now a national historical park called Puʻuhonua o Hoʻonaunau. (KILO.)

Iliʻiliʻōpae. *Heiau* at the mouth of Mapupulehu Valley, Molokaʻi. It is noted for its age, tradition, and especially its size, considered to be the largest in the Hawaiian Islands. It housed a college of *kāhuna*.

Kahuā. *Heiau* at Kohala, Hawaiʻi.

Kalepa. *Heiau* near Kamāʻili, Puna.

Kānemalohemo. *Heiau* at Kaupō, Maui.

Kaniomoku. *Heiau* at Hana, Maui, ancient and a place of refuge.

Kaunolu. *Heiau* and place of refuge at Kealia, Molokaʻi. It was half in ruins when Kamehameha visited it.

Kawaʻewaʻe. Site where Kama-puaʻa killed his father Olopana. *Heiau* site is Kāneʻohe, Oʻahu.

Kawalakiʻi. Most famous idol of Maui.

Ke alakaʻi honua. *Heiau* at Kapokea, Waiheʻe, Maui. From this *heiau* a priest led the murderous attack on the officers of the *Daedalus*.

Keikipuʻipuʻi. *Heiau* built in the 1770s by Kalani-ʻopuʻu for her war-god Kāʻili at Kailua, Kona. (KILO.)

Kūkaniloko. Place near Wahiawā, Oʻahu, where chiefs wished their children to be born. Established in the twelfth century. Kamehameha I wanted his son and heir Liholiho to be born here. Keopuolani chose not to make the trip so the heir was born in Hilo.

Kūkiʻi. *Heiau* at Kapoho, Hawaiʻi, constructed of lava blocks, a large number of which were taken by King Kalakaua for the foundation of ʻIolani Palace in 1879. One, marked Liloa, is on exhibit in the Bishop Museum Court. (KILO.)

kūkoeaʻe, kūkoaʻe. Class of *heiau* possessing a temple for purification rites and prayers for food.

Kuokala. *Heiau* on the ridge overlooking Kaena Point. It is believed that migrants from Kauaʻi constructed it.

kūpalaha. Class of Kamehameha's *heiau* in Makapala, Kohala, Hawaiʻi.

Kuʻupapaʻulau. *Heiau* at Kuʻupapaʻulau, Kohala, Hawaiʻi.

lana. Lowest floor of the oracle tower. (MALO 176.)

lanahūa. Some part of a *heiau*. (A.)

lananuʻu. Second stage in the oracle tower where the images stood.

lananuʻu mamao. Oracle tower, one of the structures of the *heiau*. It was a tall frame of wood consisting of three "floors." The lowest, where offerings were placed, was called *lana*. The middle platform, *nuʻu*, was more sacred than the *lana* level. The top platform, *mamao*, was the most sacred for it was the place from which the high priest conducted services. (MALO 176.)

Loʻaloʻa. Very large *heiau* at Kaupō, Maui.

luakini. Highest class of *heiau*, a temple for human sacrifices. Also called *poʻo kanaka*.

luapaʻū. Pit in the *luakini* where the bones of those sacrificed were deposited.

Makamau. Great *heiau*. No data. (CMH.)

Makeanehu. *Heiau* where Hua died, located in Kohala, Hawaiʻi.

mākia. Measure used for laying out a *heiau*.

mana. Largest principal house in a *luakini heiau*.

Mao. Great *heiau*. No data. (A.)

mapele. Thatched *heiau*, temple for the worship of Lono; praying for more food offerings of pigs only.

Moaʻula. *Heiau* in Waipiʻo, Kohala, Hawaiʻi, where Kāʻili, war god of Kamehameha and Kalani-ʻopuʻu before him, was kept.

Moʻokini. *Heiau* at Puʻuepa, Kohala built by Paʻao with stones passed hand to hand from 9 miles away. Its walls were 817 feet long, 20 feet high, and 8 feet across. It was the second *heiau* of Paʻao and the largest in Hawaiʻi.

noulu. Long *heiau*. (A.)

nuʻu. Raised place or second stage, in a *heiau* where the gods dwelt and where offerings were placed.

Onehana. *Heiau* at Wailua, Oʻahu.

Pāhauna. *Heiau* near Lamaloloa in Hamākua, Hawaiʻi.

Pākaʻalana. *Heiau* and place of refuge in Waipiʻo, Hawaiʻi, destroyed in 1791 by confederated forces of Maui and Kauaʻi in a war with Kamehameha I.

papahola. Court or yard on the same platform on which a *heiau* was built but in front. (2 Nal. 1:2.)

Paukahi. *Heiau* at the leper settlement of Kalaupapa, Molokaʻi, at the foot of the *pali*. Kahiwa-kaʻapu was its famous priest.

peʻa. Cross of timbers placed crosswise in the form of an X before the *heiau* as a *kapu* sign.

Polihole, polihale. *Heiau* of human sacrifice. Built on an elaborate plan with five terraces. Waimea district, Kauaʻi.

poʻopuaʻa. One of the wooden gods in a *heiau* that resembles a hog. *Lit.*, head pig.

Popoīwi. *Heiau* at Kaupō, Maui.

pou nanahua. Post near the door in a *heiau*.

pūku'i. Assembly or collection of gods at the *luakini*.

pu'uhonua. Place of refuge for one pursued; place of safety in time of war. (Nah. 35:6, 11; Isa. 25.4.)

Pu'ukohalā. *Heiau* in Kawaihae where Iwikauikaua was to be sacrificed. A noted seer predicted its completion would give undisputed sovereignty of Hawai'i to Kamehameha. It was consecrated by Lono and later restored by Kamehameha I. The *heiau* was built on a promontory above the shore at Kawaihae.

Pu'umaka-a. Noted *heiau* of *po'okanaka* class. It was consecrated in 1801 along with two others at Kaupō, Maui.

Pu'u o Mahuka. *Heiau* on Pupukea Ridge, O'ahu, of the *po'okanaka* class, 467 feet long.

Wahaule. First *heiau* consecrated by Pa'ao, this one at Pulema, Hawai'i.

Wai-'ale'ale. Most famous idol on Hawai'i. No data. (CMH.)

wai ea. Small house within a *heiau* enclosure where the *'aha,* a ceremonial cord of sennit, was stretched.

Waikaua. *Heiau* used in war. *He heiau waikaua ia na ke ali'i nui.*

Wailehua. *Heiau* at Lahaina, Maui.

HOUSE BUILDING IN EARLY HAWAI'I

The thatched house of a Hawaiian family was the product of a high degree of sophistication. Most homes were constructed with gable-end framing. The idea of hipped roofs was introduced later.

Different kinds of posts were used to support the framework, each having a name and a purpose. Plant materials were converted to make cordage and thatch. Thatch generally provided a leakproof roof and allowed a "breathing ventilation" or air conditioning considered healthful to occupants.

Hale, the Hawaiian word for house, was used as a prefix for various kinds of houses. Pukui-Elbert lists some 135 such terms, Andrews 37, and Hyde 23 (selected largely from Andrews). This book lists 26. Each family gradually built several different kinds of houses as required until a compound was created. Some villages were really only an assembly of family centers.

'aha. To stretch the cord by which the first posts of a house were set straight; general name for cordage.

'aho. General name for purlins; a thatch purlin and rafter. Thatch is lashed to this horizontal pole.

āhole, āholehole. Fish found in fresh or salt water, substituted for a human body as a sacrifice in the post hole *(pouomanu)* on a house building site before construction.

'ahu'awa. Sedge *(Cyperus javanicus)* that supplied material for cordage. (NEAL 86.)

'aka'akai. Bulrush *(Scirpus validus)* that supplied material for thatch. (NEAL 88.)

'ale'o. Lookout on a housetop.

alo. Front side of the house.

alu 'a'alu. Hard timber used for posts. No data. (CMH.)

ama. Eating house for the wife. (CMH.) See **hale 'aina.**

'ami. Hinge.

'anu'u. Steps; terrace of rocks. (1 Nal. 7:28.)

'ānu'unu'u. Stairs. (Neh. 3:15.)

'aualo. Shed or verandah for storing property such as canoes, calabashes, and other items. (A.)

'auwae. Jog cut in the top of a post of a Hawaiian house.

'auwaha. To cut forked, like the foot of a rafter on a Hawaiian house. (A.)

hākala. Gable end of a house.

halake'a. Center, upright posts in a Hawaiian house. See **pouomanu.** (RA.)

hale 'aina. Eating house for women in ancient times. See **ama.**

hale hau. House built of *hau* for the use of the gods and for healing the sick; ice house.

hale kāmala. Temporary house, booth, shed.

hale kia. Verandah supported by pillars. (1 Nal. 7:6.)

hale kipa. Inn, guesthouse.

halekoko. House, to sleep in for the *hoa ali'i* (chiefs' companions).

hale kua. Log cabin. House for women's work, *kapa* making.

hale kula. Schoolhouse.

hale lā'au. House of wood, not grass.

hale lana. Floating house. Applied to Noah's Ark.

hale lepo. House of mud, adobe.

hale lewa. Tent.

hale malu. Shaded house; shed.

hale moe. Sleeping house.

hale 'ope'ope. Chief's wardrobe house.

hale pa'ahao. Prison, house of confinement.

hale pa'ani. Theater, playhouse *(keaka).*

hale pahu. House used in the war ceremony; drum house, especially in a *heiau* where prayers were uttered. (MALO 164.)

hale papa'a. Storehouse. (Kin. 41:56.)

hale pi'o. Particular kind of house; arch.

hale pōhaku. Stone house.

hale pule. House of worship, church, chapel.

hale puna. House plastered with lime, prepared with limestone or coral.

hānā. Middle part of a house; ridge post supporting the ridgepole.

hau. Tree *(Hibiscus tiliaceus)*. Its inner bark was used in making cordage.

heiau. Temple, place for the worship of the gods.

hilo 'o 'io paki'i. Flat-braided cordage for decorative lashings in canoes and houses. (RA.)

hio. Inside corners of a grass house where ghosts were said to have congregated.

hoaka. Arch or lintel over a door. (Puk. 12:7.)

hoakake'a. Arch over the door, lintel.

holopapa. Corner shelf for storing *kapa;* rack made of sticks.

ho'oma'ema'e. To cleanse a house of contamination by sprinkling water with *'awa* and *olonā* cuttings added.

ho'omānalo. Pork, *'awa* (a red fish), a sand crab, and *makaloa* (a perennial sedge) were all buried at the site of a projected building to neutralize any evil that lurked in the ground.

ho'opōheopoheo. To shape a head or round knob on the top of a rafter on a native house.

hui. Small supporting sticks or rods both between and parallel with the posts and rafters in a thatched house frame.

'ie. Forest air plant *(Freycinetia arborea)* with aerial roots. Used in making cordage. (RA.)

'ilio. Small end pieces that hold the rafter to the crossbeam. This was the diagonal bracing device needed to achieve rigidity of the house frame. (RA.)

iwilei. Unit of measure, about a yard, from a man's collarbone to the tip of his middle finger. Used to space house posts.

kahua. Platform and floor of the house. (RA.)

kā lau. To thatch the outside of the house with *lauhala* and *kī* leaves.

kaola. Stick or beam laid across a house from rafter to rafter to strengthen it structurally. Also called a wall plate. (Kekah. 10:19.)

kauhilo. To fasten the sticks of a house with ropes while in the building process; to fasten the horizontal thatching sticks of a house with rope.

kauhuhu. Main ridgepole running lengthwise of the house to which the tops of the rafters were fastened. Also called *kaupoku*. (RA.)

kaupaku. Upper ridgepole, bonnet or cap of the house. Also called *kaupoku*.

kihihi. Door frame; side posts at the entrance way; the door itself.

kīpaepae. Stone steps to the doorway of a house.

kīpaipai. Road paved with stones, fern trunks, or other material. (A.)

kīpapa. To lay stones in a pavement.

kīpou. Post of a house set in the ground.

kohā. Trimming the corners and ridge of a thatched house. No data. (A.)

kua. Back side of a house; *kapa*-beating house, used also for storing the *kapa* tools.

kuahui. Sticks tied as braces to the thatch purlins.

kua'iole. Upper ridgepole of a house. Also called *kuai'iole*. (RA.)

kuenehale. Knowledge of house building and practice in several trades; architect.

kukuna. End post of a house; gate post; door. (RA.)

kūlana. Site of a house.

kūnana. Garden; place cleared for building a house. Similar to *kūlana*.

lala 'ama'u. Fern fronds; thatch for high chiefs' houses. (RA.)

lā'ō. Sugarcane leaf, formerly used in thatching. Also called *lau kō, lau'ō*.

lau hala. Pandanus leaf used for lining and thatch. Also called *i'o ko'o, ko'o, kī, lā'ele, muo hala, pailau ula, pala lau hala, pili-lā'ele, pū'awa, pūkani*. Sugar cane leaf used for thatch and lining is called *lāko, laukō, lau'ō*.

lauhulu. Ti leaves bundled inside banana leaves, used as thatch and for lining high chiefs' houses. (RA.)

lio. Collar or tie beam of a house frame. (A.)

lohelau. Wall plate on which rafters are fastened. (RA.) See **waha**.

lole. Thatching a house smoothly.

lolelau. Thatching and trimming a house.

lōli'i. Piece of house timber hewn with more than four sides. (A.) See **'ōpaka**.

lolo niu. Husks of the coco palm tree *(Cocos nucifera)*, used for making cordage.

lule. Pili grass *(Heteropogon contortus)*, used for thatch for houses. (NEAL 80.) Also called *maoli, kāwelu, kiolohu*. See **pili, 'uki**.

māku'eku'e. Grass used to make the best adobies.

mua. Eating house of the men.

noa. House without *kapu*. Here the family slept and gathered socially.

o'a. Rafter.

'ōhiki. To thatch in a particular manner.

ōhi'u. Stick used as a thatching needle.

'ōhua. Family of a household, usually not including master and mistress. (Kin. 12:5.)

olonā. Forest shrub *(Touchardia latifolia)*. Bark used for cordage. "Best cordage of all in Hawai'i." (RA.)

'ōpaka. Timber hewn on four or eight sides; having regular sides. See **lōli'i.**

pa'a'ā. Banana leaves used for thatch and lining on high chiefs' houses.

paehi'a. To thatch; to cover a building by thatching.

paepae puka. Threshold.

paia. Sides, walls of a house. (1 Sam. 18:11.)

pa'i hale. To thatch a house.

pākākā, pīkāka. Side or back door (not the main door); chief's entrance to a home.

pākū. Partition in a house; screen or curtain, relatively unknown in early Hawai'i.

paku'i. Tower or second story added to a house.

pāku'iku'i. To splice or join timbers to make required lengths.

pe'a. House to isolate wife for monthly period.

pe'a lau'ī. Thatch bundle for crossed ti leaf thatching and binding of the bundle to the purlins. (RA.)

pe'a lau'ī po'ohuna. Stems of the *lau'ī* (ti plant) used for concealed ti leaf thatching. (RA.)

peo. House with a rounded roof.

pīkāka. Chief's entrance to a home. Var. of *pākākā.*

pili. Grass *(Heteropogon Contortus)*, used for thatch. In early days, *pili* was pulled with roots left on. As cutting tools were introduced, the grass was cut and piled, all root ends facing one way on the ground. The grass was carried carefully to the house site, not bunched but with stalks all facing the same way. (KILO.) See **lule.**

pou. Wall posts of a house. Also called side posts.

pouhānā. Ridge post. The center, end post of a house frame to which the ridgepole was fastened. (RA.)

pou hiō. Corner post. Also called *pou kihi.*

pouomanu. Chief's post placed in a hole, which in ancient times received a human sacrifice. *Lit., post of an ancient god.*

pueo. Pole to which the ends of the house rafters are lashed.

puka. Door.

puka pākākā. Low side door in a house through which one must stoop to enter. (PE.)

pūlawalawa. Bound tightly, as a thatched house with cords and braces.

pulu niu. Coconut fiber made into sennit and coir rope. (RA.) Coir is a stiff elastic fiber extracted from the outer husk of the coconut.

pū'o'a. House with the poles meeting at the top; temporary residence. See **pū'u'o'a.**

pu'u'o'a. Small enclosure of sticks leaning together at the top in the form of a pyramid. See **pū'o'a.**

uha'i. Door frame of a house; shelter.

uhiuhi. To thatch a house with banana leaves, a poor material for such use.

'uki. Sedge grass (*Cladium* sp.) used for making cordage. See **lule.**

'uki'uki. Native Hawaiian lily *(Dianella).* Its leaves are braided into cordage for tying on thatch.

unu. Small stones used to fix the posts firmly in the ground before raising a house.

waha. Throating in the lower end of a rafter; square notch cut in the upper part of house posts in which the wall plates are placed. See **lohelau.**

wauke. Tree *(Broussonetia papyrifera),* which supplies bark for making cordage.

HOUSEHOLD ARTICLES, TOOLS, AND UTENSILS

A fair picture of household living emerges from the words in this category. Here are listed the essentials needed for a family living in its compound of thatched houses: utensils for cooking, baking, washing *kapa,* cleaning fish, making *kapa* for clothing and bedding, making mattresses and pillows, making or tending cooking fires, food storage, and so on.

Dominating the list is the calabash, with numerous terms referring to sizes, shapes, composition, and uses. The hardy shell of the gourd was indispensable.

Several words refer to the making of fire by friction. The first Hawaiians brought with them the technique of rubbing a piece of hard wood against one of softer wood, thus creating enough heat to generate a spark and fan a flame.

Among the "tools" of the household were the *lauhala* mat, valued for its numerous uses, and the *kukui* nut, needed for its oil, which was used for lighting both torches and lamps.

The important thing to remember about these tools and utensils is that all of them were made from raw materials. Hawaiians had no corner store at which to buy them. They had only their deft hands, their quick minds, the raw plant, earth materials, and themselves.

'a'aha. Netted carrier for a gourd or wooden calabash, made of sennit or *olonā* cord.

'aahi. Long bag for carrying fire-making materials.

'a'apū. Cup made of coconut shell. See **'apu.**

'ahu. Mat used as a canoe covering; fine mat used as a human covering for the upper part of the body, as a shirt, coat, cape.

'ahu'ao. Young and tender pandanus leaves used for making a fine, half-inch-mesh mat.

'ahu li'u. Heated hot, as stones in the oven.

'ahu 'o 'eno. Kaua'i mats; matting with twilled pattern.

'ahu pāwehe. Striped mat made in Ni'ihau using long, *makaloa* stems.

'aki. Pillow. See *uluna.*

'āne'ene'e. Mats, old and worn. (A.) Small mat to sit on that is carried about. (PE.)

anu'a. Pile of mats or other materials.

'apu. Coconut-shell cup for drinking *'awa* and herb medicines. See **'a'apū.**

aulama. To give out light; to light with a torch.

'aulima. Hand-held stick rubbed to produce fire. See **'aunaki, hi'a.**

'aunaki. The stick rubbed upon in producing fire.

'eo. Calabash brim full of food.

hānai. Strings knotted into a *kōkō* (net) that surrounds and supports a calabash.

hauli'ili'i. Gridiron; to broil on the gridiron. *Lit.,* little irons. Hawaiian cooks contrived this word, which they called factitious, produced artificially. (A.)

hiʻa. Rubbing two sticks together to make fire.

hikieʻe. Divan or couch, usually stationary; raised platform for sleeping.

hohana. Measure, both hands full, used in giving out food. (A.)

hōkeo. Gourd calabash for clothes when traveling in a canoe; large, high, straight gourd or calabash for the wardrobe of the chiefs.

hue. Gourd calabash for carrying water. Also called *hue wai.*

hueʻili. Animal skin container for holding liquids. (Ios. 9:4.)

hue wai. Gourd calabash for water.

hukilau. Gourd calabash for storing clothing, *kapa,* food.

iʻaloa. Mummy.

ihoiho kukui. Several strings of *kukui* nuts wound together for torches; *kukui*-nut candle.

ʻili hau. Ropes made of the inner bark of the *hau* tree.

imu. Oven in the ground. See **umu.**

ipu ʻai. Vessel, calabash, for serving food.

ipu iʻa. Meat dish or flesh pot. (Puk. 16:3.)

ipu kai. Dish for meat and gravy.

ipu kaia. Dish or bowl for fish. *O ke aloha ka mea i ʻoi aku ka maikaʻi mamua o ka ʻumeke poi a me ka ipu kaia,* love is that which excels in goodness the *poi* dish and the fish bowl.

ipu kuha. Spittoon.

kākai. Strings used in hanging up a calabash in a net.

kālana. Sieve, strainer.

kālī kukui. String of the meats of *kukui* nuts made into a flambeau. (A.)

kānana. Strainer, sieve. (Am. 9:9.) To sift, as flour; to winnow, as grain. (Ruta 3:2.)

keʻehana wāwae. Footstool.

kīʻaha. Cup, tumbler, mug.

kīkī. Roughly made basket for temporary use, as to carry food.

kilo pōhaku. Smooth black stone placed in a calabash of water; a mirror. Also called *aniani.* (Puk. 38:8.)

kilu. Small gourd or calabash usually cut lengthwise for holding choice things.

kīʻoʻe. Coconut-shell spoon.

kōʻī kukui. Bamboo splinters on which *kukui* nuts are strung. Kahananui feels a coconut-leaf midrib would be firmer but Kilolani feels the bamboo would work better.

kōkō. Carrying net of knotted cords used to hang calabashes of wood or gourd.

konaʻawa. Bowl. No data. (CMH.)

kua. Hewn anvil or log of wood on which *kapa* is beaten.

kukui. Lamp, torch, light; candlenut.

kūlono. Small holes in the bottom of the calabash where water may drop through. See **kūnono**.

kūnono. Full of small holes, as a leaky calabash. See **kūlono**.

laha. Broad, flat calabash, not high. (A.) Gourd calabash painted with patterns. (PE.)

lamakū. Large torch made by stringing the meats of roasted *kukui* nuts on a wiry stalk of grass and putting 6 to 10 of these strings together, parallel, and then binding the whole with dried banana leaves, 2 to 4 feet long. On lighting one end a large and brilliant light is produced.

lamalama. Many lights; torch fishing; torch.

la'oa. To tie up the bones of a person in a bundle; to bundle up.

mā'au'au. *Poi* calabash carried from place to place by peddlers.

makiki. Calabash for water. (A.)

makou. *Kukui* torch of three strings of nuts that burned all night.

mo'a. Cooked or baked thoroughly in any way. (Oihk. 23:17.)

moena. Mat plaited from plant fibers, as the *lau hala* leaf.

mōlī. Instrument fashioned from bone for tattooing.

mū'ā. Poor looking calabash. (A.) Bottle-necked gourd, as used for drinking. (PE.)

no'uno'u. Variety of calabash with a short fruit. Also called *paha'aha'a, pākākā*. (PE.)

ōla'i. Pumice or other stone for polishing canoes.

'ōle'ōle. Post, 5 to 6 feet high, with a notched crossbar from which were hung calabashes in *kōkō* nets.

'ōlulo. Long, water calabash.

'omo. Cover to a calabash or pot.

'ōmoki. Stopper of a calabash; cork; bung of a cask.

'ōpihipihi. Fine mat but not the best, used primarily in making sails for canoes.

paepae wāwae. Footstool.

pā ipu. Calabash in which to keep clothes dry in a canoe; set of empty calabashes.

pā ipuholoi. Washbowl. No data. (CMH.)

pākākā. Wooden calabash, large and flat; low, wide gourd calabash used for meat and fish. See **ipu kai, no'uno'u**.

pāki'i. Bowl decorated with carved figures used for baked hogs. (CMH.) Broiled as puppies that were split and laid flat. (PE.)

papa 'aina. Eating table.

pe'ahi. Fan; to fan.

pela. Mattress. Also called *pela moe.*

pōʻaha. Round ball with a hollow on one side in which to set a calabash. (A.) Round support for a calabash made of pandanus or ti leaves wrapped into a ring and bound with a cord. (PE.)

pōhue. Broken piece of calabash; water calabash.

poʻi. Upper cover of a calabash.

pūʻapuʻawa. Long, thin shell for drinking *ʻawa.* (CMH.)

pūʻawa. *Hala,* the leaves of which were made into mats. The leaves are called pūʻawa when they are young and most fit for mats.

pūlama. Torch made from *kukui* nuts.

pūneʻe. Movable divan or couch. This one contrasts with *hikieʻe,* which is not movable.

pūnuku. Halter passed over the nose of a beast.

pūpū aulama. A number of torches.

ue. Mat made with *lau hala,* untrimmed.

uluna, ununa. Pillow, in early times filled with pandanus leaves. *Kohi makau ua kau ke poʻo i ka uluna,* we thought we had laid our heads on a pillow. (Kin. 28:11.) Also called *ʻaki.*

ulu umu. Stick for extracting stones from the oven. (A.)

ʻumeke. *Poi* calabash.

umu. Oven in the ground. (Oihk. 2:4.) Place for baking food; furnace. (Neh. 3:11.) See **imu.**

HULA

This category, as compiled by Hyde, gives neither the sense nor the full story of the *hula.* David Malo wrote *Hawaiian Antiquities* under the name *Moʻolelo Hawaiʻi;* it was translated in 1898 by Nathaniel B. Emerson, and published with some footnotes and an introduction by William D. Alexander. These three men collectively contributed several paragraphs of notes on the *hula* (MALO 231.) The role of each man in unclear, but all seem to agree that the ancient *hula* was no better and no worse than other Hawaiian institutions, but even in those times they recognized a popular "worst form," which, still surviving, is the one that foreign influences have helped to keep alive. Certainly many constructive and sincere efforts are being made today to retain the beauty and historic values that the *hula* enjoyed in the days of old.

Pukui-Elbert is more expressive and reasonable on this subject.

'ai. *Hula* step.

'ai'ami. *Hula* step with little movement of the feet but not a little with the hips.

'ai kāwele, kāwele. In this *hula* step the foot makes a half circle forward and to the side not touching the floor. See **kāwelu.** (PE.)

āla'apapa. Type of ancient dramatic *hula.*

alaka'i hula. *Hula* leader.

'ami. *Hula* step with revolutions of the hips. There are three types: *'ami kāhela, 'a kūkū,* and *'a ōniu.* (PE.)

'ami kāhela. Hip rotations with weight on the right hip as the left heel raises slightly, then the reverse.

'ami kūkū. Faster revolution of the hips than in *'ami kāhela,* in groups of three.

'ami 'ōniu. Figure-eight *hula.*

'āpika. No data. (CMH.)

'aui. *Hula* step where the dancer turns to the side and points out one foot once or several times, drawing the foot well back between each pointing. See **ue.**

ha'a. Dance with knees bent. (PE.)

heke. Feathered top of an *'ulī'ulī* (*hula* rattle); upper part of two gourds composing the *hula* drum.

helo, hula helo, 'ōhelo. In this *hula* step the dancer leans over on one side, supporting himself with one hand, and with the opposite foot and arm making a sawing motion. (PE.)

hōkeo. Lower of the two gourds of a drum. (A.) Also called *'olo.*

holo. Running *hula* step to the side. Similar to *kāholo* but feet are not necessarily together. (PE.)

hue. Type of *hula* dancing used to conclude a program.

hu'elepo. Small graduation exercises for *hula* students held at noon outside in the dust *(lepo).* (PE.)

hula. *Hula* dancer; general word for dances; expression of joy.

hula 'ana. Informal *hula,* created on the spur of the moment.

hula hapa haole. Americanized *hula,* usually accompanied by English words.

hula honu. *Hula* where the dancer imitates the motions of a turtle.

hulahula. Ballroom dancing; play in which many dance and sing and a few drum and sing.

hula ki'i. Dance where the dancers imitate images; dance using marionettes.

hula kuahu. Formal *hula* as part of a ceremonial or before the altar. *Kuahu* is the altar in the *hālau hula.*

hula manō. Sitting dance carrying out the actions of a shark.

hula noho. Sitting *hula*.

hula pahu. *Hula* to a drum beat.

hula papa hehi. Treadle board *hula* that originated in Niʻihau. (PE.)

ʻili, ʻiliʻili. Pebble worn round and smooth by water. Two pebbles in each hand are used in a *hula,* clicking together with a grasping motion of the palms. *Hula ʻiliʻili,* pebble dance.

kaʻapuni. *Hula* step, called "around the island." The dancer pivots on one foot and turns a complete round putting the other foot down several times enroute.

kaʻeleloi. Rolling sound of the *hula* drum.

kāholo. See **holo**.

kālāʻau. To strike with sticks, one upon the other, marking the rhythm of the dance. Part of the accompaniment to the *hula*.

kāwele. See **ʻai kāwele**.

kāwelu. *Hula* step where one foot taps time with the heel, the toes stationary, while the other foot, flat, steps forward and a little back, twice or more, then the reverse. (PE.) See **ʻai kāwele**.

kelamoku. *Hula* step invented by a Hawaiian sailor. (PE.)

kiʻelei. *Hula* performed in a squatting position.

kiʻi. *Hula* step where one foot points to the side, front, and back, then the other foot does the same. (PE.) Also called *wāwae kiʻi*.

kōlani. A sitting *hula*.

kuhi. Motions with the hands and arms in dancing the *hula*.

kuʻi Molokaʻi. The punch, *kuʻi hula* of Molokaʻi, an ancient fast dance with stamping, head twisting, thigh slapping, knee dipping, and fist doubling. (PE.)

kumu hula. *Hula* instructor.

kuolokani. Large drum. (CMH.) Ancient musical instrument used at *hula*s; a timbrel. (A.)

kupe. *Hula* step with feet still, knees bent. The body swings down low three times to the right, over to the left, and up.

kūpeʻe. Leglet, so called because it is fastened below the knees. What were once thought to be dog's teeth were really human teeth, pierced and strung to be used later to make the *kūpeʻe*.

kūpeʻe ʻilio. Dog tooth leglet or anklet; *hula* ornaments.

Laka. Goddess of *hula*.

lele. In this *hula* step the dancer walks forward, raising a rear heel with each step, with slight inward movement. (PE.)

mea hula. *Hula* dancer.

nīpolo. Striking the drum while chanting.

'ō. *Hula* step in which the hip is thrust *('ō)* outward. Similar to the *kāwelu* except that the foot pivots while turning in the opposite direction. (PE.)

'oaeae. Solo before the *hula.* (CMH.)

'ōhelo. See **helo.**

'ōlapa. Any *hula* accompanied by chanting and the beat of a gourd drum. Also the name applied to the dancers, in contrast to the *ho'opa'a* who are the chanters and drummers.

'ōlohe. *Hula* expert. See **Occupations**

'ōlohia. No data. (CMH.)

opu. No data. (CMH.)

pahu. Drum, as related to a *hula* dance.

pahua. To dance; to go through the motions of dancing; spear dance.

pā hula. *Hula* troupe.

pahu pa'i. Small sharkskin drum, beaten for a *hula.*

pailani. No data. (CMH.)

pa'ipa'i. Shortened form of *he paipai kekahi hula,* the name of a *hula.*

pā ipu. Dance involving the gourd drum.

pa'ipunahele. Praising in detail all the beauties of a beloved in song and *hula.*

pa'iumauma. Chest-slapping *hula.*

papa hehi. See **hula papa hehi.**

pū'ili. Bamboo rattles used in rhythmic accompaniment to certain dances called *hula pū'ili.*

pūniu. Small knee drum made of a coconut shell with a tympanum of *ala* fish skin.

ue, uwe. *Hula* step where the caller announces the dance to the drummer and dancers by calling *e ue.*

'ūlili. *Hula* step similar to *'uwehe* except that only one heel is raised at a time. This step has a distinctive beat. (PE.)

'ulī'ulī. Feather gourd rattle in which a sound is produced by seeds. A dance in which such gourds are used is called a *hula 'ulī'ulī.*

'ūniki. Graduation exercises for a *hula* class.

'uwehe. *Hula* step where one foot is lifted, the weight being shifted to the opposite hip as the foot is lowered. Both knees are then pushed forward by the quick raising of the heels, with continued swaying of the hips from side to side. (PE.)

wāwae ki'i. See **ki'i.**

INSECTS AND THEIR RELATIVES

Natural scientists accompanying Captain Cook's expedition in 1778–1779 collected many insect specimens. Only two species among these specimens were described, shortly after Cook's expedition returned to England. The rest of this early collection probably has received limited attention.

Since then entomologists around the world have collected and classified insects from Hawai'i, although few scientists were interested in the Hawaiian words for them.

Not until the last twenty years of the nineteenth century were careful attempts made to establish such lists. But by then original Hawaiian names had been to some degree transferred to introduced species, which tended to obstruct research on the names once applied to native species.

More than 7,000 species of native insects lived in Hawai'i before the arrival of man, and about 2,300 other species have been introduced since the time of Captain Cook.

'a'awa. Insect that destroys sweet potatoes. No other data. (A.)

'aha. Earwig (order Dermaptera.) Possibly any of the native species *Anisolabis*. See lō.

'ami. Larva of a moth (family Geometridae) that has two pairs of prolegs and progresses by a looping movement. Hence, called looper, measuring worm, inchworm.

ana'uku. Important family, Homoptera, mostly small insects comprising the scale insects, mealy bugs and their allies, family Coccidae.

ane. Small, darkish brown or blackish beetle (family Dermestidae). Its larvae feed on dried meats, featherwork, and skins. It is known as a larder beetle, mites (as in chickens), and ringworm.

'añonanona. Ant. See naonao, nonanona.

'anuhe. General name for native cutworms or army worms (family Noctuidae). The caterpillars destroy the leaves of vegetables. Called *pe'elua* on Maui. See 'enuhe, kupa, poko.

ekikilau. Stench that draws flies.

'eleao. Plant louse, aphid (family Aphididae). Aphids generally are post-Cook in Hawai'i.

'elelū. Cockroach (family Blattidae). All cockroaches are introduced, post-Cook.

ʻelelū kea. Cockroach that sheds its skin, changing to a whitish color.

ʻelelū kīkēkē. Large American cockroach *(Periplaneta americana).*

ʻelelū laʻa loa. Cockroach, kitchen cockroach.

ʻelelū lepo. Burrowing cockroach *(Psycnoscelis surinamensis).*

ʻelelū papa. Flat, broad cockroach. (MALO 41).

ʻelelū ʻulaʻula. Two large, brown cockroaches: American *(Periplaneta americana);* Australasian *(P. australasiae),* a bit smaller.

ʻenuhe. Large, striped caterpillar of hawk or sphinx-type moths (family Sphingidae). See **ʻanuhe.**

hāʻukeʻuke. Body louse *(Pediculus humanus humanus).* Lives on the human body and lays its eggs in clothing. Also called *ʻuku kapa.*

hē. General term for caterpillar; caterpillar that eats the leaves of the coconut and palm-leaf pandanus. This may refer to the coconut leaf roller, a native insect *(Hedylepta blackburni).* See **ʻanuhe, kāhē.**

hoʻonēnē. Native singing crickets (family Gryllidae, order Orthoptera). One of these *(Paratrigonidum* spp.) is a good singer, the other *(Prognathogryllus)* is an incredible music maker. Natives showed Cook some singing snails, *pūpū kani oe,* but in reality crickets close to the snails were doing the actual singing. Specimens were taken to England and only later did scientists learn how they had been fooled. There are, of course, non-singing crickets in Hawaiʻi.

huhu. Any of the insects that bores into wood or eats cloth.

huhu ʻai lāʻau. Wood eating borer. (FOR. 4:169.)

huhuhu. Insect eaten, as wood.

hupupu. Worm or insect that eats hard bread. (A.)

ʻilo. Larva, generally a grub of beetles and weevils of the order Coleoptera.

kāhala. Refers to the anal horn found on caterpillars of the family Sphingidae. Several *Hyles* species are native to Hawaiʻi while the sweet potato hornworm *(Agrius cingulatus)* is post-Cook.

kāhē. Appearance of young caterpillars on the sweet potato vines, perhaps post-Cook.

kanapī. Crawler, class Chilopoda. Hawaiian transliteration of centipede.

kaunoʻa. Slender insect that attacks herbs or trees, making them wither. (A.)

kopena. Hornet, wasp, scorpion. This last, is almost exclusively a house scorpion. (PE.) Andrews calls this a *moʻo niho ʻawa,* viper or reptile. (Kanl. 32:33.)

kopiana. Scorpion *(Isometrus maculatus),* one of the many arachnids that constitute the order Scorpionda. This is a post-Cook species, the only one in Hawai'i. *Kopiana* is the transliteration of scorpion.

kuapa'a. Destructive caterpillar that eats vegetable plants. (A.)

kupa. Any of the native army worms *(Pseudaletia* spp.). *P. unipuncta* is the introduced species. See pe'elua.

ku'uku'u. Short-legged spider, so called because it lowers itself on a single thread.

lanalana. Large, brown spider that stands high on its legs. (A; Isa. 59:5.) See **pūnāwelewele.**

lepelepe-o-Hina. Monarch butterfly, a large, introduced butterfly known as *Danaus plexippus. Vanessa tameamea,* the Kamehameha butterfly, is one of only two native butterflies. *Tameamea* is a Russian spelling of Kamehameha. See **pulelehua.** The other native butterfly *(Vaga blackburni)* has purple on the upperside and green on the underside of the wings. It is much smaller than the brown and orange Kamehameha butterfly. (KILO.)

liha, lia. Nit; egg of the head louse.

lo. Black insect, earwig (order Dermaptera, *Anisolabis* spp.). There are several native species in this genus. See 'aha.

mahiki. A sand hopper, same as *'uku kai;* amphipod. Nicknamed back flea.

makika. Mosquito, first brought to the islands in 1823. The name is Hawaiian for mosquito. *Eng.* There are four such introduced species in Hawai'i of the Culicidae family. All post-Cook.

me'eau. Class of insects on trees. (A.) On animals. (PE.)

meli. Bee. There are native bees but they do not produce a harvestable honey. (Kin. 43:11.) See **nalo meli.** Honey is *meli* or *waimeli.*

moe one. Worm that burrows in the sand. See **pe'elua.**

mu. General name for insects that eat cloth, wood, plants. (Mat. 6:19.)

mu ai palaoa. Larva of the rusty flower beetle *(Tribolium ferrugineum)* or the rice weevil *(Sitophilus oxyzae).* Feeds on flour or meal.

mu'ai puke. Bookworm. The larva of any of the various beetles (family Anobiidae) that injure books.

mumuhi. Buzzing of mosquitoes; a whispering sound, as of people.

mumuhu. Loud buzzing of insects, as of hornets. A louder hum than that of *mumuhi* (mosquitoes).

mumulu. Swarming of insects, as flies, bees, mosquitoes; a cluster of people conversing.

nalo. Common house fly *(Musca domestica)* and others.

nalo ʻaki. Small stinging fly, as the stable fly *(Stomoxys calci-trans)*.

nalo hope ʻeha. Hornet. *Lit.,* fly-sting-hurt. (Puk. 23:28.)

nalo hue loaʻawa. Wasp. No data. (CMH.)

nalo keleawe. Fly, perhaps the hover fly (family Syrphidae) or bluebottle fly (family Calliphoridae). *Lit.,* brass or copper fly.

nalo lawe lepo. Mud wasp, such as *Sceliphron caementarium. Lit.,* dirt-carrying fly.

nalo meli. Honey bee *(Apis mellifera)*. Introduced species, post-Cook. (Kanl. 1:44.) See **meli.**

nalo meli mōʻī wahine. Queen bee.

nalo meli noho hale. Drone bee.

nalo meli paʻahana. Worker bee.

nalo nahu. Stinging fly.

nalo paka. Louse fly (family Hippoboscidae).

nalo pilau. Bluebottle fly (family Calliphoridae).

nananana. Long-legged, web-making spider. *He ʻōlelo no ke aka-mai o ka nanana i ka hana ʻupena ana,* the skill of the spider in making its web. Brown widow spider.

naonao. Winged or flying ant, different species of the family For-micidae. Introduced. See **anonanona, nonanona.**

niho ʻaki. Mandibles of insects; nippers; front teeth.

nonanona. Small, winged species of insect; gnat, ant. See **naonao.**

ʻōkai. Large night moth. Generally, butterflies fly during the day, moths at night. A few moths fly in the daytime.

ona. General term for lice or mites; mite, hen louse *(Menopon pallidum)*.

pahu meli. Beehive. Also called *pūnana meli.*

pakika. Insect that eats sweet potato leaves and destroys them. (Λ.)

peʻelua. Caterpillar; army worm *(Pseudaletia unipuncta)*. Intro-duced. See **kupa.**

peʻepeʻe makaʻole. Kauaʻi cave wolf spider *(Adelocosa anops.)*

peʻepeʻe makawalu. Large house spider. No data. (CMH.)

pinao. One of the large predacious insects (order Odonata); drag-onfly. Native.

pinao ʻula. Red damsel fly *(Megalagrion* sp.), native to Hawaiʻi.

poki. Insect that destroys vegetables. No data. (A.)

pokipoki. Sow bug, pill bug (order Isopoda). Introduced.

poko. Larger native cutworm, especially *Agrotis crinigera;* varie-gated cutworm, *Peridroma porphyrea;* and greasy cutworm,

Agrotis ypsilon. Post-Cook. See **'anuhe.** Caterpillar. (Hal. 78:76.)

pololei. Song of the cricket or locust (families Gryllidae, Tettigoniidae). *Kani kua a mauna,* singing in the mountain ridges.

pōnalo. Swarming of gnats, plant lice (family Aphidae) or leafhoppers (family Cicadellidae), also including small flies (Drosophila). These insects participate in blights, as on sweet potato and taro tops.

pu'ali. Small abdominal part of a wasp; thread waist of a wasp.

puapua. Anal horn or spike on the sphinx-moth larva; fly that bites. (A.)

pulelehua. Butterfly or moth *(Vanessa tameamea),* the Kamehameha butterfly. See **lepelepe o Hina.**

pulelehua kea. Greater Magellanic Cloud. *Lit.,* white butterfly. (PE.)

pulelehua uli. Lesser Magellanic Cloud. *Lit.,* dark butterfly. (PE.)

pūnanana. Species of house spider (Araneida); spider web.

pūnana meli. Beehive. See *pahu meli.*

pūnāwele. Fine, as threads of a spider's web.

pūnāwelewele. Spider's web. (Isa. 59:5.) Spinning spider. See **lanalana.**

'ūhini. Long-horn grasshopper (family Tettigoniidae). (Nah. 13:33). Locust (family Acrididae). (Puk. 10:14.)

'ūhini akelika, 'ūhina 'akerida. Grasshopper. (Oihk. 11:22. PE.)

'ūhini huluhulu. Cankerworm. (Nah. 3:15; Ioela 2:25; A.)

'ūhini hulu 'ole. Palmer worm, a locust named for the pilgrim palm bearer from Jerusalem; any caterpillar that suddenly appears in great numbers, devouring herbage. The Old Testament (Ioela 1:4) dramatizes the locust ritual of devastation:

> What the cutting locust left, the swarming locust has eaten.
> What the swarming locust left, the hopping locust has eaten.
> What the hopping locust has left, the destroying locust has eaten. . . .

'ūhini lele. Beetle, cricket. *Lit.,* flying grasshopper.

'ūhini pa'awale. *Lit.,* locust scorched. This term is defined by some authorities as the parent of the long-horn grasshopper *('ūhini)* or simply as an edible locust. Actually no specimens were ever collected and therefore its specific identity is not known. It can be characterized as lost. Handy writes that the *'ūhini* grasshopper fed on *kukae pua'a* sedge. The *'ūhini* were caught, strung on the flower stems of the grass, and broiled for

food. When the grassy areas were cleared and planted with sugarcane, the *ʻūhini* became extinct.

ʻūhini pua. Young of the *ʻūhini,* before it has wings. (A.)

ʻūhini wāwae ha. Bald locust. (Oihk. 11:22.)

ʻuku. Any small insects; louse, flea, mite. See *haʻukeuke.*

uku hipa. Tick, mite (order Acarina). *Lit.,* sheep louse. This may
refer to the sheep ked *(Melophagus ovinus),* a wingless fly on
sheep.

ʻuku kai. Beach sand hoppers, amphipod of the family Talitridae.
Many species. Nicknamed back flea. Also called *mahiki.* See
ʻuku limu.

ʻuku kapa. Body louse, *Pediculus humanus.* See *ʻuku poʻo,* head
louse.

ʻukulele. Flea (order Siphonaptera). *Lit.,* jumping flea. (I Sam.
24:15.)

ʻuku limu. Sand hopper, beach flea. Amphipods living on the
beach, largely family Talitridae. See **ʻuku kai.** Those living in the
sea belong to many families; some are called scuds.

ʻuku lio. Bed bug *(Cimex lectularius). Lit.,* louse horse. There are
also two kinds of horse lice in Hawaiʻi.

ʻuku noho ana. Kauaʻi cave amphipod *(Spelaeorchestia koloana).*

ʻuku papa. Crab louse *(Phthirus pubis). Lit.,* surface louse.

ʻuku pepa. Booklouse *(Liposcelis* spp.). *Lit.,* louse paper.

ʻuku poʻo. Head louse *(Pediculus humanus capitis). Liha,* egg of
the *ʻuku poʻo.*

wehi. Long black worm found in ʻEwa. No data. (CMH.)

KAMEHAMEHA I

The Lonely Warrior, the Conqueror or Puhi-kapa, Kamehameha I:
this man was the key to the unification of the people living in the
Hawaiian chain.

Entire books have been devoted to his biography; while this listing may seem meager, these are words taken from the language of
Kamehameha I's time. Although few in number, they offer a full
description of the man, referring to his law-giving, his battles
(chiefly victories), his fairness, restraint, vision, and courage.

ʻahuʻula. Feather cloak or cloak of *mamo, ʻoʻo, ʻiʻiwi* or other
birds' feathers.

'ā'ī'pala'e. In early medicine, a neck scar. Today it is called tuberculosis. See a synonym, 'ā'i āla 'āla, under **Medicine: Human Diseases.**

'aumoana. Class of Kamehameha's laws, relating to swimming in the ocean. (A.)

ha'iha'i. To dissect flesh from bones.

hāliu, haleu. What the fundament is wiped with; a word that Kamehameha applied to Keoua, when he threatened to join kings against him. (A.)

hamehame ukaki. *Ke au o Kamehameha.* Described as an anagram. (CMH.)

Hapu'u 1783 and Laupāhoehoe 1784. Two battles fought between Kamehameha I and Keawe-ma'u-hili and Keoua, Kings of Hilo and Ka'u, respectively.

Ka-'ie'ie Waho. Attempted invasion of Kaua'i in 1796 by Kamehameha, who was defeated by a strong wind *(kūlepe),* forcing his fleet back across the Kai'ei'e Waho channel to Wai'anae, O'ahu.

Kā'ili. Abbreviation of name of Kamehameha's war god, Kūkā'ilimoku; Ku, the island snatcher.

Kāleleiki. Kamehameha's raid on fishermen at Pāpa'i in Kea'au, Puna. This gave rise to the Law of the Splintered Paddle. See **māmala hoe; Pākī, Kā ehu.**

Kama'ino. Expedition of Kamehameha from Kohala to Kawaihae.

Ka na'i aupuni. Another name for Kamehameha I, the Conqueror of the Nation.

Kani'aukani. Name of Kamehameha's voyage, returning to Hawai'i by way of O'ahu, following his success in uniting the kingdom under his rule. The trip was made in 1812.

Ka peleleu. Work on digging out the hulls of a fleet of stub-nosed, broad-beamed war canoes was started in 1798. Kamehameha made much use of the fleet. He used it on his trip in 1810 to Kaua'i, to receive the island by gift from its King, Kaumuali'i, thus bringing the last of the islands under his control as a kingdom.

Kaua'awa. Second battle for Kamehameha, so called because of reverses. *Lit.,* battle bitter. He retired temporarily to Laupāhoehoe.

kekupuohi. Kamehameha's name for a red coat given him by Vancouver. When given a second he called it *keakualapu.* (A.)

Kekuwaha'ula. Sea fight or marine battle off Waipi'o, Kohala. The victory of Kamehameha was given this long name, "the red-mouthed gun," from the artillery support of John Young and Isaac Davis. (FOR 2:310–329.)

Kepaniwai. Battle fought by Kamehameha and Kalanikupule at Wailuku, Maui in 1790. In the song *"Kepaniwai o 'Iao,"* the dam in 'Iao stream was created by the bodies of the casualties.

kuhina. Highest officer next to the king.

kukaluhi, ku'ukaluhi. Rest after labor. When Kamehameha conquered the islands, he exclaimed, *"ua, kukaluhi."* (A.)

kūpalaha. *Heiau* of the Kamehameha class.

lua'ikū. Word used by Kamehameha to express contempt, meaning he will vomit.

māmala hoe, māmala hoa. Kamehameha I's Law of the Splintered Paddle, which assured safety to all, men, women, sick, and elderly. See **Kaleleiki, Pakī, Kā ehu.**

Moku-'ōhai. Kamehameha's first battle for control of Hawai'i in 1782, at Hau-ikī in Ke'ei, Kona.

Nī'au-kani, Ke nī'au-kani. Voyage by Kamehameha after the submission of Kaumuali'i who ceded Kaua'i to Hawai'i in 1812.

okaka. Term applied to foreigners in very early times, and later to the men who did business with Kamehameha. (A.)

Pai'ea. Hard-shelled crab. Loosely translated, it means star athlete, one of the often used names of Kamehameha I.

Pākī, Kā'ehu. This man, father of Bernice Pauahi Bishop, was named to commemorate Kamehameha I's escape from death at Pāpa'i, Puna, now called King's Landing. Kamehameha leaped from his canoe and went ashore alone to chase a party of fishermen. Two of the frightened men threw *(Pākī)* a shower or spray of stones *(kā ehu)*. When he stepped into a crevice and caught his foot, the two men returned and broke a canoe paddle over his head. One version of the story says that the entrapped Kamehameha picked up a handful of stones and threw them at the retreating fishermen. The stones scarred the trunk of a *noni* shrub that was pointed out to visitors for years to come. Several years later Kamehameha issued the Law of the Splintered Paddle, *māmalahoe* (or *māmalahoa*) *kānāwai* based on this incident. See **māmala hoe.**

palena. Class of men under Kamehameha at Kohala, some chiefs, others commoners. (A.)

pāpā. Class of laws of Kamehameha; to forbid, prohibit.

pūhi kāpā. Name of Kamehameha, victorious over all. (A.)

'uo'uo. Strong voiced, as Kamehameha. (A.)

wa'iōhuhūkini. Class of laws of Kamehameha.

KAPA: The Kapa Beater

Kapa manufacture was so weighted with words referring to the *kapa* beater, that this traditional category was made.

Kapa making, as an industry, demanded a great amount of time and energy from the women of old, and in the five categories of terms devoted to it, segments of Hawaiian culture will be reviewed; one of the categories covers the sending of *kapa* specimens to the great Paris Exhibition of 1889; others cover the kinds of *kapa* that were made, and the participation of women in the making of it.

'aha. Design resembling a duck's tracks carved on *kapa* beaters. (PE.) Also called *ahaana, 'ahana, kapua'i koloa.*

anuenue. Scallop-like design on a *kapa* beater and *kapa.* (PE.)

'api'i. *Kapa* beater design resembling a series of waves.

hā'ao. Kapa design. (PE.) Also called *nao ua hā'ao, ua hā'ao.*

Ha'i. Goddess of the *po'e kuku papa* (people who beat *kapa*). Ha'i is short for Ha'ina-kolo, a forest dwelling goddess of *kapa* makers.

hālu'a. Pattern on the surface of a *kapa* beater or *kapa.* It consists of two sets of parallel lines crossing at right angles.

hālu'a ko'eau. *Kapa* beater design of gently waving parallel lines.

hālu'a lei hala. *Kapa* beater design consisting of a pandanus *lei* with interlocking triangles. (PE.)

hālu'a maka'upena. *Kapa* beater design resembling a fishnet. Also called *hālu'a manamana.*

hālu'a niho mano. *Kapa* beater design, in which panels between the *hālu'a* lines are interspersed with regularly spaced triangles. *Lit.,* shark tooth design. (PE.)

hālu'a pu'ili. *Kapa* beater design. (PE.)

hālu'a pūpū. *Kapa* beater design with circular motifs.

hā'uka'uka, hā'uke'ukē. Motif on a *kapa* stamp that resembles the sea urchin.

hoa. To beat with a stick or stone, as on *kapa.*

hoahoa, hokoa. Name of a mallet with which *wauke* (mulberry bush bark) was given its first beating to make it into *kapa.*

hohoa. To smooth *kapa* by beating. This term is applied to the first process in beating. In some cases it means to beat *kapa* after coloring so that it may be soft.

hohoa kapa. To beat *kapa* on a stone with a stick; a washing stick, used after the introduction of cotton cloth.

hole iʻe. To groove or carve figures in the *iʻe* (*kapa* beater). Those who worked on the *iʻe* preparation also pounded the *kapa*.

hoʻopaʻi. Design with parallel lines on a *kapa* beater. (PE.)

hoʻopaʻi hāluʻa. Sets of parallel lines crossing each other at right angles on a *kapa* beater. (PE.)

iʻe kuku. Square carpet beater with incised designs.

iwi pūhi. Design on a carpet beater and on *kapa*, of a herringbone figure with a long ridge in the center. *Lit.,* bone eel.

kāwaʻu. Tree that furnished the hard wood on which *kapa* was pounded; the *kapa* anvil.

kīwaʻawaʻa. A rough *kapa* used for various purposes; a coarse *kapa*.

kīwawā. *Wauke* bark partly beaten into *kapa*.

koʻele. To strike with a mallet.

kōnane. *Kapa* beater design resembling the checker board.

kōnane hoʻopaʻi. *Kapa* beater design with twelve to eighteen ridges to the inch.

kōnane pepehi. *Kapa* beater design with up to fourteen ridges to the inch.

kōnane pūpū. *Kapa* beater design with rounded *pūpū* (pits) in the middle of each checker-board square. (PE.)

kōpili. *Wauke* bark of the mulberry bush pounded thin; the small white *kapa* placed over idols during sacred ceremonies.

kua. Hewn log or block on which *kapa* is beaten, which resembles the modern blacksmith's anvil; the house used for beating *kapa*.

kūʻau. Stick or mallet for beating *kapa*.

kuku. To pound *kapa*.

kulipuʻu. *Kapa* design using zigzag stripes. *Lit.,* bent knees. (PE.) See **niho wili hemo.**

kūʻonoʻono. Woman skilled in pounding *kapa*.

laʻi o Kona. Design on a *kapa* beater. (PE.)

lau ʻamaʻu. *Kapa* beater design. *Lit., ʻamaʻu* fern pattern.

lau maʻu. Design of a *kapa* beater suggesting a *maʻu* or *ʻamaʻu*, fern leaf.

lau niu. Design of a *kapa* beater suggesting a coconut tree motif.

lei hala. Design used on *kapa* consisting of a series of inverted triangles suggestive of a *hala lei*. (PE.)

lelepe. Toothed; sharp-pointed design used on *kapa*. (PE.)

lū lehua. Red *kapa* design. (PE.)

maka ʻupena. Quilting design, the mesh or eye of the fish net, carved on a *kapa* beater.

mole. Smooth, uncarved side of a *kapa* beater which is also used to smooth the *kapa* at the end of the beating. (PE.)

na'ena'e. Design on a *kapa* outer-sheet; the top covering *(kilohana)* on a bed.

nao. Ridge on the beating face of a *kapa* beater. This accounts in part for the grooves and streaks in *kapa*.

nao hālu'a. *Kapa* design with coarse lines.

nao ho'opa'i. *Kapa* beater design with fine lines.

nao ua hā'ao. Same as *hā'ao*; a *kapa* pattern.

nao ua hā'ao nanahuki. *Kapa* design. (PE.)

niho li'ili'i. *Kapa* design. *Lit.,* small teeth or notches. (PE.)

niho manō. *Kapa* design. *Lit.,* tooth shark.

niho wili hemo. Design on Ni'ihau mats and possibly *kapa*. See **kulipu'u.** (PE.)

'ōhiki. *Kapa* design.

pa'iniu. *Kapa* design resembling the native *pa'iniu* lily (*Astelia* spp.).

pāwehe. Geometric designs for *kapa* and mats.

pāwehe pūpū. Probably a *pāwehe* shell design used on *kapa*.

pepehi. Surface of a *kapa* beater formed of deep grooves, with the wide ridges rounded like an inverted U. Sometimes used as the name of the beater.

pua hala. Design for quilt patchwork and *kapa*. It resembles the *hala* flower or key.

pū'ili. *Kapa* beater pattern where tips of zigzag ridges in adjacent surfaces meet to form lozenges. (PE.)

pū'ili hālu'a. *Pū'ili* design with one or more ridges or strips between the panels of the beater. (PE.)

pū'ili ko'eau. Combination of *pū'ili* and *ko'eau* designs.

pūkē. To strike with a mallet.

pūpū. Any circular motif, as in a *kapa* design. (PE.)

pupupu. Temporary hut or shelter from the sun for beating *kapa*; white *kapa* used for a *pā'ū*; a heap of worthless *kapa*.

'upena hālu'a. *Kapa* beater design. (PE.)

'upena pūpū. *Kapa* beater design with meshes of net enhanced by small circles. (PE.)

KAPA: Kinds and Qualities

This list shows the full dependence on local island materials for *kapa* making. Plant fibers, bark, roots, dyes, scents, and tools all helped to produce subtle differences in the thickness, design, size, and shape of the finished material.

Many kinds of white *kapa* will be noted. Hawaiians were considerably advanced at creating original designs through techniques of printing with stamping devices. In some instances, patterns were developed by arranging certain kinds of fibers in strips, or in a kind of applique process by beating one set of fibers into and across other fibers.

Pieces of *kapa* were used primarily for clothing and bed covers. Certainly *kapa* must be classed among the Hawaiians' basic necessities, along with food and shelter.

'a'ahu ali'i. Colored *kapa* worn by persons of rank; royal dress; a cape.

'aeokahaloa. Fine *kapa* made of *wauke* and colored with charcoal, used with pebbles in divination at sacred rites. See **pālau anahu.**

'aha. Kind of *kapa* from Moloka'i; a small piece of wood wound around by a piece of *kapa* held in a priest's hand while offering sacrifices.

ahapi'i. *Kapa* dyed with bark and decorated with fine lines, for chiefs. (PE.)

'ahunāli'i. Chiefly *kapa* made with red stripes and colored with *noni* and candlenut; colored *mamaki kapa.*

'ai wauke. Finest kind of *kapa.* (CMH.)

akaaka, akaka. White and very thin *kapa.* (PE.)

'akaha ka na'i. Kind of white *kapa.* (PE.)

'akala. Pink *kapa* colored by a raspberry juice dye. *'Ākala* means raspberry *(Rubus hawaiiensis, R. macraei).* (PE.)

akeakea. Faded, grayish *kapa.* Originally red.

akoa. Snuff colored *kapa* colored with a dye from the *akoa* tree bark.

'ala'ihi. Pale pink *kapa.*

'āleuleu. Worn-out *kapa* or mats or other coverings, including old clothes.

'āpeu. Large, coarsely-made mats or *kapa* used for food carriers or food containers; same as *'āleuleu.* (KILO.)

'āpikipiki. Ancient spotted *kapa.*

'ele'ele. *Kapa* said to be from Kau-makani, Maui, dyed with candlenut, *pā'ihi,* and black mud. (PE.)

'eleuli. Rare, gray, and perfumed *kapa.* (PE.)

ha'imanawa. White *kapa,* thin and gauze-like.

hala kea. *Kapa* dyed with *niu* (coconut).

hamo ʻula. *Kapa* dyed or stained red.

hana. White *kapa* of *wauke*. See **kikama, kilohana, kuʻinakapa.**

he ae wauke. Very soft liquid wrung from *wauke*. *Ae* is a general term for all saps. The addition of *wauke* identifies the source. *Wauke* is a paper mulberry *(Broussonetia papyrifera)*. Its bark was made into a durable *kapa* for clothing and bed clothes. (PE.)

hili. Bark supplying a brown-black dye; *kapa* dyed with *hili;* general term for barks used in dyeing.

hōlei. Small tree *(Ochrosia sandwicensis)* that formerly supplied bark and root for a yellow dye for *kapa*.

honina. *Kapa* dyed with turmeric and used as a sarong. (PE.)

hoʻola. Word applied to a single *kapa;* a small piece of *kapa*. The word *hoʻola* is used in place of *kapa* on Kauaʻi.

hūlili. Kind of *kapa*. (PE.)

hunakānaʻi. *Kapa* with white and yellow dots. (PE.)

iʻe iolo kaha loa. Brown *kapa* from Wai-piʻo, Hawaiʻi.

iho. Set of four sheets of *kapa* below the *kilohana,* the top bed covering. The sheets were plain white, the outside highly decorated and all were made of the best materials.

kaʻeʻe. Hard or stiff, as new *kapa*.

kahaloa. Short form of *ʻaeokaloa,* a *kapa*. (PE.)

kaiāulu. Outside figured *kapa,* best in appearance. See **kilohana.**

kākau uʻauʻahi. *Kapa* bedcover printed with a smoky-gray color.

kalewai. Light-brown *kapa*. (PE.)

kalukalu. Very thin, gauze-like *kapa* made on Kauaʻi that is reserved for chiefs. *Pale kalukalu,* muffler; *kalukalu nui,* mantle.

kamalena. *Pāʻū* or *kapa* dyed yellow with the root of the *ʻōlena* (turmeric).

kapa peʻa. *Kapa* or dress abandoned by a menstruous woman when she returned to the family.

kapeke. *Kapa* of differing colors on its two sides, either or both of which may be exposed when blown by the wind; a *malo* made with such a *kapa*.

kāpilipili. Kind of *kapa*. (PE.)

kele wai. *Kapa* named for its appearance of mud. (CMH.) Coarse *kapa* made of *māmaki* bark or from waste of a better grade *kapa*.

kikama. White *kapa* made from the mulberry bush.

kikiko. Dotted; spotted, as on a *kapa*.

kilika'a. *Kapa* of Wai-pi'o, Hawai'i.

kilohana. Outside decorated *kapa* sheet of the *ku'inakapa* (bed coverings). The four under-layers were an undecorated white. (PE.) See **kaiāulu.**

kīwa'awa'a. Rough, coarse *kapa* used in various ways.

kōpili. Fine *kapa* made from the paper mulberry *(Broussonetia papyrifera)* called *wauke* or *poa'aha.* The bark was made into a durable paper used as cloth, leather, or paper. In Hawai'i, *kapa* was made from *wauke* for skirts, capes, loin cloths, sandals, and bed clothes. (NEAL 301.) Small white pieces of this *kapa* were placed over idols during prayers. See **'oloa.**

kuamū. *Kapa* used in sorcery ceremonies. (PE.)

kua'ula. Thick red *kapa.* (A.) Ribbed or grooved cloth made with a grooved board. (PE.)

ku'ina. Set of *kapa* sheets for sleeping, generally fine in quality; the best, the top covering.

ku'inakapa. *Kapa* bed coverings. Four inner sheets of white *(iho),* were fastened to an outer, decorated cover sheet, *(kilohana).* (PE.)

kū'oulena. Coarse *kapa.* (PE.)

kūpoepoe. Well furnished, as one wearing much *kapa;* bundled up, as in cold weather.

lawakea. People dressed in large, white, flowing *kapa.*

māhuna. Form of *kapa* like the *pa'ipa'i kukui.* (A.) Fine, scented *kapa* dyed with *noni* bark and made under strict *kapu.* When reserved for the chiefs it was called *māhunali'i.*

mālua'ula. *Kapa* stained with dye made from *kukui* bark. (PE.)

maolua. Red *kapa.* (PE.)

ma'oma'o. Green *kapa,* pounded from *māmaki* bark. Probably dyed green from the *mao (Abutilon molle),* the hairy abutilon plant. See **Colors.**

moelola. Striped *kapa;* outer sheet *(kilohana)* made as a bed cover. (PE.)

moelua. Red *kapa,* either a *malo* or *pā'ū.* (A.) Striped; of two colors of the same width and lying parallel, as in a *kapa.* (PE.)

mōmo. *Kapa* of inferior quality. (A.)

mo'omo'o. *Kapa,* second or third rate, with small sections pieced together. Same as *mōmo.*

ninikea. White *kapa,* as worn by priests during ceremonies. (PE.)

ni'o. Handsome, high-grade *kapa.* See **'oni'oni'o.** (A.)

no'eno'e. Printed or colored *kapa*. (PE.)

'ohu'ohu. Blackish kind of *kapa*. (A.) White *kapa* with dots and figures. (PE.)

'oloa. Small, white *kapa* placed over the idols during prayers. See **kopili.** *Obs.*

olomea. *Kapa* of *wauke* dyed with *'ōhi'a* bark, *hōlei,* and coconut water.

'ōma'o. Greenish *kapa*. (PE.) See **ma'o.**

'oni'oni'o. *Kapa* spotted like a leopard skin. See **kapeke.**

'ōnohi 'ula. Kind of red *kapa*.

'ō'ū holo ai. *Māmaki kapa* dyed or painted on each side with a different color and design. See **kapeke.**

'o'u holo wai o La'a. *Kapa* said to have been made at Ola'a, Hawai'i and associated with the goddess Laka. (PE.)

pā'a'ā. Early practice of using short lengths of bark to produce a poor quality *kapa*.

pa'i kukui a me 'ōlena. *Kapa* from Moloka'i, dyed yellow.

pa'ipa'i kukui. Dark *kapa* dyed with juice from *kukui* bark. (PE.)

pa'i'ula. *Kapa* made by beating *welu* (rags and pieces of torn *kapa*) with new *wauke,* which formed a red and white mixture for outer bed covers, etc. See **welu 'ula.**

pakē. Plain, uncolored *kapa;* white *kapa*.

pala'ā. *Kapa* of *māmaki* bark dyed brownish-red with *pala'ā* fern. (PE.)

pālau anahu. *Kapa*. See **'aeokahaloa.**

palalei. Act of spreading one's *kapa* over the head of a chief entering a house. (A.) *Kapa* with fringe-like edges uncut.

palenananahu. *Kapa* with a stamped design. (CMH.)

pā'ū. Woman's skirt or dress of fine *kapa* wound around the waist, reaching to the knees; poor kind of *kapa,* not of any definite color.

pa'ūpa'ū. *Kapa* that was wet during its making. (PE.)

pehu a koa. *Kapa* colored with the bark of the *koa* tree.

pele, pelehū. Choice Kaua'i-made *kapa*.

pepele. Kaua'i *kapa*.

pili. Uncolored sheets in a *ku'ina; kapa* for sleeping. (PE.)

pili moe. *Kapa* used in the game *pūhenehene.*

pilipuka. *Kapa* cover used in the *pūhenehene* game. A different one was used for each of the five periods of the night. See **Time: Watches of the Night.**

pīnauea. Kind of *kapa*. (PE.) Act of sprinkling *kapa* with water during the beating.

pōhaka. Painted or printed *kapa*. (A.)

poʻipū. Kind of *kapa*. (PE.)

poniponi. *Kapa* painted with different colors.

pua hala. *Hala* flower design on *kapa* and patchwork quilts. (PE.)

pua hala kākau meolola. Outer sheet *(kilohana)* for bed covers printed with a *pua hala* design.

puakai. *Kapa* dyed red with the juice of the *noni* to which coral lime has been added.

pualiʻi. *Kapa* used for loincloths and sarongs. (PE.)

pua niu. *Kapa* dyed with *niu* (coconut).

pūkohukohu. *Kapa* that is colored red with *noni* juice and designed as a *malo*.

pūlohiwa. Shining black *kapa*.

pūloʻu. Black *kapa* donned for concealment and used at funerals.

pūloʻuloʻu. *Kapa* on a ball at the top of a stick carried before a chief as a sign of *kapu*.

pūnana. *Kapa* where the fibers show like the twigs in a bird's nest; white *kapa*.

pūnoni. *Kapa* colored with a dye, probably the *noni* root, which is red in color.

pupupu. White *kapa* used to make a *pāʻū*.

puʻukoʻa. Reddish-brown *kapa*.

puʻukohukohu. Gray *kapa* made in Wai-piʻo, Hawaiʻi.

puʻukukui. *Kapa* made of *wauke* (paper mulberry, *Broussonetia papyrifera*) and *poule ʻulu* (male breadfruit flower).

puʻu lepo. Reddish-brown *kapa*.

ʻuʻa. Coarse *kapa*. (PE.)

uʻaniu. *Kapa* colored with *niu* (coconut). (CMH.) See **hala kea**.

ʻuaʻua. *Kapa* or *pāʻū* colored yellow. See *ʻōlena*, turmeric.

ʻulaʻula. Red *kapa*. (PE.)

ulu. *Kapa* made at Wai-piʻo, Hawaiʻi.

wailiʻiliʻi. *Kapa* decorated with thick yellow stripes.

wai palupalu. Kind of *kapa*. *Lit.*, soft dye. (PE.)

welu. Rag; piece of frayed or torn *kapa*.

welu ʻula. *Kapa* made of pieces of red *kapa* beaten with new *wauke,* making a mixture of red and white. More generally called *paʻiʻula*.

KAPA: Manufacture

This section contains mini-categories of terms involved in the making of *kapa*.

1. Kinds of bark
2. Beating and pounding
3. Coloring and dyeing
4. Printing and painting
5. Scents
6. Striping
7. Moistening and drying
8. Miscellaneous

Materials available for the manufacture of *kapa* were trees, stones, shrubs, and small plants, of which Hawaiians used bark, leaves, roots, seeds, sap, and fruit pulp. The importance of beating the *kapa* can be seen by the number of words referring to the *kapa* beater. The "cloth" produced had many uses: clothing, head coverings, bed sheets and covers, mats, curtains, funeral clothes, and quilts.

Two deified females, Lauhūki and La'ahana, supported *kapa* making as woman's work. Of two male gods, one, Maikoha, was credited with the origin of the paper mulberry plant, while the other, 'Ehu, was the god of the dyeing experts. They made, among other things, *hamo'ula, kapa* stained or dyed red; *wali'ili'i*, broad-striped *kapa;* and *u'au'a, kapa* colored yellow with *'olena.*

1. Kinds of bark

hili. Black dye made from *kōlea* bark for coloring *kapa;* general term for bark used in dyeing.

kūloli. Single mulberry tree that once grew in a cave at Kūloli, Hawai'i. (PE.) Species of *wauke* at Palilua, Hawai'i. (A.)

ma'aloa. *Māmaki,* a treelike native shrub *(Neraudia melasto-maefolia)* that supplied a strong fibrous bark for making *kapa.*

māmaki. Native Hawaiian tree *(Pipturus albidus)* with a smooth, light-brown bark with a fibrous inner layer, formerly a principal source of a firm, heavy *kapa,* durable if not wetted. (NEAL 319.)

'ōhi'a hā. Tree *(Eugenia sandwicensis),* the bark of which was used to color *kapa.*

pā'ihi. Bark of the *'ōhi'a hā* tree used in coloring *kapa* black. (A.)

pō'ulu. Bark of the tender breadfruit shoots from which a good quality *kapa* was made.

wauke. East Asian paper mulberry tree or shrub *(Broussonetia papyrifera),* which formerly supplied the best bark for the warmest, most flexible and water resistant *kapa.* Introduced to Hawai'i by the early settlers.

2. Beating and pounding

ho'omo'omo'o. To beat mulberry bark soaked in sea water into *mo'omo'o* preparatory to beating it into sheets; second- or third-grade *kapa* that has been pieced together. See **Kapa: Kapa Beater.**
kuku. To beat, as a *kapa.*
kūpalu. To mash *kapa* particles to a pulp in preparation for beating them into *kapa.*
'ou'ou. Sharp, quick sound of the *kapa* mallet.
'ukē. To strike, as with a *kapa* mallet. (A.)

3. Coloring and dyeing

'alaea. Any red coloring matter; red ochre used for dye. (Isa. 14:13.)
'awea. A red dye. (CMH.)
hala kea. *Kapa* dyed with *niu,* a coconut product.
hanina. Ancient garment, the *pā'ū,* colored with the yellow of the *'ōlena.*
kūpenu. To dye by dipping; to smooth a ruffled *kapa.* Also called *lu'u, ho'olu'u.*
lu'u. To dip into coloring matter; to dye. (Puk. 25:5.)
māhiehie. To dye with color-fast dyes; to color *kapa* with distinct spots or colors. (A.)
ma'o. Shrub of the mallow family *(Abutilon molle)* used in dyeing *kapa* green. It is velvety to the touch.
nā'ū. Dye or coloring matter producing a yellow tint, supplied by the *nā'ū* tree, the native gardenia. Also called *nānū.*
noni. Indian mulberry tree *(Morinda citrifolia).* The root bark yields a yellow dye. To get a red, coral lime is added. "I have made this yellow dye many times then have added the coral lime to turn the mixture to red." (KILO.)
paniki. Dye, coloring matter for *kapa.* (A.)
puaniu. *Kapa* colored with dye from the coconut. (A.)
pūnoni. Red dye for *kapa* from the root bark of the *noni* tree.
wai 'ele. Dark or black dye for *kapa.*

waihoʻoluʻu. Water for coloring; a dye; general term for dyes into which the entire *kapa* was to be immersed.

walaheʻe. Leaves of a shrub used to color *kapa* black. Also called *alaheʻe (Canthium odoratum).*

weʻa. A red dye; to print or color red.

4. Printing and painting

kākau. To print or paint upon *kapa,* as in former times.

kohu. Ink or any fixed coloring matter or plant juice for printing or coloring *kapa* (A.)

nao. Streaks on *kapa.* (A.)

ʻohe kākau. Bamboo prepared for printing *kapa.*

ʻohe kāpala. Piece of bamboo carved for printing on *kapa.*

omōhā. Design used in printing on *kapa.*

ʻōniʻo. *Kapa* printed in variegated colors.

pahu palapala. Ink or dye container used in printing *kapa.*

pālani. To paint lightly, as *kapa* with light shades.

palapala. To stamp or print on *kapa.*

palapalani. To paint or print *kapa* and put out to dry.

pāniʻoniʻo. To print a *kapa* in gaudy, variegated colors.

poniponi. *Kapa* painted with different colors. (A.)

pūhiʻōniʻo. To stamp *kapa* with different colors; to paint or color in a spotted manner.

weʻa. A red dye; to print or color red.

5. Scents

ʻāwapuhi. Wild ginger *(Zingiber zerumbet),* which has aromatic, knobbed, underground stems used to scent the *kapa.* (NEAL 257.)

ʻiliahi. Sandalwood *(Santalum* spp.). A hard wood sent to China for temple incense. Hawaiians sometimes perfumed *kapa* by using sandalwood in either powder form or mixed with coconut oil. (NEAL 325.)

kamani. Perfume plant *(Calophyllum inophyllum).* A hardwood tree supplying a sap for perfume.

kūpaoa. An odoriferous shrub *(Railliardia),* which produces a fragrance of jasmine used for scenting *kapa. Fig.,* what gives character to life. *O ke kūpaoa ia e hoʻopē ai i na ʻuhane,* that is the plant which gives scent to souls (i.e., their peculiar character). The root is used to scent *kapa.* (NEAL 845.)

laua'e. Fragrant fern *(Polypodium phymatodes)*. When crushed, its juice provides a scent used on *kapa*. (NEAL 37.)

maile. Straggling, climbing vine noted for the fragrance of its leaves. The scent from its crushed leaves is used for *kapa*.

mokihana. Kaua'i tree *(Pelea anisata)* with small, anise-scented fruits which, when crushed, supply a fragrance used for *kapa*. (NEAL 478.)

poni. Odoriferous, as in colored and scented *kapa*.

6. Striping

hālu'a. Pattern of stripes and ripples on the surface of a *kapa* beater or the *kapa* itself. (PE.)

kahakaha. To print parallel stripes on *kapa*.

kāni'o. A striped *kapa*.

kī'oki. Stripes like bars in a *kapa* design.

moekolu. Design of three parallel stripes of about equal width on a *kapa*.

moelua. Design of two parallel stripes of about equal width on a *kapa*.

'ōni'oni'o. Spotted, streaked with various colors, as a *kapa*.

pe'elua. *Kapa* with a striped design.

7. Moistening and drying

'ae. Very soft liquid wrung from the leaves of the *wauke* (mulberry bush). (A.)

'elo. To wet or soak *kapa* with rain. *Pulu kahi kapa i ka ua, 'elo wale,* a *kapa* was wet with rain and became soft. (A.)

ho'opulu. To soften *wauke* by soaking in water until it becomes paste-like.

ki'olena. Place for bleaching, drying, and coloring *kapa;* to spread out to dry and whiten in the sun.

kūhili. To mix the soaking *wauke* with coloring matter before pounding the mashed bark.

lauhiki. The girl who moistened the *kapa* while it was being pounded.

lena. To stretch out cloth or *kapa* to dry.

māhola. To spread out or enfold a *kapa* for drying.

palu. Soft matter of which *kapa* was made. *Wauke* or *māmaki* was soaked in water until it became *wali* (pastelike).

pulu. Soft matter of which *kapa* was made, so called when made soft by soaking it.

unahe. Thin; soft as *kapa*.

8. Miscellaneous

ʻāpikipiki. To fold up, as a piece of *kapa*.

hoʻai. To sew or stretch two pieces of *kapa* together; to thin *poi* with water in preparation for eating. (A.)

kapa kuʻina. Five sheets of *kapa* sewn together for sleeping.

kukaʻa. To roll up, as a bundle of *kapa* or cloth.

kukukapa. Work of Hawaiian women. (CMH.)

māwale. To fade, as the colors of a *kapa*. (A.)

ʻōmau. To tuck in the outer edge of the *pāʻū* to fasten it.

ʻopi. Folds or depressions made by folding *kapa*.

ʻopiʻopi. To fold, as a garment or *kapa*. (2 Nal. 2:8.)

paku. To unite two pieces of *wauke* by beating to make one *kapa*; to join or sew two pieces of *kapa*.

palaholo. Paste made of the sap from rolled-up fronds of the *ʻamaʻu* fern used in glueing two pieces of *kapa* together.

pūʻolo. Bundle of *kapa* tied up like a *paʻiʻai*; round bundle.

welu. Piece of torn *kapa*.

welu ahi. Ball of *kapa* cord used to carry fire. (PE.)

KAPA: At the Paris Exposition, 1889

The French offered the world a great exposition, the Exposition Universelle in Paris in 1889, and the Hawaiian Kingdom was invited to participate.

Members of the royal family, the Kamehameha Schools, private collectors, sugar factories, railroads, and the like joined in the project. John A. Hassinger was the leader in soliciting, transporting, and setting up the exhibition. Near the exposition's close, he prepared a *Catalogue of the Hawaiian Exhibits at the Exposition Universelle, Paris 1889,* a pamphlet of forty-eight pages printed by the Hawaiian Gazette Co. Therein are listed some thirty-eight *kapa* items, all credited to the government of Hawaiʻi. This chapter is derived from that list.

The definitions following the Hawaiian names and phrases descriptive of the *kapa* were contrived by the editor of the pamphlet.

Dr. Hyde did not attempt this, perhaps intending to publish an article on the subject. The list was not alphabetized by Hassinger.

hai manawa moelola. Beautiful, thin, delicate, white *kapa,* manufactured in a particular way. The word *moelola* means laying panels of a red *kapa* over a white *kapa* and beating the two to form a single *kapa,* an outersheet *(kilohana)* of a set of five bed covers. The design appears as a white sheet with parallel stripes of red and white covering.

hili me ka nānahu. *Kapa* dyed black of charcoal.

kākau uauahi puakai moelola. *Kapa* bed cover of charcoal background, painted with red dye after treatment as described in *hai manawa moelola* above.

kalakala moelola. Probably a rough *kalakala kapa* made from long panels beaten together.

kapa ʻala. Perfumed, spicy *kapa.* (CMH.)

kapa ʻala kukui me ka ʻōlena. Scented *kapa* dyed with yellow coloring from the *ʻōlena* and *kukui* bark, *ʻōlena a me kukui.*

kapa kukui ʻeleʻele. Probably this *kapa* originated at Kau-makani, Maui, dyed black with the root of the *kukui* tree.

kapa ʻōlena. *Kapa* dyed yellow from the root of the *ʻōlena.*

kāpalapala ʻalaea. *Kapa* printed with red coloring matter; red ochre.

kāpalapala hāʻukeʻuke. *Kapa* printed with a special motif, a sea urchin *(hāʻukeʻuke).*

kapa māhuna aliʻi. Fine, scented *kapa* from Molokaʻi, colored yellow from the *noni* bark, ascribed to chiefly use.

kea. Anything white; a white *kapa,* if speaking of a *kapa kea.*

kena me ka nānahu. No data.

keʻokeʻo moelola ʻulaʻula. White bed cover of *kapa* colored with long, red panels beaten in parallel lines on the white background.

kilohana. Folded bed cover scented with male flowers of the pandanus tree and made in the *kilohana* style.

kilohana paʻiʻula. Outer bed cover made by beating up *welu (kapa* remnants) with new *wauke,* a mixture made for coloring purposes.

kilohana pualima. Yellow bed cover. (CMH.)

kuʻīna paʻi kukui. Bed cover set of five *kapa* dyed dark with juice from *kukui* bark.

kuʻina paʻiʻula. Outer cover of a bed *kapa,* consisting of long strips joined to make a *kapa,* dyed in alternate panels of white and red.

māhuna. Fine, scented *kapa* used by chiefs.

malo paʻiʻula. Loincloth of mixed colors, white and red.

mau. *ʻAmaʻu* (fern stems) used for sizing *kapa.*

nānahu moelola. Striped *kapa* of parallel dark strips on a light background, used as the outer sheet *(kilohana)* on a set of bed covers.

niho me kā haʻukeʻuke. *Kapa* decorated with the figures of a tooth and sea urchin.

ʻōlena kākau. To print or paint *kapa* using yellow coloring matter.

ʻōlena me ka nānahu. To mix yellow coloring with charcoal in printing or painting a *kapa.*

ʻōlena moelola niho. *Kapa* bed cover with a jagged edge, made of long strips joined by beating, and yellow in color.

ʻōʻū-holo-wai-o-Laʻa. ʻOlaʻa, Hawaiʻi type of *kapa,* an outer sheet for bed covers.

pae kukui ʻala. Dark, smooth, and scented *kapa.*

paʻikukui kākau nānahu. *Kapa* colored like coal from the bark of the *kukui,* and printed.

paʻi kukui. Dark *kapa* colored with the juice of the *kukui* bark.

paʻiʻula moelola. Outer bed cover, a mixture of red and white panels joined by beating them together.

palenānahu pua-hala. Outer dress colored yellow and stamped with a design.

pāʻu māhuna kāpalapalaia. *Pāʻū* daubed and scented.

pāʻū paʻi kukui kāpalapalaia. Dark colored *kapa* dyed with *kukui* bark and printed with a design.

pua-hala kākau moelola. Bed cover with a *hala* key design, pounded and printed as in the *moelola* process.

puakaʻi. *Kapa* dyed with red coloring from *noni* juice.

KAPA: A Woman's World

The making of *kapa* was performed mostly by women. It is easy to picture them pounding and beating it with the mallet and hear the chatter and laughter amid the business of soaking and scraping lengths of bark. Men assisted in growing and harvesting the fibrous plants, in gathering the dyes, and in making all the tools, but the women dominated actual production of the "paper cloth." The industry—like fishing, raising basic foods, and building houses—was an important part of social life; however, clothing made of other materials was worn.

In Hawai'i most *kapa* was made from the bark of the shrub *wauke,* the paper mulberry *(Broussonetia papyrifera,* also called *po'a'aha),* and from the bark of a small native tree, *māmaki (Pipturus albidus).*

The bark was peeled from the stems after they had been cut and brought to the village from the *wauke* plantations. The stems might have been 6 feet long and 3 inches thick. The bark was soaked until *wali* (soft) and *pipili* (sticky). The process was called *kīkoni.*

The outer bark was stripped or scraped off with a shell or bone scraper. The inner cortex was beaten on a *kua kuku* (wooden anvil), a log about 6 feet long with a wide groove on the underside to allow it to stand firmly. This hollowness gave a reverberating sound *('ou'ou)* to the *i'i kuku (kapa* mallet) that formerly could be heard through all the waking hours.

The sprinkling of coloring on the *kapa* and beating it, *(kuku kapa pa'ipa'i)* was the work of the women. All worked zealously, from the queen down to the country commoner. A house *(hale kua)* was set apart for this work in every Hawaiian settlement.

Besides the *wauke* and *mamaki,* bark from a small native shrub, an endemic raspberry *(ākala, Rubus Hawai'iensis);* a low fern, *ma'aloa (Neraudia melastomaefolia);* and from the breadfruit, *'ulu (Artocarpus altilis)* could also be used. A peculiar variety of *wauke* is grown at Palilua, Hawai'i, called *kūloli.* This bark when soaked is called *pulu 'oloa;* when colored prior to pounding, it is called *kuhili.* The beating process is *kūpalu.* Other names for it are *'ukē, pūkē,* and *ko'ele.* The joining of the slips is called *paku* or *hoai. Lena* means to stretch the *kapa; mōhala,* to spread it out to dry and bleach.

The *kapa* mallet is called *hohoa kūa'u* or *i'e kuku;* the first word applies to the first part of the pounding *(hoa)* or to beating *kapa* on a stone to soften or smooth it. The mallets are made of *kauila (Alphitoma excelsa),* the buckthorn tree; or from *kōpiko (Straussia sp.),* a small coffee-like tree. Mallets are about 18 inches long, 2 inches square, with one end rounded for a handle. Each pattern on the mallet constitutes a kind of watermark, each of which had its own name. A collection of squeezes of the patterns can give an idea of their variety (see Peter Buck, *Arts and Crafts,* pp. 195–201).

Kapa was marked in many patterns with black or other kinds of dyes, impressed upon the *kapa* by slips of bamboo about half an inch wide, and 12 inches long. Each slip had its pattern at one end and bore a specific name. Collections of these bamboo markers, such as *lapa, 'ohe kākau, 'ohe kāpala,* and so on, can be seen in the Bishop Museum, assembled by number and name along with exhibits of mallets. This process of stamping *(palapala, palapalani),* gave Hawaiians their word for printed books and documents. The Bible is called *Palapala Hemolele;* the dye container is called *pahu palapala.*

Kapa was also dyed with *hili,* a general name for coloring matter obtained from the bark of trees, or with *kohu,* a stain from the saps and juices of plants. *Waiho'olu'u* is the general name for dyes; the process of dipping is called *kūpenupenu; pāni'oni'o* means to paint with gay colors; *mawale* refers to the fading colors of a *kapa; mahiehie* is to dye with color-fast dyes.

The various sources of dye include *'ala'ala wai nui,* small succulent herbs *(Peperomia* spp.); *'awe'a* or *we'a,* a red dye and *hili kolea,* a black dye; *hili kōlea, hili 'ahi,* and *holei,* a trio of plants whose barks yield a yellow dye.

Additionally, there is *ma'o,* a small velvety shrub belonging to the mallow family *(Malvaceae),* which supplies a green dye; *nā'ū,* a yellow gardenia *(Gardenia remyi),* whose fruit pulp was used for tinting *kapa* yellow; *noni,* Indian mulberry *(Morinda citrifolia),* whose roots supply yellow and red dyes; and *'ohi'a'ai* bark, mountain apple *(Eugenia malaccensis),* used to color *kapa* brown.

Others include *pa'ihi,* a weed *(Nasturtium sarmentosum),* used for a black dye; *'ōlena,* turmeric *(Curcuma longa),* used to color *kapa* yellow; and *wai'ele,* a black dye.

Nao is a streak or ridge made in felting. *Kapa* was sometimes varnished with a variety of gums to make it waterproof and to preserve the colors. *'A'ahu* is a general name for clothing. A *malo* is a strip of *kapa* girded about men's loins. The "girding" process is called *hume.* The *pā'ū* is a waistcloth or skirt for women. Generally five fold, it reaches to the knees and is fastened by tucking in *('ōmau)* one corner.

Kapa was folded *('opi)* by doubling over the colored side, leaving the white exposed. Pieces were stacked in an orderly pile and made into a bundle *(pū'olo)* or a roll *(kūka'a).* Forty pieces of *kapa* were called *'iako,* a word used in evidence of a person's wealth.

Lau huki was the god worshiped by the women who beat out the *kapa;* La'ahana was the patron deity of the women who printed *kapa* cloth. (MALO 82.) Ha'i ha'ina kolo was a forest-dwelling goddess of *kapa* makers.

KAPU

The word *kapu* gives us the English "taboo." The *kapu* system reflects the somewhat secondary role of women in Hawaiian society.

In the hierarchy of the gods, a scheme of restrictions and "forbiddens" was evolved to be applied, variously, to all humans. Some *kapu* restrictions were observed regularly, such as certain fruits or meats being forbidden to women. Other restraints applied to certain intervals of time such as seasons, moon phases, menstrual periods, the annual *makahiki,* and so on. The *kapu* also related to the council or assembly of the great chiefs, a social phenomenon demanding silence and quiet respect from all people nearby.

Some words coined by the Hawaiians provided for the imposition of a *kapu.* Other words refer to the breaking, or more properly, the releasing of the *kapu.* Penalties for breaking the more rigid *kapu* were severe, with death not an unusual end for the victim or offender.

The philosophy of the *kapu* was of deep significance in the lives of the people. Fundamentally, the system imposed great restraint upon their freedoms as individuals, under threat of penalty. It also provided the dimensions of social relationships serving the needs of the times.

'a'e. To break a taboo, violate the law.

'a'e ku. To break a law or taboo deliberately.

'ahi. Albacore or yellowfin tuna, fish forbidden to women. (CMH.)

'ai kapu. Rule against men and women eating together in observance of the *kapu* system. Words which mean release from *kapu* include *'ainoa, 'aipūhi'u, pūhi'u.*

'aīkū, 'aiā. To be ungodly in practice; to break a *kapu;* rejection of Hawai'i's gods.

'ainoa. To eat; released from *kapu.*

'ai pūhi'u. Released from an eating *kapu.*

alahula. Road made along a *pali* (cliff) traveled by residents but forbidden to strangers.

'āmama. The *kapu* is lifted; it is flown away!

'ānoho. Sitting *kapu.*

auali'i. *Kapu* sacred to *Kama,* ancient chief of Maui. *O ka noe kolo auali'i kapu o Kama,* this small fine rain of the mountains mixed with the thicker of the forest, sacred to Kama. (A.)

'ea. Species of turtle valued for its shell, forbidden under the *kapu* system to be eaten by women. (A.)

hāhālua. Fish forbidden to women. The same *kapu* applied to *hīhīmanu* and *'ihimanu,* large sea creatures called rays.

haohaoa lani. Royal heat, *kapu* of a chief. It is dangerous to approach a *kapu* chief.

hehi. To disobey or disregard the law.

hehikū. To trample on the rights of others; to violate a *kapu.*

hō'a'e. To violate a *kapu.*

Hoaka. One of the *kapu* days; second day of the moon. See **Time: Nights of the Lunar Month.**

ho'auwae. Not paying respect to *kapu.*

hō'iu. To lay a *kapu* upon a person, place, or thing, meaning to make sacred. *'Iu kahi o ke ali'i, ano, maka'u,* sacred is the place of the chief, it is consecrated, it is feared.

hono. *Kapu* where every man must hold his hands in a particular posture; *kapu* ceremony involving chiefs.

honu. Sea turtle or terrapin forbidden as food for women under pain of death.

ho'okapu. To place under a *kapu.* See **ko'okapu.**

ho'olāhui. To lay under a *kapu;* to consecrate.

ho'omāhanahana. Name of one of the last *kapu*s; to relax a *kapu* during a long, strenuous session. (MALO 160, 176.)

ho'omamao lani. *Kapu* of unapproachability of some high chiefs. (PE.)

ho'onoa. To free from *kapu.*

hu'a kapu. *Kapu* enclosure; *hula* area with *kapu* borders. (PE.) Rich property around the chiefs, *kapu* to common people. (A.)

huali. To commence a *kapu* of a particular kind. No data. (A.)

humu. Short for *paehumu,* a *kapu* enclosure, a confinement area.

'i'ilena. Thought to be especially grateful to the gods. (CMH.)

ili kapu. *Kapu* against contact with the bedding or clothing of others. (PE.)

'iu. Consecrated place; *kapu* restricting menstruating women to a special hut.

ka'anī'au. Freed, as from a *kapu;* passed away, as a *kapu. Noa ke kapu; he kapu ka lāua, noa ke kapu,* the *kapu* of the long gods and that of the short gods are no more. (A.)

ka'apola. *Kapu* night in the ruling chief's *heiau* in October. (PE.)

kaha pouli. *Kapu* on menstruating women, restricting them to a special house.

kahuna. One of three elements of *kapu,* a system of religion in effect in early Hawai'i. The *kahuna* with its priests of profes-

sions and occupations was one; a second was royalty or chiefs
(aliʻi); and the third was a supernatural influence of *akua* (gods
and goddesses) from all ranks and classes of people, and their
ancestors. All three together constituted a strict base for gover-
nance and control through the *kapu*. (Kin. 37:8.)

kai heheʻe. Ancient *kapu* of the chiefs connected with death. Also
called *lumalumaʻi*. (A.) *Kapu* place along the shore where
kauwā, the breakers of certain *kapu*, were drowned that they
might be offered as sacrifices. (PE.)

kakai. To stretch the *kapu* cord before the entrance of a chiefʻs
house. This cord was said to fall away if a relative appeared.
(PE.)

kalahuʻa. Ceremony of women being allowed to eat food after a
kapu has been lifted. (A.)

kama kiʻi lohelohe. Sacred sennit used in *kapu* services. (PE.)

kamakini. To impose a general *kapu*.

kapu moe, kapu a moe. Prostration *kapu*. Everyone was required
to fall prostrate when the chief bearing this *kapu* passed.

kapu noho. *Kapu* requiring all to sit in the presence of the chief or
whenever his food container, bath water, and other articles were
carried by.

kapuō. *Kapu* in honor of the god Kāʻili.

kapuwō. Cry proclaiming the *kapu* upon the approach of the
king; announcer of the *kapu*.

kapu wohi. *Kapu* of the *wohi* (chiefs), including their exemption
from the prostration *kapu*. (PE.) A *wohi* chief was a high chief
who preceded the king on public occasions to see that others
prostrated themselves. (PE.)

kauila, kauwila. *Kapu* ceremony of consecrating a temple.

kaumihau. *Kapu* instituted by a priest. Men were separated from
their wives, and a hog was baked. (A.)

koʻokapu. To forbid, strictly, on pain of death. See **hoʻokapu.**

kū. To act rudely or defiantly in one's observance of a *kapu*.

kuaʻa. Strong *kapu* applying to anyone approaching a chief from
behind. (PE.) Also called *kuakapu, kua liholiho, kualoi, kualoi-
loi*.

kuapala. *Kapu* chief possessing the right to carry a *pala* fern in
ceremonies. (PE.)

kūhiwa. To be under a *kapu* made by a chief and therefore under
his control, in distinction from the freedom of the people. (A.)

lelea. *Kapu* imposed by a priest on *ʻawa* while it was being drunk
by a chief so the feeling of the drink would fly to the gods.

lepapahu. *Kapu* marker flag.

malolo. Day of preparation before a *lā kapu;* to quit work at the beginning of a *kapu.*

malu. Awe and stillness of a *kapu;* peace and quiet under a *kapu.*

maluhia. To be quiet under a *kapu;* solemn awe and stillness that reigned during an ancient *kapu* or religious rite. Perhaps not a true peacefulness because of the presence of the *kapu.* (DK.)

manō. General name for shark and some other kinds of fish like the *'ahi* and *niuhi,* all *kapu* to women.

mau'a'e. To break *kapu.*

mau'u mae. Wilted grass; name of a ten-day *kapu* on men.

mumule. Silent gathering at a *kapu* ceremony. When people gather for a ceremony where a *kapu* is involved they must be *mumule.* Even animals had to be muzzled to insure silence was not broken.

na'auau. Remission of the strictness of a *kapu,* so that people could eat certain foods, thatch their houses, and perform other duties.

nai'a. Species of marine mammal, the porpoise. Its flesh is forbidden to women.

nīoi. Poison tree said to have grown on Lana'i and Moloka'i, under *kapu,* but which was uprooted by the sacrilegious Kaeokulani. (A.)

niu. Coconut. The eating of coconuts was forbidden to women under the *kapu* system. (A.)

niuhi. Large shark *(manō nunui),* the flesh of which was forbidden to women.

noa. Removed from the restraint of a *kapu.*

'ōhi'a. *Kapu,* as food patches during famine. *Obs.* (PE.)

paehumu, humu. *Kapu* around a chief's house or *heiau.*

pāhoa. *Kapu* sign.

pālama. Sacred and *kapu* enclosure, especially for royal women. (PE.)

papa 'ia. *Kapu.*

peleu. To break the *kapu* of a chief.

pihano. Sitting still in time of a *kapu;* still, as an assembly for worship under the *kapu* system, perhaps also with a sense of foreboding. (A.)

pī kai 'ōlena. To purify or remove a *kapu* by sprinkling with sea (salt) water and a touch of *'ōlena* root. (PE.)

po'iu. To be under the protection of someone with power under a *kapu;* consecrated, sacred.

po'iu'iu. To be very *kapu* or sacred.

pūlo'ulo'u. Symbol and insignia of *kapu;* ball of *kapa* at the end of a stick *(pahu).*

pu'ukoāmaka. *Kapu* pertaining only to the god Kahoāli'i. (PE.)

ua 'a'e lākou i luna la'a. Trespassing in a sacred place. The *kapu* was broken when one stepped on or in an area within which a chief was seated or which was considered sacred due to the fact that the area was set aside for the chief. (A.)

ulua. Vegetable under *kapu*, forbidden to women. (A.)

unūnu, unuunu. Stick erected as a sign of *kapu*.

wahi kapu. *Kapu* enclosure or place. (PE.)

KINDRED

The Hawaiians had a clear concept of relationships within the family and used many words to describe them. Of interest are the designations for younger brothers and younger sisters. These were terms of endearment.

There were also a numbered sequence of ancestors and, similarly, of descendants, by which genealogists could recite lineages back to great-great-grandparents (and beyond) and forward to grandchildren and sometimes great-grand-children.

In general, family history was a product of this oral transfer of information, giving both young and old an understanding of the succession of generations. These were genuine genealogical records. See "Hawaiian Names for Relationships," by Charles M. Hyde.

āewa. Family lineage.

ali'i kāne. Male chief; husband (polite usage), not said of one's husband or to him. (PE.)

'anakala. Uncle. *Eng.*

ānakē. Aunt. *Eng.*

auwaepili. Close relative. (MALO 199.)

haku wahine. Wife of a chief; woman of high rank.

hanahanauna. Contemporary born; of the same age. *Hauna* is the more commonly known term, a relative whose relationship was established several generations earlier.

hānau hope. Second child, younger in relation to the first, or the third in relation to the second, etc.; younger sister.

hānau kāhi. Only child. (Sol. 4:3.)

hānau kama. Bearer of children; fruitful, fertile in bearing; wife.

hānau mua. Oldest child; first-born child. See **hiapo, makahiapo.** (Puk. 12:12.)

hāpuʻu. Child.

hele mua. Older brother or sister.

hiapo. First born of parents; see **makahiapo, hānau mua.**

hoahānau. Kindred; some blood relation, brother, sister, cousin. *Lit.,* companion by birth.

hoʻokama. Adopted child, more like a godchild. Adopting parents might assume some or none of the child's or person's physical care. No adoptive papers were prepared as was often done in later times for a *hānai* child. (KILO.)

hoʻokāne. To offer oneself as a husband.

hoʻomakua kāne. To act, claim, or treat as a father. (PE.)

hoʻowahine. To take as a wife.

hua hāʻule. Illegitimate child.

hūnōna kāne. Son-in-law.

hūnōna. Daughter-in-law.

inoa ʻohana. Surname; family name. (PE.)

ʻiʻo pono. Friend whose faithfulness might be trusted; relation of one who guarded the king. (A.)

iwikuamoʻo. Trusted relative of a chief.

kaʻala. Widow or widower.

kāʻiēwe. Company of relatives following and caring for a chief.

kaikaina. Younger of two brothers or two sisters. Used by a brother when speaking of a brother, or a sister of a sister. But if a brother speaks of a sister or vice-versa, they use *kaikunāne.* See **kaikua.**

kaikamahine. Daughter.

kaikoʻeke kāne. Brother-in-law; male cousin-in-law of a male.

kaikoʻeke wahine. Sister-in-law; female cousin-in-law of a female.

kaikua. Elder of two brothers or sisters, as the second older than the third, the third older than the fourth, etc. Same as *kaikaina* but in reverse.

kaikuaʻana, kaikuʻana. Older child or cousin of the same sex; child or cousin of the same sex of the senior line, whether older or younger. (PE.)

kaikuahini, kuahini. Sister of a boy. Like *kaiʻana* and *kunāne* it may be preceded by *o, ʻo,* or *ko.*

kaikunāne. Brother or male cousin of a girl.

kaikuʻuwahine. Sister or female cousin of a boy.

kaina. Younger brother of a boy, younger sister of a girl.

kama. The first husband of a wife; children generally, as male and female children; second generation.

kamaiki. Oldest or first-born child; the most endeared or most beloved. (A.)

kama kāhi. Only or single child.

kama kāne. Son.

kāne. Husband. Also called *kāne i ka ʻili.*

kauō, kauwō. Offspring; fruit of marriage. David Malo says, "If Nahienaena had had a son, the old chiefs would say *ʻua loaʻa ke kauō;* hence, a supporter, a sustainer." (A.)

keiki. Child, female or male; son.

keiki ʻai walu. Suckling child.

keiki aliʻi. Child of a chief.

keiki ʻaluʻalu. Premature baby.

keiki hānai. Adopted child.

keiki hoʻokama. Godchild.

keiki hope loa. Youngest child.

keiki kamehaʻi. Illegitimate child whose father may not be known.

keiki manuahi. Illegitimate child. *Lit.,* child free, *gratis.*

keiki papa. Natives of descendants born in the same place, in contrast to *malihini* (stranger).

keiki papahema. Godchild.

keiki poʻo ʻole. Illegitimate child.

kōlea. Parent-in-law. *Makua kāne kōlea,* stepfather; *makua hine kōlea,* stepmother.

kuaʻana. Order of two children of the same sex. See **kaikuaʻana.**

kuakāhi. Third generation. First the parent, *makua;* second the child, *keiki;* third the grandchild, *kuakāhi. Moʻopuna kuakāhi,* grandchild.

kuakolu. Fifth in descent. *Kupuna kuakolu* great-great-great grandparent; *moʻopuna kuakolu,* great-great-great grandchild.

kualua. Fourth in descent. *Kupuna kualua* great-great grandparent; *moʻopuna kualua,* great-great grandchild.

kūʻauhau. Genealogy; to tax; to be recorded in genealogy.

kūkū, tūtū. Grandfather.

kunāne, kaikunāne. Brother of a girl.

kupuna. Grandparent, either father or mother. He/she served as a source of wisdom and moral standards.

kupuna kāne. Grandfather.

kupuna kuakāhi. Great grandfather.

kupuna wahine. Grandmother.

lei. A beloved child.

liko. Child, especially of a chief.

lūau'i makuahine. Mother.

māhoe. Twins.

makahiapo. The first-born child. *Lit.,* first-born person.

maka nua. First or oldest of a family of children.

makuahine, makawahine. Mother, aunt. *Lit.,* female parent.

makuahine hanauna. Aunt.

makuahine kōlea. Stepmother.

makuahonowai kāne. Father-in-law.

makuahonowai wahine. Mother-in-law.

makua kāne. Uncle, father, male cousin.

makua kāne kōlea. Stepfather.

makua kāne papahema. Godfather.

makua kōlea. Parent-in-law, either father or mother. *Lit.,* plover parent. (PE.)

makua lūau'i. These words, connected, mean natural parent as distinct from an adopted parent, uncle or aunt.

māmā. Mother.

māwaewae. Ceremony for a first-born child.

mo'opuna. Grandchild.

mo'opuna kāne. Grandson.

mo'opuna kuakāhi. Grandchild. (Kin. 29:5.) Descendants were distinguished as follows:

1st. *makua,* parent,
2nd. *keiki,* child.
3rd. *mo'opuna kuakāhi,* grandchild,
4th. *mo'opuna kualua,* great grandchild,
5th. *mo'opuna kuakolu,* great, great, grandchild etc. (A.)

mo'opuna wahine. Granddaughter.

mua. Older sister or brother.

muli. Last-born child.

muli. Youngest and last.

'ohana. Family.

'ohana kupe. Old family of several generations in a place.

'ōpu'u. Child, bud.

panina. Youngest born; the last.

papa. Ancestor, some generations back; native born; race; family.

pili ali'i. Chiefly relationship.

pili alo. Wife.

pili koko. Related by blood.

pili kua. Beloved husband.

pili loko. Blood relationship.

pili ma na kupūna. Distant relationship.

pili ʻohana. Blood relationship.

pilipili ʻula. Close relationship to one of high rank.

pōkʻiʻi. Youngest member of a family; younger of two children of the same sex; appellation of endearment.

pōkiʻi kaina. The very younger; a double epithet for a younger brother or sister; very dear little brother or sister.

pua. Child, descendant of a chief, progeny.

pūluna. Relationship between a husband's parents and those of his wife.

punalua. Formerly, several husbands of one wife or several wives of one husband. Now applies to wives of brothers and husbands of sisters who call each other *punalua.* There are no sexual implications.

tūtū. Grandfather.

wahine. Wife.

wahine male. Wife, married woman.

wahine manuahi. Common-law wife.

wena. Close relative; blood relative.

LAND

Land divisions in the Hawaiian Islands were similar to those created by other societies in Polynesia. They were based partly on the geography of altitude and terrain and partly on the wishes of the ruling chiefs and conditions of the changing times.

The following is a list of such divisions, in order of size of area designated: the largest area is *moku,* the smallest is *kuleana.*

moku	*ʻili kūpono*	*paukū*
kalana	*ʻili lele*	*kīhāpai*
ahupuaʻa	*lele*	*kōʻele*
ʻili	*moʻo*	*kuleana*
ʻili paʻa	*moʻoʻāina*	

This chapter contains all kinds of words relating to land.

ʻaʻali. Low place between two larger areas. *He puāli,* an isthmus.

ʻaʻalu. Ravine, small brook or valley.

ahunali'i. Land division. (PE.)

ahupua'a. Large land division extending from the ocean shore to the mountain top or ridge. It is roughly wedge-shaped because of the somewhat pie-shaped configuration of an island of which it is a part. Boundaries are marked by piles of stone *(ahu)*, which were regarded as altars for placing offerings. This division was the domain of a lesser chief.

'āina. Land, earth, ground.

'āina kū'ai. Land owned in fee simple.

'āina lei ali'i. Crown lands, those held by royalty from the Great Mahele of 1848.

'āina 'ole. Landless; without any ownership in land.

'āpa'a. Area on the side of the mountain below the *wao lā'au,* an upland, arid, and uncultivated region of tall trees; land lived on by one for a long time.

'āpana. Land division. Such a division may include several *kuleana,* a small land division.

au. This is the word representing all places where food grows, as *kaha* represents places on or near the shore where food does not grow. This applies mostly to the leeward side of the islands. (A.)

aukanaka. Inhabited place; the habited world. (Mat. 24:14.) This is in contrast to the *awakua* (region of the gods).

aupuni. Government; kingdom, the jurisdiction and dominion of the king.

'auwae'āina. Present of selected items—hogs, food, *kapa,* and nets —to the *haku 'āina* (landlord) when he, being the new owner, reinstated the workers on the land.

hā'awi 'āina. Land grant title.

hakuone. Small land division or field similar to or smaller than a *kō'ele* cultivated for a chief.

honua. Ground, land, earth.

'ili. Next smaller piece of land to the *ahupua'a.* There are thirty-three of these districts in the *ahupua'a* of Honolulu. However, there could be as few as two *'ili* in an *ahupua'a.*

'ili 'āina. Land acquired by inheritance.

'ili kūpono, 'ilikū. Semi-independent *'ili* of land within an *ahupua'a* that pays tribute to the king and not the chief of the *ahupua'a.*

'ili lele. Part of an *'ili* separated from but considered a part of it.

'ilima. Region next below the *'āpa'a* on a mountainside. (A.)

'ili pa'a. *'Ili,* complete within itself.

ka'ānani'au. Altar like the stone pile *(ahu)* bounding an *ahupua'a.*

kaha. Land where food does not grow, mostly on an island's leeward side. See **au.**

kahakai. Beach area where food does not grow.

kalana. Present-day name for country; next-sized piece of land to *moku* (island). Close in meaning to *'okana.* It contains several *ahupua'a* and is usually the domain of a high chief.

kīhāpai. Division of land smaller than a *paukū,* belonging to and cultivated by the people.

kō'ele. Division of land smaller than *kīhāpai* and cultivated by a tenant for his chief. About the same as *hakuone.*

komikina ho'onā 'āina. Land commissioner.

konohiki. Superintendent of an *ahupua'a* under a chief.

kua'āina. Back country; up the mountains where there are no chiefs.

kuahea. Region on the side of a mountain below the *kuamauna,* a protuberance of hillock on the side of the mountain. Trees grow slowly there due to the altitude.

kuahiwi. Top, or summit area of a mountain. (Nah. 3:1.)

kuakua. Small section of land like a *hakuone* or a *kō'ele.* Could be planted or cultivated for the *haku 'āina* (landlord).

kualono. Mountaintop area, place of silence. *Lit.,* place of hearing.

kuānea. Dry barren land; barren, lonely, forsaken.

kula. Open country, plain, field, pasture; land area at the base of a mountain; an area for houses and people. Opposed to wet land such as taro land. (DK.)

kuleana. One's appropriate business; a part, portion, or right to a thing. In modern times a *kuleana* usually refers to a small claim inside another's land.

kumu kuleana 'āina. Land title.

lele. Detached lots or parcels within an *'ili* or *ahupua'a. Lele* means to fly.

mahina'ai. Area larger than a *kīhāpai;* farm.

makoa. Land between the shore and interior where *koa* trees grow. (A.) Also called *wao koa.* (PE.)

mala. Garden, small plot of ground, field, or plantation, that was cultivated.

mānelo. Free, as land from stones, lava, or gravel.

moku. Island; largest of the land divisions.

mo'o. Narrow strip of land, less than an *'ili.* Also called *mo'o 'āina.*

nana'e. Small land division. *Obs.* (PE.)

'okana. Land district containing several *ahupua'a. Kalana* has about the same meaning.

one. Ground, sand, silt; term of endearment for one's native land.

pa'a 'āina. Landholder; to hold land. (PE.)

pahe'e. Land on the side of a mountain between the *'ilima* and *kula* levels.

palahe'i. Land below the *kualono. Obs.* (PE.)

palena 'āina. Land boundary.

paukū. Small area of land next in size below the *mo'o.*

wao. General term for areas of land in the interior; i.e., *wao akua, wao kanaka.*

wao akua. Region on a mountain below the *wao ma'u kele* for gods, ghosts, and hobgoblins.

wao kanaka. Region on the side of a mountain where people may live and cultivate the land. It is next below the *wao akua* and is a land believed inhabited by spirits.

wao ma'u kele. Region on the side of a mountain below the *wao'eiwa* and above the *wao akua.*

wao nahele. Covered with vegetation; wilderness on the side of a mountain; *wao akua* inhabited by gods an ghosts.

LEGENDS AND SUPERSTITIONS

This category is related to several others, especially "The Supernatural," "Worship," "Heiaus," and "Gods and Goddesses." The lists are presented essentially as Hyde organized them, although there is a fair amount of overlapping and much duplication. Still, each has its own integrity, telling some aspect of a broader story.

"Legends and Superstitions" is built around the word legends, stories which represent persistent searchings for explanations of the physical and natural phenomena observed by the Hawaiians. Happenings in the sky at night and, by day, on the ground or in the ocean, were sometimes given interpretations that evolved into codes of belief and behavior.

With the translation of the Bible in the 1830s and 1840s by scholarly missionaries, an important intellectual base was added to the prehistoric culture, and many of the Bible stories were adopted into the native lore: Jonah, Noah, and the burning bush are some examples.

Because of this background, many of the legends seem to suggest prior encounters with visitors from other cultures and seem to refer to actual experiences. Others seem to be pointless. Some, preserved only in Hyde's tiny pencilled notes, are illegible!

Legends occupy a broad spectrum of Hawaiian literature in special articles, books, textbooks, and general cultural offerings. They are popular items: for the public, legends are best sellers!

This category is far from being complete, but it does suggest the breadth of the field.

'a'alaioa. Wild, ferocious, and demented man who lived in the forest.

aku. One of the two fish that accompanied Pili on his voyage to these islands. *Aku* helped paddle the canoe and *'ōpelu* calmed the winds. (MALO 4:13.)

'Anahua, Ka'anahua. Second son of Lua-ho'omoe; god of husbandmen, a blind priest. (A.)

analipo. Place supposed to be beyond the stars, i.e., out of sight but really below the horizon.

'anu'u. Name of a ship formerly at the islands. (A.)

auhelemoa. Golden goblin cock in Pālolo Valley. (CMH.)

Aukele nui a Iku. Person associated with or resembling the Biblical Joseph (alternative spelling). The killing of the fabled bird *halulu* is also ascribed to this man. See **Wau-kele-nui-a-īku.**

'ewa'ewa iki. Imaginary voice of a female spirit who had died along with her unborn son. (A.)

haili. Spirit, ghost.

Hakalanileo. Son of Kaiheailani and nephew of Pau-makua, the husband of Hina. (A.)

hale umu. Name of Lono's house. (A.)

halulu. Fabulous bird of ancient times, killed by the Chief Wau kele nui a īkū, also called 'Aukele. FOR 4:65. (A.) Man-eating, legendary bird. (PE.)

Hewahewa. High priest of Hawai'i who was Kamehameha's *Kahuna nui,* keeper of the Kū-kā-'ili-moku (the feather god). He later became a devoted adherent to the Christian religion and influenced the destruction of the idols and their temples in 1819.

Hi'i-aka. General name of the goddesses of volcanoes and Pele's sisters. The favorite was Hi'i-aka-i-ka-poli-o-Pele, meaning Hi'i-aka in the bosom of Pele.

Hinali'i. Chief in whose time there occurred a universal deluge. His name is used in the Hawaiian expression *kai a Kihinali'i,* Noah's flood.

Hua. Chief of the Hana district of Maui who ordered the death of his seer, Lua-ho'omoe. *Kō'ele nā 'iwi o Hua ma i ka lā,* dry are the bones of Hua and his company in the sun. (A.)

'iu'iu. Place far off from, high above the earth, or beneath the ocean, sacred, as the dwelling place of the gods.

ka'ao, kē'ao. A legend, usually fictional or fanciful; a tale of ancient times; a traditional story, a fable. About this word, Donald Kilolani Mitchell says, "I was amused and puzzled in trying to find examples of *ka'ao.* Every tale or legend I mentioned was, according to my informants, historical; i.e., *Pele, Maui, Pikoi* and so on. Actually, *mo'olelo,* historical tale, is a better word than *ka'ao* for this meaning."

kaha lele pō. A famine in olden times. (A.) Famine in wartime, with persons seeking food at night for fear of being seen.

Kahiko, Kahiko-lua-mea. Name of the first man on the Hawaiian Islands. Father of Wakea. (MALO 4.)

kāhuna. Priests, descended from Pa'ao of Kahiki, who landed at Pu'uepa near the *heiau* of Mo'okini at Kohala. The *heiau* was built with stones passed hand to hand from 9 miles away. Near Mo'okini are petroglyphs of Pa'ao's canoe paddle and fish hooks. No one dared cultivate his pastures at Pololū. *Na mau'u a Pa'ao,* the grasses of *Pa'ao.*

kahuna Ka'oleioku. Priest of Laupahoehoe who put chief Hākau of Waipi'o to death and in his place put 'Umi, bastard son of Liloa, the adopted son of Ka'oleiōkū.

Kai a kahulu manu. Name of the flood yet to come. The great flood of the past is called *kai a Kahinali'i* (Noah's flood).

Kalahumoku. Famous dog of Tahiti. Also described as *aīwaīwa* (fabulous). (A.)

Kalaunui'ōhua. Ambitious chief of Hawai'i who attempted conquest of all the islands, but was defeated near Ka'ie'ie-waho and taken to Kaua'i by Kūkona as a prisoner.

Kali-mai-nu'u. Lizard woman who, while in her human form lured a young Kaua'i chief, Puna, to her home, a cave along Wailea stream in the Wai'anae mountains of O'ahu. After several months he learned her true identity and escaped. (KL. 194.)

Kama. Ancient chief of Maui. His full name is Kamalalawa or Kama-lala-walu, son of eight branches. He was killed in battle on Hawai'i by Lono-i-ka-makahiki.

Kana. Man who formerly resided at Hilo, said to have been 400 fathoms high. He stepped over the hill of Hā'upu on Moloka'i and slipped down. He also fought with Keolaewanui-a-kāmau, son of Hina, whose height was measured in paces. He stood with one foot on Oʻahu, and the other on Maui or Kauaʻi.

Kanaloa. One of the four great gods. He traveled much and is credited with the introduction of bananas and other useful trees. Believed to be a god of healing. Some refer to him as the god of the sea, suggestive of the Roman god, Neptune. He is sometimes spoken of as the "mischievous god." (DK.)

ka nalu. Order of the priests of Kū, who served at the *luakini*.

Kāneʻāpua. Brother of Pele. Also the name of a fish god on Lanaʻi.

Kāne-a-puaʻa. God of agriculture.

Kāneʻehalau. Prophet of Kauaʻi who, when on Oʻahu told Keliʻi-kupu of Puna that Pele had destroyed his land at Makahanaloa near Hilo. Keliʻikupu saw the ruins at Puna and hanged himself.

Kānehoalani. God of the sky and the father of Pele.

Kāne makua. God of the fishermen who caught the *mālolo* in their net. (A.) *Lit.,* Kāne, the parent. (RC.)

Kāne nui a kea. General name of a class of gods. (A.) God of prophets. (CMH.)

Kānepolu. Chief on the island of Oʻahu who was killed in a fall from a *pali.*

Kaʻonohi-o-ka-lā. God whose name means eyeball of the sun. He conducted the dead chiefs to the next world. "Thy name shall be Ghost, *Lapu,* thy food the butterflies," was the judgment against Kaʻonohi-o-ka-lā for his crimes.

Kaʻululāʻau. Tricky son of the Maui chief Kaka-ʻalaneo. The chief banished his son to Lanaʻi where he destroyed evil spirits.

Keʻakeʻalani. Ancient chiefess of good character *(haipule loa),* supreme over all the islands. She was an ancestor of Keawe.

Keakualapu. Ghost god. *Lit.,* the god ghost.

Keawe. Bearer. Keawe is a name frequently used among the Hawaiians, alone or in compounds. A most famous king of that name left so many progeny that a saying was often heard that the islands would always remain in the hands of the Keawes.

kinoakalau. Spirit or ghost of a person not yet dead. Formerly there were persons, mostly priests, who pretended to see the ghosts or souls of people still living. The priests would inform the living persons that they had seen their spirits and that it was a sign of some great calamity about to befall them. This sure sign of evil to come, they were told, could only be avoided by giving something valuable to the priest. (A.)

Koaʻe. Younger brother of Pele.

koa kumu ʻole. Tree of that name *mauka* of Kahikipolo, an inland

area of Kaua'i, perhaps legendary, famous for a trunkless tree
(lā'au kumu 'ole).

kole na iwi o Hua ma i ka la. Hua asked 'Uhiho'omoe, his
kahuna, for some diving birds *('ua'u)* from the mountains. His
men caught some they falsely said were from the mountains.
The priest was killed, the gods were displeased, and a terrible
famine followed. Hua traveled in the rain to avoid it but died in
the *heiau* of Māke anihu in Kohala.

Kū a hailo. God of the swarming maggots who was invoked by
the *kahuna* 'Ana'ana for consulting divinations.

Kūali'i. Chief on O'ahu about 1600 A.D. whose bones were
pulverized, mixed with *poi,* and then used as food. He is listed
in the genealogy of Kumu Uli, and reportedly lived to 175 years.

kūhiwa. *Pali* between Nāhiku and Hana, Maui. Two men who
had passed over the road earlier and found plenty of water, on
their return jumped from the *pali* supposing there was water as
before. Alas! They saw too late that they were jumping onto a
bed of rocks. The average annual rainfall at Kūhiwa is 365
inches.

Kū kā'ili moku. War god who snatched the islands *(kā'ili);* Kamehameha's feather god.

kū lani hāko'i. Supposed place in the heavens that is the source of
the rains. A gulch in the Ma'alaea area of Maui is named the
pond in the sky.

Kumu-honua. God with three sons. The second was slain by the
first. (A.) Beginning of the world. (PE.)

Kūpule. Ten generations after Nau, grandfather of *Kini lau a
manō,* whose twelve children founded twelve tribes. The *menehune* are descended from one of these tribes.

La'amai-Kahiki. High chief from Tahiti who established dynasties
in both Tahiti and Hawai'i. He introduced the *pahu* drum and
the *kā'eke'eke* into Hawai'i.

lapu. Apparition, ghost; the appearance of the supposed spirit of a
deceased person.

lau kapalili. Name of the first *kalo* (taro) leaf that grew in the
Hawaiian Islands; trembling leaves.

Lilinoe. Goddess of Haleakalā; fine mist, rain.

Lō. Name of certain chiefs, probably from Melanesia, who lived
on the mountain Helemano, O'ahu, and ate men. (A.)

Lonopele. Brother of Pa'ao. His son was killed by Pa'ao in retalia-
tion for accusing Pa'ao's son of cheating.

Luaipo. Ancient progenitor before Wakea. His co-contemporaries were called *he poe ʻike ʻole* (knowledgeable) and *he poe naʻaupō* (ignorant).

Makaliʻi. Person who brought cooked food to the rainbow. (A.) Chief of Waimea, Kauaʻi; father-in-law of Mano-ka-lani-pō, who was famous as an agriculturist. (PE.)

manawainuikaioʻo. Name of a fabled whirlpool. (A.)

mānele. Palanquin. *Cap.,* a certain chief of Kauaʻi, very corpulent and very crabbed to his people, who made them carry him up and down a *pali* until, weary with his petulance, they allowed him to fall. (2 Sam. 3:31.)

manini. Several places called Koholā in Hawaiʻi, one of them a fishpond at Kua-loa, Oʻahu attributed to the *menehune*s. *Lit.,* whale leaping.

Mau. God believed to have been created of red earth mixed with the spittle of Kāne, with his head made of whitish clay. He was called Kumu honua. Woman, created from his rib, was called Keolakuhonua. She was placed in Paradise, Pali-uli. In Paradise was a lake containing the living water of Kāne, which would restore the dead to life. It was Kanaloa who crept into Pali-uli in the form of a *moʻo* (lizard). This legend is one of several relatively recent Bible-oriented versions of the creation of man and woman. Kamakau relates another (p. 21) in which the major gods make the first man, Kānehulihonua, from red soil and the first woman, Ke-aka-hulilani, from his shadow *(aka)*. "Somehow, I prefer the woman made from the man's shadow, not his rib, *ʻiwi ʻaoʻao*." (KILO.)

Māui. Famous demigod who was a trickster. There are various stories about him. As he bathed, one relates, he trod with his feet in the depths of the ocean while his hair was moistened with the vapor of the clouds. According to another, he made the sun move more slowly so his mother, Hina, could dry her *kapa*. Folklorists credit seven great and even more minor deeds to Māui. (KILO.)

Māui hope. Priestly class, last of the seven daughters of Hina, who captured the demigod in the form of the *ulua* fish, Pīmoe.

Māuiakalana. Māui, son of Akalana, a demigod in search of fire, found the *ʻalae* bird with skin on top of its bill. He caused the head to bleed to get the secret of fire, hence the red spot. The bird is now called *ʻalaeʻula*.

Maukaleʻoleʻo. Giant friend of ʻŪmi, who with his feet on the ground could reach the coconuts of standing trees.

Milu. Chief noted for his wickedness on earth, now known in

Hawaiian mythology as the lord of the lower regions. He is the Pluto of the Hawaiians.

Mōʻīkeha. Son of a migrant from Kahiki. The migration is told in a chant: "The father of Kila, settled on Kauaʻi." In his day rulers were not called "king." They were merely chiefs—sometimes high chiefs.

moʻo kūʻauhau. Story, history, or genealogy of ancestors. Heading the list is Kumulipo. Others include Palikū, Olōlo, Puanue, Kapohiki, and Kalākaua. Genealogy determines a person's rank on the list.

Mū. Legendary people who lived in the country above Lāʻau-haele-mai, Kauaʻi. They were sometimes called banana eaters, *Mū-ʻai-maiʻa*. Public executioners were also called *mū* but were in no sense legendary people. Public executioners were used to procure victims for sacrifice and execution; *kapu* breakers were sacrificed when a new *heiau* was dedicated or a house was built.

Naio-ʻai-kae. Name of a famine of early times. Also called *kaiʻole-kaʻa*. (A.)

Nanamaoa. Powerful chief from the Society Islands who arrived in Hawaiʻi about 1000 A.D. and established his family in Hawaiʻi, Maui, and Oʻahu.

Nānāulu. First person to arrive from the southern hemisphere islands, one of two sons of Kū. He became chief of Oʻahu, Kauaʻi, and Molokaʻi. This line of chiefs was finally absorbed in the Kamehameha family. (A.) This genealogy begins with Wā-kea and Papa, whose progeny were Hāloa and Hoʻohōkūkalani. (DK.)

ʻōkuʻu. Great pestilence on Oʻahu in 1807. It was called *ʻōkuʻu* because the people squatted to relieve themselves anywhere they happened to be in their misery and because they freely dismissed their souls and died, *ʻokuʻu wale aku no i ka ʻuhane.*

one lauʻena. Imaginary land from whence the god Kāne came.

ʻōpelu. One of the two fishes that accompanied Pili when he came to the islands.

ʻŌpelunui-kau-haʻalilo. Son of Pele and Kamapuaʻa, who became a god; god of thieves and medical practitioners.

ʻowā. Word given and constantly used by Kukuaokalalau for seizing his prey. (A.)

Paʻao. Man who came from Upolu, Tahiti. He landed at Puna and built the Moʻo-kini *heiau* in Kohala, Hawaiʻi. He also introduced human sacrifice, walled *heiau*s, the prostrating *kapu*, and the feather god Kāʻili.

Pahulu. Goddess who conceived and brought forth Lanaʻi.

palikū. Ancient order of priests on Hawaiʻi who are said to have come from Palikū, a foreign country; priests of Lono; initial point of a genealogy line.

Papa. Wife of Wākea, superior in caste to her husband; fabled mother of the islands and the men on them.

Pau-makua. Arrived in Hawaiʻi in 1090 A.D. in early reign of Pili on Maui.

Pele. Goddess of volcanoes who is now believed to reside in Kilauea on Hawaiʻi. Her story is recorded by William Ellis, David Kālakaua, William D. Westervelt, and many others. She is credited with five brothers and eight sisters. The brothers were:

Ka-moho-aliʻi, known as king of the sharks and god of steam and vapor;

Ka-poho-i-kāhi-ola, god of explosions in life;

Ke-ua-a-ke-po, rain of the night;

Kāne-kahili, Kāne of the thunder;

Ke-o-ahi-Kama-kaua, fire thrusting child of war. Of the eight sisters only one, usually credited as being the youngest, is named: *Hiʻi-aka-i-ka-poli-o-Pele*, Hiʻiaka, in the bosom of Pele. She is the supreme goddess of the *hula* as Laka is the patron. (KILO.)

pilikaekae. Man sent by *Paʻao*, who became chief of Hawaiʻi.

polalawahi. A darkness over all the islands in olden times. It might have been a haze from a volcano.

Poliʻahu. Snow goddess of Mauna Kea.

pōliukua. Imaginary place in the back part of the heavens, where the stars are fixed; a dark place.

puapua lenalena. Dog that brought back the stolen *kihapū* (conch shell).

pueoaliʻi. Monstrous bird (killed in Nuʻu-anu by Kaululaʻau) that was inhabited by the spirit of Hilo a lakapu, a chief of Hawaiʻi who invaded Oʻahu.

Ulu. One of two sons of Kiʻi, a chief of Maui and Hawaiʻi, finally replaced by the Paʻao line. Nānā-ulu was his brother.

wailua. Ghost or spirit of someone seen before or after death, separate from the body. Kinowailua is a poetical name for a ghost or spirit of someone who is living, seen distinct from and in a different place from his body.

Wākea. Man who found favor with Hina after his marriage to

Papa. Hina is said to have given birth to Moloka'i. Wākea is spoken of as the ancestor of all Hawaiians.

Wau-kele-nui-a-īku. Chief who killed the fabled bird *halulu;* the young of the bird that waited on Kiwa'a. See **Aukele nui a Iku.**

MANNERS AND CUSTOMS

The scope of this category is understandably broad, extending from the exchange of affectionate greetings all the way to death by poisoning. A variety of routine household operations and activities is listed such as washing clothes, making *kapa,* splitting wood, baking and cooking, mummifying and burying, and fire-making.

The social order, as portrayed through these words, was that of a rigid caste system in which lesser persons crawled in the presence of the king and chiefs, a system demanding sacrifices and even requiring peculiar shapes of haircuts for specific purposes. And always the *kapu* was in control.

Social custom was a mixture of harshness on the one hand—infanticide, suicide, dirges over slain victims—and benevolence on the other—loyalty and obedience to the chief, sanctuary in a place of refuge, care and affection for children. In addition, it was a society concerned with the recitation of legends, personal adornment and decoration, and genealogy.

'aha'aina make. Food offered to guests at services for a deceased person.

'āhai. Name of a pillar, wood, or stone, set up by a chief in memory of some great exploit. A *pao* was the arch, prop, or excavation.

'aiahulu. To pray or poison to death. The agent of the intrigue was called *kālai'ino, ni'ani'a,* or *pa'opa'onohoni'a.*

'aiau. To pray or poison to death, as formerly practiced.

'ai kapu. Custom of observing a *kapu* concerned with men and women eating separately. This custom was completely overthrown prior to the arrival of the missionaries.

'ai noa. Freedom from the restraints of the *kapu.*

ala'alai. A *kalo* (taro) patch, formed by bending rushes down and covering them with earth ready for irrigating. Hence, argillaceous earth or clay, called *kipi* or mound taro, in Hilo.

ala niho. Long stripes of tattoo made on the skin using a shark's tooth.

ana'ina ho'olewa. Prefuneral vigil. (PE.)

'ano launa. Manners.

'āo'o. Sharp bone used to destroy the foetus; abortion stick. Also called *koholua*.

'apu kōheoheo. Cup of deadly ingredients, as offered to prisoners or other victims.

'auhuhu, 'auhola, hola. Neal lists the three together as a perennial herb with more or less woody stems and slender branches *(Tephrosia purpurea)*. Some distinctions can be suggested: I use *'auhuhu* as the name of the stupefying or poisoning plant. *Hola* is the name of the method of killing fish by poisoning. *'Auhola* would designate the plant for this specific purpose. (KILO.)

aukū. To swim uprightly. *Lit.,* to swim standing.

'aulima. Name of the stick held in the hand while rubbing to produce fire. *Hi'a* is the action of rubbing two sticks together.

'aunaki. Stick rubbed for friction in making fire.

'auwae'āina. Present made out of respect to the landowner or land manager *(haku 'āina)* who reinstated the workers when land was transferred. The gifts were selected hogs, fruits, and so on.

E pa'i na lima, ae nā waha. To clap hands and say yes; a covenant.

ha'akualiki. Name of an officer among the followers of the king; an officer who preceded a chief and his train to announce his rank and the purpose of his visit, *ha'akualiki*.

haiā wahine. United assemblage of a number of wives of one man exclusive of the favorite; a harem.

ha'iha'i. Flesh dissected from the bones. A burial custom.

ha'i kupuna. To recite genealogy; a chant about one's ancestors.

hākā 'ōlelo. One employed by the chief to report the errors of the people. Some chiefs were slow learners, so they engaged such a person as an advisor.

haku 'āina. To manage land for and under a chief; landlord, land owner.

hale pe'a. Special house to which women retired during their menstrual period.

hale poki. *Heiau* where the bones of the king were deposited, for example, Hale-o-Keawe at Hōnaunau, Kona, Hawai'i.

hao. To despoil, plunder. Formerly it was the practice to punish offenders for crimes other than death by stripping them of their property. This practice continued until the issuance of a code of written laws.

hāʻuke. Act of hunting for lice.

heʻa. Sacrifice of blood.

hema. South. In marking cardinal points of the compass, Hawaiians placed their backs to the east, so their right indicated the north and their left the south.

he pepehi make ʻana ia ia iho. Suicide.

hia. To rub two sticks together for friction and fire.

hiaka. To recite legends; a particular kind of *mele* (song). (A.)

hikoni. Errant servant marked on the forehead; tattoo brand on the forehead of a *kauwa* (outcast).

hoʻāu. To beat, as in washing clothes; to set a net; to swim.

hoʻi. State of marriage among chiefs; to intermarry, as a chief marrying the daughter of a brother or sister in order to increase the rank of the offspring.

hoʻohānau. To bring forth a baby. This word was mostly used in connection with the application of medicines designed to effect premature parturition.

hoʻohike. To vow, swear an oath.

hoʻohiwahiwa. To treat as an important friend; to honor; to adorn.

hoʻoholoi. To pretend to wash.

hoʻokahakaha. To pile *kapa* in a heap for one to sit on or be carried about; to make a display; to exhibit finery.

hoʻokāhiko. To deck out in finery.

hoʻokoholua. Sharp stick of fishbone or wood; abortion stick.

hoʻokonokono. To set on, as dogs or men; to fight.

hoʻolewa. Funeral. (PE.)

hoʻoluʻuluakua. To pretend to be a god. (CMH.)

hoʻomoʻa. To be cooked or thoroughly baked.

hoʻonani. To adorn, decorate; to honor, glorify.

hoʻoniau. To leave one's company secretly and go away, generally for some evil purpose. (A.)

hoʻopālau. To engage to marry; to betroth, as parents a daughter or a son.

hoʻopāpālima. To touch, join, or shake hands, as confirmatory of a previous engagement. An ancient practice.

hoʻouwēuwē. To sound, as a bell; a wailing dirge.

hoʻowehiwehi. To adorn; to decorate, as with flowers.

hume. To bind around the loins, as a *malo;* to gird on, as a sash. *Ina hume ke kanaka i ko ke aliʻi malo e make no ia,* should one bind on a chief's *malo* the penalty would be death.

hūnākele. To bury a corpse secretly to guard against theft.

iʻaloa. To mummify. The visceral organs were removed from the body cavity and perhaps also the brain and other such soft spots. The remaining flesh was salted and bathed in herbal concoctions including *ʻuhaloa.* The body thus treated was taken to a very dry place. The flesh mumified. (KILO.)

ihu. Nose. Hawaiians kissed by touching noses. *E hō mai i ka ihu,* give me a kiss.

ʻilieʻe. Roots of a vine, wild plumbago *(Plumbago zeylanica).* Its sap was used to blacken scars or tattoo marks in mourning for the dead, *kūmākena.*

ʻili hau. Bark of the *hau* tree used for making rope and modern grass skirts.

imu loa. Long oven used as a sweat bath; oven used for baking men, perhaps a sorcery cure.

kāʻalā. Ancient art of slings; hurling stones with a sling. *He nui ka poʻe aʻo i ke kākā lāʻau me ke kāʻalā,* many persons learned to use slings.

kahi. Hair formerly cut with bamboo knives; to cut longitudinally, shave, comb, press, scrape; a comb. Hair of the head was also cut by placing the locks on a turtle shell plate and cutting across it with a shark's tooth. This was less apt to pull than in using the bamboo knife. (KILO.)

kahi lauoho. Comb for hair of the head.

kahi ʻuku. Comb to remove lice.

kaka. To wash clothes by beating them; to rinse and clean. (PE.)

kākā. To split wood by striking it on a stone. (A.)

kake. Artificial language made by transposing syllables. It was used in speaking, writing, and in chants. The purpose of the garbled communication was to hide the meaning from any but the initiates.

kākele. To besmear the skin, as with oil; to anoint.

kakuʻai. To sacrifice food to the gods; to feed the spirits of the dead, mostly with bananas.

kala hewahewa. To give away property like a man demented.

kālai ʻino. To concoct mischief; to plan evil against another person; to work in secret to use sorcery to a wrong end.

kāliʻi. Ceremony where the high chief lands from a voyage with his people and his god. It was customary to hurl spears at the chief to test his dexterity in parrying them.

kālolo. Name given to the first liquor run off in distillation. See **kāwae.**

kālua. To cook underground. It was customary to cook or steam certain foods underground. Sometimes food was broiled over coals or hot ashes.

kama. Children, either natural or adopted into the family of another; a person. *Keiki hānai* is a child, usually related, adopted into a family as one's own. The family assumes all care and training. Today the relationship is legalized so the adopted child can inherit property. A *keiki hoʻokama* is like a godchild. William and Emily Taylor adopted a *hoʻokama*. They provided no support but were interested in this person and taught him things Hawaiian. This was Kilolani. See **Kindred: hoʻokama.** It was a custom to adopt a child of a relative, a grandchild, or orphan. *Keiki makua ʻole* means child or children without parents.

kanikau. Dirge, mourning song, lamentation, elegy.

ka noho ʻana nihinihi. Genteel manners. (PE.)

kanu. To bury, cover up in the earth; burial.

kapa lau. Covering leaves in which the body of a chief was bound prior to burial.

kaualae paʻakauana. Most offensive language. When used, instant fighting was the immediate consequence. (A.)

kauʻoʻe. Officer in the king's train; bodyguard.

kauwā lepo. Order of men who sacrificed themselves on the death of a chief. (A.)

kāwae. Last running of liquor from distillation. See **kālolo.** (A.)

kāwelewele. Person at the end of a long rope where many persons were pulling a canoe or other heavy substance. *Kama* was the person or god holding the rope at the one end. *O Kama ke akua i ke kāwelewele.*

keiki papa. Natives of descendants born in the same place. Contrasts with *malihini* (stranger).

kiʻikiʻi. To paint the hair on the forehead white.

kīkanu. To bury, cover over.

kikiko. To tattoo.

kikiwi. To weave along while walking, as if intoxicated.

koholua. A sharp lance or bone-stick; abortion stick.

koʻihonua. To recite genealogy; genealogical chant.

koʻi i ke kukui. Splinter of bamboo on which roasted *kukui* nuts were strung for burning, as a candle.

kolo. To crawl. No common person was allowed to address a chief for a favor unless on all fours.

kōpili. Gift customarily presented to a child at its birth.

kuaʻāina. Backwoods people; countrified; to act like one from the country.

kuahaua. To proclaim; to call together, as the people of a chief; to call the people together on business; to assemble all the people.

kū'ai. To barter one thing for another.

kuapōla'o. Name of a small pile of *waiwai* (goods or property) collected for the king.

kū'auhau. Genealogy; to recite genealogy.

ku hele leloa. A person, banished to live where he can, stripped of everything.

ku'iku'iwale. A pounding or bruising to death; an ancient method of killing. (A.)

kūkaenalo. Unbleached muslin or brown cotton cloth.

kukui. Tree and its nut. The nut was used to burn for light; the tree produced gum *(pīlali)* for resin and wax. The body of the tree was occasionally made into canoes; the bark of the root was used in coloring canoes black.

kūmākena. General mourning at death of the king or high chief, when people wailed, knocked out their teeth, lacerated their bodies, and fell in prostration.

kuni. To burn and sear the skin in mourning; to practice sorcery; to burn as a sacrifice.

kūnihi. To stand up prominently, as an uncut ridge of hair on the head.

kūpina'i. Great wailing or general lamentation, the sound coming and going.

kupu. One whose ancestors were born where he himself was born and vice versa.

lā'au mākai. Badge of a constable under the first code of laws. It was a square club of wood 6 inches long with 1-inch sides, each with one-third of the length turned for a handle.

lā'au pā. Ancient drug given to produce abortion, cause miscarriage, or prevent pregnancy.

lamakū. Torch with bamboo handle and the bundle of strings of roasted *kukui* nuts strung on a sliver or strip of bamboo or on a *nī'au* (coco leaflet midrib). (KILO.)

laoa. To tie up the bones of a person in a bundle. (A.)

lehu. Largest number in Hawaiian counting: 400,000; numerous, very many.

lei. Garland, string of beads; a necklace; a wreath of green leaves or flowers, etc. One much esteemed was the ripe *hala* nut or key *lei* on account of its odoriferous qualities. It was worn around the neck or on the head.

lele kāwa. To jump into the sea feet first. Making a splashless entry into the water was considered a great feat and rated a pastime. This act of jumping from a precipice may have had the purpose of suicide but it was a popular pastime also. The great ruler Kahekili was famed for his skill in leaping from great heights into the water. Leaping spots on several islands bear his name today. (KILO.)

lele pali. Pastime or suicide of jumping from a precipice.

loina. Customs, manners.

lua. General name for the early hand-to-hand fighting, which included possible death.

lula. Manners. *He kanaka lula 'ole,* a man without manners.

luma. To kill another person by holding his head under water. Also called *luma'i. Kauwā* were often killed in this way.

lu'oni. Person or chief who delivers a person, condemned to die, to the altar.

mā'ewa'ewa. Irregular cutting of hair due to the death of a chief or relative. (A.)

maihuli. Presents made at the birth of a child.

maka'āinana. Laboring class, in distinction from the chiefs; common people, as opposed to chiefs.

māka'i. Constable always found in the king's train.

mālolo kai. Cry of robbers on the heights as they saw only a few people passing and dared to rob them. (CMH.) The cliffs at Mākaha, O'ahu were noted for robbers who gave this cry.

mama. Food chewed by an adult or parent for a child; to feed a child pre-chewed food.

māmaka. Stick on which Hawaiians carried burdens across their shoulders. Also called *'auamo, 'aumaka. E hele huaka'i,* to travel in company, to go in bands.

māna. To chew food for infants.

mānele. Sedan chair or palanquin carried on the shoulders of four men.

mano'i. Scented coconut oil. Probably a Tahitian word.

mele kanikau. Song of mourning, dirge.

melu. Act of pulling out the beard, as the Hawaiians did formerly.

moena pāwehe. Fine braided, dark trimmed, colored mat from Ni'ihau.

mōhai. Offering of a hog by a mother in weaning a child; sacrificial offering to atone for a sin.

mōhai ahi. Offering made by fire.

mōhai hala. Offering for the sin of trespass.

mōhai ho'okō. Sacrifice upon performing a vow. (Nah. 15:3.)

mōhai mililani. Sacrifice of thanksgiving. (Hal. 116:17.)

mōhai ola. Sacrifice of one's life; to offer one's life.

mōhai poni. Offering of consecration. (Oihk. 7:37.)

mōhai puhi. Offering by fire. (Oihk. 2:3.)

mōlī. Sharp, bone instrument used to print on the skin; tattooing needle. (A.) Straight line separating tattoo patterns. (PE.)

mōlia. Child or children dedicated by their parents before a priest to some special occupation.

mōliaola. One who sacrifices himself that others may live; sacrifice and prayer for life and safety.

molimolī. To use the *moli* (tattoo needle) in puncturing the skin to make letters or figures.

muku. Measure of length from the fingers of one hand to the elbow of the opposite arm extended. Another measure, *kīkoʻo,* is the span made by the thumb and forefinger.

naʻau. Small intestines of humans thought by the Hawaiians to be the seat of intellect, affection, and moral power. There are many compounds using *naʻau.*

naʻauʻauā. Suicide or desire for it on account of the death of a friend; extreme grief.

neʻe. To crawl in the presence of chiefs. (CMH.) To move along horizontally; to hitch along, to work along.

niʻaniʻa. To accuse, then produce no evidence; blasphemy; malicious gossip.

nīheu. Person whose hair was fancifully dressed.

niho. Tooth; a shark's tooth used for haircutting; any tooth.

niholoko. Tattoo marks. (CMH.)

niho ʻoki. To cut hair; to carve.

noʻūnoʻūnea. To rub or paint the cheeks to increase beauty. (A.) Rubbing cheeks with *limu kala* to redden them. (DK.)

ʻōkolehao. Liquor distilled from the *kī* root.

ʻōlapa. The fish *āholehole,* used as a sacrifice in love sorcery; magic that sends an evil spirit to harass another. (PE.)

olomea. Native tree *(Perrottetia sandvicensis).* It supplies a hard wood used with the soft wood, *hau,* to produce friction and fire.

ʻopūao. Knowledgeable person; intelligence; knowledge.

paʻa kūʻauhau. Versed in genealogy.

pāʻewaʻewa. Fantastic or irregular cutting of the hair, formerly practiced on the death of a friend. (A.)

pahu kapa. Sanctuary; place forbidden to a visitor or anyone passing by.

paikauleia. Abandoned woman wearing a *lei* to signify she is for sale.

pālala. Tax paid on the birth of a child to a chief, generally consisting of *kapa, poi,* etc.

palalei. The spreading of one's *kapa* over the head of a chief on his entering the house.

pana poʻo. To scratch or strike one's head in order to help remember something forgotten.

pana pua. To shoot arrows. Among early Hawaiians, the greatest contempt a person could show his enemy was to procure some of his bones after death, and make them into arrow tips for shooting rats.

paʻopaʻo noho niʻa. Envy, ill-will; indulging in bad feelings toward others. (A.) Blunt or proud speech caused by jealousy. (PE.)

peʻapeʻahi. To sweep; to brush a floor, as in former times, by striking a *kapa* down upon it. (A.)

pela. Any mass of putrid flesh and bowels of a dead chief. After the bones were separated, it was thrown into the sea.

piʻi. *Ina e piʻi ke aka o kanaka maluna o ke aliʻi, make ke kanaka,* if the shadow of a common man should fall upon a chief, the man must die.

piliwaiwai. Gambling. Hawaiians were reportedly great gamblers. Sometimes they even wagered their bones.

pinika. Intoxicating drink of fermented molasses and water.

pōkinahua. An *ʻaha* (assembly) for honoring a chief.

poʻo kēpa. One-sided head. It was customary among Hawaiians, in mourning for the loss of friends, to cut the hair in very different shapes as a sign of sorrow.

pōpō kāpaʻi. Ball for *lomi*-ing or massaging the sick; medical herbs used in a ball for massaging the sick.

pouomanu, pouamanu. House post readied for a previously dug hole in which the body of a man was to be placed as a sacrifice before the post was set in.

pūʻā. Custom or manner of baby feeding among Hawaiians. Food was chewed by an adult and put in a baby's mouth.

puaʻakumulau. Woman whose husband has gambled her away with all his property. (A.)

puaʻa ohi. Children whose father has gambled them away. (A.)

puana. Opening bars of *himeni* (hymns) or other songs. The songs would be quickly recognized by an assembly which would then join in.

pūkai. To whiten the color of hair with lime; hair bleached reddish-brown with lime. Chiefesses often whitened a narrow band of their hair just above the forehead. Coral from the sea was baked, ground, and made into a paste. This lime changed the dark hair to mahogany-brown or lighter with more applications. Reddish-brown hair was known as *'eheu*. The application of lime paste to the hair killed lice as well. (KILO.)

pūkani lua. To be hard, severe, in actions; to be large, plump, and full. These qualities were often combined in the same person, especially in the second, third, and fourth grade of chiefs. (A.)

pūleholeho. Calloused shoulders from carrying. Callouses resembled the *leho* (cowry shell).

pūlimu. Fire kindled for the benefit of a sick person, the practice of the ancient physicians. (MALO 110.)

punalua. To have in common several wives or husbands; one of two wives, or favorites of a chief.

pūne'e. To hitch along on hands and knees and kneel to a chief.

puopelu. Heap of roadside stones convenient as resting places for heavily-loaded travelers.

pu'u. To draw lots by using a knotted string; habit, custom; when a chief died, some of his people, for love's sake, wished to die also.

pu'u 'ili'ili. To draw lots using a pile of pebbles.

pu'ukaula. To set one's husband or wife up as a stake in gambling.

'uhane. Dirge, song of lamentation; soul, spirit of a person.

uhemo. To divorce, as a man and wife. Wākea may have set the example when he spat in Papa's face. They were divorced! (A.)

uho'i. To unite; to live and sleep together, as a man and wife once separated.

'uki. Sedge leaves sometimes used to thatch house interiors. *Pili* was used on exteriors.

uko'o. Human sacrifice.

ukuhi. To wean, as a child from breast feeding.

ukuho'opane'e. Usury; interest on money lent. *Lit.*, deferred payment. (Isa. 24:2.)

ulaia, 'ūlala. To live as a hermit because of disappointment.

'umi kamali'i. Practice of infanticide.

'umi keiki. Infanticide.

walewale. One set apart, as a woman who has given birth to a child. In her condition she was called *walewale*. (A.)

walina, welina. Reply to a salutation, as *aloha* or *'ano'ai*. It applied to persons of the house when addressed by a stranger. (A.)

waloīna. To call to a chief in a voice of praise and admiration.

MATS

There were many qualities and kinds of mats. Most were woven, or better, plaited of pandanus leaves. The several islands gave their names to certain distinctive mats. There is general agreement that the finest mats were produced on Niʻihau. *Pāwehe,* geometric designs of very close weave, were in wide use there, and the resulting softness of Niʻihau mats made them famous.

The plaiting, braiding, or weaving of mats became quite an art. Pandanus leaves were collected and properly dried. Then they were cut into strips of the desired width, and both the strips and rolled up leaves were stored.

Mats were used as floor coverings, foundations for beds, body coverings, baskets, canoe covers, sails, and even fishnets. Some mats were exhibited at the Paris Exposition of 1889. See **KAPA: At the Paris Exposition, 1889.**

ʻaʻahu. To cover with *kapa;* to cover, as with a cloak. The *ʻaʻahu* was an early kind of *kapa.*

ʻahu. Upper body garment, shirt, cape, coat; fine, soft mat used as a cape or body covering; mat used as a cover for canoes.

ʻahuʻao. A choice mat with a half-inch mesh woven from young, tender leaves of *hala* (pandanus). See **moena ʻahuʻao.**

ʻahu moena. Fine patterned mat, plaited with materials in different colors.

ʻahuʻoʻeno. Kauaʻi mat made with reeds or ribbons to create diagonals or ribs in the design.

ʻahu pāwehe. Striped mat with geometric designs, a Niʻihau product. See **pāwehe.**

alahiʻi. Border or hem, as on a plaited mat or hat.

ʻaleuleu. Old, worn-out mats, *kapa,* or clothing. See **ʻāpeu.**

ʻaneʻeneʻe. Mats, old and worn, used for outdoor sitting; old clothing.

anuʻa. A stack of mats piled one on another, also *nuʻa.*

ao. A kind of choice mat.

ʻāpeu, ʻāpeupeu. Large but very poor mats used for holding food. See **ʻaleuleu.**

ʻekeʻeke. Mat plaited in a herringbone design. (PE.)

hale. *Pāwehe* mat pattern using a large central lozenge enclosing a rectangular figure of red on alternate weft crossings.

hoehoe pākea. Niʻihau *pāwehe* design for plaiting. (PE.)

hōkū helele'i. Design used on Ni'ihau mats. *Lit.,* stars falling. (PE.)

honu. Design for a Ni'ihau mat. (PE.)

hu'a moena. Pile of mats. See **kūmoena, p'a'ahu.**

humu. Head of a mat; starting place to interweave strips or reeds of sedges, grasses, etc., to form a firm edge; to start plaiting a mat.

humuniki. Pattern in *pāwehe* plaiting consisting of a continuous row of red lozenges; squares joined in the pattern. See **kumumiki.**

ke'eke'e. Zigzag and bent lines, as in a mat motif. A favorite form of mat.

kūka'a. Bundle of *kapa* or cloth; rolled pack, as of pandanus leaves ready for mats; wholesale.

kukanū. Mat motif incorporating red bands internally enhanced with a continuous row of white lozenges. (PE.)

kūmoena. Pile of mats spread out, as a mat or scenic backdrop. See **hula moena, pa'ahu.**

kumumiki. Mat design with a continuous row of red lozenges with their lateral angles touching. (PE.) See **humuniki.**

kumunu'a. sleeping mat thicker at one end to serve as a pillow.

lau lama. Design of a Ni'ihau mat. *Lit.,* many torches. (PE.)

lolopili. Ni'ihau mat design.

makali'i. Exceedingly fine mesh with very narrow strands, made of the tender young leaves of the *hala,* used in mat making.

maka'opihi. Fine mat of quarter-inch pandanus strips. *Lit.,* fine mesh. (PE.)

moena. General name applied to floor and *moe* (sleeping mats).

moena 'ahu 'ao. Fine mat woven from strands of the *lauhala* (pandanus leaf), with a half-inch mesh. See **'ahu 'ao.**

moena 'aka'akai. Mats of coarse sedge made from the great bulrush *(Scirpus validus)* that grows to 9 feet. After the plant material was prepared, it was woven into mats. Used for house thatch, bed bottom coverings, etc.

moena alolua. Double mat with two, smooth-faced sides, achieved by using a double weft in plaiting.

moena lau. Coarse mat. A Kā'ū name for mats with a very wide weft.

moena makaloa. Perennial sedge *(Cyperus laevigatus)* growing on all the islands. The finest mats of it were made only on Ni'ihau. Soft and pliable, the mats (also called *moena Ni'ihau),* were intended and known chiefly as sleeping mats. They were almost all decorated with plaited geometric designs. See **pāwehe.**

moena maka pepe. Mat with a medium-sized mesh.

moena pāwehe. Fine mat, colored, checkered, patterned, and designed on Niʻihau.

moena puʻao. Mat with a finger-sized mesh (quarter to half inch).

nananuʻu. *Pāwehe* design on Niʻihau mats featuring alternating solid and white triangles.

neki. Mat made of the young shoots of the great bulrush, *Scirpus validus.*

nēnē. Mat pattern of two vertical rows of triangles with the bases below and the points touching the bases above; flying-geese motif.

niho wili hemo. Design on Niʻihau mats consisting of a series of pointed notches. Also included were zigzag stripes called *kulipuʻu* (*Lit.*, knees bent). Used in *kapa* and quilt patterns.

nuʻa, anuʻa. Heap of mats, perhaps eight or ten, piled one on top of another.

olowahia. *Pāwehe* mat pattern. A favorite was that of a saw.

ʻopihi. Design for *kapa* and mats with small triangles, perhaps named for the limpet.

opihipihi. Above average kind of mat. (A.) Mat used for sails. (PE.)

ʻōpuʻu. Mat taking its name from the pattern with rounding edges resembling flower buds.

pʻaʻahu, paʻaʻahu. Pile of mats; carrier of mats. See **huʻa moena, kūmoena.**

pahakū. Design on Niʻihau mats consisting of squares with corners touching, forming a line.(PE.)

pakapaka. Large, coarse mats plaited from large *hala* leaves.

pākaukau. Long mat on which *kaukau* (food) was placed for a meal. Usually preceded by *ke.*

pālau. Old and worn mat, usually small, used to sit on by the fireplace; mat for wrapping things to carry.

pālaulau. Ordinary floor mat; mat for carrying produce; wrapper.

pālau ʻula. Thick mat of ripe *hala* leaves with very wide mesh.

pale haliʻi moena. Coarse mat, as one spread on the ground; demeaning epithet for a low person.

papa ʻaina. Dinner mat placed on the floor; dining or eating table. (Puk. 25:23.)

papa kōnane. Mat design based on a checkerboard.

papa ʻula. Mat design using a row of opposing triangles with their apices touching. (PE.)

pāʻū. Mat made as a canoe covering with a provision, if desire, for slits for the heads of the paddlers. (MALO 134.)

pāwehe. Geometric motifs employed in making the *makaloa* mats chiefly of Niʻihau. These motifs included the use of lines, zigzags, triangles and lozenges in various combinations.

poho mōkoi. Design used in Niʻihau mats.

puahala hīnano. Famed mat of Puna, made with the tender young bracts of the male *hala.*

ʻuʻa. Coarse mat.

ue. Mat made with no trimming, the *lau hala,* allowing the ends to stick out irregularly.

MEDICINE: Anatomy; Body Parts

The first of the medical categories is devoted to the human body—its parts and functions. It owes much to the list incorporated in Handy, Pukui, and Livermore's "Outline of Hawaiian Physical Therapeutics."

The sheer bulk of these six categories attests to the Hawaiian peoples' capacity for observation and their concern for the body's construction and well being.

ā. Jawbone.

ʻaʻa. Vein, artery, muscle, tendon, nerve; envelope of the foetus. (Ioba 14:17.)

aʻalele. Pulse; an artery, from its motion. *Lit.,* vein jumping.

aʻalolo. Nerve. *Lit.,* vein brain.

āʻaopo. Sinews and flesh on the neck.

aʻapū. Valve of a vein.

aʻa puʻupuʻu. Capsular ligament.

ʻae. Saliva.

ʻahalike. Square bone in the wrist joint.

ʻaha maha. Part of the face in front of the ears.

aho. Breath.

ʻāʻī. Neck.

aka. Knuckle joints of the hands or ankles; joints of the backbone.

ake. Liver.

akeloa. Spleen.

akemamā. Lungs.

akenīʻau. Spleen.

akepaʻa. Liver. (Oihk. 3:4.)

akepahaōla, akepāhōla. Lungs.

ālaea. Forepart of the thigh; long, narrow muscle of the thigh.

alalo. Man's lower jaw.

alelo. Tongue. (2 Sam. 23:2.)

alo. Breast, stomach, front, face. (Kin. 3:8.)

'alu. Lines of the hand; to be connected, as the joints in the human body; muscles of the eye.

'āluna. Upper jaw.

'ami. Joint. *Ihu'ami,* nose with irregular bridge.

amo, imo. To wink. (Hal. 35:19.) To twinkle, as a star; contraction of the anal muscles. (PE.)

'ao'ao. Human rib.

'āpo'opo'o. Hollow of the foot, instep. Also called *poho wāwae, poli wāwae.*

'auwae. Chin. *Auwae, kahi malalo o ka waha,* the *auwae* is the place beneath the mouth.

awāwa. Space between the fingers of the hand or the toes of the foot.

ea. Breath, life. See **hānō, hanu.**

'e'e. Armpit. Also called *pō'ae'ae.* See **kapo'o, po'e'e.**

ēlemu. Buttocks.

ēwe. Aorta; navel string; abdominal aorta.

hā'ae. Saliva; spittle.

ha'i. Joint of a limb. *Ka ha'i a mawe,* the elbow joint.

ha'ilima. Elbow, wrist.

hakelo. Mucus.

haku. Ball of the eye.

haku'ōnohi. Eyeball.

hane. Soul; spirit, of a person. See **'uhane.** (Oihk. 5:1.)

hānō. Breath, asthma. See **ea, hanu.**

hanu. Breath, in the sense of existence; life. See **ea, hānō.**

haoa. Bile; pungent, bitter matter heaved from the stomach.

haupo. Lower end of the breast bone where the ribs unite. (A.)

helehelena. External appearance of a person; contour, form, face. (Iak. 1:23.)

hena. Hollow of the thigh; human anatomy.

hoehoe. Shoulder blade, so called from its resemblance to a canoe paddle.

hoko. Fleshy, movable part of a fat man; buttocks.

hokua. Lower and back part of the neck where it joins the shoulders.

hono. Back of the neck.

honowā. Excrement contained in the intestines.

hoʻōpū. Stomach. No data. (CMH.)

houpo. Thorax, region of the heart. (Isa. 60:5.)

hua. Testicles. (Oihk. 21:20.)

hua. Round-ended bone; head of femur, entering the hip socket. See **iwi hua.**

hulu. Human body hair. *Lauoho,* hair of the human head. *Lit.,* leaf head.

hulu kuʻemaka. Eyebrows.

humuhumu. Dark spot on the body, mole; birthmark believed caused by the pregnant mother eating the *humuhumu* fish. (PE.)

ʻiēwe, ʻieʻiēwi. Placenta; navel string.

ihu. Nose. (Isa. 65:5.)

ihu kūmene. Blunt or flat-nosed. Also called *ʻūmene, ʻūpepe.*

ila. Small, permanent mark on the skin; birthmark, mole.

ʻili. Skin.

ʻili kea. Fair skin. *ʻIli kou,* medium skin. *ʻIli hāuli,* dark skin.

ʻimo. To wink. (Hal. 35:19.) See **ʻamo.**

ʻiʻo huki. Muscle.

ʻiʻo maha. Temple muscle.

iwi. Bone.

iwi ā. Jawbone.

iwi alalo. Lower jawbone, mandible bone.

iwi ʻāluna. Upper jawbone, superior maxillary bone. (Hal. 137:5.)

iwi ʻaoʻao. Rib, rib bone. (2 Sam. 2:23.)

iwi elelo. Hyoid bone at the base of the tongue in the anterior neck.

iwi hilo. Thighbone, femur.

iwi hoehoe. Shoulder blade; scapula.

iwi hope. Occipital bone; bone that forms the posterior segment of the skull.

iwi hua. Hip bone, a large irregular bone belonging to the pelvis and forming the principal prominence of the hip. See **hua.**

iwi kā. Part of the hip bone, ischium, on which the body rests when sitting; seat bone.

iwi kanaka. Human bone, skeleton.

iwi kano. Preaxial bone of the forearm.

iwikū. Tibia, the bone of the lower leg.

iwikuamoʻo. Spine, backbone.

iwi lae. Bone of the forehead.

iwi lei. Shoulder blade, collarbone, clavicle.

iwi maha. Cheekbone.

iwi 'ōpe'ape'a. Two paired bones between the occipital and frontal bones of the cranium, the parietal bones.

iwi pili. Fibula; double or united bones of arm or leg.

iwi pona. Hollow bone, as the eye socket; a joint into which the round end of a bone fits.

iwi po'o. Skull, headbone. (Lunk. 9:53.) Also called *iwi puniu.*

iwi pūhaka. Pelvic bone.

iwi puniu. Same as *iwi po'o,* skull.

iwi uluna. Humerus, bone of upper arm or forelimb.

iwi umauma. Breastbone, sternum.

kaenako'i. Anus.

kāhā po'ohiwi. Fat or muscle on the shoulder blade.

kai ko'ako'a. Watery fluid of the bowels.

kaka'a. To shift or roll the eyes; to squint. See 'ōleha.

ka mai a māwe. Elbow joint. (DMH.)

kani'ā'ī. Windpipe.

kano. Forearm, lower legbone.

kāpakapaka. Labia of the female; crotch of the male.

kapo'o. Armpit.

kapo'ohiwi. Shoulder.

kapua'i. Sole of the foot.

kapua'i wāwae. Foot.

kauha. Rectum.

keahakahaka. Abdomen.

ke'apa'a. Human chest.

ke'awa'awa'a. Upper part of the thorax. (CMH.)

kihi po'ohiwi. Generally the same as *po'ohiwi* (shoulder); but really means the corners, points, or sides of the shoulder.

ki'i 'ōnihi. Pupil of the eye.

kīkala. Hollow of the back between the hips; coccyx bone, hip, buttocks, posterior.

kīleo. Larynx; palate of the mouth. (Ioba 34:3; 29:10.)

kino. Body.

ki'ona. Anus, fundament. See *'ōkole.*

kō'ala. Womb, placenta, uterus. See *pū'ao.*

ko'ana. Bladder.

kohe. Anatomic structure; *Vagina feminarum.* (RKB.)

koko. Blood.

kokuli. Ear wax.

kōnāhua. Kidney. (Puk. 29:13.)

kowaū. Testicles. See **hua.**

kua. Back.

kuahiwi. Shoulder.

kuāhua. Hunchback. See **kuapuʻu, lanai.** (Oihk. 21:20.)

kua maha. Side of the head; bones back of the ear.

kuamoʻo. Of or pertaining to the backbone.

kuamoʻo loa. Backbone. (CMH.)

kuapoʻi. Kneepan, patella; bone in arm or hand.

kuapuʻu. Hunchback; hunchbacked. See **kuāhua, lanai.** (Oihk. 21:20.)

kuʻekuʻe. Joint, knuckle, wristbone, elbow.

kuʻekuʻe lima. Elbow.

kuʻekuʻemi. Inner corner of the eye, next to the nose. See **luaʻu-hane.** (CMH.)

kuʻekuʻe wāwae. Heel; ankle joint.

kuʻemaka. Eyebrow.

kuha. Saliva, spittle.

kuʻi. Large back tooth, molar.

kukuli. Kneepan, knee joint.

kuli. Knee.

kumuhele. Crotch.

kumumumu. Cartilage; something between bone and meat. Also called *pīlali.*

kumu pepeiao. Mastoid process; ear bone.

kumu ūhā. Groin; joining of leg and torso. (PE.)

lae. Forehead, brow. (1 Sam. 17:49.)

lae koʻi. Sharp or projecting forehead.

laho. Testes of the male.

lanai. Hunchback. See **kuāhua, kuapuʻu.**

lapawāwae. Shin.

lauoho. Hair of the head. See **oho.** (Nah. 6:5.)

lehelehe. Lips.

lemu. Underpart of the thigh; buttocks.

lihilihi. Eyelashes.

lima. Hand, arm.

lima nui. Thumb.

loko. Internal organs.

lolo. Brains, bone marrow.

lolo iwi. Bone marrow.

lolo poʻo. Brain.

luaʻuhane. Inner corner of the eye, next to the nose.

maiʻao. Nail of finger or toe; hoof; claw. (Isa. 5:28.)

maka. Eye, organ of sight.

maka akau. Right eye.

makahakahaka. Deep-set eyeballs.

maka hema. Left eye.

makalua. Socket for the eyeball.

maka 'upena. Midriff, that which covers the bowels; anterior abdominal wall.

mālama. Pancreas.

mana. Limb of the body.

manamana lima. Finger. (Puk. 29:12.)

manamana nui. Big toe; thumb.

manamana wāwae. Toe.

manawa. Soft place in an infant's skull; anterior fontanel in the head of a small child. Also called *po'opu'ali.*

manea. Ball of the foot.

meukeu. Knuckles of a fist when the hand is doubled up. (AP.)

mimi. Urine; water from the bladder.

momi. Hard center of the eye; fish eyeball; yellowish tissue elevated between the cornea and the inner canthus of the eye. Usually caused from irritation by wind and dust, not formed from fat. The medical term is pinguecula.

na'ana'au. Small intestines; stomach.

na'au. Intestines, bowels.

na'au li'ili'i. Entrails. (CMH.)

niho. Tooth.

nikiniki. Sheath covering the bowels.

niuniu. Skull, head.

nuku. Mouth. See **waha.**

oho. Hair of the head.

'ōkole. Anus, buttocks. *'Ōkole maluna,* bottoms up, a modern drinking idiom. See **'ēlemu.**

'ōleha. To set the eyes in a squinting manner; to squint. See **kaka'a.**

olonā. Ligament, muscle, sinew, tendon, hamstring. (Kol. 2:19.)

'olo'olonā. Cords and ligaments that bind bones and muscles together.

'olo'olo wāwae. Calf of the leg.

'ōnohi. Center of the eye; eyeball.

ōpe'a. Testicle, scrotum.

'ōpū. Stomach, abdomen, bladder.

'ōpū mimi. Bladder. *Lit.,* belly urine.

'ūpu'uu'u lima. Knuckles.

pa'i a'a. Incipient arteries or veins of an embryo branching out from the heart.

pakapaka. Wrinkles; wrinkled skin of the eye.

pana. Heartbeat, pulse.

pane. Joining the head with the bones of the neck.

panepo'o. Occiput or hinder part of the head.

papa 'auwae. Lower jaw.

pāpākole. Hipbone, hip; joining of the hipbone with the socket bone.

papālina. Cheeks, cheek. (Kanl. 18:3.)

pe'ahi. Bones of the hand as distinct from those of the arm.

pe'ahi lima. Palm of the hand.

pepeiao. Ear.

piko. Navel, navel string.

pipi. Center of the eye; pupil.

poe'e. Armpit. Same as *po'ae'ae.* (Ier. 38:12.)

poho lima. Palm of the hand. (Isa. 49:16.)

poholua. Cavity of anus or vagina.

poho wāwae. Hollow of the foot. See *āpo'opo'o, poli wāwae.*

poli. A slight hollow, as the lap when sitting; bosom. (Ruta 4:16.)

poli wāwae. Hollow of the foot; instep. See **'āpo'opo'o.**

pona. Joints, as of the spine and fingers.

po'o. Head.

po'ohiwi. Shoulder.

pū'ā'ī. Projection formed by the thyroid cartilage in the inside of the neck; Adam's apple.

puana'i. Front of the neck and throat.

pū'ao. Ostincae or orifice of the womb.

pūhaka. Loins.

pūhi. Uncircumsized foreskin.

pukaihu. Nostril.

pūlima. Wrist; wristbones and knuckles.

pūniu. Skull of a man which resembles a coconut *(niu).* (2 Nal. 9:35.)

puniuhui. Place on the top of the head where the bones unite.

pu'u. Ankle joint, knuckles; Adam's apple of the throat, hence, the throat.

pu'u koko. Clot of blood; heart.

pu'u kole. *Mons veneris.* See **Earthy Expressions.**

pu'ulima. Wrist joints; knuckles and wrist bones; palm of the hand; fist.

pu'upa'a. Kidneys. (Hal. 7:9.)

pu'upu'u wāwae. Ankle, ankle bones.

pu'uwai. Heart. *Lit.,* lump water.

ʻuala, ʻuwala. Large muscles of the upper arm.

uha. Alimentary canal.

ʻūhā. Thigh.

ʻuhane. Soul. (Oihk. 5:1.)

uhao. Line of lean flesh on each side of but outside the backbone.

ʻulapaʻa. Virgin.

ule. Penis.

ulu. Muscles in the calf of the leg.

uluna. Upper part of the shoulders where they unite with the neck.

umauma. Chest, breast, bosom. (Puk. 4:6.)

ʻūmene. Flat nosed. Same as *ʻūpepe.*

ʻumiʻumi. Beard; hair on the chin; whiskers; mustache.

ʻūpā. Action of the heart in receiving and sending out blood.

ʻūpē. Mucus or secretions from the nose.

ʻūpepe. Flat nosed. Also *ʻūmene, ihu kūmene.*

uwala. Large muscles of the upper arm.

waʻawaʻa. Upper part of the thorax; lower part of the throat.

waha. Mouth.

wai au. Bile. (CMH.)

waimaka. Tears.

wai mimi. Urine. (2 Nal. 18:27.)

waiū. Breast, breast milk.

wale. Phlegm.

wāwae. Leg, foot.

MEDICINE: Human Diseases

The Hawaiian language is notably replete with words for human diseases. Early treatment was bound to be less successful than modern methods and yet among certain individuals there was an efficacy, a power to produce effects, that led them to become *kahuna lapaʻau,* or medical practitioners.

Diagnoses, based on careful scrutiny of the sick patients, led to remedial attempts that resulted in a fair degree of success.

ʻāʻā. To stutter or stammer, as a dumb person; inability to speak intelligibly; dwarf or small person. (Oihk. 21:20.)

aʻahuʻi. Aching vein or tendon. (A.)

ʻaʻai. Spreading sores or lesions; to increase or grow, as an ulcer.

'ahē. Hacking cough; to cough in short, broken surges.

'ahē'ahē. Hacking cough. *I ka manawa 'ahē'ahē; ke kau 'ahē'ahē make o Kahalaia ma laua o Humehume,* in the time of coughing, a deadly cough seized upon Kahalaia and Humehume.

ai'a. Watery eye. See **'ōnohiāi'a.**

'ā'i 'ala'ala, 'ala'ala. Scrofula scar, now believed to represent tuberculous lymphadenitis, due to the specific organism, *Mycobacterium tuberculosis.* Scrofula is a medieval term for ulcerating neck lymph nodes. Tuberculosis, as an illness, was unknown in Hawai'i before Captain Cook.

'aīkū. Spasmodic affection of the muscles of the neck, which draws the head to the affected side; croup or transient myositis, stiff neck. It can also refer to another very different ailment, the progressive sternomastoid muscle shortening, torticollis or wry neck.

'ā'īkukuku. Swelling and soreness of the mouth, neck, or legs; large itch. May be fatal. (A.)

'ā'ili. To struggle for breath; to breathe convulsively, gasp, pant, draw short, labored breaths. (HPL.)

'ā'ī 'o'ole'a. Stiff-necked. (HPL.)

'ai 'uha'uha. Wry neck, torticollis. (HPL.)

'āka'aka'a. Peeling or falling off of the scarf skin after a sunburn or a course of drinking *'awa* (kava); lean, reduced in flesh, tired. (HPL.)

akepau. Consumption, an obsolete term for tuberculosis used before the causative germ, *Mycobacterium tuberculosis,* was discovered by R. Koch in 1882. *Lit.,* liver finished. Tuberculosis rarely involves the liver.

'aki. Sharp, recurring pain in the head or stomach; headache. To begin to heal or scar over, as a wound. (HPL.)

'ako, 'ako'ako. Infectious venereal disease. Called *'ako* in women, *waikī* in men.

'aku'e. Manner of walking due to pedal malformation, said of anyone with deformed feet. (HPL.)

'ala'ala. See **'ā'ī 'ala'ala.**

'alalehe. Sick, weak, fretful, as a child from hunger; disease relating to breathing, which affects the lips, mouth, and throat. (HPL.)

'alaneo. Disease in which the patient suffers swelling greatly in every part except the face; dropsy, kidney disease.

'ālina. Scar, blemish. This could refer to a keloid, an abnormally large, ugly scar from any cause, occurring in certain persons.

'**āmokumoku.** Intermittent. No data. (CMH.)

'**anako'i.** Inflammatory swelling of the lymph gland; venereal tumor; bubo. Also called *'auko'i, auwaihiki, 'āwai, 'ēwai, haha'i.*

'**ānuhenuhe.** Rough with cold. *'Ānuhenuhe kā 'ili i ke anu,* the skin is pimpled with cold; wrinkled, furrowed, shriveled.

'**ānu'u.** Traumatic stretch injury to muscle, tendon, or ligament without dislocation.

'**auko'i.** Swelling in the groin, a bubo. Same as *'awaiāhiki.*

'**auwaihiki, 'āwai.** See '**awaiāhiki.**

'**awaiāhiki.** Swelling in the groin, bubo. See '**auko'i, 'auwaihiki, 'āwai, 'ēwai, haha'i.**

aweawe. Tenacious, sticky, threadlike; metaphorical reference to the sliminess of feces in some diseases.

'**eha.** Pain, ache, hurt; to suffer such.

'**eha'eha.** Same as *'eha;* great pain, many small pains.

ehaha. To breathe hard or spasmodically; to gasp, pant.

'**ehē'ehē.** Unproductive cough; to cough slightly; hard dry cough. Also called *ma'i 'ehē'ehē.*

'**eho.** Sore or ulcerous swelling, as from friction under the arm.

'**eke'eke.** Piercing, stinging pain; to be pained, as the bowels with pressure. (A.)

'**ekemu.** To act as a cathartic.

eu. Peculiar sensation of the skin; creeping numbness. (A.)

'**ēwai.** Swelling under the axilla, armpit, or groin. See '**awaiāhiki, 'āwai.**

ha'akōhi. Travail, labor pains; to suffer labor pains. (Kin. 35:16.)

ha'akokōhi. Strong labor pains of a female. (1 Tes. 5:3.)

hā'awe'awe. Sharp abdominal pains.

haha'i. Swelling in the groin; bubo. Same as *'awaiāhiki.*

haho. To become poor in flesh; to fail; to want strength.

hahu. Bowels in a purged state.

haikala. Severe cramp, often fatal. *Waikī* was the medicine: an enema made of the juice of the poisonous gourd, water, salt, and other matter—drastic and painful.

haikala muku. Cramps, still potentially fatal, but less severe than *haikala. Waikī* was also used.

hailepo. Ash-gray pallor; ailment of earlier times probably related to the bowel processes; any such illness causing one to be wan or pale, a sign, but not a disease, of amnesia, shock, or impaired perfusion.

hakakai. Excessive fat; swollen.

hākanelo. Thin, spare in flesh.

hakanene. To be weak, infirm, from protracted illness.

hākau. To look slim and tall, as a person whose flesh is wasted from his limbs. (A.)

hākea. Pale, as one sick.

hākelo. Mucus hanging from the nose of a child; slimy, snotty.

hākuʻekuʻe. Ringworm. See **hāʻukaʻuka, hāʻukeʻuke.**

hākuʻi. To be sickish, nauseated; to palpitate, as the heart.

hākumakuma. To be rough or pitted, as from the scars of small-pox.

halahalawai. Wet, watery, as a sore eye.

hālaʻo. To suffer pain from a mote lodged in the eye.

haloke. Sprained or broken, as a limb. (HPL.) To rub against each other, as the ends of broken bones. (A.)

hālulelule. To be weak from overweight; to walk unsteadily from weakness.

hanahemo. Feeble state of health; state of weakness. (A.)

hanapilo, hanopilo. Speak with a wheezy, hoarse voice, as with a cold or sore throat.

hanawai. To menstruate, urinate.

hānō. Asthma; to cough or wheeze.

hanou. To breathe with difficulty; asthma. See **hōkiʻi, nae.** (A.)

hanu. To sniff, smell, breathe; breath, breathing.

hānunanuna. Hard breathing from stoppage of the nose.

hanunu. Bent over, stooped, round-shouldered.

hanu paʻa. Head cold, catarrh; choked with breathing.

hanu pau. Gasping of a dying person; giving up of the spirit.

hanu pilo. Offensive breath.

haoa. Sour stomach, nausea, heartburn.

hapakuʻe. Crippled, deformed; to speak with an impediment.

hāpauea. Wanting in strength; debilitated with old age.

hāpōpō. Almost blind; bleary-eyed.

hāʻukaʻuka, hāʻukeʻuke. Ringworm, fungus skin ailment.

hauʻoki. Palsy or stiffness of the bones, as one chilled to the bone or stiff with cold.

haupuʻu. Bunionlike enlargement on the joints.

haupuʻupuʻu. Disease of the joints, which develops nodules or little bone-like knots on joints or fingers.

hea. To be red or sore, as inflamed eyes.

heʻewale. Miscarriage.

heha. Sore, red, as inflamed eyes.

hēhē. Boil, running sore; ulcerous. (Kanl. 28:27.)

hehe'e. With *ma'i,* a running sore; boil furuncle. Central nidus of viscous matter which may or may not drain. (Oihk. 13:18.)

hehena. To be crazy, mad, insane. (Ier. 25:16.)

hela. Redness of eyelids; partial blindness.

helei. Inflammatory disease of the eye.

hemo'ē. Last extremity of life before death; dying breath.

hepa. Palsy; shaking of the limbs; partial paralysis of the vocal organs causing indistinct speech; slight form of dementia; imbecile.

hewahewa. Crazy, demented. (Ier. 29:26.)

hī. Dysentery, diarrhea; a flowing away, a purging. (Oih. 28:8.)

hīkoko. Flowing of blood; dysentery, hemorrhoids. (Kanl. 28:27.)

hiliō'ū. Ailment of stomach or bowels, accompanied by gas pains.

hilo. Gonorrhea, a running sore. (Oihk. 15:23.)

hīnawenawe. Tall, thin, feeble, debilitated.

hinipoa. Feeble, debilitated, weak.

hō. To wheeze, breathe hard; asthma.

hō'ā īpuka hale. Ruptured appendix.

hoaka kai. Ailment, possibly appendicitis.

hoaka kākala. Ailment, possibly a ruptured appendix. (PE.)

hoaka kū. Probably appendicitis. This, and the three preceding words are based on the prefix *hoaka* meaning acute abdominal ailment. (A.) A ruptured appendix was probably always fatal. In ancient days, the only remedy suggested was an enema *(waikī)* concocted of the juice of the poisonous gourd, water, salt, and other ingredients.

hōhule. Baldheaded. Also called *'ōhule.*

hōkale. Hard secretion in the flesh; kernel.

hōki'i. Pining sickness; low in flesh; phthisis, consumption, tuberculosis. (Isa. 10:18; Oihk. 26:16.) See **hanou, nae.**

hoku. Thin in flesh; asthma.

honea. Dirt; matter in the intestines not voided.

ho'oā, ho'owa. To retch, vomit; to heave with nausea.

ho'okakani. To have the itch. See **maiau, me'eau, mane'o, mene'o.**

ho'okihe. To cause to sneeze.

ho'oki'iki'i. To cause to swell out, as the breast or stomach. (HPL.)

ho'okilo. Wasted in flesh by illness; to waste away, as by consumption.

ho'okuhō. To cough, as in whooping cough.

ho'okuloukulou. To bend over, as in sorrow or pain.

hoʻokunu. To cause to cough.

hoʻokūʻoha. Venereal disease.

hoʻokūʻoʻi. To limp, walk with unequal steps. (HPL.)

hoʻokuolo. To shake, as with the palsy.

hoʻolāʻau. Cramp; to be afflicted with a cramp.

hoʻolapa. Swelling or rising of a blister.

hoʻolihaliha. Nauseated; to be sick in the stomach after eating fatty food.

hoʻoluaʻi. To vomit; to expel from the stomach; to cause vomiting.

hoʻomāio. To cause thinness; to have little flesh on the bones; to be lame in the hip joint; to be weak in the muscles of the thigh; sore caused by friction of the *malo* over the hip.

hoʻomakou. To be bloodshot, as the eyes from salt water.

hoʻomauiui. To bruise a previous bone break or renew an old sprain.

hoʻonahunahu. To be in labor pains.

hoʻonini. To revive from fainting; to convalesce, as a sick person.

hoʻopailua. To nauseate, induce nausea.

hoʻopohā. To burst, as the contents of a boil.

hoʻopuʻua. To choke; to be in labor, as in childbirth.

hōpilo. To relapse after a partial recovery from sickness.

houpo. Palpitation or fluttering of the heart.

hūʻalu. Slight viscous membrane that covers the eye.

huene. Asthmatic breathing; wheezy.

huʻi. Inflammatory pain of the muscles; ache in any physical organ.

hukihelei. Skin about the eye drawn down showing an abnormal eversion, especially of the eyelids; ectropion.

hula. Swelling under arm or thigh; to palpitate, as the heart; to throb, as an artery.

hupe. Mucus from the nose.

hūpekōle. Catarrh; running nose.

ikiiki. Severe pain; to pant for breath, as one dying.

ilikona. Wart; small, hard protuberance on the skin.

ʻīloli. Unpleasant sensations of pregnancy.

ʻīʻo kupu. Polyp in the nose; gumboil.

kaʻahē. To be feeble, near dying.

kaʻakua, kaʻakukua. Headache accompanied by a severe dizziness.

kaʻalele. To walk unsteadily, as with palsy or dizziness.

kāʻaweʻawe. Chest stricture, stomach sickness, strangling sensation; nonspecific angina.

kaea. Having no appetite, no relish for food.

kaha ea. Disease of the scalp, which can advance over the human body.

kahe koko. Flow of blood, commonly in higher altitudes; hemmorrhage.

ka'i. Loose or decayed tooth that requires removal; toothache.

kā'ihi. Dizziness; to be dizzy.

kāiki'alamea. Wasting disease; emaciation. (PE.)

kā'iliponi. To die suddenly; apoplexy, stroke, accident.

kāka'a. Condition of the eyes in which the muscles that serve the eyeballs suffer partial paralysis.

kakani. Itch; little pimples on the arm, a nonspecific skin lesion. See **maiau, mane'o, me'eau, meau, kāki'o.**

kāki'o. Itch; itching pustules, recurring or persistent on the leg, leaving scars. (Kanl. 28:27.)

kālawa. Intermittent pains in neck of sides; inflammation of the nerve. May be neuritis.

kalea. Choking; whooping cough.

kālilo. Fatal disease or sickness so great that the patient is at death's door.

kāmau ea. Barely holding onto the breath life.

kāmokumoku. To move the bowels in diarrhea at intervals.

kane. Fungus skin disease; tinea.

kanea. Loss of appetite; nausea; slight sickness.

kaokao. Syphilis.

kapakapa. Lameness in the hip joint, aggravated by friction between the ball and socket of the hip joint from long, hard walks. (DK.)

kapeke. Limb out of joint.

kauhola. To lose consciousness, as in a seizure, stroke, or heart attack.

kauhua. State of pregnancy; to conceive; to be full of child. (Hal. 7:14.)

ka'uka'u. Piles, hemorrhoid; an obstruction to evacuation.

kau'oku'u. Pestilence that swept over the islands in 1804, believed to be cholera. It was marked by acute vomiting and a diarrheal illness, and called by this name because people were almost continuously *'ōku'u,* squatting at stool.

ke'a. Tightness in the chest; pleuritis, usually acute. See **pani.**

kio. Bubo, in the inguinal region of the groin; lymph node enlargement. Earlier considered to be a manifestation of syphilis.

kī'opa, kī'ope. Lame, limp. Also called *kā'opa, kā'ope.* See **'o'opa, 'opa.**

kohe ʻako. Ravished vagina; dysuria, painful urination. Not specifically for venereal disease.

kohekohe papa. Sore, ulcerated throat; an eating sore. (HPL.) Bilateral tonsillitis. (PE.)

kohepopo. Venereal disease; form of pulmonary consumption. (HPL.)

kōhoko. Disease of the womb. Also called *ōpū lauoho*. (HPL.) Luetic infection, nonspecific syphilis. (PE.)

kokōhi. Pains of childbirth; to hold back.

kokoni. Twisting, jerking, throbbing of the muscles, accompanied by pain.

kole. Inflamed, red, as a raw wound.

komokomo. Epilepsy, associated in early times with sorcery. See **maʻi kau, maʻi kuhewa.**

kōnui. To be smitten with great heat, as from the sun.

kuākaikai, kūhākakai. Swelling of the cheek and abdomen; adiposity, tendency of being fat.

kuakoko. Pain, distress, as a woman in childbirth.

kuanaka. Abscess on the back. The actual ailment described as a "disease up and down the back" is a matter of speculation. Osteomyelitis, tuberculosis of the spine, and rheumatoid spondylitis are possibilities.

kuapuhi. Abscess on the back. *Lit.,* back burst. Also called *kuapuki.*

kuawehi. Burn on the back and shoulders by the rays of the sun.

kuhewa. Stroke, as with heart failure; apoplexy.

kukuʻe. Club footed; lame person; one deformed and twisted.

kukuku. Piles. (A.) Pimply. (PE.)

kulu. Dysentery, gonorrhea.

kumakuma. Rough or pitted, as the skin after smallpox; ravished, as by leprosy. Also called *hākuma.*

kunakuna. Itch, scabies, scabby skin condition. (PE.)

kuni. Fever, ague.

kunu. Cough; to cough.

kunukalea. Whooping cough.

laina. Eruption on the body like shingles; rash similar to prickly heat or hives but more serious.

lanakea, nanakea. Pale, wan; whiteness from long sickness; general debility.

laʻo. Mote moving in the eye causing pain.

laʻolaʻo. Discomfort arising from inflammation of a membranous tissue, as an eye suffering from a mote, or the bowels from a tendency to colic. (HPL.)

lawa. Disease about which it is said, *pa'apū ka 'ōpū i nā iwi 'ao'ao,* the abdomen or stomach is stifled by the ribs. (A.)

leho. Bunch or swelling like the shell of a *leho,* caused by carrying a burden on the shoulder or back.

leholeho. To be calloused, as one whose skin is largely toughened by friction.

leiowī. Phthisis, consumption, tuberculosis; a disease of the lungs.

lelehu. Partially blind; able to see with difficulty. (A.)

lena. Complaint of the bowels; jaundice; bile.

lī. Ague; to tremble from fever. (Kanl. 28:22.)

liha. Nauseated with oily food.

lihaliha, liliha. Anything causing stomach sickness; nauseated after much rich food; to vomit.

li'i. Anguish; sick of a fever and the ague.

lilio. Acute, darting pain; to have the sensation of eating too much.

loio. Thin, poor, reduced in flesh.

loku. Extreme pain, physical or mental; distress.

lokuloku. Pain, distress; numbness of limbs.

lola. Lame, stiff, paralyzed; palsied person.

lōlō. Palsied, unable to use one's limbs, paralyzed, numb. *Ma'i lōlō,* paralyzing illness.

lolohi. One slowed up by disease, as from palsy.

loloka'a. Dizziness with spinning head, affecting the eyes.

lolokuli. Deaf from disease.

lololoa. Feeling of an arm or leg when blood ceases to circulate. (HPL.)

lonu. To swell up, as in a disease; to groan in pain.

lou. Pain in the side; stitch.

lua'i. To vomit.

lua'i koko. Vomiting of blood; hemorrhage.

luea. Dizziness, nausea, seasickness.

lūmanawahua. Internal pain; pain in the bowels accompanied by frequent evacuations; gas and looseness of the bowels. See **manawahua.**

mae. Wasting disease, said of any prolonged, consuming sickness.

mā'e'ele. Benumbed; void of feeling, as in a leg or arm in which circulation is stopped.

māhuna. Scaly appearance of the skin after drinking *'awa* (kava).

maiahulau. General sickness among the people; pestilence. (Ezek. 12:16.) *Lit.,* sickness pestilence.

Maiau, me'eau. The itch, *kāki'o.* (Kanl. 28:27.)

maihehe. Boil, running sore. (HPL.)

maʻi hilo. Venereal disease, gonorrhea.

maʻikakai. Form of syphilitic infection. (HPL.)

maʻi kau. Chronic or recurring disease.

maʻi keiki. Pregnancy sickness.

maʻi kuhewa. Epilepsy. (CMH.)

maʻi kuni. Typhus fever.

māilo. Thin; wasted away, as a sick person.

maʻi lōʻihi. Any chronic ailment; an invalid. (HPL.)

maʻimaʻi. To be sick, feeble, weak; chronically ill.

maio. Disease reducing a person's flesh, like tuberculosis.

maʻi pūhā. Ulcer, running sore.

maʻi puʻu puʻu kuna. Dangerous kind of itch. (CMH.)

maʻi puʻu puʻu liʻiliʻi. Smallpox.

maʻi wili. Incessant pain; running sore; venereal disease.

makaʻaha. Covered with sores; full of pimples, as with the itch; leprous.

makaha. Inflamed and running eye.

maka helei. Eye so inflamed or diseased that the eyelid is turned out; abnormal eversion, especially that of the eyelids.

maka momi. Small, yellowish swelling near the inner or outer margins of the cornea, occurring especially in older people. It is usually caused by irritation from dust or wind and is not formed from fat. *Pinquecula. Momi* is the hard center of the eyeball or the eye of a fish.

maka pala. Soft, ripe; ready to burst, as a boil.

maka pela. Eyes with an offensive smell; sticky, dirty eyes.

maka pōniuniu. Faintness or dizziness resulting from hunger. (Lunk. 8:4.)

maka pula. Mote in the eye; matter in a corner of the eye.

mākole, mōkole. Sore watery eyes, brought on by swimming too long in salt water. Also called *maka kole.*

makuʻu. Involuntary bowel or stool discharges, as after eating great quantities of *walu,* a fish.

mala lua. To swell, as anything blistered.

manawaea. Hard breathing; impediment in breathing; panting for breath.

manawahua. Unpleasant state of the bowels related to gas or diarrhea; loss of appetite. See **lūmanawahua.**

manene. Affected with dizziness in walking.

maneʻo, meneʻo. Itch; itchy; itchy pain. Also called *maiau, meʻeau.*

manunu. To break, as bones; to crack or creak against each other, as broken bones.

maoa, ma'oha. Sore caused by friction of *malo* between the legs from a long journey.

mauā, mauwā. Lame, sore, stiff.

maui. Sprain or bruise; pain from a broken limb.

maule. To be faint through fasting; to be weak through dizziness.

mauleho. Callous on the shoulder from carrying heavy burdens; calloused.

mauli'awa. Hiccough; gasping for breath; hard breathing; dying breath.

maumanaha. Perhaps meaning heartburn. (A.)

mene'o. Var. of *mane'o.*

me'ome'o. Reddish, as a feverish swelling on one's finger.

moekuhua. Viscous matter in the eyes; sore-eyed, so that on waking the eyes cannot be opened.

mu'umu'u. Lame person; one who has lost or never enjoyed use of the limbs; primarily one who creeps, halts, or limps.

nae. Disease marked by hard or short breathing; asthma. See **hanou, hōki'i.**

naeiki. Breathing but little; almost exhausted, near death.

naenae. Difficult breathing; phthisis; asthma.

nae-'oai-ku. Disease in which hard breathing causes one to stretch out the neck; throat disease; croup. (HPL.) Severe asthma. (PE.)

nāhoahoa. Wound on the head and the resulting pain; effect of a sunstroke on the head; intense headache.

nahu kuakoko. Labor pains. (Mika 4:9.)

nahunahu. Birth pains of females. (Ioba 29:3.)

nakanaka. The shakes, *delirium tremens.*

nakinaki. Tightness in the chest; ailment of the respiratory organs; difficult breathing, as during an asthma attack.

nalulu. Severe sharp pain in the head; dull pain in the abdomen.

nanae. Swollen abdomen and depressed stomach; disease that causes difficulty in breathing.

nanahe. Empty bowels from fasting or sickness.

nanakea. Thin in flesh; pale, as a sickly person.

nananakea. Weakly, thin in flesh, pale.

nananananaiea. Weak, feeble, frail.

nao. Spittle, phlegm; mucus from the nose.

nau. Pain or distress, but to a lesser degree than *hu'i.*

nāwali. Sickly, feeble, weak.

nāwaliwali. Weak, feeble, sick; want of strength.

newa. To be dizzy; to reel or stagger with vertigo.

newanewa. Vertigo, dizziness.

niho hu'i. Toothache.

niho kaʻi. Aching tooth.

nīpoa. Headache, mostly in the area of the temples; dizziness; dullness or numbness of the body.

nīpolo. Sick and faint, as one dying.

niua. Vertigo; distortion of the eyes.

nunu. To swell up, as in some forms of leprosy. (CMH.)

ʻō. Sharp pain in the body; keen darting pain in the side of the chest.

ʻoāʻoā, ʻowāʻowa. To sicken, vomit.

ʻohākulaʻi. Tumor on a joint of the human body; protuberance in the flesh.

ʻōhao, ʻōhaohao. Distended, full, as the bowels with wind or water.

ʻōhemo. Illness likely to occur in a little child when deprived of its mother's milk.

ʻohune. Eruptive disease resembling chickenpox.

ʻoikipuahola. Pestilence that occurred in the time of Wala.

ʻōlala. To become lean, as a fleshy person; to pine away. (Ezek. 33:10.)

ʻōmali. Weak, feeble with sickness.

ʻomī. To droop, to lose flesh, as a person.

ʻona. Kind of nettling or pricking of the skin, attended by some pimples; dizziness.

ʻōnohiāiʻa. Watery or sore eye; cataract of the eye. See **aiʻa.**

onū. Swelling; wen on the head or neck.

ʻoʻolā. Blister on the foot; stone bruise on the bottom of the foot.

ʻoʻopa, ʻopa, ʻopaʻopa. Lame person. (Mat. 11:15.) Person, lame from walking, having lost a foot or overstrained an arm.

ʻōpikopiko. Form of syphilis in which the skin becomes spotted.

ʻōpilo. Relapse in the course recovery from a disease.

ʻōpū haʻo. Abdominal pains due to prolonged fasting.

ʻōpūʻōhao. Abdomen enlarged to hardness, limbs weakened.

ʻowaikū, ʻoaikū. Worst form of asthma.

ʻōwali. Weak, infirm.

paʻa mua. Movement of gas in the bowels.

pāʻaoʻao. Childhood disease leading to physical weakness.

pahāha. Swollen, as the neck with mumps.

paholehole. Break or bruise of the skin leaving a raw surface.

pahuhu. To ooze or gush out, as blood from a wound.

pailua. Nausea.

pākea. Pale or gray, as from illness or age.

pākoni. Throbbing toothache.

pakū. To burst out or break open, as with a boil.

pala. Syphilis.

palahēhē. Pus.

palahī. Discharge of liquid matter from the bowels; diarrhea.

palakiʻo. Form of venereal disease.

palalalo. Applied to persons sick with venereal disease.

palapū. Soft, as a boil ready for lancing.

paloke. Broken, as a joint.

pāmake. Death; epidemic attended with a large death rate.

pānauea. Poor or thin in flesh.

pani. Choking sensation; severe pain at the solar plexus. See **keʻa.**

papakū. Disease caused by costiveness, constipation, accompanied by vomiting, back pains, sore eyes.

papālinanui. Large, fleshy, and weak.

paunakalike. Scales, as from the flesh; baldness. (Isa. 40:12.)

pēheuheu. Plump or swollen, as the neck from mumps.

pehu, pepehu. Dropsy; swollen; a blain. (Oihk. 13:2.)

pehu pala. Scurvy. (Kanl. 28:27.)

piapia. Thick, white, viscid matter from sore eyes.

piele. Mattery eruptions or eczema of the scalp.

pīheka. Inflamed, as the eyes.

pihi. A venereal disease; scab or scar; itch.

piliʻaikū. Stiff neck, numbness.

pili wale. Poor or thin in flesh.

poʻa. Castrated, emasculated, despoiled of virility.

pohā. To burst or break out, as a boil. (Puk. 9:9.)

pohala. To be healed; to recover from sickness; to revive from fainting.

pōhānō. Hoarse or unnatural voice from a cold or other cause; hard breathing.

pōheʻepali, poʻoheʻepali. To die mysteriously; to fall alone from a *pali* (cliff).

pohole. Severe wound, break, or scrape of the skin; bruise.

poholo. To cast, as a female, her young; to miscarry by premature birth.

pohona. Contraction of muscles in disease; sinking in or down with pain.

pōhukuhu. Copious overflowing of phlegm with a severe cold.

pokoke. Disease affecting excretions from the kidney; urinary incontinence.

polapola. Bright, as the face of one recovered from illness.

polokawae. Gradual wasting away; long sickness.

poluā, poluwā. Nausea, dizziness, sickness. *Lit.,* heads two.

ponanā. Lame, sore from walking, applied only to the calf of the legs.

pōniniu, poniu. That which causes dizziness or vertigo.

pōniuniu, po'oniuniu. Vertigo, dizziness, sickness.

po'ohe'epali. Unexpected or accidental death; sudden death.

po'ohū. Wound, particularly if swollen; bruise.

po'o hua'i. Neuralgic pain in the head; splitting headache.

po'olopū. Blister; rising of the skin.

po'opo'o. Sunken, as the eyes of a sick person.

puahilohilo. Breaking or cracking of skin from disease; scaly appearance of the scarfskin.

pua'i. A vomiting, spitting, heaving from stomach sickness.

puakī. Thin, spare, poor in flesh.

puapua. Nauseous.

puawai. Spittle of someone with a sore mouth, as if salivated.

pūehuehu. Rough, ragged, as the skin after drinking much *'awa;* skin flaked, cracked, and peeling, as from sunburn.

pūhā. Broken or burst open, as a sore or boil; an issue, a running sore; abscess; gonorrhea.

puhikaokao. To burst open and break the skin, as the *kaokao,* a venereal disease.

pūhō. To be broken out in ulcers; to burst a sore, develop an abscess.

pula. Mote or particle in the eye; mucus in the corner of the eye.

puleholeho. Knot or calloused place on the shoulder from carrying burdens.

pūlele. Neck sore, tuberculous lymphadenitis. The medieval term for tuberculosis is scrofula, King's evil.

punia. Cold in the head; pain in the head above the eyes.

pupu'u anu. Goose pimples from cold. (CMH.)

pu'u. Prominence, pimple, wart, knuckles; joints of the ankles; Adam's apple.

pu'ua, pu'uwa. To be choked or suffocated in swallowing food; to stick in the throat.

pu'uhau. Calcium deposits growing into lumps, particularly on the joints; hard bunch growing on the flesh.

pu'ulele. Rupture, hernia. *Lit.,* falling round object.

pu'upau. Cancer of the throat.

pu'upu'u. Full of blotches or pimples; to break out into blisters and boils.

ua 'ena loa ka'ula o ka ma'i. Sick person in bed with heat, high fever.

uakaka, uauakaka. Stiffness of the cords of the neck.

uanaoa. Having no relish for food; to be squeamish at the sight of food; to be sick in the stomach; nausea.

uha. To belch; to hawk up mucus or phlegm.

uhaki. Fracture; to break, as the bones.

uhalu. Weak; exhausted from illness.

uhaluhalu. Having a pale or sickly hue; pallid; languid from illness.

ukokole. Sore, inflamed, as the eyes.

ule hilo. Gonorrhea.

uleule. Sty on the edge of the eyelid; hordeolum.

ulu. Increase in any way; to spread, as a disease on the skin.

umalei. Apoplectic disease involving sudden loss of consciousness from effusion of blood in the lungs or brain. Also called *kokolana*. *Lit.,* rush of blood. *Obs.*

'umi. Strangled, suffocated, choked to death.

'ūmi'i. Sharp body pain in the side, like the piercing of a needle.

unea. Nausea; sickness of the stomach.

uneunea. Sick to the stomach; having no relish for food. (A.)

unouno'o. Red, inflamed, as the eyes.

upehupehu. Swollen, bloated, fleshy, but weak, as a fat man.

'ū'ū. To stutter, stammer; speech impediment.

'u'u'u. Hoarse; stammering; unable to speak intelligibly.

waiiki. Kidney disease that impedes urination. Anuria vs. urinary retention. (RKB.)

wai ke'oke'o. Fluor, a disease of women; leucorrhea. *Lit.,* liquid white.

wai 'ōpua. Disease, similar to pulmonary tuberculosis.

walania. Stinging pain, as a burn.

wale kea. An eye disease; exudation from a sore eye; white mucus.

wekaweka. Foul stomach.

welawela. Burning, as of a fever; feverish sore.

wili. Gonorrhea. See **ma'i-wili.**

wīwī. Lean; to grow poor in flesh, as a person. (Zek. 14:12.)

MEDICINE: Preparations

This category underscores the predominance in the Hawaiian language of words devoted to purgatives and cathartics. It also shows the dependence on prescriptions relying on plant, mineral, and animal sources with which Hawaiians created a veritable cornucopia of vital health products.

Marie C. Neal states: "A final, accurate correlation of native names of medicinal plants with their botanical identities must await the future completion of a collection of plants . . . used and named by competent Hawaiian informants." This represents a great challenge and is a necessity for a correct understanding of the Hawaiian language's medicinal terms.

'akukapihe. Juice of the shrub *koko* or *akoko* (*Euphorbia rockii* Forbes) used as a cathartic and for debility. (NEAL 516.)

'ape. Large taro-like plant *(Alocasia macrorrhiza),* a main ingredient for treating burns. Its leaves are used in relieving headaches and neuralgia; its milky sap to relieve nettle stings. In addition, it helped ward off evil spirits, and its potion could stimulate love. (NEAL 156.)

'apu. General name for medical potions, as made of taro, yams, or herbs. The drink takes its name from the coconut-shell cup.

'auhuhu. Shrub *(Tephrosia purpurea)* used to poison or intoxicate fish. Dorothy Kahananui reports that her family used to catch *'o'opu* by pounding the *'auhuhu* and scattering the leaves in a pool or ditch temporarily closed downstream, to allow catching fish bare handed. (NEAL 448.) See **Manners and Customs: 'auhuhu.**

'awa. *Piper methysticum,* called *kava* on other Pacific islands. It is a narcotic used to induce sleep, as a tonic for anxiety and tiredness, to ease passage of urine, relieve headaches and lung troubles, and assist in a displaced womb. (BHK.)

'awapuhi kuahiwi. Wild ginger (*Zingerber zerumbet*). Its roots supply materials for all medicines derived from this plant. They are washed, then ground, water is added, and the mixture strained through *makaloa* fibers and drunk to relieve a headache. (BHK; NEAL 257.)

'awī'awī. Herbaceous weed *(Centaurium sebaeoides).* A plant used to stop bleeding. (NEAL 684.)

'āwikiwiki. Blackberries used as an emetic and cathartic in medicine. (A.)

hā ipu. Stem of a gourd leaf used for medicine.

hala or pā hala. Pandanus or screwpine *(Pandanus odoratissimus).* Its root tips were mixed with other plants and sugarcane juice and then heated as a tonic for mothers weak from bearing many children. The soft, lower part of the flower was chewed by the mother and given to little children as a laxative. Also used by adults. (BHK; NEAL 51.)

hau. Hibiscus *(Hibiscus tilliaceus).* Medicinal ingredient is the slimy juice or sap in its bark and flower buds. It is used as a laxative by infants and adults. Buds are chewed for dry-throat; the bark of the stem for congested chests and to facilitate the delivery of a baby. (BHK; NEAL 559.)

hauʻoki. Medicine given to women in labor, made from the bark of the *hau* tree. Similar to slippery elm.

hinahina. Native heliotrope *(Heliotropicum anomalum),* a low spreading beach plant. The traditional flower of Kahoʻolawe, used for both tea and medicine. (NEAL 717.)

hoʻopioloolo. Fruit of the Indian mulberry *(Morinda citrifolia),* the *noni* tree. Its fruit is crushed and used as a poultice. (CMH.)

ʻihi. Yellow wood sorrel *(Oxalis corniculata).* The leaves and bulbous roots of the *ʻihi* and *ʻihi maka ʻula* supply a cathartic.

ʻiliau. Woody plant *(Argyroxiphium gymnoxephium)* of the dry, western slopes of Kauaʻi, related to the silversword; a medicinal plant.

ʻilieʻe, hilieʻe. Wild plumbago *(Plumbago zeylanica),* growing in dry regions near the coast. Its roots contain poison, the bark supplies a stimulant, the leaves are used for medicine, and the sap supplies a black coloring for tattoo marks. (NEAL 667.)

ʻilima. Flower of Oʻahu *(Sida fallax).* A variety called *kanaka maikaʻi* supplies a juice squeezed from the flower buds that is chewed by mothers and given to children as a laxative. Flowers mixed with other flowers are used for "womb" trouble. A concoction of the root bark mixed with other plants is pounded, mixed with water then strained, and taken as a tonic. Also used for asthma. (BHK; NEAL 552.)

ʻinikō. Indigo *(Indigofera suffruticosa).* The whole plant was used. It was mixed with other plants, pounded, the juice squeezed out and used for backaches and rheumatism. A tablespoonful drunk by a female relieved "womb" trouble. Also used for a hard, dry cough. (BHK; NEAL 447.)

kāʻeʻe. Sea bean *(Mucuna gigantea).* A tall tree with black-spotted or brown seeds in pods, which were processed for use as a cathartic. The seeds are called *pēkaʻa.* (NEAL 462.)

kāhili kāpopo. Concoction of juices of the gourd and the *puʻukaʻa* grass *(Cyperus auriculatus)*. Used medicinally.

kalikali. Plant or tree used for medicine. No data. (A.)

kalo. Taro *(Colocasia esculenta)*. Used raw in medicines. A laxative was made from grating the root and mixing this juice with sugarcane juice and other plants. The mixture was then pounded, squeezed, and strained. The liquid was usually drunk, but if constipation were severe, a suppository made from a core cut from the root was inserted. (BHK; NEAL 157.)

kāmanamana. Bitter-tasting, weedy plant *(Adenostemma lavenia)*. In Hawaiʻi the leaves were used to treat fever. (NEAL 829.)

kāmanomano. Polynesian grass-weed *(Cenchrus calyculatus)*. The leaves were used in love magic.

kanawao. Small tree *(Broussaisia)* with berry-like fruits, which were of medicinal value. An old belief says that eating this fruit aids fecundity. (NEAL 380.)

kāpaʻi. Pod of medicinal herbs used for rubbing on the skin; to apply such as a poultice.

kī. Ti plant *(Cordyline terminalis)*. Its flowers were pounded and mixed with ginger root and other plants, squeezed, strained, and made into little balls with *pulu* (tree fern). When a ball became saturated, its vapor was inhaled for growths in the nose. A mixture of its flowers and young leaves was used for asthma, and its leaves, dipped in cold water and placed on the forehead, helped with fever and headache. Hot stones wrapped in ti leaves served sore backs. (BHK; NEAL 203.)

kiʻikea. Bark of the breadfruit tree *(Artocarpus incisus)*, used to make an ointment for relieving pain.

kipa. Name of a medicine given to a mad man. See **pēkaʻa, pīpā.**

kiʻukiʻu. Medicine used as a drink from the sap of the *ʻakoko* shrub *(Euphorbia rockii)*. (NEAL 516.)

kō. Sugarcane *(Saccharum officinarum)*. Known for its sap squeezed from the pulp of the stem and used to sweeten "bad-tasting" medicines. Juice also squeezed out of a charcoal-baked concoction of young shoots and applied to cuts. (BHK; NEAL 77.)

koa. Koa tree *(Acacia koa)* the leaves of which were spread evenly over a bed of sleeping mats where a feverish patient lay. Heat from the body and the leaves made the patient sweat and fall asleep. (NEAL 408.)

koali, kowali. Morning-glory *(Ipomoea,* spp.), generally herbs with twining stems and erect shrubs; the convulvus plant. Used as a cathartic for wounds, fractures, and injections. (NEAL 703.)

koheoheo. Poisonous drug, causing death. See **'auhuhu.**

kokomai'a. Juice of bananas, used to relieve *'ea* (coated tongue).

ko'oko'olau or kī nehe. Beggar's tick or Spanish needle *(Bidens pilosa).* Used in plant mixtures for throat and stomach troubles and for asthma. Young leaves were used fresh or dry for tea of various strengths, as a tonic adjusted to age. (BHK; NEAL 844.)

kuawa. Guava *(Psidium guajava).* The juice of this plant mixed with that of others was applied directly to deep cuts, sprains, and other injured parts. Its roots were mixed, pounded, and heated. The strained liquid was drunk to stop bowel bleeding. (BHK; NEAL 632.)

kukui. Candlenut tree *(Aleurites moluccana).* Supplied many medicinal items: the rich, uncooked nut was used as a drastic purge; juice of the bark was a therapy for asthma; a mouthwash was prepared from the very bitter juice of the shell of an unripe nut; and a concoction similarly gave relief to *'ea* (coated tongue).

kū pali'i. Species of a forest herb *(Peperomia* spp.), a medicinal plant. Another species is called *'ala'ala wai nui.*

kūpele. Concoction of herb juices mixed with *poi,* mashed potatoes, and other foods. *Kūpele,* as a medical term, is difficult to define. (BHK.)

kupukupu'ula. Plant used in the process of scarifying the skin.

lā'au. Medicine.

lā'au ho'opē. Medicine given to prevent fecundity. (PE.)

lā'au ho'opi'i. Emetic. *Lit.,* medicine ascend. Also called *lā'au lua'i, lā'au pi'i.*

lā'au nāha. Cathartic.

lapa'au. General term for medicine; medical practice. *Kauka lapa'au,* western medical doctor.

lau kāhi. Broad-leafed plantain *(Plantago major),* the seeds of which are a *mawai* (cathartic) to infants. Its purpose is to carry off the meconium. (A.) This broad-leafed plantain was used externally to "ripen" and heal boils, internally for diabetes and other ailments. (BHK; NEAL 792.)

limu kala. Seaweed *(Sargassum echinocarpum).* It was mixed with *limu līpoa* and given to children to help them gain strength.

lū. Small seeds of the *maula* plant, beaten into a juice and used as a purgative. See **pua-kala.**

mai‘a. Banana (*Musa* spp.). Sap or juice from cut flower buds was used to strengthen the body or clear the *‘ea* (coated tongue) of sores. The flower bud was pounded and mixed with other things, then the juice was squeezed and strained and taken to relieve stomach cramps. As an aid for constipation, boiled, ripe bananas were mashed, mixed with other ground-up plants and water, and then strained. The ripe fruit was also eaten for arthritis. (BHK; NEAL 245.)

manena. Medicinal herb *(Pelea cinera)* related to *mokihana*.

manewa. Grass, probably used for a medicinal tea.

ma‘o. Native cotton *(Gossypium sandvicense)*. Its flowers were partly dried and eaten along with other plants for relief from stomach cramps. A tea, made from *ma‘o* bark mixed with other roots and barks, was used to relieve stomach cramps. (BHK; NEAL 566.)

maulaili. Poisonous plant used to burn and scarify the skin. (CMH.)

māwai. Cathartic made from seeds of the *lau kāhi* plant. Given to children and infants.

milo. Fruit of the tree *Thespesia populnea,* which contained seeds used as a cathartic. (NEAL 563.)

moa. Name of a plant *(Psilotum nudum),* the stems of which were cathartic in effect when drunk in a tea. Its fine white spores were used in talcum powder. (NEAL 1.)

naule. Medicinal plant *(Argemone alba),* the seeds of which provided juice for a purgative. (NEAL 365.)

nini. Balm or ointment used for external application for wounds.

nīoi. Tree from Lana‘i and Moloka‘i, said to be fatal if touched. Legend has it that it was entered by the god Kālai-pāhoa o Kahuila-o-ka-lani, and thence became a poison tree that was worshiped as a god. (A.)

noni. Indian mulberry *(Morinda citrifolia)*. Its unripe fruit were pounded with salt and the mixture applied to deep cuts and broken bones. The juice of this mixture was used for the same purpose. Ripe fruit was used as a poultice to clear out the matter and core from an infected boil.

nonolau, lonolau. Bitter calabash used in medicine; *‘o‘opu hue,* name of the bitter calabash. (A.)

‘ōhia lehua, lehua. Variety of *lehua* tree *(Metrosideros collina)* popular in Hawai‘i. A mixture of slimy sap of a *hau* branch, several lehua blossoms, and water, were strained through coconut fibers, placed in a coconut shell, and then given to a woman in childbirth to ease labor pains. (BHK; NEAL 637.)

ʻoʻopu hue. Bitter calabash. (A.) Strong concoction made of green gourd and *kukui* nut used as an enema. (PE.)

paʻaliʻi. Medicine derived from the morning glory. (PE.)

pa-nini ʻawaʻawa. Aloe or star cactus *(Aloe vera)*. It looks like a cactus *(pa-nini)* and can be used as a medicine like *ʻawaʻawa*. When a leaf is cut a thick, sticky juice oozes out that can be used on burns. Or the leaf can be peeled and the juice inside placed on the burn. Sap or juice of the leaves is used for insect bites, sunburn, athlete's foot, and arthritis. (BHK; NEAL 196.)

papaʻa. Scab of a sore; red sugarcane, the juice of which was thought to be a love potion.

pāʻū o hiʻiaka. Vine like the *koali*, used as a cathartic. (A.) Pukui-Elbert records that Pele, one, found that this spreading vine had covered her baby sister Hiʻiaka from the sun.

pēkaʻa. Sea bean of the *kaeʻe* vine *(Mucuna gigantea)*, native to a large area from India to Polynesia. In Hawaiʻi, it is found at low elevations. The seeds are used in powder form as a purgative, or strung for making leis. (NEAL 462.) See **kipa, pīpā.**

pia. Arrowroot *(Tacca leontopetaloides)*. When ground to a fine powder it was used for a bleeding ulcer, bowel disorders, and as talcum powder.

pīhelehele. Grated, as a potato that the sick may swallow more easily; to mash, pulverize.

pīholoholo. Thin, watery *poi* made of *kalo* or potatoes, suitable for consumption by the sick. (A.)

piʻi. Any medicine acting as an emetic, *he lāʻau piʻi.*

piʻikū. Drink made from the leaves, branches, and fruit of the *kukui* tree and used as a medicine; a gargle.

pili kai. Morning-glory type of vine, the seeds of which were used for medicinal purposes; cathartic for children.

pīōʻō. To force into the mouth of a sick person, too ill to feed himself, a medicine made of potatoes, taro, and seasoned with herbs.

pīpā. Seed of the *kāʻeʻe* vine and the medicine made from it, like a bean. See **kipa, pēkaʻa.**

pōpolo. Black nightshade *(Solanum nigrum* or *S. nodiflorum)*, a smooth, cosmopolitan herb that has a history of interbreeding with poisonous plants but is also a valued source of medicines. The fruit was used for infants subject to a disease called the thrush. Roots were chewed for colds, and the juice was used in cataract operations. Inflamed tendons could be treated by rubbing with this juice. Bruised leaves were rubbed over the stomach area to relieve digestive problems. (NEAL 744.)

pua-kala. Prickly poppy or beach poppy *(Argemone glauca).* Its yellow sap or juice was used to lessen pain from toothaches, neuralgia, and ulcers. (BHK; NEAL 367.)

'uala. Sweet potato *(Ipomoea batatas).* Its tuber, scraped and mixed with the scrapings of a ti stem, then warmed and strained, induces vomiting. (BHK; NEAL 706.)

'uha loa or hi'a loa. Waltheria *(Waltheria americana).* Bark of the native roots was chewed and swallowed for sore throats. Roots, leaves, buds, and flowers were mixed with other plants and then pounded. The juice was squeezed out, strained, and heated, to be taken for asthma. (BHK; NEAL 575.)

'ulu. Breadfruit *(Artocarpus altilis).* All parts of the tree give a milky sap used alone or in a mixture with other plants to give relief for skin diseases, cuts, scaly skin, or mouth sores. (BHK; NEAL 302.)

MEDICINE: Treatment

This category deals with therapy for the ill and their convalescence. It reflects a mixture of modern medicines and native equivalents, involving the priestly procedures of the *kahuna lapa'au.*

In practice, Hawaiians created a rich lore of medicine production and a routine of diagnosis and treatment that was quite advanced. The object of their study, of course, was the human body. Their medicines were derived from plants—trees, seeds, leaves, stems, fruits, roots, and bark—and from animals and minerals.

Probably the most frequent regimen of treatment called for cathartics, and these they had in ample supply, all derived from natural sources.

The medicines ran the gamut from nauseating to acrid to modestly palatable. But the practitioners of old depended more on a holistic approach, trusting their invocations to the gods rather than medicines in their efforts to achieve a restoration of harmony between man and nature.

'ana. Kind of light, siliceous sponge found in the sea, used by nurses to treat the *'ea,* the white fur or thrush on a child's tongue.

'ao'o. Hard, polished bone used in ancient times for infanticide. See **koholua.**

hahano. To use the syringe; to give an injection, as an enema (*hano*).

hailepo. To evacuate the bowels; an ancient pestilence; diarrhea.

hakahaka. Empty feeling in the abdomen after birth. This was relieved with hot broth and herbs including a hot tea, *kauna'oa pehu* or *ko'oko'olau*.

hau'oki. Medicine given to women in labor, made of *hau* bark.

he akua pua. Kind of deity supposed to reside in some person who was called Kahupua and who had power to send Pua to do injury to others. *He akua pua* was applied to some kinds of sickness, inducing delirium, a sickness supposed to be sent by someone in anger. (A.)

hehu. To purge from the effects of medicine with water and juice; enema.

hoene. Medicine for abortion; abortion; to use a douche or enema for cleansing purposes.

hohahuhahu. To cause frequent bowel evacuations; to purge.

ho'ohahu. To purge, as with a cathartic.

ho'okahikahi. To rub salve or ointment on the body; to *lomilomi* (rub) gently.

ho'okakekake. To mix medicine with food to ease its taking.

ho'onahā. To clean the bowels with a purgative.

ho'opapa. Condition of a woman with a board tied to her abdomen to secure conception.

ho'opi'opi'o. To perform ceremonies with medicine sorcery in order to kill. The god to whom such a prayer was made was Pua. (A.) A form of sorcery in which the practitioner touched a part of his own body in the same place as the victim's pain. Were the victim to see him doing this, he could imitate the action and send the black magic back. (PE.)

ho'opohala. To recover from illness through rest and quiet.

huaale. Pill; medicine in the form of a little ball to be swallowed whole. *Lit.,* seed to swallow.

imu loa. Long oven used for sweating the sick. A thick layer of greenery was placed over hot coals, and the patient laid thereon with a coverlet of *kapa* which confined the steam. The practice of exorcism was performed with prayers to Lono and Hina.

kaha ea. To operate, as on the sick.

kahe. To subincise the foreskin.

kahikahi. Gentle massage performed by those skilled in *lomilomi;* to draw thumb and fingers with a slight pressure over any part of the body.

kāhinu. To rub over with oil; to anoint.

kahuna hāhā. Second highest, after the *kahuna lapaʻau* and an expert diagnostician and healer. He explored the body with his palpating hands to detect and treat illnesses.

kahuna lapaʻau. Top man among *kahuna* specialists. Kindly in temperament, apt in counsel, he represented the highest form of healing. Such a specialist started study at five years, learning the medical herbs and the causes and remedies of illnesses.

kanawao. Tree (Broussaisia) which, according to an old belief, aided fecundity. (PE.)

kāpaʻi. Any remedy prepared for rubbing externally; to pound gently, as on one's flesh to promote circulation.

kīkoni. To pierce or incise a swelling.

kīpola. To apply a warm wrapper to a sick person to assist in treatment. Also called *kīpolapola*.

koholua. Instrument of polished stone for abortion. See **ʻaōʻō.**

kōkō. To press, as in massaging; to set a broken bone by applying pressure.

komohia. Quarantined. (CMH.)

konekonea. Convalescing; restored to health.

konini. To revive after fainting; convalescent.

kualima. Medicine of "fives," for example, three *opae* (shrimp) mixed with two dips of *poi* to fill the vacancy of an extracted tooth. (CMH.) This word refers to doing something five times: medicine given for five days, or five times in one day, and so on.

kupukupuʻule. Plant used to scarify the skin. (A.)

lāʻau hoʻohiamoe. Narcotic; medicine to induce sleep. See **lāʻau moe.**

lāʻau lapaʻau. Medicine, as herbs, roots, or other compounds for relief of the sick.

lāʻau make. Name common to all poisonous herbs.

lāʻau moe. Medicine causing sleep; opiate. See **lāʻau hoʻohiamoe.**

lāʻau nahā. Cathartic medicine.

lāʻau pā. Ancient drug given to produce abortion or prevent fecundation.

lāʻau piʻi, lāʻau hoʻopiʻi. Emetic. *Lit.,* medicine to cause vomiting.

lapa. Bamboo instrument used in infanticide, before or at the birth of a child. (A.)

lomi, lomilomi. To massage or chafe the limbs and body of one weary or in pain.

māhola. Spreading out and distending of the stomach. For example, squid *(heʻe)* might be fed to a patient, in the belief that relief would follow and cause the illness to flee.

mālena. Medical bark; ashes of bamboo or *makaloa* sedge used for medicine.

māwai. Any cathartic medicine.

nini. Medicine for external wounds; balm or ointment. (Ier. 46:11.)

ʻōmilo. Medicine or operation to effect abortion.

ʻōpā. To rub or knead the body.

pakelo. To make an injection; to prepare an enema of *hau* bark for imbibing.

pale keiki. One who acts as a midwife; to deliver a child. (Kin. 38:28.)

pani pūpū. Operculum of a small marine shell used to remove a foreign body, thus its name, "eye-stone." It is put into the inner corner of the eye under the lid and works its way to and out of the outer corner, usually bringing out the foreign body.

papakiʻipiʻipiʻi. Massive accumulation in the large, stationary bowel. It is treated by insertion of a hollow bamboo syringe to blow water into the bowel.

piʻi. Any substance acting as an emetic.

pīōʻō. To force into the mouth of a sick person a medicine made of potatoes, *kalo,* and other things, with something fragrant such as herbs. This technique is used with those too ill to feed themselves. (A.)

pōʻahā. Ball wound with a hollow on one side to apply to a swelling. (A.) A ring, as of *kapa,* about a sore to prevent friction. (PE.)

pōʻala. Medicine prepared in a form to be swallowed whole, as pills or capsules; to gargle.

pohala. To be healed; to recover from sickness; to revive after fainting.

pōhuehue. Beach morning glory *(Ipomoea pes-caprae).* Its leaves were crushed for rubbing over the abdomen of a mother after childbirth. A clean blossom of the flower was often placed over a circumcision wound serving as a protective cap and helpful to healing.

polapola. Bright, as the face of one recovered from illness.

pōpolo. Plant *(Solanum nodiflorum)* used as a medicine, formerly valued for ceremonies. The leaves were pounded, placed in thin cloth, and positioned on the fontanel of a child in treating a cold. (DK.) Leaves were also cooked and eaten as a pot herb.

puahilohilo. Breaking or cracking of the skin from disease; scaly appearance of the scarfskin.

pua ʻilima. Cathartic medicine from the *ʻilima* blossom. Mothers chewed the flowers and fed them to babies.

pūholoholo. To take a sweat bath. Perspiration was produced by steam coming from a thick carpet of greenery laid over a fire on rocks in the ground. The patient stayed close to this steam heat covered with a *kapa* or mat.

pūlima. Fire kindled for the benefit of a sick person, a practice of ancient physicians. (A.)

pūlimu. Ceremonial cleansing for the sick at which *kapu* food was burned.

pūliʻuliʻu. Small gourd in which the *lāʻau waiike* (medicine) was made. (A.) Kidney disease that impeded urination.

uha loa. Native downey weed *(Waltheria indica)* that grows in tropical areas. (A.) The bitter root is used medicinally by Hawaiians for tea. The juice relieves a sore throat with action similar to aspirin. (NEAL 575.)

ʻūpī. To inject fluid into a narrow orifice; syringe.

waianuʻukole. Soft, porous stone used in the practice of medicine, or for squid sinkers. (MALO 19.) *Obs.* (PE.)

waikī. Medicine made of *ipu ʻawaʻawa,* the bitter calabash gourd, for injections. Also called *ipu ʻawahia, pīpā, welo.*

walehau. Medicine from the slippery sap of the *hau* tree, chewed to relieve constipation. (PE.)

welo. Native medicine; also *waikī, ipu ʻawahia, pīpā.*

MEDICINE: Well-Being and Distress

An important class of specialists—the *kahuna lapaʻau,* or medical practitioner (*Lit.,* treatment expert)—was the product of an evolving, centuries-long study and observation of human anatomy, physical processes, and mental characteristics. The terms in this category and others support the claim that, despite their devotion to their gods and superstitions, these *kahuna lapaʻau* had developed a profession worthy of attention from modern physicians.

The role of the missionaries in creating a written form for the Hawaiian language seems to have been especially significant for medical terminology.

ʻaʻā. Dumb person; to be dumb. (Puk. 4:11.) Dwarf, small person. (Oihk. 21:20.)

'aka. To laugh, deride.

'amo. To wink, as the eye. (2 Kor. 15:52.) To twinkle. See **'imo.**

'api. To throb, beat, as a pulse.

haha. To breathe hard, pant for breath, as if in haste.

hāhā. To feel, palpate; to grope, as a blind person. (Kin. 27:12, 21.)

hakakē. To stand on stilts; to stand, as a spider on long legs.

hanunu. Bent-over, stooped, stoop-shouldered. See **nanai.**

hāpauea. Short of breath, as applied to invalids and the aged; the feebleness of old age.

heana. Corpse, especially of a casualty in battle. (Kanl. 28:26.)

helehelena. Appearance of a person; one's form, contours, and especially face. (Dan. 10:6.)

hilikau. Tripping in one's walk; to stumble.

hohopa. Spare in frame, as a man. *He kanaka hohopa,* a thin, spare man.

hoko. Fat or fleshy, as buttocks or thighs.

honi. To smell, as an odor; to sniff, as a perfume.

ho'okē. To blow the nose.

hulahula. Involuntary twitching of the eyelid, taken by some as a prediction of rain or personal unhappiness.

hulilī. To shiver, as with wet and cold.

ihu kūmene. Blunt nosed, short nosed, pug-nosed.

'imo. To wink, twinkle; winking, twinkling. See **'amo.**

kana. The outside of the neck; protuberance of the windpipe; Adam's apple.

kani'ā'ī. Throat; Adam's apple; *Lit.,* hard neck.

ke'ehi. To stamp with the feet; to kick; to brace with the feet; to "put one's foot down."

kīkala. Hollow of the back between the hips; coccyx, bone, hip. (Lunk. 15:8.)

koe. To spit, discharge phlegm.

kō'ele. Tall man.

kōnāhua. Fat, fleshy, as a man. (Lunk. 3:17.) Kidneys. (Puk. 29:13.)

kuhinia. To eat to the full; to be satiated with food, hence, to be fat.

kumu pepeiao. Mastoid process behind the ear; ear bone.

kūnewa. Sleep, heaviness for want of sleep; fatigued.

mane'o. Ticklish, itchy; pricklying sensation.

manunu. To crack or break against each other, as with bones; tremor, as in an earthquake. Also called *'u'ina, 'u'u'ina.*

mimilo. Curling of hair on top of the head.

muku. Distance from the ends of the fingers of one hand to the elbow of the opposite arm when extended. See **paukū.**

naʻau. Small male intestines, which the Hawaiians supposed to be the seat of thought, intellect, and the affections. See **ʻōpū.**

nahenahe. Gentle mannered, soft-spoken.

nahu. To bite, as a human, dog, or serpent; to gnaw, to bite off, as a shark; to sting, as beating rain.

nakinaki. Stricture, difficulty in breathing, as with an attack of asthma.

nanai. Difficult to climb, as a cliff; humped over as a result of stiffness. See **hanunu.**

nū. To cough, sigh, groan; mentally disturbed, worried, agitated.

okuʻu. To sit hunched up with a covering over the shoulder, arms across the breast, as if cold; to sit in any position to keep the head up; to squat.

ʻolāʻolā. To snore while sleeping; to gargle.

ʻōʻōhu. Round-shouldered or bent with age; stoop-shouldered man.

ʻōpū. Abdomen, the seat of thought. See **naʻau.**

pākole. Short. Also called *pākolekole, pōkole.*

paukū. Distance from the fingertips of one hand to other elbow extended. See **muku.**

peku. To kick with the foot. See **keʻehi.**

pepeiao. Ear; to hear.

pōkole. Short. See **pākole.**

pōnaha. Arms bent akimbo, as in a circle or arc of a circle.

poupou. Short and stocky of stature. See **ʻaʻa.**

pula. Eye affected by a small bit of foreign matter.

ʻūhekeheke. Full, plump, as applied to the cheeks; large, fleshy, and weak, as a fat man.

ʻūpehupehu. Large, fleshy, but weak, as a fat man.

ʻuʻulukai. Swollen, dropsical, fleshy, weak.

MENTAL HEALTH: Feelings and Concerns

This category concerns a wide range of human reactions and is remarkable for the unusual number of Hawaiian words for each of several English words: for example, anger, desire, fear, grief, hate, and opposition. There is a certain subjectivity in these emotions, but intellectual Hawaiians were able to coin appropriate words and to use them with clarity and precision.

'ā. Anger. *Ua ho'a 'ia kona 'ā,* his anger was aroused.

'a'ā. To burn, as anger. (Kin. 30:2.) To be silent, still, lonely; to send love in compliment.

'a'ahuwā. To speak contemptuously; to deride.

ahonui 'ole. Impatient. Without *'ole* the word means patient, enduring, or forbearing.

'aiā. Unbelieving, irreligious; unprincipled or ungodly person. (Hal. 14:1.)

akamai. Wise, smart, expert, witty; *akamai ma ka na'au.* (Puk. 28:3.)

ake. To desire or yearn for something. (Nah. 23:10.) *Ake nui no lakou e ha'ule ka ua,* they greatly desired that rain should fall.

ālai. To oppose, obstruct. *Ua ālai e ka hilahila a hiki 'ole ke pane aku,* he/she was hindered by shame and could not answer.

'alalehe. Fretful, plaintive, as a child who is weak or hungry.

aloha. Love, sympathy, charity, salutation, gratitude.

'ālunu. Covetous, greedy of gain. *Waiwai 'ālunu,* property taken unlawfully. (Puk. 18:21.)

'āna'anea. Foolish; stupid, as one influenced by sorcery.

'āniha. Hardhearted, unfriendly, angry.

ano. Awe, reverence, fear. See **ho'āno.**

'ano'i. To desire very strongly; to covet.

'ānoni. To doubt, be in suspense; confused in making a judgment. Also called *'ānoninoni.*

'āpaha. To doubt; a doubter.

'ā'ume'ume. To act with opposition; to pull away in contention. *'Ā'ume'ume na kānaka i ka ia,* the people contended for the fish.

aumihi. To sorrow, repent; to grieve for the loss of something.

aumoa. To care for.

'auwaepu'u. To oppose; laziness, indifference.

auwē. Expression of wonder, surprise, fear, pity, or affection. *Auwē kākou,* alas for us. (1 Sam. 4:7, 8.)

'e'ehia. Awe, dread, fear, reverence. (Kin. 28:17.)

'ele'ele. Hate.

'eleu. Bustling, moving.

'eli'eli. Reverence.

'ena. Angry, raging.

'eno. To be afraid, fearful.

ha'aheo. Proud, lofty, haughty, magnificent. (Oihk. 26:19.)

ha'akei. Proud, naughty, vain, scornful. (Hal. 1:1.)

ha'akoi. To brag, show off; egotistical.

hae. Deep affection for another. *Aloha hae hae,* from the yearning, breaking, or tearing of the heart.

haehae. To be moved with compassion; to sympathize with one in want. (Kanl. 28:32.)

haha. Proud; to strut.

haili. Something fondly remembered; thoughts of absent friends.

hakanū. Struck dumb with fright or astonishment; silent.

hakupehe. Careful and slow in speaking as to truth and propriety; hesitation in walking.

hāmau. Silent; silence. *E hāmau,* to keep silence as an act of worship. (Zep. 1:7.)

ha'oha'o. To wonder at; to be astonished. (Isa. 52:14.)

hapuka, hapukū. To be crowded together, as thoughts in the mind; to gather together indiscriminately or in haste. *Hapuka 'ohi'ohi,* to talk foolishly.

hāpu'uu'u. To be undecided as to what someone has said; to be uncertain as to the meaning of something said.

hāupu, hāu'upu. Yearning or strong feeling for someone; thought of remembrance.

hauwawā. Confused noise of a multitude talking all at once; to talk in vain; confused or in disorder.

hauwene. To be fretful; to cry.

hāwāwā. Blundering, unskilled, awkward, foolish; without energy or intelligence to attain any success.

hema. Left-handed.

hemahema. Awkward, unskilled, dull in comprehension.

heo. Proud, haughty.

hewa. Blunder, mistake, error; to be wrong; to transgress. (Isa. 43:27.)

hia. To desire, take delight in; to think, reflect.

hihipe'a. Someone entangled, as in a thicket; and so, bewildered and in grief.

hili hewa. Entangled, confused; to stumble, fall.

hili na'i. To believe or trust in; to have confidence in one's word. (2 Nal. 18:19, 20.)

hili na'i 'ole. Unbelieving.

ho'āno. Awe, reverence. See **ano.**

ho'ēmiemi. To hesitate, doubt; to shrink back, as the mind.

hō'ihi. Reverence.

hōkai. To blunder along; nuisance.

hole hele. To move about busily.

hoʻohalahala. To complain, find fault, criticize.

hoʻohehelo. Proud, particularly of one's dress or appearance.

hoʻoheno. To love, cherish.

hoʻohihiu. To cause fear; to make afraid, hence, to make wild, untamed.

hoʻohopohopo. To cause doubt, fear, anxiety.

hoʻoipoipo. To court, woo, make love.

hoʻokaʻau. Witty, clever, entertaining. *Hoʻokaʻauʻana,* time spent pleasantly.

hoʻohākālia. To delay, draw out the time.

hoʻokāpūhi. Witty, smart. This word is said to have been peculiar to Oʻahu.

hoʻokehakeha. To be proud, high-minded; to imitate a chief in manners and dignity.

hoʻokoko. To spill blood; to flow, as blood; angry.

hoʻokupaianaha. To amaze, surprise, to seem wonderful, strange, extraordinary.

hoʻolauaʻe. To cherish, as a memorable person or occasion.

hoʻolohe. To cause to hear; to listen, obey.

hoʻolono. To listen, obey, keep; obedient.

hoʻomāikeike. To cause to know well; to make known and understandable.

hoʻomainaina. To anger, cause anger.

hoʻomakaʻu. To cause one to fear; to frighten, make afraid, terrify.

hoʻomākeʻaka. To make laughter; to exercise wit; witty.

hoʻomalu. To bring under the protection of; to shelter, care for.

hoʻonāhili. To waste time by blundering or wandering off; to linger, hesitate.

hoʻonē. To be fretful; to ask for food, as a child; teasing, nagging.

hoʻononohuwā. To hate; to create jealousy and ill will.

hoʻopalai. Confused; to cause one to turn his face away; ashamed.

hoʻopūʻiwa. To be scared suddenly; to be startled, astonished.

hoʻopulakaumaka. Person with ambivalent feelings toward another, cherishing or wishing to injure.

hoʻoukiuki. To insult or offend, hence, to irritate.

hoʻouluhua. To annoy, weary, irritate.

hopo. To fear, be afraid.

hopohopo. Fear, fright, anxiety, uncertainty.

hūʻeu. Bold, fearless man; one who excites to action, good or bad. (A.) Witty, humorous, fun loving. (PE.)

huhū. Angry, indignant.

huikau. Confused, mixed-up, without order.

hūpō. To be in mental darkness; ignorant, savage, wild, idiot-like. (Hal. 119:130.)

'iha'iha. Anxiety of somone needing to answer a call to nature but restrained by the presence of another.

ihi. Feeling of respect or reverence for someone or something held sacred or majestic. In earlier days, this feeling applied to high chiefs. (Hal. 72:19.)

'ihi lani. Reverence for a chief; glory and beauty of heaven.

ihu ku. To turn up the nose in anger; contemptuous.

ihu pi'i. To turn up the nose in contempt.

'i'ini. To desire, yearn for, long for. (Kin. 31:30.) *Ka 'i'ini nui,* to greatly love one. Also called *'i'i.*

'ike. Sense of hearing or sight; to perceive mentally; to know, understand. (Kanl. 4:6.)

ikiiki. Grief, pain, suffering, as from pressure; to be weary of refraining from. (Ier. 20:9.)

ilihia. Overcome with awe and reverence at a happening; to be in great fear or dread with such.

'iloli. Unpleasant sensations of pregnancy; intense yearning and desire.

inaina. Angry, wrathful, hateful.

'ino. A strong intensive, used in both a good and bad sense. It expresses very great feelings of affection or hatred.

ioiole'a. Angry, quick-tempered, brisk, lively.

ka'alokuloku. Fearless.

kaena. To boast, glorify; to make pretences about what one has done. (2 Oihn. 28:19.)

ka'eo. Indignant or angry with negative or wrong activity.

kahaha. To wonder or marvel at; to be surprised with an idea or a thing; expression of displeasure, contempt; to doubt or be perplexed with a thing or idea that seems strange.

kahu ka 'ena. Anger.

kalalī. To walk proudly or stiffly; to walk or talk in a brisk, haughty way.

kali. To wait, hesitate, tarry; hesitancy in speech.

kānalua. To be in doubt; to hesistate between two things. See **ku'ihē.**

kani'āu. Deep-seated sorrow; to move about in sadness and grief.

kani 'uhu. To sigh, complain, groan, bemoan. Groaning, trouble, sorrow. (Isa. 30:6.) Groaning from oppression. (Lunk. 2:18.)

kapake'u, kāpēke'u. To complain vigorously, quarrel, disagree; to be on unfriendly terms.

ka'uka'u. To slow down, hesitate, delay.

ka'ulua. To be remiss in keeping a promise; slack, hesitant.

kāunu. To make love; the thrill of love. (PE.) To provoke feelings of jealousy. (A.)

ka wawa lapuwale. Foolishness, vanity; babbling, vain, foolish talking. (1 Tim. 6:20.)

kē. To oppose, struggle against, shove, criticize.

ke'eo, ka'eo. Displeasure; indignant at something wrong; resentful.

kekene. Jealous, envious.

kēueue. To push against, treat harshly, oppose someone.

kīna'una'u. To scold, threaten; to be evil and internally vile.

kīpona maka'u. Intense fear.

koa. Fearless.

kōanoano. Fearful.

kohi. To hold back, hinder; fear.

ko'i'i. To desire.

kolokolohai. Thoughtful, kind, humble. A term of respect for a chief or a commoner whose character is respected for probity and good conduct.

konā. Contemptuous, unyielding, haughty, angry, blustering.

kū'aki. Impatient, intolerant, annoyed.

kuano'o. Thoughtful, meditative, understanding.

kū'ē. To oppose; to be contrary; opposition, commotion, strife.

kūhili. To blunder, mistake.

ku'ihē. To hesitate, doubt; unbelieving, undecided. *Alaila, ku'ihē iho la kela no ke aloha i na mākua,* then she hesitated on account of love to her parents. See **kanalua.**

ku ka ihu. Proud.

kuko. Strong desire, good or evil; to lust, desire. *Kuko 'imi 'ole,* unrestrained desire. (2 Tim. 3:3.)

kūmākene. To grieve, lament, mourn, as for a deceased person.

kūnānā. Undecided, puzzled, hesitant, bewildered.

kūo'o. Fearless, ready, prompt in action; earnest, dignified, serious. (1 Pet. 1:13.)

kūpau. Fearful.

kūpiki'ō. To be agitated, as the sea; to be troubled, as the mind. (Isa. 57:20.) Largely the same as *kūpikipikio.*

lālama. Fearless, daring, adventurous, as a mountain climber.

lalau. Mistake, error, blunder. (Ioba 19:4.) To go astray; to wander.

lana ka mana'o. Thoughtful.

laukōnā. Angry, heartless, unfriendly.

laukua. Incoherent in speech; things put together irregularly or in confusion.

laupaʻapaʻani. Witty, playful, jolly, humorous. A word used by chiefs in flattering each other.

leho. Covetous. Also called *lekia, maka leho.*

lelehua. Thinker, planner; able to apply good mental powers.

leoleowā, leoleoā. To yell in a vociferous manner, noisily. To wish evil; to curse; to consign someone to death.

leo ʻole. Uncomplaining; considerate of others; giving generously; silent. *Lit.,* voice no.

liʻa. Thinking intensely on some subject; strong desire.

liha, liliha. Dreadful, fearful.

lili. Jealous, proud, overbearing; troubled by criticism. See **nini.**

loea. Ingenuity, skill, cleverness in planning and executing a project.

loheʻana. Hearing.

lohena. Hearing; to obey.

loka. Doubt, misbelief; state of mind, as disbelief in religious truth. See **maloka.** (1 Kor. 7:12.)

loloā. To fret.

luaahi. Fearful.

luhina. To care for.

luʻuluʻu. To be oppressed with sorrow. (Mat. 26:37.) To be troubled in mind. (Ioane 13:21.) Bent over from toil, pain, and sorrow.

makāʻeo. Anger.

makahahi. Wonder, amazement. *Ua haka mai lākou iaʻu me ka makahahi,* they stared at me in wonder. (Hal. 22:17.)

makahehi. To desire, admire.

makani. Angry; to show anger.

makaʻu. Fearful, afraid; causing fear or dread.

makaua. Vexed, troubled, afraid, harassed.

makaʻu kūhewa. Sudden fear; panic.

makauliʻi. To desire, covet.

makaʻu loa. Fearful.

makaʻu ʻole. Fearless.

makaʻūpē. Grief.

make. Desire, want.

makeʻe. Covetous, greedy.

makemake. Desire, want, wish.

makoa. Fearless, aggressive; to be hard with people; to be close, stingy.

mālama. To reverence; to obey, as a command; to care for.

mālama pono ʻia. Well cared for.

maloka. Disbelieving; to treat sacred things with contempt; to disregard the commands of a chief. See **loka.**

malu. Quiet, without care or anxiety; state of quietness and peace with others; favored with enjoyments and privileges; comfortable, as in the protecting shade.

manaʻo. Idea, concept, thinking, view, impression, feeling. *Manaʻo akamai,* spirit of wisdom. (Puk. 28:3.)

manaʻo ʻino. Evil feeling of hatred.

manaʻo ʻoʻio. To have confidence in. (Puk. 14:31.) To believe; to credit what one says.

manaʻo ʻonaʻo. Grief, sadness on parting with friends; to lament, mourn, pity.

manawahua. To grieve over the loss of a loved one.

manawahūwā. Jealous disposition.

manewanewa. Grief, mourning.

manini. Anger, wrath.

manuea. Blundering, slipshod, indifferent.

manukā. Slow, careless, blundering.

maopopo. To understand; to see clearly and plainly.

mehameha. Loneliness, aloneness, solitude. These are the last four syllables of the name Kamehameha I, "the lonely warrior."

memeki. Anger.

menemene. To have compassion upon; to pity. (Roma 9:15.) To fear for someone lest evil befall him.

mihi, mimihi. To be sorry; to regret, repent; a breaking away from a sinful course.

mīkolelehua. Power of reflecting; thoughtful.

minamina. To be sorry; to regret the loss of something; to have sympathy for; sorrow for others' misdoings. (Hos. 11:8.)

moakaka, mōakaaka. Clear, plain, intelligible, as the expression of a thought. See **mōlaʻelaʻe.**

mōhala, mōhola. To open or calm the mind; to be devoid of fear, as one in danger. (Kin. 40:10.)

mokuāhua. Grief, sorrow; to yearn with pity for someone; to be moved with affection toward someone. (Kin. 43:30.)

mōlaʻelaʻe. Easily understood; clear, explicit. See **moakaka.**

mū. To shut the lips and make no answer; silent.

mumule. Silent; to hold one's peace through grief and affliction. (Hal. 39:2.)

naʻanaʻa. Confused, complicated, perplexed.

na'au ali'i. Kindly, forgiving.

na'au'auwā. Depressed in spirit; deep anguish, intense grief.

na'au kūhili. Disposition to carelessness; blundering, indifferent.

na'au lua. Undecided, in doubt.

na'aupō. Dark-hearted; ignorant; to be willingly ignorant.

nāhili. To act awkwardly; to blunder, lag behind; confused.

na'ina'i. Sour, crabbed, as one's disposition; to oppose; to be ill-disposed.

nalu. To be in doubt or suspense; to wonder at; to search after any truth or fact.

namunamu. To complain, mutter unintelligibly.

nānā. To care for, take care of; to comfort one who mourns.

nauki. To cherish ill-will, stir up anger, fret, complain; to be impatient, irritating.

nāukiuki. Vexed, ill-tempered.

nāulu. To vex, provoke, anger. (Kanl. 9:22.)

nē. To fret, tease, nag; to cry for food persistently, as a child.

neku'e. Angry.

nēnē. To cherish; to think of, as with affection.

nini. Jealous. See **lili.**

nipo. To desire, yearn for, love.

no'eau. Wise, prudent. (Sol. 12:23.) Skillful, dexterous.

none. To fret, tease, nag, annoy.

noni. Confused, troubled, perplexed.

no'ono'o. Thinking, planning, reflecting; thoughtful, meditative.

nū. To think, reflect upon, ruminate.

nūkuke. Silent; refusing to speak.

nunu. To covet, as the property of another; greedy.

nunu'a. Confused; persons assembling informally, as a crowd.

ohaoha. To greet; fond recollection of a friend; strong affection; joy.

'ōhio. Reflection upon an absent loved one.

'ōhumu. To complain of or find fault with the conduct of a person or of something done. (Neh. 5:1.)

'ōkaikai. Angry, as the sea.

'ōkalakala. Boisterous, gruff, enraged, angry.

'ōnēnē. Fretful, complaining.

'ōnihi'ula. Angry, furious.

'ōpikopiko. Anxiety; to be concerned and depressed about impending danger; syphilis.

pahilolo. Tall, strutting; proud in one's movements.

pa'i a uma. Strong affection; lamenting or sorrowing over the absence of a loved one; endearing attachment to one dead or long absent; to slap the chest in grief.

pākuʻi. To oppose.

pālola. Palsied, stiff, awkward, useless.

pānewanewa. Grief, mourning.

pauaho wale. Impatient.

paulele. Confidence, trust; to have faith; to believe fully.

paumākō. Deep grief; mourning the loss of a friend. *I ka paumākō o koʻu naʻau,* when my heart is overwhelmed.

pihano. Silent; weak of voice; sitting still under *kapu* with no noise.

pīhoihoi. Anxious, worried, astonished. (Dan. 5:6.)

piʻilae. Vain, haughty.

pilihua. Silent from sorrow; warm feeling or attachment; astonished with fear and wonder. (Ier. 14:9.)

pilikia. To be in straits, difficulty; to be entangled in any way; lack of means or instruments for doing a thing; crowded with no room. (2 Nal. 6:1.)

piliwi. To believe.

piʻoloke. Confused, without order. *ʻE heʻe piʻoloke,* to flee in disorder. (Lunk. 20:41.) Noisy confrontation; to gabble; to be excited; to commit a blunder. *Hoʻo piʻoloke,* to disturb, to vex. (Ezek. 32:9.)

pohihi. Obscure, as language; puzzling, as a question; entangled, mysterious; hard questions. (1 Nal. 10:1.)

pōkaʻakaʻa. Confused; overcome by the weight of work.

polohina. Grief.

pololoa. To blunder, act awkwardly, go astray.

pōnaʻanaʻa. Bewildered, confused.

pūhili. Frustrated, confused.

pūʻiwa. To meet with surprise from any source; speechless from sudden excitement; startled, amazed, frightened.

pūkalaki. Gruff.

pūkani lua. Strong, energetic; severe in discipline; to oppose, as authority of a chief or leader; to contend, as from anger.

pūlama. To cherish, care for.

pumehana, pumahana. Warm, warmhearted, warmth of feeling or attachment. *Me ke aloha pumehana,* with warm *aloha.*

puni. To covet, desire; to be devoted, to be fond of.

punihai. Addicted to running; cowardly, fearful, afraid.

pupuāhulu. To be in a fluster, in a hurry about readying everything to be away; not prepared for a duty; bustling.

'ū. To grieve, mourn; expression of affection; unwillingness; not disposed to cooperate.

ui. To ask one or a series of questions; to inquire; to interrogate.

uilani. Restless under discipline; to be averse to restraint. *'A'ole anei he uilani?* Is he not in difficulty?

ukiuki. To be offended, vexed, provoked and very angry. (Neh. 4:1.) To be angry with and contemptuous of someone. (Kanl. 19:6.) To treat vengefully, to hate. (Kin. 50:15.)

uluhua. Vexed, annoyed, displeased. (1 Nal. 20:43.)

'upu. To desire strongly; to be strongly attached to a person.

wae. To choose, pick out; to sort the good from the bad. (Puk. 12:21.)

waha kole. Clamorous, noisy, boisterous, obstreperous, contradictory in speech. *Lit.,* raw speech.

walama. Mental distress; anguish, deep pain at something said. Also called *walania, walenia.*

weli. Fear, trembling; afraid, fear-stricken. Also called *weliweli.*

wiwo. Fearful, modest, timid, obedient.

wiwo 'ole. Bold, fearless. (Oih. 4:13.)

MOTION

Not unexpectedly, the words of motion found in this category apply more to humans than to inanimate objects and materials.

'a'alo. To dodge this way and that; to dodge a stone. A more common spelling is *'alo.* (1 Sam. 18:11.)

'a'ama. Motion of the hands as a person tries to seize hold of something, as a crab scampering down a steep rock; large black crab, edible, living on a rocky shore.

'a'e. To cross over. (CMH.) To pass, physically or mentally, from one state, condition, or place to another.

'āha'i. To flee, run away, carry off, chase.

akahele. To walk with measured tread in doing a thing; to go carefully. (A.) E hikiwawe mai i ka lohe, e ahele ho'i i ka 'ōlelo, "Be quick to hear, but slow to speak." (PE.)

akaholo. To sail or run cautiously.

'alakē. To jump; to run from one place to another.

alakō. To drag; to drag along the ground.

'alelele. To go or act as a messenger; to jump or skip.

'alo. To dodge, elude.

'alo'alo. To dodge or run, as from a shower; to turn this way or that; to dodge quickly.

alualu. To chase, follow, pursue. (Kanl. 32:30; Ios. 23:10.)

'apakau. To seize upon; to hold on to, as in falling.

au. Movement of any kind; eddy, tide; walking, floating, hurrying.

'au. To swim.

auau. To walk swiftly.

'aui. To shun a blow by inclining the head.

'au like. To swim evenly; to swim abreast, as two or more persons.

'āwala. To pull steadily on a fishline; to work steadily with energy.

'āwīwī. To walk easily and swiftly.

'e'e. To climb up, climb aboard; to mount a horse.

e manahalo a 'ike i ke 'au. Paddle until you know how to swim.

'eu. To crawl; crawling; to be sitting and rise to a standing position.

ha'alulu. To tremble with fear; to be troubled; to shake.

hā'awe. To carry a burden on the back; to put upon the back or shoulders for carrying.

hahai. To chase, pursue, hunt.

hahao. To place in a basket. (CMH.) To thrust in, cram down; to put into, as a person in prison; to put into one's head, as a suggestion.

hālalo. To lift from beneath.

hālāwai. To assemble, as people for worship or assembly; church, association, and committee meetings.

hāli'i. To spread out, as a sheet or mat. (CMH.) *Hāli'i i ka pākaukau 'aina,* set the eating table. (DK.)

halo. Motion of rubbing or polishing; to spread out, as the hands in swimming; motion, as the fins of fish in swimming. (Isa. 25:11.)

hamo. To stroke gently with the hand; to whitewash; to wash, rub, or brush, as in cleaning clothes; to plaster, anoint, smear.

hau. To strike, hit, beat.

hā'ule. To fall, drop from a height, tumble.

hei. Motion of the hands and fingers, as with dying persons and deaf-mutes; pastime of string figures or cat's cradle.

heihei. To run in a foot, horse, or canoe race; to dash, race.

hele. To walk; to walk lightly and swiftly.

hele kū. To walk upright.

hele mālie. To walk quietly, slowly.

hele wāwae. To walk, go afoot.

hiʻi. To lift up; to bear upon the hips and support a child, as with the arms. (A.) Hawaiians did not carry children unrelated to them, and commoners did not touch a chiefʻs child. (PE.) Finishing off the weaving of anything plaited, as a hat or mat. (DK.)

hīkākā. To stagger or reel, as a drunken man or a man carrying a burden. (Isa. 19:14.)

hīkau. To throw stones; to pelt. Also called *hiʻikau.*

hina. To topple, tumble.

hiolo. To tumble down, as a wall; to stumble or fall down, as a horse; to roll away and pass into oblivion; to void, set aside, as a law.

hoʻalo. To dodge, avoid, pass by.

hohi. To bend, as a bow. (CMH.)

hoʻi. To return, go back.

hoka. To squeeze or strain, as liquids through fibers; to press, take hold of, gather up.

holo. To move swiftly.

holo hīkī. To run swiftly, headlong.

holoholo. To take a walk.

holo māmā. To run fast, dash.

ho mai. Bring here; hand this way; give this way. (Ruta 3:15; A.)

hone. To prick, as a sharp thing. *Me ke wahi kaikele la ia e hone nei iloko o ka manaʻo,* like a needle it pierces into thought.

hoʻohala. To dodge, turn aside.

hoʻoheihei. To run swiftly, take part in a race.

hoʻoholo. To move swiftly.

hoʻohuli. To turn over; to cause an overturn; to convert.

hoʻokāwala. To throw with force.

hoʻokiʻekiʻe. To lift up.

hoʻokiwi. To stagger, as in drunkenness.

hoʻokuʻekuʻene. To move back and forth, as a fan in cooling; to wait on someone; to cool with a fan.

hoʻokuke. To drive off, throw away, banish.

hoʻomuʻu. To heap together; to make a collection. (A.) To miss, as in shooting marbles. (PE.)

hoʻopahūpahū. To do a thing quickly; a drumming or thrumming on a *pahu* or a drum. *Pahūpahū ke kūlina,* the corn explodes or crackles.

hoʻopālaha. To cause to fall; to push over.

hoʻopiʻipiʻi. To beat against the wind, as in a sailboat; to ascend, go up; to raise the cud, as ruminating animals.

hoʻopuehu. To scatter, disperse, rout.

hopu. To seize upon, as something escaping; to arrest, take as a prisoner. (Lunk. 21:21.)

huli. To turn; to curl over, as a wave; to change, as one's opinion; to turn, as pages of a book.

ʻiamo. To leap into water and not make a splash. Also called *lele kawa*.

ʻiliki. To dash; to strike against, as in war, or rain in a storm, or water in a torrent.

ilo. To creep.

kā. To strike or hit, as with one quick, hard stroke.

kaʻahina. To fall down and roll.

kaʻaholo. To move swiftly.

kaʻakaʻa. To open, as the eyes; to look upon, watch over.

kaʻalo. To pass to and fro; to cause to pass.

kaʻa niau. To walk quietly, slowly.

kaʻawale. To roll freely but with no control.

kaha. To pass by; to turn and go on.

kahi. To rub or press, as in a massage; to cut, comb.

kaʻi hele. To walk unsteadily.

ka i ka hoe. To pull on a paddle.

kākā. To cut and split or break wood, done anciently by striking sticks against stones or rocks; to strike, dash, beat, whip; to strike flint or steel for fire.

kakaʻa. To roll or turn this way or that; to stare or gaze in wonder; to squint.

kalalī. To walk proudly, briskly.

kanaliʻo. To stagger, walk like a drunkard.

kapalili. To vibrate, as a leaf in the wind; trembling or palpitation, as the heart in fear or joy.

kaukolo. To creep, follow, chase.

kauō. To pull, drag, or draw along; to escort, as a prisoner.

kauwo waʻa. To drag a canoe, particularly one shaped in the mountains and taken to the shore for finishing.

kiau. To walk swiftly and lightly.

kīkahakaha. To walk proudly.

kīkīʻalo. To dodge easily and quickly.

kikihi. To dodge quickly, especially with quick turns around corners.

kikī holo. To run fast.

kōʻai. To creep; to stir with a circular motion of the hand.

koene. To creep or back away; to move cautiously and carefully.

kohi. To dig a hole, as in the ground or for a well. (Puk. 7:24.)

kokolo. To creep, crawl.

kolo. To creep or crawl, as an infant; to crouch as an inferior.

komi. To massage.

koʻo. To push off, as with an oar or setting pole; to brace up anything likely to fall; to loosen, unbind.

kua. To strike down, as an image. (Oihk. 26:30.)

kue. To push with arms and shoulders.

kuemi. To walk backward or step backward, as from the presence of a chief.

kuʻi. To strike, hit.

kuia ka wāwae. To stumble.

kuʻi lima. To strike with the fist.

kuke ku. To push with arms and shoulders, as forcing a way through a crowd.

kūlapa. To jump, skip, or frolic about, as in sport.

kulipeʻe. To creep along, as a sick person; to walk awkwardly, stumbling along.

kūnaʻina. To push over, conquer.

kūnewa. To stagger, reel, totter with weariness.

kūʻoʻili. To climb steeply.

kuoni. To walk quietly, slowly.

kūpehe. To walk slowly, unsteadily, as a sick person.

kūpou. To walk downhill; to stagger because of the slope.

lēhei, lēkei. To jump, as a goat over a wall.

lele. To jump, fly; to depart, as the spirit of a dying person.

lele kawa. To leap into water from a cliff feet first without splashing, or with the least possible splash.

lele kīkoʻo. To take a flying leap.

lele koali. To jump rope; to swing on a morning glory vine *(koali)*.

lelele. To jump.

lele oʻo. To leap feet first into water. *Lit.,* piercing leap.

lele pā. To jump over a fence.

lomi. To massage.

lū. To scatter.

lūlū. To scatter, as seeds; to shake, as an earthquake, to fan, winnow; to disperse, as a people; to flap or flutter, as a sail.

māʻalo. To pass by, alongside.

mahiki. To jump, hop, leap, teeter, seesaw.

mahikihiki. To jump or fly; to vibrate rapidly, as the tongue; to shake, as an earthquake; to overturn, upset.

mākaʻikaʻi. To take a walk. (PE.)

makolo. To creep.

malo kai. To go swimming.

mōhala. To evolve; to unfold, as the leaves of a growing plant; to blossom; to be loosened or set free, applied to that which has been bound, coiled, or drawn up tight.

nāhoahoa. Wound on the head and the pain connected with it; effect of a sunstroke on the head.

nanai. To walk, as with a stiff back.

ne'e. To move along horizontally; to hitch along; to move off.

ne'e mōkio. Movement.

neku'e. To rub with one's elbows.

newa. To stagger.

nihi ka hele. To walk quietly.

nou. To throw a stone; to cast stones.

nounou. To throw stones, as two persons at each other, back and forth.

'ōkupe. To stumble; to trip in walking; to sprain an ankle.

'oni. Movement, motion.

'ō'ō ihe. To throw a spear.

pāhi'a. To jump in an oblique manner from a height into the water, so that when rising to the surface the feet come up first.

pahu. To push over or down; to tramp down, as opposition; to hurl a spear; to burst forth with noise; to blunt.

pakī. To strike with the palm of the hand; to spatter, as water; to dash in pieces, as plopping a melon on the ground.

pakīpakī. To sail along; to divide the water, as the keel of a ship; to move sideways. (A.)

pālaha. To stumble; to trip and fall.

pane'e. To move along, drive back, push out; to shove along, as a canoe on the sand. *Pane'e i kua,* to progress.

paopao. To beat or bruise, generally. (Isa. 53:5.)

pehi. To throw; to pelt with stones.

pepehi. To strike, hit, beat, kill.

peu. To push up, thrust up, uproot.

pi'i. To walk up a hill or mountain; to ascend, climb.

pi'i mauna. To climb mountains.

pi'ina. To climb, ascend. The gatehouse at the Kamehameha Schools is called *Hale Pi'ina,* House of the Ascending Way.

pīnana. To climb, as a cat; to climb, as a mischievous child; to crook; to bend out of shape.

pipika. To rush against the sides of any confining object; to thrust or push against a wall; to flow or overflow, as a stream over a bank; turning aside.

pōhai. To go around, encircle; circle or group of people; gathering.

pulelo. To float in the air, as a flag; to hang loosely.

pūneʻe. To crawl or move humbly, as in the presence of a chief in earlier times.

punohu. To arise, as a high flame or column of fire or smoke; to fill out, as the sails of a ship. *He hina me ha nāhi ia no ka lua o Pele,* the gray-like smoke or steam of the volcano.

uhai. To chase.

uhai a holo. Eager pursuit.

unuhi. To draw out in numerous ways; to subtract, as in arithmetic; to unsheath, as a sword; to remove, as a ring from a finger; to translate from one language to another.

ʻūpoi. To sink, as in water; to cover, as a bird with its wing; waves breaking in quick succession.

wāwae. One who is afoot.

MUSIC: Instruments

There were only some sixteen or seventeen sources of music and sound in ancient times, but these sources developed to a good measure of refinement—despite the lack of contact with other cultures and the limited number of creative materials and tools. Most musical instruments were played with hands, feet, nose, or mouth. The chromatic scale and sophisticated solo and choral singing accompanied by modern Western instruments started only after Cook's discovery of the islands. Many words relating to the post-Cook period are included in this listing.

In the course of teaching native Hawaiians to sing hymns, the missionaries supplied the alphabet, compiled a dictionary, and published hymn books—some with music, others with words only. This was a prodigious accomplishment which had great influence in adapting ancient music to the new culture of music.

ʻakoleana. Accordion. See **koliana, pilaʻumeʻume.**

hapa. Harp. See **kinola, lila.**

hoehoe. Sorrowful sound, as played on a nose flute.

hōkeo kani. Wind instrument, as in a band.

hōkio. Small gourd whistle; musical pipe played with the mouth. (1 Sam. 10:5.)

hōkiokio. Wind instrument, pipe, gourd; to whistle. (Isa. 5:12.)

'ili'ili. Pebbles used in dances to make rhythmic clicks.

ipu heke. Drum made either of the single gourd or two large gourds of unequal size fixed with a smaller atop the larger. The top gourd was the *heke,* the lower was the *'olo.*

ipu heke 'ole. Drum made of a single gourd with no top section.

ipu hula. Dance drum of two gourds fastened together with glue and *olonā* cord.

ipu pa'i. Gourd drum. *Lit.,* drum pound.

kā'eke'eke. 1. Anciently, a drum made of the hollowed trunk of a coconut tree covered with sharkskin, said to have been introduced by La'amaikahiki when he returned from Kahiki, Tahiti. (A.) 2. Bamboo pipes of varying lengths, representing the chromatic scale, tapped on a hard surface to produce soft, well-rounded notes. (PE.) The first commercial revival of this long unremembered art was initiated by Ken Darby for Capital Records when he researched the "hollow tubes" in the Bishop Museum. He hired Hawaiians to prepare bamboo trunks to fit the chromatic scale, trained a group of Kamehameha Schools students to play them, and marketed the results in a recording, *Ports of Paradise.*

kā'eleloi. Sound of a roll or ruffle, as made on a drum.

kā lā'au. Hardwood sticks used to produce rhythmic sounds to accompany dancing.

kaleoneke, kalionete. Clarinet.

kī hoalu, kī ho'oku'u. Slack key, where the outside strings of a guitar are turned to D, not E. The unchorded strings are picked individually.

kīkā. Guitar.

kīkā kila. Steel guitar, a modern instrument invented by a student at the Kamehameha School for Boys.

kinola, kinora. Harp. See also hapa, lila and autoharp, pila hapa.

kōheoheo. Alternate name for the nose flute; one of the instruments used in courting.

koliana. Accordion. See 'akoleana, pila'ume'ume.

kumepala. Cymbal. *Kumepala wala'au,* tinkling cymbal. (1 Kor. 13:1.)

kuolo. Small drum, timbrel. (Hal. 92:3.) Resonate, as the voice of a chanter. *Hula kuolo,* a dance or hula drum.

kuolokani. Ancient musical instrument used at *hula* dances; timbrel. (Puk. 15:20.) Psaltery. (2 Oihn. 9:11.)

kūpe'e niho 'ilio. Dance leglets.

lila. Harp. See hapa, kinola.

melokiana. Melodeon.

niāukani. Rude Jew's harp made of the midrib of a coconut leaf. (A.) True Jew's harp made of a thin, one-by-four-inch piece of wood, with a coconut midrib or bamboo strip lashed lengthwise. (PE.)

oeoe. Roarer.

'ohe. Musical instrument of the flute family.

'ohe hano ihu. Nose flute. Also called *hano*.

'ohe kani. Flute. *Lit.*, bamboo playing.

'ohe puluka. Nose flute. *Lit.*, bamboo flute.

'ōkani. Organ.

pahu. Hollowed-out coconut tree trunk with a sharkskin fastened tightly over the upper end of a tympanum. See **pūniu**.

papa hehi. Platter-shaped board on which the *hula* dancer placed his foot while standing on the other. The center of the board was held above the ground by a wooden rod placed under it. The dancer moved his foot as a treadle to rock the board, or *papa hehi*. While doing this the dancer also beat out the rhythm with a pair of sticks (*kā lā'au*) one held in each hand. (KILO.)

piano. Piano. *Eng.*

pila. Early name for a fiddle; any musical instrument. See **waiolina**.

pila hapa. Autoharp. *Lit.*, fiddle harp.

pilapuhipuhi. Harmonica, mouth organ.

pila'ume'ume. Accordion. See **'akoleana, koliana**.

pū. Any musical instrument that would make a large sound by blowing upon it; trumpet, conch shell, bugle. *I na pū kiwi hipa 'ehiku*, seven trumpets of rams' horns. (Ios. 6:4.)

puhi'ohe. Flute; to play a flute.

pū'ili. Rattles of split bamboo used for tempo and rhythm for dancing.

pū kani. Trumpet; any wind instrument. (1 Oihn. 13:8)

pū lā'ī. Trumpet made by twisting or rolling up a ti leaf. (CMH.) Ti-leaf whistle. (PE.) *Pū lā'ī* is a contraction for *pū lau kī,* the leaf of the ti. *Lau kī* became *lā'ī* and has to be a ti leaf. (KILO.)

pū lau niu. Whistle made from the rolled-up coconut leaf.

puluka. Flute. *Eng.*

pūniu. Small knee drum made of a coconut shell covered with the skin of the *kala* fish as a tympanum. The drum was tied to the thigh of the player who performed on both it and the large drum. The *pahu* and *pūniu* produced different drum sounds. See **pahu**.

pū puhi. Wind instrument, conch shell, horn, trumpet.

'ūkēkē. Narrow bow up to two feet long with two or three strings. It was held at the "tuning" end between the lips, and while the strings were strummed and with the mouth cavity as a resonator chamber, a muffled message could be heard. This instrument was used for amusement and in love making. (H. Roberts, Dover ed. 25.)

'ūkēkē hahau. Jew's harp, a small lyre-shaped instrument. When placed between the teeth and strummed it gives a pulsating sound. (1 Sam. 10:5.)

'ūkēkē hao. Jew's harp. *Lit.,* metal musical bow. (PE.)

'ūkikē. Ancient musical instrument; kind of Jew's harp. (A.)

'ūkulele. Ukulele. *Lit.,* jumping flea.

'ūlili. Musical instrument made of three small gourds pierced by a stick. A string was wound around the stick after passing through the center gourd, pulled, and released like a yo-yo. This caused the outer gourds to whirl creating the musical sound. Also called *'ūli'uli'u.*

'ulī'ulī. Gourd topped with feathers and partially filled with dried seeds, used as a *hula* rattle.

'ūpoho. Bagpipe.

waiolina. Violin. See **pila.**

waiolina kū nui. Bass violin.

MUSIC: Notes

This category is in some respects a glossary. The chromatic scale with its notes (most Europeans called them, do, re, mi, and so on) is defined. Also included are many noises described as musical sounds. There are references to pipe and nose flute playing, rattling of stones, striking of sticks, beating of drums, along with some allusions to modern music from Western countries. Today, with the infusion of other cultures into the Hawaiian culture, music has reached glorious heights of expression in Hawaiian, English, and other languages, in song, dance, and instrumental ensembles.

alapi'i mele. Musical scale—*pā, kō, lī, hā, nō, lā, mī, pā.* See **pākōlī.**

'anu'u. Interval in music; interval of a major second. See **pale, wā.**

hā. Fourth note in the scale, fa.

ha'a. To dance, here connected by Hawaiians with singing. (A.) A dance with knees bent. (PE; 1 Sam. 18:6.)

hapa. Half note in music.

hekili. Thunder; to thunder; voice from the clouds.

heluhelu. To read music.

hoʻoheihei. To drum; to beat the *heiau* drum; a playing of the drum.

hoʻokani pila. To play a musical instrument; to make a musical sound; to ring a bell; to sing for joy.

hoʻopaʻa. Drummer who chanted and drummed for the *olapa hula* dancers.

hoʻopahu. To beat the *pahu* (drum).

hua. Term for a note in music; to read music.

hua hapa. Half note in music.

hua liʻiliʻi. Grace note.

hua mele. To read music.

hua ʻōkoa. Whole note in music.

kā lāʻau. Striking two rhythm sticks together, as in *hula* music; stick dancing.

kani ka pila! Play music! (PE.)

kawewe. To clatter, as in the movement of plates; to make a rustling noise.

kāwōwō. To roar, as a waterfall; to give a rushing sound, as a strong wind; to rumble, rattle.

keha. To sing or repeat a song. Also called *kehaluha*. (A.)

kio. To blow on a pipe; to blow on a leaf across the lips, producing a sound through vibration. *Kiokio* means to play on a pipe or other wind instrument. (A.)

kō. Second note of the musical scale, re.

koʻele. Slight knocking or tapping.

koheoheo. Nose flute, less used than *ʻohe hano ipu.*

koʻokoʻo. Staff or five lines on which music is written.

kumu pākōlī. Three of the syllables used in solmization in practicing vocal music; staff or five lines on which music is written.

lā. Sixth note of the musical scale, la.

leo mele. Song; musical sounds; vocal music generally.

lī. Third note in the musical scale, mi.

mea himeni. Singer of hymns. (PE.)

mele. Vocal music; chant, song; words of a song, poem. To sing in chorus, singly or with others. (Puk. 15:1.)

mī. Seventh note in the musical scale, ti.

mūki. To play on the *hōkiokio* or pipe, a wind instrument.

nākolo. Sound of rain on dry leaves; squeak of new boots; rumbling of thunder; roaring of the surf.

nīpolo. Striking the drum while chanting.

nō. Fifth note on the musical scale, la.

'olē. *Pū* or conch shell *(Charonia tritonis);* any wind instrument, as a trumpet, horn, cornet.

pā. First and eighth notes of the musical scale, do.

pākōlī. Musical scale. Coined as a short form to identify the scale, using the first three notes, *pā, kō, lī.* See **alapi'i mele.**

palalī. To sound softly, as a flute or gourd pipe. (A.) Any shrill, flutelike sound. (PE.)

pale. Musical term; interval of time or bar in music. See **'anu'u, wā.**

pihe. Wailing with a voice of sorrow; crying; confusion of voices.

pila ho'okani. Instrumental music.

po'o. Whole note.

po'olima. Half note.

pu'ukani. Pleasant; sweet, as the sound of a pleasing voice singing.

'uwalā'au. To make a noise, as a multitude; tumultuous sound; shout. (A.)

wā. Musical term, interval. See **'anu'u, pale.**

OCCUPATIONS

It would appear from the words and pertinent terms listed in this category, that government in the early days was overloaded with functionaries. Most of those positions related to the king, his supporting chiefs, staff, family, and followers.

Not all occupations are included here, but those appearing give evidence of a complex, well-structured social order, even though its people still lived in a stone-age civilization. But even with the limitation of material resources, a race of intelligent, articulate, and imaginative people was evolving in these islands.

'alihi kaua. General, commander; one who directs in battle.

a'o. Reading book or manual; to teach reading.

a'oa'o. To teach; to give instructions on how to act on occasion. (A.)

a'oheluhelu. To teach reading.

a'o hokū. To teach astronomy.

a'o kepela. To teach spelling; spelling book.

aʻo kilo. To teach punctuation; manual of punctuation.

aʻo loko. An inspiring teacher.

aʻo palapala. To teach writing.

aʻo piliʻōlelo. A grammar; to instruct in grammar.

apo hao. Formerly the king's guard; one of the followers of the king.

aumoaha. Sailor; to travel the open sea.

elele. Messenger; one who carried news.

haʻakualiki. Officer of the king's train who walked ahead of the royal party on a journey and made known the identity of the king and his purposes.

haʻakuʻe. Person who swung the fly brush over the king when he slept. (A.) Kahili-bearer for a chief or chiefess of the same sex. (PE.)

halepai pāpākāhi manuia. Captain of a white vessel. (CMH.) No data. (DK.)

hikoni. Indentifying mark on the forehead of a *kauwā* (slave).

hīpuka, kīpuka. Snare for catching birds.

hole ʻie. To peel the bark from the *ʻie,* vine for basket making; one who carved figures on the *kapa* beater.

holomoku. Sailor, seaman, passenger; anyone who sails.

hoʻokele waʻa. Steersman, helmsman.

hoʻomikanele. To act like a missionary. (CMH; PE.)

hulipahu. Second mate of a vessel. *Lit.,* binnacle turner. (PE.)

ʻīlio ʻaukai. Experienced sailor; seadog; a nickname.

ʻiʻo pono. Person entrusted with the care of the king, his person and effects, protecting him against their misuse in his possibly being prayed to death; blood relative, relation of a trusted friend.

kaʻa kaua. One skilled in warfare.

kaha keleawe. Worker in copper or brass; engraver.

kaha kiʻi. Artist; one who paints or draws; to draw or paint.

kaha kiʻi hale. Architect; to draw plans for buildings.

kahu. Pastor, guardian, keeper.

kahu kālai waʻa. Canoe builder.

kahu maʻi. Nurse.

kahu mālama. Custodian, caretaker.

kahu mālama hale. Housekeeper.

kahuna. Priest.

kahuna lapaʻau. Medical practitioner.

kahuna nui. High priest.

kahu pipi. Cattle rancher.

kaka ʻōlelo. Counselor, adviser, lawgiver, scribe, orator; one skillful in language.

kākoʻi. Adze maker.

kala. Public crier; one who summons people and chiefs to a special meeting or emergency.

kālai pōhaku. Stonecutter.

kālai waʻa. Canoe maker or carver.

kalawaiʻa. Fisherman; a professional. See **lawaiʻa.** (Mat. 4:18.)

kā luʻu wana. *Wana* (diver); the one who dives for *wana;* sea-egg, size of a turnip; sea urchin.

kamanā. Carpenter. (Mar. 6:3.)

kamanā kāpili moku. Shipwright.

kanaka ʻako lauoho. Barber; to trim, cut, shear, as hair.

kanaka hana. Worker, servant.

kanaka paeāea. Fisherman.

kanaka paʻi. Printer.

kāpili manu. Art of catching birds with lime or bird gum.

kauka. Doctor; medical doctor.

kauka lapaʻau. Medical doctor.

kawili lāʻau. Apothecary, pharmacist.

kealia. Place where salt water was brought or caused to flow inland, the sea then shut out, and the water evaporated. The salt remained; *aliapaʻakai,* salt. (A.)

kelamoku. Sailor.

kiaʻi. Guard, watchman. (1 Sam. 14:16.)

kiaʻi poʻo. Head guard; person who guarded the king; bodyguard.

kiaʻi puka. Porter; guard at the gate. (Ioane 10:3.)

kīkoni. Art or trade of finishing off canoes once they were dug out and shaped. See **hole ʻie.**

kīpuka. Snare for catching birds; sliding noose.

koe. Wool carder.

kualanapuhi. Officer who kept the flies away from the sleeping king. He waved the *kāhili,* a brush made of feathers bound on a handle.

kualapehu. Officer in the king's train; pugilist.

kūhea. Hunter, as of birds; one who imitated the whistling of birds, thus summoning them into his snare.

kumu. Teacher.

kumu aʻo. Teacher; source of learning.

lawaiʻa, lowaiʻa. Fisherman; expert. See **kalawaiʻa.** (Mat. 4:18.)

lawaiʻamanu. Hunter and catcher of birds; fowler. *Lit.,* to fish birds.

lawe hana. Workman.

limahana. Worker.

loea kālai'āina. Politician.

loio. Lawyer, attorney; to act the lawyer.

lolo. Lawyer.

lopā. Tenant farmer; one dependent on others for his livelihood.

luna kānāwai. Judge.

mahi'ai. Cultivator of the soil; tiller of the land; husbandman.

makālae. Fishing.

mākilo. Beggar.

mālama. Caretaker, custodian.

mālama hale. Custodian of a house.

mea ana 'āina. Surveyor.

mea pena. House painter.

ōlohe. Man who is a robber and yet skillful at the *lua,* art of bone breaking in fighting. (A.) *Hula* expert.

pa'a hana. Skillful in warfare.

pa'a ipu kuha. Bearer of the king's spittoon.

pa'a kū'auhau. One versed in genealogy.

pale keiki. Midwife.

paniolo. Cowboy. This word is a Hawaiian version of the Spanish *español.* Some early cowboys on Hawai'i ranches were Spanish.

pena hale. House painter.

pi'opi'o. Practitioner in sorcery who caused injury on his victim's body by touching his own. But the tables could be turned on the sorcerer if the victim saw him in the act and touched his own body in the same place.

puaa'a. Day laborer. (CMH.)

pu'upu'uone. Fortune telling; living in a strange house called *hale pu'uone.* (A.) Beach hut used by the sorcerer in teaching and practicing his art. (PE.)

'uao, 'uawo. Referee, umpire, mediator, peacemaker.

'ūhā kākau. Office of one of the king's attendants. (A.)

wa'ewa'e. Fisherman who cared for the *kū'ula,* stone gods of the fishermen.

OCEAN

The Hawaiian fisherman's constant observation of the restless sea, with its myriad changes, brought great advantages. This observation process gradually built up a fishing lore that enabled the fisherman to greatly contribute to the food supply. Every action of surf and sea was expressed in descriptive words.

'a'ai, 'a'ei. Action of the surf at high tide, as it dashes ashore and then recedes, thus depositing sand and gravel or eroding them depending on the season.

'a'aka. Dry, as the coral of the reef at low tide.

'ae. Rising tide.

'ae'aekai. Ebbing and flowing of the sea; froth of the sea.

'ae kai. Place in the sea where the surf breaks. (A.) Water's edge where land and sea meet. (PE.)

'ae oeoe. Continued sound of the surf. (CMH.)

āhua. Any place elevated in the manner of a high path; bank formed by sand at the mouth of a river; ford or passing place across a stream.

'ako'ako. To swell up, as a wave before breaking.

'akūkū. Rising of water when wind and current meet.

alania. Smooth, as the ocean, without ripple or wave.

'ale. Wave or billow put in motion by the wind. *Ka 'ale wai hau a ke kua,* water of the snow god. It was supposed that the gods made the snow.

'ale'ale. A moving, swelling, stirring, as the waves of the sea.

aniani. Winds. *Aniani,* blow softly; *aheahe,* a gentle wind; *nahe,* a gentle breeze; *Malanai,* one name of the northeast trade wind.

au. The current in the ocean.

'aui. To swell, as the sea in great rollers; to pitch.

'aui'ale. Swell of the sea, so called from the motion, passing by; not a small wave. (A.)

'aui'aui. To roll up, as a high sea.

aukaka. Place far out at sea where fish are caught with a hook. (A.)

aukūkū. Swelling up of the waters of the sea. (A.)

auwiliaku. Ebb tide. (CMH.)

hakukai. Stormy sea. (A.)

hālelelo. Caves presumed to be in the ocean; coral sea caverns.

hālu'a. Ripple on the water; the rising up of water from the wind.

hāo'eo'e. Chopping sea; uneven, as waves of the sea. (A.) The seas at Hōpoe, Puna, and Hawai'i were noted for their roughness. (PE.)

haukau. Choppy sea, something like the *kai kūpiki'o* (raging sea), very difficult to urge a canoe through.

hāuliuli. Rippling of the sea when the wind just begins to blow. (A.)

hī aku. Area in the sea beyond the *kohola* (reef flats) and inside the *kaiule* (the deep blue sea); a casting area for bonito.

hohonu. The deep (i.e., the sea).

holu. Depth of the sea; the deep ocean; flood tide. (A.) Ripple, as waves. (PE.)

hōlūlū. Mid-tide.

hoʻokahela. To come along, as the swell of the sea when it comes along the western coast of Hawaiʻi from the south; to flow along, as a high swell of the sea. Also called *kāhela*.

hūlili. The rolling up of the surf before it breaks; fluttering, quivering motion of a wave. (A.)

kai. The sea; sea water; flood; a current in the sea.

kai ahula. Foamy sea, as when wind and current are contrary; raging sea.

kai a malō, kai a maloʻo. Extremely low tide that exposes the reef. *Lit.,* dry reef.

kai a Pele. Tidal wave. *Lit.,* sea of Pele.

kai apo. Rising or high tide. *Lit.,* encircling sea.

kaiʻau. Place a little way out in the sea, beyond the *kuaʻau;* shallow place in the sea; basin in the sea.

kaiāuli. In the deep blue sea, beyond the *kohola* (reef flats).

kai ea. Rising tide.

kai ʻeʻe. Tidal wave.

kai emi. Falling, ebbing tide. See **kai make.**

kai heʻenalu. Place on or near a reef, like *kohola;* sea suitable for surf riding.

ka hele ku. Sea beyond the *poʻana;* second space beyond where the surf breaks and where a footing may still be found, *kaipapau.*

kai hōʻeʻe. Surf running above the land; high sea; tidal wave. Also called *kai ʻeʻe.*

kai hoʻi. Falling or ebbing tide; low tide.

kai kī. High water; high tide. (A.) Tide beginning to flow in. (PE.)

kai kōʻele. Very shallow sea, unsuitable for canoeing in. (A.) *Lit.,* a thumping sea, because the canoe thumps the coral. (PE.)

kai koʻo. To roll in; to rage, as a high surf; a rough, strong sea.

kaīkū. Middle tide, neither high nor low. Also called *kaimaumau.*

kai lānahu ahi. Very dark or blue water of the ocean. *Lit.,* coal of fire.

kai lipolipo. Deep sea, dark blue or black.

kai lū heʻe. The deep sea; *kai uli.* (A.)

kai make. Low water, ebb tide, calm sea; the Dead Sea.

kai malolo. Shallow place in the sea near the shore where the water is at rest; place of soundings.

kai malo'o. Low tide, ebb tide; when many places on the seashore are dry, or the coral and reef are bare. Dorothy Kahananui recalls the *kai malo'o* at Miloli'i, Hawai'i and Kaupō, Maui where she looked for *'opihi* and *pipipi* (shell fish). *Lit.*, dry sea.

kai maumau. Middle tide, neither high nor low.

kai mihi. Receding sea, as before a tidal wave.

kai moku. Middle tide, i.e., when the tide begins to recede. *Lit.*, cut tide.

kai nui. High tide.

kai nunuki. Irregular ebb and flow of the sea. (A.)

kai nu'u aku. Ebbing sea. *Kai nu'u mai*, a flowing-in tide.

kai 'ōhua. Place a short way out in the sea just outside the breaking surf. (A.) *Poana*, an eroding, undermining sea. (PE.)

kai 'ōkilo he'e. Place in the sea beyond the *kua au*, like *kai au*. (A.) A place in the sea where a fisherman would look for *he'e* (octopus) after blowing chewed *kukui* nut in the water to enable him to see clearly *('ōkilo)*. (PE.)

kai pāieaea. Calm, smooth sea; calm sea after a storm. See **pohu.**

kai piha. High sea, flood tide. *Lit.*, full tide.

kai pi'i. Rising, incoming tide; high tide.

kai po'ana. Name of the sea just outside where the surf breaks. Also called *po'ana kai*.

kai pū. Mid-tide. *Lit.*, lifeless sea.

kai 'ūlala. Area far out at sea; out of sight of land. (A.)

kai uli. Dark-blue sea. Both *kai o pelu* and *kai lū he'e* are areas in the dark-blue sea. (A.)

kai ulu. High tide.

kākaha. Shallow place in the sea; strip of narrow land near the seashore; shoal.

kākala. Breaking of the surf; surf comber; to form combers.

kāna'i. Place in the sea where the water lies smooth and calm like a road.

kilo he'e. Squid looking; person who looks and fishes for squid and octopus. The place for looking is just beyond the *kua'au*, the basin inside a reef.

ki'oki'o. Anything variegated, as spots in the sea—some areas calm, some ruffled. See **kipona.**

kipona. Variegated areas in the sea; some calm, some ruffled.

kīponapona. To be variegated, as the sea—sometimes calm, sometimes rough.

kīpuka. Opening, a calm place in the high sea or deep inside a shoal.

koʻakā. Place where a retreating wave meets one coming in, as over a coral shoal. This dashing process may dislodge and move pieces of coral. See **puaʻō**.

kohola. Bare reef, reef flats; shallow place of water some distance from the shore like Kalia on Oʻahu and as at Kona, Molokaʻi.

kuaʻau. Bare reef, *ke kohola;* dry place in the sea; basin in the reef; lagoon.

kua nalu. Outside of the surf toward the sea just before it breaks. See **poʻi**.

kuapaʻa. Coral reef or rock showing itself above water, though water may flow over it. (A.)

kūhela. High, unbroken swell of the sea as it moves along. See **kāhela**.

kūlana. Sea in a calm immediately after a high wind; state of the sea when wind and current are opposite. (A.)

kūʻono. Bay, gulf; indentation of the sea into the land. (Isa. 11:15.)

kūpikiʻō. To rage; to be in commotion, as water agitated by the wind; to be troubled mentally. (Ioba 30:27.)

kūpikipikiʻō. To rage, as the sea when wind and the water current are opposite. Early name for Black Point, Oʻahu.

lālahalaha. To rise and swell and move along, as the surf before it breaks. See **hoʻokahela**.

lipo. Deep water in the sea. *Moana lipo loa,* blue or black from the depth of the sea.

lipolipo. Great depth of the ocean gives the impression of deep blue or black.

lūlā. To be smooth, as the sea. To be still and calm, as the surface of the sea unruffled by the wind.

lulu. Calm area leeward of an island; protected.

malau. Calm place in the sea.

malina. Calm smooth place in the sea. (A.)

malino. Calm, as the surface of the water without wind.

malolo. To ebb and flow, as the ocean, much more than usual. (A.) Low as applied to a tide. (PE.)

manawahua kai koʻo. Great agitation of the sea with wind and sea current contrary; tidal wave. (A.)

manono. Sea as the surf dashes across the rocks. (Isa. 8:7.)

mimiki. To recede, as a wave from the shore; collision of one returning wave with another; undertow; to suck in, as a whirlpool.

mimilo. Whirlpool.

moana. Ocean; open sea.

mole. Bottom of the sea. (A; Hab. 3:13.)

nā kai ʻewalu. The "eight seas," a poetic expression for the channels separating the eight inhabited islands of Hawaiʻi.

nalunalu. Roaring, as a high surf; appearing rough, as a high sea.

nao. Slight ripple on the water. (A.)

niania. Calm and smooth sea.

niohe. Turn of the tide.

oe. Continued sound of the surf. Also called *oeoe*. (A.)

ʻōhū. Roller, comber, or swell that does not break.

ʻōkaikai. Heaving; rough, as the sea. (CMH; PE.)

ʻoʻolokū. Choppy sea, when the current of the sea and wind are opposite; blustering, stormy, boisterous sea.

pāeaea. Smooth, unruffled, as a calm sea.

pāpakea. Action of the ocean current against the wind when the waves stand up; *kūpihipihiʻō*. (A.) White spray of the sea; white caps. (PE.)

papakū. Ocean floor. (PE.)

pāpaʻu. To flow off, as the sea at low tide leaving shallow water on the rocks; to be at low tide. *Kahi pāpaʻu,* a fording place.

poʻana. Name of the sea outside the line of the breaking surf. Also called *puʻeone*. This is the area where eroding and undermining takes place.

poʻanakai. Same as *kai poʻana*.

pohu. Calm, quiet, as the sea after a storm; calm, still water out of the wind. *Makemake nui ko Hilo poʻe aliʻi ia Kona, no ka pohu,* the Hilo chiefs greatly desired for the calm water of the sea.

poʻi. To curve and break over the top, as high surf; the top of a curling surf when it breaks.

pō manomano. Place where pointed clouds arise out of the ocean. See **pōpuakiʻi**.

popoʻi. Area where the surf, on approaching the shore, rises high and breaks with roaring noise; combing of the surf.

pōpuakiʻi. Place where pointed clouds or clusters of them arise out of the ocean. See **pō manomano**.

puaʻō. Commotion caused by a retreating wave meeting one coming in. See **koʻakā**. (A.)

puʻeone. Place in the sea outside of where the surf breaks. Also called *poʻana kai*. (A.) Sand dune; sandbar. (PE.)

puʻewai. Waves made at the mouth of a stream as the stream rushes into the ocean. (A.) Agitated water, as at the base of a waterfall or at the meeting of stream and sea. (PE.)

puhi. Place in the sea where the water is black from depth or from deep holes in the rock. (A.) *Lua puhi,* blowhole. (PE.)

pūkō. To be rough like the sea.

pūkoʻa. Sunken rocks; coral rocks of the ocean. (A.) Coral head that wrecks canoes. *Pūkoʻa kani ʻāina,* a reef that makes the land ring [a great and invulnerable fighter]. (PE.)

pūkoʻawāwāhi waʻa. Canoe and net snagging tree-like coral growing in the sea, of great annoyance to fishermen.

puʻunohu. Motion of waves succeeding each other. (A.) Rising mist, spray, or cloud. (PE.)

ulana. Lying still or calm, as the surface of the water unruffled by the wind.

ulukū. To be restless, as the sea, *kūpikiʻō.*

PLACES: Names

The modest number of site descriptions in this category cannot rival the recent edition of *Place Names of Hawaii* by Pukui, Elbert, and Mookini. That book presents approximately five thousand entries, while the Edwin H. Bryan, Jr. collections number above twenty-five thousand! This category lists about a hundred place names.

The roster contains a variety of "places": gulches, streets, points, streams, channels, churches, schools, mountains, hills, cinder cones, towns, villages, cities, *heiau,* valleys, surfing areas, parks, and so on.

ʻAʻahoaka. *Kīpuka* near Lihue, Kauaʻi. There are uncounted numbers of them among the lava flows of the islands. Each was created by a lava flow encountering an obstacle in its path causing it to flow around on both sides, the split flow joining again to make a lava-walled oasis. These were sometimes used as corrals for stock. Vegetation could grow undisturbed.

ʻAʻawa iki, ʻAʻawa nui. Tiny islands off the land division, Kahapu-loa on the west coast of Maui.

Ahu-o-Laka. Tiny island off Kaha-luʻu, Kāneʻohe, Oʻahu; altar of Laka, goddess of *hula,* and the *maile, ʻieʻie,* and other plants.

ʻĀina-hau. Home and land with beautiful gardens that stood on the site now occupied by the Princess Kaʻiulani Hotel, Waikīkī, Honolulu. Kaʻiulani was visited by Robert Louis Stevenson who immortalized her in his poetry.

'Āina-moana. State park built on a sand and rock fill at the Diamond Head end of Ala Moana Park. The area is now called Magic Island.

'Ākaka Falls. State park near Hilo, Hawai'i. The falls have an elevation of 422 feet.

'Alani. Mountain of Lana'i. (A.)

'Ālia-pa'akai. Salt Lake, O'ahu, generally below Tripler Hospital. Now developed and filled in, it was once a scenic wonder. The salt is said to have been laid there by Pele's tears as she was traveling on the island.

Aloha Kuakini. Aloha Temple of the Shrine organization of North America which operates the Shriners Hospital for Crippled Children on Punahou Street. The Shriners also have a country home at Waimanalo, O'ahu.

'Analu. Street, in Pu'unui, Honolulu named for Lorrin Andrews, a justice of the Supreme Court and author of a Hawaiian dictionary and grammar. His credit in this dictionary of categories is the letter A. His scholarly work has been significant in this dictionary. (HWK.)

Haika. Hawaiian name for Dr. Charles McEwen Hyde whose monuments in Hawai'i include a share in the work of Punahou School and a massive hand in the development of the Kamehameha Schools. He founded the Social Science Association and the Hawaiian Historical Society and was head of the North Pacific Missionary Institute. (HWK.)

Hale-a-ka-lā. Dormant volcano covering a large area of southeast Maui. The crater is some 13 miles in diameter. The famous and rare silversword plant can be found in sheltered spots below the crater rim on the north side. *Hale-a-ka-lā* was also the name of the home of Mr. and Mrs. Charles Reed Bishop on King and Bishop Streets where the Bishop Trust Building now stands.

Hale-hō'ike'ike o Kamehameha. Museum in the Kalihi area of Honolulu donated by Charles Reed Bishop in honor of his late wife, Princess Bernice Pauahi of the royal Kamehameha line. He authorized the first three buildings: Polynesian Hall, 1894; Hawaiian Hall, 1903; and Pākī Hall, 1911. This may now be said to be the greatest museum in the world in the field of Polynesian collections and operations. Its official name is Bernice Pauahi Bishop Museum.

Hale-kū-lani. Waikīkī hotel erected on the beach in 1917. It replaced the Robert Lewers family home and Hau Tree Hotel. The great tradition of the Clifford Kimball family hospitality marked the Halekūlani operation for more than sixty years.

Hale-ma'uma'u. Crater or firepit of Ki-lau-ea Crater, about 30 miles above Hilo to the southeast. *Lit.*, house fern.

Hāmākua. Name of two land areas on the northeastern side of Maui: Hāmākua Loa District (*lit.*, long Hāmākua) and Hāmākua Poko District (*lit.*, short Hāmākua). On the northeastern slope of Hawai'i there is another Hāmākua District.

Hānai-a-ka-malama. Queen Emma's summer home in upper Nu'uanu, Honolulu. Now operated by the Daughters of Hawai'i as a museum.

Hanamanioa. Lighthouse on a cape in southwest Maui near Mākena Village. It has a Fresnel lens made with refracting prisms, invented by French physicist A. J. Fresnel about 1812. Most lighthouses in Hawaiian waters are equipped with such lenses.

Hawai'i. Largest island in the Hawaiian chain, called the Big Island. Hilo is the main town and also the county seat. Area about 4,000 square miles. Population about 80,000. The largest and highest mountains, Mauna Kea and Mauna Loa, close to 14,000 feet each and formed of lava, are in the central part of the county. Mauna Kea has long been a burgeoning beacon to astronomers and their instruments due to clear air and the absence of local lights at night.

Hi'i-lawa. Waterfalls in Wai-pi'o Valley, the highest free-fall in the state. Located on Hawai'i island.

Honolulu. Capital city, largest in Hawai'i. Old names for the harbor were Hou and Mamāla. Its most famous landmark is Diamond Head Crater; another is the National Cemetery of the Pacific; and a third might be the Aloha Tower on the waterfront.

Hualāla'i. Volcanic crater, mountain, on the western side of Hawai'i island.

Hu'ehu'e. Name of the water on Hualāla'i where the last eruption occurred. Also name of a ranch.

Hui Malū Kuakini. Masonic Temple on Makiki Street near Beretania Street, Honolulu. There are other Masonic Temples at Hilo, Maui, and Schofield Barracks, O'ahu.

Huli-he'e. Palace at Kai-lua, Kona, Hawai'i, built on the site Ka-lāke'e by Kuakini in 1838. He was governor of Hawai'i island. Royalty used it as a summer residence. Now operated as a museum by the Daughters of Hawai'i.

'Io-lani. The present Royal Palace, presently fully restored, is the second of this name. In 1879 a cornerstone laying ceremony was held for this palace and as of today its location is unknown. The building was authorized by King Kalakaua. The first official dinner was a Masonic banquet with the proceedings printed on sheets of silk. It is managed by the Friends of 'Io-lani Palace.

Ka-ako-pua. A "picking flowers" district in Honolulu, site of Princess Ruth Ke'elikolani's home, Ki-o-ua-hale, now the site of Central Intermediate School.

Ka'ala. Highest mountain (about 4,000 feet) on O'ahu.

Kaha-ka-'au-lana. Early name for Sand Island, Honolulu. *Lit.,* floating swimmers passing by. An earlier name was Ka-moku-'ākulikuli, "succulent plant" island.

Kahana. Districts on the island, each with a stream and valley: Waimea, Kaua'i; Wai-kanē and Kahana, O'ahu.

Ka-hana-moku. Beautiful beach in front of the Hilton Hawaiian Village Hotel, named for Duke Kahanamoku, the world-famed Olympic swimmer. The Duke of Edinburgh visited the Charles Reed Bishops in their King Street, Honolulu home in 1869. A son was born to a retainer on the premises while the visitors were there and they were asked to name the child. Mrs. Bishop suggested Duke (Kahanamoku). A grandson was born in the same house August 26, 1890. He was named Duke and became the olympic swimmer.

Ka-hau-nui. Land section of Fort Shafter, O'ahu. *Lit.,* the *hau* tree large.

Kahua-i-lana-wai. Last stream of water in Nu'uanu Valley Road, O'ahu, before coming to the Pali. Formerly the site of a fishpond for Makalei, the celebrated fish log [*sic*] of ancient times. *Lit.,* fruits that fly about in the waters.

Ka-'ie'iewaho. Channel between Kaua'i and O'ahu. *Moana o kai,* ocean down below. *Lit.,* Ka'ie'ie outer.

Kā'ili'ili. Narrow valley near the top of Wai'ale'ale, Kaua'i, a resting place for kings and queens in ancient times.

Kaimana-Hila. Diamond Head Crater, a famous landmark on O'ahu. Heavily fortified during World War I, less so in World War II. It was named for calcite crystals in the rocks that were taken for diamonds.

Kaimuohema. The oven of Hema in Nu'uanu Valley, Honolulu, where a chief was baked. *Lit.,* oven of Hema.

Kakana'ena'e. Open spot near the summit of Wai'ale'ale, Kaua'i.

Ka Lae. Hawaiian name for South Point, Hawai'i, the southernmost point of all of the United States. Holes in the lava at the water's edge were used to anchor canoes in ancient times.

Ka-lalau. Lookout on an eminence at the head of Ka-lalau Valley, Kaua'i, from which one can gaze down into the valley and out onto the ocean. The lookout, at the edge of the *pali,* is guarded by a fenced walkway.

Kalalea. Sharp-pointed mountain above Anahola, Kaua'i, marked by an easily visible hole pierced through the top below its jagged ridge. It was pecked open by Hulu, a supernatural bird. A later legendary version has Kaua'i hero Ka-welo hurling his spear through the hole, an incredible feat!

Ka-lani-kāula. *Kukui* grove and hill at Hālawa, Moloka'i. Also the name of a seer or *mo'o*-slaying prophet who lived here. In later days a grove of *kamani* was planted by Albert F. Judd, a trustee of the Bishop Estate. Both groves are considered sacred.

Kala-pana. Black sand beach on Hawai'i island. A great tourist attraction.

Kaleokumu'u. Place near the summit of Wai'ale'ale, Kaua'i.

Ka-liu-wa'a. Hawaiian name for Sacred Falls near Hau-'ula, O'ahu. A park and stream are part of the area, all included in the state park.

Kaminaka. Hawaiian name for Chaminade, a college operated by the Brothers of Mary, located *mauka* of Waialae Avenue above the campus of St. Louis High School. The Order of the Society of Mary was founded in 1817.

Kana'ana Hou. Successor church to Siloama, built in Kalaupapa as the people and buildings concentrated there away from Kala-wao in the leper settlement. Formed in 1885. The name means New Canaan.

Kau'i-ke-o-lani. Children's Hospital in the Nu'uanu area, founded by Albert S. Wilcox. It has now merged (appropriately) with Kapiolani Maternity Hospital.

Kau-ke-ano. Hawaiian name for Central Union Church, Punahou area, Honolulu. Earlier locations at Fort and Beretania and Richards and Beretania. It was originally a merger of Bethel Church (1856) and Fort Street Church (1856) in 1892. Present site at Punahou and Beretania streets was donated by the Dillingham family. It is one of the largest Congregational Churches in the United Church of Christ. *Lit.,* awe inspiring.

Kaunakakai. Principal town of Moloka'i made famous by the late Hilo Hattie, a Hawaiian entertainer who featured the song, "The Cockeyed Mayor of Kaunakakai."

Ka-wai-a-ha'o. Congregational (Hawaiian) Church in downtown Honolulu. A beautiful coral edifice with a spacious cemetery to its right and a missionary cemetery at its rear. A chapel with the coffin of King Lunalilo is on the right as one enters the compound. This is Hawai'i's most noted church, rich in the history of the Congregational missionaries.

Ke'ākū. Cave on the eastern side of Ka'ili'ili, a narrow valley near the top of Wai'ale'ale. Also the name of a cave on the south slope of Haleakalā, Maui.

Ke-ala-i-Kahiki. Channel between Lāna'i and Ka-ho'olawe where the canoe fleets assembled in ancient times to venture the trip to Tahiti. *Lit.,* the ocean road to Kahiki.

Ke-ana-kāko'i. Ancient adze quarry at about 12,000 feet on Mauna Kea, Hawai'i.

Ke'elikōlani. State office building, Honolulu, named for Princess Ruth Ke'elikōlani. Her will in 1883 provided the bulk of the lands eventually inherited by the Bernice P. Bishop Estate/ Kamehameha Schools.

Kekaha. Land given by Liloa to high priest Laeanui on North Kona, Hawai'i island.

Kekohia Hui Malū Kuakini. Scottish Rite Cathedral, Wilder and Kewalo Streets, Honolulu.

Ke-one-kani-o-Nohili. Barking sands, beaches in the Waimea district, Kaua'i. *Lit.,* sounding sands (cinders) (PE), because of the cause of the crunchy sound when one walks over the beach. The U.S. Navy has an important tracking facility based here.

Ke-o-ua-hale. Princess Ruth's home on Queen Emma Street, Honolulu. Central Intermediate School occupies the site now.

Kī-lau-ea. Intermittently live crater and volcano on the northeastern flank of Mauna Loa. It is part of a National Park. It is composed of two craters, Kīlauea and Kīlauea Iki, separated by a flat-topped ridge called Byron's Ridge. It was named for Lord Byron (George Anson), a cousin of the poet and Captain of the HMS *Blonde* which in 1824 returned the bodies of Kamehameha II and his Queen Kamāmalu who had died in England. (PE.)

Koko Crater, Koko Head. Modern names for two volcanic craters, landmarks to the Waimanalo side of Diamond Head.

Koliaka. School Street between Nu'uanu Avenue and Fort Streets. (CMH.)

Kuakini. Hospital on Kuakini Street near Nu'uanu Avenue. Kuakini was named for Ka-'ahu-manu's brother. He built many public buildings, including churches such as Moku-'ai-kaua in Kailua, Kona.

ku'emaka. Brow of a hill. *Ku'emaka pali,* brow of a cliff.

Kumu-kāhi. Easternmost cape of Hawai'i, named for a wandering hero from Tahiti and associated with a red stone.

Kunawai. Spring between Liliha Street and the old insane asylum. Considered sacred by early Hawaiians. It was the residence of a *mo'o* (water spirit) named for a fresh water eel *(kuna)* that lived in the spring-fed pond *(wai)* where wild ducks never lived. (PE.)

Kupa-nihi. Old name for Pacific Heights. It is the name of a legendary pig that gave birth to a human child. The child later became a celebrated warrior and consequently the ancestor of some of O'ahu's bravest warriors and high chiefs. *Lit.,* native treated with respect.

Lahaina. Restoration Foundation of Maui, based on the restoration of the Dr. Dwight Baldwin home and related buildings. Other elements were added: Seaman's Hospital, Petroyglyph Wall, Hale Pa'i printshop at Lahainaluna School, Baldwin Museum, and others. This author was one of three incorporators and a director for many years.

Lahainaluna. Public high school for boarding and day students, a short ride above Lahaina town. The first Hawaiian newspaper was published on the school press from 1834, Hale Pa'i.

Lāna'i. Island west of Maui. *Lāna'i Kaululā'au,* Lāna'i of Kaululā'au. (PE.)

La Pietra. Home of Walter F. Dillingham, on the slope (town-side) of Diamond Head. Now the home of the Hawai'i School for Girls.

Lehua. Island of about 300 acres just west of Ni'ihau. The name is also well known as a flower, a breeze, a hardwood, and terms for shellfish, and *kalo*. The island is also a bird refuge.

Līlīnoi. Mountain peak, 12,956 feet high in the Mauna Kea area of Hawai'i island. Also called Pu'ulīlīnoe after a goddess of mists, Līlīnoe, sister of the more famous Poli-ahu, goddess of snow. (PE.)

Maka-weli. Land division of the southern coastal region of Kaua'i. It is a valley and river joining the Waimea valley and a branch of the Waimea river to flow into the Pacific Ocean at Waimea town. The Maka-weli area is noted for several generations of the Robinson family, the owners of Ni'ihau island.

Malia-ka-malū. Catholic Cathedral at Fort Street Mall and Beretania Street, Honolulu. *Lit.,* Mary (at) peace.

Māmalahoa. Belt road in Hawai'i. Likely named for the law of the splintered paddle *(māmalahoe)* of which Kamehameha I was the sponsor.

Manamana. Site of Queen's Hospital, O'ahu.

Maui. Second largest island in the Hawaiian chain at 728 square miles. Maui county includes Lāna'i, Kaho'olawe, and Moloka'i.

Mauna-'ala. Site of the Royal Mausoleum in lower Nu'uanu, Honolulu. Here are buried royal members of the Kalakaua and Kamehameha dynasties.

Mauna Kea. Highest mountain in Hawai'i on the island of Hawai'i, 13,796 feet. It is part of a state park and is the site of a number of observatories sponsored by scientific societies from many nations. It is probably the greatest such settlement in the world, and more observatories are planned.

Mauna Loa. Companion mountain to Mauna Kea, elevation 13,677 feet. It is not as high but it has the much larger land mass of the two.

Milo-li'i. Fishing village on the Kona side of South Point. Noted for its 'opihi. Located about 5 miles below the *mauka* road.

Moana-lua. State park near Fort Shafter, O'ahu, with a rich history of early ownerships. Mrs. Bernice Pauahi Bishop willed 3,000 acres here to Samuel M. Damon in 1884. In 1974 Damon's heirs presented the lands, with their beautiful gardens of native flora, historical sites, and Japanese buildings, to the people of Hawai'i.

Moku-'ai-kaua. Hawaiian Congregational Church in Kailua-Kona, Hawai'i. The first building was constructed by Kua-kini, governor of Hawai'i. After a fire in 1835 it was rebuilt with coral. Attendance in the early days may have reached 4,000 on a Sunday.

Moku-ola. Island in Hilo Bay, Hawai'i. Its modern name is Coconut Island. Another island of this name is in Kāne'ohe Bay, formerly the home of Chris Holmes; now a marine biology station of the University of Hawai'i.

Moku-'ume'ume. Old name for Ford Island in Pearl Harbor, named for a Honolulu physician Dr. S. P. Ford (1818–1866). Still earlier it was called Poka 'Ailana. The *Arizona* Memorial of World War II, although anchored over the U.S.S. *Arizona,* touches the island.

Moloka'i. Island said to have been brought forth by a woman named Hina, who was ever after regarded as the mother of Moloka'i. A poetic reference is made to this: *Moloka'i-nui-a-Hina,* great Moloka'i, child of *Hina.* The island has an area of about 260 square miles.

Molokama, nā molo kama. Mountain in Hanalei District, Kaua'i. In singing a *mele* a suffix, *aka,* is added to *molokama.*

Ni'ihau. Privately owned island southwest of Kaua'i, inhabited largely by native Hawaiians whose dialect carries a Tahitian influence. Permission to visit is rarely granted.

O'ahu. Island with an area of 608 square miles, and the location of Hawai'i's capital, Honolulu, the island's most populous city.

'Ohe'o. Seven Sacred Pools near Kīpahulu, Maui. Now part of a national preservation project.

Olokele. Name of a stream, canyon, sugar plantation, and school. The Olokele river joins the Maka-weli and eventually a branch of the Waimea river, all on Kaua'i.

Olowā pupu'u. Place where many hillocks stand near each other. *Kinikini pu'u,* many *pu'u* or hillocks standing close together. (A.)

Our Lady of Peace Cathedral. Catholic Cathedral facing Fort Street Mall near Beretania Street, Honolulu. Constructed in 1843.

Pahauna. *Heiau* near Lamaloloa in Hāmākua, Hawai'i.

Pā-o-Pelekane. Site at Beretania Street in Honolulu, location of St. Andrews Cathedral and Priory. Once the site of the home of Kamehameha III. The land was given to St. Andrews Cathedral, Church of England.

Pelekikena Hale. President's home at the Kamehameha Schools. Known as the Master's Hale.

Pilomena. St. Philomena Catholic Church at Kalawao, Kalaupapa, Moloka'i. This is the church largely constructed by and associated with Father Damien.

Pōhai-nani. Retirement home, Kāne'ohe, O'ahu. *Lit.,* surrounded beauty.

Polynesian Cultural Center, Lā'ie, O'ahu. This is devoted to native cultures of the Pacific and is operated by the Church of Jesus Christ of Latter Day Saints, which also sponsors the Hawai'i Campus of Brigham Young University, located adjacent to the center. The school dates from 1955, the center from 1963.

Prince Jonah Kuhio Kalanianaole. Federal building recently opened to replace an earlier building. Named after Prince Kuhio, an early delegate to the U.S. Congress. Located close to the waterfront on the edge of downtown Honolulu, the monolithic building is two blocks long and one block deep.

Punahou. Private school at Punahou and Wilder Streets. Established by Hiram Bingham in 1841. Present enrollment about 3,700.

Pu-o-waena. Punchbowl, a crater above downtown Honolulu that contains the National Cemetery of the Pacific. *Lit.,* hill placing human sacrifices.

Puʻuloa. Queen's Bath, a large, warm spring pool at Puna, Hawaiʻi.

Puʻu-o-Kila. Lookout in Kōkeʻe State Park, Kauaʻi. *Lit.,* hill Kila.

Siloama. Church of the Healing Spring, Congregational. The first house of worship in the leper settlement at Kalawao, Molokaʻi, 1866. It is only used now on annual and special occasions. Its successor church at Kalaupapa is called Kanaʻana Hou. From Siloam, Biblical springs.

ʻUala-kaʻa. Old name for Round Top, Honolulu. *Lit.,* sweet potato rolling.

Uwapo o Haʻalili-a-manu. Bridge spanning Nuʻuanu Stream at Hotel Street, Honolulu.

Wai-alae. Golf and country club near the Kahala Hilton Hotel, Honolulu. *Lit.,* water mudhen.

Wai-alae iki. Bishop Estate subdivision of four areas above the Kahala golf course, Honolulu. The old name was Wiliwili nui.

Wai-ʻaleʻale. Highest mountain on Kauaʻi. It is also the name of a spring near the summit. *Lit.,* water rippling or overflowing. This general area is among the wettest in the world.

Wai-ka-kaʻa. Waterfall, on Kauaʻi, 150 feet high. (A.)

Wai-lenalena. Small valley near the top of Wai-ʻaleʻale famous for its huge-leafed *ʻapeʻape* forest of permanent herbs. *Lit.,* yellow water.

Wailupe. Pond fill made of coral dug out of the reef off ʻĀina-Haina in the Kahala area, Honolulu. Piled a few feet above sea level, it made a subdivision in the shape of a half circle.

Wai-niha. Stream near the top of Wai-ʻaleʻale, Hanalei district, Kauaʻi.

Wai-o-kila. Area in the *haku-loa* full of precipices and ravines, on Maui. *Lit.,* water of Kila. Perhaps this is Kila, a son of Moʻikeha who journeyed to Kahiki to fetch Laʻa-mai-Kahiki. (PE.)

PLACES: Miscellany of Poetic References

In this section the listed phrases and clauses are treated as poetic versions of place names. Hawaiians seemed to find the use of such phrases natural, even in common talk. Some of these items probably originated from students of Dr. Charles M. Hyde in his North Pacific Missionary Institute sessions on the Hawaiian language. Some expressions are familiar, others may be hitherto unknown.

Ehuehu ka nalu o Kailua, Kailua's waves are majestic/powerful/violent.

'Ele'ele Hilo e ho'opanopano i ka ua lā, Hilo is black, darkened by the rain.

E nā one ku'ilima laulā o 'Ewa nei, the broad hand holding the sands of 'Ewa [refers to being united].

Hāmākua mai ka pali o Ka'ula a Honoke'ā, from the cliff of Ka'ula to Honoke'ā.

Hāna mai ka wai o ka 'o'opu a inu i ka wai o Manawainui i ahiki nui, Hāna, from the waters of the goby fish till one drinks the waters of Manawainui [north Moloka'i].

Hāna mai Ko'olau ā Kaupō, Hāna from Ko'olau to Kaupō.

Hawai'i o Keawe, island of the Keawe line of chiefs.

He ua moaniani lehua o Puna, the rain with the *lehua* wind bearing fragrance to Puna.

Hīlea i ke kalo 'eka'eka, Hīlea, village of the dirty *kalo*. A saying applied to anyone careless or inefficient in his work. Kā'u, Hawai'i.

Hilo, mai Māwae o ka pali o Ka'ula, from Hilo to the cliffs of Ka'ula [islet off Ni'ihau].

Huli ka 'eka makai, the *'eka* wind of Kona has moved to the sea below.

Īnu-wai koli'uli'u o Hilo, the dim, distant, water-drinking sea breeze of Hilo.

'I waho o ka nuku o Māmala kehi i ku ai, anchors outside the mouth of Māmala [entrance channel of Honolulu Harbor].

Ka 'āina kai mā'oki'oki i ka hau a Kona, streaked sea of many colors, in the waters off Kona.

Ka 'āina ua lani ha'aha'a, land of the heaven-low rain [it hangs low over the land, as at Hāna, Maui].

Ka alanui pali o 'A'alaloa, a heavily traveled path between Wailuku and Lāhainā. The macrons indicate this form means cruel sun, the old name. Lahainaluna School does not use the macrons. It has not been generally accepted although perhaps it should be. (KILO.) Inez Ashdown wrote the booklet "Ke Alaloa o Maui," [Long Road Around Maui], 1971.

Kai malino o 'ehu, kaimā'oki'oki o Kona, calm sea of *'ehu* [sea foam], the many colored sea of streaks in the waters off Kona.

Ka ipukukui pio 'ole i ka makani Kaua'ula, the light lamp of the Red Rain cannot be extinguished. This wind, especially strong over Lahaina, Maui, is caused by the trade winds when they break over the hills behind Lahainaluna.

Ka kapakahi ka lā ma Wai'anae, the sun looks or stands lopsided at Wai'anae [O'ahu].

Ka kāua mea i 'au mai nei i kēia mau kai 'ewalu, that for which we swam these eight seas.

Ka lā ikiiki lā o Honolulu, the stifling hot sun of Honolulu.

Ka lā ko'ehāna o Lahainaluna, the sunny weather [the warmth] of Lahainaluna.

Kama'āina i ka i'a hāmau leo, acquainted with the silent voiced fish [oyster].

Kama'āina i ka i'a makani, acquainted with the Kaiaulu wind [of Wai'anae, O'ahu].

Ka makani 'akipohe o Waihe'e, the wind that nips the fingers at Waihe'e. The Waihe'e wind.

Ka makani i ka ua o Ko'olau, the rain-bearing wind of Ko'olau [O'ahu]. This phrase is mentioned in the song about the first electric lights in Kāne'ohe, O'ahu.

Ka makani kūlōlia o Hāmākua, the gusty wind at Hāmākua [Hawai'i].

Ka makani mā'ā'ā o Lahaina, famous sea breeze at Lahaina [Maui]. Also called *'a'a.*

Ka malu hēkuawa o Wailuku, the shaded valley of Wailuku [Maui].

Ka malu 'ulu o Lele, the shelter and quiet of the breadfruit tree at Lele [Lahaina, Maui].

Ka nalu o huia ma Hilo, the surfing wave at Hilo.

Ka nalu o Kalehua-wehe ma Wai-kīkī, the shelter of Kalehua-wehe near [Queen's Surf] Wai-kīkī [O'ahu].

Ka papa kahulihuli o Wailuku, the unstable foundation of Wailuku [meaning the rank of fighters on flat land].

Ka ua hāli'i i ka nahele, the rain that spreads in the *ka nahele* [the woods or woody region].

Ka ua he'enehu, name of a misty rain off the Hilo coast when the *nehu,* fish, are running.

Ka ua kea o Hāna, the misty, white rain of Hāna.

Ka ua kīpū iluna o Pueo, the misty rain which holds back over Pueo.

Ka ua kīpu'upu'u o Waimea i ka la'i, the chilly wind and rain for which Waimea, Hawai'i, is famous.

Ka ua kūkala hale o Honolulu, a local rain in Honolulu.

Ka ua lani haʻahaʻa, a close down rain of Hāna, Maui.

Ka ua lani pāina o ʻUlupalakua, the crackling rain of ʻUlupalakua [Maui].

Ka ua līlī-lehua o Pana-ʻewa, the wind and rain, chilling but wafted with the fragrance of *lehua* blossoms to Pana-ʻewa, Hawaiʻi; Pālolo, Oʻahu; and Wai-ehu, Maui.

Ka ua lū lehua o Waipiʻo, to scatter *lehua* blossoms at Waipiʻo [said poetically of rain].

Ka ua nāulu o Honua-ʻula, the sudden shower of Honua-ʻula.

Ka ua nāulu o Kawaihae-uka o Honua-ʻula, the sudden shower of upper inland over the *heiau* for human sacrifices in Waipiʻo Valley, Hawaiʻi.

Ka ua niu lokuloku o Wai-ʻoli, the rain downpour of Wai-oli, Kauaʻi.

Ka ua nounou ili o Waimea, the wind which blows the gales of Waimea, [Hawaiʻi].

Ka ua o Kawaohio, the rain of Kawaohio, Hawaiʻi.

Ka ua peʻeʻeʻepōhaku o Kaupō, rain on the moss-covered stones of Kaupō.

Ka ua popokapa o Nuʻuanu, Nuʻuanu rain. Those caught in the rain would roll up their *kapa* so it could not get wet and hold it in a way to protect it. When the rain stopped the *kapa* was unrolled and put back on.

Kaʻū o Kaua o Haʻao, the Haʻao rain of Waiohinu, Kaʻū, Hawaiʻi.

Kaupō ʻai loli. *Loli* means sea cucumber or sea-slug eaters. Said of the people of Kaupō.

Ka wai a ka pāoʻo i Lehua, the waters in which *ʻoʻopu,* varieties of fish, abound along the coast of Lehua.

Ka wai hālau o Hanalei, expansive waters of Hanalei [Kauaʻi].

Ka wai hālau o Wailua, expansive waters of Wailua [Kauaʻi].

Ka wai hiʻuhiʻu o Wailuku, the pelting rain of Wailuku [Hilo, Hawaiʻi].

Ka wai hoʻihoʻi lani o ʻEleile, the delighting waters of ʻEleile; water that turns upward. (CMH.)

Ka wai puka iki o Helani, the blow hole at Helani [Kona, Hawaiʻi].

Keanini ma Kapueokāhi, the varying waves of the sea at Kapueokāhi [Hāna, Maui].

Ke awa hanupanupa o Mahu-kona, the surging channel of Mahu-kona [Kawaihae, Hawaiʻi].

Ke awa laʻi lulu o Kou nei, the calm, sheltered channel or harbor of Kou, which is the old name for the area of Honolulu Harbor. *Awa* means an entrance between two reefs, a harbor. *He awa o*

Kou ma O'ahu, he awa ku moku, he nui na awa ho'okomo wa'a, there is the harbor of Kou [Honolulu] on O'ahu, where ships anchor.

Ka awa lau o 'Ewa, the many lochs of 'Ewa. There were also many lochs in Pu'uloa, Pearl Harbor.

Ke kai hanupanupa la o Ale-nui-hāhā, the surging channel of Ale-nui-hāhā [between Hawai'i and Maui]. The name speaks of the heavy waves or billows that endanger shipping of water traffic of any kind.

Ke kai malino i ka pohu la'i o Kona, the peaceful sea in the calm silence of Kona.

Ke kai malino mai Kekaha a hiki i Miloli'i, the peaceful sea from Kekaha to Miloli'i.

Ke kai wawalo o ka wahine i ke one, the roaring sea of the woman on the sand.

Ke kalukalu moe ipo o Kapa'a, a chief, covered with a thin gauze-like *kapa,* sleeps with his beloved of Kapa'a [Kaua'i].

Ke kawalele ma'opu o Pi'ikea, the precipice from which Pi'ikea, daughter of Pi'ilani, a Maui chief, was wont to dive.

Ke keiki awāwa o ka ua Kuahine o Mānoa, the valley child of the Kuahine rain of Mānoa.

Ke kula o Lele, the plain of Lele [Maui].

Ke mau nei nō ka loku 'ana o ka ua kinai lehua o Pana-'ewa, ke hālalo nei i luna o ka lau 'ōhi'a, the rain that destroys the *lehua* of Pana-'ewa continues to pour and it centers on the 'ōhia leaves.

Ke one wali o Hilo, the fine sand of Hilo.

Kohala i ka naulu, Kohala [Hawai'i] of the sudden shower. More commonly associated with the area next to Kohala, Kawaihae.

Kohala mai Honoke'ā a Keahulono, from Kohala to Honoke'ā to Keahulono.

Kona akau mai Keahulono a Pu'uohau, Kona is to the north of Keahulono of Pu'uohau.

Lahaina ka malu ulu o Lele, breadfruit grove of Lele an old name of Lahaina.

lau 'awa, first two *kalo* leaves, as offered with kava leaves with prayers for a good supply.

Mai ka lā hiki a ka lā kau, from sunrise to sunset [a whole day or a lifespan].

Mai ka lā oni a'e ma Makanoni i ka lae kaulana o Kumu-kāhi, a ka lā welo i ka 'ilikai malalo aku o ka mole olu o Lehua i ka wai huna a ka Pāo'o, from the rising of the sun over the famous promontory of Kumu-kāhi, to the last lingering rays as it sinks below the waves behind the lovely, lonely isle of Lehua.

Mai ka limu kā kanaka o Manuʻa-kepa i Hanalei a hiki aku i ka wai ʻula ʻiliahi o Wai-mea, from the man-striking moss of Manuʻa-kepa to the red sandalwood water of Wai-mea.

Mai ka pali o Nuʻuanu a i ke kai o ʻĀinahou, from the Nuʻuanu *pali* to the beach at ʻĀinahou.

Mai ka wai o ʻOʻopuloa a Keʻehuaiea, from the waters of ʻOʻopuloa to Keʻehuaiea.

Makawao o ka ua ūkiʻukiʻu, rain of the gentle breeze of Makawao.

Maui o Kamalālāwalu, Maui, land of Kamalālāwalu.

Molokaʻi o Hina, Molokaʻi, child of Hina.

Nā ale ʻāpipiʻi o nā kai ʻewalu, the tempestuous waves of the eight seas.

Nā ale hanupanupa o Pāilolo, the surging waves of Pāilolo Channel [between Maui and Molokaʻi].

Nā ʻale uliuli a ke kōwā kai hānupanupa ʻAlenuihāhā, the surging, green waves of the ʻAlenuihāhā Channel [between Hawaiʻi and Maui].

Nā Kona kai ʻōpua i ka laʻi, the cloud banks on the horizon above Kona [Hawaiʻi].

Nā nalu huikumu o ʻUo, the surfing waves of ʻUo [in ancient Lahaina].

Nā pali hāuliuli o Koʻolau, the green hills of Koʻolau.

Nā ula momona o Kaluaʻeleʻele, the fat lobsters of Kaluaʻeleʻele.

Nā ʻulu o Lele, the breadfruit trees of Lele [Lahaina].

Nā waʻa e huli lua nei i ka makani, canoes which shift with the wind [a person who cannot make up his mind].

Nā Waiʻehā mai ka polio Kapulehu a i ka pali o ʻAʻalaloa, from the four waters of Waiʻehā [poetic name for Wai-luku, Wai-ehu, Wai-heʻe, and Wai-kapū, Maui] and the dark torments of Kapulehu to the cliff of ʻAʻalaloa [great fragrance].

Nā wai hale o Kahaluʻu, the prison of Kahaluʻu.

Nā wana momona a aʻe o kōkōliʻi, the fat sea urchins like the dark clouds of the northeast trade winds.

Oʻahu o Kākuhihewa, Oʻahu isle of Kākuhihewa [an old time powerful chief].

ʻO ʻEwa, ʻone kai ʻula i ka lepo, ʻEwa, where the sand is reddened by dirt.

ʻO Hāmākua ʻāina pali loloa, Hāmākua, land of long hills and tall cliffs.

ʻO Hilo nahele paoa i he ʻala, Hilo wild wood with strong heady fragrance.

ʻO ka ʻehu kai o Puaʻena, the sea spray of Puaʻena [Waialua, Oʻahu].

ʻO ka nalu o paiāhaʻa, Kaʻū, the waves of Paiāhaʻa [an ancient surfing area of] Kaʻū. *Lit.*, lift and sway, waves. *Paiāhaʻa* means surging.

ʻO Kaʻū niu Kua makani, windy back. Probably refers to the hills of Kaʻū.

ʻO ka wai e ʻauʻau ai, o ka wai hū o Kauila, the water to bathe in, the gushing spring of Kauila.

ʻŌ Kīʻope ka wai e ʻauʻau ai. Kīʻope is the name of a pond on the grounds of Huliheʻe Palace, Kona, Hawaiʻi, where chiefs used to bathe.

ʻO Kona kai ʻōpua i ka laʻi, ʻōpua hīnano kau i ka mālie, Kona with its cloud billows and sea in the calm, puffy clouds white like hīnano blossoms resting in the quiet. (PE.)

ʻO Puna, kai nehe i ka ulu hala, Puna whose sea rustles in the *hala* grove. The *hala* (pandanus) grows near the sea.

ʻO Puna, nahele ulu hala, Puna, land of *hala* (pandanus) groves.

Pāhala i ka ʻāina lepo haʻaheo i na maka, Pāhala, cultivation by burning mulch, prideful to the eyes.

Ua heʻeia nā nalu o Hilo, people have surfed on Hilo's waves.

Ua hoʻopaʻa ʻo Laʻamaomao i kāna ipu makani a pō iā lā, Laʻamaomao kept her wind calabash closed all that day.

Ua kani lehua o Hilo, the *lehua*-rustling rain of Hilo.

Ua ma ke awa ma Lahaina, rain in the harbor of Lahaina.

Ua o Kōʻiʻopulepule a me ka wai, the rain of Kōʻiʻopulepule supplies its water.

Ua o Wailuku, nona ka papakāhulihuli, the rain of Wailuku provides a soft, unstable foundation to the land.

Ua pupū hale o Hāmākua, the rain stays close to the houses at Hāmākua.

Uliuli ka pali o Kahikinui e kokolo mai lā ka ohu heino, the shadow of the *pali* of Kahikinui creeps there, toward the *heino* mist.

Waikapū i ka makani, Waikapū, land of the gusty wind.

Wailuku i ka malu he kuawa, Wailuku in the shelter of the valley.

PLANTS

Before their discovery in 1778 by Captain James Cook, the Hawaiian Islands were isolated—except for the Polynesian migration, and possibly a few unconfirmed incidental "touchings" by Portuguese or Spanish explorers on journeys across the Pacific. In these circumstances plant life had opportunities to develop unique forms which Hawaiian settlers recognized and named. The species introduced after Cook's visit were in turn called by the names they bore in their homelands, or adaptations of these accommodating the Hawaiian alphabet.

All of the plant categories include both native and introduced plants. Herbs, grasses, mosses, vines, and even seaweeds may be listed more than once under two or more headings. For example, an herb may also be in the grass, vine, or moss category. This is not a special problem, but the reader should be aware of some repetition within the categories.

PLANTS: Elements and Parts

This category, short and easy to read and understand, offers a preview, unintended, of the many references to trunks, leaves, roots, flowers, and seeds in the listings that follow.

ʻaʻa. Small roots of plants and trees.

ʻaʻa niu. Coarse, clothlike sheath at the base of the coconut and other palm leaves; coconut cloth.

ahuahu. Young sprouts or shoots from layers, as from sugar cane; to grow rapidly, thrive.

ʻāhui. Bunch or cluster of fruit, as bananas, grapes, or whole pandanus fruit.

ʻanoʻano. Seeds of fruit, as apples, melons, onions.

ʻauʻau. Name of a certain stick *(aho)* to be thatched first in the construction of a *heiau;* the stalk of the *loulu* palm made into a spear. (A.)

ʻaweʻaweʻa. Seeds of green fruit, as squashes, melons, and the like. (A.)

ēulu. Branch cut off to be planted again; a layer; to crop or trim off top branches.

hilohilo. Sweet juice of the steamed or roasted *kī* root, especially enjoyed since there is so little of it.

hīnalo, hīna'alo, hīnano. Male flower of the pandanus about a foot long surrounded by white, pointed, edible bracts.

hūka'a. General name for pitch, resin, or gum from a tree; any resinous substance.

kaikea. Sap of a tree; outer white layers of wood resembling in color the fat of animals. (A.)

koaha. Soft mulberry fiber used for making a fine white *kapa;* young shoots of the mulberry used for medicine.

kumulā'au. Trunk or stump of a tree.

lā'ī. Ti leaf, a contraction of *lau kī.*

lau kapalili. Name of the *kalo* that grew on the first *kalo* plant of the Hawaiian Islands. This is the legendary expression for the trembling leaf of that first *kalo* plant, said to have emerged from the burial site of Holoa-naka, son of *Wākea.* (MALO 244.) The leaf was called *lau kapalili* and the *kalo* stem was called *haloa.*

lolo. Sheath covering the coconut flower. (A.) Pithy, white sponge in a sprouting coconut.

lolokia. Stem of a coconut.

nonohina. White blossoms of the *olopua* tree in the olive family.

'ohā. Small plantlets of *kalo* that grow on the sides of the older corms; the suckers which are transplanted.

oho. Leaves of the coconut tree, so called from their resemblance to hair; to leaf or sprout out.

'ōmu'omu'o. Upper and youngest leaves of the sugarcane; youngest leaves of most plants.

pa'a'ā, pā'ā. Fiber, as of sugarcane stalk or banana sheath.

palula. Leaf of the sweet potato; a dish of food made by roasting sweet potato leaves with hot stones.

pīkoi. Core of the breadfruit or pandanus.

pīlali. Gum of the *kukui* tree; gum or any sticky substance of any tree.

pola. Lower end of the banana *(mai'a)* inflorescence consisting of the blossom and subtending sheath.

polokā. Bunch of *hala* fruit, especially the lower end of the bunch.

polope'a. Thick stem of a pandanus *(hala)* or banana bunch.

pona. That part of a stalk of sugarcane between the joints; the joints themselves of sugarcane or bamboo.

pōule. Stamen of the male flower of the breadfruit.

pōule'ulu. Stamen of the breadfruit flower; something that grows on the extreme branches of the *ulu* or breadfruit tree. It was pounded into *kapa* for use in making a *malo*.

pua kō. Top tassle of the sugarcane.

pua lei. Top leaf or branch of a tree when the lower ones are cut off. (A.) Flowers used in making *leis*.

pū 'awa. Root of the *'awa* plant.

pū hala. Pandanus tree, with special reference to its body. (A.)

pūlumi nī 'au. A later word for *pūpū nī'au;* a broom.

punako. Joints of sugarcane. (CMH.)

pūpū nī 'au. Broom made of coconut midribs tied together at one end. Later called *pūlumi nī'au*. (PE.)

wekea. Top of a tree. Also called *wēkiu*.

PLANTS: Fruits

Hawai'i has been host to numerous introduced, fruit-bearing plants, but they seem to have perished or adapted because of pests or economics. Many have survived—and fame, if not fortune, has come to Hawai'i in the blossoms of the pineapple, papaya, guava, passion fruit, and mango. Our varieties are among the best in the world. The islands, in a sense, are one great fruit farm.

'ākala. Two species of native raspberries, *Rubus hawaiiensis* and *R. macraei*. (NEAL 391.) See **Plants: Uses.**

'apelekoka. Apricot (*Prunus armeniaca.* L.). Grows at above 3,500 feet. (NEAL 396.)

hala kahiki. Pineapple *(Ananas comosus),* the species best known for its delectable fruit. After years of importations, experiments and all, James D. Dole raised and canned pineapple with great success. Today Hawai'i is a leading world producer. (NEAL 176.)

hē'ī. The papaya *(Carica papaya),* tree and fruit, a favorite in Hawai'i. Native of tropical America. Also called *mīkana, papa-ia*. (NEAL 600.)

kanawao. Small endemic fruit tree *(Broussaisia arguta)* of the mountains. Currants, gooseberries, and some ornamentals such as hydrangea are in the same family. An old belief was that eating the fruit helped in fecundity. The increase of chiefs was compared to a fruiting *kanawao*. (NEAL 380.)

kuawa, puawa. Guava *(Psidium guajava)*. Grows on a small evergreen tree native to tropical America. The outside of the fruit resembles a lemon, while the pulp is cream colored or solid pink, with numerous hard seeds, and is pleasantly acidic. Jelly, jam, and juice are made from it. It is about equal to an orange in vitamin C content. (NEAL 632.)

kukane. Variety of introduced lemon *(Citrus limonia)*. The rough outer skin is liked for its fragrance, but the sour pulp is not eaten. Named after two great Hawaiian gods, Kū and Kāne. (NEAL 482.)

laikī. Litchi *(Litchi chinensis)*, an introduced member of the soapberry family, is a fruit with a hard, scaly covering containing a large hard seed. Flesh is white, watery, transparent, and a popular food item in Hawai'i. (NEAL 534.)

lemi. Lemon, lime tree *(Citrus limonia* and *C. aurantifolia)*. Small trees native to Asia. Hawai'i varieties of lemons include Rough, Ponderosa, Meyer, and Villa Franca. *Kukane* (names of two Hawaiian gods, Kū and Kāne) is the local name for the rough lemon. Hawaiians like it for the fragrance of the skin but do not eat the pulp. (NEAL 482.)

mai'a. All kinds of bananas. The Hawaiians introduced the first bananas from which many cultivars were developed. In the post-Cook era many more species of *Musa* were introduced from the tropics of the old world. In Hawai'i, the fruit ripens throughout the year since few diseases or pests disturb the growth. One use of the banana stock and leaves is as containers for *lei*s or plants to be transported. They can also be used for thatching, stringing *lei*s, and tying and plaiting into clothing. (NEAL 245.)

manakō. Mango *(Mangifera indica)*. A large fruit tree import from India. Its large, somewhat fibrous, sweet, juicy fruit with orange flesh is a favorite fruit in the islands. (NEAL 521.)

momona. Fruit of the cherimoya *(Annona cherimola)*, a small fruit tree from tropical America related to the custard-apple. It has greenish, pleasant-tasting fruits that may be eaten raw. Seeds are used as an insecticide, and medicinally as an emetic. (NEAL 359.)

niu. The coconut, tree and palm *(Cocos nucifera)*. Widely distributed around the world and in Hawai'i. It thrives in sandy soils along tropical beaches. (NEAL 119.) See **Plants: Uses.**

'ōhelo. Whortleberry *(Vaccinium reticulatum)*, an endemic member of the cranberry, blueberry, and huckleberry family. Common around the volcano area on Hawai'i island. Edible raw and cooked. (NEAL 662.)

'ōhelo 'ele'ele. Blackberry *(Rubus penetrans)*. Introduced in

Hawai'i in 1894, it has been thriving ever since as roadside weed on most of the islands at 3,000–4,000 feet and above. It bears an abundance of seedy, purple-black, juicy fruits, ¾ inch long. (NEAL 392.)

'ōhelo papa. Strawberry *(Fragaria chiloensis,* var. *sandwicensis),* native to Hawai'i, growing on Hawai'i island and East Maui between 3,500 and 6,000 feet. *'Ōhelo* means berry and *papa,* flat spreading. The fruit is globose, red, and edible but smaller than the cultivated variety *(F. chiloensis* var. *ananassa)* which bears a red juicy fruit, a rich source of vitamin C. (NEAL 393.)

'ōhi'a 'ai. Mountain apple *(Eugenia malaccensis),* a forest tree up to 50 feet in height, belonging to the myrtle family. Grows in shady valleys. A thin, deep crimson skin covers a crisp, pure white pulp that has a slightly sweet taste. The fruit is eaten both raw and pickled. (NEAL 636.)

'ōhi'a-hā, hā. Edible fruit related to the mountain apple *(E. sandwicensis).* The fruit is globose, a third of an inch in diameter, red, with a little edible pulp. (NEAL 635.)

'olohua. Fruit of the *pōpolo* plant *(Solanum nigrum),* the black nightshade. In cultivated form it is the garden huckleberry with large fruits used in pies and preserves. It is valuable in medicines, formerly useful in ceremonies. Berries and stem tips are edible. *'Olohua* is also called *hua 'olohua.* (NEAL 744.)

palama. Methley plum *(Prunus cerasifera* X *salicina),* an import from Natal, South Africa. It has sweet, small, red-purple fruit. (NEAL 396.) *Eng.*

pā-nini, pā-pipi. Prickly pear *(Opuntia megacantha),* native to Mexico. This species of *Opuntia* bears the best fruits for food. In Mexico, in season, it can be a principal human food, eaten raw, dried, or cooked into a paste or candy. The Hawaiians made a fermented drink from the fruits. (NEAL 607.)

pī'ai. Candlenut *(Aleurites moluccana),* also known as the *kukui* tree. It produces the nut of either name with many uses: it can be made into a black dye, polished and strung as a necklace or *lei;* eaten ground and uncooked as a purgative; used as a drying oil in varnishes and fertilizer. But the edible part to man is the relish *('inamona)* made of crushed, roasted nut kernels with salt and chili pepper added. (KILO.)

piki. Peach tree *(Prunus persica).* Probably introduced from China, it has never flourished in Hawai'i. It made quite an impression with its fruit of velvety, whitish, yellow or red skin and thick, juicy, edible, white or yellow flesh around a wrinkled stone. One discouragement to this peach tree is the Mediterranean fruit fly. (NEAL 395.)

pohā. Cape gooseberry *(Physalis peruviana),* an introduced perennial herb of the tomato family. A small shrub, it grows wild on mountain slopes to 5,500 feet. The fruit is globose with an orange skin covering a sweet, juicy, many-seeded pulp and is edible raw or cooked for jam. It is enclosed in a papery sack. There is a fair market for this jam in Hawai'i. (NEAL 740.) Called *pa'ina* on Hawai'i island.

pōpō'ulu. Plantain bearing a short, round banana. *Mai'a pōpō-'ulu,* cooking banana. The root of the young plant was formerly used medicinally. Its fruit is rounded and yellow. Edible raw but preferred baked. *Lit.,* banana ball breadfruit. (HP 177.)

'ulu. Breadfruit *(Artocarpus altilis).* Early Polynesians brought the breadfruit tree from Tahiti, an attractive tropical tree 30 to 60 feet in height. Its ripe fruit is brownish in tone, 5 to 8 inches in diameter, and weighs up to 10 pounds. It has a sweet, mealy pulp somewhat like the sweet potato. (NEAL 302.)

waiawī. Yellow strawberry guava *(Psidium cattleianum* f. *lucidum),* called the Cattley guava. A handsome tree bearing large, yellow fruit. (NEAL 634.)

waiawī 'ula'ula. Purple strawberry guava *(Psidium cattleianum).* A shrubby tree from Brazil, with purplish red fruit about an inch in diameter and white pulp that is eaten raw or made into jam or jelly. It tastes somewhat like strawberries. (NEAL 633–634.)

PLANTS: Grasses and Sedges

Grasses were seemingly everywhere in ancient Hawai'i. They could be fashioned into almost anything: hats, mats, cloth, purses, baskets, tablecloths, fans, and other items.

Today these grasses serve equally well as putting greens, lawns, beach-binders, and sand-retainers. They also overcome and choke off other growth.

'ahu'awa. A sedge *(Cyperus javanicus),* 1 to 4 feet high with a basal tuft of long, narrow leaves and a radiating inflorescence borne at the tip of a long, slender stem. (NEAL 86.)

'aka'akai. Great bulrush *(Scirpus validus).* (NEAL 88.) See **Plants: Uses.**

ʻakiʻaki. Seashore rush grass *(Sporobolus virginicus).* A coarse grass growing on sandy beaches, said to have been used by exorcists. (NEAL 66.) See **mahiki, mānienie ʻakiʻaki, m. haole, m. maoli.**

ʻakiʻaki haole. Buffalo grass, St. Augustine grass *(Stenotaphrum secundatum).* (NEAL 72.) See **mānienie haole, manienie maoli.**

ʻemo loa. Native grass *(Eragrostis variabilis),* an endemic Hawaiian tufted perennial grass. This wind-blown plant is easily seen at Nuʻuanu Pali. See **kāwelu, kalamalō.**

heʻu pueo. Reedlike grass, a bent grass *(Agrostis avenacea),* native to Australia. Another species is cocoos bent *(A. palustris),* a creeping bent, propagated from seed. Used for putting greens. (NEAL 66.)

kākonakona. Native species of grass *(Panicum torridum)* that thrives in dry places where it gives good forage. Characterized by a thick covering of long, silky hairs. (NEAL 73.)

kalamalō. The swollen finger *mauʻu lei (Chloris inflata),* is conspicuous for its ten or more spikes in the stem, which are used for hat *lei*s. (NEAL 69.) See **ʻemo loa, kāwelu.**

kaluhā. Papyrus *(Cyperus papyrus),* an ancient sedge most familiar because of its importance to Egypt. In Hawaiʻi it is used in flower arrangements. Its name, *kaluhā,* was first used in the Hawaiian Bible. (NEAL 83.)

kāmanomano. A Hawaiian grass *(Cenchrus agrimonioides)* bearing a spike of spiny flowers. The leaves, used in love sorcery, are called *hoʻomano.*

kāwelu. Wind-blown grass *(Eragrostis variabilis),* a word frequently used in *meles* (songs) of Nuʻuanu Pali. See **ʻemo loa, kalamalō.** (NEAL 64.)

kiliʻoʻopu. Nut grass *(Cyperus rotundus),* a perennial sedge and a troublesome cosmopolitan weed in Hawaiʻi since 1850. It is difficult to eradicate as the roots bear tubers at about 5-inch intervals, successively, each able to produce new plants. (NEAL 84.)

kō. Sugarcane *(Saccharum officinarum).* See **Plants: Uses.**

konakona. Native tufted grass *(Panicum nephelophilum).* It grows to 4 feet with a large, open-flowering panicle.

kualohia. Said to be a grass used in thatching. (PE.)

kūkae kōloa. Species of long grass which takes its name from Kōloa, a district of Kauaʻi. Early writers mention Job's tears being strung and used for ear drops in the South Pacific. (NEAL 81.) See **pūʻoheʻohe.**

kūkae puaʻa. Small, weedy, creeping grass, one of three species

(Digitaria adscendens, D. sanguinalis, D. pruriens), all of which are called *kūkae puaʻa*. They are crabgrass, invaders of lawns. Formerly, Hawaiians used these grasses for offerings to the gods instead of pigs. *Lit.*, pig excreta. (NEAL 72.)

kūkae pueo. Species of grass; a weed. *Lit.*, owl excreta.

kukū. Small thorn or bur that fastens readily on clothes; the thorn bush.

kūlina, kurina. Corn, maize (*Zea Mays* L. Corn), with no wild forms but including several races: sweet, pop, dent, and flint. It is grown increasingly in Hawaiʻi with emphasis on seed corn. (NEAL 81.)

kuolohia. Probably all endemic species of a genus of sedges *(Rhynchospora)*, with tufted stems, numerous narrow leaves, and clusters of small brown spikelets. (NEAL 465.)

lāpine. Lemon grass *(Cymbapogon citratus)*, a grass with the odor of lemon, fragrant leaves with sharp edges. Also called *lūkini*. (NEAL 79.)

lau mauʻu. Blade of grass.

lili. Variety of *pili* grass. (PE.)

lūkini. Same as *lāpine*, lemon grass. (NEAL 79.)

mahiki. Thick, tall grass *(Sporobolus virginicus)*, a turf-forming, sand-binding rush grass, common on beaches of Hawaiʻi. It is also used as lawn grass around beach houses. Same as *ʻakiʻaki*, a grass used to exorcise evil spirits, especially when *mahiki* shrimps were not available. (NEAL 66.) See **mānienie ʻakiʻaki.**

makaloa, makoloa. Perennial sedge *(Cyperus laevigatus)*. (NEAL 86.) See **Plants: Uses.**

mākuakua. Species of grass growing in bunches; bunch grass. (A.)

mānewanewa. A beach grass, used for making *lei*s on Lanaʻi.

mānienie. Bermuda grass *(Cynodon dactylon)*. A fine-leafed, cosmopolitan grass, much used for lawns in Hawaiʻi. Its name refers to the plant's creeping habit. (NEAL 68.)

mānienie ʻakiʻaki. Seashore rush grass *(Sporobolus virginicus)*. This is a turf-forming, sand-binding rush grass. The Hawaiian word *ʻakiʻaki* refers to the supposed power of this grass to exorcise evil spirits. (NEAL 66.) See **mahiki.**

mānienie aliʻi. Wire grass *(Eleusine indica)*. A weed found in lawns and waste places. Introduced to Hawaiʻi about 1840. It has strong stems and many tenacious but shallow roots. Young plants may be eaten by stock. (NEAL 67.)

mānienie haole. Buffalo grass, St. Augustine grass, *(Stenotaphrum secundatum)*. A native of the United States, it is a creeping perennial of Hawai'i. Propagated by cutlets. Planted for lawns in Hawai'i. See **'aki'aki haole.**

mānienie maoli. Buffalo grass *(Stenotaphrum secundatum).* A creeping perennial commonly planted for lawns in Hawai'i. Like the seashore rush grass it was supposed to have the power to exorcise evil spirits. See **'aki'aki haole.**

mānienie 'ula. Small, stiff, weedy grass *(Chrysopogon aciculatus).* It tends to mat thickly. It produces barbed spikelets which stick to humans' clothes and animals' skin or fur.

mau'u. General name for grasses, sedges, rushes, and herbs.

mau'u kepanī. Velvet grass *(Zoisia tenuifolia),* a turf-forming grass. It is a dense, fine, dark-green grass that forms hummocks soon after planting. Called Japanese grass in Hawai'i. (NEAL 67.)

mau'u kukū. Bur or prickly grass *(Cenchrus echinatus).* A weedy grass bearing round burs that stick to anything passing by. See **'ume'alu.** (NEAL 76.)

mau'u laiki. Rice grass *(Paspalum orbiculare),* a coarse, tufted perennial grass used like *pili* to thatch houses. (NEAL 73.)

mokae. Plant resembling nut grass *(Cyperus rotundus).* (NEAL 84.) See **kili'o'opu.**

'ohe. All kinds of bamboo in Hawai'i are known as *'ohe.* Vigorous underground stems, growing horizontally in crowded clumps, supply the base for shrub or tree growth. Eight genera are represented in Hawai'i. (NEAL 66.)

pālāmoe. Grass. No data. Used in *Unwritten Literature* by Emerson.

pili. A grass, tanglehead *(Heteropogon contortus),* once used for thatching houses, both walls and roof. It was preferred because of its pleasant odor, brown color, and neat appearance. In a warm, dry climate a thatching job would last for ten years.

pilipili'ula, mānienie 'ula. Small, stiff, weedy grass *(Chrysopogon aciculatus),* from southeastern Asia. It forms mats and bears a narrow head of reddish, barbed spikelets, which stick to people's clothes and animals' coats. (NEAL 80.)

pīpī wai. All species of sedge of the genus *Eleocharis.* Also called *kohekohe.* (NEAL 87.) See **Plants: Rushes.**

pū'ohe'ohe. Job's tears *(Coix lachryma - jobi),* a coarse, branched grass growing in tropical areas. An annual resembling Indian corn. The seeds or beads are the plant's most interesting feature. They are worn for rosaries, sometimes for curative purposes. In Hawai'i mats, purses, *leis,* and so on were also made from the seeds. See **pūpū kōlea.** (NEAL 80.)

pūpū. Clump of grass.

pūpū kōlea. A grass, also a periwinkle. Early writers mention Job's tears as being strung and used for ear drops in the South Pacific. See **pūohe'ohe.** (NEAL 80.)

'uki. Coarse sedge (all species of *Cladium*) with pointed, leathery leaves, up to 3 feet long by ½ inch wide. Used for dry flower arrangements. The Hawaiians called it *'aha niu* (coconut sennit) because the leaves were used for tying. (NEAL 89.)

'ume'alu. Bur grass *(Cenchrus echinatus)*. Also called *ma'au kūkū.* (NEAL 76.)

weuweu. General name for grasses and herbs. (Kanl. 11:15.)

PLANTS: Growth

The words in this category are concerned primarily with young plants. Examples are not confined to any one variety of plant.

ahihi. Any plant with extensive runners or long creepers, as cup of gold *(Solandra hartwegii)*. (NEAL 748.)

ahuahu. To grow fast, thrive. *Ulu ahu,* to grow vigorously and rapidly. See **ehuehu.**

aūlu. To grow; *ulu,* to grow, increase.

ehuehu. Healthy and vigorous growth. See **ahuahu,** a more common term.

hā'awe'awe. Potato growths from rootlets after harvesting. In fact, Dorothy M. Kahananui says, "We used to coil potato vines after harvesting and cover a portion with soil which produced another crop."

haupu'upu'u, hāpu'upu'u, hā'apu'apu. Sprouts from sweet potato vines. If the potato vines are left for awhile, roots will grow from the nodes. Early Hawaiians did not grow sweet potatoes from sprouts, only vine cuttings or slips.

heu. To sprout, as seedlings.

hō'i'o. To grow thick. The Hawaiian *hō'i'o* ferns grow so thickly that it is difficult to walk through the matted growth. (NEAL 745; KILO.)

ho'oheu. To grow, sprout, germinate.

ho'okokōhi. Stunted, slow to grow.

ho'opiha. To fill out in growing.

ho'opulapula. To propagate by planting cuttings; to start seedlings.

ho'oūlu. To grow, sprout.

kā. Vine that branches, spreads, and runs. (A.) Vine, as of a sweet potato; to send out a vine; to grow into a vine. (PE.) See **ke-kā-ulu-ohi.**

kā'aha'aha. To grow thriftily, of plants. (PE.)

kā hiwa. Sacred vine.

kāi'oi'o. To have a scrubby irregular growth; to be untrimmed or unpruned; to be uncared for.

kākiwi. To layer a plant; to start a new plant or growth.

kālī. Long vine, as of a sweet potato.

kālina. Roots of the sweet potato which form at the ends of a vine segment and grow new crops; long vine, as that of a sweet potato.

ke kā ulu ohi. Growing vine, as the sweet potato in shoots; young growth. *Ke-kā-ulu-ohi* is the name of Lunalilo's mother and of a dormitory on the Kamehameha School's upper campus. Pukui-Elbert translates it as the vine that flourishes. (KILO.)

kīkī holo. To grow fast.

kolokolo. Any creeping vine.

kupa li'i. Slow, retarded growth.

kupu. To sprout, spring up, grow, as vegetables. See **nopu.**

kupuna. Starting point for growing.

kupuohi. To grow vigorously, wild and lush.

lā'au hihi. Creeping vine.

lau nahele. Plants, forest growth, leaves.

mākua, māhua. To attain full growth; to reach maturity; a growing. (Puk. 1:12.)

māohiohi. To grow vigorously. See **ohiohi.**

mūnō. Retarded, imperfect growth, as with plants occasionally.

nene'e. To grow low, as a creeping, spreading vine.

nopu. To spring up, as a seed planted. See **kupu.**

oha. Thriving; spreading, as vines; to grow with lushness.

ohiohi. To grow vigorously; to flourish, as plants.

'ōhulu. To grow, especially from broken or torn bits of sweet potato vines; sprouts from old potatoes; second growth potatoes.

'ōkupu. To sprout; to show forth roots, as the ti plant.

'olūlu. Growth.

ōpū. To expand, as a flower opening from a bud.

'ououo. To grow thriftily, as plants.

polopoloūa. Unripe but still growing *hala* fruit from the pandanus tree.

pōlumu. General name for trailing vines.

pūhili. Wild and lush plant growth.

pulapula. Sugarcane stems cut for planting.

'uali kahiki. White or Irish potato *(Solanum tuberosum)*, grown from eyes or buds of the very edible potato itself. Even here the botanist calls the Irish potato an underground stem. (KILO.)

ulu. Growth. See **'aūlu,** to grow.

uluāhewa. Wild and lush in growth; luxuriantly.

uluaō'a. Growing in wild profusion, as in a rainforest or jungle.

ulu'āwiawi. To grow rapidly.

PLANTS: Herbs

This is a fascinating listing, revealing the wealth of beautiful Hawaiian words representing native reactions to these plants— which are beautiful as well as practical.

'a'ao. A banana, tall, wild and uncultivated. No data.

'āhewa. O'ahu name for the *mānā* fern *(Pteris irregularis)*. (NEAL 17.) See **Plants: Uses.**

'āhinahina. Florida moss; the long moss *(Tillandsia usneoides)*. See **hinahina.** (NEAL 170.)

'āhina kuahiwi. Herbaceous, native fern *(Cyrtomium caryotideum)*, that grows in many mountain areas of Hawai'i. It is a remedy for general debility and stomach ache.

'ahu'awa, 'ehu'awa. A sedge *(Cyperus javanicus)*. (NEAL 86.) See **Plants: Uses.**

aka'aka'awa. Endemic Hawaiian plant *(Hillebrandia sandwicensis)*, a member of the begonia family. Rarely found and then in damp ravines at altitudes of between 2,000 and 4,000 feet. Called *pua maka nui* on Kaua'i. (NEAL 602.)

akiahala, kanawao, pu'aha nui. Small, endemic trees *(Broussaisia arguta)*. This genus is native to Hawai'i. Useful plants related to it are currants and gooseberries. An old belief was that eating these fruits helped in fecundity. (NEAL 380.)

'ākōlea. Native fern *(Athyrium microphyllum)*, having large, beautiful, lacy fronds. (NEAL 25.)

'ākōloa. Species of fern. No data. (A.)

'ākulikuli. Wild, prostrate, coastal herb *(Sesuvium portulacastrum)*, known in many countries. Looks much like purslane. (NEAL 340.)

'ākulikuli kula. Purslane *(Portulaca oleracea)*. Also called pigweed. It is a smooth plant growing close to the ground that bears small, flat, succulent, reddish to dull green leaves. A few portulacas are native to Hawai'i but most are rarely seen. (NEAL 342.)

'ākulikuli lei. Noon flowers *(Lampranthus glomeratus)*. The species with the rose-pink flower is considered the best known in Hawai'i. The flowers are popular in *leis*. This rose-pink form is a succulent, low-spreading, shrubby plant. It grows largely in Waimea, Hawai'i; Koke'e, Kaua'i; and Wahiawa, O'ahu. The flowers open around noon in the sunshine. (NEAL 341.)

'ala'ala wai nui. All species of *Peperomia,* a small succulent forest herb related to *'awa.* Qualified by *kāne* on O'ahu and *kupa li'i* on Hawai'i. (NEAL 293; PE 15.)

ali'ipoe. Ornamental canna *(Canna indica).* (NEAL 263.) See **Plants: Uses.**

'ape. Large, taro-shaped plant *(Alocasia macrorrhiza).* (NEAL 156.) See **Plants: Uses.**

'auko'i. Coffee senna *(Cassia occidentalis).* (NEAL 422.) See **Plants: Uses.**

'awapuhi 'ai. Same as *'awapuhi Pākē.* (NEAL 257.) See **Plants: Uses.**

'awapuhi ke'oke'o. White ginger *(Hedychium coronarium).* (NEAL 252.) See **Plants: Uses.**

'awapuhi ko'oko'o. Torch ginger *(Phaeomeria speciosa).* (NEAL 258.) See **Plants: Uses.**

'awapuhi luheluhe. Shell ginger *(Catimbium speciosum),* a highly ornamental plant. Also called porcelain ginger. *Lit.,* drooping ginger. (NEAL 259.)

'awapuhi melemele. Yellow or cream ginger *(Hedychium flavescens).* (NEAL 252.) See **Plants: Uses.**

'awapuhi Pākē. Ginger *(Zingiber officinalis).* (NEAL 257.) Also called *'awapuhi 'ai.* See **Plants: Uses.**

'awapuhi 'ula'ula. Red ginger *(Alpinia purpurata),* a native of some of the Pacific islands and a common ornamental in Hawai'i. Grows from 4 to 15 feet. (NEAL 260.)

'aweoweo. Native herb or shrub *(Chenopodium oahuense).* Also called *'aheahea,* lambsquarters. (NEAL 331.) See **Plants: Uses.**

'aweuweu. Variety of taro, often growing wild. It is good for *poi* but too acrid for table taro. Also called *ma'auea.* (PE.)

'ēkaha, 'ākaha. Bird's nest fern *(Asplenium nidus).* In the vernacular it might be termed a tree fern for its usual perch is as a large dark green rosette of fronds on tree trunks and branches. Many native species of *Asplenium* grow wild in Hawai'i. (NEAL 21.) See **Plants: Uses.**

ha'uoi, ha'uōwī, ōwī, oi. Weedy verbena *(Verbena litoralis).* (NEAL 721.) See **Plants: Uses.**

hihialou. Plant with small yellow flowers. No data. (A.)

hinahina. Florida moss *(Tillandsia usneoides),* an herb that grows on tree branches with slender, gray, flexible hanging stems and leaves resembling the beard of Sanford B. Dole, the "grand old man of Hawai'i." See **'umi'umi-o-Dole.** (NEAL 170.)

hō'i'o. Large native fern *(Athyrium arnottii).* (NEAL 25.) See **Plants: Uses.**

honohono. Wandering Jew *(Commelina diffusa).* (NEAL 185.) See **Plants: Uses.**

huna kai. White-flowered beach morning glory *(Ipomea stolonifera).* Distributed in tropical regions, it bears white flowers with yellow centers. (NEAL 705.)

'ihi. Yellow wood sorrel *(Oxalis corniculata).* Wood sorrels are all oxalis. This one is a creeping perennial herb. Flowers have a pleasant, sour taste due to oxalic acid. (NEAL 473.) See **Plants: Uses.**

'ihi-mākole. Kind of *'ihi,* with yellow flowers and red stems and leaves. (NEAL 473.) See **Plants: Uses.**

'i'i. Short for *hāpu'u 'i'i,* a Hawaiian tree fern *(Cibotium chamissoi),* cultivated as an ornamental. Similar to the *hāpu'u* with similar characteristics and uses. (NEAL 10.)

'ili ahi. Small tree or shrub *(Santalum* spp.). (NEAL 325.) See **Plants: Uses.**

iliau. Native Hawaiian plant *(Wilkesia gymnoxiphium)* found only on the dry leeward slopes of Kaua'i. A woody single-stem plant that grows to 12 feet. (NEAL 845.)

'ilima. Various forms of *'ilima* plants *(Sida* spp.). (NEAL 552.) See **Plants: Uses.**

'iwa'iwa. Maidenhair ferns *(Adianum* spp.). (NEAL 17.) See **Plants: Uses.**

kāhili. *Kāhili* ginger *(Hedychium gardnerianum),* a close and famous relative of the *'awapuhi* gingers. Its yellow flowers project out on stalks from the central spike commonly thought to resemble the *kāhili,* symbol of royalty. It has a flower similar to that of the yellow ginger. (NEAL 253.)

kakakē, kake. Species of potato. (A.) Variety of sweet potato; poor quality, as of taro not fit for *poi.* (PE.)

kalo. Taro *(Colocasia esculenta).* (NEAL 157.) See **Plants: Uses.**

kaluhā. Papyrus *(Cyperus papyrus)*. (NEAL 83.) See **Plants: Uses.**

kalukalu. Kind of rush or grass like the sedge, *kaluha*. Well known around Kaua'i shores and beaches, especially at Kapa'a.

kāmole. 1. The primrose willow *(Ludwigia octivalvis)*, a perennial herb growing up to 4 feet high. It is widely distributed in tropical regions and grows as a weed in wet places. Its flowers are yellow. The plant is used medicinally. (NEAL 648.) 2. Name of a plant *(Polygonum glabrum)*. Common around *kalo* patches and running water. A member of the buckwheat family.

kaua lau, mai'a kaua lau. Hawaiian variety of banana or plantain, a cooking banana *(Musa paradisica* var. *normalis)*. Grows to a height of 25 feet. Flour is made from the fruit. (NEAL 249.)

kauna'oa. Native Hawaiian dodder *(Cuscuta sandwichiana)*. Grows on roadsides and in uncultivated fields. It is a parasite. Plants are used as orange *leis*, and they represent Lana'i in the "Song of the Islands." In old literature it is called the "motherless plant." (NEAL 710.)

kī. Shrubby ti plant *(Cordyline terminalis)*. (NEAL 203.) See **Plants: Uses.**

kīkānia. Cocklebur *(Xanthium* spp.), a coarse herb bearing tenacious burs 1 inch long. (NEAL 838.)

kīkānia pīpili. Spanish clover *(Desmodium uncinatum)*, a long established perennial herb on roadsides and in pastures in Hawai'i. The fruit sticks to clothing and the coats of animals. (NEAL 451.)

kikawaiō. Native fern *(Cyclosorus cyatheoides)*. (NEAL 21.) See **Plants: Uses.**

kīlau. Bracken fern *(Pteridium aquilinum)*, a cosmopolitan plant collected at up to 9,500 feet but most common at 4,000. (NEAL 15.)

kō. Sugarcane *(Saccharum officinarum)*. (NEAL 77.) See **Plants: Uses.**

kō'āweoweo. Sugarcane species with joints striped white and red. No other data. (A.)

kō kea; kea. Variety of sugarcane. One of the best known and most used canes, especially in medicine. (PE.)

kōloa. Long cane. *Lit.,* cane long, the reason why a district in Kaua'i is so named. No other data. (A.)

ko'oko'olau. Beggar tick, Spanish needle *(Bidens* spp.). (NEAL 844.) See **Plants: Uses.**

kulu'ī. Endemic shrub, amaranth family. Contains a genus called *kulu'ī (Nototrichium* spp.), with flowers in downy, catkin-like spikes $\frac{1}{2}$ to 2 inches long. (NEAL 332.)

kupa li'i. See **'ala'ala'wai nui.**

kupukupu. General name for ferns with a single stem, as the sword fern *(Nephrolepis exaltata),* sometimes placed on the *hula* altar to Laka; to gain knowledge; to sprout. Also called *ni'ani'au, 'ōkupukupu.*

kupukupu 'ala. Rose geranium *(Pelargonium graveolens).* (NEAL 471.) See **Plants: Uses.**

la'alā'au. Herbs, shrubs, green things; that class of vegetation between grasses and trees. (Mat. 13:32.)

lā'au iki 'ai. General names for herbs. (Roma 14:2; A.)

lā'au iki 'ai 'ia. Edible herb. (Roma 14:2; PE.)

lā'au palupalu. Herbs, tender vegetables. (PE.)

laiki, raisi. Rice *(Oryza sativa)* (NEAL 69.) See **Plants: Uses.**

laua'e, lauwa'e. Aromatic herb, fragrant fern *(Phymatosorus scolopendria),* with a sweet smell that suggests the *maile,* a twining shrub. (NEAL 27.)

lau lele. 1. Butterfly weed, milkweed, blood flower *(Asclepias curassavica).* (NEAL 697.) See **Plants: Uses. 2.** Dandelion *(Taraxacum officinale).* (NEAL 860.) See **Plants: Uses.**

lau nahele. Herbs generally. (Kin. 1:11.)

launahele hou. Tender herbs. (Kanl. 32:2; A.)

lilina. Flax or linseed *(Linum usitatissimum).* (NEAL 475.) See **Plants: Uses.**

līpoa. Much branched, brown seaweeds of the three most edible kinds.

mai'a. Banana *(Musa paradisica).* Introduced by the Hawaiians. A staple food from earliest days. (NEAL 249.)

mākeke. Black mustard *(Brassica nigra).* A cosmopolitan herb, a weed in Hawai'i, once cultivated for seeds, the main source of table mustard. (NEAL 370; Mat. 13:31.) *Hua mākeke,* mustard seed. See **Plants: Uses.**

makou. 1. All native and introduced species of buttercups *(Ranunculus)* of which there are two native upland species with small yellow flowers and many stamens, pistils, and seeds. (NEAL 351.) **2.** Native perennial herb *(Peucedanum sandwicense)* of the parsley family, with coarse leaves and tuberous roots, used medicinally. It has a smooth skin and rather slimy juice used as a laxative prenatally and continuing usually for the first year with the infant. Looks like giant celery leaves.

malina. Sisal *(Agave sisalana).* (NEAL 224.) See **Plants: Uses.**

mamauea, manauea. Wild *kalo* growing in uncultivated places. See *'āweuweu,* a native variety of *kalo* also often growing wild. Both are good for *poi* but too acrid for table taro.

mānā. Fern *(Pteris irregularis)* found on all islands usually in woods and deep gullies. *Mānā* is its Oʻahu name.

māʻohiʻohi. Member of the mint family *(Stenogyne rugosa),* native to Hawaiʻi. Not uncommon from 2,000 to 8,000 feet.

melekule, melekula. Pot marigold *(Calendula officinalis).* (NEAL 855.) See **Plants: Uses.**

miki nalo. Insectivorous herb *(Drosera anglica)* found in the Alakaʻi Swamp at the 4,000 foot level. Its miniature spoonlike leaves have little hairs at the ends, each with a drop of sticky liquid at its end. Insects become entangled on the hairs and are absorbed by the plant, furnishing necessary nutrients for growth. It is called a "fly catcher." *Lit.,* to suck flies. (NEAL 374.)

moa. Tufted, green, leafless plants *(Psilotum nudum).* (NEAL 1.) See **Plants: Uses.**

mohihio. Name of a plant. No data. (A.)

nani ahiahi. Four o'clocks *(Mirabilis jalapa).* (NEAL 335.) See **Plants: Uses.**

naunau. Name of several acrid plants such as wild horseradish, cresses, and peppergrass. All are used medicinally.

nehe. Prostrate or perennial herbs and small shrubs *(Lipochaeta* spp.). Twenty-six species of *Lipochaeta* are known, twenty-four of which are native to Hawaiʻi. (NEAL 840.)

nena. Seaside heliotrope *(Heliotropium curassavicum),* a prostrate, smooth, perennial herb, 1 to 2 feet long. The plant is native to Hawaiʻi and America. It is found near the sea and in salt marshes. Formerly it was dried, and tea brewed from it was used as a tonic. (NEAL 718.)

nohu. Hoary prostrate perennial *(Tribulus cistoides),* found on coasts of tropical regions around the world. It is considered a weed, because its spiny fruits stick to the coats of animals and injure their feet. It has yellow flowers. It is called "carpet weed" because its growth of silvery-green leaves completely covers large areas. (NEAL 477.)

ōī, ōwī, haʻuōwī. Tropical plant *(Verbena litoralis).* (NEAL 721.)

ʻōlena. Turmeric *(Curcuma domestica).* (NEAL 255.) See **Plants: Uses.**

paha. Wild sweet potato or morning glory with enlarged tuber eaten in time of famine. (PE.) The leaf of a plant eaten in time of scarcity. (A.) Also called *kūpala.*

paʻiniu. Native Hawaiian lily *(Astelia* spp.) with long, narrow, silvery leaves forming rosette-shaped plants growing on the ground or perched in trees. Flowers are small, yellowish or greenish. Formerly, on visiting Kīlauea Crater, Hawaiians selected leaves of a kind of *pa'iniu* growing there *(Astelia menziesiana)*, removed the translucent outer layer, and braided it into hat *leis*, as a sign they had visited the volcano. (NEAL 192.)

paka. Tobacco *(Nicotiana tabacum)*. (NEAL 752.) See **Plants: Uses.**

pakai. Spleen amaranth *(Amaranthus dubius)*, a coarse, erect, spineless, weedy, tropical herb. It looks much like Chinese spinach. Formerly seeds were ground into meal and cooked. Young, tender parts of the plant were cooked and eaten. (NEAL 334.)

pala. Native fern *(Marattia douglasii)*. (NEAL 6.) See **Plants: Uses.**

pala'a, palapala'a. Lace fern *(Sphenomeris chinensis)*, one of the commonest wild Hawaiian ferns. Formerly Hawaiians extracted a dark brown dye from the lacy fronds. (NEAL 15.)

pāla'au. Healing herb; to heal with herbs. Hi'i-aka, the goddess of healing.

palai, palapalai. Hairy, native Hawaiian fern *(Microlepia setosa)*. (NEAL 12.) See **Plants: Uses.**

palani. Sugarcane *(Saccharum officinarum)*. *Palani* is a purple variety, growing more in the higher and exposed highlands. This was the sugarcane of the early Hawaiians. There are at least forty Hawaiian words for varieties of sugarcane. One is *ho'opa'apa'a* (quarreling) because two men quarreled about naming it. Another is *manu lele,* (flying bird) involving the return of a wife's love for her husband. (NEAL 77–79.) See **Plants: Uses.**

palaoa. Wheat *(Triticum aestivum)* was formerly cultivated on the highlands of East Maui and Hawai'i, but growers lost out to competition from California. The grain contained so much gluten that it required the addition of foreign flour to make light bread.

palau. Maui name for fern.

pale, bale. Barley *(Hordeum vulgare)*, a tufted annual 2 to 4 feet tall, a native of the Old World. It is cultivated for grain but in the islands is usually seen in pastures. First seen in 1906.

palunu. Creeping plant like the *koali*. No data. (PE; A.)

pepeiao akua. Tree fungus *(Auricularia auricula)*. Jew's-ear, a fungus or touch-wood that grows on dead trees and also on *hau* and *kukui*. Used as a delicacy by the Chinese. (A.)

pia. Polynesian arrowroot *(Tacca leontopetaloides)*. (NEAL 228.) See **Plants: Uses.**

poʻe. Native purslane *(Portulaca sclerocarpa)* with narrow leaves and whitish flowers. (PE.) Also called *ʻihi-mākole.*

puaʻa kuhinia, pākahakaha. Native fern *(Pleopeltis thunbergiana)* with related forms in Asia. Common to trees and rocks.

pua lele. Sow thistle *(Sonchus oleraceus),* an annual weedy herb. (NEAL 860.) See **Plants: Uses.**

pua makahiki. Annual flower. No data. (PE.)

puapākē. *Chrysanthemum,* a genus, from the eastern hemisphere, annual or perennial herbs. Flower heads are red, yellow, and purple. A member of the daisy family. (NEAL 850.)

pua pilipili. Spanish clover *(Desmodium uncinatum),* a long established herb in Hawaiʻi. Grows to 3 feet. Used for fodder and ground cover. The plant fruits stick to clothing and coats of animals. (NEAL 451.)

uhauhakō, pāwale. Native dock *(Rumex* spp.). Some are weedy herbs such as sorrel and dock of the buckwheat family. (NEAL 328.)

uiui. Arrowroot, a slender high herb *(Maranta arundinacea).* (NEAL 271.) See **Plants: Uses.**

ʻukiʻuki. Native lily *(Dianella sandwicensis)* with smooth leathery leaves. They form a two-row cluster along a short, erect stem from which a loosely branching flower cluster rises. Flowers are small and whitish or blue. The fruits, conspicuous light or dark blue, long persistent berries, are the chief attraction of the plant. Formerly, Hawaiians extracted a blue dye from the berries for *kapa.* This Hawaiian lily is seen wild in the woods around Kīlauea Crater. (NEAL 191.) See **Plants: Uses.**

uluhe. False staghorn fern *(Dicranopteris* spp., *Hicriopteris* sp. and *Sticherus* sp.), found in Hawaiʻi between 500 and 5,000 feet in dense thickets. It smothers plants and prevents growth of other vegetation. It advances by means of underground root stocks and raises wiry fronds. It is of little value as part of the natural succession of eroded areas. (NEAL 9.)

ʻumiʻumi-o-Dole. Dole's whiskers. See **hinahina.**

wāwae ʻiole. Cosmopolitan tropical club moss *(Lycopodium cernuum).* This Hawaiian name means rat's foot. It is a far-creeping moss-like plant growing well at the edge of woods. It is gathered to make Christmas wreaths and is inserted in *lei*s. This plant is a descendant of the giant club mosses of the United States mainland which changed into the coal beds of today. (NEAL 2.)

weleweka. The coleus *(Coleus blumei),* an ornamental perennial from Java. *Weleweka* means velvet in English. (NEAL 734.)

weuweu. General name for herbage; grass; green grass; a clump of grass or greenery, as placed on the altar honoring the goddess Laka. (PE.)

PLANTS: Limu

The Hawaiian word for marine algae is *limu*. Seaweed is an English synonym.

At the national level in the field of *limu* studies, special notice has been taken of a graduate from the class of 1937 at the Kamehameha School for Girls, Honolulu, Hawai'i, who in early youth, developed a flair for botany: Isabella Aiona Abbott. Her interest was cultivated by the school's principal, Miss Maude Shaeffer. She obtained her B.A., M.S., and Ph.D. degrees in botany. Now she spends alternate semesters as Professor of Botany at the University of Hawaii in Honolulu and Professor of Biology at Stanford University in California. Her special interest in *limu* has extended to folk taxonomy and a single genus of *limu,* liagora. In both areas she has gained widespread recognition.

'a'ala'ula. Edible seaweed *(Codium reediae),* called *a'ala* on Kaua'i. It is more familiar on all islands as *limu wāwae'iole (Codium edule),* a creeping species covering coral rocks with branched, spongy, felt-like mats. As *'ala'ula* it is known for its fragrance.

'āka 'ako'a. Species of seaweed *(Ectocarpus indicus)* plentiful along shallow coastal waters. Used for food.

'aki'aki. Succulent, brittle, brownish-red alga *(Ahnfeltia concinna),* thus called on Hawai'i and Maui; perhaps called *kō'ele'ele* on Kaua'i and Hawai'i; *'eleau* was its name on Maui. Grows on lava. A popular food with raw fish, as a relish and in soup. A good source of gelatin.

alani. Two brown seaweeds *(Dictyota acutiloba* and *D. baratayresii),* both very branched. They attach themselves to other algae. Native Hawaiians disliked their bitterness.

amansia. Common alga *(Amansia glomerata)* forming patches of dull brownish or bright red rosettes when under overhanging rocks. Used for food if seaweed is clean. Also called *līpepeiao* and *limu hā'ula.*

'anapanapa. Edible seaweed, reddish and stiff. It is tenacious, holding fast to the exposed lava rocks near the tide line in rough water, where it is washed constantly by the surf. Especially liked by the natives of Kaua'i and Maui. Also called *limu loloa,* perhaps *Gelidium* spp.

'ānuhenuhe. Species of seaweed. No data. (A.)

'āpe'epe'e. Species of *limu (Laurencia nidifica).* Lives in shallow water along coral reefs. All species are used for food and when prepared are marketed. Abbott and Williamson give eight to ten *Laurencia* spp. under these common Hawaiian names. Also called *līpe'e, līpe'epe'e* for the finer forms, and *māneoneo* for the coarser, shorter species.

'ēkaha, ēkahakaha. Two plants, one a green-colored seaweed *(Pterocladia caerulesceus);* the other, a land plant, the bird's nest fern *(Asplenium nidis).* Both are very similar except in size. Each has a segment of five "leaves" attached to a stem, each having the shape of long oblong fronds. The seaweed is tiny in contrast to the fern. But both wave their fronds similarly in their respective environments of seawater currents or free air movements. It can be said that the keen-eyed natives saw in the bird's nest fern frond the same shape and waving actions they had always seen in the seaweed *'ēkaha;* hence, the name. And hence perhaps, the first pairing of a sea plant and a land plant as described in the *Hawaiian Hymn of Creation* in the *Kumulipo.* (KL.)

'ele'ele. Edible alga *(Enteromorpha prolifera),* a black *limu.* It lives in fresh brackish or salt water. Eaten with raw fish and in stew. Some of the species are very popular at *lu'au* tables. See **hulu'īlio.**

hāwane. Small red seaweed *(Polysiphonia* spp.), with branching filaments growing into dense tufts. Not popular for food.

huluhuluwaena. Irregularly branching, dark-red seaweed *(Grateloupia Filicina),* so called on Hawai'i. Called *pakele a wa'a* on Maui and Moloka'i. It is abundant in shallow water within the coral reef and on submerged rocks. Used in beef stew with octopus and especially beef liver *(ake).*

hulu'īlio. 1. A seaweed *(Centroceras clavulatum),* red in color and forming dense tufts. 2. Seaweed called *'ele'ele (Enteromorpha prolifera).* 3. Branching green seaweed *(Cladophora* spp.) occurring in mountain streams and pools.

hulu manu. Green seaweed *(Caulerpa* spp.) with roots. Also called *hulu moa, līmoa.*

hulu pua'a. Small, matted seaweed *(Spyridia spinella).* Its branches are covered with short bristles. Eaten mostly in South Hawai'i.

huna. Alga *(Hypnea cervicornis)*. At one time a commonly eaten Hawaiian seaweed, especially when cooked. It has a fine quality of gelatin when boiled. See **limu huna.**

īlioha'a. Sea lettuce, seaweed *(Ulva* spp.). Two of the three species in Hawai'i are common in shallows along the coasts and coral reefs. *Ufasciata* is known as *limu pahapaha* or *līpahapaha; Ulactuca,* as *palahalaha* or *pakaiea.* All grow in quiet waters near the shore and are easily gathered.

kākanakana. Species of *limu, limu kākanakana,* smooth and slippery. (A.) This word probably replaced by *limu kā kanaka.* (PE.)

kaupau. Edible brown seaweed *(Chnoospora Minima).* Magruder and Hunt list two more *Chnoospora* but with no Hawaiian names. Also called *wāwāhi wa'a.*

kihe. Red seaweed *(Chylocladia* spp.) with narrow, cylindrical, branching stems. Also called *akuila.* Unknown to AW.

kō'ele'ele. 1. Small, edible seaweed *(Gymnogongrus* spp.) with fronds and thick, flattened stems and branches. Also called *'āwikiwiki.* **2.** Seaweed with brownish-red fronds, horny and irregularly branched *(Ahnfeltia concina).* Called *'aki'aki* on Maui and Hawai'i, *kō'ele'ele* on Kaua'i and Hawai'i.

limu. Hawaiian word for alga, a general name for seaweed, sea moss, sea lettuce, land mosses, and freshwater algae.

limu akuila. A seaweed *(Chylocladia* spp.), one of which, with branching stems is called *limu kihe,* an edible alga. Unknown to AW.

limu huna. Fine, common seaweed *(Hypnea nidifica),* liked especially when boiled with octopus.

limu kā kanaka. Blue-green alga *(Nostoc commune).* A freshwater weed common on damp soils, around water troughs and dripping tanks. In the wet season it covers the ground, making it slippery. Referred to in Hawaiian songs. (PE.)

limu kala. Long, rough, brown seaweed *(Sargassum* spp.), gathered in shallow to deep water along the reefs. It is more abundant than any other seaweed in most places and is usually used as a typical *limu* in talks and lectures. Eaten in a mixture of seaweeds, raw.

limu kīkī. Edible seaweed. (CMH.) Name given a seaweed. (PE.)

limu kohu. Red seaweed resembling a miniature pink tree *(Asparagopsis taxiformis).* It is succulent, cylindric, and tufted, found attached to coral reefs in feathery, tree-like tufts. A very popular and widely used alga and the original one used in *poke.*

limu lūʻau. Red seaweed (*Porphyra* spp.), a highly prized delicacy. Found on exposed rocks, making it difficult to gather. Scarce also due to short seasons. It is a beautiful purple in color. See **līpaheʻe.**

līpahapaha. Edible seaweed *(Ulva fasciata),* called by the general name of sea lettuce. Other names include *pahapaha,* young taro leaves from Kauaʻi, and *pakaiea,* ruffled, heart-shaped leaves from Hawaiʻi. Found on all islands, usually on lava rock and old coral.

līpaheʻe. Same as *pāheʻeheʻe,* seaweed which is called *līpāhoe* on Maui. Same as seaweed *limu lūʻau* of Kauaʻi.

lipalaʻō. Edible alga (*Pithophora* spp.). Other native names are *limu pālāwai* or *līpālāwai,* general names as applied to fresh and brackish water algae listed as *Stigeoclonium* spp. Both live in pools, streams, and taro patches.

līpeʻepeʻe. A seaweed (*Laurensia* spp.) *kapu* to those learning *hula* because *peʻe* means to hide and the gods did not want anyone to see them eating this seaweed. Also called *līpaʻa* on Hawaiʻi.

līpehu. Salty seaweed that is pounded. Also called *limu paʻakai, lipaʻakai, paʻakai.*

līpepeiao. Small, red seaweed *(Amansia glomerata).* The deep rosettes of this alga are found in deep, shady holes and crevices in the coral reefs. Edible.

līpoa. Two species of widely branched brown seaweed (*Dictyopteris plagiogramma* and *D.* Australis), considered very palatable. Referred to commonly as *limu,* they appeal as a delicacy of crunchy crispness at a Hawaiian *lūʻau.* They are widely distributed on Oʻahu, growing far out on the outer margin of coral reefs.

līpūpū. Edible seaweed that grows attached to a shell.

lī puʻupuʻu. Edible seaweed *(Valonia utricularis)* that grows in clusters along the coral reefs.

loloa. Edible seaweeds (*Gelidium* spp.).

manauea. Small, red seaweed (*Gracilaria coronopifolia*), an all-seasons alga. Extensively used for food; a specialty is cooking it with octopus. It has a clear, fine gelatin. A similar seaweed has a Japanese name, *ogo (Gracilaria bursa-pastoris),* popular with Japanese in Hawaiʻi.

māneoneo. Shorter, coarser red alga (*Laurencia* spp.) than the *peʻepeʻe,* which has longer, finer stems and fronds. Also called *lipuʻupuʻu (Valonia utricularis).* All species are used for food, and all are sold in the market. See **ʻāpeʻepeʻe.**

mo‘opuna. Short for *mo‘opuna a ka līpoa,* a fine red seaweed (*Griffithsia* sp.) used for food on Maui and south Hawai‘i.

nanue. Edible seaweed. No data. (CMH.) *Nenue* is a variant of *nanue.* (PE.)

‘ō‘ōlu. Two common, edible, fragile seaweeds (*Champia parvula, Chondria tenuissima),* pink to purple in color, gelatinous. They must be quickly prepared and soon eaten.

pahe‘e, pāhe‘ehe‘e. Green, cushion-shaped, solid seaweed (*Dictyosphaeria versluysii).* Also called *līpahe‘e, līpahe‘ehe‘e, līpahoe, pāhe‘e.* On Maui it is called *līpāhoe.*

pakele a wa‘a. See **huluhulu waena.**

pālahalaha. Edible seaweed (*Ulva fasciata)* of Moloka‘i and Maui. Called *pahapaha* on Kaua‘i and O‘ahu, *pakaiea* on Hawai‘i.

pāpa‘akea. A seaweed (*Liagora valida)* related to *puakī.*

pe‘epe‘e. Same as *līpe‘epe‘e,* a seaweed of Maui.

pipīlani. Species of green seaweeds (*Enteromorpha* spp.). This is the Maui name. Also called *‘ele‘ele.*

pohāpohā. Green seaweed (*Dictyosphaeria cavernosa),* small, round, and hollow that bursts with a pop when stepped on.

puakī. Red alga (*Liagora maxima),* somewhat calcified but flexible, branched. Not edible. Related to *pāpa‘akea.*

wāwae‘iole. Same as *‘a‘ala‘ala.*

PLANTS: Mosses

In their quiet unobtrusive way mosses often pass unnoticed—unlike their neighbors, trees, shrubs, vines, herbs, grasses, and such—but the subject holds even more satisfaction because of that fact.

‘ēkaha. Moss that grows on rotted trees. Also called *limu ‘ēkaha.*

huluhulu a ‘īlio. Green, velvety, carpet-like mountain moss. Lit., fur like a dog's. (PE.)

hulu o Ka‘au hele moa. A moss said to grow only in Pālolo Valley, Honolulu. It was named after a legendary cock defeated in battle by a hen. According to the story she pulled out his feathers, which fell and became moss. It is used in *lei*s. (PE.)

iliohe. Green, freshwater moss.

kale maka pi‘i. Bright-green, native moss (*Thuidium hawaiiense)* with lacy, flat, mat-forming fronds. See **mākole mākōpi‘i.** (PE.)

limu. General name for all kinds of plants living under water, both fresh and salt. This includes mosses.

limu ʻahuʻula. An upland moss.

limu ʻēkaha. Another name for the moss ʻēkaha.

limu hau lāʻau. General term for mosses growing on trees, which also refers to tiny ferns, lichens, and liverworts.

limu holo a wai. Freshwater moss. (PE.)

limu kele. Moss growing on trees in rain forests. (PE.)

mākole mākopiʻi. A native moss, *(Thuidium hawaiiense)*, whose branches are in one plane looking like small ferns. (PE.)

ʻōnohi awa. Black moss found in fresh water. (PE.)

ʻowau, ʻoau. Species of moss.

peʻepeʻe. Species of moss. This seaweed was *kapu* to *hula* learners because *peʻe* means to hide and the gods would hide their secrets from those eating the seaweed. (PE.) Also called *līpeʻepeʻe,* a seaweed of Maui.

pōpōʻolimu. Moss that grows on stones, especially on mountains where rainfall is abundant. *Heʻiō no ka pō.* (A.)

ʻumiʻumi. Moss that fastens the *nahawele,* a bivalve, to the rocks. (A.) Suckers that fasten bivalves to rocks. (PE.)

ʻumiʻumi o Dole. Florida moss, Spanish moss or long moss *(Tillandsia usneoides). Lit.,* Dole's whiskers. Also called *hinahina.* (NEAL 170.) This is not a true moss but a member of the pineapple family *(Bromeliaceae).* See **Plants: Fruits, hala kahiki.** (NEAL 176; KILO.)

PLANTS: Odoriferous

Odoriferous plants are among the more memorable charms of Hawaiʻi Nei for visitors and locals alike. Fragrances and perfumes come from trees, shrubs, and vines, emanating from their roots, bark, wood, blossoms, or fruits. Their fragrance is captured by crafted or natural processes, whereby breezes and winds waft welcome scents over the land.

ʻawapuhi, ʻawaphui kuahiwi. Wild ginger *(Zingiber zerumbet).* (NEAL 257.) *Lit.,* root fragrant. See **Plants: Uses.**

ʻawapuhi keʻokeʻo. White or butterfly ginger *(Hedychium coronarium).* Also known as the ginger lily. Highly prized as flowers for *leis,* it has a delicate aroma. (NEAL 252.)

hala. Pandanus tree *(Pandanus odoratissimus,* synonym *P. tectorius),* a native from Hawai'i to southern Asia. It is distinguished by its aerial roots which grow out from the trunk like stilts, looking as if the tree were walking on them; hence, the name "walking trees." Tips of the young aerial roots were formerly used medicinally. *Lau hala* leaves, which are tough and pliable, were (and are) plaited into many durable articles: floor and sleeping mats, baskets, fans, sandals for lava walking. In Hawai'i the blind are taught to plait *lau hala.* The fragrant flowers were used in many ways to take advantage of the much desired scent, as is shown by this expression of Puna, Hawai'i: *Puna paia 'ala i ka hala,* Puna, its walls fragrant with pandanus. Drupe of the *hala,* usually orange in color, is a fragrant material for *leis.* (NEAL 51.)

ihu anu. Odoriferous shrub or tree found at Kawelo. (CMH.)

'ili ahi. Sandalwood, trees or shrubs *(Santalum* spp.). Its heartwood is fragrant. (NEAL 335.) See **Plants: Uses.**

kiele. Gardenia, a shrub *(Gardenia augusta).* A native of China, it is grown for its handsome, fragrant flowers. It is popular on the mainland United States as a conservatory plant. Some choice *leis* are made of the flower in Hawai'i. (NEAL 799.)

kolū. Thorny, weedy shrub *(Acacia farnesiana)* that supplies a superior gum named *kolū* after the shrub. This makes a better glue than the well-known Arabic gum. The orange-yellow flower balls yield a penetrating but pleasant odor of perfume. Swollen pods supply a tannin for dye, ink, and tanning; its green fruit is an astringent used medicinally. (NEAL 406.)

kūpaoa. Night cestrum *(Cestrum nocturnum)* and other strong-smelling plants, such as *Peperomia* spp., a scentless plant, and *Railliardia* spp., a genus of plants with a slight resinous odor. Also a plant used to scent *kapa.* (NEAL 751.)

laua'e. Maile-scented fern *(Microsorium scolopendria),* found both wild and cultivated in Hawai'i, creeping over ground and tree trunks. One form has a vanilla-like fragrance, similar to that of the *maile,* popular for *leis.* (NEAL 27.)

lei kolona, lei korona. Rosary, prayer beads. The term is rather new, introduced probably after Catholicism settled in Hawai'i. The rosary looked like a necklace that the Hawaiians called *lei* or *lei'a'i.* (DK.)

maile. A favorite native plant *(Alyxia olivaeformis).* The fragrant bark of its stems and the fragrant, oval, pointed leaves with their vanilla-like odor are more or less indispensable at festive times for decorations and *lei*s. It grows as a straggly, twining shrub in native forests of the lower and middle mountain regions. Much used in songs, hulas, chants, and dirges. Laka, goddess of the *hula,* was invoked as the goddess of the *maile.* (NEAL 690.)

maile haʻi wale. *Maile* vine *(Alyxia olivaeformis)* that has small rounded leaves. *Lit., maile* that breaks easily. (NEAL 690.)

maile kā kahiki. *Maile with an unpleasant odor (Paederia foetida).* Stink vine, native to southern India and environs. *Lit., maile* of Tahiti or *maile* from afar. Also called *maile pilau.* (NEAL 794.)

maile kaluhea. This vine *(Alyxia olivaeformis* var.) grows along cliffs. Its odor is very agreeable. It is useful as a remedy for ulcers and infected sores. *Lit., maile* fragrant. (NEAL 685.)

maile lau liʻi. *Maile* vine *(Alyxia olivaeformis f. augusta)* with sharp, pointed leaves. *Lit., maile* small leaf.

mānele. Soapberry tree *(Sapindus saponaria).* A plant of many useful parts, among them its spherical seeds which are widely used for making rosaries. (NEAL 532.)

manoʻi. Coconut oil scented; perfume. (Isa. 57:9.)

mokihana. Tree *(Pelea anisata),* one of about eighty native species called *alani,* well known in Hawaiian legends. The name *Pelea* is derived from the Hawaiian goddess of volcanoes, Pele. Its fragrant fruits are symbolic of Kauaʻi, the only island on which this species is found. All parts of the tree are anise-scented. The fruit is a leathery, cube-shaped capsule, which is strung into the *mokihana lei* representing Kauaʻi. (NEAL 478.)

naʻenaʻe. Many resinous shrubs and small trees *(Dubautia* including *Railliardia)* confined to Hawaiʻi and growing most commonly in the native forests. Belonging to the daisy family, the plants have narrow leaves and small orange or purple flowers, with heads borne in large, cone-shaped clusters. The Hawaiian name means "pleasant odor." (NEAL 845.)

naio. Bastard sandalwood *(Myoporum sandwicense),* found at levels between the seashore and 10,000 feet in Hawaiʻi. The wood is hard, dark yellow-green, and scented like sandalwood. In the waning sandalwood trade it was often substituted for the actual wood. (NEAL 791.)

pakaha. Native herb *(Lepechinia hastata),* a mint. Its flowers are clustered, narrow, and reddish, and it has gray foliage. Used for kitchen herbs, perfume, insect repellent, flavoring, and medicine. (NEAL 732.)

pala. Fern *(Marattia douglasii),* which the natives ate raw for its laxative effect. In time of famine the thick bases of this fern were cooked for food. The *pala* fronds were wound with *maile* to bring out its fragrance for *leis.* It was also used in *heiau* ceremonies. This fern is now rare. (NEAL 6.)

pīkake. Arabian jasmine *(Jasminum sambac),* a fragrant-flowered shrub with white, tubular flowers. The double flowers resemble small, white roses and are used in *leis.* The flowers were called *pīkake* the name for peacock because Princess Ka'iulani was fond of both. She had white peacocks in her gardens in Waikīkī. The flower is used as a design on quilts and its scent is extracted for perfume. (NEAL 680.)

pō. Heady perfume; fragrance as of the pandanus, gardenia, jasmine, ginger, or night cestrum.

poni. Wood used in ceremony of anointing; to anoint. (Ioane 12:3.) To consecrate by anointing, as a priest. (Puk. 23:41.) To annoint, as a king. (Lunk. 9:8; A.) Probably not a reference to a Hawaiian wood but possibly to a wood distillate used in biblical times to anoint a monarch. (KILO.)

PLANTS: Rushes

Rushes and sedges are quite alike: they look alike, they are closely related, and they are chiefly wind-pollinated. Only a few sedges are included in this category.

The rush family is called Juncaceae, while the sedge family is named Cyneraceae.

kohekohe. Species of sedge *(Eleocharis dulcis)* called water chestnut, a popular vegetable in Chinese dishes. The plant, which grows in water, looks something like an onion. In some countries the stems are made into mats, baskets, and hats. Shorter, finer-stemmed species of *Eleocharis* grow as weeds in some damp spots in Hawai'i. Hawaiians called every kind *kohekohe* or *pipi wai.* (NEAL 87.)

makaloa. Kind of rush out of which mats are made. (A.) A perennial sedge *(Cyperus laevigatus).* (NEAL 86.) See **Plants: Uses.**

māku'eku'e. Bunch grass with which good adobies are made. No data.

naku. Great bulrush, *'aka'akai (Scirpus validus)*, growing at the edges of brackish-water marshes in Hawai'i. The erect stem grows to 9 feet. Formerly Hawaiians used stems of bulrushes like grass or ti leaves for house thatch, for plaited mats for lower layers of *hikie'e* (beds), or for some temporary purposes as the material is not durable. (NEAL 88.)

pīpī wai. Species of the genus *Eleocharis,* of the family of sedges. This is perhaps more like a grass, having a long stem with a little fuzzy ball for a flower. The stem was often used as a thread for stringing ginger flowers. (DK; NEAL 87.)

PLANTS: Shrubs

This category acquaints the reader with glorious, flower-bearing shrubs such as *pīkake,* hibiscus, wild plumbago, *'ilima,* and China rose. Other plants in this group are well known for their uses or ornamental value, and still others for their fragrance. Then there are those with less pleasant qualities: some have sharp spikelets or burs; others emit disagreeable odors; and still others have almost uncontrollable growth.

'a'ala pū loa. 1. American shrub *(Spiraea tomentosa)* with rusty tomentose leaves and dense terminal panicles of pink (rarely white) flowers like the hard hack. **2.** Bridal wreath *(S. prunifolia),* a shrub having copious umbels, flat or well-rounded clusters of small white flowers. Also called St. Peter's wreath.

'āheahea. Member of the goosefoot family *(Chenopodium oahuense),* known as lambs'-quarters. The young plants are used as greens. (NEAL 331.) This plant does not have a particularly agreeable odor.

ahewa. 1. O'ahu name for the *mānā* fern. Also called *'āweoweo.* (PE; CMH.) **2.** Slender mimosa *(Desmanthus virgatus),* a low, smooth, or downy American shrub, brought to Hawai'i in the early 1900s. Eaten by stock. A serious pest in sugar fields. (NEAL 413.)

'āhihi, 'ahihi lehua. 1. Cup of gold *(Solandra hartwegii),* a large, smooth, woody shrub enjoyed for its large, showy, yellow flowers blooming January through March. Watching a bud as it opens is interesting. Kamehameha Schools supplied cuttings for the slopes looking down into Punchbowl. (NEAL 748.) **2.** Low-spreading bush in Nuʻuanu Valley; variety of *lehua,* noted for its blossoms. Name ʻahihi means entangled.

ʻāhinahina. 1. Small shrub *(Artemisia australis).* (NEAL 852.) See **Plants: Uses. 2.** Silversword *(Argyroxiphium sandwicense),* a compact plant, a shrub, native to Hawaiʻi. Found only on Haleakalā, east Maui, and on high mountains on the island of Hawaiʻi between 6,000 and 12,250 feet. Well known for its unique and beautiful appearance. (NEAL 845.)

ʻākala. Hawaiian raspberry *(Rubus hawaiiensis* and *R. macrae),* a trailing shrub. Grows at 4,000 to 7,000 feet in forests. (NEAL 391.) See **Plants: Uses.**

ʻākia. Endemic shrub or small tree (*Wikstroemia* spp.). (NEAL 615.) See **Plants: Uses.**

ʻakiohala, ʻakiahala. Native pink hibiscus *(Hibiscus youngianus).* See **hau hele.**

ʻakoko. Endemic shrub *(Euphorbia* spp.) with jointed stems; opposite, oblong leaves; and milky sap. Another species of ʻakoko *(E. rockii)* is a native of Oʻahu mountains. It has shiny, dark-green leaves and bears red or pink fruiting capsules at branch tips, hence the name ʻakoko, meaning blood-colored. (NEAL 515.) See **koko.**

ʻākulikuli kai. This low trailing shrub *(Batis maritima)* was discovered in 1859 in salty marshes near Honolulu. It spread its bright green masses to many low places, covering Sand Island to the degree that it became known as ʻAkulikuli Island. It is smooth and woody-stemmed. Its leaves contain a salty juice that smells like pickles; hence the local name, pickleweed. (NEAL 339.)

ʻalaʻala pū loa. Small native shrub *(Waltheria indica),* a down-covered plant with a woody base and small yellow flowers. The bitter inner bark of the root is used to relieve a sore throat. (NEAL 575.) Also called *hiʻa loa, kanaka loa.*

ʻalaʻala wai nui. 1. All species of genus *Peperomia,* small, native, succulent forest herbs. Related to ʻawa. Used as ornamentals. (NEAL 736.) **2.** Small weed herb *(Plectranthus parviflorus)* in the mint family from Australia and the Pacific Islands. (NEAL 736.) ʻAlaʻala wai nui may be qualified by adding *kāne.*

ʻalaea. Annatto dye plant *(Bixa orellana).* (NEAL 589.) See **Plants: Uses.**

alaheʻe. Large native shrub or small tree *(Canthium odoratum).* (NEAL 797.) See **Plants: Uses.**

ʻamaʻu. Tree fern *(Sadleria* spp.). (NEAL 22.) See **Plants: Uses.**

ʻāmaumau. Tree fern, *ʻamau* in a group called *āmaʻumaʻu*, found on all the Hawaiian islands. (NEAL 22.)

ʻānapanapa. Smooth shrub *(Colubrina asiatica)*. (NEAL 541.) See **Plants: Uses.** See **kukuku.**

ʻauhola, ʻauhuhu. Small, slender shrub *(Tephrosia purpurea)*. (NEAL 448.) See **Plants: Uses.**

ʻawa. The kava *(Piper methysticum)*. (NEAL 291.) See **Plants: Uses.**

ʻāwiwi. Native Hawaiian gentian *(Centaurium sabaeoides,* synonym, *Erythraes sabaeoides)* with pale pink flowers in the gentian family. (NEAL 864.)

ʻēkaha, ʻākaka. Bird's nest fern *(Asplenium nidus)*. (NEAL 21.) See **Plants: Uses.**

hāhā. Native member of the lobelia family *(Brighamia* spp.). The flowers of all Hawaiian species are curved like the beak of native nectar-feeding birds, which suck honey from them. Also called *ālula*. (NEAL 815.)

hau hele. Native pink hibiscus *(Hibiscus youngiamus),* found most commonly in marsh land. It has few branches and grows to 7 feet or more. Also found in abandoned taro patches on all islands as, for example, Kapalama, Oʻahu. See **ʻakiohala.** (NEAL 560.)

heau. Native shrub or tree of Hawaiʻi *(Exocarpus* spp.), the *heau* of the sandalwood family. (NEAL 325.)

hōʻawa. All Hawaiian species of the genus *Pittosporum*. (NEAL 382.) See **Plants: Uses.**

huahekili. Beach *naupaka (Scaevola taccada)*. (NEAL 820.) See **Plants: Uses, naupaka kahakai.**

huahekili uka. Small native *naupaka (Scaevola kilaueae)*. A shrub found only on Mauna Loa and most commonly around Kīlauea Volcano. Formerly used to dye *kapa*. Also called *papaʻa hekili*. (NEAL 819.)

huna olonā. Waste and refuse of the small shrub *Touchardia latifolia*. (NEAL 319.) See **Plants: Uses.**

iliau. Native Hawaiian woody plant *(Wilkesia gymnoxiphium)*, found on the dry western mountain slopes of Kauaʻi. Related to the *ʻāhinahina*, silversword *(Argyroxiphium sandwicense)*, a native plant found on Haleakalā, east Maui, and on high mountains of Hawaiʻi island, a rare and protected treasure of Hawaiʻi. (NEAL 845.)

ʻilieʻe, ʻileheʻe, hilieʻe. Wild plumbago *(Plumbago zeylanicum)*, native from the tropics of the eastern hemisphere to Hawaiʻi. Its flowers are ½ inch long and white. (NEAL 667.) See **Plants: Uses.**

'ilima. Various forms of *'ilima* plants (*Sida* spp.). (NEAL 552.) See **Plants: Uses.**

'inikō. Indigo *(Indigofera suffruticosa),* a 3-foot shrub from the West Indies, introduced around 1850. While the introduced plant did not succeed in establishing an industry for blue dye, it became naturalized and today is found as a weed at low altitudes. (NEAL 447.)

kī. Shrubby ti plant *(Cordyline terminalis).* (NEAL 203.) See **Plants: Uses.**

kīkānia haole. Jimson weed, a shrub *(Datura stramonium).* Also called *lā'auhānō.* (NEAL 750.) See **Plants: Uses.**

kili. Shrub or grass. No data. (CMH.)

koko. Native shrubs or trees (*Euphorbia* spp.) take the name from the capsules which are deep red to green to brown. *Koko* means blood and *'akoko,* blood-colored. The species has potential use as a poison or medicine. See **'akoko.** (NEAL 516.)

kolī. Castor bean, castor oil plant *(Ricinus communis),* a shrub that grows to 30 feet. (NEAL 509.) See **Plants: Uses.**

koli'i. Native lobelia shrub *(Trematolobelia macrostachys),* growing to 6 feet. Commonly called *'oha* or tree lobelias. It lives in native forests or along wet ridges. (NEAL 815.) See **Plants: Uses.**

kolomona. Shrub or small tree *(Cassia surattensis),* as important as the indigenous *kolomona (Cassia gaudichaudii).* (NEAL 427.) See **Plants: Uses.**

ko'oko'olau. Native herbs or shrubs (*Bidens* spp.). (NEAL 844.) See **Plants: Uses.**

kopa. Native shrub *(Hedyotis glaucifolia),* found only on Kaua'i. Its fruit is made into beads.

kowaha, koaha. Kind of *wauke;* young shoots of the mulberry plant used for medicine; soft mulberry fiber used for making a fine white *kapa. Obs.*

kukū. *Lā'au kukū,* brambles or thicket. (1 Sam. 13:6.)

kukuku. *'Ānapanapa,* a smooth shrub, *Colubrina asiatica.* (NEAL 541.) See **Plants: Uses, 'ānapanapa.**

kūloli. Person who has no wife or children is called *kūloli,* a name derived from a lone mulberry shrub or small tree, *wauke,* growing in a cave at Kūloli, Kona, Hawai'i. (PE.) A *wauke* at Palilua, Hawai'i. (CMH.)

lani wela. Canada fleabane *(Conyza eanadensis).* Herbaceous weed. An aromatic insect repellent oil is derived from the plant. (NEAL 834.) See **'uwī'uwi.**

loke. Rose (*Rosa* spp.), a low altitude favorite in Hawai'i, but it needs care: fertilizer, pruning, and regular spraying. A few varieties grown in Hawai'i include the China rose with crimson or pink flowers, the green rose with narrow green leaves for petals, and a white rose with pink forms. The flower of Maui is the double "a" pink or the Damask rose, known as *lokelani.* (NEAL 394.)

luhea. *Sesbania tomentosa.* Listed as an endangered species. Grown in Waonahele, Hawaiian garden, Kamehameha Schools campus. *Ka lau o luhea o ka 'ōhai o Mānā,* the drooping leaves of the *'ōhai* of Mānā [Kaua'i]. (KILO.)

ma'aloa, ma'oloa. Low native shrub *(Neraudia melastomaefolia),* related to the *māmaki.* Used for making *kapa.* Also called *'oloa.*

maiapilo. Caper bush *(Capparis spinosa).* (NEAL 368.) See **Plants: Uses.**

maiele. Small shrub *(Styphelia* spp.). (NEAL 663.) See **Plants: Uses.**

makaloa. Perennial sedge *(Cyperus laevigatus).* (NEAL 86.) See **Plants: Uses.**

māmaki. Small native trees *(Pipturus* spp.), the bark of which has a fibrous inner layer. Formerly a principal source of *kapa.* This was durable *kapa* when dry but torn easily, as paper, when wetted. (NEAL 318.)

manu o palekaiko. Bird of Paradise *(Strelitzia reginae* Banks), an herbaceous perennial used as an ornamental. Its leaves are used for a brownish dye. Also called a crane's bill. (NEAL 242.)

mao. Native cotton *(Gossypium sandvicense),* a shrub of the hibiscus family. It has seed cases containing seeds wrapped in short, brownish, cotton fibers. But it also has glands that attract the boll weevil. This plant has potential value if it could be genetically bred as a strain with long staple fibers and a few glands, less susceptible to boll weevil damage. Also called *huluhulu.* (NEAL 566.)

na'ena'e. Pleasant odor from the genus *Dubautia,* which is confined to Hawai'i. This is a resinous shrub or small tree. (NEAL 845.)

naupaka. Native shrubs *(Scaevola sericeaea)* that grow on beaches and in mountains. In both places, white half flowers distinguish these shrubs. The physical separation of its two habitats and its seemingly divided flowers have been focused on in chants, leg-

ends, and stories of lovers, whose agonies of parting are represented by the half flowers of the youth blooming above in the
mountains and those of the maiden below on the beach. (NEAL
819.)

naupaka kahakai. Beach *naupaka (Scaevola taccada),* a smooth,
spreading, succulent shrub, which grows from 3 to 10 feet high.
See **naupaka.** (NEAL 820.) See **Plants: Uses.**

naupaka kuahiwi. Mountain *naupaka (Scaevola gaudichaudi-
ana).* It reaches 4 to 6 feet in height and is commonly found on
the Koʻolau Range of Oʻahu. Most have small black berries,
some white, formerly used to dye *kapa.* See **naupaka.** (NEAL
819.) Not all species belong to the genus *Scaevola.*

nīnika. Member of the crepe myrtle family (Lythraceae), a prostrate or erect, smooth perennial growing wild well above sea
level. See **pūkamōle.** (NEAL 617.)

nīoi. Red pepper *(Capsicum annuum).* (NEAL 741.) See **Plants:
Uses.**

ʻōhai. Native shrub *(Sesbania tomentosa).* It is prostrate with
silky, wool-covered branches and leaves, red to orange, inch
long flowers, and narrow pods 5 to 7 inches long. (NEAL 450.)
See **Plants: Uses.**

ʻōhā wai. Native lobelia (family Lobeliaceae), one of the most
interesting and characteristic groups of plants in the whole
island flora. They are shrubs and small trees, probably survi-
vors of an ancient flora. Hawaiians recognized their striking
form and gave names to most of the species. One of the most
common is *ʻōhāwai,* applied indiscriminately to species of the
more abundant genus *Clermontia.* They are known as plants
from which the old-time bird catchers made a sticky glue for
capturing birds. (NEAL 815.)

ohenaupaka. Native *naupaka (Scaevola glabra),* a shrub found in
the mountains of Kauaʻi and Oʻahu. It has yellow, curved, tubular flowers about 1 inch long.

ōlena, lena. Turmeric *(Curcuma domestica).* (NEAL 255.) See
Plants: Uses.

olomea. Native shrub or tree *(Perrottetia sandwicensis).* (NEAL
530.) A plant form of the pig-god Kama-puaʻa. Also called
waimea.

olonā. Native shrub *(Touchardia latifolia).* (NEAL 319.) See
Plants: Uses.

ōpūʻōhai. *ʻŌpū* refers to a bundle, bunch, or clump formed by a
natural spreading out of young shoots or sprouts. Hence,

ōpū'ōhai, a bundle of '*ōhai* shrubs *(Sesbania tomentosa)*. (NEAL 450.)

pāmakani. Native violet, an upright, branching shrub *(Viola chamissoniana)* 3 to 5 feet high with woody stems. Found on all islands between 1,000 and 3,000 feet. It has pale, purple flowers. (NEAL 591.)

pōhinahina, kolokolo kahakai. The beach vitex *(Vitex ovata)*. Distributed from eastern Asia to Hawai'i, it is an aromatic shrub, a beach creeper. (NEAL 728.)

pua kala. Prickly poppy *(Argemone glauca).* (NEAL 367.) See **Plants: Uses.**

pu'e. Lobelia *(Lobelia gaudichaudii* var. *kauaensis)*, found only on mountains on Kaua'i. It has large whitish flowers streaked with purple. (PE 321.)

pūkāmole. Low shrubby plant *(Lythrum maritimum)*, a smooth perennial. It grows well above sea level in Hawai'i. A member of the crepe myrtle family. (NEAL 617.)

pūkiawe. Shrub at lower levels, a small tree or shrub at higher elevations *(Styphelia* spp.). The trunk is rather twisted in a finely corrugated brown bark. It occurs on all islands. Legend has it that a chief who wished to mingle with his people would shut himself in a little house and smudge himself from a fire of the *pūkiawe* shrub. See **maiele.** (NEAL 663.)

'ūlei. Native Hawaiian evergreen *(Osteomeles anthyllidifolia)*. (NEAL 387.) See **Plants: Uses.**

'uwī'uwi. Tall, slender, coarse, introduced weeds of the daisy family *(Erigeron* spp.). Used medicinally. (NEAL 834.) Also called *ilioha.* See **lani wela.**

wahine noho kula. Native shrub *(Isodendrion hawaiiense)* of the violet family, an endemic genus. *Lit.,* woman plains dweller. (NEAL 591.)

walahe'e. Small shrub or tree *(Canthium odoratum)*. (NEAL 797.) See **Plants: Uses.**

PLANTS: Trees

The larger share of the trees in this list appeared in *Hae Hawai'i,* March 14 and 17, 1860, and a companion list was published in Thrum's *Hawaiian Annual and Almanac* for 1891.

aʻaahi. Scion or shoot of the sandalwood tree, *ʻili ahi* (*Santalum* spp.). The mature tree was the base of the sandalwood traffic between the Orient and Hawaiʻi from about 1790 to 1830. (NEAL 325.)

ʻaʻaka. Wood of the *naio,* bastard sandalwood *(Myoporum sandwicense).* (NEAL 791.) See **Plants: Uses, naio.**

ʻaʻaliʻi. Native hardwood trees (*Dodonaea* spp.). (NEAL 536.) See **Plants: Uses.**

ʻaʻawa, ʻaʻawa hua kukui, hoʻawa. Native tree *(Pittosporum hosmeri)* growing to about 20 feet. It has woody or leathery valved fruits, the outer layer of which was pounded up and used medicinally to apply externally to sores. (NEAL 382.)

aʻe. Aromatic trees (*Zanthoxylum* spp.) that supplied a yellowish, hard wood for spears and digging sticks. Its round, black seeds were strung for *lei*s. Also called *mānele (Sapindus saponaria).* (NEAL 532–533.)

akoa. Small tree resembling the *koa.* A dye from this tree was used to give *kapa* a snuff color. (A.)

ʻakūʻakū. Endemic lobelia *(Cyanea rollandioides).* (NEAL 815.) See **Plants: Uses.**

ʻālaʻa. Several species of this tree (*Planchonella* spp.) are found in Hawaiʻi. (NEAL 668.) See **Plants: Uses.**

alahiʻi. Species of bastard sandalwood. (A.)

āneho. *Hala* tree. No data. (CMH.)

ʻaoa. Sandalwood (*Santalum* spp.), better known as *ʻili ahi.* A small tree. (NEAL 325.) Andrews defines *ʻaoa* vaguely as "the name of a tree not found in these islands, but in some foreign country; often spoken of in the ancient meles."

ʻapelika kulehe. African tulip (*Spathodea campanulata),* a showy ornamental tree, growing to 70 feet. Scarlet or gold flowers are crowded in erect clusters at branch tips. It has fine-lobed leaves. Blossoms and leaves are used in preparing dyes. (NEAL 769.)

ʻau hau. Stalk of the *hau (Hibiscus tiliaceus)* tree; light wood used in making spears for casting firebrands from the *Mahuiki pali, ka ʻau hau welo i no pali.*

ʻaukala. Umbrella tree, octopus tree *(Schefflera actinophylla).* Reaches a height of 40 feet. An Australian ornamental tree, it sometimes germinates on other trees and sends clasping roots to the grounds. Though the wood is soft and not durable, it is not attacked by insects. (NEAL 653.)

hā, ʻohiʻa hā. Native forest tree *(Eugenia sandwicensis)* with inverted ovate leaves, small, clustered flowers, red, globose fruit with a little edible pulp. Reported by Thrum as *kauokahiki;* and by Rock as *pā'ihi* on Maui only. (NEAL 635.)

hae. Species of wood. No data. (CMH.)

hala. Pandanus or screw pine *(Pandanus odoratissimuss)*, native to Hawai'i with wide branches and long aerial roots. Substantial crafts were built around its products. (NEAL 51.) See **Plants: Uses.**

hala pepe. Native tree of the lily family *(Dracena* spp.). (NEAL 204.) See **Plants: Uses.**

hala pia. White *hala.* No data. (A.) Indigenous variety of pandanus. The plant is used in medical prescriptions and exorcizing evil spirits. Much prized for *leis.* (PE.)

hāmau. Species of *'ōhi'a* tree. (A.) Similar to the *lehua hāmau,* a poetic reference to the *lehua* tree. *Lit.,* the silent *lehua,* so called because bird catchers were silent among the branches while snaring birds. (PE.)

hame, ha'a. Two native species of *Antidesma.* (NEAL 500.) See **Plants: Uses.**

hao. All native species of a genus of small trees *(Rauvolfia)* related to *maile* and *hōlei.* (PE; NEAL 691.)

hāpu'u. Hawaiian tree fern *(Cibotum chamissoi),* a tree, not a shrub. (NEAL 10.) See **Plants: Uses.**

hau. Much-branched tree, not a shrub *(Hibiscus tiliaceus).* (NEAL 559.) See **Plants: Uses.**

hō'awa, ha'awa. Genus *Pittosporum,* twenty-three or more species of which are in Hawai'i. (NEAL 382.) See **Plants: Uses.**

'ili ahi. Small tree or shrub, sandalwood *(Santalum* spp.). (NEAL 325.) See **Plants: Uses.**

'inia. Pride of India *(Melia azedarach).* (NEAL 491.) See **Plants: Uses.**

kai waina. Sea grape *(Coccoloba uvifera),* a wind-twisted tree, used as a windbreak close to beaches. It has broad, round leaves and fragrant flowers. The pear-shaped, reddish, astringent fruits hang in clusters, each fruit with a large, globose nut. Roots, also astringent, are used to cure dysentery. The wood is hard and polishes well for cabinet work. It supplies fuel and when boiled yields a red dye. Gum from the bark is used for tanning, and medicinally for throat ailments. (NEAL 330.)

kālai pāhoa. Name of three woods *(kauila, nīoi, 'ohe),* believed to be the tree forms of two male gods (Kāne-i-kaulana-'ula and Ka-huila-o-ka-lani) and one goddess *(Kapo).* Small pieces of the woods and roots were used in black magic. The three trees were found in Mauna-loa, Moloka'i. (PE.)

kalia. Member of the linden family *(Elaeocarpus bifidus).* (NEAL 545.) See **Plants: Uses.**

kamani. Tall, handsome tree *(Calophyllum inophyllum),* probably brought in by early Polynesians. (NEAL 585.) See **Plants: Uses.**

kamani ‘ula. False *kamani (Terminalia catappa).* (NEAL 627.) Also called *kamani haole.* See **Plants: Uses.**

ka‘uhi‘uhi. Forest tree, the timber of which is used for *holua* boards and *‘ō‘ō* (digging sticks). (A.) See **uhiuhi.** (NEAL 615.) Also called *‘ākia.*

kauila, kauwila. Two native trees bear this Hawaiian name. Both are rare, both sink in water. *Colubrina oppositifolia* is found only on Hawai‘i and O‘ahu. Its wood was formerly valued for making spears and *kapa* beaters and is even harder than that of the *Alphitonia ponderosa,* which grows on the largest islands. (NEAL 541.) Also a tree on Kaua‘i, the *pu‘ukapele.* (A.)

kauokahiki, ‘ōhi‘a hā. Native tree *(Eugenia sandwicensis).* The name *‘ōhi‘a hā* was reported by Thrum as *kauokahiki* and by Rock as *pā‘ihi,* on Maui only. Andrews says that "out of this timber the god was made for the *heiau.*" (NEAL 635.)

kāwa‘u. Native tree *(Ilex anomala).* It is a handsome tree growing to between 20 and 40 feet. It is common on all islands, chiefly in the rain forests. The tree is seldom bothered by insects. Its wood is whitish and rather soft. (NEAL 528.)

kilikā. Black mulberry *(Morus nigra).* Its Hawaiian name comes from the English, silk. The tree is cultivated for its abundant, juicy, dark-red to black fruits. Its leaves provide food for silkworms. The tree is used for hedges. (NEAL 300.)

koa. Largest of native forest trees *(Acacia koa).* (NEAL 408.) See **Plants: Uses.**

koai‘e. Native tree *(Acacia koaia).* (NEAL 405.) See **Plants: Uses.**

koa kumu ‘ole, koa makua ‘ole. Famous and legendary tree *mauka* of Kahihikolo, Kaua‘i, a tree associated with Kamapua‘a. *Lit., koa* without a trunk (without a parent). (A.)

koa lau kani. Species of *koa* used specifically in carving gods. (A.) Kind of *koa* tree regarded by Hawaiians as male. *Lit.,* strong *koa.* (PE.)

koki‘o, hau hele ‘ula. Native Hawaiian genus *(Kokia).* It includes four species that grow wild on the islands and are sometimes cultivated. Produces red flowers. (NEAL 567.)

kōlea. Small native tree *(Myrsine* spp.). (NEAL 664.) See **Plants: Uses.**

koli‘i. Native lobelia *(Tremato lobelia).* Grows to 6 feet. Ordinarily called *'oha* or tree lobelia. This tree lives in a native forest. (NEAL 815.) See **Plants: Uses.**

kopela. Camphor tree *(Cinnamomum camphora)*. (NEAL 361.) See **Plants: Uses.**

kōpiko. About thirteen native species of this name belong to a genus *(Psychotria)* in the coffee family. (NEAL 794.) See **Plants: Uses.**

kou. Evergreen tree *(Cordia subcordata)*. (NEAL 714.) See **Plants. Uses.**

kuawa. Guava *(Psidium guajava)*. (NEAL 632.) See **Plants: Uses.**

kukane. Lemon tree *(Citron limonia)*. Called rough lemon in Hawaii, it is known for its fragrant skin and bitter taste. Varieties in Hawai'i include Ponderosa, Meyer, and Villa Franca. Kukane is a combination form of the names of two Hawaiian gods, *Kū* and *Kāne*. (NEAL 482.)

kukui. Candlenut tree *(Aleurites moluccana)*. (NEAL 504.) See **Plants: Uses.**

kulu'ī. One of two native genera of the amaranth family *(Nototrichium* spp.). The other is called *pāpala (Charpentiera)*. (NEAL 332.) See **Plants: Uses.**

kupukupu'ala. Rose geranium *(Pelargonium graveolens)*. (NEAL 471.) See **Plants: Uses.**

laholio. India rubber tree *(Ficus elastica)*. (NEAL 312.) See **Plants: Uses.**

lama. Two native species *(Diospyros* synonym *Maba)* are forest trees. (NEAL 674.) See **Plants: Uses.**

lapalapa. Native genus *(Cheirodendron)* with six endemic species known as *'ōlapa* and *lapalapa*. It has opposite leaves which flutter in the slightest breeze. Member of the *Panax* family. (NEAL 652.)

lehua. A favorite tree *(Metrosideros collina)* that thrives between 1,000 and 9,000 feet in some forests. On the slopes of Mauna Kea and Mauna Loa, the trees reach 100 feet, and around Kīlauea Volcano they are associated with the tree fern. Its flowers are full of honey, which is the food of the *'i'iwi*, a small bird matching in scarlet plumage the color of the flowers. Stories and legends are based on the flower. Also called *'ōhia*. (NEAL 561.)

lehua 'āpane. Kind of *lehua* tree bearing dark-red flowers.

lehua hāmau. Poetic reference to the *lehua* tree. Bird catchers were silent when snaring birds on the branches of this tree. *Lit.,* silent *lehua.*

leleu. Fruit tree. No data. (CMH.)

loulu, noulu. Fan palm (*Pritchardia* spp.) with a smooth trunk. In its wild state it grows in secluded places in the forests to 3,000 feet. One species is the *loulu lelo,* a native of Moloka'i. Another, the *loulu hiwa,* grows only on O'ahu. It is the only genus of palms native to Hawai'i. (NEAL 97.) Also called *uli, wahale.* (A.)

māmane. Native leguminous tree *(Sophora chrysophylla).* (NEAL 442.) See **Plants: Uses.**

maua. Tree good for making boards (genus *Xylosma,* family *Flacourtia*), a native forest tree. (NEAL 592.)

milikana, mīkana. Papaya *(Carica papaya).* (NEAL 600.) Also called *papaia.* See **Plants: Uses.**

mimoka. Mimosa tree.

momona. Fruit tree *(Annona cherimola).* (NEAL 359.) See **Plants: Uses.**

nahele. Verdure of trees; thicket or grove of trees.

naio. Bastard sandalwood tree *(Myoporum sandwicense).* Found at sea level to 10,000 feet. An unwelcome substitute for sandalwood when the supply ran out. As a firewood it burns like pitch pine. It is a strong timber used in buildings' main timbers. (NEAL 791.)

nanapau. *Kou* tree, perhaps *Cordia subcordata; lā'au,* tree or forest. (A.)

neleau, neneleau. Wild, native Hawaiian sumach *(Rhus chinensis* var. *sandwicensis).* Its wood is soft, light, tough, and yellowish gray. (NEAL 525.)

noni. Indian mulberry *(Morinda citrifolia).* (NEAL 804.) See **Plants: Uses.**

noulu, loulu. *Noulu is a var. of loulu,* a palm. See **loulu.**

o'a. Maui name for the *kauila* tree *(Columbrina oppositifolia).* (NEAL 541.) See **Plants: Uses.**

'ōhai, pū 'ōhai. Monkeypod or rain tree *(Samanea saman).* (NEAL 401.) See **Plants: Uses.**

'ohe. Peculiar Hawaiian tree *(Reynoldsia sandwicensis).* It resembles the *wiliwili* in that both shed their leaves during the summer months or arid season. Grows to 80 feet. It is peculiar to the very dry districts of the lowland zone, especially the *'a'a* lava fields where the heat is intense and rain infrequent. The soft, whitish wood has no commercial value but was used for making *kukulūae'o* (stilts) employed by early Hawaiians in a game of the same name. (NEAL 652.)

'ōhi'a'ai. Mountain apple *(Eugenia malaccensis).* This handsome tree is a native of India and Malaya and was introduced to Hawai'i by early Polynesians. In Hawai'i it grows to 50 feet in height at elevations up to 1800 feet. Flowers lay a bright red carpet on the ground underneath. The tree starts fruiting when it is six or seven years old. The fruit is eaten both raw and pickled. (NEAL 636.)

'ōhia'āpane. Same as *'ōhi'a lehua,* except the blossom is dark red.

'ōhi'a lehua, lehua. *Lehua (Metrosideros collina),* a favorite native tree growing between the 1,000 and 9,000 foot levels. The flowers are full of honey, food of the *'i'iwi,* a bird matching in scarlet plumage the color of the blossoms. On the slopes of Mauna Kea and Mauna Loa the tree grows to 100 feet. *Leis,* quilt designs, stories, and legends are all based on the *lehua.* (NEAL 637.)

'ōlapa. Member of the *Panax* family, native species of a Pacific genus *(Cheirodendron).* The opposite leaves of *'ōlapa* and *lapalapa* flutter in the breeze. See **lapalapa.** (NEAL 652.)

'oliwa, 'oliana. Oleander *(Nerium oleander* and var. *indicum),* native to the region from Southern Europe to Japan. Common ornamental shrubs in Hawai'i. (NEAL 695.)

olomea. Native shrub or small tree *(Perrottetia sandwicensis).* The wood is hard and was formerly used with the *hau* wood to produce fire by friction. It is one of the plant forms of the pig god, Kama-pua'a. Also called *wai-mea.* (NEAL 530.)

'ōpiko, kōpiko. Genus of the coffee family, one of perhaps ten genera native to Hawai'i (Psychotria hawaiiensis var.). It grows on Hawai'i island on the slopes of Mauna Loa in the botanically rich Kīpuka Paaulu, source of new finds because of its isolation in the midst of lava flows. (NEAL 794.)

'opiuma. Manila tamarind *(Pithecellobium dulce).* (NEAL 399.) See **Plants: Uses.**

paina. Word applied to conifers generally.

pā makani. Native white hibiscus *(Hibiscus arnottianus).* Usually a small to medium sized tree growing wild between 1,000 and 2,000 feet. Its flowers have a subtle fragrance. This species is one of the parents in producing new hybrids. It was formerly more common than now, as many references were made to it in old Hawaiian songs and legends. (NEAL 561.) Also called *koki'o ke'oke'o.*

papaia. See **milikana.**

pāpala. Amaranth tree (genus *pāpala, Charpentiera* spp.) with light, inflammable wood used by early Hawaiians on the north coast of Kaua'i. On dark nights pieces of wood were lighted as firebrands and hurled from the cliffs into the wind, which tossed them about or let them float gently downward. (NEAL 332.)

pā'ula. Tree that achieves a red color in its wood when mature. *Lit.,* touched red. (A.)

po'a'aha, pō'aha. Small tree in Hawai'i *(Broussonetia papyrifera).* (NEAL 301.) Also called *wauke.* See **Plants: Uses.**

pō'ala. Name of a tree. No data. (A.)

pōhai. To be surrounded and gathered into an enclosure or circle, as of people or trees.

pō'ola. Small tree of soft wood *(Claoxylon sandwicense).* Grows from 18 to 20 feet, with pale, spreading branches. It is fairly common in the lava fields of Haleakalā, Maui, and Pu'uwa-'awa'a, Hawai'i. There are two native species in Hawai'i. (NEAL 499.)

pua. Large native tree *(Osmanthus sandwicensis).* (NEAL 676.) See **Plants: Uses.**

pū'aha nui. Tree *(Broussaisia arguta)* found in all rain forests from 1,000 to 3,000 feet elevation. Its native names are *pū'aha nui* and *kanawao.* It is never found in dry districts. The family *(Saxifragaceae)* is widely distributed except in Hawai'i, where it is represented by this one genus with a single species. (NEAL 380.)

pū'aloalo, pua aloalo, aloalo. Hibiscus, a favorite flower of Hawai'i and commonly grown in most gardens. More than 5,000 varieties have been produced using native and introduced species. Some are edible, some produce fiber. The *aloalo* is the state flower of Hawai'i. (NEAL 556.)

pulu, pulupulu. Material that grows on and is collected from species of large ferns *(Cibotium* spp.) from the base of the stalks. The *pulu* resembles that of the *'ama'u* and has been similarly used to stuff pillows and mattresses. Hawaiians also stuffed the bodies of their dead after removing the vital organs. Young fronds were used to make hats. Tree trunks were made into fences. (NEAL 10.) See **Plants: Uses,** hāpu'u.

pu'ukapele. Tree on Kaua'i, the *kauwila.* See **kauila.** (A.)

uhiuhi. Endemic leguminous tree *(Mezoneuron kavaiense).* (NEAL 435.) See **Plants: Uses.**

uli. Coconut fan leaf palm. See **loulu.**

'ulu. Breadfruit *(Artocarpus altilis).* (NEAL 302.) See **Plants: Uses.**

ulu'eo. Very durable timber tree, even more so than *uhiuhi.* (A.)

'ulukahiki. Foreign breadfruit *(Artocarpus altilis).* (NEAL 302.)

unū. Breadfruit tree. (A.) Young *'ōhi'a* timber, as used in making images. (PE.)

unuunu, ununu. Young *'ōhi'a* timber as used in making images. (AP.)

'uo'uolea. Species of *'ōhi'a.* No data. (A.)

'uwo'uwo. Species of *'ōhi'a* on the hills. No data. (A.)

wahale. Same as the *loulu,* palm tree. (A.)

waokele. Long, tall *'ōhi'a* tree. No data. (A.)

wauke. See **po'a'aha.** (NEAL 301.)

weleweka. Coleus *(Coleus blumei),* an ornamental perennial from Java. *Weleweka* comes from the English velvet. (NEAL 732.)

wī. 1. Wī tree *(Spondias dulcis),* a smooth, gray-barked import from the South Pacific belonging to the mango family. (NEAL 523.) 2. Tamarind *(Tamarindus indica),* probably a native of Africa and Asia. It grows to medium size and is noted for its shade and fruit. (NEAL 417.) Bernice Pauahi Bishop quite regularly "held court" among her Hawaiian people under a tamarind tree planted on her birthday in front of the Bishops' home on King Street in Honolulu. Also called *wī'awa'awa.*

wiliwili. Native Hawaiian tree *(Erythrina sandwicensis).* (NEAL 548.) See **Plants: Uses.**

PLANTS: Uses

The impressive thing about this category is not the number of entries or the wide variety. It is the almost unbelievably close attention and observation applied by the early Hawaiians to research among the myriad of plants: grasses and sedges, small plants and shrubs, ornamental and fruit trees, and more. This research involved the searching out, discovery, and study of barks, gums, leaves, inner woods, and roots; the analysis of these materials; and finally the experimental application of each as a medicine, dye, lumber or perfume product, and so on. These were the achievements of early Hawaiians in an era where products were manufactured by hard stone instruments and written language did not yet exist; these were the people whose intelligence and patience carried them far beyond survival into a creditable culture of unstoried heights.

'a'ali'i. Native hardwood shrubs and small trees (*Dodonaea* spp.) of which four species and their variants are found in Hawai'i between sea level and 8,000 feet. Its fruits are red, yellow, or brown capsules. Trees with long, straight trunks were formerly used for house posts. Its leaves were used for medicinal purposes. Seed clusters were made into leis, combined with leaves or ferns, and worn in the hair. (NEAL 536.)

a'e. Native trees (*Xanthoxylum* spp.) supplied a yellowish wood for spears and digging sticks. Their large, round, black seeds were used in making leis and rosaries. Also called *mānele*. (PE.)

'ahakēa. Tree of an endemic genus *(Bobea)*. Its wood was used for canoe rims or gunwales, *poi* boards, *mo'o,* and canoe paddles. See **Canoes: Construction and Parts.**

'āhewa. O'ahu name for the *mānā* fern *(Pteris irregularis),* which has large, bright green, subdivided fronds. (NEAL 17.) Also listed as a mimosa tree. (PE; CMH.)

āhinahina. Small shrub *(Artemesia australis)* usually found on dry cliffs. Its pounded leaves were used as remedies for high fever, lung trouble, and asthma. Also called *hinahina*. (NEAL 852.)

'ahu 'ao. Fine mats made of narrow strands of young pandanus leaves using a $\frac{1}{2}$-inch mesh.

'ahu'awa, 'ehu'awa. Sedge (*Cyperus javanicus*) found in or near marshes and taro patches. Its fiber, stripped from the stem, was used to strain *'awa* and make cordage. The leaves were fashioned into hats. (NEAL 86.)

'aiea. All five species of the genus *Nothocestrum* are known in Hawai'i as *'aiea*. All are soft wooded. Slender stems are used for thatching, *'aho,* sticks, and firemaking in friction with a hard wood. The town of 'Aiea, O'ahu, was named for these trees. (NEAL 738.)

'aka'akai. Great bulrush *(Scirpus validus),* which grows on the edge of fresh- or brackish-water marshes. Formerly the natives used grass stems or *kī* leaves for house thatch or plaited them into mats for lower layers of *hikie'e* (beds). They are used today to tie vegetables into bunches. (NEAL 88.)

'ākala. Two species of native raspberries *(Rubus hawaiiensis* and *R. macraei),* which grow in open areas in forests. Both are *'ākala* (pink), and both are edible. One has red fruit, the other red or yellow. The juice was used as a dye. Their ashes were used as remedies for scaly scalp, heartburn, and vomiting. (NEAL 391.)

'ākia. Endemic shrub or small tree (*Wikstroemia* spp.) with small leaves, tiny yellowish flowers, and yellow to red fruits. The roots, bark, and leaves are thought to contain poison and formerly were pounded in a porous container and sunk in salt water to narcotize fish. No part of the plant has been found poisonous to mammals. The bark made an excellent fiber for cordage. (NEAL 615.)

akoa. Small tree resembling the *koa*. A dye from the bark of this tree was used to give *kapa* a snuff color.

'ākoko. Endemic shrub (*Euphorbia* spp.) with jointed stems, opposite, oblong leaves, and milky sap. Another species of *'ākoko (E. rockii)*, a native of the mountains of O'ahu, has shiny, dark-green leaves and bears red or pink fruiting capsules at branch tips; hence, the name *'ākoko,* meaning blood-colored. (NEAL 515.)

'akū'akū. Endemic lobelia *(Cynea rollandioides),* a small tree or shrub. Its leaves were cooked like cabbage, taro tops, or sweet potato leaves with salt beef or pork.

'āla'a. Several species of this tree (*Planchonella* spp.) are found in Hawai'i. Its milky sap was used to trap birds, and its wood for spears, digging sticks, and house building. (NEAL 668.)

'alaea. Annotto dye plant *(Bixa orellana),* an evergreen shrub. The scarlet to orange seed coat was used to color butter, cheese, candy, cloth, soap, and paint. Its bark supplied a fiber for cordage, the stems a gum like gum Arabic. Also known as the lipstick plant. (NEAL 589.)

alahe'e. Large, native shrub or small tree *(Canthium odoratum)*. It grows up to 20 feet in height and is found in the lowlands up to 2,000 feet. The wood is handsome, hard, and durable. It was used by Hawaiians to make the *'ō'ō* (cultivating stick) and was also used medicinally. (NEAL 797.)

alani. One of the largest trees of the genus *Pelea*. It grows in O'ahu's wet forests. The wood is used for *kapa* beaters, the leaves for scenting *kapa,* and the bark for medicine. (NEAL 477.)

ali'ipoe. Ornamental canna *(Canna indica),* a large tropical herb native to tropical America. Its round black seeds called *li'ipoe* are used in leis and placed in shells of the *la'amia,* fruit of the calabash tree, for *hula* rattles. The leaves are used for wrapping food and the plants themselves as ornamentals. (NEAL 263.)

'ama'u, ma'u (pl. 'ama'uma'u). Tree fern (*Sadleria* spp.) living on all Hawaiian islands. It is common in the mountains of O'ahu and on the lava flows around Kīlauea. It grows to about 5 feet, and is crowned with a cluster of smooth, leathery fronds. At the base of the frond stems is buried a mass of *pulu,* used as stuffing for pillows and mattresses. The almost tasteless pith of the trunk was cooked and eaten in time of famine. *Lau hala* (thatched houses) were sometimes trimmed with this fern. Its stems were used in sizing *kapa* and the fronds to mulch dryland *taro.* Halema'uma'u is the pit in Kīlauea Crater, home of the *'ama'uma'u* fern. (NEAL 22–23.)

'ānapanapa. Smooth shrub *(Colubrina asiatica)* with twining stems reaching up to 20 feet. Its leaves, which form a lather in the water, have long been used as soap. The plant is also used medicinally and is not poisonous as once supposed. It is mostly found near the coast. Its name means glistening. Also called *kukuku.* (NEAL 541.)

'āpane. Kind of *'ōhi'a lehua* with dark red blossoms. Its nectar provides a food service for birds.

'ape. Large, taro-shaped plant *(Xanthosoma robustum)* with huge, heart-shaped shiny green leaves. At one time cultivated in small patches of dry land in the mountains. In times of scarcity the Hawaiians cooked the coarse underground stem for food. The milky juice of the plant is said to relieve nettle stings. Native stinging nettle is rare. (NEAL 162.)

'auhau. Stalk of a *hau* tree; spear made of *hau* wood.

'auhola, 'auhuhu. Small, slender shrub *(Tephrosia purpurea)* used as a poison to catch fish. The plant was pounded up and thrown in the tidal pools causing the affected fish to float to the surface. (NEAL 448.)

'au kī. Stem of a ti plant. See **kī.**

'auko'i. Coffee senna *(Cassia occidentalis),* an herb used medicinally for ringworm and skin diseases generally. The bark supplies tannin. Also called *'au'auko'i, mikipalaoa.* (NEAL 422.)

'awa. Kava or *'awa* plant *(Piper methysticum),* growing to 12 feet and valued as a source of a narcotic drink and for medicine. It has long played a part in the life of the people through ceremonies and festivals, and is always a sign of good will. It is closely related to pepper *(Piper nigrum),* a climbing shrub, the fruits of which yield black and white pepper. (NEAL 291.)

'awapuhi. Wild ginger *(Zingiber zerumbet),* a forest herb found in the lower parts of damp forests. A native of India, it also is distributed throughout Polynesia. The plant forms a continuous ground cover and has large, aromatic, underground stems, formerly used to scent *kapa.* A sudsy juice, squeezed out of mature flower heads, was used for shampooing and as a thirst quencher in earlier times. Also called *'awapuhi kuahiwi.* (NEAL 257.)

'awapuhi 'ai. See **'awapuhi pākē.** (NEAL 257.)

'awapuhi ke'oke'o. White or butterfly ginger *(Hedychium coronarium),* also known as ginger lily. Its flowers are highly prized for *lei*s and perfume. (NEAL 252.)

'awapuhi ko'oko'o. Torch ginger *(Phaeomeria speciosa),* a large herb from the East Indies, grown in Hawai'i for its ornamental pink or red, cone-shaped flower heads. *Lit.,* walking stick ginger.

'awapuhi melemele. Yellow or cream ginger *(Hedychium flavescens).* Similar to white ginger but its blossoms are yellow. This ginger grows wild in damp, low, open parts of forests in Hawai'i. The flowers are threaded into *lei*s. (NEAL 252.)

'awapuhi Pākē. Ginger *(Zingiber officinalis),* known around the world for its root spice. In Hawai'i it is largely cultivated for home consumption and for shipping to the mainland United States. Green roots are used for ginger ale. Also called *'awapuhi 'ai.* (NEAL 257.)

'aweoweo. Native shrub *(Chenopodium oahuense)* resembling pigweed, called lamb's quarters. It is endemic to Hawai'i, where it grows in arid or salty soil. The leaves are cooked as a pot herb. Also called *'aheahea.* (NEAL 331.)

'āwikiwiki. Climbing herbs *(Canavalia* spp.) cultivated for screens, flowers, or for green manure. Used as small, temporary fish traps. (NEAL 464.)

'ehu'awa. See **'ahu'awa.**

'ēkaha. Bird's-nest fern *(Asplenium nidus),* which perches, as a large, dark-green rosette of fronds, on tree trunks and branches. The dark, shining outer layer of the midrib has long been used by Hawaiians to decorate small mats and other plaited *hala.* In the old ceremony of cutting a tree for a canoe, it was necessary to cover the stump with a bird's-nest fern before the trunk could be adzed. (NEAL 21.)

hākona. Scorched or dried black, as breadfruit which hangs on a tree long after the season is over. One side becomes parched and black from the sun.

hala. Pandanus or screw pine *(Pandanus* spp.), native to the region from southern Asia to Hawai'i. Its base is supported by a clump of slanting aerial roots. It has many uses: its leaves *(lau hala)* are made into mats, baskets, and hats; the red to yellow fruit sections are used for *lei*s; male flowers, to scent *kapa;*

leaflike bracts, to plait mats. Fragrant flowers of the *hala* were placed indoors under the mats and in the thatch of the walls to maintain a sweet-scented and airy effect in the house. (NEAL 51.)

hala pepe. Tree with golden flowers (*Dracaena* spp.) that grows to a height of 35 feet. It is a dry district-loving tree, found at an elevation of between 1,000 and 2,000 feet, commonly in Kona and Ka'u, Hawai'i. Its wood is white with reddish streaks and is extemely soft. It was used by the natives in carving their images. Sap of some species was used formerly for varied medicinal needs and today is used for varnish. (NEAL 204.)

hame, ha'ā, mehame. Two native species of *hame (Antidesma)* bear much fruit. Hawaiians used the hard, brown wood for anvils on which to scrape *olonā* fiber. Berries were used to color *kapa* red. The wood is very resistant to shipworms, the best according to Dr. C. H. Edmondson. (NEAL 500.)

hāpu'u. Hawaiian tree fern *(Cibotium chamissoi),* native to Hawai'i. On Hawai'i island, in association with *'ōhi'a lehua,* it forms forests in dry or in damp regions, especially in Puna and near Kīlauea Volcano. Some years ago there were an estimated 400,000 acres of tree ferns up to 16 feet high. Its *pulu* resembles the *'ama'u* and was used to fill mattresses and pillows. Stems of the young, partly unfurled fronds were used to make hats. These stems were also mealy and fed to hogs. A food, nearly pure starch, was produced from the core of the tree and used during famine or as pig feed. (NEAL 10.)

hau. Branching tree *(Hibiscus tiliaceus)* that can be erect, gnarled, or spreading horizontally over the ground making an impenetrable thicket. The rounded, heart-shaped leaves are leathery. Flowers grow in profusion and open as bright yellow cups, changing to dull orange, and dull red by night. Formerly the *hau* was a useful tree. Its light, tough wood was used for outriggers of canoes, cross sticks of kites, and was rubbed with the harder *olomea* wood to obtain fire. Flowers were used for medicine and the fiber of inner bark for ropes, bags, and *kapa.* (NEAL 559.) Examples of *hau* can be seen along the Waialua River, Kaua'i, and above the oceanside restaurant of the Halekūlani Hotel, Honolulu.

ha'uoi, ha'uōwī, ōwī, oi. Weedy verbena *(Verbena litoralis),* a tropical American plant. It grows to 6 feet, with paired, long-stalked, narrow heads bearing tiny blue flowers. Hawaiians used the plants medicinally for skin ailments, applying the juice externally, and later sprinkling the affected area with powdered *pia* root. (NEAL 721.)

hāwane. Nut of the *loulu*, the fan palm tree, considered a delicacy. Also called *wāhane*.

hihiawai. Swamp fern *(Ceratopteris thalictroides)*, a somewhat succulent species that may be eaten raw or cooked as greens. Young fronds are eaten with freshwater shrimp. (NEAL 12.)

hinahina. Native heliotrope *(Heliotropicum anomalum)*, a low-spreading beach plant with small, white, fragrant blossoms. It is the *lei* flower of Kahoʻolawe. Used for tea and medicines. (NEAL 717.)

hōʻawa. All Hawaiian species of the genus *Pittosporum*. They are trees and shrubs with narrow leaves clustered at branch ends, and thick-valved fruits containing two to many smooth seeds surrounded by a thick, sticky liquid. The Hawaiians used the outer layer of the fruit valves medicinally, pounding it up for application externally to sores. (NEAL 382.) There are twenty-three species of genus *Pittosporum* in Hawaiʻi, and perhaps more.

hōʻiʻo. Large native fern *(Athyrium arnottii)* with subdivided fronds. The young unrolled fronds can be eaten raw with freshwater shrimp or with salted salmon. *Pohole* is the Maui name. (NEAL 25.)

hōlei. Rare Hawaiian tree *(Ochrosia compta)*, related to the *hao* *(Rauvolfia* spp.). A yellow dye for *kapa* was once extracted from the bark and roots. (NEAL 691.)

honohono. Wandering Jew *(Commelina diffusa)*, a low-creeping weed with small, irregularly-shaped, bright blue, paired flowers. They last but a day. In Hawaiʻi it is a rapid-growing, succulent plant, covering the ground even in the shade. *Honohono* is relished by cattle and is used as food in dairies. It is sometimes eaten raw or cooked by humans. (NEAL 185.)

hōpue. Native tree *(Urera sandvicensis)* related to the *olonā*. It once supplied bark fiber used for fishnets. Also called *ōpuhe*. (NEAL 320.)

huahekili. Hailstones. See **naupaka kahakai.**

huehue. Native climbing vine *(Cocculus ferrandianus)* that spreads like a thrifty vine. Flexible stems were used for twine and for funnel-mouth fish traps. (NEAL 354.)

huna olonā. Waste and refuse of the shrub *olonā (Touchardia latifolia)* after its bark has been treated for its fiber. Formerly sought for fishnets and rope to make them more resistant to sea water. *Huna* has a biblical equivalent in the word "tow," impoverished or ground to dust. (Isa. 1:31; NEAL 319.) See **olonā.**

'ie'ie. Native Hawaiian vine *(Freycinetia arborea)* growing between the 1,000 and 2,000 foot levels. Its brittle, woody stems are about an inch in diameter. The long aerial roots formerly had many uses: providing material for the famous Hawaiian twined baskets; close fitting coverings around gourds, calabashes, and bottles; fish and shrimp traps; feathered images and helmets. Lā'ie (shortened form for *lau i'e*), the O'ahu town, means "leaf of the *'ie'ie.*" (NEAL 54.)

'ihi. Mountain plant. The root is slightly cathartic. (A.) Yellow wood sorrel *(Oxalis corniculata),* a weedy oxalis, a creeping perennial herb. It has a sour taste due to the presence of oxalic acid. This plant, and a form with red stems and leaves and orange flowers, *'ihi-maka-'ula* or *'ihi-mākole,* is used medicinally by Hawaiians. (NEAL 473.)

'ili ahi. Sandalwood, a shrub or small tree *(Santalum* spp.) with a deeply scented heartwood. Formerly a wood of foreign trade where the scent as well as the grain were preserved in beautiful furniture, chests, and boxes. In early times the Hawaiian scented *kapa.* The Hawaiian islands were largely stripped of sandalwood in a frenzied China trade between 1790 and 1830. (NEAL 325.)

ilie'e, hilie'e. Wild plumbago *(Plumbago zeylanica)* native to the tropics from Indonesia to Hawai'i. Grows in a dry area near any leeward coast. This plant is not as poisonous as the red- or blue-flowered species and has a long history of medical use. The sap was used to blacken tattoo marks, often a form of mourning for the dead. It was used internally as a cathartic, externally as a poultice. (NEAL 667.)

'ilima. Various forms of *'ilima* plants *(Sida* spp.) growing from sea level to more than 2,000 feet. They may be anywhere from 4 feet in height to nearly prostrate. Flowers vary from bright yellow to rich orange to dull red. Some forms are cultivated for *lei*s, which, when twined with *maile,* are a favorite sign of farewell or welcome. The *'ilima* flower is the official flower of O'ahu. (NEAL 552.)

'inalua. Balloon vine *(Cardiospermum halicacabum),* a variable, herbaceous vine that climbs to 10 feet. Roots and leaves are used as medicine to treat rheumatism and digestive and pulmonary disorders. (NEAL 532.) See **Plants: Vines, 'inalua, pōniu.**

'inia. Pride of India *(Melia azedarach),* found in warm parts of the

Old World. It grows to 60 feet in Hawai'i. Often called the chinaberry tree. It has delicate, lilac-colored flowers. The wood is used for musical instruments and seeds yield oil. Some parts of the tree have medicinal value. Its leaves, placed in books, may keep insects away. (NEAL 491.)

ipu 'awa'awa. Variety of gourd *(Lagenaria siceraria).* One form was called *ipu 'awa'awa* by the Hawaiians from its bitter, even poisonous pulp, which was used medicinally. There is a non-poisonous, nonbitter pulp form, *ipu mānalo.* (NEAL 812.) See **Plants: Vines.**

'iwa'iwa. Maidenhair fern *(Adiantum* spp.), known in many forms in Hawai'i. Most species originated in warm climate areas of America. Stems are used by Hawaiians to decorate plaited *lau hala* purses. (NEAL 17.)

ka'a. Any foreign timber except oak. No other data. (A.)

kā'e'e, kā'e'e'e. Sea bean *(Mucuna gigantea),* a high climber containing flat seeds in large pods. In Hawai'i powdered seeds are used for their strong purgative effect. Seeds are also used in making *leis.* (NEAL 462.)

kāhipi, kāpiki. Inferior grade of *poi;* Hawaiian word for cabbage.

ka'i'i'i. Vegetable growing on the mountains, eaten as food in time of famine. No other data. (A.)

kākalaioa. Gray nickers *(Caesalpinia major),* a large, weedy bramble that climbs. Its name, *kākalaioa,* means "prickly." Hawaiians string the seeds in *leis,* and children play with them as marbles. Powdered seeds supply a strong purgative. (NEAL 433.)

kalia. Member of the linden family *(Elaeocarpus bifidus).* Formerly used for fire-making and constructing grass houses. Bark was used for cordage. (NEAL 545.)

kalo. Taro *(Colocasia esculenta),* cultivated for food since ancient times in the tropics and subtropics. Nearly three hundred Hawaiian forms have been recorded. Its uses are many. Food, chiefly *poi,* is made from the roots and *lū'au* greens from its leaves. Once certain varieties were reserved for medicines and a few choice forms as food for chiefs. Two types are cultivated: wetland, grown along streams, in irrigated marshy land and flooded terraces; and dry taro, grown in rain-watered uplands without irrigation. (NEAL 157.)

kaluhā. Papyrus *(Cyperus papyrus),* the well-known Egyptian sedge, is used in Hawai'i as an ornamental in water gardens and in flower arrangements. It is a tall perennial sedge. The name *kaluhā* is the Biblical Hawaiian word. (Ioba 41:2; NEAL 83.)

kamani. Tall, handsome tree *(Calophyllum inophyllum)*, from the shores of the Indian and western Pacific oceans. Grows somewhat crookedly to 60 feet. The flowers suggest orange blossoms. Its seed, the "Punnai" nut, a commercial name, yields an oil used medicinally and for lights. It is a hardwood used for calabashes, special furniture, and wood carvings. Considered a sacred tree in many places. (NEAL 585.)

kamani ula. False *kamani,* Indian almond *(Terminalia catappa).* Among the green leaves during certain seasons there is a scattering of red leaves. Timber is reddish, strong, elastic, and good for building boats and houses. Roots, bark, leaves, and fruit are used medicinally and for tanning skins; kernels of the fruit can be eaten raw or roasted; the fruit also yields a dye and an ink. (NEAL 627.)

keki. Shrub or small tree whose fruit was eaten in time of food scarcity. No other data. (A.)

kī. Shrubby ti plant *(Cordyline terminalis),* found from Asia and Australia to Hawai'i. Ornamental varieties and hybrids are common and widely used. The plant is useful: its leaves make whistles, house thatch, raincapes, sandals, *hula* skirts, eating plates, food wrappings, fodder for horses, and sliding material for children enjoying a downhill sport. Its large white root supplies *'ōkolehao,* a high-grade, transparent brandy. (NEAL 203.)

kīkānia haole. Jimson weed *(Datura stramonium),* a narcotic plant and strongly poisonous to man and beast. A drug called stramonium is extracted from dried leaves and flower tops and used medicinally to treat asthma. Also called *lā'au hānō.* (NEAL 750.)

kikawaiō. Native fern *(Cyclosorus cyatheoides).* Used for food and medicines. Its roots are grated and salted to taste. Also called *pakikawa'iō.* (NEAL 21.)

kō. Sugarcane *(Saccharum officinarum).* Yields one of the five most valuable plant products in the world. It is a perennial grass known only in cultivation. Cane was introduced in Hawai'i by early Polynesians. Sugar is the principal product. Valuable by-products include molasses, alcohol, bagasse, canec, plastics, and fertilizer. There are many proverbs and maxims involving sugarcane. (NEAL 77.)

koa. Largest of native forest trees *(Acacia koa).* It has a fine red wood, once used for canoes, surfboards, and calabashes. Now it is more often used for furniture and ukuleles. (NEAL 408.)

koai'e. Native tree *(Acacia koaia),* growing on Moloka'i, Maui, and Hawai'i. Harder than the *koa,* it is used for house posts, shark hooks, spears, paddles, *kapa* beaters and, more lately, furniture and machine-turned calabashes. Its grain is gnarled and twisted. (NEAL 405.)

koali, kowali. Morning glory vine (*Ipomoea* spp.), a tough perennial, bitter to the taste. Pounded stems and roots are used to relieve pains and aches. It may be too strong as a cathartic. Hawaiian legends speak of the use of the vine as a rope. The vines were used for *kōkō* (nets) and *lele koali* (swings). (NEAL 703.)

koali ʻai. Morning glory *(Ipomoea cairica),* a trailing herbaceous vine. Its tuberous roots and stems provided food and their juice was used medicinally. Some varieties of this plant are native. (NEAL 708.)

koali ʻawa. Morning glory *(Ipomoea indica).* A common, pretty flower in Hawaiʻi, beginning the day with blue-violet petals that change to pink by late afternoon. Its vine structure makes it usable as a swing. Bitter tasting stems and roots are good for external treatment of bruises and broken bones. Cordage is another product. (NEAL 708.)

kōlea. Small native tree (*Myrsine* spp.), found in bogs and wet summit forests. Charcoal from the wood and its red sap were used to dye *kapa.* The wood itself was used for houses and the logs on which to beat *kapa.* (NEAL 664.)

kolī. Castor bean, castor oil plant *(Ricinus communis),* more commonly a shrub and likely a native of Africa. It grows to 30 feet. Seeds have a high proportion of oil *(ʻaila kolī)* used for lubrication, lighting, medicinally as a cathartic, in soap, and as a leather softener. The waste makes good fertilizer but it is poisonous to eat. (NEAL 509.)

koliʻi. Native lobelia shrub *(Trematololobelia macrostachys).* Grows to 6 feet and bears pink flowers. (NEAL 815.)

kolomona. Shrub or small tree *(Cassia glauca)* growing wild in Hawaiʻi. It is used ornamentally, sometimes for hedges. It has clumps of orange-yellow flowers and thin brown pods. The bark is used medicinally by diabetic patients. Another similar plant *(C. gaudichaudii),* native to Hawaiʻi, is also called *kolomona,* "Solomon in all his glory." (NEAL 427.)

koʻokoʻolau. Native herbs or shrubs (*Bidens* spp.). The weedy introduced ones are called beggar's tick or Spanish needle. They grow up to 3 feet and are common in Hawaiʻi. Some have been used medicinally by the Hawaiians as a tonic in tea, and the plants and leaves are still gathered, dried, and used for tea.

(NEAL 844.) Some seventy species and varieties are endemic to the various islands in Hawai'i. (KILO.)

kopela. Camphor tree *(Cinnamomum camphora)* of China and Japan, grows to 40 feet. When crushed, leaves and other parts of the tree have the odor of camphor, believed to be deterrent against insects. When distilled or boiled, the chopped wood, roots, twigs, and leaves yield an aromatic, white, volatile gum that is used medicinally, for perfume, and in the manufacture of nitrocellulose compounds. (NEAL 361.)

kōpiko, 'ōpiko. Native genus *(Psychotria)* in the coffee family, with thirteen species ranging from large shrubs to trees. It is cultivated and its berries processed and sold commercially, largely as a blend ingredient. The wood is used for anvil making, *kua,* on which *kapa* is beaten, and *pulu,* used in quilting. The most common species *(Coffea arabica)* is grown for market. (NEAL 794.)

kou. Evergreen tree *(Cordia subcordata).* Grows to 30 feet, found on ocean shores from East Africa to Polynesia. Hawaiians used its soft but lasting wood for cups, dishes, and calabashes. It was a favorite shade tree and supplied the finest cabinet wood. (NEAL 714.)

kuawa. Guava *(Psidium guajava),* a tree growing to 25 feet, native of tropical America. Gauvas, raw or cooked, contain iron, calcium, and phosphorous and are about equal to oranges in vitamin content. Hawaiians distinguish a few varieties such as *kuawa lemi,* with sour, pink pulp; *kuawa momona,* with larger seeds and a sweet, pink pulp; *kuawa ke'oke'o,* with a whitish pulp. A medicinal tea is made from the leaves. (NEAL 632.)

kukui. Candlenut tree *(Aleurites moluccana),* common in Hawai'i. Its flowers and seeds are popularly used for *leis.* The rind of the green nut is used to make a black dye. Formerly, the oily kernels were dried and strung for candles, and the oil was burned in stone lamps. The rich, uncooked nut is a drastic purge. Oil cake is a good fertilizer. The crushed kernels make an excellent drying oil for varnish and medicine. Canoes were made of the soft wood. The *kukui* is the state tree of Hawai'i. (NEAL 504; KILO.)

kulu'ī. One of two endemic Hawaiian genera *(Nototrichium)* of the amaranth family.

kupukupu 'ala. Rose geranium *(Pelargonium graveolens).* In Hawai'i the leaves are used in *leis.* The flowers are pink, the leaves fragrant. (NEAL 471.)

laholio. India rubber tree *(Ficus elastica)* of South Asia. In Hawai'i some specimens have had time in one hundred years to become medium-sized trees. From smooth, gray bark comes an elastic substance, caoutchouc, which is one-third the weight of the milky sap. (NEAL 312.)

laiki, raisi. Rice *(Oryza sativa),* one of six tropical species in the genus of rather tall annual and perennial swamp grasses. It is the chief food of more than half the world's people. Besides food, rice grains provide fermented liquor, a nondrying oil, and a laundry starch. Its straw supplies hats and shoes. (NEAL 69.)

lama. Forest trees, both native species of Hawai'i *(Diospyros* synonym *Maba).* The hard, brown-red wood was highly prized by the ancient Hawaiians who used it in building temples. A piece of it, wrapped in yellow *kapa,* was used in the temple of Laka, goddess of the *hula. Lama* means light. (NEAL 674.)

lā'ō. Leaf of the sugarcane, formerly used in thatching. Also called *lākō, lau kō, lau'ō.*

lau kāhi. Broad-leafed plantain, *(Plantago major),* probably a Eurasian native, now a cosmopolitan weed in Hawai'i. Used internally for diabetes and to clear the system, externally as a poultice for boils. Its seeds and leaves are used for fodder. There are more than twenty varieties of *lau kāhi* native to Hawai'i. (NEAL 792; KILO.)

lau lele. 1. Butterfly weed, milkweed, blood flower *(Asclepias curassavica),* a host of the Monarch butterfly. Long known in Hawai'i as both a weed and an ornamental. The floss of its seeds is used to stuff pillows. Fiber from its stems can be spun. (NEAL 697.) 2. Dandelion *(Taraxacum officinale),* a widely distributed perennial. Young, mild-tasting leaves are eaten as greens; roots are used medicinally as a tonic. When ripe the fruiting head is a globose puffball. (NEAL 860.)

lilina. Flax or linseed *(Linum usitatissimum),* widely cultivated both for its fiber, which has been used for five thousand years, and for linseed oil. It is a slender, erect annual growing at least 1 foot high and having blue or white flowers. (NEAL 476.) Linen. *Eng.*

maiapilo. 1. Native shrub with bad smelling fruit *(Capparis sandwichiana)* resembling the night-blooming cereus. In Hawai'i the plant has long been used medicinally, as a cure for broken bones. The whole plant is pounded and applied to body joints, but not directly to the injured area. The blossoms, which open only at night, are fragrant. (NEAL 368.) 2. Caper bush *(Cap-*

paris spinosa), a spring shrub of the Mediterranean region. Pungent buds of the flower are pickled and eaten. Same uses as **1.** (NEAL 368.)

maiele. Small shrub (*Styphelia* spp.) found chiefly in Australia, New Zealand, and Hawai'i, where it is called *maiele* or *pūki-awe.* It is common near Kīlauea Volcano. Hawaiians add its bright fruits to *leis.* In ancient times the wood was used for cremating outlaws. Also the smoke from the burning wood freed a chief from a *kapu* so he could mingle without harm with his people. (NEAL 663.)

makaloa, makoloa. Perennial sedge *(Cyperus laevigatus)* found in or near fresh or salt water. It supplied a material, *makaloa,* from which the finest mats were made by the early Hawaiians. Young plants yielded the best stems for such plaiting. Floor and bed covers, clothing, capes, cloaks, and *pa'u* skirts were made. (NEAL 86.)

mākeke. Black mustard *(Brassica nigra),* a cosmopolitan herb. A weed in Hawai'i formerly cultivated for the seeds, which are the main source of table mustard. *Hua mākeke,* mustard seed. (Mat. 13:31; NEAL 379.)

malina. Sisal *(Agave sisalana),* so named because of its export town, Sisal, Yucatan. A perennial herb. Marine ropes were made from the fibers. *Malina* is a Hawaiian version of marine. The plant looks like the century plant; it forms a rosette of stiff, straight, 6 foot leaves and in nine or more years grows flowering stalks up to 30 feet tall. It is used for twine, rope, and to make *hula* skirts. The waste is high in mineral content, thus making good fertilizer. (NEAL 224.)

māmane. Native leguminous tree *(Sophora chrysophylla),* which grows up to the tree line, as on Mauna Kea and Mauna Loa. It has yellow flowers. The wood is used for spades and sled runners. (NEAL 442.)

mānele. Soapberry *(Sapindus saponaria),* native and deciduous in Hawai'i, native and evergreen in America. Its wood is white and used for fuel; the fruit (37 per cent saponin) forms lather when mixed with water; seeds are used for *leis,* and the kernel medicinally for fevers and rheumatism. (NEAL 532.) Also called *a'e.*

manono. Shrub, occasionally a tree, whose timber was used for some parts of canoes. (A.) Block set athwart a canoe to which the *'iako* (outrigger booms) are attached. (PE.)

ma'u. All species of the endemic genus of ferns *(Sadleria),* very common about Kīlauea. Also the starchy pith formerly eaten in time of famine. Some state it is the fern referred to in the name of the crater pit Halema'uma'u. See 'ama'u. (NEAL 22.)

mau'u la'ili. Yellow flowers, a relative of the perhaps one hundred species of blue-eyed iris *(Sisyrinchium acre)*, a native of Hawai'i. The juice was once used by the Hawaiians to stain the skin with bluish designs to prove they had visited Kīlauea Crater where the plant grew profusely. (NEAL 232.)

melekule, melekula. Pot marigold *(Calendula officinalis)*, a hairy, branching, variable annual up to 2 feet in height. A native of southern Europe, it is grown for its flowers, the heads of which are used to flavor stews. *Melekule* is the Hawaiian equivalent for marigold, but it applies only to the generic word, *Calendula*. (NEAL 855.)

milikani, mikana. Papaya *(Carica papaya)*, a small tree that reaches up to 25 feet. The date of introduction is unknown. The fruit is globose to ovoid, with five shallow grooves; its pulp is white to orange or red, sweet and juicy with a central space lined with small, hard, knobby, black seeds. The fresh fruit is a good source of calcium, sugar, and vitamins A, C, and G. The milky juices have many medicinal uses. (NEAL 600.)

milo. Tree *(Thespesia populnea)*, a native of the coasts of the eastern tropics. It grows around houses as a shade tree. A better tree and wood than its relative, the *kou*, it was once widely used for tannin dye, medicine, oil, and gum. The young leaves are edible. (NEAL 563.)

moa. A slender, tufted perennial *(Psilotum nudum)*, growing up to a foot high. It grows wild and is also grown ornamentally. A tea with cathartic properties was brewed using the whole plant. It was used as a purge, and its spores were made into talcum powder. Hawaiian children played a game of interlocking the branches and then pulling them apart. (NEAL 1.)

momona. Fruit tree *(Annona cherimola)*, growing to 25 feet. Seeds are used as an insecticide, and medicinally as an emetic. (NEAL 359.)

naio. Bastard sandalwood tree *(Myoporum sandwicense)*. This tree supplied a substitute wood, *'a'aka*, to the sandalwood trade when the true sandalwood tree had disappeared commercially. The Chinese merchants would not accept it. Timbers of the *naio* were used as posts in the Hawaiian house. The yellow-green heartwood has a fragrance somewhat similar to the original *'ili ahi*. (KILO.)

nani ahiahi. Four o'clock *(Mirabilis jalapa)*. In Hawai'i, four o'clocks, which are from tropical America, grow wild and also are cultivated. They make good hedges, and the popular flower is used for *leis.* The Hawaiian name means "beauty of the evening." Roots have a purgative value, boiled leaves are used as poultices, and the black seeds—in a white, powdery form—are used as a cosmetic. (NEAL 335.)

nā'ū. Shrub *(Gardenia brighami),* one of four species of the genus *Gardenia* native to Hawai'i. *Na'u* grows in dry areas and has fragrant, white flowers. Yellow pulp of the fruit was used to dye *kapa.* Another species, *nānū (G. remyi),* is a tall tree (up to 40 feet) growing in a variety of places in Hawai'i. (NEAL 800.)

naupaka kahakai. Beach *naupaka (Scaevola taccada),* a plant that grows to 10 feet, wild, on Hawai'i beaches. Its white flowers appear to be split with only half flowers remaining. The half flowers on beach and mountain have given rise to many romantic and sad love stories. For uses: it is sometimes planted at beach houses for ornament, windbreaks, or soil-sand binding. The bitter leaves and bark are used for indigestion and beriberi, the leaves for poultices and cooked greens. Its white berries created the Hawaiian word *huahekili* (hailstones) as a rare name for the plant. (NEAL 820.)

nioi. Red pepper *(Capsicum annuum),* a small, tropical American shrub. Fruits are podlike berries with many seeds, commonly red and globose to long and narrow. Some are grown for their hot fruits, which are used for their flavoring or as a vegetable. Since about 1815 a red pepper with narrow, inch-long, cone-shaped fruits has been growing in Hawai'i. The peppery, red fruits are used to flavor food. (NEAL 741.)

niu. Coconut tree *(Cocos nucifera).* The coco palm is the best known palm in the world. It may grow to 100 feet. Flowers and fruit start in about six years; nuts ripen in nine to ten months. The palm is planted ornamentally but has many uses: coconut shells are used for buckles, buttons, and lamp stands; charcoal for gas masks and automobile fuel; the fresh white pulp for food; wood for cabinets; husks for cordage, mats, brushes, and stuffing; fresh young leaves for hats and baskets. Leaves generally are plaited into screens. (NEAL 119.)

niu hiwa. Variety of coconut with a black shell and dark-green fruit, used for rituals but off-limits to women. It is also used in other ceremonies, medicinally, and in cooking. (PE.)

niu lelo. Coconut *kapu* to women. (A.) Coconut used in many ways but not ceremonially or medicinally. (PE.)

noni. Indian mulberry *(Morinda citrifolia),* a small evergreen tree of the coffee family. In Hawai'i the *noni* grows in open lowlands and at the edges of forests. It was brought to Hawai'i by the early Polynesians who found it useful. The roots supplied a yellow dye that turned red when coral lime was added; the fruit was eaten when food was scarce; leaves, fruit, and bark yielded medicines. (NEAL 804; KILO.)

nonolau, lonolau. Bitter calabash used in medicine. (A.) Strong concoction made of green gourd and *kukui* nut, used as an enema. (PE.) See **'o'opu hue.**

o'a. Maui name for the *kauila* tree *(Colubrina oppositifolia). O'a* is a rare, native Hawaiian specimen with hard, dark-red, heavy wood, and it sinks in water. It was once valued for making spears and *kapa* beaters. The wood resembles mahogany except in grain. (NEAL 541.)

'ōhai, pū 'ōhai. Monkeypod or rain tree *(Samanea saman),* a favorite shade tree of tropical America. It rivals the elephant's ear in spread and height, growing to 80 feet. A monkeypod planted by Mark Twain was a landmark in Ka'u, Hawai'i. The tree's pods yield seeds for leis, and its wood is prized for hand-made calabashes, platters, and other products. (NEAL 401.)

'ōhia. See **'ōhi'a 'ai** and **'ōhi'a lehua.** See **Plants: Trees.**

'ōlaelae. Bitter gourd *(Lagenoria siceraria),* a variety of bitter gourd with bitter-tasting pulp. Used medicinally. (NEAL 812.)

'ōlena. Turmeric *(Curcuma domestica),* a ginger found from India to Australia. In Hawai'i the *'ōlena,* once found wild in damp forested valleys, is now rare. It had ceremonial value for it was used in purifying persons, places, and things. The steamed root was eaten as medicine by consumptives; the raw juice relieved earache and sinusitis and also supplied a yellow dye for *kapa.* (NEAL 255.)

'oliwa, 'oliana. Oleander *(Nerium oleander),* a common ornamental in Hawai'i that grows to a height of 20 feet. Its flowers, foliage, bark, roots and wood seem to be poisonous to insects, humans, and livestock. The milky sap is used in small amounts as a medicine for skin disease. This species is difficult to distinguish from *N. indicum.* (NEAL 695.)

olomea. Shrub or tree *(Perrottetia sandwicensis).* Its hard wood was once used with soft *hau* to make fire through friction by the plough method. (NEAL 530.)

olonā. Native shrub *(Touchardia latifolia)* related to the *māmaki* in the nettle family. Six-foot strips of bark were soaked in water for many days, the long fibers removed, bleached in the sun, and then braided into cord, rope, or even cable in a desired diameter. This was the famous *olonā*—strong, long wearing, no kinks. It was used for binding needs, fishnets, container nets, as a woven base for feather capes and helmets and ti-leaf coats, as rope for rigging on ships and cable to move canoes. Even the fiber thread was used to sew body incisions after embalming. Another use was in a swinging bed of sennit mesh, *'ahamaka* (hammock). (NEAL 319.)

'o'opu hue. Bitter calabash. (A.) Strong concoction made of green gourd and *kukui* nut, used as an enema. (PE.) See **nonolau.**

'opiuma. Manila tamarind *(Pithecellobium dulce)*, native to tropical America. Used in Hawai'i for landscape planting. Its black seeds are used in making *lei*s. The wood is strong and resilient and supplies lumber for building, posts, and fuel. Wood is turned on a lathe for calabashes and hand worked for other items. Its seeds resemble commercial opium, hence, the Hawaiian word *'opiuma*. (NEAL 399.)

ōwī. See **oi** in **Plants: Herbs.**

pā'ē. To strip the bark from a tree; a bunch of cleaned bark, as from an *olonā* tree. See **olonā.**

pā'ihi. Weedy herb *(Nasturtium sarmentosum)* distributed throughout the Pacific islands, including Hawai'i. Hawaiians used the plant medicinally and as a *kapa* dye. It is related to the watercress. (NEAL 372.)

paka. Tobacco *(Nicotiana tabacum)*, a native of tropical America, the source of commercial tobacco. A large, sticky, hairy herb that grows to 6 feet. It has been in Hawai'i since 1812, where it has been tried in plantings in Kona and elsewhere but without success. Plants are both wild and grown as ornamentals. (NEAL 752.)

pala. Native fern *(Marattia douglasii)*. Its large, long-stemmed green fronds were eaten raw for their laxative effect. The Hawaiians used the thick, spongy bases of frond stems, or the liquid resulting from slicing and soaking them in water, for medicinal purposes after draining the mix. Fronds were used for their fragrance by twining or winding them in *lei*s. The fern was also used in *heiau* ceremonies. (NEAL 6.)

palaholo. Paste made from the *'āma'uma'u* fern, needed in pasting sheets of *kapa* together.

palai, palapalai. Hairy native Hawaiian fern *(Microlepia setosa)* found on the edges of forests and used as border edges. It grows up to 4 feet in height. This is one of the plants used on the *hula* altar built for Laka, goddess of the *hula* (other plants were *lehua, maile, halapepe,* and *'ie'ie*). (NEAL 12.)

palakea. Variety of *kalo,* usually not made into *poi.* It was once used as a substitute for bread and eaten in time of famine. Also used medicinally.

palani. Sugarcane *(Saccharum officinarum).* Aside from raw sugar, which brought the agricultural list its top competitor, sugarcane has many by-products: molasses, alcohol, bagasse, canec, plastics, and fertilizer. In addition, cane tops can be used as cattle feed, flower heads for home decoration, and leaves for house thatching. Today, sugarcane is munched like candy. (NEAL 77.)

pāpala. Endemic Hawaiian genus *(Charpentiera)* of the amaranth family. Its light, flammable wood was used by early Hawaiians for firework displays. On dark nights pieces were lighted and thrown into the wind from cliffs on Kaua'i's north coast where they floated gently down. In Hawai'i the leaves are used for *leis.* Its flowers are pink, the leaves fragrant. (NEAL 471.)

pāpapa. Hyacinth bean *(Dolichos lablab),* a smooth perennial or annual vine with whitish or pinkish flowers. The seeds are cooked and eaten when green or white. Plants are used for fodder or green manure. (NEAL 468; 2 Sam. 17:28.)

pā'ū o Hi'i-aka. Attractive, native beach plant *(Jacquemontia sandwicensis).* The involved Hawaiian name refers to Hi'i-aka's skirt which was given by Pele because this vine protected her baby sister, Hi'i-aka, from the sun while lying on the beach. Similar to the *koali,* used medicinally. (NEAL 710.)

pia. Polynesian arrowroot *(Tacca leontopetaloids).* Its tubers are good food, high in starch, but rarely cultivated in Hawai'i today. Medicinally it was used for diarrhea and dysentery. (NEAL 228.)

pili kai. Wood rose *(Operculina tuberosa),* another member of the morning glory family. It is grown ornamentally in Hawai'i for its dry, brown, rose-shaped fruit. (NEAL 709.)

po'a'aha, po'āha. Small tree *(Broussonetia papyrifera),* well known for its usefulness. Bark was turned into a durable paper which could serve as cloth, leather, or paper depending on the process of preparation. *Kapa* made from it was valued for bed clothes and clothing of all sorts. *Po'a'aha* is also called *wauke,* which as a source of fiber for *kapa* was much preferred for its warm, flexible, and water-resistant qualities. (NEAL 301.) *Wauke,* as another name for *po'a'aha,* is actually better known.

There are slight differences: *wauke* has one- to three-lobed leaves; *poʻaʻaha* has entire round leaves, no lobes. (KILO.)

pōhuehue. Beach morning glory *(Ipomea pes-caprae),* a vigorous creeping vine. Flowers are a dusky pink. The fruit is a capsule with seeds having some cathartic value. Hawaiians formerly ate roots and stems in time of famine. They also used the vines to whip fish into nets and also to whip the sea into higher waves for surfing. (NEAL 709.)

pōpō kāpaʻi. Medical herbs rolled into a ball for rubbing or massaging the body.

pōʻulu. Bark of young and tender breadfruit shoots, used for making *kapa.*

pua. Large native tree *(Osmanthus sandwicensis),* growing to 60 feet in most forests but at low altitudes. The wood is dark brown with black stripes, hard, heavy, and strong. It was formerly used for spears, adze handles, and digging sticks for cultivating the soil. Also called *olopua.* (NEAL 676.)

pua kala. Prickly poppy *(Argemone glauca),* a species peculiar to Hawaiʻi, where it grows in dry, rocky soil from sea coast up to 1,000 feet. It is a conspicuous, attractive, wild annual up to 4 feet in height. Seeds that can resist fire are scattered from prickly capsules about an inch long, creating new plants springing up from burned-over ground. Formerly used for toothache, neuralgia, and ulcers, all because of a narcotic in the yellowish juice. (NEAL 367.)

pua lele. Sow thistle *(Sanchus oleraceus),* an annual weedy herb that grows to 10 feet. Flower heads are clustered and yellow. Flat fruits are tipped with a large, white, hairy tuft or pappus. Leaves and roots are used medicinally as a tonic and for indigestion. *Lit.,* flying flowers. (NEAL 860.)

pulapula. Seedlings, sprouts, cuttings, as of sugarcane; tops of sugarcane used for planting.

pulu. Soft, yellow "wool" found at the base of the leaf stalks of the large tree fern *(Cibotium* spp.). The plant is most common in the area of the upper part of the Hilo-Kīlauea highway on Hawaiʻi. *Pulu* is collected and exported to California where it is still used to stuff pillows and mattresses.

pū maiʻa. Banana stalk.

ʻuha loa. Small, down-covered plant *(Waltheria indica).* Its bitter root is used medicinally; its juice is used to relieve the throat. Also called *hiʻaloa, kanaka loa.* (NEAL 575.)

uhiuhi. Endemic leguminous tree *(Mezoneuron kavaiense).* A beautiful tree, it grows to a height of 30 feet, its trunk reaching 1 foot in diameter. The tree is scarce on Kaua'i, its first home. It inhabits the leeward side of the islands, especially lava fields. On Maui, above Kaupō, it is called *kea*. Its wood is extremely hard, close-grained, and almost black. Bark and young leaves were used for purifying the blood, the wood for spears and the *holua* (sleds). (NEAL 435.)

uiui. Arrowroot *(Maranta arundinacea),* a slender high herb. It is called arrowroot because the juice of its thick roots was used as an antidote for wounds from poisonous arrows. It also counter-acts insect stings. Sometimes Oriental markets in Hawai'i sell young arrowroots, which can be eaten like sweet potatoes. (NEAL 271; A.)

'uki'uki. Perennial herb *(Dianella sandwichensis),* a native member of the lily family found in forest undergrowth. The fruit was used as a pale-blue dye; the leaves were twisted into cordage for use in thatching houses. (NEAL 191.) "The grass house in the Bishop Museum has the *pili* grass tied on with *'uki'uki* cordage. The long tough leaves make good cordage but are too narrow for thatch." (KILO.)

'ūlei. Native Hawaiian evergreen shrub *(Osteomeles anthyllidifolia),* which grows in dry areas up to 1,000 feet. The wood is hard and was once used for fish spears and a native musical instrument, *'ūkēkē.* Sometimes flexible branches were bent into hoops for fishnets. (NEAL 387.)

'ūlili. Musical instrument made of three small gourds or coconuts pierced by a stick. The instrument was operated with a string twined around the stick. The outer gourds were glued fast to the stick while the center one rotated freely. A cord fastened to the stick passed through a hole in the side of the center gourd. The string was pulled, then released to cause the outer gourds to whirl. (DK; KILO.)

'ulu. Breadfruit *(Artocarpus altilis).* Early migrations of Polynesians brought the first breadfruit trees from Tahiti. Rather common in Hawai'i, the tree ranges from 30 to 60 feet in height. It has many uses: the wood is light and good for canoes; the smooth, gray bark is fibrous and one source of *kapa;* the milky sap was used for filling seams of canoes, as a lime for catching birds, and as a chewing gum; fruit is baked or boiled to make its sweet, starchy pulp edible; *poi* is made by pounding up this pulp. (NEAL 302.)

walahe'e. Small shrub or tree *(Canthium odoratum),* reaching up to 20 feet in height. It grows in dry woodlands. The wood is hard and used for ʻōʻō sticks and also employed medicinally. Also called *alaheʻe, oheʻe.* (NEAL 737.)

wiliwili. Native Hawaiian tree *(Erythrina sandwicensis)* that grows from sea level to 2,000 feet in dry regions on all islands. The wood is the lightest of Hawaiian woods and once was used for surfboards, canoe outriggers, and floats for nets. Seeds were strung in *leis.* (NEAL 458.)

PLANTS: Vegetables Introduced

There is no Hawaiian equivalent for the word vegetable, but there are Hawaiian names for introduced vegetables, most of which are in this category. (The sweet potato *[ʻuala]* enjoys its own category.) Examples of English words adapted to Hawaiian needs include *kalohe* (carrot) and *kelaki* (celery).

ʻakaʻakai. Onion *(Allium cepa),* grown for its large bulbs; leek *(A. porrum)* with a small bulb; chive *(A. shoenoprasum),* used in Hawaiʻi for flavoring food; green onion *(A. fistulosum),* good for food. *ʻAkaʻakai mahina,* wild onion, the leaves of which are used to relieve a sore throat. *ʻAkaʻakai pilau,* garlic *(A. sativum),* which has a bulb divided into several cloves with a strong persistent odor. (NEAL 198.)

anunū. Turnip.

ipu kālaua. Autumn and winter squashes *(Cucurbita maxima* Duch), a vine differing from the pumpkin mainly by its softer stems and leaves that are rounded, heart-shaped, and not lobed. The pumpkins and squashes are for baking. (NEAL 813.) See **pū kualau.**

ipu pū. Autumn and winter squashes for baking *(Cucurbita maxima).* The vine differs from the pumpkin mainly by its softer stems and leaves that are rounded, heart-shaped, and lobed. (NEAL 813.)

kaloke. Carrot *(Daucus carota),* a biennial or annual cultivated for 2,000 years as a vegetable. Carrots are high in carbohydrate and are good food for stock and humans. Use is made not only of the thick, orange taproot but also of the young leaves, which are eaten as greens. (NEAL 660.)

kamako. Tomato *(Lycopersicon esculenium),* introduced from

South America. The common tomato (var. *commune* Bailey) has globose fruits flattened on the ends. See **'ōhi'a lomi.**

kāpiki. Cabbage *(Brassica oleracea* var. *capitata).*

kāpiki 'ai maka. Lettuce. *Lit.,* cabbage eaten raw.

kelaki, keraki. Celery *(Apium graveolena).* This is the "vegetable of commerce." Roots can be cooked as a vegetable; seeds are used for spice and supply a base for perfume. The plant has medicinal value. (NEAL 659.)

kua hulu. Wild vegetable eaten in time of famine. (A.; PE.) This is the *koali kua hulu,* a wild morning glory eaten in time of famine. (KILO.)

kūlina, kurina. Indian corn, maize *(Zea mays),* a valued annual crop of the United States. There are no wild forms today. Several races have developed, the chief ones being sweet, pop, dent, and flint corn. Besides yielding fodder and a popular vegetable, corn is a source of flour, cornstarch, syrup, alcohol, oil, hominy, wallboard, paper, breakfast foods, and fuel. (NEAL 81.)

kūlina 'ono. Sweet corn *(Zea mays* var. *rugosa).* This has been grown more commonly of late in Hawai'i due to development of resistant strains. (NEAL 81.)

kūlina pohāpohā. Pop corn *(Zea mays* var. *everta).* (NEAL 81.)

laulele. Butterfly weed, milkweed, blood flower *(Asclepius curassavica),* a tropical American perennial herb. It has erect, podlike fruits containing numerous round, flat seeds each bearing a tuft of long, silky hairs. This floss is used for stuffing pillows; fiber from the stem can be spun. Leaves are eaten in time of famine. The plant is a host of the Monarch butterfly. (NEAL 697.)

leluke. Lettuce *(Lactuca sativa),* a smooth annual herb with milky juice, long cultivated for its edible leaves. (NEAL 861.)

'ōhi'a. Tomato. See **'ōhi'a lomi.**

'ōhi'a lomi. Common table tomato *(Lycopersicon esculentum* var. *commune* Bailey). See **kamako.**

'ōhi'a ma kanahele. Currant tomato *(L. pimpinellifolium* Mill), a weak, downy herb with red, globose fruits half an inch in diameter. Introduced from Peru, it grows wild in Hawai'i.

pakanika. Parsnip *(Pastinaca sativa),* a plant brought from Europe. Its roots are white; the leaves once divided are narrow and ovate. (NEAL 659.)

pala 'ai. Field pumpkin *(Cucurbita pepo).* Originally, along with the squash, this plant was named *pala 'ai* for its resemblance to a long extinct gourd. It is grown for its edible fruits. It is commonly used in pies and is popular at Halloween. (NEAL 813.)

pī. Beans, peas, lentils. (2 Sam. 17:28.)

pū. General name for pumpkin. See **ipu pū**. (NEAL 813.)

pū kualau. Winter crookneck squash (*Cucurbita moschata* Duch).

'ualu pilau. Turnip. *Lit.*, potato smelly.

uhi. Yam *(Discorea alata)*, a vegetable from southeast Asia. Commonly eaten by Captain Cook's crewmen on his visits to Hawai'i. (NEAL 229.)

PLANTS: Vines

Vines, taken collectively, supply an amazing variety of needs. For example, the *maile* is associated with *leis* for VIPs; the *koali,* with its tough, flexible, and slender stem, is used as a rope in swings; and the roots, leaves, and stems of many other vines are involved one way or another in medicines. Even the lowliest of vines, *pūhilihili,* serves as a sand cover on beach-house lawns.

āhihi Mehiko. Mexican creeper, mountain rose, chain of love *(Antigonon leptopus)*. It flowers much of the year in Hawai'i, producing pink and white blossoms. The leaves are used for dye. The plant produces edible tubers. (NEAL 329.)

'ai 'a ka nēnē. Scandent shrub or vine (genus *Comprosma*). Around Kīlauea it is also called *kūkae nēnē, nēnē*. (NEAL 803.)

'āwikiwiki. 1. Leguminous vine *(Canavalia cathartica)* common on all islands. It is popular for its pink to lavender, 1½-inch-long flowers, which are long lasting and beautiful in *leis*. Seeds are brown to black. (NEAL 464.) 2. Climbing herb *(Canavalia* spp.), cultivated for screens, flowers, or green manure. (NEAL 463.)

hoi. Bitter yam *(Dioscorea bulbifera),* a vine with a round stem, heart-shaped leaves, small tuberous roots, and round aerial tubers *('ala'ala)* at the leaf axils. Neither the root nor aerial tuber were commonly eaten except in time of famine. (NEAL 230.)

huehue. Native climbing vine *(Cocculus ferrandianus)*. (NEAL 354.) See **Plants: Uses.**

'ie'ie. Native climbing liana *(Freycinetia arborea),* a native of Hawai'i growing in woods between the 1,000 and 2,000 foot levels. It not only climbs to tree tops but forms a luxuriant, impenetrable cover on the ground. (NEAL 54.) See **Plants: Uses.**

'**inalua.** Balloon vine *(Cardiospermum halicacabum)*, a variable, slender-stemmed, herbaceous plant that climbs to about 10 feet. An inflated, ovoid capsule contains three pea-sized seeds, each black with a white, heart-shaped scar on one end. Superstition has it that a *lei* of the plant worn on the head and then thrown into the sea will rid one of a headache. See **pōniu.** (NEAL 532.) See **Plants: Uses.**

ipu'awa'awa. Variety of gourd *(Lagenaria siceraria)*, a downy annual with a wide-spreading vine. Fruit is smooth, green, and mottled to white, ranging in shape from thick and short-globose to 4 feet by 1 foot. The pulp is white, the seeds light in color. It is known as the bottle gourd. (NEAL 812.) See **Plants: Uses.**

kā'e'e, kā'e'e'e. Sea bean *(Mucuna gigantea)*, a vine found in the valley back of Hawai'i beaches, grown from floating seeds washed up by high surf. The seeds, covered by nearly hairless pods, are flat, brown with black lines, and edged with a long black line. (NEAL 462.) See **Plants: Uses.**

kākalaioa. Gray nickers *(Caesalpinia major)*, a large, weedy bramble that climbs and straggles in dry lowlands of Hawai'i. The word means prickly. (NEAL 433.) See **Plants: Uses.**

koali, kowali. Morning glory vine *(Ipomoea* spp.). It numbers nearly twenty species in Hawai'i in both annual and perennial forms, some of which, including the sweet potato, have swollen roots. The name of the genus, *Ipomoea,* refers to their twining habits. (NEAL 703.)

koali'ai. Morning glory *(Ipomoea cairica).* (NEAL 708.) See **Plants: Uses.**

koali'awa. Morning glory *(Ipomoea indica).* (NEAL 708.) See **Plants: Uses.**

maile. Shrub *(Alyxia olivaeformis)*, a favorite native vine noted for its vanilla-like odor and popular as a special *lei* for special people. (NEAL 690.) See **Plants: Odoriferous** for several compounds of *maile.*

mauna loa. 1. Sea bean *(Dioclea wilsonii)*, a tall climbing vine from Brazil. Formerly Hawaiians made *lei*s from the blue or white flowers and used the beans for medicine. Today the similar and more common flowers of a *Canavalia* are made into *mauna loa lei*s. (NEAL 463.) 2. Fast-growing annual vine *(Canavalia cathartica)*, popular for its pink to lavender flowers used for decoration and *lei* making. (NEAL 464.)

mōhihihi. Herbaceous vine *(Vigna marina)*, possibly from the Eastern Hemisphere. Its yellow flowers are $\frac{1}{2}$ inch long; pods are 2 inches long by $\frac{1}{4}$ inch thick with three to six brown, ovoid seeds. (NEAL 467.) Also called *'ōkole makili*. See **nanea, pūhili-hili.**

nanea. Annual herb *(Vigna marina)* established on most shores of the tropical world. With its roots in the sand, it serves as a ground cover on the beach and around a beach house. (NEAL 467.)

nēnē. Woody, trailing plant *(Coprosma ernodeoides)* that grows prostrate over lava rocks on the islands of Maui and Hawai'i only. The fruit is a black berry. Also called *kūkae nēnē*, dung goose; *lepo nēnē*, filth goose. See **'ai a ka nēnē.** *Lit.*, food goose.

nuku 'i'iwi. Woody climbing legume *(Strongylodon ruber)*, a native vine that grows in forests. It has red flowers shaped like the narrow beaks of the *'i'iwi* bird. The pods are flattened, thick, and smooth. Also called *ka 'i'iwi*. (NEAL 461.)

'ōkole makili. Herbaceous vine *(Vigna marina)*, an annual that grows in the sand, spreading itself as cover. It serves as a ground cover around beach houses. It is used for asthma, boils, and broken skin. See **mōhihihi, nanea, pūhilihili.** (NEAL 467.) *Lit.*, buttocks cracked.

'ōlaelae. Bitter gourd *(Lagenaria siceraria)*. (NEAL 812.) See **Plants: Uses.**

pāpapa. Hyacinth bean *(Dolichos lablab)*, an annual that grows to over 15 feet. It has whitish-pinkish flowers and pods that are $2\frac{1}{2}$ to 5 inches long, enclosing three to five dark, thick, oval seeds. (NEAL 468.) See **Plants: Uses.**

pili kai. 1. Vine *(Stictocardia tiliaefolia)* that resembles the silver morning glory. The rose-purple flowers are funnel-shaped with $\frac{1}{2}$ inch sepals that increase to 2 inches in length. (NEAL 702.) **2.** Wood rose *(Operculina tuberosa)*, another member of the morning glory family. Its dry, stiff, brown sepals enclose the fruiting capsule. Together they are used for dry bouquets. (NEAL 709.)

pi'oi. Kaua'i name for the bitter yam, *hoi (Dioscorea bulbifera)*. It has a stem and leaves similar to the *uhi* and often bears tubers. Aerial tubers of the bitter yam are called *'ala'ala*. (NEAL 230.)

pōhue. Climbing legume *(Canavalia sericea)*, which is cultivated for screens, flowers, or green manure. Pods are tan, flowers rose-colored. The *pōhue* originated in the South Pacific. (NEAL 464.)

pōhuehue. Vine *(Ipomoea pes-caprae)*, a beach morning glory, a vigorous creeping plant. Its thick leaves, notched at the tips, are shaped like a goat's foot *(pes-caprae)*. (NEAL 709.) See **Plants: Uses.**

pōniu. Balloon vine, heartseed *(Cardiospermum halicacabum)*, a slender-stemmed herbaceous plant that grows to 10 feet. It has small white flowers and balloonlike fruit. It is used in its entirety as a head *lei,* which was believed to have healing power, especially for headaches (hence, the name *pōniu* meaning spinning, dizziness). Lengths of the vine were twisted or plaited into a round *lei* that was placed on the head. The plants were grown for vegetables; leaves were used medicinally for rheumatism or digestive and pulmonary disorders. (NEAL 532.) See ʻinalua.

pua kalakoa. Calico bush *(Aristolochia littoralis),* a Brazilian vine which produces the calico flower *(pua kalakoa).* It is cultivated for its brown-purple, veined flowers, which somewhat resemble a bent pitcher in shape. (NEAL 326.)

pūhilihili. Herbaceous vine *(Vigna marina)* established on most shores of the tropical world. Leaves are three-parted, flowers yellow. When growing in the sand it provides a cover for the beach. (NEAL 467.) Same as *mohihihi.* See also **nanea, ʻōkole makili.**

waina. Isabella grape *(Vitis labruscana),* the first grapevine in Hawaiʻi (1792). This is a strong climber with dark-purple to blue flowers. The fruit is skinned loose from the pulp. Slow in catching on commercially, it is the best of the grapes in the islands. It is excellent raw and in grape juice, jams, and jellies. (NEAL 542.)

POETIC REFERENCES

This category includes words and expressions that in some way can be termed "poetic." A number would also merit the adjective "practical." This listing hints at the power and influence of the newly written Hawaiian language, not only as a means for the transition to new requirements in communication, but also by giving the art of language a more effective role in Hawaiian culture. The examples herein speak to the beauty of figurative language, but the literal meanings too are picturesque and delightful.

Questions might be raised about the appropriateness of including four words: *iwi hoe hoe, iwi kano, iwikuamoʻo,* and *iwi uluna.* The poetic implications are present in each definition, although often this consists of just the literal meaning.

This category was assembled by Charles M. Hyde.

'a'a hu'i. Pain, ache; desire for pleasure attended with some sense of pain. *Pau ke 'a'a hu'i, ke a'a koni oloko,* the painful desire within has ceased. (A.)

'a'a koni. Throbbing heart. *Lit.,* vein throb; hence, perhaps, artery. (A.)

'ai'ē. To eat or enjoy a thing before paying for it (from the custom of paying for work before it was done, payment being something consumed); to owe. *Lit.,* eat beforehand.

'aki'aki. To pilfer, nibble; to bite in two; to bite again and again.

'auana, 'auwana. To float, wander away. This word has its origin in the overturning of a canoe, when men and cargo float off in scattered directions.

'āwala. To pull steadily and carefully, as a fisherman wanting to hold his fish on the line or in the net.

'ehu ahiahi. Red of the evening, a name for old age.

'ehu kakahiaka. Red of the morning, a name for youth.

hālokoloko. Small pools of water standing after a rain; tears as they well up in one's eyes; to be about to weep.

haole. White person of any nationality (German, American, Portuguese, Frenchman, Englishman, etc.); formerly, a person from any foreign country; alien.

he kupa 'ai au. See **kupa 'ai au.**

he ulu lā'au. "It is a forest," exclaimed the natives on first sighting the ships of Captain James Cook. *Ua nei ae la iloko o ke kai,* "it has moved into the sea. A habitation of wild beasts." (Ios. 17:18.)

he wahi kūnono mana'o iki no nae. A small idea; insignificant. *Lit.,* a leaky calabash full of little holes. Also *kūlono.*

hiki ku. Place of the sun's rising; poetically, the east.

hikina. The full form of this word is *ka hiki 'ana o ka lā,* the coming of the sun, i.e., the east.

hōkū huelo lō'ihi. Long-tailed star; comet.

hōkū puhi baka. Comet. *Lit.,* tobacco-smoking star, obviously because the trailing smoke of tobacco resembles the tail of the comet.

hōkū welowelo. Comet, from its tail of light. *Lit.,* streaming star.

homa. To be thin in flesh; to be disappointed or baffled in one's efforts to do something.

ho'ohiala. To cram down food; to eat with greediness; to swallow down iniquity, in a moral sense. (A.)

ho'okolokolo. To call to account; to try in court; to investigate by questioning.

hoʻomanawanui. To take plenty of time; a good time is coming; be patient.

huahekili. Hail, hailstone. *Lit.*, fruit thunder or egg thunder. It generally thunders during mountain storms in Hawaiʻi, hence the belief that hail was produced by thunder.

ipu wai ʻauʻau. Washbowl. This was an epithet applied to those who washed or kept clean the genealogies of the chiefs, thus keeping their lives and reputations unsullied.

iwi. Bone, used figuratively for near kindred. *Alaila pōmaikaʻi kāua, ola nā iwi iloko o ko kāua mau lā ʻelemakule,* then we two shall be happy, our descendants shall live in the days of our old age.

iwi hoehoe. Bone of the shoulder, shoulder blade. *Lit.*, bone paddle.

iwi kano. Bone of the forearm. *Lit.*, bone handle.

iwikuamoʻo. Backbone; a close trusted relative who attended the person of a high chief and executed his private orders. *Lit.*, bone lizard.

iwi uluna. Bone of the upper arm. *Lit.*, bone pillow.

kahua o Maliʻo. First dawn of morning light. *Lit.*, source of light and comfort. Figuratively, the source of life's enjoyments such as food, fish, mats, and all the fruits of the land. A mythical woman noted for her music and love magic.

kaiakahinaliʻi. A flood in the days of the celebrated chief Hinaliʻi that was named after him. By tradition this flood covered the whole earth (i.e., the Hawaiian Islands). This is the word used for Noah's flood. (Kin. 6:17.)

kaiāulu. The *kilohana,* the outside and best of the *pāʻū kapa* and usually with the best design(s). *Fig.*, something rather remarkable in appearance.

kakahiaka. Morning breaking the shades of night; morning. *Kakahiaka nui,* early morning.

kamaʻāina. Child of the land; resident; a native, born of Hawaiʻi.

kamani. Tree producing beautiful leaves and wood. *Hoʻokamani,* hypocrite. (Mat. 15:7.) The inside wood of the *kamani* is prized for wood turning and carving.

kānāwai. Regulations governing the lives of the ancient Hawaiians which derived from ownership and use of flowing water. Laws of modern Hawaiʻi are called by this name.

kapae. To turn a thing from its designed use. This word was formerly used as applied to the management of a chief's property, a species of embezzling. It was also applied when a commander ordered a soldier to throw a spear at a friend. The soldier would throw his spear where it would do no hurt. He thus would be said to *kapae* the spear. (A.)

kilohana. Outside *kapa* of a *pā'ū*, which was the best in material and design; a top bedcover.

kōko'olua. Staff or cane; hence, a second, assistant, or helper; companion or partner, always consisting of two.

kolekole kou maka. "Down! you see that you are up a stump." Said when the corner of your eye is red or even raw, a poetic taunt.

kuamo'o. Place, such as a road or frequented path (as meant on Hawai'i). *Lit.*, back lizard. *Alanui* is used now.

kūikawā. Word signifying independence in a person who does not take sides. It is similar in meaning to the English expression "on the fence." *Lit.*, to stand in space. (1 Kor. 9:1.)

kūkaheu. To stand up, as the bristles of a hog when angry. The word is applied to someone whose face seems flushed with anger. (A.)

kukui. Tree favored for the usefulness of its parts. The nut was formerly crushed for oil that was widely used as fuel for lamps. The body of the tree was occasionally made into canoes. Bark supplied the gum *pilali*. It is now the official state tree of Hawai'i.

kupa 'ai au. Someone who is native-born, who eats and enjoys the land. Also called *he kupa 'ai au*.

lehua. A word frequently used figuratively for a person highly esteemed. *Ku'u lehua 'ala a Ko'olau,* my sweet-scented *lehua,* (very dear friend) of Ko'olau.

lelo. Tongue. *Ka hoe uli o ka 'ōlelo ma ka waha,* the rudder of speech in the mouth.

loko. Inner part; that which is within, as applied to persons or internal organs. Often used in songs to refer to one's inner feelings. The Hawaiians believed moral powers or dispositions had their base in the small intestines.

mā'e'ele. Benumbed. Hawaiians express a strong feeling of love for a person in using this word.

mā'eha'eha. Twilight; dusk of the evening, when it is painful to see with the eyes.

māmala hoe. Kamehameha I's famous law of the splintered paddle. *Lit.,* piece of a paddle, which granted safety on the trails and roads to women and children, the ill and the elderly. The name was based on the fact that Kamehameha almost lost his life from a paddle broken over his head. The law is also known as *māmala hoa kanawai*.

ma'oha. Appearing gray or whitish, as tops of mountains at a distance; applied also to a person whose hair turns gray.

mauha'alele. Shadow of death; signs of death.

naio 'ai kae. Pinworm that causes an itch in the anus; contemptuous term for a backbiter or slanderer.

'ohina. To have one's property completely swept or taken away. *Fig.*, a man loses his surfboard while swimming, *'ohina 'aupapa;* hence, he lost his property, the mainstay of his independence.

'ōlemu ka'a. Epithet of a man who often moves from place to place, gathers no property and never becomes *kū'ono'ono* (quietly settled); "A rolling stone gathers no moss." *Lit.*, thigh rolling.

'ōpala. Refuse, rubbish, litter. *Fig.*, the rabble; people without character; people of no account.

pa'akai. Salt; any encrustation, as in the corners of the eyes.

pepeiao akua. Edible touchwood or fungus *(Auriclaria auriculajudae)* that grows from the bark of the trees in damp forests; god's ears, Jew's-ear. Also called *akua pepeiao. Lit.,* god ear.

pilihua. To stick fast, as words in a person's mouth when afraid or admonished; speechless.

pili pū. To shut one's mouth; to be confounded and unanswering through astonishment; to cease making a reply.

unuhi. To draw out in various ways; to take a ring, as from a finger; to unsheath, as a sword; to let fall from a bundle; to subtract, as in arithmetic; to translate from one language to another.

wilikōi. Substances that are gathered up in the center of a whirlwind. *Me he kanaka la no ka wilikōī,* like a person before the whirlwind. (DK.)

PROVERBS AND GNOMIC UTTERANCES

Two collections of Hawaiian proverbs were published in the *Hawaiian Annual and Almanac* for 1883. One was compiled by H. S. Sheldon, the other by Charles M. Hyde. A careful review of both suggests the propriety of limiting this category to Hyde's collection.

Most of his list was developed at his Mid-Pacific Missionary Institute in group discussions with his Hawaiian students. Entries in this category are not alphabetized, since all items are arranged in prose form in a loose series of titles. There are a few proverbs and some gnomic maxims; other items are slang phrases or historical allusions; still others are quotations from old *meles* or poems and have become bywords. Many gained general currency, the rest remained local.

In English such words or phrases may be grouped under the terms adage, aphorism, apothegm, and axiom. Hawaiians call them *'olelo ho'o na'auao, poeko, poleko, mikololohua, palolo hua, loea, ho'oka'au, ho'ohuake 'eo, ma'a,* or *kuluma.*

1. Expressions of admiration

Uene ke kolopā, The crowbar rings sharply. Applied to successful effort.

Pali ke kua, mahina ke alo, A back straight as a precipice, a front round as a moon. A favorite phrase in praise of a well-formed person.

Oni kalakea ke kū a ka lā'au loa, The top of the tall pine waves proudly. Spoken in praise of good scholarship.

Līlā ka mai'a 'e'a, wili o ka 'ōka'i, The banana looks withered, but it has an excellent flavor. Similar to the English allusion to singed cats, better than they seem.

Ma'ema'e i ke kai ka pua o ka hala, The pandanus blossom is fairest by the sea. Similar to our common saying, "The rose that all are praising. Oh! that's the rose for me."

Kī'ilīlī pua hau o Kalena, Well dressed, as the flowers of Kalena [Hill at Makawao, Mau, near Ki'owai, a beautiful sheet of water].

Ke 'a'ali'i kūmakani o Hōpoe, The stately tree of Hōpoe [a famous rock in Puna, the laudatory epithet of a well-formed man].

Niniu Puna pō i ke ala, Puna renowned for its loveliness.

2. Flattering chiefly title

Kaulilua'ikeanu, Dark blue mountain top. A favorite name for Wai'ale'ale on Kaua'i, an allusion to "dandified" Kalākaua.

3. An esteem for certain places

Ke kai wehi poli o ka 'Ie'iewaho. Name of the sea between O'ahu and Kaua'i.

Ke kai malino mai Kekaha a hiki i Miloli'i, Calm, smooth water between *Kekaha and Miloli'i* [*South Kona, Hawai'i*].

Ke kai hāwanawana o Kawaihae, Whispering sea of Kawaihae.

Malihini au i ke kai o Kuloloia, I don't know much about the harbor of Honolulu. The harbor is simply a deep basin with precipitous sides in a shallow, girdling reef.

Ke ʻehukai o Puaʻena, Gray sea spray or foam of Waialua Bay. *Lit.,* issue hot. *Pele* lived at Waialua Bay before going to Hawaiʻi.

Pulu ʻelo i ka ua Kanilehua, Drenched by the rain that patters on lehua blossoms. Hilo rain.

Huaʻi ka malu ʻulu o Lele i ka malie, The grove of breadfruit trees rises in grateful warmth. Praise for Lahaina.

Ka puʻu pānoa i ka lā, Hillside lying bare in the glare of the sun. Said of Lahainaluna.

Ka makani ku loio o Hamakua, Brings to mind the strong trade wind that blows over Hāmākua.

Ka ua Kipuʻupuʻu, Waimea is equally well known for its drenching rain.

Wailuku i aloha nui ʻia o ke malu he kūawa, Wailuku, its shaded valley greeted by the westering sun.

4. Nationalities and their epithets

Nā ahi maka kēpau o Maikonisia, The glaring eyes of the Micronesians.

Nā hiena lehelehe ʻeuʻeu o Fiji, Projecting lips. This is characteristic of the people of Fiji. *Lit.,* animated lips of the natives of Fiji.

Ka poe Pākē o Waʻapaʻa, The soft and weak (!) people of Waʻapaʻa. Pākē is a universal nickname.

5. Taunting allusions

Kolekole kou maka, Your eyes are red. A common taunt when anyone has asked a favor and been denied.

E kū no ia ma ka puka o ka hoka, He will stand at the door of disappointment. Said of anyone doomed to defeat.

I ke alo iho no ka ʻulu, a hala, The maika stone was right in front, but it missed. Reference to the ancient game of *maika.*

Haumanumanu e ka ipu ʻinoʻino, How full of holes is that dirty calabash. Spoken of an ugly, ill-favored person.

Kamaliʻi ike ʻole i ka helu malama, The child does not know the number of months. Said to shame a child's ignorance.

Aia i ka mole kamaliʻi, Children always begin at the foundation. Meaning that the action of children is no matter for astonishment.

Ka poʻe unaunahi heʻe o Kula, The country people of Kula, who tried to scale the squid. The squid or octopus has suckers but not scales, an allusion to uninformed persons.

Ka heʻe o kai uli, kā pae ka ʻalaʻala, The squid of the deep blue sea has a peculiar bulge. Said to poke fun at excessive corpulence.

Ka pūhi o ke ʻAle, ʻalu ka ʻolo, That eel from ʻAle is all wrinkled. Said of a man with a double chin.

6. Bald heads: witticisms

Wehea iho maluna o Hīhīmanu, Mount Hīhīmanu is all clear on top. Reference to a bald-headed man.

Ka iʻa nui a kāua i kahaone, Our big fish is on that spot of shining sand.

Ka na poʻokea i ke oho o ke kīwainui, The hoar-frost has fallen on the top of this big kī plant.

Kapuahi heu ia e ka pueo, The owl's oven. An allusion to the fact that a bald head is smooth and clear, just as the owl scratches bare the place where she makes her nest.

7. References to quarrelsome people

Lele liʻiliʻi ka lehu o kapuahi, He is scattering the ashes of the fireplace.

Ku ke ʻehu o nā wahi ʻau waʻa liʻiliʻi, How the spray dashes up before that fleet of little canoes. An allusion to the "tempest in a teapot."

Piʻi ka ihu o ka naiʻa i ka makani, The porpoise holds his nose up to windward. An allusion to manifestations of anger.

E o mai ana ka ua līpuʻupuʻu lipalawai o Waimea, The rain of Waimea will wet through. Said of quarrels that hurt both parties.

I hoʻoluʻu hoʻohualei ʻia e ka makani, The wind will stir up all the loose dust. An allusion to the fact that angry people will tell what would be better kept concealed.

8. Problems of travel

Maloʻo nā iwi o Hua mā i ka lā, The bones of Hua and company are dry in the sun. Reference to a war party that died from volcanic fumes, an allusion to disappointment in one's schemes.

Ka au waʻa pānānā kau i Kapua, The flat-bottomed fleet has to land at Kapua [i.e., it cannot beat to windward]. Kapua was the landing place for Kapiolani Park, leeward of Leahi, O'ahu.

Mai pi'i 'oe i ka lapa manu 'ole, Don't go to the ridge where there are no birds. Similar to the English saying, "don't go on a wild goose chase."

'Awapuhi lau pala wale, The ginger root has a leaf that rots quickly.

Hele po'āla i ke anu o Waimea. An allusion to wandering around and around, retracing one's tracks, in going to Waimea in the fog. See **Ho'iho'i ka pa'akai i Waimea.**

Ho'iho'i ka pa'akai i Waimea, Oh ho! you are taking your salt back to Waimea. The Waimea people were taking *poi* to the seaside to exchange for salt, but got lost in the fog and returned to Waimea, of course without the salt.

9. Pride

He lani i luna, he honua ilalo, 'oni'oni ia kūlana ā pa'a, Heaven above, earth below and his own position firmly fixed. The natives' way of applauding a thrifty man.

Ke lino a nei ke kēhau o Wai-'ōpua, He glistens with the fine dew of a pleasant breeze. Applied to a man once poor but subsequently wealthy.

Ke kaha pili a ka Iakea. An allusion to a poverty-stricken place on Moloka'i, come to grief.

'Eli'eli kūlana o 'Āina'ike. A place on Kaua'i famous for good living and a thrifty man. Similar to the expression, *"He was born with a silver spoon in his mouth."*

Ka-la'i-a-ka-manu. A place near Kaunakakai, Moloka'i that may be the site of Kamehameha I's home. Similar in meaning to *'Eli'eli kūlana o 'Āina'ike.*

10. Phrases of encouragement

'Umi 'ia i nui keaho, Press hard and take a long breath.

Alu ka pule a Hakalau, Let us join in the prayer of Hakalau (an old Hawaiian known for the fervency and efficacy of his prayers).

'A'ohe keiki hele wale o Kohala, Your Kohala boys don't travel without making suitable provision for contingencies.

Hāhā pō'ele ka pāpa'i o Honolulu, Honolulu people know how to feel for crabs. Reference to their muddy water.

E ku'i ka māmā i loa'a o Kaohele, You must hurry if you would catch Kaohele [a famous runner of ancient times].

'A'ohe Hana a Kauhikoa, ua kau nā wa'a i ke 'aki, Kauhikoa has done his work of placing the canoes back on their stools [everything is lovely and "the goose hangs high"].

Ha'a ka mikioi i ke kai o Lehua, It takes a skillful sailor to go to Lehua. A warning not to undertake what cannot be accomplished.

Ka ikaika i ke kī, e ku'u pōki'i, lā ola, Pull hard at the kī root my boys, you'll get it at last. This is the Lahainaluna scholars' expression to persevere for mastery, something like "grubbing at Greek roots."

Ako Nu'uanu i ka hale halauloa o ka makani, People thatch their houses in Nu'uanu even if the wind does blow. Proverb commending perseverance.

Ako Mānoa i ka hale a ka ohu, People of Manoa thatch their houses in spite of the mist. A call for perseverance.

11. Racy proverbs

O ke aloha ka mea i 'oi aku ka maika'i mamua o ka 'umeke poi a me ke ipu kai i'a, Love is far better than the calabash of poi or the bowl of fish.

He kapa malo'o ka 'ili, The skin is a kapa that does not wet through. Similar to the English saying, "If it rains I am neither sugar nor salt."

Kau ke po'o, i ka uluna, o Welehu ka malāma, Put your head on your arm, this is the month of November. Reference to the rainy season, which keeps people inside giving them time to indulge their laziness.

Maka'ala ke kanaka kūhea manu, He must be quick-motioned who would snare birds. Allusion to a favorite occupation.

E nihi ka hele i ka uka o Puna, Step carefully when you travel inland from Puna. The Puna region is full of cavities and pitfalls for the unwary traveler.

E pūpūkāhi ka mana'o, Be of one mind. *Lit.,* only one shell for all.

Paki ke kēpau, o'o ka 'ulu, When the gum exudes, the breadfruit is ripe. Similar to the English expression, *"He has cut his wisdom tooth."*

Pulu 'elo i ka ua o ka hōli'o e, Wet with the rain of distilled liquors. A drunkard, euphemistically speaking.

Noho i ka hale Kāmala. A man who has committed some offense and has run away, is sometimes said "to have gone to Texas." Foreigners, when sent to the Honolulu prison, say they "are going on the reef."

Huli ka ua kapakea, huli i Mololani, When a wife leaves her husband and goes off with a handsomer man.

Nani ka 'ōiwi o ka lā'au i ka luaiele 'ia e ka makani, How beautiful that tree is, even when stripped by the wind. If the husband finds no fault with such a fickle wife he is accorded the above commendation.

Pua ka wiliwili, nānahu ka manō, While the wiliwili is in blossom the sharks will bite. Applied to those who run the risk of illicit love and find themselves in the hands of the law.

O ka pohole i ka 'iniki a ka ipo, he hao kuni ia a ke aloha, This is the brand-mark of love. Reference to pinching or biting the neck, an allusion to the custom of branding cattle on the neck.

12. Allusions to mountains and air space activities

'Ua ko'oko'oū i ke anu nā mauna, The chilling storm is on the mountains. This designates a time of sorrow.

Kukulu kala'ihi a ka lā i Mānā. The mirage at Mānā supplies a simile for the discomfiture of pretentious persons, boasters.

Hanohano Pali-uli i ka ua moe, Glorious is Pali-uli in the misty rain. This expression is similar to the English saying, "Blooming roses will never fade." Said in admiration of a man.

13. Some similes from the fisherman's work

Nānā ke'e ka i'a i ka maunu 'eka'eka, The fish looks sideways at the filthy bait. Expression applied to a poor sermon. The Hawaiians were good judges of preaching.

Hauhili ka 'ai a ke kāwelē'a, We've lost our chance at a kāwelē'a. The fish made off with the bait during a squabble on the boat. The kāwelē'a (Sphyraena helleri) was a prize fish to catch. A smaller relative of the barracuda, kākū.

'A'ohe hemahema iki o Ho'ohila, We're all safe on the Ho'ohila [a rock on the shore of Kaua'i]. Strangers walking on the shore find safety on this rock at high tide.

He make no ke kalo a ola aku i ka naio, The kalo root is dead [but] there are live maggots enough. Formerly applied to battles in which the bravest had perished. In recent times has been applied by scoffers to the overthrow of paganism and the growth of Christianity in its place.

PUNCTUATION

The missionaries who transformed Hawaiians words into writing had no difficulty in employing English punctuation for pauses or stops, using the period, comma, colon, and semi-colon. But one great problem was not so easily solved. They were very much frustrated with what we call today the "glottal stop." It was finally recognized as a consonant (or better, as a stopped consonant), the second most used of all consonants, and was given two Hawaiian names, 'okina and 'u'ina.

ha'i'ano. Adjective.
ha'iinoa. Noun.
ha'ina. Verb.
ho'opōkole. To abbreviate.
ho'opōkole 'ana. Abbreviation.
hopuna'ōlelo. Syllable, paragraph, enunciation, pronunciation. (PE.) Sentence. (CMH.)
hua hō'ailona. Abbreviation.
hua leo hui. Consonant.
hua leo kāhi. Vowel, a letter representing a sound. There are five vowels in the Hawaiian language a, e, i, o, u.
hua palapala. Letter of the alphabet. *Lit.,* writing letter.
hua palapala iki. Small letter; lower case in printed matter.
hua palapala leo hui. Consonant. See **hua leo hui.**
hua palapala leo kāhi. Vowel. See **hua leo kahi.**
hua palapala nui. Capital letter.
kahaapo. Parentheses, brackets.
kahamaha. Dash.
kahamoe. Hyphen.
kauna koma. Quotation marks.
kiko ho'omaha. Period, comma, colon, semi-colon. All mark pauses in reading.
kiki ho'ōho. Exclamation mark.
kiko koma. Semi-colon, sign of a pause in reading. *Lit.,* point comma.
kiko moe. Hyphen. *Lit.,* mark lying down.
kiko pū'iwa. Exclamation mark.
kolona. Colon. Name of a pause in reading.
koma luna. Apostrophe, glottal stop. *Lit.,* comma above. It signifies a consonant has been dropped. See **'okina.**
leokanipū. Consonant.

māmala'ōlelo. Sentence, clause, phrase.

'okina. Glottal stop; separation, a cutting off. In punctuation it took the form of a reverse single apostrophe although Samuel H. Elbert and Mary Kawena Pukui in their *Hawaiian Grammar* state that the modern, vertical apostrophe is entirely acceptable.

palehalapa, paregarapa. Paragraph.

paniinoa. Pronoun.

paukū. Paragraph.

'u'ina. Glottal stop. Andrews refers to this as a sound such as the gutteral pronunciation break between two vowels.

QUALITIES: Human, Positive

Dr. Charles McEwen Hyde could be called a "qualities" man. He pursued words for each category of qualities with a firm tilt to his pen. His interest in human qualities was that of a teacher or a missionary; and he was aware of all of them—positive and negative, moral, unmoral, and amoral—as the basic materials of his profession.

Being fair-minded, Hyde included all the words he could discover. As a result a disproportion sets in: there are more "negative" words than "positive" words in the lists. This imbalance may reflect the emphasis in earlier times on the *kapu* and punishment.

The two categories of positive and negative human qualities are generally filled with subjective words and subjective meanings freighted with a load of Christian morality.

a'iwa'iwa. A remarkable person or animal, applied to the fabulous dog Kaiahumoku of Tahiti. *A'iwa'iwa* refers to the excess of character, very good or very bad: a kind hearted chief, a mischievous child; very proficient or skilled, very bad or ignorant.

'auli'ikolomanu. A well-formed person of good advantages, commended as being skillful, expert, or reflecting.

hiehie. Neat, tidy, good, lively, distinguished in manner. The word also means proud, as associated with haughty; self-dignified, overbearing.

hilu. Still, quiet, reserved, dignified. Also neat, elegant, powerful, magnificent.

ho'ohiahia. Outward appearance of gentle-heartedness without the substance; to be good; honorable; noble in aspect and deportment. (A.)

hoʻopī. Persons economical in their use of food, in contrast to those who were wasteful.

hukailoa. A person who has always lived with one particular chief.

kahiau. To give away lavishly; to give away generously from the heart, expecting nothing in return.

kihikau. To give lavishly and until all is gone.

koapaka. Valiant, brave; successful as a combatant.

koa paki. A soldier well cared for; an active soldier. (A.)

kuapapanui. Deep and substantial peace in government; quiet, tranquillity, calm. To enjoy quietness and satisfaction under the same ruler; to be quiet, as the effect of a virtuous life. (Isa. 32:17.)

kūkapu. A person never sick in youth, but taken sick when grown up. (A.) Chastity; chaste. (PE.)

kūoʻo. Fearless, ready, vigilant, prompt. Also serious, dignified, earnest, solemn. (1 Pet. 1:13, 4:7.)

loia. Skillful, ingenious, or dexterous, as applied to women. Similar to *maiau* which is applied to men.

lōkāhi. Agreement in mind or opinion; unanimity of sentiment; unity of feeling; oneness.

lokomaikaʻi. Grace, good will, special favor. To feel and act benevolently; to be kindly disposed toward someone; to be favorable to someone.

maiau. Men ready and expert in speaking and in work; natural skill, wisdom, ingenuity. This word involves chiefly men. A similar meaning or word for women is *loia* or *loea*.

miki. Energetic, active, ready to act, diligent. (Sol. 22:29.)

mikiʻala. Early; on hand and ready for business; punctual.

mimiki. To be industrious; to be constantly at work; to be quick and spry. (A.) To work with a will. (PE.)

nākuʻi, nakue. Cheerful, thrilled, hopeful; diligent in business. (A.)

ʻoʻoleʻa. Physically hard and unyielding; morally rough and perhaps selfish in manners; stern justice.

pāʻihiʻihi. Neat, tidy, well dressed.

pākiko. To eat but little; to be temperate; to be abstemious in diet. *ʻAi pākiko,* to eat moderately; *inu pākiko,* to drink temperately. (Puk. 4:21.)

pākūʻei. To be present before time to start work; to commence a job before the time.

pālawaīki. Nice, polite; neatly done, done with taste.

pūlawalawa. Prepared; having a supply of what is necessary;

ready for an emergency. Energetic; active for work, as a man. (A.)

pūnihi. Lofty, majestic, dignified.

QUALITIES: Human, Negative

This category contains words dealing with dawdling, indifference, stinginess, mischief-making, and fickleness. Collectively, they outnumber the positive listings four to one. And yet our acquaintance with Hawaiians does not support this negative image. For example, more words refer to the trait of stinginess than to any other. Yet, a closer look shows how these words have refined the concept. This suggests that such emphasis allowed people to avoid being stingy, and in that way led to the strengthening of one of this people's finest traits: generosity, a positive quality.

'a'ana. To speak angrily, abusively; to fret, revile.

'a'apa. Presumptuous, as a drunken man who lies on the edge of a precipice or *pali;* illiberal, fault-finding, meddling, officious.

'aikena. To compel someone to work when already fatigued; to cause a groaning or complaint for hard usage.

'akihi. To walk off without paying attention to directions. (CMH.)

'alamakāhinu. Name of a stone at Mai'ao, flat and shining; applied to a disobedient child or a greased forehead. (A.)

'alapahi. Slanderous, demagogical; to deceive, falsify, slander.

'alihi. Ready to work for the sake of gain but otherwise absent.

'āna'anea. Stupid, foolish, as one subjected to sorcery. Also called *palaka.*

'ānihaniha. Easily provoked; captious, caviling.

'apa. Meddling, officious, careless. See **'a'apa.**

'apa'apa. Unsettled, unstable, irresolute.

'āpane. Red on the flesh when burned; hence, applied to anger; red with anger.

'āpo'o. Idle, lazy person; to go from house to house but doing no work.

'au'a. Close, hard, stingy, parsimonious.

'awahua, 'awa'awahua. Surly, obstinate, bitter; unwilling to tend to one's duty regardless of obligation.

'elekū, 'ele'elekū. Homely, lean or insignificant person; coal-black in color.

hae. Furiously angry.

haukaʻe. Slovenly, foul, wicked; babbler; trifling talker; mean fellow. (Oih. 17:18.)

hāwaʻe kai nui. Sea urchin with much juice and little meat; hence, *fig.,* useless; awkward in diving and overly spattering the water.

hewa. Error, wrong, sin; to transgress, sin, condemn; to be under a curse; to be viciously inclined.

hewahewa. Sullen silence; derangement of the mind from sickness; mad. (Ier. 29:26.)

hiliau. To wander, go astray morally, do wrong. *He ikaika hiliau,* strong to do evil.

hōʻaʻano. Presumptuous; defying punishment; proud, daring, obstinate, self-confident.

hohono. To smell strongly, as tar; odor of perspiration; strong, offensive smell; stench.

hōʻiʻi. Stingy, close dealer, parsimonious; oppressive of the weak and poor.

holowale. Coward, one fleeing without cause. (A.)

hone. To be saucy; to tease, play pranks.

honehone. Playing tricks, teasing, fretting; not letting someone alone.

honekoa. To rail; to be saucy. *Lit.,* to be bold. (A.)

hoʻoauwaepuʻu. To jut out the chin and twist the lips to the side, or stick the tongue under the lip to form a lump—a gesture of contempt or refusal. (PE.)

hoʻohehelo. To be deceitful, proud; to be proud of one's appearance or dress.

hoʻohie. To be proud, haughty, and carry a high head. (A.)

hoʻokaha. Someone guilty of extortion, who strips people of their property, perhaps with their knowledge but not their consent. (A.) To extort. (PE.)

hoʻokananuha, hoʻokolonuha. To cause sulkiness; hearing impaired. (Heb. 5:4.)

hoʻokano. haughtiness, pride, self-sufficiency, conceit. (Ezek. 3:7.)

hoʻokaʻulua. To procrastinate; to be slow in obeying a command; to postpone a work; to cause to delay.

hoʻokē. To crowd at the door of a house; to elbow one's way; to force oneself into possession, as a foreigner.

hoʻokehakeha. To be puffed up with pride; to be self-glorifying. (A.) To act proudly; pride, dignity. (PE.)

hoʻokei. To set oneself literally above others; to be self-exalted; to take a higher seat. (A.) To take pride in; dignified, full of pride. (PE.)

hoʻokiʻekiʻe. Pride, haughtiness; overwhelming in conduct. (Nah. 15:30; A.) Overbearing, disrespectful to older people. (PE.)

hoʻokiʻi. Thin; lean in flesh; close, parsimonious. (Isa. 34:4.)

hoʻokuli. To bribe someone to disobedience; to give one's property away for an evil purpose; to turn away from hearing; to feign deafness.

hoʻokuʻoʻi. To feel jealous of another for some real or imagined advantage. (CMH.) To limp with unequal steps.

hoʻolana. Indifference to moral principles. (A.) Cheerful, unworrying; to encourage. (Mat. 14:27; PE.)

hoʻomakakiu. To watch with a jealous eye; to lie in wait to do evil with a design to surprise. (A.) To spy, watch, reconnoiter. (PE.)

hoʻomakauliʻi. One who feigns friendship and eats with another while he awaits an opportunity to injure him; one acting with cunning and duplicity.

hoʻopilimeaʻaʻi. A person serving another merely for a living.

hopepe. Humble, depressed, downtrodden, as the people of a hard, cruel chief. *Lit.,* to mash fine. (A.)

hua, hūwā. Envy, jealousy; an envious disposition; quick to find fault.

huahualau. An endeavor to ensnare someone by questioning; to try to deceive; to question captiously.

huoi. To overflow with anger; to be jealous, suspicious.

ʻilihelo. Class of farmers who worked but little, and not skillfully.

ʻīnana. To loaf about, walk idly. For a moral quality, a positive definition, see PE.

ʻino. Depravity, wickedness, iniquity; sinful, vile, immoral. *Mea ʻino,* an abomination. *ʻIno* is a strong intensive, used in both a good and bad sense: affection or hatred, love or contempt, etc.

kāʻape. Disobedient to orders; obstinate, headstrong.

kahua ʻole. Good-for-nothing person; someone useless. (A.) An ignoramus; someone without background, trade, or profession. *Lit.,* foundation not. (PE.)

kaialile. To be indolent, indifferent, contemptuous; unskilled, awkward.

kāʻili wale. Seizing the property of another; a plunder, robbery.

kamani. To deal falsely. (Oihk. 19:11.) To dissemble; to profess to be what one is not; a hypocrite.

kāpae. To pervert; to turn aside from moral rectitude. (1 Nal. 9:6.) To turn aside from obedience to law. (Kanl. 9:12.)

kāpekepeke. To be unsettled in mind or opinion; inconstant, fickle, hesitant; to walk unsteadily; to totter.

kāpulu. To be unfaithful in business; to be slovenly, careless. (Ier. 4:22.)

kīke'eke'e. Wrong, perverted, as in a moral sense. This is the opposite of *pololei,* to be correct, naturally or morally.

kilohi. To act with complacency; to exhibit vanity in any way; to be opinionated.

kīmopō. Secret assassinations at night; secret rebellions. *Lit.,* strike in the night.

kīnā. Sin, wickedness, error; blemish, as in a person. (Kanl. 15:21.)

kīpē. To bribe; to secretly offer a reward for some wrongdoing. (Ioba 15:34.)

kuamuamu. To blaspheme, curse, reproach; a reviling of sacred things by word or song. (Kanl. 28:37.)

kūka'i. To cheat in various ways. (A.)

kupu. One who is mischievous or lawless.

ku'ulala. Stupid, lascivious, lawless; a want of common sense; free to do as one wants, right or wrong.

lalau. Mischievous, wicked; violating good morals; generally bad; to wander, go astray, blunder. (Mat. 22:29.)

lanaha'akei. Pride and haughtiness in bearing, conduct, and treatment of others. (Isa. 2:11, 3:16). *Lit.,* proudly floating.

lawehala. To commit an offense; to sin against someone; to transgress; one who breaks a covenant.

lili. Proud, haughty, overbearing, jealous, hateful; a disregard of others' rights.

loko 'ino. To act wickedly, cruelly, malevolently, mercilessly.

lōlō moe hālau. A man, woman, or child who is lazy, indisposed to work.

lomaloma 'ai halalē. Lazy and eating the food of others through idleness. *'A'ole e loa'a kēia mea, o ka na'auao, i ka mea manāka, 'a'ole hoi i ka mea kaialile lomaloma 'ai halalē,* this thing, knowledge, cannot be obtained by the easily discouraged nor by the indolently awkward.

lua'āpana. To live idly or in pleasure; to live wantonly. (A.) A jester; hilarity, sport. (PE.)

mahuakala. Disobedient to the gods; contemptuous of good things; wicked. (A.) Disbelieving, skeptical of religion; atheistic. (PE.)

mākaha. To extort property, seize what is another's; to rob, plunder. (A.) *Kā'u mākaha,* fierce Ka'ū, a story of the people killing several oppressive chiefs. (PE.)

mōkoi. Cruel, hard, stingy; to provoke, anger.

mokuāhua. Evil minded; sad at the evil of another; grief, sorrow, pity.

molowā, moloa. Laziness, slackness, indifference, carelessness.

moluna. To steal, rob, plunder, take by force.

nukunuku. To complain of someone behind his back.

'ōhi'ohi'o. To stagger, reel, as one intoxicated; tipsy.

'onou. Seduction, enticement, generally for an evil purpose.

'ōpū 'ino'ino. Evil disposition; wickedness, depravity, malevolence. (1 Pet. 2:1.)

'ōpūke'emoa. An evil disposition; inclination to meanness.

pāhau. To embezzle secondhandedly. Applied to property intended for use of a chief's people, such as fish, *kapa,* etc.

pākaha. To extort, cheat, oppress; to be dishonest in any way.

pakaulei. To change one's residence continually; to live freely with one female or another.

palaualelo. Indolent, idle; having no incentive to work. (A.) Lazy, especially true of a verbose person. *Lit.,* lying tongue. (PE.)

pūhalaua. Covetous person.

pūhali. Stinginess, covetousness; small, delicate sea shell.

punihai. Running in fear; afraid, cowardly.

puni kālā. One greedy for money; a strong desire for property; covetousness. (Heb. 13:5.)

punikoko. Blood-thirsty person; inclined to crime, as murder. (Sol. 29:16.)

punipuni. To deceive; to tell a lie; to act treacherously in any way as to deceive one.

pūniu. A cheat; dishonest gambler, who refuses to give up what he has won in a game. (A.)

uhinu. To take advantage of a man's ignorance in a bargain. (A.)

ukiuki. To treat vindictively, with contempt; to be angry, offended, vexed. (Neh. 4:1.)

wahahe'e. To lie, speak falsely, deceive in speaking. *Lit.,* mouth wily.

waha koko. Tale bearing; slandering one's own blood. *Lit.,* mouth blood.

QUALITIES: Moral, Good

Early Hawaiians could grasp the objectivity of good moral traits and formulated words to convey their meanings. The variety of words and phrases coined to give meaning to a concept testifies to the complexity as well as resourcefulness of the language and the people.

Anyone seeking assistance to describe persons in obituaries, memorials, testimonials, praises or honors of any description can find appropriate Hawaiian words in this category.

alamimo. Quick. *Na kapuaʻi alamimo o na kini maka lehua o na ʻōpio,* nimble soles [dancing feet] of the many *lehua* blossoms of youth. (PE.) Straightness, uprightness, what is normally good; to be gentle; without noise or confusion; easy in manner. See **ʻelemimo.**

ʻeaʻea. Dignified, honorable, highly placed. (A.)

ʻelemimo. Straightness, uprightness, what is morally good; to be gentle, without noise or confusion, easy in one's manners. See **alamimo.**

haʻahaʻa. To be humble; to live quietly.

haipule. Pious, devout, religious; religiously disposed.

haohaoalani. Reverence and affection formerly felt by the people for their chiefs. (A.)

hemolele. Perfect in a moral sense; virtue, holiness, a state of glory. (Oih. 3:12.) *Baibala Hemolele,* Holy Bible.

hiluhilu. The excellent, the glorious, the powerful; beautiful, nice, excellent.

kalaʻihi. Proud, exalted on account of one's office or nearness to a chief. (A.)

kamahoi. Glorious, splendid. *He aliʻi kamahoi,* a glorious chief.

kāmau. Endurance, perseverance, especially in uncertainty; constant, as a friend or relative. (A.)

kaʻokoʻa. To separate oneself from wrongdoing; to be whole, undivided.

kapukapu. Honor, praise, dignity; separation from what is common; entitled to respect and reverence.

kapukawai. To be handsome, noble. (A.)

kohukohu. To be harmonious in opinion. *Hoʻohokuhoku, a kanaka ihe ia kekahi poʻe no ke Akua,* a certain company agreed together and acted like men towards God. Noble, honorable, dignified.

kolokolohai. Chief or a common person whose character is respected for probity and virtuous conduct.

kū. To be proper, fit.

kuapapa. To be united, as people under one chief; to be at peace; to live quietly, free of turbulence and anarchy.

kūhaʻo. To stand firm, as iron; to stand firm and not alone.

lokomaikaʻi. Disposed in feeling and action to do good; benevolent, generous, obliging.

maʻalea. Prudent, having foresight, wise; crafty, cunning, deceitful. *Maʻa* "accustomed" and *lea* "very" make the literal meaning practiced or skillful, which may be used for good or evil, and in this case both.

makauliʻi. A person careful to save the property of a chief; to fear, i.e., to serve a chief in order to obtain favors, to follow him from motives of self advantage.

manawaleʻa. Bestowing freely upon the needy; generous, giving to the undeserving. *Hui manawaleʻa,* relief society. To give willingly, cheerfully, and liberally. (1 Sam. 25:27.)

mikioi. Anything excellently, carefully, and neatly made, by good workmanship.

mokumokuāhua. To yearn; to be moved with affection or pity for someone.

naʻau pono. To be upright, just, right-minded.

nakue. Diligent in business; active, not lazy.

nakuluʻai. Perfect, good, upright praiseworthy.

nonohe. A beautiful, virtuous, modest young woman.

ʻōheke. Shy, modest, bashful. *He ʻōheke wale ko ke kuaʻāina kanaka,* the country people are modest and diffident; *he ʻōhekeʻole kanaka wahi aliʻi,* the people about the chief are without modesty.

pākiko. To eat quietly or cautiously; to think beforehand and not follow the appetite; to be temperate in diet. *Pākiko* is the opposite of *pākela,* spoken in reference to taking. *Kiko ana,* here a little and there a little. (Puk. 4:21.)

pakuʻei. To be present before time to start work; to commence a job before the time.

palawaiki. nice; neatly done; polite; done with taste.

pulawalawa. Prepared; having a supply of what is necessary; ready for an emergency; energetic; active for work, as a man. (A.)

punihi. Lofty, majestic, dignified.

QUALITIES: Moral, Negative

This list of so-called negative moral qualities emphasizes such substantives as blasphemy, covetousness, extortion, false pride, idleness, lying and deceit, and wickedness generally. There is a subjective nature to these words, just as there is to the positive words.

It is interesting to note the fair number of words that, while not exactly carrying double meanings, can have both positive as well as negative implications.

'a'amo. Female insatiable in lust.

'aiā. Unprincipled or ungodly person; irreligious; careless in observance of the *kapu*. (Ier. 23:11.)

'aiāhua. Term applied to those who disregard the *kapu* while others observe it; hypocrite.

'aihalalē. To be lazy; to do nothing; to be the reproach of others; to eat the food of others without work. Also called *lomaloma 'aihalalē; Lit.,* awkward eat gluttonlike.

'ai noa. General disregard of the *kapu* in eating and manner of living.

akena. Puffed up with pride, haughtiness; feeling of superiority over others. See **ha'ano'u.**

'alapahi. To spread false reports; to slander, deceive, as would a demagogue.

'ala'uka. Vile, bad, worthless, slovenly, negligent.

'ālina. Loss of respect for marrying someone of low birth. Could be applied to a chief who so married and consequently had children of low order. To be disgraced, implicated in sin.

alolua. With two sides or two faces. Applied to men and objects. *Moena alolua,* a double mat having a finished side on the front and back.

'ama'ama. To reveal secrets; to speak of another's faults, to slander. *'Ama'ama ka waha i ka ha'i,* a mouth gossiping about others.

'ānulu. To be covetous or greedy; *'ālunu,* a covetous or greedy person.

'āpani. To go from house to house tattling and doing nothing noteworthy. *Lit.,* to block or shut.

'āpapa. To deceive. (A.)

'āpiki. Crafty, roguish, mischievous; to sport at another's expense; to beg; to live at the expense of others; of or belonging to yellow flowers, the *'ilima,* etc.

'āpua. Man who disregards or disobeys the orders of his chief; disloyal, disobedient, rebellious.

'āpuapaleleo. Chief who would not obey the command of a priest; *Lit., 'āpua,* disobey; *pale,* to reject; *leo,* voice or order.

'āpuka. Deceit, treachery. In law it means forgery.

'aweka. Deceit, dishonesty; one who refuses to pay a forfeit. (A.) To hide rather than share wealth. (PE.)

'e'epa, 'epa. Forgery, deceit, treachery.

'epa. One who is false to his trust; an act of villainy, fraud, or forgery; to steal, backbite.

eu. To steal; to be disobedient, mischievous, naughty, as a child; a roguish scamp.

ha'ano'u. Puffed up with pride. *'Ōlelo ha'ano'u,* boasting language. See **akena.**

haheo, ha'aheo. Proud; proud of dress or anything gaudy; haughty in manner; to put on airs of superiority.

ha'iha'i. Proud, haughty; to break or breach the law; to tease, vex; to follow, pursue.

haihaiā. Ungodliness; unholy, wicked, profane, unreasonable.

hā'ili'ili. To revile the gods; to swear profanely, curse, blaspheme. (Puk. 21:17.)

hāloli'ili. Lazy, idle; useless, as a canoe in the mountains, which lies there and rots.

hānēnē. To blackguard; to use low, vulgar language. (A.)

hā'upu. To excite, stir up, as the affection or passion; to suffer from anxiety; to suddenly rise up in the mind, as a thought.

ho'omalimali. To flatter. (Hal. 38:76.)

ho'omaloka. To be sluggish mentally; to be stupid; to be unbelieving; to disobey the command of a chief. (1 Kor. 7:12.)

ho'omano. To tease and pursue importunity. (A.)

ho'omauakala. To be lazy; to go about doing nothing; to laugh with scorn; to accuse falsely.

ho'omauleho. To oppress; to make someone work long hours and every day without wages.

ho'omo'o. To persist in levying taxes upon the people; to urge or force people to give their property for such purposes as the rulers needed. (A.)

hūhā. A large, weak, indolent, and lazy person, man, woman, or child. (A.)

hupō. To be ignorant, wild, savage, dark, idiot-like. *Lit.,* swelling darkness. (Hal. 119:130.)

ikepenalonalo. Stupid. (CMH.)

ipu lei. Kohala people having large bodies and short legs, a term of reproach; *lei* container.

kaena. Self-opinionated, proud; to make pretenses; to boast of accomplishments; to be conceited.

kāʻiʻī. To walk buttoned up tightly; to strut; to be vain; to be stingy or closefisted.

kakana. To speak sneeringly or contemptuously.

kalauae. Indisposed to work; lazy; loitering.

kāmukumuku. To work and stop; a self-made schedule of work dallying.

kananuha. To be dull in listening to a story; to sit in sullen silence, giving no reply; stupid, surly, sulky. (Heb. 5:11.)

kapukapulani. To frown or to repel someone by our looks; to be distant and ill-natured. (A.)

kehakeha. Arrogant, wasteful, proud, dignified. (Isa. 2:13.)

kī. Parsimonious.

kīhoe. To do a little here and there; to hip-skip; to do things irregularly; to reprove indiscriminately; to lead a roving life.

kiʻipua. Going about, as a person without business; more or less inclined to mischief. Pua was the goddess of mischief and sorcery.

kipa wale. To go in and sit unbidden in another's house; to take another's property without right.

koeʻā. Self-willed, disobedient, taciturn, indolent.

kōʻehaʻeha. One who is hard, unobliging, or morose; discomfort, physical distress.

kohelemu. Dull, disobedient, inactive, inattentive.

kokoko. Like a person with his blood up; raging with anger.

kolohe. Mischievous, roguish, troublesome; pollution, defilement, evil.

kopekope. Silent, taciturn, ill-natured, morose.

kuānea. Dry, barren land; unprofitable land; hence, by association, an awkward, ignorant person.

kuhilani. Proud, haughty, high-minded. To dominate others.

kūhili. To blunder, mistake.

kūliʻu. One who is quick and violent tempered; one given to quick revenge. (A.) Deep, penetrating, as a voice; profound, as thoughts. (PE.)

kūlōʻihi. To take a long time about doing something.

lauwili. Changeable, as the wind; turning this way and that, as leaves in the wind; hence, fickle, inconstant, unstable; to be double-tongued or double-minded.

liki. A boast or boasting. *Kanaka liki,* braggart.

limulimu. Opposite of open and honest in conduct; trickish, dissembling, trifling.

linu. Close, tight-fisted, ungenerous, ungracious.

loha. To fade, wilt, wither, as vegetables; hence, sullen, dumpish, indisposed to speak or act, spiritless.

lohi. Tardy, lingering, slow. *A lohi aku la maua mahope me ka hele mālie,* we two lingered behind by walking very slowly.

lohiʻau. To make blunders; to be slow in doing a thing. *Lohiʻau Puna i ke akua wahine,* Puna was slow, even retarded by the goddess.

lōiele. Slowness in doing a thing; to linger. *Ka! manomano ka lōiele ia oe,* astonishing, the slowness of you.

loko hāiki. Parsimonious, tight-fisted, hardhearted.

lokolinu. Parsimonious, close.

loko liʻu. To be insipid, without strength, bitter; cross, angry, indifferent.

lolelua. Changeable, fickle, double-minded, unstable.

loma. Indolent, idle, awkward, slow.

lomaloma. Idleness, indolence, awkwardness.

lōpālauʻeka. A slovenly man, worthless squatter.

luhe. Proud; exhibiting one's haughtiness; making a show.

mahaʻoi, maʻoi. To be bold, impertinent in asking questions, immodest in asking favors.

maīhiʻili. One who strips another of all he has; skinflint; to lay a tax so as to take all the people have. (A.)

mākonā. An unpeaceful disposition; implacable, mean, hard.

malauea. An indolent person, indisposed to work; lazy.

maloka. Disobedient to the chief and unbelieving in his word; treating sacred things with contempt; sluggish mentally.

manaka. Faintheartedness, boredom, laziness, indifference.

maua. Close, stingy, illiberal; lame, sore, stiff, as with walking; large; many.

māunauna. Wasteful, extravagant.

melomelo. Lazy, unemployed; lying in the house. (A.)

mōkoi. To be stingy; to provoke to anger; to tempt, deceive, as fish. See **mākonā.**

molohai. Used by the proud and foolish for *molowā,* laziness, heaviness of head. Drowsy, sleepy.

mulea. To be bitter, as the water of Mulea; to be bitter, as herbs; insipid. (Puk. 15:23.)

naʻanaʻa. Sour, unsocial, crabbed. (A.) Confused, bewildered.

naʻau keʻemoa. An evil disposition; a general disposition to wickedness; perverseness.

naʻau kopekope. Surliness, perverseness, a bad disposition.

naʻau kūhili. A disposition to carelessness, inattention, or indifference.

naʻaupō. Benighted, ignorant, dark-hearted, awkward, brutish.

naua. Cold, distant, unyielding, unaccommodating, angry.

nohili. Tedious, slow, of a long time.

noke. Peevish, angry, stubborn; to continue, persist, persevere.

ʻōlemu kaʻa. "The rolling stone gathers no moss." Thriftless. *Lit.,* the rolling thigh.

ʻōlena. Fickle. (CMH.)

ʻōlēʻolē. Idiot; to grin like an idol, widemouthed.

ʻonana. Weak, awkward, unskilled.

oʻoʻo. To be very careful of one's person or property; parsimonious.

opohokano. Stingy, close, not willing to part with anything good. (A.)

ōpū. To live idly, lazily; to sit bunched up with the knees drawn close.

paikauhale. Vagabond owning no home; house-to-house wanderer.

pākela. To overindulge in eating or drinking; to abound in wickedness; to excel, do better than another. *Lit.,* to shoot out.

pākiki. To be hard or solid, as with substances; to be obdurant, inflexible, as applied to the mind.

palaka. Dull, stupid, indifferent. See **ʻānaʻanea.**

palaleha. To lift the eyes slowly; hence, to be lazy; to be faint-hearted; to be slothful, careless, listless. *Lit.,* to lift the eyes.

palani. Word of contempt applied to persons seeming dirty and filthy, probably from the fish *palani* that stinks abominably.

palaualelo. Idleness, indolence; to neglect to cultivate land; low, ill-bred; a verbose person. *Lit.,* lying tongue.

palela. Lazy; contemptuous of work; to saunter along as if bored. (Puk. 5:17.)

palupalu. Tender, soft, flexible, weak, feeble, pliable, limber. *ʻŌlelo palupalu,* soft-spoken, gentle in speech.

pāpalalē. To speak indistinctly; to make blunders in speaking; unthinking, unreflecting, inexpert.

pāwaʻa. Wild, rude, rough in manners and habits; the incivility of uncultured persons.

pī. Stingy, close, parsimonious; to be hard upon the poor.

pō'ele'ele. Blackness, darkness, as applied to the mind; ignorant, bewildered. *Aloha pō'ele'ele,* Good night [on a black night].

polohana'ole. A woman who refuses to work but lives on her husband's earnings is called by this name. (A.)

pouli. This word speaks of the effects of love; ignorance, generally expressed by *na'aupō. Fig.,* to be affected with silence and sadness. *Lit.,* black night, darkness.

pū. To sit with hands on knees; idle, indolent, lazy. (CMH.)

pūhaluo. Stingy, parsimonious. (CMH.)

pūkani. Stingy, hard, severe, unfeeling for others. (A.)

pulelo. To float in the air, as a flag; to wave to and fro in the wind; to hang loosely; changeable, unstable.

pūlewa. To be changeable; to turn this way and that; to float here and there, as one of unstable opinion; swinging, as a ship at anchor.

pūnihaniha. To refuse; to be stingy; to be hard to trade with; sullen, cross.

pupuka. Epithet of reproach, signifying good-for-nothing; anything full of holes, hence, worthless; having an unsightly appearance. *Lit.,* vain, without substance.

'uha'uha. To live in a wasteful manner; to live in every indulgence of passion, moral folly, and madness.

waha kole. Clamorous, obstreperous, contradicting. *Lit.,* mouth red, raw.

wahapa'a. A noisy, clamoring, or raving person. *Lit.,* mouth hard.

waha pu'u. Unintelligible in conversation, as of one who has had a stroke. *Lit.,* throat swollen.

waha'uha'uha. Hoggish in one's eating manner; filthy.

wekaweka. Stingy, close, hard; refusing to fulfill a contract.

QUALITIES: Unmoral

Negativeness is not a accurate characterization of the words in this category. Many of them are negative in the sense of fat, ugly, wrinkled, confused, cold, worn out, unwashed, uneasy, and so on. These qualities are not condemnatory, and in some cases can be said to be positive. They are not really involved in morality.

'ā'ā. Dumbness, inability to speak intelligibly; silent. (Puk. 4:11.)

'a'a'ā. Uninhabited, as a house or village; lonely. (A.)

'a'ala. Fragrant, odoriferous. *Fig.*, of high or royal rank. *He 'a'ala no o Ka'ahu-manu,* Ka'ahu-manu is of sweet royal rank.

'a'alakai. Large, plump, full-fleshed.

a'alinanui. Large, fat, and weak, as a fat man.

'a'ao. Greedy, voracious.

'ā'aua. Coarse, as wrinkled or blotched skin. (PE.)

ahuwale. To be in plain sight, conspicuous, exposed.

a'ia'i. Bright, clear, pure, clean, as moonlight; white, clean, as linen. (Hoik. 19:8.) Pure, as gold. (Hoik. 21:21.)

'alakai. Large, potbellied, plump. See 'a'alakai.

'ālapa. Ugly, poor, thin in flesh. (A.) Athletic, active; epithet for Kamehameha I. (PE.)

'ala'uka. Ugly, slovenly, vile.

'ālu'a. One who is old and wrinkled.

'amumū. Blunt, dull.

ania. Smooth, even.

āniania. Smooth and still.

'ānoninoni. To be in doubt, suspense; confused mind.

anu. Cold, absence of warmth.

anuanu. Chilly, as the morning; air from the mountain.

'ape'ape. Full of knots, as a string; of stones, as a road. (A.)

'āpulu. Worn out, as a garment. *He wahi 'āpulu kapa,* a remnant of a garment.

'auhaka. Man with long, spindling legs, like the legs of a horse.

'auli'ikolo manu. A beautiful, well-formed person.

'eko. Dirty, as in former times, when it may have been *kapu* to bathe. Also called *uweko, weko.*

'eko'eko. Unwashed; dirt, filth.

'eleu. Alert, nimble, prompt.

hai'malulu, ha'imalule. Effeminate; deliberate in work; soft, weak.

hakahaka. To be full of holes or open spaces. *Fig.*, want, loss, deficiency.

hana walea. Self-satisfaction, contentment, quietness.

hānonono. Cracked, full of holes. See hakahaka.

hāpapa. Rocky area covered with a thin layer of soil; not deeply planted, as with seed.

hāpa'upa'u. Besmeared, dirty, as glass; sooty.

hauhili. Carelessness in doing something; diverging from the straight path; blundering; not to be depended upon for the truth.

hauna. Offensive to the smell, as spoiled food.

haunama. Offensive smell, but less so than *hauna.*

hinu. To anoint or besmear, as with oil or grease; to be smooth, shining.

hinuhinu. Glittering, as polished stones. Bright, shining, splendid.

hipa, hepa. To blunder in speaking.

hipū. Knot, fastening, anything tied.

hipuʻu. Knotty, as a string tied up in knots; tied fast.

hīpuʻupuʻu. To tie up, as a bundle; tied, fastened.

hōʻalo. To dodge, shun, escape from; working in spells.

hoʻokahēkahē. To wash dishes slovenly; to water, as land; to drain, as land; to cause to flow.

hoʻokamalani. To be partial; to make one a favorite; seeming to be worthless to everyone except the chief; to lavish favors on a mischievous child.

hoʻopāpalalē. To speak imperfectly, as one with a foreign accent or a speech impairment.

hūʻeu. Bold man, fearless and energetic when in action, good or bad. (A.) Witty, funny, amusing, mischievous. (PE.)

ikiiki. Close and stifling, as a confined room.

ʻīnea. Hard to obtain; costing much time and labor with chance of losing. *O kuʻu hoa pili, hoa ʻīnea,* my companion, a friend hard to be obtained.

kaʻapeha. Man of large size, as a chief; one of great influence.

kaekae. Young, fresh, and smooth, as an unmarried woman who is much in demand.

kakale. Thin, greatly diluted with water, as thin *poi.*

kakāuha. To stretch out, as the arm with muscles taut; to exhibit great strength; hence, to oppress, punish, bring under bondage.

kākiwi. Crooked sword, knife, or sickle; to strike suddenly from the side; to bend the body, as in bowing; to nod, as one going to sleep.

kālaʻe. Clear, pure atmosphere, calm and unclouded.

kalakaka, kalakala. Rough, thorny, scraggy, knotty.

kāwalawala. To speak in an unintelligible manner. *ʻŌlelo kāwalawala,* speech of which only a word here and there is understood.

kena. To be weary; to suffer under hard labor; to grieve.

kikiki. Very hot and close, as a tight room filled with people. *Ikiiki,* stifling.

kīkoʻolā. Topsy-turvy, mixed together, confusedly entangled.

kila. Strong, stout, able, bold.

kilakila. Great, tall, imposing, admirable, as applied to a person.

kīʻoki. Plump, fat, rolling, muscular.

kīpalalē. A rushing, a rapid flow, as a swollen stream of water.

I na kīpalalē a na waiahulu, by the rushing of muddy water. To talk or work quickly and incoherently.

kiwi. To turn from a natural position; to fall, tumble, bend; to be crooked; to nod, walk crookedly.

koi. To urge, to entreat someone to do or not do something. *Koi ae la lākou iāia, Liholiho e ʻaiʻē,* they urged him, Liholiho, to go into debt.

koʻikoʻi. To urge; to be hard upon; to entreat with perseverance; responsibility, weight; to stress, emphasize.

kōliliʻu. Dimly seen, as by persons of defective vision. Also called *kōliʻuliʻu.*

kukule. To be dumpish, loath to move, as with some diseases; listless, downcast.

kūliʻa. Young, handsome, desired, and sought after beauty.

kūlolalola. To be paralyzed; to act as an idiot in drooling or slobbering; to be weak, slow, or awkward.

kūmūmū. To make blunt, dull, or short.

kūnāhihi. Weak, as from shock; to have the hair stand up, as a wild man; to stand shivering with the cold, bristling up.

kūpa liʻi. Diminutive, as a dwarfish person.

laʻelaʻe. Bright, clear; a light; calm and pleasant weather.

lauʻeka. Awkward, not skilled in work. *Lōpālauʻeka,* a man slovenly, awkward, and unskillful in his work; a worthless, shiftless squatter.

laulā. Broad, wide. *He keʻena laulā,* a wide room. Liberal, widely known.

leho ʻula. Very precious, as the red-shell cowry.

lelehua. Skillful, able in applying mental processes and powers.

linolino. Brightness that dazzles and blinds one; calm, unruffled, as the sea with no wind.

lipi. Sharp, tapering down, as the edge of an axe; sharp mountain ridge.

loia. Ingenious, skillful woman, handy and expert at any business.

lola. Paralyzed or palsied person; idle, neglected.

luʻaluʻa. Secondhand garment, soft and worn; hence, to be old, as garments; to be much used and worn. (Heb. 1:11.)

luhi. Weary, fatigued, tired. Weighed down with labor, burden, grief, oppression. (Isa. 56:11.)

mahūmahū. To be silent, as a weak dying man. Often said of a dying man or tasteless *poi.*

maiau. Industrious, ingenious, expert; ready and ingenious. Applies to men.

makali'i. Small, diminutive, tiny.

makamae. Precious, valuable, much desired, as a stone (2 Sam. 12:30); as a beloved child or servant (Isa. 43:4); as a darling or loved one. (Hal. 22:20.)

makepono. Cheap, reasonable in price; bargain. (PE.)

māluhiluhi. Weary, fatigued.

maniania. A sensation of shuddering, dizziness; a grating on the nerves; drowsy, sleepy, dull; straight, even, smooth, as a surface.

mano. Thick, numerous, many; the number 4,000, a large unit in Hawaiian counting.

manomano. Great in number, magnificent, powerful. (Hal. 86:5.)

manu'u. Great, immeasurable, multitudinous, vast, manifold. *Manu'unu'u.*

maopopo. Clear; plain to the senses, understanding; clearness, that which is explicit, as a moral or natural truth; not to be doubted.

mauna. Large, swelling; mountain. On all the islands, the land rises on all sides from the sea to the central parts of the island. This is called the *mauna.*

meumeu. To be blunt, dull, as an instrument whose edge or end is beaten off to roundness.

mīkolelehua. Thoughtful and skillful in reflection; eloquent and moving in speech.

mikomiko. Relishable, as well seasoned food; to be instructive and pleasant in conversation.

mūkā. Tasteless, insipid. (A.) Sound of lips popped open; to smack the lips, as in eating. (PE.)

mulemule. Bitter, as herbs; to taste sharp.

mūmū. To hum, make an indistinct sound; confused sound of a multitude at a distance.

nahe. Soft and slow, as the voice of music; soft, as a fine cloth; blowing softly, as a gentle breeze. Also called *nahenahe.*

nanea. Ease, quietude, comfort, joy; relaxed at leisure; absorbed in an interest.

neanea, neoneo. Lonely, desolate, empty worthless.

ni'ani'a. Smooth surface; calm and smooth sea.

nunu. Taciturn, unsocial, sullen, displeased. Applies only to men. (A.) Greed; to covet, extort. (PE.)

nunuha. Unsocial, still, sulky, sullen. Applied to persons.

oe. Word for a beautiful woman; long, applied to the neck of a person.

ōheahea. Warm, tasteless, as lukewarm water. (A.) Drowsy, as weather. (PE.)

'ōkolo. Slippery, here one is likely to fall. (A.)

'ōlala. Lean, poor in flesh, (Isa. 17:4.)

'ōmole. Round and smooth, as a bottle, cruse, or phial.

'ōnaha. Crooked, bending, as an aged person. *'Ōnaha na kihi o ka mahina*, the points of the moon bend round.

onaona. Beautiful, graceful. *Ka wehiwehi i ka onaona i ke 'ala,* beautiful, as applied to the eyes and face, rosy cheeks. Odoriferous, as a rose; pleasant fragrance or perfume.

'onipa'a. To be fixed, firmly bound together, steadfast, immovable, persevering. This word was a key to the characters of Kamehameha V and Queen Lili'u'okalani. (Hal. 140:11.)

'ono. Sweet, palatable, savory, delicious. *Lit.,* the throat craves. (Oihk. 1:9.)

'o'ohu. A stoop-shouldered man, as a mechanic or carpenter from long labor bent over.

'ōpilopilo. Dirty, bad smelling, as a soft, muddy road or stagnant water.

pahe'e. Smoothed, polished, slippery; shining, as a polished surface. (Hal. 73:18.)

pakelo. To slip out of the grasp of a person; slippery, sliding; to thrust, as a spear; to speak, as with a slippery tongue.

pakika. Polished, smoothed, as a thing polished.

pālahalaha. To spread or broaden out; to spread a report; to extend far and wide; breadth or extent of a country.

pālakahuki. Putrid, soft, overcooked.

palanehe. Gentle, good, without noise or confusion.

panonono. Full of holes or cracks.

paupauoho. Breathless, as a panting person; to be discouraged through fear; to be faint through great exertion.

pelupelu. To double over and over; to recapitulate. (A.)

pihi. Blunt, dull, as a wooden digging stick. Also called *pihipihi.*

pi'o. Extinguished, quenched, as a fire or lamp; bent, crooked, arched; to have disappeared, as a ship at sea.

pōhaha. Round, circular, and deep, as a sore, pit, or crater. See **pōnaha.**

pōheoheo. Round and plump, as a woman wearing many folds of *kapa.* Also called *puheheo.*

pōka'o. Very poor, as one destitute of decent clothing; naked.

poko, pōkole. Short, a word often applied to the small division of a mountain range; e.g., *Ko'olau Poko* (short) plus *Ko'olau Loa* (long) make up the Koʻolau mountain range. Similarly, *Hāmā-kua Poko,* etc.

pōkole. Insufficient for a purpose, incompetent for a place; low, humble.

polohuku. Large, plump, bulging, wealthy, prosperous. Also called *ponohuku, pōkeokeo, poʻokeokeo.*

polupolu. Large, fat, and weak, as a man; fat, gross, and heavy, as a very fleshy person.

pōnaha. Round, circular, and deep, as a volcano, a pit, or a sore. See **pōhaha.**

poni. To consecrate by anointing, as a priest; to anoint, as a king. (Lunk. 9:8.) To rub in some odoriferous substance to cause a pleasant odor.

ponunu. Short, stumpy, thick, clumsy.

popopo. Rot, as of timber; deterioration, as of cloth or paper; decayed, as teeth.

poupou. Short in stature, low, short generally. Different from *poʻopoʻo,* deep down.

pūekōlea. Round and plump, as a *kōlea* or plover.

pūhaʻuhaʻu. Large and fat, as some men.

pūhulalu. Fat and weak, as some men. (A.)

puʻipuʻi. Corpulent, thickset, stout. (Lunk. 3:29.)

pukapuka. Full of holes, cracks, chinks. *ʻEke pukapuka,* a bag full of holes. (Hag. 1:6). Porous stone; pockmarked.

pululuhi. Hazy, foggy, dull, as the weather; dull, as a person waking from sleep.

pupuku. Wrinkled, frowning, contracted; curled, as hair. Also called *pukupuku.*

uila kanaka. A brilliant man.

waʻawaʻa. Plump, muscled, as the shoulders of a young man.

walea. Accustomed to doing a thing from frequent efforts at it.

QUALITIES: Impersonal

In general, the words in this category deal with the elements (such as wind, sea, and water), with action, light and darkness, bad odors, eyesight, and others.

ʻaʻanapuʻu. To work; to bend in different directions; to be small and large, i.e., to be uneven in size, as rope made of native materials.

a'ea'e. Dark or obscure, as a vision seen indistinctly. *Pō a'ea'e,* a night of indistinct vision, not totally dark, i.e., light and darkness mixed.

ahe. Anything quiet, gentle, or soft, as a light breeze.

aheahe. Gentle breeze accompanied by a faint whispering sound.

'āheahea. Warm, as water from standing in the sun; to wilt, as a plant.

'ai ha'a. Standing but bending the back; *hula* step danced with bended knees. *Lit.,* style low.

akaka. To be plain, clear, as a thought or the expression of an idea; to be distinct and intelligible, as language. Also called *akaaka.*

akenawale. Clamor against hard times. (CMH.)

'ala. Perfumed, fragrant.

'alā. Smooth and round, as a waterworn pebble. *'Alā o ka ma'a,* sling stone. (Zek. 9:15.)

'ala pāku'i. Exceedingly fragrant, too much so, or too strong to be pleasant; sickishly sweet.

'ālohilohi. Splendor, brightness; to shine brightly, to shine, as light. *Maka 'ālohilohi,* bright eyes; *malamalama 'ālohilohi,* bright light. (Ioba 37:31.)

'āmokumoku. Intermittent. (CMH.) Full of stumps or abounding in islets or rocks. (PE.)

aniani. Agreeable, cool, refreshing; to flow gently, as a wind.

anoano. Solemn stillness, a sacred, hallowed place; solitary, still, retired.

anu. To be and feel cold. *Ua anu au i kāhi kapa'ole,* I am cold, having no clothes.

anuanu. Cold, as temperature; coolness. *Hu'i, hu'ihu'i,* cold, cool, chilly, as the morning air from the mountain.

'a'ole okana mai ka nui. No end to the number; unusually large such.

'āpa'apa'a. Firm, compact, as a well-made road. *'Āpa'apa'a,* name of a strong wind at Kohala.

'auli'i kolo manu. Beautiful, well-formed person; any article beautifully made. (CMH.)

'awa'awa. Pungent, as rum, orange skin, pepper, etc; sour, bitter, sharp; brackish water.

'awahia. Bitterness, sourness; bitter, like gall; cold mountain rain, fog, mist. *'Awahia noho'i ka ōlelo,* what embittered words!

aweawe. Beautiful, handsome, as applied to both men and women; curling water in the wake of a ship; tentacles of a squid.

'ekeke'i. Short, too short, shorter than something else. Applied to clothes, strings, etc.

ʻeleʻelepī. Dashing different ways, as waves affected by various winds; agitated, tumultuous, rough.

ʻelo. To wet or soak, as *kapa* with rain.

ʻeloʻelo. Very wet, soaked, drenched; to moisten, dampen. *Ua pulu ʻeloʻelo wale ko lakou aʻahu i ka waimaka,* their robes were soaked soft with their tears.

ʻeʻolani. Stretching or reaching up to the heavens; hence, very high, *ʻeʻolani na kia i kamoku kiekie.*

hao. Iron. After seeing iron in many uses on and off the ships of Captain Cook, the natives eagerly sought "samples." Certain phrases illustrate subsequent uses: *hao na kēpā,* spurs of iron applied to hurry a horse; *hao na pōlena,* the bowlines are iron, applied to a swift sailing ship; *hao kilou,* an iron hook.

haumanumanu. Full of cracks and holes; something worthless. (A.) Rough, irregular, bruised. (PE.)

hohonu. Deep, profound. *He kanaka hohonu o kea ʻike,* a man with profound knowledge. (PE.)

kaʻeʻe. Hard or stiff, as new *kapa;* to dry up, as water in the sun.

mania. To be affected, as the nerves with any sudden noise; dizziness on looking down a great height; drowsiness, an inclination to sleep.

moakaka, mōakaaka. Clear, plain, intelligible, as the expression of a thought or idea; transparent, as glass; distinct, as colors.

nahe. Soft, slow, gentle, as the voice of music; to blow softly, as a gentle breeze. Also called *nahenahe.*

nokeʻa. Stuffed full, as with food; filled to the brim, as a cup.

nuʻa. Road much traveled; mats and *lei*s stacked in thick piles; surging, rising in swells, as the ocean.

nuʻanuʻa. Large, soft, fleshy; a heap of mats; *lei*s piled up; waves pushed in on the shore.

ʻoā, ʻowʻā. To split, as a log or board; timber in a ship's hull; five parallel lines on which music is written.

ʻohaʻoha. To grow thriftily, as plants.

ohiohi. Wavy like the grains of certain woods, mahogany, curl-maple, curly *koa.*

ʻōnuhenuhea. Very fat, shaking with fat. Applied to men when bloated.

ʻoʻoma. Open, as the spout of a pitcher; flaring bonnet, a name given to the bonnets of the early missionary wives.

pāʻepaʻewa. Incorrect or irregular in judging. (CMH.)

pepeʻe. Deformed, crooked, twisted, out of shape.

piʻipiʻi. Curls of hair; wavy, as hair.

pōahiahi. Dim, obscure.

pōholoholo. Ill fitting, loose fitting, as with clothes or shoes; adhering only slightly; separating easily; sinking.

pōwehiwehi. Dim, obscure, indistinct, as vision; twilight.

pū'ili. That which gives temporary delight; to clasp, embrace. *E pū'ili me ka lima,* to hold fast with the hand. Bamboo rattles.

pu'uiki. Small, squat. (CMH.)

ueueko, uweko. Bad smell, stench. See **'ui'uikō.**

uihā, uiha'a. Weary with long distances; idle, i.e., without work; burdened with work, but desiring it.

'ui'uikō. Unpleasant smell. See **ueueko.**

uluhua. To be vexed with any matter; to be weary with life; to be angry, discontented, displeased.

'uo'uo. Soft, pastelike, as *poi* wet with water; clear, fine, without lumps.

uweka, ueka. Crying child; dirty, bleary, as the eyes.

wī. Poor in flesh, lean, famishing; barren, as land.

wini. Sharp, as a point. *Ho'owini,* reduce to a point.

winiwini. Sharp point.

wīwī. Poor in flesh; slender, feeble. (Kin. 41:6.)

RAINS: Names

The names of the rains listed here make specific reference to their well-known characteristics, such as a topographical area or an association with a particular kind of cloud or wind.

A mellifluous arrangement of syllables in a word or words produces descriptive terms much relished by Hawaiian lovers of nature. These names are also a testimonial to their careful observation of the many subtle variations in the activities of Mother Nature.

'Āpuakea. See **Ua-'Āpuakea.**

'Awa. Fine, light rain like *noe.* See **Rains: Glossary.**

Hā'ao. Rain at 'Au-'au-lele, Ka'ū, Hawai'i, and Nu'uanu, O'ahu, called this because its showers follow one another down their respective valleys like members of a chief's retinue.

Ho'olua. Rain that accompanies the north wind, *ke ua Ho'olua, he ua nui no ia.*

Ka-na-'ula. Special rain in Lahaina, Maui.

Kani-lehua. Well-known misty rain of Hilo. *Lit.,* rain that *lehua* flowers drink. (PE.)

Ka ua nāulu o Kawaihae. Sudden shower of Kawaihae. (PE.)

Kea. Rain or mist at Hana or Koʻolau, Maui. (A.)

Kili. Wind at Waiheʻe, Maui.

Kilikili noe. Fine, cold, misty rain of Kēkē.

Kio wao. Name of the mist or cloud that frequently settles in the hills of Oʻahu.

Kīpuʻupuʻu. Chilly rain at Waimea, Hawaiʻi; rain like small shot at Waimea.

Kona. Rain accompanying the southwest wind, a leeward rain of Kona.

Kona hea. Cold rainstorm of Kona.

Kona-hili-maiʻa. Cold rains in the mountains of Kona; drawn out, protracted rains.

Kona-kū. Heavy Kona rain in the mountains. (MALO 14.)

Kona-lani. Kind of Kona rain; fine, light, showery rains. (MALO 14.)

Kona-moe. Class of Kona rains. *Kona-hea,* a cold rain.

Līlī-lehua. Rain and wind well known at Pālolo, Oʻahu, and Waiehu, Maui.

Mololani. Name of a wind at Kahaluʻu, Oʻahu; rain over a crater of that name on Mō-kapu peninsula, Oʻahu.

Nahua. Fine rain that accompanies the northeast trade winds along the northern part of Maui. (A.)

Noenoe. Fine mist, fog, or rain. *Uakea o Hāna,* the fine mist of Hana.

Pōpō-ua. A rain. Lit., *kapa* bundle rain. Also called Ua-pōpō-kapa.

Ua-a-kalīpoa. Light, cold rain. *Lit.,* rain by the *līpoa* (seaweed).

Ua-ʻĀpuakea. Famous rain of Koʻolau-poko, Oʻahu, said to be named after a beautiful woman, ʻĀpuakea, who was changed to rain by the goddess Hiʻi-aka.

Ua-heʻe-nehu. Misty rain seen off the Hilo coast when the *nehu* are running.

Ua hehi pua hala o Poʻo-kū. Rain that treads on the pandanus flowers of Poʻo-kū, Hanalei, Kauaʻi.

Ua-kaʻau. Fine rain in Kohala, Hawaiʻi.

Ua kāʻele-loli. Rain at Makiki, Oʻahu.

Ua-kani-koʻo. Rain that accompanies the Koʻolau wind. *Lit.,* rain cane-tapping (PE.)

Uakea. Well-known mist at Hana, Maui. *Lit.,* rain white.

Ua kinai lehua o Pana-'ewa. Rain at Pana-'ewa that quenches the *lehua* flowers.

Ua-kini-maka-lehua. Mountain rain; rain of countless *lehua* blossom faces. (PE.)

Ua-kī-o-wao. Well-known rain in Nu'uanu Valley, O'ahu.

Ua-kuahine. Misty rain familiar in Manoa Valley, O'ahu, named after Kuahine, who turned to rain upon the death of her daughter.

Ua-kūkala-hale. Rain familiar to Honolulu.

Ua lani ha'aha'a Hāna. Rain well known in Hāna, Maui.

Ua'lani-pa'ina. Rain of Ulu-pala-kua, Maui. *Lit.,* crackling rain. (PE.)

Ua-lēhei. Rain local to Makawao. *Lit.,* leaping rain. (PE.)

Ua-lena. Rain tinted yellow from Hanalei, Kaua'i.

Ua-lū-lau-kō. Rain at Limu-nui, Kaua'i. *Lit.,* rain that scatters sugarcane leaves. (PE.)

Ua-ma-ka-lau-koa. Rain of Nu'uanu.

Ua-moaniani-lehua. Rain at Puna, Hawai'i. *Lit.,* rain that carries the fragrance of the *lehua* blossoms. (PE.)

Ua-pa'ū-pili. Rain that moistens the *pili* grass at Lahaina.

Ua-pōa'i-hala, ua-pōa'i-hale. Rain famous at Kaha-lu'u, O'ahu. *Lit.,* rain surrounding pandanus. (PE.) See **Winds: Ka-ua-pōa'i-hale o Kaha-lu'u.**

Ua-po'o-lipilipi. Rain of Kalihi, O'ahu. *Lit.,* adze-like head, so named since the heavy rain caused people to sleep so much their heads looked as if sharpened by an adze. (PE.)

Ua-po'o-nui. Light, steady rain. *Lit.,* a rain head big.

Ua-pōpō-kapa. A rain. *Lit.,* *kapa* bundle rain. *Kapa* was rolled into a bundle and covered to keep it dry.

Ua-pupū-hale. Well-known rain at Hāmākua, Hawai'i. *Lit.,* rain standing near house. (PE.)

Ua-'ula-lena. Rain at Pi'i-hole, Maui. *Lit.,* rain red yellow.

'Ula-lena. Rain of reddish hue. *Lit.,* reddish yellow. *Kapu ka luna o Ka'ala i ka ua 'Ula-lena,* the uplands of Ka'ala mountain are sacred to the red-yellow rain (chant).

Wa'ahila. Rains of Manoa and Nu'uanu Valleys. *Ola ke kai o Kou i ka Ua-wa'ahila,* the land Kou, Honolulu, lives by the Wa'ahila rain. (PE.)

Waikaloa. Cold rains at Honolulu. (CMH.)

RAINS: Glossary

This listing describes different kinds of rains and includes a few terms dealing with mist. Other weather categories—"Winds," "Clouds," and "The sky"—provide interesting comparisons.

'alo'alo kiki. To dodge the rain quickly, as one in a hurry.

ana ua. Rain gauge.

anuenue kau pō. Lunar rainbow.

aokū. Rain cloud, mist, rain.

'awa. Fine rain or mist.

'awa'awa. Fine, misty rain that frequently can be cold.

ha'akō'ihe. Waterspout. (CMH.) See **waikō'ihe, waipu'ilani.**

hau. Snow, ice, frost, (Nah. 12:10.)

hekili. Thunder; to thunder. (Hal. 29:3.)

hekili pāmalō. Thunder and no rain.

he ua hu'ehu'e ia no uli. Spreading over, as a rain.

he ua lanipali. Shower reaching to heaven, i.e., a very heavy shower.

ho'oilo. Rainy season or wintry months in contrast to *kau,* the summer season. (Kin. 1:14.)

ho'okili. Fine, gentle rain, a form much beloved.

ililani. Unexpected rain; rain from a seemingly clear sky.

kaha'ea. Cloud reaching over the heavens, composed frequently of several colors such as black variegated, white, and blue. A frequent sign of rain.

kahakikī. To pour down violently with a roar, as rain or rushing water.

kaka'i. Cloud that lies near the horizon.

kawa. To rain heavily. See **pulepe.**

kēhau. Mist; cold, fine rain floating in the air, usually in mountains.

kēwai. Mist merging with rain some distance off.

kili. Fine, light rain; peal of thunder; raindrops.

kili hau. To fall gently, as a cold, soft shower; to stop falling and fade away, as rain at the end of a shower.

kilihuna, kilihune. Scattered into small drops, as fine rain or mist; fine windblown rain, a much beloved rain.

kilikili noe, kilikili oe. Fine, misty rain.

kili nahe. Soft, gentle and fine rain.

kili noe. Fine misty rain.

ki'o wao. Cool, mountain rain accompanied by wind and fog.

ko'iawe. Light moving shower.

ko'i'ula. Rainbow hued rain; rising cloud.

koko. Falling rain with light looking reddish as it shines through.

kuāua. Season of rains; frequent, fertilizing rains.

kuāua hope. Spring rains. (Ioba 29:23.)

kū'aukahi. Summer rains.

kūlipolipo. Dark, deep water in mountain pools.

kūlokuloku. Falling rain or flowing water.

la'a ua. Rainy season.

leleaka. Light, wind-blown rain or mist.

lelehuna, lelehune. Fine, wind-blown rain or mist.

leleua. Fine, gentle rain.

līhau. Gentle, cool rain believed to bring luck to fishermen.

lihau pua i ka wai. Raindrops larger than *moe* or *kilihuna* but smaller than *paka ua*.

lilinoe. Fine, sprinkling rain or mist. *He ua lilinoe.*

luahoana. Rainbow or halo around the sun or moon.

ma'au. Rain in the upland forest; rain forest.

ma'ukele. Rain forest. *Ka wao ma'u kele,* the upland damp region. (KL 618.)

nākikiki'i. Slanting rain.

nāulu. Sudden shower of fine rain without seeming benefit of cloud or clouds.

noe. Mist or fine rain, spray or fog; to sprinkle a little, as fine rain; to be damp, as fog; to rain, yet be scarcely discernible.

noe kolo. Small fine rain of the mountains that mixes with the thicker rain of the forests. (A.) Creeping mist. (PE.)

noenoe. Fine mist, fog, or rain.

noe 'ula. Red eyed or sore eyed from going in the rain or the sea.

'ohu. Fog, mist, cloud. *Ka 'ohu e uhe ana i ke kuahiwi,* the light cloud that covers the mountain.

pa'apūhea. Mist, fine rain; fine, cloud-like fog. (A.)

paka. Raindrops. See **pakapaka.**

pakakū. Rain falling in large drops.

pakapaka. Heavy shower of large rain drops; spattering noise that such drops make on a hollow or dry substance, as on dry leaves.

paka ua. Raindrops making a nose as they spatter on dry leaves.

pāki'o. Showery rain.

pāki'oki'o. Showery rain; to rain in short showers and often.

pali koa. Overhanging cloud, one that lies near the shore.

pīpinoke. To rain continuously. (PE.)

pōhina. Fine mist or fog; light rain; thin cloud; whitish, grayish.

pulepe, pulu pē. To rain heavily; to be drenched. See **kawa.**

puneʻeneʻe. To move along, as a shower of rain.

ua. General word for rain; to rain.

ua ʻawa. Chilly rain, cold and bitter.

ua hānai. Rain that nurtures the earth. (PE.)

ua hekili. Rain in large drops.

uahi wai. Mist, spray. *Wawai,* a well watered land.

ua hōʻeʻele. Drenching rain; to make black, darken.

ua hōʻokina. Continuous rainfall.

ua kea. See **ʻĀpuakea, Rain: Names.**

ua koko. Low-lying rainbow; rain sparkling with a rainbow; heavy rain that turns the streams and the nearby ocean a red-brown color with runoff from the hills.

ua lanipili. Several-days downpour; heavy rain, cloudburst.

ua limua. Period of constant rain. *Lit.,* moss-growing rain.

ua loa. Long rainy period.

ua loku. Downpour of rain.

ua nāulu. Showery rain.

uaoa. Mist or light rain.

ua poko. Short rain.

ua poʻo nui. Light, steady rain. *Lit.,* big-head rain. (PE.)

ua pūnohu. Rain, red in the sunshine.

waikōʻihe. Waterspout.

wai puʻilani. Waterspout. See **haʻakoʻihe, waikōʻihe.**

wao kele. Rain forest; rain belt.

wā ua. Rainy season.

RANK AND CLASS

The relationships between a chief and all others around him—aside from ties of blood—were based primarily on vocations. Many men served the king or the chief, and these attendants ranged all the way from lesser chiefs down to the *auwa* (outcasts).

The king's retinue was a kind of catchall for positions and jobs. Several people were identified as being merely officers in the king's train. This category spreads before us the whole cast of participants in royal rule. It was a well-organized establishment of loyal subjects largely devoted to service or to security, or to both, for the sake of the ruling chief.

aha aliʻi. Agency that settles questions of rank and lineage. (CMH.)

ahupuaʻa. Division of land, such as Wailuku, made up of several sub-divisions descending in size. The *ahupuaʻa* extended from the ocean to the highest uplands. This division, usually placed under a lesser chief for control, was roughly shaped like a segment of pie, very wide on the ocean side and coming to a point or narrow boundary at the top. An *ahupuaʻa* often included one or more fishponds.

ʻaialo. Prince or princess of the royal court. They had the privilege of eating with the chiefs of their sex.

ʻai moku. Holding the rank of a chief or acting for him. (A.) Ruler of a *moku,* island. (PE.)

ʻāʻīpuʻupuʻu. Steward, cook, servant, in preparing food for and waiting on a chief. Originally applied to stewards of chiefs. (A.)

ʻalaea. Clan; descendants of servants; tribe; people in a district who have intermarried.

ʻalihi kaua. General, commander; one who directed in battle. (1 Nal. 16:16.)

aliʻiʻai ahupuaʻa. Chief who rules an *ahupuaʻa.*

aliʻi papa. Person whose mother is a high chiefess and father a commoner.

ʻāneʻe. To hitch along; to move along, as a cripple; to go from house to house to tell fortunes; to beg; fortune teller; beggar.

haʻakuʻe. Name of the person who swings the fly brush over the chief when he sleeps. The motion of to and fro, back and forth, as a *kāhili,* or as the tide with sand.

hāiki. Suffering for want of food; pinched with hunger. (Mar. 2:25.)

haku. Owner, overseer, lord, master, ruler, pastor. (Oihk. 21:4.)

hamohamo. Name of an office handled by one of the servants of the king; to touch, rub with oil, anoint.

hamuʻili. Distinct class of persons about a king; personal attendant of a chief, as a taster.

haui. Title of a chief, as noble, a descendant of kings. (A.)

hoaliʻi, hoa aliʻi. Companion of a chief; a fellow chief. (FOR 6:266.)

hoʻokohu. Favorite or chosen one; one appointed first to a post of duty. (A.)

hu. Class of common people. Closely synonymous with *makaʻainana. Lit.,* people that cultivate the soil.

hulu-manu. Court favorites of the king.

'iele. Chief, king.

ikū nu'u. Rank below *ikū pau;* collateral branch with temporal power.

ikū pau. Priests, direct descendants of the god *Kāne,* the highest personage of all. (FOR 6:266.)

'ilihelo. Class of farmers who worked vicariously; unskilled workers.

'io. Herald; forerunner who announced the approach of a chief.

'i'o pono. Persons of a class formerly entrusted with the care of the king. Their business was to guard his person and his effects lest someone should obtain his spittle and his garments and then have the power to pray him to death. The *poe 'i'opono* were generally high chiefs.

ipu kuha. Spittoon.

iwikuamo'o. Trusted person who attended a high chief, cared for his needs and effects, and executed his orders.

ka'a kaua. War chariot. (Puk. 14:25.) One skilled in managing war operations and maneuvers; class of chiefs consulted by the king in times of difficulty.

ka'apeha. Large-sized person of influence, importance, and distinction. (A.)

kahu. Pastor, attendant of honor, guardian.

kahu ali'i. Royal guardian in the family of a high chief.

kahuna. Priest or person who offered sacrifices; sorcerer, teacher, expert.

kahuna ki'i. Guide and director of the high chief or king in matters relating to war; caretaker of images.

kala. Public crier who assembled people in time of war, using lamps or torches.

kālai'āina. One who divides, manages, or directs the affairs of the land. Minister of the Interior, *Kuhina Kālai'āina.*

kālaimoku. One who administers or manages the affairs of an island *(moku),* generally one whose advice is valued in managing a people.

kāpi'i. Office in the king's retinue.

kauali'i. A low, not a high chief; commoner raised to chieftainship by the king. See **kaukauali'i.**

kaukauali'i. Class of chiefs below the king, the father a high chief and the mother above a commoner but not a chiefess.

kāula. Prophet; one who preaches or announces future events. (Oih. 3:24.)

kau'o'e. Office in the king's train; bodyguard.

kauwā. Servant of no rank; slave; menial; outcast.

kauwā lepo. Order of men who sacrificed themselves on the death of a king. (A.)

kia'ipo'o. Guard of the king or chief who was asleep; bodyguard. *Lit.*, guard head.

konohiki. Manager of the land of an *ahupua'a* under the chief.

kualanapuhi. Officer who waved the flies off the resting king with his fly brush or *kāhili*.

kualapehu. Officer in the king's train; a personal defender; pugilist.

kuene. Steward, waiter, treasurer; layout man for a building site.

ku'iaumoe. Name given by those about the chiefs to those below them in privilege, though perhaps the better persons.

kūkae pōpolo. Somewhat demeaning term for a chief whose mother was a commoner. *Lit.*, excreta from greens.

kūkini. Fleet runner or messenger who was valued in proportion to his speed.

kuku'i wana'ao. Persons about the king who talked and told stories all night.

kūlua. Person whose father was a chief and mother was not. See **kūkae pōpolo, waikī.** (A.)

lanika'e. People who ate with the king at sundown; name of the *kālaimoku* when there was only one chief.

lawa. Office in the king's train; strong man, as in a king's retinue.

loa. Officer who has universal charge of the taxes; name of the tax.

lomilomi. Servant whose duty it was to take care of the spittle and excrements of the chief; the masseur of the chief.

lōpā. Man who cultivates land under a commoner-farmer but was a tenant; poor, shiftless worker.

lōpāho'opili wale. Low grade of farmers who obtained their living by clinging to the *lōpā,* tenants working under farmers.

luna. Executive officer of any type; person, generally, who was over others as director or supervisor; herald sent on business by the chief; ambassador.

maka'ainana. Laboring class, which was resident on the land they worked and transferred with it when ownership changed; commoners, in distinction from chiefs.

makawela. Servant marked on the forehead. This term is applied to the *kauwā,* outcast or despised.

mālalaioa. Office in the king's train. Probably filled by one skilled in an occupation or craft.

mālama ukana. Person in charge of provisions and supplies on a trip.

mūkī. To suck into the mouth, as in lighting a pipe.

mūkī baka. Suck, puff, or kiss given by the pipe bearer to keep the *baka* (tobacco) always lighted.

muki'i. Pipe lighter to the king or chief. See **mūkī baka.**

nī'aupi'o. Highest or superior chief; to cohabit at that level, as a brother with a sister; child of such a union. *Lit.,* a coconut leaf midrib bent, i.e., of the same stalk.

niho mauole. Office in the king's train. *Lit.,* teeth worn, a figurative term for a chief who has outlived his usefulness.

noanoa. Common man, country man, laborer; one whose ancestors were laboring people.

nohi'ialo. Person who was born with a chief and continued to live with him. (A.)

nohi'ikua. People who are born and live on the back part of an island. (A.)

nopohokano. One who manages a district or an island *(moku)* under two chiefs. See **kālaimoku,** counselor.

nou. Servant born of a common person and a *kauwa 'aumakuā.* (A.)

'ohina. To have one's property swept away by debt. (A.)

oma. Ranking officer below the king.

pa'a ipu kuha. Chief's spittoon bearer.

pa'akāhili. Office of a high chief, bearer of the royal feather standard.

pa'aua. Laborer, worker, hired man. (Isa. 19:10.)

pākeokeo. People of chiefly ancestry who ate with the chief, as the *'aialo.*

palani. To stink, a word applied to servants in distinction from chiefs.

pio. See **nī'aupi'o.**

po'oho'olewa. Very high chief, always carried by his people. Even his shadow might not fall upon himself or any other. Pukui-Elbert states that he was carried about by night. *Lit.,* head carried.

po'okela. Chief; prince or chief among men; a superior by birth or exploit. (Ier. 13:18.)

puali'i, pua ali'i. Descendant of a chief. (PE.) One who lived idly with a chief. (A.) *Lit.,* flower chief.

pūlo'ulo'u. Stick capped with a ball covered with *kapa* borne before a chief, as a sign of *kapu.*

pu'ukū. One entrusted with care of the gods. (Kin. 15:20.) Steward. (1 Nal. 16:9.)

'ūhā kākau. Office of one of the king's attendants. *Lit.,* tattooed thighs.

ukali. To follow; to follow after, as in the train of a chief.

uli. One of the king's special servants, a steersman for his canoes.

wahi. Favorite or high servant of the king. (A.)

waikī. Person whose father was a chief but whose mother was not. See kūlua, kūkae pololo. Each of these bears a sense of contempt.

SHELLFISH

A shellfish may be defined as an invertebrate animal having a shell, especially a mollusk—such as an oyster, clam, snail, whelk, or limpet—or a crustacean, such as a crab or lobster.

All Hawaiian islands abound in shellfish, which scientists have been studying for more than a century. Their findings—resulting from individual aquatic observations and organized expeditions, such as that of the *Albatross*—have initiated and supplemented museum collections around the world, including those of the Bernice Pauahi Bishop Museum and public and private collections representing these islands.

Two respected Hawai'i women published manuscripts about shellfish during the preparation of this manuscript: E. Alison Kay, Professor of Zoology, University of Hawaii, and the late Margaret Titcomb, former Head Librarian, Bishop Museum.

'a'ama. Edible black crab *(Grapsus tenuicrustatus)* that lives among the shore rocks.

ālealea. Small, sharp, light to dark brown shell *(Laemodonta octanfracta)* found in certain places in East Loch, Pearl Harbor. Found in supraspray zones under rocks and rubble.

'alinalina. Yellow-foot *opihi (Cellana sandwicensis).* These *opihi* are common along the basalt shores of all windward islands where the surf breaks.

aloalo. Squilla or mantis shrimp *(Pseudosquilla ciliata),* highly desired as food. It is found in shallow water under stones or in holes in dead coral blocks. It looks like a four-footed animal of the sea.

'aoa. Snail *(Melampus castaneus)*. Small shellfish, typical inhabitant of the high shoreline. It has a smooth, brown, polished shell, often strung on leis. See **ālealea, maka'aoa.** (EAK 491.)

'āpa'apa'a. Lobster. *He ula 'āpa'apa'a,* a red macrurid crustacean.

'au wa'a lā lua. Paper nautilus *(Argonauta argo)*. This is a cosmopolitan species of warm and temperate waters. *Lit.,* fleet of canoes with two sails. (EAK 491.)

'e'eke. Species of small black crab, a four-footed animal of the sea. See **'elemihi.**

'elemihi, alamihi. Small black crab *(M. messor)* common under stones on muddy, flat reefs near river mouths. Also called *'e'eke, 'ēlepi.*

hā'uke'uke. Sea urchin or sea egg *(Colobocentrotus atratus)*. Large shells growing up to 3 inches. Lives on rocky shores washed by surf. See **hāwa'e, 'opihi, wana.**

hā'uke'uke'ula'ula. Smooth-spined sea urchin *(Heterocentrolus mamillatus)*. The spines were used as slate pencils. A large specimen may be 4 inches long.

hāwa'e. Sea egg or pinchushion urchin *(Tripneustes gratilla),* a Hawaiian shoal-water form, 4 to 5 inches in diameter. Edible, but not as flavorful as other urchins. Not a poisonous species.

hawa'ewa'e. General name for small lobsters.

he'e. Squid, octopus *(Octopus* spp.). This word has the meaning of slipperiness; hence also called *he'ehe'e.* (EAK 589.)

he'e'ala'ala pū loa. Long-headed night squid prized for its livers *('ala'ala),* which are salted, dried, and eaten.

he'e 'āpa'apa'a. Inedible squid. No data.

he'e makōko. Large, reddish squid *(Octopus ornatus),* bitter to human taste but effective as medicine. A night squid that forages after dark. Also called *puloa,* which is used for bait rather than food.

he'e mākole. Squid used with salt, reddish in color. The salt was a protective seasoning.

he'e mauli. Day squid *(Octopus cyanea)*. It lives on reef flats, foraging during the day. (EAK 589.)

honumaoli. Native sea turtle. Its flesh is forbidden to women.

ko'e. Angleworm (family Lumbricidae), valuable for loosening soil.

kohekohe. Shellfish that grows on the sides of a ship at sea. Not the same as *'ōkohekohe* (barnacle). (A.)

kuanaka. Chinese umbrella shell *(Umbraculum sinicum)*. It is a mollusk, like the *kua po'i.* Large specimens are up to 5 inches long. These opisthobranchs are common, found beneath ledges and in crevices on basalt shorelines. (EAK 446.)

kuapaʻa. The chiton *(Acanthochiton viridis)*. A small sea creature used in the *māwaewae* ceremony for babies, but not edible. This is the largest Hawaiʻi species. It is greenish, and a large specimen can be 1 inch long. It is found in holes and under rubble in tide pools.

kūhonu. Edible spotted-back crab *(Portunus sanguinolentus)*. This swimming crab carries barnacles. A large specimen may measure $1\frac{1}{2}$ inches between the tips of the long lateral spines. This species is popular in Honolulu markets.

kūkūau. Large grapsid crab *(Metopograpsus messor)*, which may measure $1\frac{1}{2}$ inches across the carapace. It is gray to dark green or black. It is common under stones on muddy, flat reefs near river mouths.

kukuma. Crab (perhaps *Aphanodactylus edmondsoni*), whitish, of the *paiʻea* species. This small crab lives as a commensal in the tube of a large terebellid worm.

kūnounou. Sea cucumber, Hawaiian or oriental. Also called *hula-ki, loli*.

leho. General name for cowry shells *(Cypraea spp.)*.

leho kupa. Serpent-head cowry *(Cypraea caputserpentis)*. Most common of the Hawaiian cowries, it is chiefly herbivorous. *Lit.,* cowry native. (EAK 189.)

leho lei. White money cowry *(Cypraea moneta)*. Rare in Hawaiʻi. The scientific name *moneta* comes from its use as money or barter in other Pacific Isles. I am told that Queen Kapiolani wore a *lei* of these in London when she attended Queen Victoria's Jubilee. The white shells were held over smoke to give them an ivory hue. (KILO.; EAK 196.)

leho ʻōmaʻo. Greenish cowry, *leho* series. This description might fit a diseased shell.

leho-paʻa. Brown, humpbacked-cowry shell *(Cypraea mauritiana)*. Commonly found in shallow water under ledges and in crevices of basalt outcrops. (EAK 196.)

leho pāuhu. Cowry *(Cypraea schilderorum)*. These sea animals occur in moderately deep water from Fiji throughout Polynesia. (EAK 196.)

leho pouli. Very dark brown cowry *(Cypraea mauritiana)*. See **leho-paʻa.**

leho ʻuala. Dark-yellow money cowry *(Cypraea moneta)*. *Lit.,* sweet potato cowry. See **leho lei.**

leho ʻula. Red-shelled *leho,* rare and treasured cowry. It is a good color for octopus fishing.

lepelepe o Hina. Red, soft-bodied marine mollusk, classified as an opisthobranch. *Hina* is a reference to the goddess, protectress of Molokaʻi.

luheʻe. Fishing for octopus with a line and a cowry lure. Also the name of the lure.

mahina. Eye of a snail in the end of its horn.

makaʻaoa. Shellfish *(Melampus castaneus).* Known throughout the tropical Pacific. Found with *Laemondonta* and *Pedipes* in the supraspray zone under rocks and rubble. See *ʻaoa.* (EAK 491.)

moʻala. Edible crab *(Podophthalmus vigil)* found in shallow waters. One of the largest swimming crabs in Hawaiʻi, up to 5 inches broad. It is used for food and is available in fish markets.

moamoa waʻa. Paper nautilus *(Argonauta argo). Lit.,* fleet of canoes with two sails. See *ʻau waʻa lā lua.*

muheʻe. Squid *(Septioteuthus lessoniana)* that moves two ways like a crab. It is caught in nets and is a common squid in the Hawaiʻi market. (EAK 588.)

nahanawele, nahawele. Edible shellfish (family Isognomonidae), a bivalve. Also called *nakawele, mahawele;* Toothed pearl shells.

naka. Mollusk similar to *kua poi.* Also a general name for sea creatures.

ʻōhiki. Sand crab or sandpiper *(Ocypode ceratophthalma),* a sand burrower.

ʻōhiki ʻau moana. Crab found in the open sea (subfamily Grapsinae). *Lit.,* ocean swimming *ʻōhiki.*

ʻōkala. Shellfish *(Cypraea granulata),* a cowry. *Lit.,* rough cowry. This species is endemic to the Hawaiian Islands and prized in collections. Also called *leho ʻōkala.* (EAK 193.)

ʻōkalekale. Probably a reduplicate of *ʻōkala.*

ʻōkohekohe. Small barnacle that attaches itself to the wood of a ship's hull, floating logs, or timber generally.

ʻōkole emiemi. Sea anemone. *Lit.,* contracting *ʻōkole.*

ʻōkole hāwele. Sea anemone. *Lit.,* bound up *ʻōkole.*

ʻōle. Conch shell *(Charonia tritonis).* Also called *pū kani,* speaking trumpet. (EAK 215.)

ʻōlepe. Bivalve that resembles the *pipi (Pinctada radiata),* the Hawaiian pearl oyster. A common shallow water species along shores of the main Hawaiian islands. Once plentiful in Pearl Harbor and Kaneohe Bay. (EAK 518.)

'ōlopelope. Species of small shrimp found in taro patches; larva of the dragonfly.

'ōpae. General name for shrimps, fresh- and saltwater.

'ōpae kala 'ole. Freshwater spineless shrimp. Also called *'ōpae kuahiwi,* mountain shrimp.

'ōpae 'oeha'a. Clawed shrimp *(Macrobrachium grandimanus)*, found in mountain streams and ponds. *Lit.,* shrimp crooked walking.

'opihi. Shellfish *(Cellana sandwicensis, C. exarata,* and *C. talcosa)* or limpet. Said to be the most commonly eaten shellfish. Associated with the helmet urchin *(Colobocentrotus atratus).* Common along shores of all windward islands. (EAK 46.)

ōunauna. Hermit crab (family Paguridae). The crab occupies the empty shell of gastropods. See **unauna.**

'owā'owaka, 'oā oaha. Bivalve mollusk *(Isognomon* spp.). *Lit.,* open-shut mouth. (EAK 521.)

pā. Mother-of-pearl shellfish *(Pinctada margaritifera)*. Once common in Pearl and Hermes Reef in the leeward islands, now rare. It is the shiny shell-lure on the bonito or *aku* hook. (EAK 518.)

pai. Snail poisonous to the touch.

pai'ea. Soft-shell crab (family Grapsidae). Edible. Pai'ea was one of the names of Kamehameha I. See **'a'ama, kuapa'a.**

pa'imalau, po'imalau. Portuguese man-of-war *(Physalia utriculus)*, a jellyfish, with a float having a powerful sting in its long, stringlike tentacles. It floats in the ocean like the *'au wa'a lā lua* (paper nautilus).

panapanapuhi. Thick-shelled, gray rock oyster *(Spondylus tenebrosus).* (EAK 532.) Hawai'i's largest bivalve, it was once abundant in Pearl Harbor. It is the most common Hawaiian spondyli and is found in tide pools and reef fringes.

pāpa'i. General name for crabs.

pāpa'i 'āloa. Small reddish crab from the mud flats. Also called *maka'āloa.*

pāpa'i kuapā. Hard-shell crab of the *pai'ea* group.

pāpa'i kūhonu. Edible spotted-back crab *(Portunus sanguinolentus).* It can be eaten raw or cooked. *Lit.,* turtle back.

pāpa'i Lāna'i. Name of a small crab. (A.)

pāpaua. Bivalve *(Isognomon* spp.) found attached to stones submerged in shallow water. (EAK 521.)

paua. Rare bivalve, clam. Also called *pāpaua.*

pāuhu. Cowry shell *(Cypraea schilderorum)* used on the octopus lure. See **leho pāuhu.**

pauiwa. Bivalve, oyster. See **pāpaua.**

pe'a. Starfish, an echinoderm (class Asteroidiae). Also called *hōkūkai, 'ōpe'ape'a, pe'ape'a.*

pe'eone. Sand crab *(Hippa pacifica)* that hides itself by going into the sand backwards. *Lit.,* sand hiding.

pī'oe'oe. Bivalve (family Isognomonidae). (EAK 520.) General term for barnacles. Also called *mahawele, nahawele.*

pipi. Hawaiian pearl oyster *(Pinctada margaritifera).* In songs it is best known as *i'a hāmau leo o 'Ewa,* Ewa's silent sea creature, as it was believed that talking would cause a breeze to ripple the water and frighten the *pipi.* (EAK 516.)

pipipi. General name for small edible mollusks (including *Nerita picea, N. theodoxus*). After cooking, the flesh was removed with a bone pick. (EAK 63.)

po'apo'ai. Wormlike marine mollusk (family Vermetidae), a small, coiling shellfish. Most of the species listed by E. Allison Kay are "described" from the Hawaiian Islands.

pōhaku hele, pōhaku hali. Crab (family Leucosiidae). *Lit.,* stone fetcher.

pokipoki, popoki. Hard-shell, gray box-crab *(Calappa hepatica),* not preferred for eating.

pololei kāhuli. Tree shells, land shells, called descriptively *kani kua mauna,* singing on the mountain ridges, and *pūpū kani oe,* singing shells. These small, colorful mollusks have no vocal organs. The chirping sounds are made by crickets living inconspicuously in the trees near the shells. Chants, songs, and *hula* have been composed about the *kāhuli.*

po'o palaoa. Cream-white nerita or *kūpe'e* shell. *Lit.,* head covering, head ivory. The *kūpe'e* was an emblem of mourning for the *ali'i* (chiefs). Shells of *Nerita polita* were used for adornment. (EAK 65.)

popoki. Crab, var. of *pokipoki.*

pūhali. Small, delicate seashell (family Janthinidae). Three species are recorded in Hawai'i. They are associated with the Portuguese man-of-war *(Vellela* and *Physalia)* on which they feed and with which they are cast upon shores after a storm. Floats readily. *Lit.,* a seashell carried. (EAK 157.)

pū ho'okani. Shell trumpet, conch shell *(Charonia tritonis),* second in size of all gastropods in the Indo-West Pacific. Feeds on starfish and sea urchins. *Lit.,* triton shell sounding. (EAK 215.)

pūleho. Small shellfish; long, slender cowry *(Cypraea isabella),* used in *lei* making. A shallow water species, well known and widely distributed. (EAK 193.)

pūpū. General name for sea and land shells; a snail. The meat of the larger ones is relished by the Hawaiians. (Hal. 58:8.)

pūpū alea alea. Snakehead cowry *(Cypraea caputserpentis).* A Kauaʻi name. Most common species of the genus in the Hawaiian Islands. Found in shallow water under loose rocks and boulders along the shoreline. (EAK 215.)

pūpūʻawa. Seashell *(Drupa ricina)* abundant in the intertidal zones. It feeds on worms and mollusks. Well known throughout the Indo-West Pacific. (EAK 241.) The word *ʻawa* warns that it is bitter when eaten raw, but some people enjoy the flavor. The bitterness is destroyed in cooking. Also called *aupūpū* and *makaloa.*

pūpū hakuli. Class of small shells. (A.)

pūpū lo loa. Auger shell (Terebridae family), so called from its long, spiral form. *Lit.,* shell long.

pūpū ʻōa ʻoaka, ʻowaka. Shellfish, bivalve (family Isognomonidae). *Lit.,* shell open-shut mouth.

pūpū poapoʻai. Wormlike shell *(Dendropoma* or *Vermelis* spp.). The coiled shells are found cemented to boulders and on reefs.

ʻuala, ʻuwale. Sweet potato cowry shell. Rare, dark-yellow form of the money cowry shell. Also called *lehoʻuala.* (EAK 196.)

uhi. Large mother-of-pearl oyster. The shell is used in making *aku* hooks called *pā (Pinctada nebulosa).* See **paua.** (EAK 518.)

ula. Hawaiian lobster *(Panulirus japonicus).* Large specimens may reach up to 15 inches long.

ula hiwa. Dark-colored lobster; delicious, choice.

ula pāpapa. Gray crayfish *(Paribaccus antarcticus). Lit., ula* flat.

unauna, ōunauna, pāpaʻi iwi pūpū. Hermit crabs in general.

wana. Sea egg, sea urchin *(Centrechinus paucispinus).* In the adult stage it has long black spines equal in length to the diameter of the shell—nearly 4 inches. This species can produce painful injuries.

SKIES

Hawaiians felt great admiration and respect for the wonders of nature. This interest shows in their coining of words to describe the objects and happenings of nature.

Their choices were graphic and styled appropriately, using from one to several syllables arranged in clauses and phrases.

Sometimes they could not account for certain natural phenomena, as, for example, the blue sky. They thought of it in terms of a blue cloud, compounded from *ao* (daylight) and *uli,* the dark blue of a blue-black cloud.

Most of the Hawaiian words or phrases in this category are based on David Malo's *Hawaiian Antiquities.*

aoūli. Blue cloud; sky, firmament.

halenale. Clear moonlight.

hiki ku. Portion of the sky above the horizon.

kahiki kapu i holani ke kuina. Sky directly overhead; meeting place. (MALO 10.) *Lit.,* sacred *kahiki* at *holani.*

kahiki ke papa lani. Region in the sky just below *kahiki kapu i holani ke kuina.* (MALO 10.)

kahiki ke papa nu'u. Region in the sky just below the *kahiki ke papa lani.* (MALO 10.)

kahiki kū. Lowest of the four layers of the sky; place of the sun's rising; poetically, the east; generally the circle of the sky that bends upward from the horizon. (MALO 10.)

kahiki moe. Circle or zone of the earth's surface, whether sea or land, that the eye scans in looking to the horizon. *Lit.,* prostrate *kahiki.* (MALO 10.)

kālanipa'a. Broad blue sky; the fixed, strong firmament.

kama ku i kāhi lewa. Sky just below the zenith.

kapa'ailalo. Any place below the heaven, even below the earth.

kapa'ailuna. Arch of heaven above, supposed to be firm and strong.

kūkulu o kahonua. Circle of the horizon encompassing the earth at the borders of the ocean, where the sea meets the base of the heavens. (MALO 10.)

kūkulu o kalani. Border of the sky where it meets the ocean horizon; the walls of heaven. (MALO 10.)

kumulani. Horizon; bottom of the sky.

lani. Sky, heaven.

lani ha'aha'a. Low sky.

lewa. Foundation of the sky.

lewa ho'omakua. Space in the sky just above the earth; lowest atmosphere.

lewa lani. Highest stratum in the sky; the heavens.

lewa lani lewa. Atmospheric zone just above the *lewa ho'omakua.*

lewa nu'u. Atmospheric zone just below the *lewa lani.* (MALO 10.)

mahina. Moon; lunar month.

nae. Upper regions of the air; place from which the winds come.

pā, paʻa. To blow, as the wind.

palamea. Pure, clear atmosphere; appearance of the heavenly bodies with the beautiful blue of the sky. (A.)

papa lani. General term for the upper atmosphere; upper heavens.

pā uliuli. Dark blue, as the sky in the evening near the horizon. Such a sky is one of the signs of a *kai koʻo* or high surf.

pawa. Sky; blue expanse of the sky; darkness before dawn.

uila. Lightning.

STARS AND CONSTELLATIONS

The Hawaiians had names for all the planets (with the possible exception of Neptune) and for constellations such as the Big Dipper, Pleiades, Aquila, and the twins, Castor and Pollux.

They were intrigued with meteors, comets, and the Milky Way, but although approaching an understanding of these phenomena, they lacked some of the tools needed to improve on their observations. They had already begun to see the reoccurrence of certain phenomena and to probe the mystery of repetition. Had they been able to maintain written records over many years, they would have developed even greater competency in star watching.

This category only hints at the number of stars bearing Hawaiian names. Pukui-Elbert lists 216; Johnson and Mahelona, in *Nā Inoa Hōkū,* list over 300, less than half of which have been identified with the stars recognized by astronomers today.

ʻalepa. Alpha. Some star, usually the brightest in a constellation, would be designated Alpha. For example, in the constellation Lyra, the star might be Vega.

analipo. Place supposed to be beyond the stars, out of sight but really below the horizon.

ʻAua. Betelgeuse.

Au-haele. Name of a star, companion to Hōkū-ula and Paikauhale. The three may be Sigma, Antares, and Tau Scorpii.

Heleekela, Hereekela. Planet Uranus. Its name in Hawaiian derives from that of its discoverer, Sir William Herschel. *Eng.*

hoaka. Crescent of the new moon.

Hōkū-ʻaeʻa. Moving star, meaning a planet. *Lit.,* star wandering.

Hōkū-'ai-'aina. Navigator star. *Lit.*, star ruling land.

Hōkū-ao. Morning star. Applied to the planet Venus when it is in the proper position. It was used in navigation to Hawai'i from Tahiti. Also called *Hōkū-ali'i, Hōkū-loa.*

Hōkū-ho'okele-wa'a. Sirius. Its appearance was the signal for sailing on a voyage. *Lit.*, star canoe-guiding.

Hōkū-hue-lō'ihi. Long-tailed star. See **hōkū-puhi-paka, hōkū-welowelo.**

Hōkū-'iwa. Hawaiian constellation. *Lit.*, star frigate-bird. (PE.) Perhaps the constellation Bootes.

Hōkū-kau 'ōpae. Sirius; evening star. *Lit.*, star for placing shrimps.

Hōkū-ke'a. Southern Cross. See **Newa, Newe.** *Lit.*, star cross.

Hōkū-komohana. Morning star; Venus. *Lit.*, star western.

Hōkū-le'a. Arcturus, the zenith star for Hawai'i. It moves directly overhead in Hawai'i. *Lit.*, star clear or joyful.

Hōkū-lele. Meteor; shooting star.

Hōkū-lewa. Star in motion; planet.

Hōkū-makapa. Sobriquet for the star Polo-ahi-lani, said to be associated with Polo-ula and Mūlehu in a triangle. May be Alpha, Beta, and Gamma—Cassiopeia.

Hōkū-noho-aupuni. Milky Way. Also *Kau, Lele-aka, Leileona, Pae-loa-hiki.*

Hōkū-pā. Constellation Leo. *Lit.*, star fence.

Hōkū pa'a. North star. *Lit.*, the star fixed or unmoving. See **Kio-pa'a.**

hōkū puhi paka (baka). Comet, called by the Hawaiians a tobacco-smoking star.

hōkū-ukali. Following or satellite star. See **Ukali.**

Hōkū-'ula. *Lit.*, red star. In tradition it might be Mercury, but from the Hawaiian meaning, red star, it might be Antares, principal star of Scorpio. Also called Scorpio's Heart.

hōkū-welowelo. Comet, from its tail of light. *Lit.*, star streaming.

Holoholo-pīna'au. Planet Mars. See **Mareka.**

Ho'omañalonalo. Planets Venus and Jupiter. Other names are Iao (Morning star); Ikiiki (Jupiter); Ikaika (Jupiter); Mānalo, name reported for both Venus and Jupiter.

Hukui. Cluster; the Pleiades of seven stars. Also called *Huhui, Huihui.* The common name is Makali'i. Also *Kūpuku.*

Humama. Cluster of three stars in a row in the constellation Aquila.

Humu. Altair, a star of the first magnitude in Aquila, a southern constellation in the Milky Way; the Eagle.

Ī'a. Galaxy or Milky Way.

'imo 'imo. Twinkling star.

Īupita, Īupika. Jupiter. The earliest name was Ka'ā-wela, a name which may now apply to either the planet Venus or Jupiter.

Ka'a-wela. Planet Venus. This name was originally used for Jupiter.

Kaekae. Name of a star. No data.

Kamahana. Constellation Gemini. *Lit.,* twins. Also called Nā mahoe. The twins are Nānā-mua, Castor (*Lit.,* looking ahead); Nānā-hope, Pollux (*Lit.,* looking back). Donald Kilolani Mitchell reports his membership on a committee that funded the purchase of two 'iako (outrigger booms) on the twin-hulled Hōkūle'a. His suggestion resulted in the booms' names, Nānā-mua and Nānā-hope.

kaoma'aikū. Aldebaran, a red star of the first magnitude, in the eye of the constellation Taurus, the Bull's Eye. It is the brightest star in the Hyades.

Kao-makali'i. Dart of Makali'i, a constellation. (KEP. 79.)

Kape'a. Constellation named Crux or the Southern Cross. *Lit.,* the cross. See **Newa.**

Kaua-mea. Constellation, possibly Corona Borealis.

ke alanui a ke ku'uku'u. Term for equator. *Lit.,* the path of the spider which follows a single string. Also called *Ka Piko o Wākea,* the way to the navel of Wākea.

ke alanui ma'awe-'ula a Kanaloa, road of the scarlet footprint of Kanaloa. Reference to the western sky. (PE.)

ke alanui polohiwa a Kanaloa, the dark path of Kanaloa. Reference to the southern limit of the sun, the Tropic of Capricorn.

ke alanui polohiwa a Kāne, the dark path of Kāne. Reference to the northern limit of the sun, the Tropic of Cancer.

ke alaula a Kāne, the flaming path of Kāne. Reference to the eastern sky.

Keoe. Constellation Lyra with its brightest star, Vega.

Kio-pa'a. North star. *Lit.,* fixed projection. See **Hōkū-pa'a.**

kiwikiwi. Horns, as of the new moon. (CMH.)

koili. To set, go down, as the moon, seemingly, on the surface of the sea.

koli. Something moving through the air; meteor.

Ku-loa, Hōkū-loa, Hōkū-ao. Morning star, Venus.

Lawai'a. Name of a group of seven stars.

lele. To move through the air, as a meteor.

Lele-aka. White belt of stars in the heavens, the Milky Way. See **Hōkū-noho-aupuni.**

Leleiona. Milky Way.

lele piʻo. To fly in a curve *(piʻo)*, as a meteor through the sky; to move along, as a comet showing its tail.

Lono-muku. Woman of the Moon. When Hina-i-ka-malama leaped from earth for the moon, her husband caught her leg and broke *(muku)* it off. She has ever since been called Lono-muku.

lua hoana. Rainbow or halo around the moon or sun. *Lit.,* pit polished.

lua kālai. Halo around the sun or moon in cloudy or hazy weather.

mahina. Moon; lunar month.

Maka-holo-waʻa. North Star.

Maka-ʻimoʻimo. Constellation in the Milky Way. *Lit.,* eyes twinkling.

Maka-ʻio-lani. Name of a star. *Lit.,* eye of the royal hawk.

Makaliʻi. Pleiades. This is the preferred name all over the Pacific.

Makeaupeʻa. Name of a constellation that, because *peʻa* refers to cross, may be the Southern Cross.

Makulu. Planet Saturn.

Mānanalo. Planet Venus. See **Kaʻā-wela.**

Mareka. Hawaiianized word for the planet Mars. See **Holoholo-pīnaʻau.**

Nāhiku. Big Dipper, constellation with seven stars. Also called Kīaha. *Lit.,* the seven.

Nā-hōkū mahana. The twins: Castor (Nānā-mua) and Pollux (Nānā-hope).

Nāholoholo. Hawaiian name for the planet Venus, as it appears in the morning sky. See **Hōkū-ao.**

Nā-kao. Belt and sword in the constellation of Orion. See **ʻOliona.** (Ioba 9:9.) *Lit.,* the darts.

nakoʻo. Constellation with five stars. (CMH.)

Nā-mahoe. Castor and Pollux.

napoʻo. The going down or setting of the sun.

Newa, Newe. Southern Cross; a boat-steering star. Also refers to Keoe, a constellation of Lyra including Vega. See **Hōkū-keʻa.**

Nuʻu-anu. Name of a star. No data.

ʻOliona, Oriona. Orion. (Ioba 9:9.) See **Nā-kao.**

ʻōnahanaha. Halo of the moon.

papawai. Name of a cluster of stars. No data. (CMH.)

piko-o-Wākea. Equator.

Puana-kau. Rigel, a star; tutelary star of West Maui. (PE.)

Puʻuwepa. Name of a star. No data. (PE.)

Saturena. Hawaiianized word for the planet Saturn. See **Makulu.**

Ukali, Ukali-aliʻi. Planet Mercury, so called from its following close after the sun. *Lit.,* following the chief.

STONES, METALS, AND EARTH

There was a real dearth of workable metals in Hawaiʻi, but earth of various kinds was plentiful; there was sand, limestone, clay, and coral, in addition to the basic lavas; and stones of all sizes and shapes were abundant.

Aside from *heiau* platforms and *imu* cooking, stones were used chiefly for the *koʻi* (adze); the *maika,* the very smooth, rounded disks for bowling; and the soft, porous stones used for rubbing and polishing articles made of wood and bone.

Hao (iron) was introduced to Hawaiʻi natives through the nails, knives, pieces of scrap-iron, carpenters' tools, ships' hardware, muskets, cannon, and a great miscellany of the metal articles aboard Captain Cook's ships. This gave rise to a mini-industrial revolution in the islands.

ʻaʻā. Lava rough to walk on and work in. This rough lava consists of jagged clinkers and cinders.

ʻākoakoa. Horned coral; coral generally; a precious stone. (Ioba 28:18.)

ʻalā. A hard rock found at Kaneleau, Puna, which was turned into smooth ovoid stones for slingstones. The *wiliau,* with its circular eddying motion in the ocean, shaped pieces of rock for this purpose. *ʻĀla o ka maʻa,* slingstone. (Zek. 9:15.)

ʻalaea. Water-soluble dirt or clay, a red ochre. *Kuʻi ʻalaea,* priests who used this colored earth to mark land limits. Due to the presence of iron oxide, it was used as pigmentation in salt, medicine, and dye.

ʻalahinuhinu. A bright, lustrous, and polished stone used as a mirror.

ʻalāmea. Hard stone of volcanic origin used in making the adze *(koʻi).*

ʻalamole. Species of stone. No data. (A.)

ʻāla o kamaʻa. Slingstone. (Zek. 9:15.)

alaʻula. Kind of red chalk, sterile for growth; red dust in a road; red dust, generally.

'ana. Pumice found in the sea, used by nurses to clean the tongues of children by rubbing off *'ea,* a white fur caused by the thrush disease. Also used in rubbing and polishing canoes.

aniani. Mirror, glass.

aniani kilohi. Mirror, looking glass.

aniani pa'alima. Hand mirror.

au. Pumice; soft, porous stone.

'awali'i. Hard stone used for making the adze. See **'alāmea, ehuehu, hai'ali'i.**

ehō. Stone pile; *imu* stones; pillar. (FOR 5:65.)

ehuehu. Kind of hard rock used to make the adze. (MALO 19.)

'eku'ekū. To dig up and turn over earth, as for planting.

'elekū. A coarse, brittle stone, *he pōhaku 'elekū.*

'elikū. Porous black lava, used in the earth oven. (CMH.)

gula, kula. Gold.

hai'ali'i. Hard stone used to make the adze. (MALO 19.)

haku. Name of several pieces of hard stone used in making the adze.

haku kā ko'i. Stone for chipping.

hāpou. Pumice, a soft, porous stone. Also called *'ōla'i.*

hau'ele. The native Glauber salts dug from caverns on Hawai'i island; sulphate of soda.

hauone. Soft limestone.

hāwena. Chalk or similar substance. (A.) White lime used for dressing hair. (PE.)

hiena. A soft, porous stone used to polish wood articles and utensils. *'Ana,* a lighter stone than *hiena,* was used to cure *'ea* (coated tongue). Also used in rubbing and polishing canoes.

honokeana. A soft, porous stone.

ho'ōne. Pumice; to rub and polish with sand. (PE.)

huipa. A hard, black stone used in making the *maika,* a flat, round sliding stone; an ancient Hawaiian game suggestive of bowling; the game of *maika.*

hule'ia. A soft, porous stone. See **'ana.**

humu'ula. Red jasper, a very hard stone of which the *ko'i* (adze) was made.

ihi makua. Stone for making the *maika* stones. See **ulu maika.**

'ili'ili. Waterworn pebbles, rounded stones.

'ili'ili hānau. Birth pebbles of Kō-loa, Punalu'u, Ka'ū, which were believed to reproduce themselves. Some of the smooth stones were considered male, the porous stones female.

'ili'ili nemonemo. The smooth *'ili'ili hānau* pebbles, considered the male type. (CMH.)

'ili'ili puka. The porous female type of *'ili'ili hānau* pebbles.

ipu hao. Iron pot.

ipu lepo. Earthen pot.

kā'alā. Species of porous stone.

ka'au'aupu'u. Hard rock used in shaping the *maika* stone.

kahua pa'a. Solid earth, *terra firma.*

kalai pōhaku. Stone; stone cutter. (2 Sam. 5:11.)

kāla ke'oke'o. Silver money.

kalama'ula. Stone for making the *maika.* See **humu'ula.**

kanawao. Hard, heavy stone found in brooks and streams, used in war with a sling.

kaua 'ula. A soft, porous stone used for rubbing and polishing; stone sinker used as a squid lure.

ka'ulaīhi. Smooth, pinkish, slightly porous stone.

kāwa'ewa'e. Stone for polishing canoes.

ka wahine 'ai honua. Pele, the earth-devouring woman. (PE.)

ke'e. Hard stone for shaping an adze.

kei. Hard stone for making an adze.

keleawe. Copper, tin, brass. *Kui keleawe,* an artificer in these metals.

kēpau. Lead, pewter.

kepue. Hard stone used for the adze. Also called *humu'ula.*

kihikihi. Coin of the California gold rush period, so called because of its crescent shape. (PE.)

kīpōpō. Stone used for chipping the *ko'i* (adze, axe).

ko'a. Coral rock, *'āko'ako'a.*

kohenalo. Stone with coarse striations, used in smoothing wood or stone.

kolekole. Red earth or clay.

kuakea. To be white, as chalk or salt on or about salt ponds; to bleach white.

kui. Pointed instrument of metal or wood.

kumuma'oma'o. Green stone from which the *maika* could be made.

kumuone. Sandstone for making a *maika. Lit.,* sand base.

kūpaoa. Porous stone from which octopus sinkers were made. (PE.)

lau kea. Hard, gray stone from which adzes were made.

lei ole. Soft, porous stone; a pumice used for polishing and medicine.

lepo. General term for dirt, earth, ground.

lepo hī'aha. Clay prepared for pottery. (Isa. 45:9.)

lepo kāwilī. Adobe, clay. (Isa. 41:25.)

lepo pa'a. Solid earth.

lepo pohō. Marshy ground; marsh. (Ioba 8:11.)

lepo ʻulaʻula. Marshy ground; marsh. (Ioba 8:11.)

loaʻā. Rough, scraggy coral rock or lava slab.

luehu. A soft, porous, brittle rock.

lūheʻe. A material unlike any other. Used in making cowry octopus lures.

maheu. Porous stone used to scour, rub, and polish.

māʻili. Pebble used as a sinker in squid fishing.

mākā. A very hard stone from which the *maika* was shaped.

makaʻāwela, makawela, makawelawela. Soft, porous stone out of which sinkers for cowry octopus lures were made.

makiki. Soft, porous stone used in making the *maika,* sinkers for octopus lures, adzes.

māpala, māpela. Marble.

māʻulaʻula. Red earth or clay used in coloring that was obtained in deep ravines.

mauna. Hard stone for making the *koʻi* (adze).

mekala, metala. Metal.

melemele. Brass. (CMH.)

nohu, nohunohu. Soft, porous stone used for scouring.

noninui. Soft, pinkish, porous stone used in polishing.

ʻōahi. Rough stone or pumice, used in polishing the calabash, canoe, and surfboard.

ʻōʻio. Stone for polishing canoes and calabashes.

one. Sand; *hoʻōne,* to rub and polish with sand.

ʻoʻolopua. Stone of which the *maika* was made. (CMH.)

paʻakea. Stone out of which the *maika* was shaped. (A.) Limestone or coral beds found on the leeward sides of the islands. *Lit.,* hardness white. (PE.)

paea. Flint. Probably a modern word. It is the Hawaiian pronunciation for fire, which is connected with flint. (Isa. 50:7.)

pāhoehoe. Smooth, unbroken, flat lava. It contrasts with *ʻaʻā,* the rough lava. These two words are commonly accepted and used to describe the lavas by scientists writing textbooks in any language in the world. When so used they are written *aa* and *pahoehoe,* omitting the diacritical marks.

pākea. White stone found at Wai-mea, Hawaiʻi.

pālolo. Adhesive mud; whitish clay; clay mortar. (Puk. 1:14.)

papa. Stone used as a sinker for *lūheʻe* (octopus lure). (MALO 138.)

pāpaʻakea. Soft, white stone found above Lahaina, Maui; limestone. See **paʻakea.**

pā pōhaku. Stone wall; soft stone.

pī wai. Hard rock from which the adze was made. (FOR 5:319.)

pōhā kea. White stone; limestone.

pōhaku. General name for stones, rocks, pebbles. *Pali pōhaku,* large stones; *pōhakū uʻuku,* lesser stones; *ʻiliʻili,* small stones worn smooth in the water; *ʻaʻā,* melted rocks.

pōhaku keʻokeʻo. Marble. *Lit.,* white stone. (Hoik. 18:12.)

pōhaku paʻa. General name for solid hard stones. (Ioba 28:9.)

pōhaku paea. Flint. (Ezek. 3:9.)

poho. Chalky, white earth; chalk.

pōhuehue. Stone used in polishing canoes.

polipoli. Soft, porous stone used for polishing and rounding an adze. Also used for polishing sinkers for squid lures.

puna. Unburned lime; mortar, coral, stone. (Oihk. 14:42.)

puna kea. White coral sand thrown up on the beach by a high surf.

puʻupā. Stone out of which the *maika* is made. See **ʻulu maika.**

ʻūlikalika. To adhere to like wax, or any gluey substance like mud or clay; like *kalo* that is *loliloli* (water-soaked).

ʻulu maika. Name of the ancient bowling game played on a flat surface or a roadway. This phrase is used interchangeably with the biconvex rolling stone, *maika.* Each is the name of the game and the stone.

unu. Small stones between *ʻiliʻili* and *makaliʻi* in size; small chips or stones for propping up and sustaining large ones or wedging posts in the ground.

waianuʻukole. Soft, porous stone used in medicine or for squid sinkers. (MALO 19.)

waiehu. File or rough stone; any substance that will grind or polish iron.

waimano. Name of a soft porous stone. Octopus sinkers were made of this. (MALO 19.)

SUGARCANE

Sugarcane is native to tropical regions of the world, India, and New Guinea, from where it was taken northward to China and Japan. Some consider New Guinea to be its original home. Hawaiʻi received it from the Marquesas Islands and Tahiti.

The list that follows includes those varieties known to Hawaiians that were listed by Daniel K. Kamakea in January 1872 and published in the *Fornander Collection of Folklore* (Bishop Museum Memoirs, 1918–1919, Vol. V, pp. 522–88.)

The distinguishing of the Badila and Laukona Groups, as mentioned below, was accomplished in a paper presented by W. W. G. Moir before the Society of Sugar Technologists Fourth Congress, Bulletin No. 7, 1932.

Polynesian Sugarcane: Group I

kō. Sugarcane, *Saccharum officinarum*. Below are varieties.

A. *'Aki-lolo* family.

'aki lolo. Cane named after the bird wrasse fish *(Gomphasus varius)* for its coloration. Striped green and deep purplish-red when young, yellow and deep red on older exposed stalks. Leaf sheath striped with purple.

nānahu. Red mutant of *'aki lolo*. Solid purple leaf sheath and fairly heavy purple cast to the leaves.

'ōhi'a. Coloration same as the *'ōhi'a 'ai* tree from whence it derives its name. Deep red and green striped, becoming bronze-red and yellow-brown on exposure. Leaves somewhat variegated.

pakaweli, hou, pailolo. Certain islands have different names for this cane. Deep purple-red and green-striped, much like the *'aki lolo*. It produces mutants of yellow and solid red similar to *nānahu* and *pili-mai*. Named after the *hou,* surge wrasse fish *(Thalassoma pupureum)* for its coloration.

pili mai. Yellow-green mutant of *'aki lolo,* very similar to *'aki lolo* in appearance. This *pili mai* (cuddling) was used to promote a short but temporary love affair by a *kahuna*. His patient drank the recommended juice to enhance his charms.

B. *'Akoki* family.

'akoki. This cane has a very dark-brown pith. The top is very heavy and the leaves somewhat larger than *'aki lolo*. Stalks are usually larger and plants more vigorous in appearance, especially in wetter districts where *'aki lolo* does not thrive. Kamakea: Deep red and green when young, changing to purple and yellow on exposure. Insipid when eaten.

maka'a. Faint, green-striped mutant of *'uala*. Named after a fish *(Carangus politus)* because of its markings.

papa'a. Deep red or purple mutant of *'akoki,* with large stalks and a purple-striped leaf sheath that contrasts with the solid color of *nānahu*. Has an odor similar to burnt sugar. Kamakea: This cane was first named *papa'a* from a land called Kā-papa'a, used by a *kahuna* to nurture a life-lasting love affair.

'uala. Yellow mutant of *'akoki*. It has very large stalks, and is often called *pili mai* because of a close similarity, but it is a stronger cane.

C. *Manulele* family.

honua-'ula. Variety of sugarcane, a dark brown-red mutant of *manulele*. The leaf sheath and leaves are purple. Newly striped stalks are a dirty brown. It was formerly used as a medicine and is one of the best canes for eating raw. It was one of the early canes used in love making. *Lit.*, red earth.

manulele. Variety of sugarcane with dark brown pith. Has opposite buds on medium height stalks. It is yellow-brown with red-brown stripes underlaid with green, changing to buff-brown and maroon on exposed stalks. *Lit.*, flying bird. Kamakea: Leaves have a purplish cast striped with white. Used in sorcery to establish a life-long love. Valuable medicinally. (NEAL 79.)

mīkokoi. Lighter brown mutant of *manulele*, but no purple cast to leaves or sheath.

D. *'Aina kea* family. This cane family may be related to the *'Akohi* family.

'aina-kea. Cane with opposite buds, pith generally dark. Striped maroon-red when young, changing to purplish-red and yellow when mature. It is a pretty cane. It could be mistaken for *'ōhi'a* when young. The leaves are somewhat variegated, and leaf sheaths are distinctly striped with white. Used medicinally.

yellow 'aina kea. Yellow mutant of *'aina kea*. The pith is dark brown. Very similar to *'uala*.

E. *'Āwela* family, *Holocentrus*.

alaihi. Deep-red cane with a purple leaf sheath. Leaves have a purple cast. Named for the squirrel fish *(Adioyx lacteoguttatus)*.

'āwela, pua 'ole. Flowerless cane, yellow and green striped, that becomes flushed with rose in the sun. The leaves are variegated, the leaf sheath striped with white. Named for the *'āwela* fish because of its markings. (HP 221, 224.)

uluhui, ule'ohi'u. Bronze-yellow mutant of *'āwela* (or vice versa). On exposure to the sun it takes on a deep, reddish-bronze cast over the yellow-like gold. Kamakea: Discovered by Kalua and Paiaalani. The latter suggested he use the cane juice to cover his boils and sores: boil it in hot water, drink some, and rub it in the skin. Insipid when eaten. Also soft.

F. *Palani* or Moloka'i *'akoki* family. A markedly *Badila* type with dark pith, short stalks, and buds not opposite.

Moloka'i 'akoki. Brownish-purple sugarcane with deep, olive-green stripes; leaves a flush of purple.

palani. Cane with deep, olive-green cast changing to reddish-yellow on exposure to the sun. Leaves and sheath are green. Probably the parent of the Moloka'i *'akoki* and not its mutant. Named after the surgeonfish *(Hepatus dussumieri)* because of its markings.

Lahaina Type Canes: Group II

Canes of the Lahaina type of growth, in contrast to the *Badila,* are usually free tasseling, heavy stooling, rather semi-erect, with large, long, heavy tops.

G. *Laukōnā* family. Vigorous growing, heavy stooling, canes of medium size, dark-brown pith, susceptible to mosaic, eye-spot, and brown stripe diseases. Tassels are long, open, and light.

laukōnā, or manini. The name *laukōnā* refers to its use in the *kahuna* profession, *manini* to its resemblance to the striped fish of this name. It is orange-yellow with light-green stripes changing to pea-green when young or with a rose flush overall. Leaves and sheath are variegated. It frequently mutates to a solid yellow-green named *lahi.* Kamakea: This cane was used in sorcery to reverse earlier magic and break the influence of the *hana aloha* (love magic), turning love into hate.

lahi or 'uala-lehu. The second name was applied later to the yellow bamboo. This one is the yellow mutation of *laukōnā,* the same as *laukōnā* except for variegations and stripes, and very much more robust in growth.

pink striped lahi. A thin, pink cane of light red-striped mutations of *lahi.* Otherwise same as *lahi.*

H. *Māikoiko* family. A very common cane, relished for chewing. Medium stalks; vigorous stooler and grower; opposite buds, very dark brown pith; light yellowish-green leaves with a tinge of red; sheath deep red. This cane seldom tassels.

māikoiko. Named after the *maiko* fish *(Hepatus atramentatus)* for its coloration. *Kō-'ele'ele,* black cane; *kauila,* Niger cane, the blackest cane of the group when exposed to the sun.

striped māikoiko. Buff-brown and maroon striped when young, becoming olive-brown and very deep purple upon exposure. Mutates readily to *māikoiko.*

I. *Uahi-a-Pele* family. Heavy stooling cane; opposite buds; susceptible to eye-spot diseases, heavy tasseler.

pōhina. Smoky cane, almost identical to *uahi-a-Pele* but less vigorous. Dies back after tasseling, which it does freely. Has practically no wax bloom, which gives it a dirty-red to brown color.

uahi-a-Pele. Volcano smoke. A light, red-purple cane with a heavy wax bloom. Also called *na'aukake* (sausagelike) for the shape of the internodes.

J. *Opukea-Halāi'i* family. A vigorous stock cane of the *lahaina* type. Heavy stooler, distinct wax band, not a free tasseler, white pith. Probably the best of all Hawaiian canes.

halāli'i, wehe hala, uku hala. All these names refer to the top of the cane, like a small *hala* tree *(Pandanus odoratissimus)*. Ni'ihau natives saw it growing in the dunes when shifting sands covered the stalks except for the green tops. Lately called *pua'ole* after its red, yellow, and green stripes.

'opukea. Solid yellow cane, the mutant of *halali'i*. It takes on a rosy-red flush on exposure. A celebrated early native found this cane at Laupāhoehoe.

K. *Kea* family. This is the only other family group besides *halāli'i* that has white pith. Erect growth; smallish-sized stalks of greenish yellow; heavy stoolers; compact, green tops; opposite buds.

'ili 'ōpua. This cane is identical to *kea* but never attains its stature, always remaining small. Medium susceptibility to eye-spot and borer.

kea. Best known and most used cane in these listings. Limited height. The erect compact stooling of this cane with its clinging trash leaves the stool in such shape one cannot see through it. Pith is white and dense.

Miscellaneous Canes of Group I

lau loa. Yellow-green, striped with light yellow-brown when young; with exposure it turns a deep olive, striped with dark brown-red. Broad, long green leaves, large-sized stalks. A more robust looking cane than others of this type.

'ōhi'a. Deep red and green stripes when young, becoming bronze-red and yellow-brown on exposure. Colors are the same as the leaves and flowers of the *'ōhi'a-'ai* from which it got its name. The leaf sheath is striped with white, which is usually flushed with pink. Position of buds same as in the *'aki lolo* family to which it is related. Pith very dark brown, opposite buds.

pili ko'a. Yellow-green, with pale-brown stripes when young, changing to deep bronze-yellow with darker red-brown stripes on exposure. Position of buds as in the *'aki lolo* family; pith colored in segments as in *'aina kea*. Named for a fish because of its coloration.

uhu. Dirty-red cane very similar to *lau loa* in general appearance and probably related to it. Deep brown pith.

'ula'ula. A deep claret-red cane of medium size when young, changing to black-purple on exposure. Has a purple leaf sheath and leaves with a strong purple cast. Pith is deep orange-brown.

wai-'ōhi'a. Deep olive-brown striped with dull red. Dark-colored pith. Leaves have no purple cast. Eyes are positioned as in the *'aki lolo* family. A fairly vigorous grower but with small stalks.

Miscellaneous Canes of Group II

hinahina. This cane may be a member of the *laukōnā* group. It is a grayish-green cane with a rosy flush, the whole covered with a very heavy wax bloom. Susceptible to mosaic and eye-spot. General appearance like *lahi*.

lehu. Hairy bamboo cane, a recent arrival. Given the name *lehu* (ashes) because the stunted, mature canes look like dead stalks except for their green leaves. Pith is a green white.

moano. A red cane that becomes dark brown on exposure. Not like the *Badila* canes in cast of color, erectness, or stiffness. Pith is dark brown. Named after the *moano* fish.

'oliana. Cane similar in appearance to *lahaina* in type of growth and color. Pith is very dark brown and the leaf sheath is covered with long, red-brown hairs. Cane is hard.

Miscellaneous Canes: Ungrouped

'āweoweo. This cane was "discovered" during the battle between Kamehameha I and Kīwala'ō at Moku-'ōhai. Formerly it was called *'ōhi'a* but since it was eaten by the hungry in the battle its name was changed. Named for the fish *'āweoaweo (Pricanthus cruentatus)* for its stripings and coloration.

lahaina. Variety of cane. Usually free tasseling; heavy stooling; semi-erect to recumbent growth; large, long, heavy tops. Brought by Captain Pardee Edwards by whaler from the Marquesas.

mālolo. Cane earlier known as *puahala,* said to be a tough cane. Used by bird catchers as an offering upon snaring their first bird. Kamakea: It was named after the fish *mālolo (Evolantia microptera),* the flying fish.

SUPERNATURAL: Sorcery and Spirits

There is much more to the "pagan" theology of the Hawaiians than can be attributed to superstition. The mystery of the supernatural, of the stars in their constellations, of the winds, rains, and clouds, so interested the Hawaiians that they expressed the wondrousness of what they were witnessing.

As for spirits, ghosts, and gods, Hawaiians usually—as did the Greeks with their deities—ascribed to them the shape and characteristics of humans, birds, animals, and fish. But Hawaiians also considered them much like humans, only slightly removed from mortal flesh.

In ancient times most beliefs among commoners were relatively simple, but grew more complex with time, at least for the priestly intellectuals. By the time Christian missionaries arrived in 1820, Hawaiian theology had achieved a high degree of sophistication.

'āhai. Pillar of wood or stone set up by a chief in memory of some great exploit.

akalau. Ghost that appears to some people but not to others; ghost or spirit of a living person seen by others, a sign of calamity. *Lit.,* shadows many.

akua lapu. Ghost, apparition, evil spirit. According to the older people, the *poe akua lapu* were spirits of deceased persons seen in the night in burying places and elsewhere. Their purpose was to frighten people.

'āpuni. Name of a day supposedly inauspicious to one's enemies; to have a quarrel; to be angry; to curse, scold, or threaten a person but depart without fighting.

aumiha. To float off in the air, as miasma; contagion; evil influence supposedly attending the graves of the dead.

awaloa. Place where the bones of chiefs may be hidden, as a cave. *Lit.,* haven eternal.

'ewe'ewe. Love and affection for the place of ones birth, where the first years were spent. (A.) Cry of 'Ewe'ewe iki, a legendary woman who died in childbirth, which is followed by a *nā* cry like that of an infant, an omen of an imminent birth. (PE.)

haihaiā. To use various arts, as the gathering of herbs and medicines and offerings, to prevent the gods from hearing another's prayers. (2 Tim. 2:16.)

haili. Spirit, ghost; the impression of something fondly remembered which brought a solemnity as if a spirit rested upon one.

hale poki. *Heiau* where the bones of the chief were deposited, as the Hale-o-Keawe at Kona, Hawai'i. (MALO 106.)

hanehane. Wailing of the spirits; the air was filled with lamentation and crying out.

hipu lau'ī. *Lei* for warding off danger. (CMH.)

hiu. To practice sorcery. (A.)

hua'i mai lā Kahiki i ko ipu makani, Kahiki, thou didst open thy wind-box.

'ili'ili. Pebble, stone. If the *'ili'ili puka,* female pebble, and the *nemonemo,* the male pebble, are put together it is believed they will generate offspring—other stones. They are found at the beach at Ko-loa, Puna-lu'u, Ka'u, Hawai'i.

kaha 'akua. Track of a god in a desert place.

kāhoaka. Spirit or soul of a person still living. Such spirits presumably could be seen by priests.

kāhuli. Motion of land shells as they turn and sway along the plant leaves and twigs; also the name of the snails. Since they supposedly sang or chirped they were called *pūpū kani oe.* Crickets, usually hidden among the leaves, made the sounds believed to come from the shells.

kāina. A session to practice sorcery; the practice of sorcery.

kākāola. Soul or spirit of a living person, as seen or claimed to have been seen by the *kahuna kilokilo* or juggling priest.

kālai pāhoa. Name of three woods—*kauila, nīoi, 'ohe*—believed to be the tree forms of two male gods and one goddess named Kāne-i-kaulana-'ula, Kahuila-o-ka-lani, and Kapo. The wood was considered deadly poisonous at Mauna-loa, Moloka'i only. (PE.)

kāpilialo. Unknown land inhabited by unknown people. (A.)

kāpilikua. Imagined country with imagined people. (A.)

kāwa'a. Voice of the curlew bird on Moloka'i, which seems to say

"I kāwa'a, e holo, uā nui ke kai o ke aumoe, let's sail, do canoe net fishing for the sea is high at midnight." (A; trans. PE.)

kīhae. To be inspired or possessed of some god; to become a god and go above.

kilo. Sorcerer, astrologer, stargazer; predictor of events by observation of the stars, the barking of dogs, the crowing of cocks.

kilokilo. Practicing enchantment, divining, fortune telling; to examine carefully; to predict concerning future events.

kilokilo hōkū. Astrologer, stargazer.

kilokilo'uhane. To foretell the condition of one's soul, as living or about to suffer; necromancy based on falsehood, practiced in early times. (A.)

kinoakalau. Spirit or ghost of a person not yet dead. See **akalau, kino wailua.** *Lit.,* shadows many.

kino wailua. Poetic name for a spirit or ghost of a living person, distinct from and in a different place than his body. See **kākāola, kinoakalau.** (A.)

koa kumu 'ole. Tree *mauka* (toward the mountain) of Kahikikolo, Kaua'i, devoted to Kamapua'a. *Lit.,* tree trunkless.

ku lani hāko'i. What is above or on high; supposed place in the heavens. Pukui-Elbert calls it "mythical lake or pond in the sky from which waters of rain came"; the windows of heaven. *Lit.,* stands lowering in the sky.

kuoha. Prayer used to cause a man to love his wife and a wife to love her husband.

lapu. Apparition, ghost; the appearance of the supposed spirit of a deceased person. (Hal. 88:10; Isa. 34:14.)

lawaa'ea'e. Name of a white fowl, particularly a cock.

lawakea. White cock. (A.)

Leina a ka 'uhane. *Lit.,* leaping place of ghosts. A place of departing ghosts said to be leaping to the netherworld. Such places are located on each island: Hanapepe no Kaua'i, Hilo no Hawai'i, Hōkūnui no Lāna'i, Ka'a no Maui, Kai-mololo no O'ahu, Kapapaki'iki'i no Ni'ihau, Kulae o ka Maomao no Maui, Mau-loku no Lehua, Pa-lehua no Hawai'i, Wai'anae no O'ahu, Wai-pi'o no Hawai'i.

māhola. Describes certain medicines used in the ancient practice of the *kahuna.*

maliu. Chief deified and become an *'aumakua,* a family or personal god; to be accepted as an offering. (Oihk. 1:4.)

malu ko'i. Shadow of death; deep gloom. *Lit., kapu* adze.

malu make. Shadow of death. (Ioba 24:16.)

mana. Worship, reverence, adoration. Supernatural power, such as was supposed and believed to be an attribute of the gods. Applied under the Christians as divine power.

mauha‘alele. Shadow of death; death shade.

maunu. Objects or property of a person, which another could obtain, such as his *kapa,* hair, spittle, etc., and by means of them pray him to death.

meha‘i, kāmeha‘i. Some hair or *kapa* or other article brought to the sorcerer, by which he might procure that person's death. (A.) Portion of the body of a person killed by sorcery, placed in a spot where the supposed murderer will contact it and be killed. (PE.)

mōlulolea. Voice or wail of a ghost.

mūki ke akua. If a ghost is heard, to make a noise with the mouth.

nē. To whisper as the gods do; to murmur, talk low.

nihi. To abstain from doing certain things through fear of offending the gods; to do a thing quietly, silently, or secretly, i.e., unseen.

‘oi‘o. Company or troop of ghosts; the same in respect to ghosts as *kuākai* is in respect of men.

‘ōka‘ihau. Name given to a sledge obtained from Captain James Cook. It is an object of worship for the natives.

pilikua. Land existing only in the imaginations of men. (A.)

pi‘opi‘o. Practitioner of sorcery or witchcraft. (Hoik. 22:15.) Old form of prayer, *he pule‘ana‘ana.*

pō kinikini. Place where the wicked dwell forever; eternal night. Also called *pō manomano,* a prayer used by the priests.

pō liukua. Imaginary place in the back part of the heavens where the stars are fixed; a very dark place. *Lit.,* back mystery.

po‘oko‘i. One skilled in sorcery; persons having a sharp projecting forehead who supposedly had something supernatural about them and had the power of using the *pule ‘āna‘āna,* power of praying people to death.

pouomanu. Post hole of the chief's house into which first a man was placed as a sacrifice, followed by a post, an ancient custom.

pu‘upu‘uone. Fortune telling; living in a beach hut called *hale pu‘uone.* Here was taught and practiced the divination called *pu‘uone.*

‘uhane. Spirit, applied to the third person of the Trinity. (Ioane 1:32.) Hawaiians supposed that men had two souls each, that one died with the body, the other lived on—either visible or invisible as might be—but having no more connection with the deceased than his shadow. These ghosts could talk, cry, complain, whisper, and so on. Some persons were skillful in trapping them.

ūkō. Offering that one carried to lay before Wākea when he died. (A.) Fulfilled. (PE.)

ulana. Prophecy or expression of the *kilokilo* (fortune teller) when looking upon a person in good health, indicating that he will soon die.

wao kele. Shadow of death.

SWEET POTATO: Glossary

The *'uala* (sweet potato) was a staple of diet for hundreds of years in the Marquesas and other parts of Polynesia. Very likely it was brought to Hawai'i a thousand years before Captain Cook's expedition first touched land at Kaua'i in 1778. The *'uala* has been a staple food down to the present time.

Captain Cook had found it a wholesome staple for his crew at earlier stops in other island groups. He asked about the sweet potato, learned its Hawaiian name, and the Hawaiians supplied his ship with generous amounts. Yams were also provided freely.

The plant grows almost anywhere so easily that it can establish new varieties quickly and in bewildering array. A list of these varieties can be found in the next category, *"Sweet Potato: Varieties."*

'a'awa. Insect that destroys the sweet potato plant, perhaps a caterpillar or even a blight.

ālālā. Sweet potato that grows on the vine part of the plant.

'anani'o, 'amoki'i. Stem or tuber that holds the potato to the main root.

'āni'uni'u. Root connecting the sweet potato to the vine.

'ao. Baked sweet potatoes, dried and hung in baskets to dehydrate.

au. Small, poor-quality potatoes that grow from a vine.

apoapo. Hill of potatoes.

'āpu'epu'e. Hill of potatoes. (A.)

hahae. Culling or thinning of the small potatoes as an aid to the growth of others. (NP 132.)

hale papa'a. Storehouse; floor built up off the ground for sweet potatoes and general storage. *Lit.,* house secure. (PE; Kin. 41:56.)

hāpuʻupuʻu, hāʻupuʻupuʻu. Sweet potato sprouts.

hāwaʻe. Sprouts from sweet potatoes.

hoʻopuʻe. To hill up potatoes. (CMH.)

hua hāʻule lani. Species of wild potato that was believed to have been started by seeds falling from heaven.

kāhala. Cutworms; caudal or anal horn, as on caterpillars. (NP 133.)

kahili. Exhausted potato patch that is called worthless, meaning it is about time to prepare it for planting. (HP 149.)

kāhuli. Sport or mutant. (HP 141.)

kāʻioʻio. Second crop of potatoes ready for harvesting. (NP 133.)

kaiue. To soften the earth and bed it down around the plants. (NP 131.)

kālina. Old vines remaining in the ground; long vine. (NP 133.)

kauaīki. Harvesting the first crop of small new potatoes, allowing those remaining a full growth. (NP 133.)

kīkī. Baskets of loose plaiting (for circulation of air), made of any available material, for handling potatoes—from digging and carrying to storing. (HP 150.)

kilo. Word applying to digging potatoes. (NP 133.)

kiʻo. Part of the sweet potato plant that branches off from the main rootlet; rootlet.

kiʻoʻe pālau. Small spoon of coconut shell. *Kiʻoʻe,* spoon; *pālau,* sweet potato *poi.* (NP 136.)

kōāʻā, kōʻā. To be unproductive, as plants in dry ground.

koloaha. Sweet potato with fine roots but a watery interior.

kuaiwi. Wall about 2 feet high to enclose rocky planting patches. (NP 131.)

kūʻōʻō. Broken or torn fragments of a sweet potato, from contact with a digging stick or other sharp object.

kūpuʻu. Preparation of sweet potatoes by baking, but no pounding into *poi* or mixing with coconut cream.

lālā. Branch vines of the sweet potato which bear fruit.

lau. Sweet potato slip, vine, or cutting used for propagation. (NP 127.)

lau kanu. Planted sweet potato vine. (HP.)

lau manamana. Species of sweet potato with slim, much divided leaves. *Lit.,* leaf divided.

lau ʻuala. Sweet potatoes propagated from cuttings. (NP 129.)

maka. Little rootlets, the "eyes" of the sweet potato, growing on the vine below the petiole. Growth at this point is closely watched. (NP 132.)

makaili. Patches of sweet potatoes in stony places. (NP 129.)

mala. Patch cleared by burning grass and shrubs, with the soil thoroughly turned over. (NP 129.)

moku pawa. To furrow a sweet potato field. (NP 141.)

mū. Weevils that attack the stems, roots, and tubers of the sweet potato. (NP 133.)

olohi'o. Weeding; to weed, cultivate. (NP 132.)

'ō'ō. Digging stick used to make holes for the slips, vines, or cuttings of the sweet potato. (NP 136.)

'ōo'o'a. Stringy sweet potatoes. (CMH.)

pāhoehoe. Hollow areas in the lava used for planting. They were prepared with soil and later walled in. (NP 132.)

pahulu. Second growth sweet potatoes or "volunteer potatoes"; rattoon crop; replanted patch. (NP 129.)

pālau. Digging stick used to make vertical holes for planting slips or cuttings. (NP 130.) Pudding of sweet potatoes and coconut cream. (NP 136.) Also called *ko'elepālau*.

pao, pā'ōō. Species of sweet potato plant; sprouting pieces of those broken or thrown away.

pe'elua. Caterpillar that destroys the sweet potato leaves. (NP 133.)

piele'uala. Sweet potato mashed, mixed with coconut milk, and steamed. (NP 135.)

poko. Cutworms, a serious pest of the sweet potato. (NP 133.)

pōnalo. Yellowing of leaves, which indicates dry rot; the dying or drying up of potato tops. (NP 133; A.)

pū. Variety of sweet potato. Its flesh is used as *palu* (bait) in feeding and attracting *'ōpelu* in their breeding places. (NP 135.)

pu'e. Hill, as of sweet potatoes. The ancients planted potatoes in mounds. (NP 132.)

pu'epu'e. High mounding of sweet potatoes in hills, which made for a symmetrical arrangement. (NP 131.)

puepuelu. Hard, tough, as applied to certain sweet potatoes. (A.)

puku kālina. Vines of sweet potatoes gathered for planting.

pu'u-kōlea. Plover's dunghill. This is a poetic (?) name for the condition of a potato patch before the burning of old tubers and vines in preparation for planting. (NP 134.)

'uala 'awa'awa. Sweet potato beer. (NP 135.)

wela. Patch of freshly turned soil. (NP 129.)

wiliwili. Turning under the vines when good growth is noted. Each vine is *wili* (twisted) around its own base to restrain excess runners. (NP 132.)

SWEET POTATO: Varieties

The sweet potato, *'uala* or *'uwala (Ipomoea* sp.), is discussed here more in terms of its variety; scientific names and precise definitions are not given. Dr. E. S. Craighill Handy, in his book *The Hawaiian Planter,* says that the "naming of sweet potatoes is not consistent, and therefore much duplication is encountered. The plant is plastic, mutates rapidly, and is readily transferable from place to place." Hence, we see in this category only terse definitions, a Hawaiian name, infrequently an English name, and perhaps a brief comment on roots, stems, leaves, and other parts.

See Pukui-Elbert (p. 334) for a list of many varieties (with the prefix *'uala*) and also (p. 15) a simple but comprehensive list of Hawaiian words for sweet potato. Handy lists about two hundred in his two editions of *The Hawaiian Planter.*

'a'anali'i, 'anali'i. Small, stunted sweet potato. Also called *kakana-li'i.* (NP 126.)

'ae'a hauka'e. Wild potato that was found in many places before ranching days. Purple-green leaves, purple stem, and light-purple tuber. Good as pig feed.

'aina. Variety of sweet potato. (CMH.)

'ākala. Pink sweet potato variety. (NP 127.)

ākea. Sweet potato with a wide leaf. (NP 126.)

'alamea. Variety of sweet potato. (HP 141.)

aliolio. Variety of sweet potato. (HP 141.)

'āpō. Ancient variety of sweet potato. Reddish tuber, deep-purple stem, deep-purple leaves. Raised at Kalaupapa, Moloka'i. (HP 141.)

'aumakiki. Variety of sweet potato. (HP 141.)

'auono. Variety of sweet potato. (HP 141.)

'awa'awa'a. Sweet potato with grooved roots. (NP 126.)

e'epu'u. Variety of sweet potato. (HP 141.)

'ele'ele. Variety of sweet potato with light-purple stems and veins, and purplish-green, channeled roots. (NP 127.)

euau. Variety of sweet potato. (HP 141.)

hā'ele-lepo. Variety of sweet potato. (HP 141.)

hākala. Sweet potato. The kinds are qualified by the colors *ke'oke'o* and *poni.* (PE.)

hākeakea. Sweet potato, dirty white in color. (NP 126.)

hālenalena. Sweet potato, yellowish in color. (NP 127.)

hā-loa. Variety of sweet potato.

hālona-ipu. Variety of sweet potato. (HP 141.)

hāʻulaʻula. Sweet potato, reddish to pink in color. (NP 127.)

haule-lani, hua-hāʻule-lani. Variety of sweet potato. *Lit.,* seeds fallen from the sky. (HP 141.)

hāuliuli. Sweet potato, dark in color. (NP 126.)

hā-wai. Variety of sweet potato. (HP 141.)

hoiki. Sweet potato with a narrow leaf. (NP 126.)

hōkeo. Variety of sweet potato. (HP 141.)

hōlei. Variety of sweet potato. (HP 141.)

holili. Sweet potato with underdeveloped vine. (NP 126.)

hoʻokamo, kamo. Variety of sweet potato. (HP 141.)

huamoa. Sweet potato, so called because in size and color the cooked tuber suggests the yellow of a hen's egg. It is said to have the odor of an egg when raw. An ancient variety. (HP 141.)

hua ʻono. Variety of sweet potato. (HP 141.)

ihumai. Variety of sweet potato. (CMH.)

kaʻe-umu. Variety of sweet potato. (HP 141.)

kakaka-ʻili-paheʻe. Sweet potato with a soft, smooth skin. (HP 141.)

kakaka-o-Keawe. Variety of sweet potato. (HP 141.)

kake, kakakē. Variety of sweet potato. (HP 141.)

kala. Ancient Hawaiian variety of sweet potato. It has pink and green leaves, a light yellow tuber with a pink spot, and deeply indented leaves. (HP 141.)

kala. Sweet potato plant with pointed leaves. An ancient variety. (HP 133.)

kala Pele. Variety of sweet potato called Pele's smoke, named after the goddess for its dusky, smoky-looking foliage.

kaleponi. Old Hawaiian sweet potato. Its name means purple *kala* and, coincidentally, California. There is a variety of sweet potato on Maui specifically called after the state. (NP 135.)

kalinaloa. Long sweet potato vines.

kālonaipu. Dark variety of sweet potato, formerly sold at seaports on Molokaʻi. Raised in Ka-laupapa.

kāne ʻohe. Variety of sweet potato named for Kāneohe, Oʻahu. It has the most indented of all leaf forms. (HP 135.)

kāne ʻohe, keʻokeʻo. White *kāne ʻohe* with light-green foliage and vines. (HP 135.)

kāne ʻulaʻula. Red *kāne ʻohe* having some purple coloring in vines and foliage. (HP 135.)

Kāpena-Keoe. Variety of sweet potato, possibly introduced by a sea captain. (HP 142.)

kawelo. Variety of sweet potato that matures in six to eight months. An identical variety of sweet potato in Kona was introduced by a man named Tommy. (HP 133.)

kawowo. Variety of sweet potato. An ancient plant. (HP 133.)

kea. White variety of sweet potato. (NP 126.)

keiki. Sweet potato variety with a vine sprout and a bud mutant. (NP 126.)

ke'oke'o. Tuber universal throughout the Hawaiian islands, with white flesh and skin and a green vine with green wings. Used only for food, not medicine. (NP 126.)

kihe. Sweet potato variety that matures in three months. Ancient. (HP 133.)

kihi. Variety of sweet potato. (HP 141.)

kihikihi. Variety of sweet potato having leaves with sharp points and corners. (NP 126.)

kihikihi poepoe. Variety of sweet potato that takes its name from the shape of its leaves—round with corners. An ancient potato. (HP 142.)

kihi-lau-nui. Variety of sweet potato. *Lit.,* large-leafed sweet potato. (HP 142.)

ki'i-hekekē. Variety of sweet potato. (HP 142.)

kipawale. Variety of sweet potato. (HP 142.)

kipoe. Variety of sweet potato. (CMH.)

kokoko'ohā. Very small sweet potatoes with red veins and often soggy tubers.

koume, koumi. Variety of sweet potato. (HP 142.)

ku'i popo. Ancient variety of sweet potato. *Lit.,* decayed molar. (HP 142.)

kupa. Sweet potato that grows wild in the uplands of eastern Maui above Nāhiku. Ancient Hawaiian variety. (HP 142.)

lalo loa. Variety of sweet potato. *Lit.,* deep down. (HP 142.)

lapa. Variety of sweet potato. (HP 142.)

lau manamana. Species of sweet potato with slim, much divided, leaves.

lau 'ula'ula. Variety of sweet potato. (HP 142.)

lenalena. Tubers that are bright green like the turmeric. (NP 127.)

lihilihi palu. Variety of sweet potato. (HP 142.)

liko lehua. Dark variety of sweet potato, raised at Ka-laupapa, Moloka'i. Formerly sold at seaports. (HP 142.)

loloa. Variety of sweet potato with a long root. (NP 126.)

lupalupa. Variety of sweet potato with a vigorous, growing vine. (NP 126.)

mahina. Variety of sweet potato. (HP 142.)

mahina kēkau. Variety of sweet potato of ancient vintage. (HP 142.)

mā'i. Variety of sweet potato. (HP 142.)

maka nui. Variety of sweet potato. *Lit.,* big eyes.

māku'e. Variety of sweet potato, generally dark-red in color. (NP 127.)

malihini aka wai. Variety of sweet potato. (HP; CMH.)

mānalo. Variety of sweet potato having a root with a certain sweetness. (NP 126.)

manamana. Variety of sweet potato. Sometimes qualified by *ke'oke'o* (white). (NP 126.)

mauna pōhaku. *Mauna* probably refers to the Rocky Mountains. The Mormons may have brought this sweet potato to Hawai'i in the 1860s. It is called *lahaina* on Maui, *kahului* on Maui and Moloka'i, and *maui* on Hawai'i. Noted for vigor, adaptability, and productivity. It has a large tuber with brownish skin, a thick vine, and a large, heart-shaped leaf. Favored by Hawaiians. (NP 128, 134.)

melemele. Variety of sweet potato, with a divided, fingered leaf. (NP 127.)

mohihi. Quick growing variety that requires a great deal of rain. Matures in six months. It is the most popular variety for making *'uala 'awa'awa* (sweet potato beer). Sometimes qualified by *ke'oke'o* or *'ula'ula.* (NP 128.)

mokiawe. Variety of sweet potato.

momona. Variety of sweet potato. (HP 126.)

nā'ū. Variety of sweet potato. (HP 142.)

ne'ene'e. Variety of sweet potato. (HP 142.)

nemonemo. Variety of sweet potato with a smooth root. (NP 126.)

nika. Nigger, formerly called *pā'ele,* is a sweet potato of Kona with broad, deeply indented five-point leaves, green veins, white flesh when raw and dark after cooking. (HP 142.)

nui. Variety of sweet potato with many leaves. (NP 126.)

nukilani. Ancient *kali-poni* planted first at Kaupō, Maui. It has heart-shaped leaves, yellowish skin, and white flesh. The name means New Zealand. (HP 137.)

nukukau. Variety of sweet potato. (HP 142.)

nukulehu. Variety of sweet potato. (HP 142.)

nunui. Large leaf variety of sweet potato. (NP 126.)

'ōma'oma'o. Greenish variety of sweet potato. (NP 127.)

pa'akiki. Variety of sweet potato with hard roots. (NP 126.)

pa'apa'aina. Variety of sweet potato. (HP 142.)

pā'ele hili mānoaoa. Variety of sweet potato. Also called *nika*. (HP 142.)

paha. Variety of sweet potato much like *koali 'uala* with a heart-shaped leaf. Roots were generally used only as hog feed but were cooked for humans in time of famine. (HP 133.) A wild sweet potato; name of a plant eaten in time of scarcity. Also called *kahala, kūhala*. (A.; PE.)

pākeke. Ancient variety of sweet potato. The name comes from the English, potato. (HP 133.)

pala. Variety of sweet potato, an ancient plant. (HP 133, 142.)

palaai. Variety of sweet potato. (HP 133.)

palahalaha. Variety of sweet potato with a flat root. (NP 126.)

pala-mahiki. Variety of sweet potato. (HP 142.)

palupalu. Variety of sweet potato with a soft root. (NP 126.)

pani kohe. Variety of sweet potato. (HP 142.)

pa nini. Ancient variety of sweet potato. (HP 133.)

panioe'e. Variety of sweet potato. (HP 142.)

pā'ū-o-Hi'i-aka. Variety of sweet potato, dusty and smoky in color. Matures in four to six months. *Lit.*, skirt of Hi'i-aka. (HP 133.)

pa'ū'ū. Variety of sweet potato that matures in four months. (HP 134.)

pehu. Variety of sweet potato. (HP 142.)

pia. This pure white tuber resembles in color and consistency the *pia* (arrowroot). (HP 133.)

piapia. Variety of sweet potato. (HP 142.)

piko. Variety of sweet potato. (HP 142.)

piko ha'o. Slow-maturing sweet potato. Latex from the raw tuber was widely used as a medicine for throat and stomach ailments. Ancient variety. (HP 142.)

piko nui. Ancient variety of sweet potato, flattish and round like a swollen navel. *Lit.*, great navel. (HP 133.)

pili mai. Variety of sweet potato. (HP 142.)

poepoe. Variety of sweet potato with round roots and stems. (NP 126.)

pōhina. Ancient variety of sweet potato. (HP 133.)

pokopoko. Variety of sweet potato, with short roots and vines. (NP 126.)

pōko'u. Variety of sweet potato with short roots and vines. (NP 126.)

poni. Variety of sweet potato, most of its parts colored some shade of purple. (NP 126.)

pū. Most of this variety used as *palu* (bait) in feeding and attracting *'ōpelu* in their breeding places offshore. (HP 139.)

pua Kawai-hae. Variety of sweet potato. (HP 142.)

punapuna. Variety of sweet potato with a mealy root. (NP 126.)

uahi a Pele. Variety of sweet potato with a smoky, dusky leaf coloration. Matures in four to six months. *Lit.,* Pele's smoke. (HP 133.)

'uala helelei. Variety of sweet potato. (CMH.)

'uala 'ula kīna'u. Variety of reddish sweet potato. (PE.)

ulaula. Variety of sweet potato with red coloration. (NP 126.)

uliuli. Variety of sweet potato, dark or dusky in coloration. (NP 126.)

unahi uhu. Variety of sweet potato. (HP 143.)

wai aniani. Variety of sweet potato named moloka'i. It gets its name from the transparency of its white flesh. The vine and foliage are light green throughout. *Lit.,* window pane. (HP 143.)

wailua. Ancient variety of sweet potato, probably transferred from Wailua, Kaua'i. (HP 143.)

wehiwa. Variety of sweet potato. (HP 143.)

TIME: General

This category and the three which follow deal with time in the sense of months of the year, nights of the lunar month, and week days.

Before the coming of Captain Cook, the Hawaiians had observed the regular appearance of the moon in its phases and had created a thirty-day lunar month or cycle. This became a framework for *kapu* days: fishing, planting, cultivating, harvesting, and worshiping in the *heiau.*

Hawaiians must have enjoyed the early hours of the day, for a large share of words speak of breaking dawn, the colors of the dawn, glimmering early dawn, and breaking light. Evening hours, on the other hand, are described by fewer terms.

ahiahi. Later part of the day; toward night; late afternoon; evening; gloaming.

ao. Day; to become light or day, as in the morning; dawn.

'a'ole 'emo. No time at all.

au. Period of time; era; age; passing of time; to pass time.

'auinalā. To decline, as the sun in the afternoon; afternoon. (1 Nal. 18:29.)

aumoe. Late at night, specifically, midnight. *Lit.,* time to sleep. (Puk. 11:4.)

awakea. Noon; when the sun is at its highest. Name of the god who opened the gate of the sun, Awakea.

hai manawa. School book used at Lahainaluna Boarding School in teaching chronology.

hanana. Certain time; certain event; certain occasion.

hola. O'clock, hour, time. *Hola 'ehia keia?* What time is it?

ho'oilo, ho'īlo. Rainy or wintry months, in contrast to *kau,* the summer season.

ho'okā'au. To pass time pleasantly and entertainingly.

ho'onanea. To pass time pleasantly; to relax; to be contented and at peace.

ho'opaumanawa. To waste time.

ka au moe. Midnight; time of deep slumber.

kahua o Mali'o. First dawn of morning light; *fig.,* the source of life's enjoyments, such as food, fish, mats, and all the fruits of the land; place of happiness, comfort, and pleasure, named for Mali'o, a mythical woman renowned for entertaining with music and for her mastery of love magic.

kakahiaka. Morning. *Lit.,* breaking the shade of morning. *Kakahiaka nui,* early in the morning.

ka līulā. Dusk; day draining away, *lālīu.*

ka pe'a ma. First sunrays; herald beams, *mea ma.* The Greeks had the same simile.

kau. The summer or warm season, in contrast to *ho'oilo,* the winter months.

ke wa lā ula. Pre-sunrise glow; rosy interval.

koloku. High noon; when the sun stands at the zenith.

konale. Bright, clear, unobscured, white; quiet, still, like moonlight in a calm night.

kōnane, kōnale. Bright, moonlit nights.

kuluaumoe. Near midnight.

la'a'ula. Autumn. *Lit.,* red time of leaves.

lā ho'omalolo. Day before *lā kapu;* hence under the Christian system, Saturday, the day before the Sabbath. (Mat. 27:62.) *Pō'aōno* the sixth night.

lehu. The number 40,000; highest specific number.

li'u, li'uli'u. A long time; taking a long time.

luakaha. To pass time pleasantly.

mahina. Lunar moon month in contrast to a solar light month.

mākole. Time of day when the sun is high or fiercely hot, perhaps from eight in the morning to three in the afternoon.

mālama. Solar month.

mālehaleha. Appearance of the sky at evening; the time of evening; twilight. (Isa. 5:11.)

mālehulehu, mōlehulehu. Appearance of the sky at dawn of day; twilight of the morning. Webster's International Dictionary defines twilight as "the light from the sky between full night and sunrise, or between sunset and full night."

maliʻo. Earliest morning light, as it pierces the shadows of night. See **kahua o Maliʻō.**

mamuaiho o Ke Wakea. Forenoon, just before noon.

manawa. Time, season; in no time, immediately.

manawaʻole. No time at all.

mōhalu. Day of the month when the moon begins to round.

mōlehulehu. Shade of the morning or evening. (Ier. 6:4.) When sky is ashy.

ʻowakawaka. Breaking or opening of day.

pau ka pouli. Day.

pawa. Breaking of the dawn; darkness just before dawn.

pō. Night, darkness; time when the sun gives no light; chaos.

pohā mai ka lā. Dawn.

polehulehu. Between darkness and light; in a state of twilight; partial light; twilight of morning or evening.

pō manomano. Excessive darkness; the place where the wicked dwell in separation forever; eternal night.

poniponi. Early dawn of the morning, so called because of the mixture of colors; hence, purple.

pō uli. Dark.

pualena. Glimmering or first dawn of morning; yellow light at dawn.

puka o ka lā. Sunrise.

ua huli ka lā. Past midnight.

ua poʻo ka lā. Sunset.

wa. Period of time; era, epoch, season, age.

walea. A quiet time, free of effort.

wanaʻao, waʻanaʻao. To dawn, as the first light of morning; to appear, as the dawn. *Lit.,* light appears. False dawn; prophecy of daylight.

TIME: Months of the Year

This category hints at the number of Hawaiian words for the cycle of twelve months. There are many different sets of words, each with its own term for each month; there are many kinds of sets as well: ancient, ceremonial, those used only on a single island, and assorted patterns used elsewhere in Polynesia. There are also Hawaiianized versions of the English terms.

Malo filled a section of his valued *Hawaiian Antiquities* with the several versions at hand when he wrote his manuscript. Kepelino too, had his choice of lists, but he prepared his own, and published it in the *Hawaiian Kuahoa*, December 23, 1890. This grouping, also known as "the Maui list," is used in this book, along with five other groupings—those used on the islands of O'ahu and Hawai'i, phonetic Hawaiian, the introduced Tahitian, and the English versions. For a textual explanation of each of the names, see *Kepelino's Traditions of Hawai'i* as originally prepared, edited by Martha Warren Beckwith (pp. 84–96). See listing on opposite page.

TIME: Nights of the Lunar Month

Na pō Hawai'i a me Nā Ao, nights and days of Hawai'i, lists many alternative words, with some versions repeating the same words (or some of them) in another of the "thirty nights." *Kepelino's Traditions of Hawai'i* (pp. 101–112) carries a comprehensive review of the Hawaiian names and meanings of the "thirty nights." The accompanying texts emphasize the major occupations of the early Hawaiians—largely agriculture and fishing.

The Hawaiians were impressed with the complicated regularity of movement of the stars, sun, and moon and the recurring patterns of daily, monthly, seasonal, and annual happenings in tides. They were on the brink of creating a calendar incorporating a cyclical correction factor in the manner of the Western leap-year. It is likely that the waves of Polynesians who first settled the Hawaiian Islands brought with them a relatively advanced thinking on these matters, forming the base on which the Hawaiians continued to build.

Kepelino or Maui	Oʻahu	Hawaiʻi	Phonetic Hawaiian	Introduced Tahitian	English
Makaliʻi	Nana	Kāʻelo	Ianuali	Ianuari	January
Kāʻelo	Welo	Kaulua	Pepeluali	Feberuari	February
Kaulua	Ikiiki	Nana	Malaki	Maraki	March
Nana	Kaʻaona	Welo	ʻApelila	Aperila	April
Welo	Hinaiaʻeleʻele	Ikiiki	Mei	Mei	May
Ikiiki	Mahoemua	Kaʻaōna	Iune	Iune	June
Kaʻaōna	Mahoehope	Hinaiaʻeleʻele	Iulai	Iulai	July
Hinaiaʻeleʻele	ʻIkuwā	Mahoemua	ʻAukake	Augake	August
Mahoemua	Welehu	Mahoehope	Kepakēmapa	Sepatemaba	September
Mahoehope	Makaliʻi	ʻIkuwa	ʻOkakopa	Okatoba	October
ʻIkuwā	Kāʻelo	Welehu	Nowemapa	Nowemaba	November
Welehu	Kaulua	Makaliʻi	Kēkemapa	Dekemaba	December

Prior to adopting our reckoning* the Hawaiians allotted thirty nights to each lunar month, showing no favor to any. The first night was called *Hilo*, to twist, because the moon was a mere curved line. The second night was *Hoaka*, a crescent. The following nights were *Kū-kahi, Kulua*, etc. When the sharp points of the crescent were lost it was called *Huna*, to conceal.

"When the moon became convex it was *Mōhalu*, to spread out. As it still waxed it was called *Hua*, to increase; and when quite round it became *Akua*, clear.

"The three nights of almost full moon were *Hoku, Mahea-lani* and *Kulu*. Then as it diminished night by night it was known as *Lā'au'ku-kāhai, Ole-ku-lua, Kāloa-pau* and so on until it had almost disappeared when it was called *Mauli*, or over-shadowed. When it finally vanished the moonless night was named *Muku*, cutoff."

Hilo. First night of the lunar month. The new moon "looks like a twisted thread," *o Hilo ka pō mua no ka puāhilo ana o ka mahina.*

Hoaka. Second night of the lunar month, with a crescent-shaped moon, a *kapu* day. A favorable day for planting. *Lit.,* clear.

Ku-kāhi. Third night. This word (and those that follow, Kulua, Ku-kolu, and Ku-pau) is one of the four *kapu* days of Kū. On this day a man is sacrificed; it is also the day of a very low tide.

Ku-lua. Fourth night. Day of freedom from *kapu*.

Ku-kolu. Fifth night. First night of the rising moon. It is a good fishing day. Sand is exposed, the day is clear, and the sea calm.

Ku-pau. Sixth night. Day of low tide.

'Ole-ku-kāhi. Seventh night. The rough sea bares the beach and rocks. On this night it is light after the moon sets.

'Ole-ku-lua. Eighth night. Rough seas continue. It is disliked for planting, but considered a good night for torch-fishing.

'Ole-ku-kolu. Ninth night, with rough seas, some torch-fishing. Farmers think little of the day.

'Ole-ku-pau. Tenth night, when farmers plant. It is the fourth in this group of nights, the last day of the rough seas.

Huna. Eleventh night, a day much liked by the farmers. The tide is low and the fishing good. Ho'aō is the day of the night of Huna.

Fire Fountains, by Gordon Cumming (W. Blackwood & Sons, Edinburgh 1883).

Mōhalu. Twelfth night. The moon begins to round. This night was liked for planting flowers because it was believed they would be round and perfect like the moon.

Hua. Thirteenth night. Anything that bears fruit is planted on this day, formerly a day of prayer. The moon is rounded like *hua* (egg).

Akua. Fourteenth night, with a perfectly round moon. The day is *kapu* as is the night.

Hoku. Fifteenth night, a day that succeeds the night of the full moon. It is well liked by farmers.

Māhea-lani. Sixteenth night, when the full moon begins to wane. This day is liked by the farmers; it is a day of low tide.

Ku-lua. Seventeenth night, when the moon seems to dip into the ocean. Farmers trust this day; the sea gathers up and replaces the sand.

Lā'au-ku-kāhi. Eighteenth night. This day is avoided for planting.

Lā'au-ku-lua. Nineteenth night, considered favorable for planting. The sea is rough.

Lā'au-pau. Twentieth night, a day for planting. Also a day for boisterousness.

'Ole-ku-kāhi. Twenty-first night. "Nothing to be had from the sea." These were the days for planting potato slips, banana suckers, and gourd seeds.

'Ole-ku-lua. Twenty-second night, a good day for planting. Also a day of rough seas.

'Ole-pau. Twenty-third night. A planting day with rough seas.

Kāloa-ku-kāhi. Twenty-fourth night, a *kapu* day. High seas; also a planting day.

Kāloa-ku-lua. Twenty-fifth night, a *kapu* free day.

Kāloa-pau. Twenty-sixth night. *Lit., Kāloa,* last.

Kāne. Twenty-seventh night, when the moon diminishes. A potato planting day. *Kapu Kāne, kapu* nights of *Kāne* and *Lono.*

Lono. Twenty-eighth night, a day of prayer followed by a free day. Favorable for men fishing with lines and for girls diving for sea urchins.

Mauli. Twenty-ninth night, the last night the moon is visible. The sea gathers up the sand and returns it to its place.

Muku. Thirtieth night. The moon has entirely disappeared; end of the lunar month. *Lit.,* over shadowed, cut off.

TIME: Watches of the Night

Each of the words in this category refers to one of five successive three-hour periods starting with first watch at approximately 6:00 P.M., "when evening awaited the darkness." The periods that followed at three-hour intervals were similarly named: second watch, third watch, and so on. Collectively, they were called watches of the night.

Hawaiians probably observed the formalities at the changes of the watch aboard the ships of Captain Cook and later explorers, and were intrigued by those naval rituals. To European mariners, the sequence was simply a security measure. But some of the prurient-minded natives regarded the sequence as a framework adaptable to other purposes. They gave names of their own devising to the five bundles of *kapa* usually placed in a line between two rows of players in the game of *pūhenehene: kihi moe, pilipuka, kau* (middle bundle), *kihi puka, pili moe.* The familiar trappings of the daytime game of *pūhenehene* were still present: five bundles of *kapa,* the "ready" call of *pūheoheo,* the *maile* wand, the *hoʻo pāpā* of repartee, the *kapa* covering sheet, and the hidden *noʻa* which when found lifted the *kapu* of restraint. Added were adult players, nighttime scheduling, and more interest in forfeits than scores. See **Amusements and Games.**

kihi moe. Commencement of evening, *ke kihi o ka pō.* First watch of the night beginning with the coming of darkness at about 6:00 P.M. This was also the name of the first bundle of *kapa.* The piles of *kapa* and the persons sitting in front of them were hiding places for the *noʻa* during each watch.

pilipuka. Second watch of the night. *Ka pili o ke ahiahi,* at the end of the evening, i.e., nightfall, approximately 9:00 P.M. This watch ran from 9:00 P.M. to midnight.

kau. Third watch of the night. This was the name of the middle bundle of *kapa.* The *noʻa* could have been hidden in any pile or on any person across the way. The watch starts at midnight and goes to 3:00 A.M.

kihi puka. Fourth watch of the night, approximately 3:00 A.M., *ka pili o ka wanaʻo,* the approach of dawn. More generally, it is considered to be between midnight and dawn. This is the fourth pile of *kapa.*

pili moe. Fifth watch of the night, extending from about 6:00 A.M. to an indefinite period. This is the last pile of *kapa.*

TIME: Week Days

Time was also reckoned by the Hawaiians in nights and days. They began their week with Monday night. They consistently added the prefix *pō* (night) to each night except Sunday, perhaps because, although it certainly was a day of the week, it was not strictly considered a week day. It was also a special day. See **Pōehiku.**

Pō'akāhi. First day of the week. Monede. *Eng.*

Pō'alua. Second day of the week. Tusede. *Eng.*

Pō'akolu. Third day of the week. Wenede. *Eng.*

Pō'ahā. Fourth day of the week. Tarede. *Eng.*

Pō'alima. Fifth day of the week. Kō'ele, a work day for commoners.

Pō'aōno. Sixth day of the week. Sabati. *Eng. Lā Ho'omalolo,* day before *lā kapu,* day of *kapu.*

Pō'ehiku. Seventh night of the week. Sunede. *Eng.* Pō lā o Haku, the Lord's Day, has been widely used. Also Lāpule, day of prayer. *Lit.,* day prayer.

TOOLS AND IMPLEMENTS

This category concerns all occupations involved in the production and transportation of food. Thus, the homely task of smoothing and polishing a canoe to be used in fishing is included, as are the building of thatch houses and the manufacture of the 'ō'ō (digging stick) and the *ko'i* (adze).

Special significance is assigned to the 'ō'ō, which, in its supreme simplicity, proved its worth as perhaps the leading agricultural tool. The *ko'i* was also important for its usefulness in cutting, hewing, and shaping wood, bone, and stone. *Ko'i* were first fashioned from wood and later from the hardest forms of lava. The use of pumice, high-density coral, and other hard stones indicates Hawaiians' absolute dependence on such non-metallic materials.

'aha. Cord braided from the husk of the coconut, sennit; cord made from human hair and intestines of animals.

'ahakū. Cord used in laying out lines for a house or an *'ulu maika* field.

ala ūlili. Ladder. (Kin. 28:12.) Also called *alahaka*.

'ana, ane. Pumice, a soft stone used in polishing canoes and calabashes.

apuapu. File or rasp.

'auamo. Stick or pole for carrying burdens across the shoulders; yoke. *Lit.,* handle carrying. See **mamaka**.

'aumaka. Pole or stick for carrying a burden across the shoulders. See **'auamo, māmaka**.

hale. Tool house or workshop; any house.

hāmale, hamare. Hammer. (Lunk. 4:21.)

hāmale ki'u hao. Sledge hammer. *Lit.,* hammer driving iron.

hāmale lā'au. Wooden mallet.

hānui. Butt of a coconut leaf used in firming the sides of a taro patch. (CMH.)

hao hou puka. Metal punch.

he mau mea pa'ahana. Tools.

hoana. Hone, whetstone, grindstone.

hole. Rasp.

ho'okala. Sharpener, whetstone.

ho'o'oma. Carpenter's gouge.

hula. Polynesian drill. No data. (CMH.)

'iliki. Varnish made of *kukui* (candlenut tree) bark, *lauī kī* (root) *'ōpu'u maia* (parts of the banana tree), and other items.

'īliwai like. Carpenter's or surveyor's level.

iwiole. Adze made of bone; eyetooth. *Lit.,* bone fang.

ka'a lio. Horse-drawn wagon.

kāhei. Bit for a carpenter's drill.

kāhele. Name of the common adze. (A.)

kahi. Scraper, as for *olonā* fiber.

kalaweka. Cultivator.

kalepa. Scraper.

kaula. Rope or strong cord.

kāwa'ewa'e. Stone used in polishing canoes.

kepue. Hard stone from which adzes were shaped.

kia. Spike or nail. See **meki**.

kila. Chisel.

kipikua. Pickaxe. *Lit.,* dig strike.

koholua. Hard polished stone for feticide, a practice of early Hawai'i.

ko'i. Adze.

ko'i holu. Broad adze for smoothing a canoe. *Lit.,* adze bent.

ko'i kahi. Carpenter's plane; adze shaving.

ko'i kēlai. Adze used for carving.

ko'i lipi. Axe or hatchet; tapering edge; instrument for hewing stones. *Lit.*, adze sharp. (Puk. 20:22.) Any tool. (Kanl. 27:5.)

ko'i 'ōwili. Adze made with the blade held by a socket. When twisted a quarter turn it was like a hatchet.

kolopā. Crowbar.

kua. Anvil.

kua lā'au. Anvil.

kui. Sharp-pointed needle; general name for small pointed instruments.

kui kala. Screwdriver.

kuke. Thin, chisel-shaped adze.

kūpā. Swivel adze, named for a god of canoe makers.

kūpele. To hollow out the inside of a log for a canoe.

lā'au ana. Yardstick; ruler.

lā'au pālau. Wooden tool used for cutting *kalo* tops; war club. (A.)

lanalana. Coconut cords for tying the *ko'i* (cutting blade) to the *'aulima* (handle) of the adze. These cords also served as canoe lashings.

lauohe. Bamboo leaf used in polishing wooden calabashes.

lipi hoehoe. Adze or chisel with a wide, flat blade. This is one of several shapes of cutting instruments in which the term *lipi* is combined with another.

lōhai. Lever used for prying up heavy materials. See **une.**

lōkea. Long, pointed knife with a white handle.

lopu. *Ko'i* adze used in sacrifice.

lula. Ruler; measuring stick.

mahiki. Fulcrum for a lever.

maka ole. Point of the *'ō'ō* (digging stick). *Lit.*, eye tooth.

māmaka. Stick for carrying burdens placed as a yoke on the shoulders. See **'auamo, 'aumaka.**

mānai. Needle used in stringing *lei*s.

mea hana. Tool.

mea ho'okala. Sharpener.

mea pa'ahana. Tool, implement.

meki. Nail or spike; an ancient name for iron, modern name is *hao.* See **kia.**

mikini kaomi. Press, as for clamping material.

mōlī. Tattooing needle made of albatross bone, used to print on the skin. *Hahau iho la ka mōlī, pahukū ae la ke koko,* the *mōlī* is struck on and the blood flows out. (A.)

na mea hoʻohana. Tools, general term.

nao wili. Drill and bit.

nī ʻauniu. Hawaiian broom made from midribs of coconut fronds.

ʻoahi. Pumice stone used in polishing canoes and calabashes.

ʻoʻe. To probe, prick, jab, as with a stick, for example.

ʻōhākālai. To polish lightly, as a spear; stick for polishing. (AP.)

ʻolokeʻa. Scaffold.

olo mea. Small hardwood tree *(Perrottetia sandwicensis)* used in rubbing on the soft *hau* wood to make fire by friction.

ʻoma. Small, gouge-shaped adze.

ʻōʻō. Digging sticks made of various woods. **1.** *alaheʻe,* a large, native hardwood shrub *(Canthium odoratum).* (NEAL 797). **2.** *kauila,* a native of the buckthorn family supplying a very hard wood. (NEAL 541). **3.** *ʻūlei,* a native spreading shrub *(Osteomeles anthyllidifolia)* noted for its toughness. (NEAL 387.)

ʻōʻō hao. Digging stick made partly of iron.

pahi. Knife; any knifelike cutting tool.

pahi olo. Saw.

pānānā. Compass.

pao. Chisel.

pelu. Jackknife. (A.)

pia. Kind of stone used in adzes; kind of stone hammer.

pipi. Lower part or blade of an adze.

pōhaku kuinoni. Stone for pounding *noni.*

pōhaku ʻoahi. Stone, pumice used for polishing canoes and scraping bristles from pigs.

pōhuehue. Stone, pumice, used in polishing canoes.

poʻi kāpīpi. Substance for sprinkling, as with salt; or scattering, as with sand.

polipoli. Soft, porous stone used for polishing. (AP.)

pono hana. Tools, general term.

pūʻili. Smallish type of rope. (A.)

pūlumi. Broom; to sweep.

pūpū nīʻau. Broom made from midribs of coconut leaflets. See **niʻauniu.**

ʻūmii. Clamp, vise.

une. Lever for prying up. See **lōhai.**

ʻūpā. Any instrument that opens and closes in the manner of shears, bellows; compass, tongs. Early tools of this type were made of shark's teeth.

ʻūpa ahi. Tongs for hot coals. (Puk. 25:38.)

ʻūpa niho manō. Hair cutting tool made of shark's teeth. The person cutting would hold a length of hair out taut from the head and with a quick slice whisk it off at the desired length, repeating until all the hair was cut.

'ūpā nui. Shears.

'ūpā 'ūmi'i. Pliers.

waiehu, waiahu. File. Any rough stone or substance was used earlier to grind or polish iron.

wa'u. Scraper or grater.

wili. To bore, as with an auger or gimlet. (Nal. 12:10.)

wili kāhei. Bit for boring rocks; bit of any kind for boring.

wili nui. Auger.

wili pua'a. Corkscrew, gimlet, auger, hand drill. Also called *ulepua'a.*

WAR AND WEAPONS

The words in this category are no longer used. Hawaiian warfare among competitive chiefs came to an end in December 1819 following skirmishes by Hawaiians protesting Kamehameha II's abolition of the *kapu* system (although a later battle was fought on Kaua'i in 1834 involving an attack on the fort at the mouth of the Waimea River). It was this confrontation among partisan forces that led to the first constitution of the nation.

The weapons used were spears, daggers, clubs, tripping cords, slingstones, and shark-tooth knives. Such weapons, shaped by stone adzes, dictated the strategy and circumstances of warfare. A battle was little more than hand-to-hand conflict, punctuated by offensive and defensive flurries.

In Hawai'i bows and arrows were used only in sport.

'a'a pua. Arrow case, quiver; sports equipment. (Ioba 39:23.)

ahi ka nanā. Champion. (CMH.) *Ka pūkaua ahi ka nanā,* a warrior, fierce as the *ahi* [fish]. (PE.)

'ai pahuna. Spear thrust.

'alā o ka ma'a. Slingstone.

ana. Cave; shelter for the women and children during wartime and for the retreating vanquished; place where the conquered may be found. (Kin. 19:30.)

'au. Handle or helve of an axe. (Kanl. 19:5.) Staff of a spear (1 Sam. 17:7.) Handle of a sword (Lunk. 3:22.)

ʻauʻau. Stalk of the *loulu* palm made into a spear. Its outer end may have been trimmed with shark teeth.

ʻau hau. Spear made of *hau* wood.

ʻelau. Point of a spear or bayonet; spear of hibiscus wood; pointed spear.

hae. In early times a torn piece of *kapa* was used for a signal; hence, in modern times, a flag or banner.

hahau. To strike, smash, or scourge using a sword, rod, or staff; to hit with a club.

hai. To offer human sacrifice; particular form of gathering slain warriors in war.

hale pahu. Drum house used in war ceremonies in the *heiau;* place of refuge in time of war.

hau. To club, strike, beat. See **hahau.**

haua. To strike, apply stripes, chastise. (Sol. 19:18.)

hāuna lāʻau. Stroke or thrust of a war club. (PE.)

hē. Weapon used in war, a swishing, sweeping whip.

hoa. To strike, as in fighting; to club with a stick or rod.

hohoa. War club or *kapa* beater used as a club; to strike, as in fighting. See **pāhoa.**

hoʻomoe. To club down an opponent.

hoʻoūka. To attack, rush upon, as in a battle. *La hoʻoūka,* day of battle.

hūlili. Garrison; fort or strong place; ladder, plank, or bridge used to cross a defile.

ihe. Spear, javelin. *Ihe paheʻe a me na ihe ʻō,* the hand staves and the spears.

ihe hulali. Shining spear.

ihe paheʻe. Short spear; sliding spear.

kaʻa kaua. Tactician in war.

kāʻalā. To sling, hurl stones with a sling.

kaʻa lāʻau. To brandish a war club.

kā aliʻi. Hurling spears at a chief, not only to test his dexterity in avoiding them but to better one's own skill.

kāhiko kaua. Chief's war dress; *mahiole,* helmet; *ʻahuʻula,* cape.

kakaka. Crossbow, bow for shooting arrows; sport or game.

kanawao. Hard, heavy stone used in war with a sling. This stone is like a pebble found in some brook or stream.

kao. Dart, javelin; firebrand thrown on grass houses in time of war.

kaua. War; army drawn up for battle. (2 Nal. 28:5.)

kaua kūloko. Civil, internal war.

kekui'elua. Weapon used in war. (A.)

kiko'o. Bent bow. (1 Sam. 2:4.) Sport.

kīmopō. To kill in the night; to waylay in the dark; to attack unexpectedly.

kokōhikū, kōhikū. To lay waste in time of war; to destroy food.

kū'aupa'a. Bundle of *pololū,* spears carried by the chief going into battle.

ku'ia. Small, flat, pointed spear.

kui'elua, kui'alua. Ancient game, a form of *lua* fighting, more often practiced by bodyguards of the chiefs than used in war; art of wrestling and bone breaking. (KILO.)

ku'ikē. To destroy completely, as in war; to raze or level to the ground.

kūlana. Place in a *hūlili,* fortification or tower, where warriors stood to throw spears.

kūpololū. Stabbing or striking with a *pololū* (spear). (A.) Vaulting with a *pololū.* (PE.)

lā'au. Wooden club; blow with a club.

lā'au māka'i. Constable's badge, club.

lā'au pālau. Instrument of offense used in war; long club; *ihe* or *pololū* (spears); war club; lance, 12 to 20 feet long; sword or saw, the edge set with shark's teeth.

lau'au'a. Maneuvers in battle. See **ka'a kaua.** (A.)

laumeki. Barbed spear.

leiomano. Shark-tooth weapons. Teeth are fastened securely into wooden, bone, or fiber handles.

lua. Watchword given by Hoapili prior to his last Kaua'i battle; form of wrestling called *kaialua.*

luahi. Person or persons captured in battle or whipped in a single fight. *Lua ahi,* pit of fire; hell.

lua huna. Cave or pit in which property was concealed, as in time of war; similarly for hiding bones of the dead.

ma'a. Sling, an offensive weapon used by Hawaiians in war. *Ma'akū,* to cast a stone with a sling.

mahiole. War cap or helmet; officer's cap. (1 Sam. 17:5.) Feather helmet. *'A'ahu a po'o,* a head defense in battle, a shield in wartime; *pale kaua,* a shield, defensive armor. (1 Sam. 17:41.)

maka. Edge or point of an instrument, as a sword. *Maka o ka pahi kaua,* blade of a sword. (Lunk. 3:22.)

maka'ākiu. To lie in wait to kill; to spy out the land; to act as a spy on an enemy.

makalau. Medley of spears.

māmakakaua. A principal man in battle who bears the brunt of the fighting. (A.) Company of warriors. (PE.)

mamo. Endemic honeycreeper, now extinct. It was the source of the black and yellow feathers used in the choicest featherwork, including the all-yellow cloak of Kamehameha I made around 1800 from some half million of these feathers. (KILO.)

mea hōʻeha. Someone who causes damage.

mea kaua. Person or weapon relating to war.

mea make. Someone defeated and killed in action.

newa. War club, cudgel. Warriors would strike with the blunt club and stab or pierce with the sharp pointed *pāhoa*.

ʻō. Piercing spear.

ʻoala, ʻowala. War club; to swing, whirl, or brandish a war club.

ohokuʻi. Awkwardly made wig, once used in war. The wig in the Bishop Museum is not "awkwardly made" as Parker wrote, only less stylish than those of his time. (KILO.)

oma. Space between two armies where sacrifices were offered; preparations prior to war; first man killed in battle. (A.)

ʻoumuamua. Name of the foremost soldier in battle or the front rank of the battle.

pahelo, pakelo. To escape or slip out to freedom from the grasp of a captor.

pahiʻoi. Sharp sword or knife. (Ios. 5:3.)

pāhoa. Short wooden sword or dagger, used for thrusting and stabbing.

pahu. To throw or hurl, as a spear. *Fig.,* to overthrow, as an enemy.

pahukū. Reserve force of an army; rear guard and reinforcement.

paikau. To exercise in march, drill, and parade; to practice with firearms. Vancouver taught Kamehameha's men the manual of arms and other drills.

paʻi wale. Drawn battle, when neither side had the victory.

pālau. War club.

pana pua. To shoot with bow and arrow; archer.

papa a poʻo. Company of men dispatched as an early striking force to plunder and kill. Such an act was understood to be a commencement of hostilities and a declaration of war.

papa kaua. Division of warriors, so named upon going into battle.

pīkoi. Tripping club consisting of a long rope with a stone at the end. This was thrown at the foe, encircling his arms and thus rendering him helpless. (FOR 5:55.)

poʻi pō. Ambuscade; to attack at night.

polokāwaʻe. Long spear.

polulu. Long spear. This is listed elsewhere as an item of war dress, a shield. It was not so considered in early Hawai'i. (KILO.)

pua. Arrow used with a bow. *Pū'ā, pu'e,* to besiege. (2 Sam. 11:1.) War in the Biblical reference, sport in early Hawai'i.

pu'e. To thrust a spear; to attack; to besiege a village or town.

puwalu, pualu. Ancient flag of the Hawaiians, placed on the triangular canoe sail.

uhau. To whip, scourge. (Oih. 12:23.)

'unua. To thrust a spear into an enemy.

wa'a kaua. Army division about to enter battle; war canoe.

waikaua. Robe worn in battle; temple in a *heiau* devoted to sacrifice in war.

waikī. In ancient times, a ball of stone projected from a squirtgun. Hawaiians supposed at first that the noise of a gun, *kani pū,* had some effect on the projectile. (A.)

WINDS: Names and Characteristics

Words in this list describe the varying intensities of wind, directional breezes and winds, compass readings, land and sea breezes, as well as those connected with particular places. Things connected with the wind are also covered, such as *nū,* the sound of a storm; *palo'o,* thunder without rain; *ulu aunui,* a wind bad for anchoring, as in Hilo harbor; *La'amaomao,* goddess of Hawaiian winds. (See the tall calabash in Bishop Museum *"Ka ipu makani o La'amaomao."*)

Other interesting words are *wiliwili,* trash sucked up by whirlwinds and borne spiraling away; and *welowelo,* sails flapping in wind-rippled water.

'A'a. Sea breeze at Lahaina. See **Ma'a, Ma'a'a.**

'a'au. Calm sea, mildly rippled, as in a slight breeze.

'Ae. Northeast trade wind. See **Moa'e.**

A'e-loa. Regular trade wind. In Hawai'i "regular" means northeast trade winds.

ahe. Anything soft, gentle, or light, as a gentle breeze; wind.

'Āhiu. Wind well known in the mountains of Kahana, O'ahu.

akakū, akaku'u. To grow calm; to abate, as wind, rain, or surf. *Ua akakū mai ka makani,* the wind has abated.

'ākiukiu. Penetrating, searching wind. *A me ka makani 'ākiukiu* *kīpē pua hala o Puakei,* the searching wind pelting the pandanus blossoms of Puakei.

Ala-honua. Light, gentle breeze at Hilo. *Lit.,* fragrance land. (PE.)

ālani. Land breeze on Lana'i named after a mountain of the same name on that island.

alau. Place at Hāna, Maui, where the east wind is divided or parted. General word for any such situation.

ani. To blow gently, softly, as a wind. See **aniani, 'ōnini.**

aniani. An agreeable, cool, refreshing breeze. See **kōaniani.**

'Ao'aoa. Pleasant sea breeze at Honolulu.

'Āpa'a. Wind strong enough to knock a person down. *I kuipeia e ka makani 'Āpa'a,* he was knocked flat by the wind 'Āpa'a. (A.)

'Āpa'apa'a. Strong wind at Kohala, Hawai'i.

'Āpapa. Strong wind that blows over Kohala point.

aūlu. Rough, raging sea wind. (PE.)

'E'elekoa. Storm driven upon Waimea, Hawai'i, from the northeast.

ehuehu. Wind of great strength and fury.

'Eka. Sea breeze at Kona, Hawai'i.

'ēlau. Beginning of first feeling of a breeze.

ha'alelewa. Flying or driven with the wind. (CMH.)

hāla'i. Lulling of a strong wind; calm.

hālūlā. Calm, stillness, as a sea without wind. See **kāha'u.**

hau. Land breeze that blows at night; hence, any cool breeze.

Hau-o-Ma'ihi. Land breeze that blows down a valley in middle Kona across the *mauka* road at a point close above Keauhou, Kona.

hea. Cold rain created by a chilling wind. *Kona-hea,* a cold Kona storm.

hikina. Gentle breeze out of the east.

Hikina 'ākau. Northeast wind. (CMH.)

Hikina hema. Southwest wind. (CMH.)

hiō. Slanting wind, i.e., a wind down a hill. (A.)

hono. Place where a wind meets an obstacle and is reflected back. (A.)

Ho'olua. Strong north wind; name of the rain accompanying said wind, made famous in a song.

ho'oluluhi. Thickening weather; heavy and dark clouds gathering before a storm.

ho'opuehu. Scattered, as a fleet of canoes in a storm; to be blown away, as dust in a wind; to be routed, as an army in retreat; gone.

hu'ihu'i. Cold, chilly air of the morning, as from the mountain.

Īhu-anu. Wind upland of Kawela, Oʻahu.

Īnu-wai. Sea breeze at Lehua on Kauaʻi.

Ipu makani o ka maumau. Gourd of the constant winds. On a still day in Hilo, Maui wished to fly a huge new kite. He called loudly to the *kahuna,* Kaleiiola, keeper of the gourd, who dwelled in Waipiʻo Valley, Hawaiʻi:

> O winds, winds of Waipiʻo
> In the calabash of Kaleiiola
> Come from the gourd of winds
> O wind, the wind of Hilo
> Come quickly, come with power.

The winds blew with gale force, tossed the kite about, and broke the heavy *olonā* cord allowing it to fly to distant Kaʻū. Maui's footprints, made as he tried to restrain the kite, may be seen in the lava rock on the banks of the Wailuku River.

ka ahe Puʻu-lena o ka hia. Cold but gentle wind at Kīlauea Crater, Hawaiʻi.

kāʻao. To be calm in one place while the wind blows in another; to be smooth, as the sea in a calm, but not a dead calm.

kāhaʻu. To abate, as the wind or a stream of water. See **hālūlā.**

Kaiāulu. Northeast trade wind off Wai-ʻanae, Oʻahu, famous in a song.

Kani-lehua. Well-known misty rain of Hilo. It starts a rustle among the *lehua* blossoms.

kanoenoe. To blow strongly, applied to the northeast trade winds. See **noe, noenoe.**

Kaomi. Northeast trade wind blowing at the east side of Lanaʻi, Maui, and other areas.

ka ua pōʻai hale o Kahaluʻu. Rain that whisked about on all sides of a house at Kahaluʻu. Hiʻiaka sang the song while walking along Kaneohe Bay. The "whisking rain" was also described as "the house circling rain of Kahaluʻu." (PE.) This phenomenon of course was caused by the wind. See **Ua pōʻai hala.** (KILO.)

Kaua-ʻula. Strong wind from the mountains, occasioned by the breaking over of the northeast trade wind. Often destructive at Lahaina. (A.) *Ke kukui pio ʻole i ke Kaua ʻula,* the light which the Kaua-ʻula cannot blow out. Said of Lahainaluna School. (PE.)

kēhau. Mountain breeze in the morning, anywhere; gentle land breeze, as of West Hawaiʻi.

kēwai. Wind from a place of rain; mist connected with rain some distance off. *He makani kēwai,* a wind laden with moisture.

kīkīao. Sudden gust of wind; squall; strong wind.

Kiliʻoʻopu. Wind at Waiheʻe, Maui.

Kiu. Strong wind at Honuaʻula, Maui, occasioned by trades breaking over the mountain; northwest wind at Hāna, Kaupō, and elsewhere, very similar to those at Hoʻolua, Mālualua, and Malua-kiʻi-wai.

kōaniani. To blow softly or gently, creating coolness; to make a breeze, as with a fan; place cooled by a gentle breeze. Also called *kōaheahe.*

Kolo-ʻapuʻupuʻu. Wind, well known at Waimea, Hawaiʻi. *Lit.,* creeping rough.

kolokolonahe, kolonahe. Very gentle and pleasant breeze. *Lit.,* creeping gentle.

kololio. Very strong wind that would swamp canoes at sea; gust.

Komohana ʻākau. Northwest wind.

Kona. Southwest wind; south wind; name given to a wind blowing on the leeward side of any of the islands.

kualau. Wind of gale strength; wind and rain on the ocean.

kūlepe. To blow, as the wind in the middle of a channel.

Kumu maʻomaʻo. Easterly wind on Oʻahu.

kunu. To blow softly or gently, as the wind.

kūpapaūla. To blow directly on, as the wind; to have the wind ahead or in front.

Laʻamaomao. Name of a goddess of the winds, characterized as the Aeolus (a Greek god) of the Hawaiian Islands. Laʻamaomao possessed a deep, slender, wooden calabash containing the bones of her mother. This she gave to her son Pakaʻa. It was called Laʻamaomao and is in the Bishop Museum. The possessor could control the winds by lifting the lid and chanting the proper wind. Kalakaua was so intrigued with this *"ipu"* that he had gold bands put on it and a special stand made to hold it. (KILO.)

laʻelaʻe. Calm, pleasant weather.

laʻi. Calm, still place in the sea, meaning little or no wind.

Lauʻauʻa, Lauʻawa. Name of a local wind at Hāna, Maui. (A.)

lauwili, lauili. To turn or whiffle about, as the wind; whirlwind. Short form of *makani lauwili.*

lūlā. Smooth, as the surface of the sea unruffled by the wind; a diminishing or calming of a storm.

luli. To roll, as a ship with the wind; to shake, as a bush in the wind. (Mat. 11:7.)

lulu. To lie still, as a ship in a harbor; to be calm, as the sea. See **mālie, mālia.**

Maʻa, Maʻaʻa. Sea breeze at Lahaina. See **ʻAʻa.**

Maʻaʻa-kua-lapu. Wind at Kahaluʻu, Hawaiʻi.

Maʻaʻa paʻimalau. Name of a wind.

maʻahe. Light breeze. See **ahe.**

makani. General term for wind(s); wind, breeze, air in motion. *Makani ʻOla,* winds of life (name of the author's home, Wai-ʻalae Iki Ridge, Honolulu, Hawaiʻi).

Māla. East wind; gentle breeze. See **Aʻe-loa, hikina.**

mālaʻe. Clear, calm, as a windless sky.

Malana. Fine rain from the northeast at Waimea, Hawaiʻi, as it moves along before the trade wind. (CMH.)

Malanai, Mananai. Gentle blowing of the northeast trade wind.

mālie, mālia. Clear, calm, serene. *Mālie ke kai me ka makani,* the sea and wind are calm. (PE.)

Mālua-hele. Northwest wind on Kauaʻi. *Lit.,* sea breeze traveling.

Mālua-kele. Local wind blowing on Kauaʻi. *Lit.,* sea breeze damp.

Malualua. Northwest wind at Lahaina, Maui; a north wind on Oʻahu.

māpu. Moving, as a gentle wind; floating, as odoriferous matter in the breeze; name of a wind.

Maununu. Sea breeze at Puʻuloa on Oʻahu.

miha. To pass, as a slight breeze over still water.

Moaʻe. Usual name of a trade wind.

Moaʻe kū. Foreign wind or a wind from a foreign country; a strong wind; strong *Moaʻe* trade wind.

Moaʻe-Lehua. Wind that shakes the *lehua* tree; trade wind.

Moaʻe pehu. Swelling wind.

Moani. Wind at Puna, Hawaiʻi; a breeze, usually associated with fragrance.

Moani lehua. Name of a wind; the *lehua* breeze; wind-borne fragrance of *lehua* blossoms.

Moʻoaʻe. North wind at Honolulu. (A.)

moʻolio. To breeze on one side. See **kololio.**

mumuku. Wind blowing over land between two mountains, as if cut off from the main wind. (A.) Strong wind at Kawai-hae. (PE.)

Muʻululū. South wind at Honolulu. (A.)

nahe, nahenahe. To blow softly, as a gentle breeze.

nahenahe. Same as *nahe;* stronger than *aheahe* and *aniani.*

Nahua. Wind from overland at Lahaina; fine rain that comes with the northeast trade winds on the northern part of Maui.

nāulu. Heavy mists; shower of fine rain, apparently without clouds or with but a single cloud; sea breeze at Wai-mea, Kauaʻi.

Noe. Northeast trade winds, from overland at Lahaina; unusual name for trade winds.

noenoe. To blow, as the wind. Also called *nōnoenoe*.

nou. To blow hard, as a gale of wind; puff or blast of wind.

nū. Roar or sound of a strong wind.

'olu. To be cool, as with a salubrious breeze; a cool breeze, *kōaniani*.

'ōnini. First beginning of a sea breeze; puff of wind, applied to a gentle wind when it covers the sea with ripples. (Isa. 57:12.)

'o'olokū. Stormy, tempestuous; state of the sea when the current and wind are opposite; to act like a choppy sea.

'ōuli. Token of the approach of a storm with high wind, as a northwest wind generally preceding a Kona storm.

pa'a. To blow, as the wind; to strike suddenly, as a gust of wind.

pāhili. To blow on different sides, as a flickering wind. (A.) To lash, as in a storm. (PE.)

Pailua. Wind from Kamiloloa, Moloka'i. (A.)

Pakai'elelū. Name of a strong wind, the northeast trade wind, off Wai-'anae, O'ahu.

pāku'i. To beat against, as an opposing wind. (Mat. 6:48.)

pāku'iku'i. To beat against, to be contrary to, as a contrary wind.

pālo'o. Thunder without rain, especially if the weather is good. Also called *pāmalo, pāmalo'o*.

pālūlā. Quiet, as in the lull of the wind.

papāukiuki. Name of a very fierce, strong wind.

pe'ahi. Gentle fanning breeze; a soft wind, as though made with a fan. (A.)

pilia'a. Strong, heavy wind in gusts or woolies off Kawai'hae. See **mumuku.** (CMH.)

pohu. Calm, still, as the sea or wind after a storm; the wind lulled greatly.

polinahe. To blow softly, as a gentle breeze; gentle as a zephyr.

pōlua. Disturbance produced by conflicting currents of air; wind.

puahiohio. Whirlwind.

puaia. To blow gently, as the wind.

puakaiāulu. Light, gentle breeze; dying breeze of the trade wind. (A.)

puehu. Flurry of wind which scatters whatever cannot resist it, as small dust particles or bits of paper.

puhi. To blow, as the wind.

pūkīkī. Strong, boisterous wind; a heavy storm.

puku kālina. Sweeping, as a small whirling wind that scatters small things.

Pūlena. Southeast wind at Hilo, Wai-mea; softly blowing, as a gentle wind.

pulihi. Whirlwind.

pūnonohuʻula. Blowing the dust; raising the dust, as a strong wind.

pupuhi. To blow violently, as a strong wind. (Puk. 15:10.)

Puʻu-lena. Cold wind on the mountains or at the volcano, Kīlauea, Hawaiʻi. (A.) *Ke ano laʻi aloha a ka Puʻulena,* the peaceful, loving mystery of the Puʻulena wind. (PE.)

Ua-pōʻai-hala. Rain famous at Kaha-luʻu, Oʻahu. *Lit.,* rain surrounding pandanus. (PE.) See **ka ua pōʻai hala.**

ʻŪkiu, ʻŪkiukiu. North wind and rain from the sea at Haiku, Maui. Similar to the Hoʻolua. (A.) Diminutive ʻŪkiu wind; to blow gently, as the ʻŪkiu wind. (PE.)

ʻūkiʻuki. Strong blowing wind.

ʻUlu aunui. Wind of Hilo; a bad wind for anchoring in Hilo harbor; the north wind attended by rain. (A.)

Ulu-mano. Strong wind that blows from the south and other quarters in the night only, on the west side of Hawaiʻi. Kamehameha and his party were shipwrecked by this wind off Nawawa. A whole village was burned to light them ashore—Hawaiʻi's first lighthouse!

ʻUmihau. Strong east wind that blows all before it. (A.)

Unūnu. Wind breeze at Puʻuloa, Oʻahu. (HP.)

Waiakoloa. Northwest wind at Honolulu and Molokaʻi. (CMH.)

Wai pao. Well-known land breeze at Wai-mea, Kauaʻi. *Lit.,* water scooped.

Wai-puhia. Windblown water, as of a waterfall; name of the upside-down waterfalls in upper Nuuʻanu valley, Oʻahu. Here many slender, rain-filled falls are interrupted at a high level along a hard lava projection on the *pali* wall by ascending winds, causing the water to seem to be falling upwards.

welowelo. To flutter, flap, or float in the wind, as a kite tail or a flag; hair, streaming behind a runner.

wilikoʻī. Materials, trash, etc., blown up by a wind and whirled away.

WORDS: Meaning and Application

Finding an appropriate name for this category has been difficult. In her notes on this book Dorothy Kahananui said, "I wondered why Dr. Hyde listed these words as 'peculiar'. . . . Many of the words are still used and nobody I know considers them peculiar." Hyde's original title was "Peculiar Words."

These words are concerned with early times; the list then is of historical and sociological significance. There is emphasis on words referring to emotions and relationships. Many terms express the status of a chief in the thoughts of his followers.

'a'ama, 'ama. Person who speaks rapidly, concealing from one person and communicating to another; talkative; tattling. *He waha 'ama iā ha'i,* a mouth revealing secrets to others.

a e 'ae 'oia ia'u, and he shall say "yes" to me.

'ai'ililoko. To possess land less than an *ahupua'a* in size.

'aikola, 'akola. To triumph over the ills and misfortunes of another. *Lolo,* it serves you right, an expression of triumph over the ills of another.

'ā'ī oeoe. Long neck. An appellation applied to wives in missionary families on account of the shape of their bonnets (ca. 1820?), which made them appear to have long necks.

'aki lou. Thief who stole with hooked rods. *Lit.,* hook biter. To secretly eat the food of another.

alama'aweiki. Small, narrow, and indistinct path. Applies to the departure of the soul when one dies since it traverses the "untrodden" path *(ala 'ololī).*

alapapi'imo'okū. Mean man of no character who goes before the king.

'alihi. To be ready to work for the sake of gain but be otherwise absent.

ali'i papa. Name of a child whose mother is a chiefess but whose father has no rank.

'ālina. Defiled, as a chief by marrying a commoner of low birth.

'ālualua. Name given to the multiplication table from saying, *elua lua 'ahā.*

anahulu. Period of ten days used to measure activities. This was used in place of the English week, which of course the pre-Cook natives knew nothing about.

'apakau. To give thoughtlessly, as a man who gives away his food until all is gone.

'āpali. To go into the presence of a chief and, on account of shame, return without making a request.

'elemakule. Old man, mostly applied to men. See **luahine.**

hālau. Hen that has had chickens; long house with the end at the front, used mostly for canoe storage *(hālau waʻa)* and *hula* instruction *(hālau hula)*.

hāliʻaliʻa. Rising of a fond recollection of a friend in the mind; beloved; cherished.

halolani. Flight of a bird that sails round and round but with little motion of the wings.

hana wale. To work gratuitously; to do for the sake of doing; a benefaction.

hao. Hard like iron; to strain tightly; to come with force, as wind or rain.

haole. Formerly a foreign person. Now commonly applied to whites (Caucasians): French, Portuguese, American, German, Scandinavian, and others.

hele aku la ʻoia i ke ala maʻawe iki a ke aloha, he [or she] has gone on the path of the narrow and small footprint of the beloved one, in death.

hele wale. To go about naked; to go anywhere with unfixed purpose.

He ulu lāʻau, ua nei ae la iloko o ke kai, it is a forest, it has moved into the sea! The exclamation of the natives on first sighting the ships of Captain Cook.

hiwa. Black, a very acceptable color for a sacrifice to the gods, including, of all things, a *keiki hiwahiwa.* (1 Tes. 2:8.)

hoʻohānau. This word was mostly used in connection with medicine designed to effect premature parturition. In modern times it carries the sense to beget or cause to be born, although it is not used in this sense by the Hawaiians themselves. Midwife; obstetrician.

hoʻoholoholo. To hold court; judiciary; trial. *Lit.,* to crawl on hands and knees, a posture of humility in ancient times.

hoʻoiloilo. To predict disaster, misfortune, and especially evil.

hoʻokēʻai. To fast; to push away food.

hoʻokuʻekuʻemaka nui. To grin horribly with rage or anger; to frown severely; to scowl.

hōʻupuʻupu. To tell lies, as in giving a false alarm or accusing another in order to clear oneself of suspicion. (CMH.)

hulaʻana. To swim past a cliff that projects into the ocean obstructing passage along the beach.

ʻilihelo, ʻiliholo. Class of farmers that worked but little; those who worked at *mahiʻai* (tillage) only part of the day.

ʻili pilo. Farmers who worked till dark; smelly skin, said of industrious farmers.

ka'au. The number forty used in counting.

kā'ili ke aho. The breath being snatched away from the person who died. (Kin. 35:18.)

kainoa, kainō. I thought (impersonal verb). *Kainoa ua pau loa na kanaka Hawai'i i ka ike 'au,* I thought all the people of Hawai'i knew how to swim.

kake. Kind of artificial language, used both in speaking and writing. It is designed as a kind of secret communication only for the initiated. It might be called the secret language of the chiefs.

kamakonākahikūlani. Without love or affection for someone; lack of understanding among people and chiefs, parents and children; no communication.

kanale'o. To try to walk straight when partially drunk; to attempt self-possession when intoxicated. (A.) To mislead, deceive, act the hypocrite. (PE.)

kānāwai. Laws. Literally pertained to water rights, which were the commonality of all laws. In modern times the term applies to all laws.

kāpae. To pervert; to turn aside from moral rectitude; to turn a thing from its intended use or object; to pretend not to understand what is said. (1 Nal. 9:6.)

kapu. Prohibited; sacred; consecrated; forbidden; general name of the system of religion in Hawai'i based on restrictions, most of which served to hold the commoners in obedience to the chiefs and priests.

kapu a moe. *Kapu* requiring all to prostrate themselves when the chief of highest rank passed.

kapu a noho. *Kapu* requiring everyone to sit when a lesser chief or his calabash and other articles were carried by.

kapuni. Name of a chief who was born, grew up, became old, and died in the same place.

kapu nī'aupi'o. Chief whose father and mother were both high chief and chiefess respectively and were also brother and sister or half-brother and half-sister.

kapuō, kapuwō. *Kapu* in honor of the god Kū-kā'ili moku; *kapu* proclamation of the approach of a sacred person; the announcer of this *kapu. Kapuō e moe,* prostrate yourselves.

kapu wohi. *Kapu* of *wohi* ranked chiefs (one rank below *kapu nī'aupi'o),* which includes exemption from the prostration order.

kau holopapa. Shelf or rack on which *kapa* and other articles were placed. Person of chiefly blood who was entitled to place his belongings on a separate rack so that they might not be defiled by the possessions of others. (Malo 56.)

kauōlani, kauwōlani. To express admiration of a chief, as in a chant.

kauwālupe, kauālupe. To carry, as a man wounded in battle, intoxicated, or sick, with arms around the shoulders of two persons. *Lit.,* place like a kite.

kēpau. Word used by Hawaiians for printer's type. *O ke kēpau i paiia'i ke mana'o o ke kanaka,* the types by which the thoughts of men are printed.

kia'āina. Governor of an island; ruler. *Lit.,* the pillar or support of the land.

kinikini. Multitude; a number indefinitely large.

kīpapa. To turn sideways, as on a surfboard; to protect and support when another condemns; to pave; to lay a pavement of stones.

kipa wale. To enter and sit unbidden in another's house; to seize and take another's property; to intrude.

kīpu'upu'u. Thought that arises in the mind upon hearing that someone has slandered or spoken evil of oneself. *Kipu'upu'u,* a cold wet wind of Wai-mea, Hawai'i.

kōkēkōkē. To punish or strike someone for an offense, real or imaginary.

kokoko. Raging with anger, like a person with his blood up.

kū'aki. To be annoyed at the loss of a bet in gambling; impatient, irritated.

kuapa'a. Breadfruit, parched with one side exposed to the sun (referring to the fruit that remains on the tree after the season has ended); a human back, hard and calloused, from carrying heavy burdens and performing hard labor; slavish, oppressed, severe.

kuapo'i. Weatherboard fore and aft on a canoe; young birds fully fledged.

kuapuiwi, kula'īwi. Long residence in a place; homeland; native land.

kuhinia. To eat until full; to be satiated with food; hence, to be fat, plump, or round.

ku'ikāhi. To make peace among contending parties; convenant or treaty of peace. *Ku'i* means to unite and *kāhi,* one; hence, to have things and interests united in one.

kuku'i 'ōlelo. Company of people full of talk and noise at night when they should be asleep; to narrate, recount; to join words coherently. *Lit.,* joining speech.

kukuʻi wanaʻao. People around a chief who talk and sing and tell stories all night. *Lit.,* spreading tales dawn.

kukuni kēia lā. This day is favored; it has a fever, i.e., it is very warm.

kulāia. Festival day; feast day; commemoration of a great event.

kulaiwi, kuapuiwi. Long residence in a place.

kuleana. Portion, part, or a right to a thing; right of property that pertained to the individual. This was established in the Great Mahele of 1858. The chiefs were awarded large tracts of land called *ahupuaʻa* not including the commoners' small tracts called *kuleana.* Wherever these small isolated spots of land were located the commoners had an exit to the outside. In modern times this refers to a small land claim within a larger tract of land. See **Land.**

kuleiʻula. Expression of admiration for one's chief appearing in rainbow colored *kapas.*

kūlia. To strive, try. *Kūlia i ka nuʻu,* strive to reach the summit, Queen Kapiolani's motto. *Kūlia i ho ikaika,* exert your strength; *kūlia e loaʻa ka naʻauao,* seek to obtain wisdom. (PE.)

kuliana. Desire for a gift or present with the promise of keeping silent.

kumulau. Vegetable that produces much; tree trunk with sprouts; hen that lays eggs; sow that gives life to piglets; generally a prolific producer.

kūnihi. Ridge, as of uncut hair or along a mountain top; edge; edgeways turn; top line or crest of a helmet.

kunukunu. Anger with the *haku* for requiring too much labor; anger laid up and cherished in the mind; "nursing one's wrath to keep it warm." (Robert Burns.)

kūʻoulena. Listless, disinterested; a kind of coarse *kapa.* (AP.)

kupa. To be at home; longtime resident or native of a place. *Kupa ʻai au,* a native-born who eats [enjoys] the land.

lalowaia. Ancient history (even before *ʻUmi*) as distinct from modern times. (A.)

lanakila. To conquer; to hold dominion over; to win, triumph.

lau. The number four hundred.

laupaʻapaʻani. Word used by chiefs in flattering and caressing each other; term used to excite pleasure. (A.) Merry, jolly, playful, witty. *Lit.,* much playing. (PE.)

leho. Bunch or knotty swelling on the shoulder or back of a person like that of the *leho* (shellfish) caused by long carrying of heavy burdens. This swelling was seen on the shoulders of laboring men as late as 1840.

lolena. To be limber, flexible, as cloth; to be inefficient, impotent; to be weak or faded, as a person; a person not desired by women.

lomi. Rubbing, pressing, or squeezing of someone in pain or sick; to shampoo, comfort.

lomilomi. To rub, squeeze, and chafe the limbs of someone in pain or weary; to act upon, as the spirit of God acts upon the heart.

luahine, luwahine. Aged or old lady.

luina. Laborer on a ship; sailor; formerly a common word for foreigners. (Hoik. 18:17.)

luluāʻinaʻole. Young person who has been well cared for from childhood and has grown up handsome and agreeable. (A.) Without freckles. (DK.)

luma, lumaʻi. To drown someone by holding his head under water.

luna. Upper, higher; above. Everything above the height of a man's head is said to be *luna,* everything below is called *lalo;* overseer; executive officer; head man of a land; ambassador; leader of a yard crew.

luʻoni. Chief, or any person who delivers a victim to the sacrifice. The work of salvation as effected by Jesus Christ, called Haku Mālama by the Hawaiians.

māʻeʻele. Benumbed; deeply moved by love. Hawaiians express a strong internal glow of love by this term, equivalent to the feeling in a limb when the flow of blood has been slowed and it is said to be asleep.

mahiʻili. To take or seize property for the king. This was often done by unscrupulous officers who left nothing to the people but their skin. *Lit.,* dig skin.

maʻīhiʻili. To peel off the skin; to strip a person of all he has. (A.)

maka hinu. Unpleasant feeling of a chief when someone comes to him perhaps too frequently for a favor. (A.) Bright face, cheerful look. (PE.)

mākaia. Name of a *punahele* (favorite) of a chief, who is turned away and becomes a *punahele* of another chief. The two chiefs go to war and, through the efforts of the *mākaia,* the second chief conquers the first. Hence, betrayal, vengeance.

maka ole. Eye, eyetooth. *Fig.,* the *ʻoʻo,* (digging stick) with its sharp point.

makauliʻi. Careful, frugal person who saves the property of the chief. This person likely serves in fear. *Lit.,* fear chief.

maka lūauʻi. Parent; those whom children call *makua* or parent. Lūauʻi united with *makua* means natural parent as distinct from an adopted parent or uncle and aunt.

mano. The number four thousand or ten *lau,* four hundred.

manuahi, manuwahi. Something free, gratis, no charge; adulterous.

mauli au honua. Descendant of a line of chiefs from early times.

maumaua. To obtain property without work, the way the chiefs obtained their property in early times.

mea. Thing; an external object, condition, circumstance. In its general meaning it includes a person and a thing.

mino. Crown of the head; dimple, depression, dent. (PE.) *Mino* or *mimino* is an expression made use of with children as a caution: "cover up your nakedness."

muliwai. At the mouth of most island streams there is a bar behind which at low tide some water stands. This pool is called a *muliwai. Lit.,* remains water.

nalowale. This word identifies the area beyond the highest countable number. When one reaches this point it means any higher number is lost, or that it vanishes, or is concealed. A person can go no further in counting.

nauā, nauwā. Celebrating the birth or residence of a chief. Nauwā was adopted by King Kalakaua in the secret society that he formed for the study of the ancient Hawaiian religion and manner of living. *Hale nauwā* was the place were genealogy was scanned for eligible entrants.

nāu paha la. Phrase covering the return of a salutation.

nohea kaua. Person born under one chief but fighting for another. (CMH.)

nohiʻialo. Person born with a particular chief and ever continuing to live with him. (A.)

nohiʻikua. People who were born and lived on the back part of the island. (A.)

noho wale. To work idly; just sitting and doing nothing.

ʻōhua. Family part of a household, as children, servants, domestics, and sojourners, but not including the master and mistress. (Kin. 12:5.)

ʻō hulu. Person who sails or goes on the ocean; seal hunter. *Lit.,* spear fur.

ʻōiwi. Well-built man with bare upper body; native son.

ʻōkū. To give secretly so that another may not know.

ʻolu Ekeloa hoʻokaʻa moena. Protector of the sleeping place of the high chief as he slept; a protectress served a high chiefess likewise. Both fanned their respective subjects.

pāhola. That which is rendered useless, ineffectual, or of no account; to poison fish.

paka. Tobacco *(Nicotiana tabacum),* an annual herb from tropical

America, introduced in Hawai'i about 1810. (NEAL 664.) To criticize constructively, as in chanting; to make war, fight; to strike, as large drops of rain upon dry leaves; clearly, intelligently.

pākū'ei. To be ahead of time; to commence a job early; to finish without thoroughness.

paokoke. To betray relatives or those close, *koke*, to one.

pelu. Doubled; folded over; shut, as a knife; to bend or flex; as a joint. (A.) Hiding one's sins or wrong behavior from a chief. (CMH.)

penu. To sop up gravy; to wipe one's eyes with a *kapa* or handkerchief; to dip one's piece of fish into the gravy, to absorb as much as it can.

pilihua. To be sad, cast down; to stick fast, as words in a person's mouth when afraid; to be unable to speak through fear; astonished, perplexed.

pilimea'ai. Someone who followed a chief or other person for the sake of food or a living. Such persons were usually spoken of with contempt.

pīna'i. To adhere to a chief or rich person for the sake of food or support; repeating visits too frequently thus wearing out one's welcome.

polohana'ole. A woman who will not work but lives on her husband's earnings. (A.)

puhainānā. To look only, instead of answering someone's question.

pūhānihaniha. To rue one's part in a bargain; to pay an obligation with reluctance. (A.)

pūhe'emiki. To steal or filch and run away. When a present is made to one of two persons, the one who has not received anything seizes the gift and makes away with it.

puhi palalū. To flatter and amuse someone who has property in order to acquire such.

puni ku'uala. Anxious about the repayment of a debt; expecting gain for something loaned or given. (A.)

puni kuwala. Usurious; usurer; extortion. (PE.)

'ula'ulaīla. Child born illegitimately of a chief and a common woman.

unu pehi 'iole. Class of persons that adhered to others for sake of a home. (A.) Rat pelting pebble, insulting epithet for a person of no consequence. (PE.)

'ūpī. Noise made by walking when one's shoes are full of water; to wring water out of clothing; to squeeze, as a sponge.

'u'uluhaku. To stir up *poi,* as a lazy man; hence, his *poi* will be lumpy.

uwinihapa. Brick, named after Captain Winship who brought the first bricks to the islands. This word is the Hawaiian orthography for Winship.

'uwi'uwia. To rub or dash one person against another; to assemble closely.

wa'awa'a. To act without foresight, as giving away one's property in a moment of generosity; mischief from ignorance; stupid.

wāwae. Leg or foot of an animal or a person; foot. Hawaiians do not have a separate word for leg or foot. *Wāwae* includes both. Likewise, *lima* signifies either arm or hand.

weuweu. General name for grass, bushy or fuzzy; name of a fish caught only in the night; hence, the figurative expression, "success in night iniquity."

WORDS: Miscellaneous

This list is left largely as originally prepared by Charles M. Hyde. It was probably developed during the years he was teaching Hawaiian students in his North Pacific Missionary Institute. Collectively, those students would have represented a valuable source of primary information about their mother language. They were admitted to the Institute on a highly selective basis, the emphasis being on intelligence, character, willingness to work, and promise of leadership.

The twelve students in each four-year course produced an elite core of intellectuals. Instruction was both in English and Hawaiian. There were informal intra-class exchanges of the words and phrases in active colloquial use in the students' homes and communities. Moreover, the students represented a broad range of family groups from the major islands.

Many of their words and phrases are not attributable elsewhere. The notes for these entries were handwritten, some in Hyde's finest Spencerian hand, others in what must have been his most hurried moments!

'a'e. To cross over mentally and physically from one condition, place, or state to another; to yield assent; to grant permission; to consent, agree.

'aikena wale. A hard time of it! To cause someone to work for no apparent reason.

'ainakini, lainakini. Drab or navy-blue cloth. (PE.)

alahaka. Bridge; rough road, with many ravines or chasms; trestle, ladder. (Kin. 28:12.)

alakō. To drag along the ground. *Lit.,* path-drag.

'ale'o. A lookout on a housetop; firebell tower, a fairly modern usage.

'āmana. Gallows; two sticks crossing at oblique angles on a pole.

'āmokumoku. Intermittent. (CMH.)

'ano'ai 'oe. Greetings to you! *Aloha,* your Honor! *'Ano'ai* can be called an early form of *aloha* in usage.

apokaka. Apostate.

a pu'iwa e ka lā'au paku'iki'i o ka po'e lawai'a a hei i ka pā, 'a'ole i ka mole o he Kamaniali'i, you can be beaten with a stick like the fisherman's and frightened into the net, but not to the truth about the true genealogy of the chiefs. (CMH.)

a puka ma'o, Go through, over there.

awāwa uahi. Gray or smoky valley.

buke kānana. Blank book; writing tablet. *Kālana* is a name given by early Hawaiians to white writing paper.

dālā mā'i u'ilu i loa'a, Disgraceful! His wage is a pittance.

'ehuehu. Dust blown by the wind. (CMH.) Darkness arising from dust, fog, or vapor.

ele a Hagai. Money got by cheating. (CMH.)

elemino. Morally right. (CMH.)

e noke nei i ke kūpaka. To writhe or twist about; to be borne down or overwhelmed with sadness. (Isa. 21:3; CMH.)

e nononoke 'ana i ke 'ā ume'ume i ka 'i'o bipi, persisting in the struggle for a piece of beef.

hae. Here. (CMH.)

hai'ai. To clear up mysteries. (CMH.)

hakawai ka 'ōhua. Thirsty family members, except master and mistress. (CMH.)

hale pai pāpākāhi manuia. Captain of a white vessel. (CMH.)

hāli'ali'a. Beloved, cherished; remembered with affection; recollection.

hanai. Spokes of a wheel. (CMH.)

hana mau. Without rest. (CMH.)

helina. Recited. (CMH.)

he pōhina. Gray, as smoke.

hihi'o. Dream, vision. *E pa'a ka maka a ike ka 'uhane,* to shut the eyes and see with the soul, i.e., to have a vision. (Hoik. 1:10.)

ho'āna'ē. To set apart; to stow away for future use.

ho'auia. Opening of a new store. (CMH.)

holo kīau. To trot; to gallop swiftly.

ho'ohūa'e. To bring a wind. (CMH.) To cause to overflow; to have more than enough; to allow to escape. (CMH.)

ho'ohui. To cause a union among two or more things; club, partnership, association.

ho'okā'au. Witty, entertaining, clever, humorous. (PE.)

ho'okapalili. Trembling or palpitation of the heart; to vibrate, as a leaf or reed in the wind; to trill by vibration of the tongue.

ho'okelakela. To boast, brag; to show partiality; to show-off. (Hal. 10:30.)

ho'ola'ola. To gurgle, as water when drinking; to gargle.

ho'o mikanele 'ana. To act as a missionary.

ho'opahulu. Things seen in dreams; to cause a nightmare; to haunt; to bring bad luck. (PE.)

ho'opakika. To make slippery; to slip or slide in walking.

ho'opalaina. Blind. (CMH.) *Ho'omakapō,* to cause blindness or pretend to be blind. Turning away in embarrassment; concealing true feelings.

'ihi'ihi. Sublime, sacred, majestic.

ilihia. Breathless stillness of an audience; stricken with awe; thrilled.

kāhili kāpopo. Medical combination of juices of the gourd and the *pu'uka'a* grass. (PE.)

kake. Secret language of the chiefs, with garbled words and inverted syllables tending to confuse the uninitiated. Used not only by chiefs but by those who composed poems for chiefs.

kalālaloha. Setting sun. (CMH.)

ka nome i keia lono. Without rest, *hana mau.* (CMH.)

kapa uweke. Waterproof. (CMH.) Raincoat; sou'wester. (DK.)

ka pua o ka'awahi. Curling up. (CMH.)

kāwelu. Like wind-blown grass waving gracefully.

kena. Enough to drink; no longer thirsty.

kēnā. To give orders, to command.

kimio. Stolen property. (CMH.)

kohopono. Inference. (CMH.)

kohowale. To guess; selecting indiscriminately.

koko'olua. Companion, associate, assistant; always a pair or a union of two.

ko lākou ho'ononohua mai, they're being jealous of us; they are hating us. (DK.)

kou pu'uwai i ho'omaluea. To be made heavy; sad; sinking. (CMH.)

kuaīlo. To answer a riddle; to declare or explain something enigmatic or mysterious. (A.) Term used by someone who cannot guess the meaning of a riddle. *Kua'ilo!* I can't guess, tell me. (PE.)

kūha'u. To harangue.

kuhike'e. To blunder from one's course; to give a wrong direction. (PE.)

kuhi pu'uone, kuhikuhi pu'uone. Class of priests who gave advice concerning the location and building of the *luakini* in a *heiau*. Could be called architects.

kūlia. Young and handsome person desired and sought after; a beauty.

kulio'o. Stingy, penurious. (PE.)

kumapa'a. Family god similar to *'aumakua*.

kūmo'oali'i. Dynasty; race or line of kings.

kupulau. Spring season of the year. *Lit.,* sprouting leaf. (PE.)

lako. Rich, prosperous; well provided with every convenience.

lau wai. Full stream; an abundance of water.

leiomano. Weapon with a shark's tooth as its cutting edge; bodyguard armed with this weapon. (KILO.)

lele. Altar higher than that at Kuahu.

likini. Rope for the mast; rigging. *Eng.*

loloiāhili. Tangled in speech; to wander or stray.

luki'i. Seeds. (CMH.)

maka 'a'ā. Sparkling; wide, staring eyes. *Lit.,* glowing eye.

makahiki. Annual festival in memory of Lono's wife. (CMH.)

makani. Wind, weather, news.

makehewa. Bad bargain; to profit in vain.

makepono. Cheap. (CMH.) Reasonable, profitable; a bargain. (PE.)

mālili. To calm down, as a storm or a person in fierce anger. (A.)

māmio. Prosperous, ready, prepared. (A.)

ma na'e iho o ko mākou hale, on the windward side of our house. More accurately, on the east side of something—house, wall, any large obstruction.

mānanalo. Potable fresh water; rather tasteless or insipid; sweet, as fresh water in contrast to brackish or salt water. (Sol. 9:17.)

milika'a. Fancy work. (CMH.)

mio. Sleight-of-hand. (CMH.)

moehewa. Sleep walker; nightmare.

moe koa. Unexpressed. (CMH.)

mohoheihei a nā lio. Man selected to race horses. (CMH.)

nā'ālē'ahui. Wild waves. (CMH.)

na la i 'au ae la. Past days. *Auld Lang Syne.*

nā mea a pau loa. Things that you finished.

naneha'i. Problem in mathematics; riddle; question to be solved.

nīpu'u pa'a a ka berita (pelika). Bound fast, as in a covenant. (Kin. 9:9.)

o'ia manu i puka'amaka a'e nei, Something passed before my eyes, as a bird flying.

'oili. To lose from the pocket. (CMH.)

o ka la nokonoko. Day of sensation and nervous anticipation of a coughing spell. (PE.)

'ōlelo mīkololohua. Thinking, reflecting; skillful, wise, intelligent in affairs of difficulty; eloquent, entertaining in speech.

'olē'olē. Idiot. (CMH.) To grin like an idol.

'opi. Bend of a wave; wavy, like the grain of certain woods.

ōpū weuweu. Oasis. (CMH.)

pa'a lima. To handle; to hold in the hand. (PE.)

pā'ina maka luhi. Feast for those who prepared and served it.

pakalaki. Bad luck; unlucky. *Eng.* (CMH; PE.)

pākaneo. Poverty stricken. (CMH; PE.)

pākaukau. Table or long mat for setting out food. (CMH; PE.)

pālaha. To extend, spread out.

palakahuki. To corrupt, decay, rot; to be soft. (Sol. 10:7.)

palapu'ano malani. Partly healed sore or welt.

panapana. To shoot, as a marble or arrow; to strike lightly.

pāpahi i ka hae o ka lanakila. Banner of the victorious; to confer honors.

papa ho'onohonoho. To arrange in a series; classification board.

pili laulā. Of broad interest; of general application.

pua ehu. Numerous. (CMH.) To blow spray or dust. (PE.)

puhipuhi. To keep off evil spirits. (CMH.)

pūkonakona. Husky, muscular. (PE.)

puku'i i ka na'auao. To assemble items of knowledge; to organize one's knowledge. (DK.)

pulakaumaka na kona makua. Cynosure. (CMH.) Person one thinks of constantly with affection or hard malice. (PE.)

pūlo'ulo'u. Steam bath with head and body covered, using a *kapa* or mat.

pū'o'a. Dome. (CMH.) Pyramid; house built with poles uniting at the top in a pyramid; steeple.

pūpūkāhi. People united in purpose.

pu'u ai la. Short stop without finishing. (CMH.)

ua ho'onakalo mai la na pu kuni ahi. Thunder rattling and rolling.

uakea. Mist, white rain. *Lit.,* rain misty. (CMH; PE.)

ua limua. Long and constant rain. *Lit.,* rain moss-growing. (CMH; PE.)

ua pālina'ia. To spread mortar.

uila. Brilliant, as lightning. (CMH; PE.)

'ula'ula. Red, as a blaze seen in the night. *Lit.,* tongue of fire. (CMH.)

ulia. Sudden accident; to come upon suddenly. *He ulia pōmaika'i,* sudden good fortune. (PE.)

ulia pōino. Sudden accident, troubles, injury.

'ūlōlohi. Detention. (CMH.) To move or act slowly; to linger; to be tardy.

uluāhewa. Place where men can hide. (CMH.) Mania, delusion; deranged; sometimes believed to be possessed by a spirit. (PE.)

ūlūlohi. To snore. (CMH.)

ulupono. Progress. (CMH.) Thriving; successful; progressive. (PE.)

uwehu. To moan. (CMH.)

uwene ke kolopā, the crowbar lifts. (CMH; PE.)

Wa'ahila. Rain on Mount Ka'ala, O'ahu. (CMH.) Rains in Nu'u-anu and Manoa Valleys. Also the name of a beneficent rain in Manoa Valley.

wae 'alu'alu kopē. To separate the rind from the coffee bean. (CMH.)

waianuhea. Compliments. (CMH.) Cool, soft fragrance of the ginger plant. (PE.)

wailana. Outlaw, outcast; calm, quiet place in the sea.

WORSHIP: Ancient Times

The sheer size of this category is evidence of the importance of the system of worship in ancient times. The individual was dominated by the system of *kapu* and the chiefs and priests, and was utterly responsible to it.

Worship was a mixture of devotion to superior powers and of

descents into superstition. However, it offered a practical system of checks and balances on the behavior and thoughts of early Hawaiians, regardless of whether their motivations were based on fear or scruple.

'a'ae. Ancient form of commencing worship. (A.)

'aha. Prayer to heaven, connected with a rigid, non-interruptive *kapu,* drew its name from *'aha,* the very strong cord braided from the husk of the coconut. This sacred prayer was presumed an effective process to hold the kingdom together in time of danger.

'ailolo. Ceremony held at the end of training in the art of *lua* (hand-to-hand fighting) and *'anā'anā* (the practice of sorcery). Those taking part in the ceremony marked completion of the training by eating a portion of the head of an all-black pig.

akua ki'i. Idol; carved figure representing a god.

'alaea. Red ochre used by a class of priests of Lono to mark the boundaries of land. See **kuhi 'alaea.**

'ālana. Present made by a chief to a priest to procure his prayers; present made to a god; oblation or free-will offering. The purpose of all these presents was to gain forgiveness for a transgression.

ālia. Name of two *kauila* or *māmane* sticks carried annually by priests before the god of the *makahiki.*

'ama. To offer *'ōhi'a,* a fruit similar to the apple, and melons to the gods. Also called *'āmama, hā'ama, hō'ama.*

'āmama. Offering of a sacrifice; to finish a prayer; to pray and sacrifice. The word is like the Christian "amen," in effect ending a prayer.

'ānu'u. Tower in a *heiau* formed by long poles overhung near the top, which were tied and covered with white *'oloa kapa;* high place in the *heiau* before which the idols were placed, and where the victims of sacrifice were laid.

'aumakua. Class of ancient gods, departed spirits of deceased persons; person who provided for a chief or chiefs; trusty, steadfast servant; personal or family spirit.

ha'alelea. Man who was sacrificed at the cutting down of an *'ōhi'a* tree to make an idol.

ha'eha'e. Name of two yards adjoining a particular house of Lono. (A.)

hahauhui, uhauhui. Religious ceremony or prayer used in the practice of sorcery, *pule ho'opi'opi'o.*

hai. Sacrifice or offering at the altar; the god of the *poe kuku kapa;* particular form of gathering the dead in war.

hai ao. Sacrifice offered in the daytime as distinct from the *hai pō,* a night ceremony.

haili. Temple. (A.)

hainaki. Prayer presented as a removal of the *kapu* on property after the taxes have been paid to the tax gatherer.

hai pō. Sacrifice at night. (A.)

haku 'ōhi'a. *'Ōhi'a* tree from which an ancient idol was to be made. On the day they cut down the tree, some man would die to give virtue and force to the idol.

hālapa. To bring to pass, in prayer; to pray that a thing hoped for may be granted. (A.)

hānaipū. Title of the person who carried an image and ate the food offered to the god.

hanoalewa. Oven of the temple; place for sacrifice; temple.

he'a. To finish eating the last hog sacrificed on the eighth day of dedication of a *heiau.* Anyone unable to eat his portion would be immediately sacrificed.

hi'uwai. A ceremony of purification was observed on a night late in the year by frolicking and bathing in the cold water. It was followed by a prepared feast and games lasting most of the next day. (KEP. 97, 193–194.)

hiwa. Black, clear black. Applied mostly to that which was used to sacrifice to the gods, as a black hog.

hō'au. To bring out and present on the altar of the gods at the *heiau;* to offer a sacrifice.

ho'omanaki'i. Practice of worshiping idols; idolatry. (A.)

ho'omeha. To stay home from work. Formerly, this word was applied to a day of *kapu,* but is now used synonymously with *lā ho'omalolo,* the day before the Sabbath, i.e., Saturday.

ho'oululu akua. To pretend to be a god. (A.)

ho'oūnaūna. To send someone to perform a part in the *'anā'anā* or *ho'opi'opi'o* (sorcery).

ho'owilimo'o. Ceremony during the dedication of a *luakini* or war temple using the sacred prayers, *'aha, hulahula.*

hui. Prayer in the morning following the *'anā'anā.*

hui o Papa. Chorus of Papa, a prayer for the purification of women, uttered early in the morning at a temple reserved for them, the house of Papa.

hulahula. Name of a favorable prayer, similar to the *'aha* used at a *luakini* ceremony.

kāʻaha. Stick or rod with a bunch of leaves covered with *kapa,* held by the priest while offering a sacrifice in the temple.

kāʻai. Girdle put around the loins of the gods by the chief. It was made of vines.

kahuakua. Someone engaged about the altar; someone who has charge of the gods; priest.

kahuna hahu ʻōhiʻa. Priest, *kahuna,* in charge of the image made of ʻōhiʻa used in *luakini* ceremonies.

kahuna hale o Papa. Priest of the house of the goddess Papa.

kahuna hele honua. Priest equipped for a sudden start on a journey.

kahuna kahalaʻalaʻa. No data. (CMH.)

kahuna kapapau luʻa. Priest of human sacrifice. (CMH.)

kahuna kualea. No data. (CMH.)

kahuna lapaʻau. Physician; doctor of medicine. *Lit.,* a healing expert.

kahuna Lono. Priest of Lono.

kahuna moʻo Kū. Priests of the god Kū; priests in the lineage of Kū.

kahuna moʻo Lono. Priests of the god Lono; priests in the lineage of *Lono.*

kahuna nui. Priest and councilor to a high chief.

kahuna pule. Minister, pastor, priest; one who officiates publicly in the exercise of religion.

kai a pō kea. Name of a long prayer used after the *kauila* ceremony at the dedication of a *heiau.*

kai ʻōlena. Sea water or salt water colored yellow with the ʻōlena root, used for purifying purposes after a burial and to remove a *kapu.* This ceremony is called *pī kai ʻōlena.*

kai oloa. Tying the *malo* on a god or image, done by the women of the chief. This was a beautiful white *kapa.*

kakaʻi. To pray, as in ancient times at a great *kapu* event; a sacrament.

kakaloa, ʻaekakaloa. Name of a blue-gray *wauke kapa* used in ceremonies, as for divining with pebbles. (KILO.)

kākua. To worship the gods; to ascribe power; to offer sacrifice.

kākūʻai. The constant daily sacrifice offered at every meal; to feed the spirits of the dead. Offerings consisted mostly of bananas, fish, and ʻawa.

kālewa. Place in the *luakini* where the king and a few others stood apart from the multitude.

kāliʻi. Ceremony performed when the high chief lands from a voyage with his people and his god. This was a semi-ritual in which spears were hurled at the king to test his skill and courage in avoiding or returning them.

kalokalo. To utter a personal prayer to the gods.

kānaenae. Chanted prayer of appeal; propitiating sacrifice; offering to the gods.

kanalu. Priests of Kū who served at the *luakini*.

kapaʻau. Raised place in the *heiau* where gods, images, and offerings were set. It was believed invisible gods lived there. See **nuʻu.**

kapa paulua. A human sacrifice. (A.)

kauila, kauwila. To offer sacrifice at the end of a *kapu;* decorating ceremonially the images of the gods with feathers. Also called *kauila huluhulu.*

kauiliakua. Ceremony of redecorating with red feathers of rare birds, never performed except in time of peril or war. (CMH.)

kaukau. Heap of stones made into a rude altar; chant of lamentation.

kaumaha. To make a sacrifice or offering.

kauō, kauwō. To pray for a special blessing or favor. Applied to the worship at the time of the *makahiki.*

kauokahiki. Species of *ʻōhiʻa hā.* Gods were made for the *heiau* out of this timber.

kauwila, kauila. To set a day for consecrating the *heiau.*

kekaloakāmakamaka. Prayer used in ancient worship. (A.) *Kalokamākamaka,* name of a religious service set up for dedication of timber for a temple building. (PE.)

kia. Standing idol of worship.

kīhāpai. Ceremonies of religion. Formerly, the ceremonies of religion were divided into various departments: keeping the altar in order, offering the sacrifice, each of which was a *kīhāpai.*

kiʻi. Image of a god made of wood or stone. *Kiʻi ku,* standing idol.

kiʻimanana. Belly god. (A.)

kīpolo. Prayer used in black magic leading to the death of the desired person, such as an enemy.

koliʻi. Special prayer used in ancient times. (A.)

kōpilinui, kōpilo nui. Name of the day when altars and sacrifices were dressed out in white *kapa.*

kuaʻaha. Altar in a private house for worship of the gods.

kuawili. Prayer, a day long ceremony, at the highest order of the *heiau;* long, drawn out, repetitious. The word is used in Matthew 6:7 to exhort against vain repetition.

kuhi ʻalaea. Certain priests of Lono who marked land boundaries with *ʻalaea* coloring.

kuhikuhipuʻuone. Class of priests who were consulted in ancient times. They gave advice concerning the building of the *luakini,* including its location; architect.

ku'ikepa. Work of making the image of the god Lono mahua; sculpturing, carving, shaping.

kuili. Prayer that lasted all night at temple dedicatory ceremonies. According to Malo it was memorized and recited in unison. (MALO 171.)

kūkawowo. To pray with strength and earnestness; a sorcerer's prayer.

kūkoea'e, kūkoa'e. Name of a *heiau;* temple of purification ceremonies. (MALO 151–152.)

kuku. Standing image or idol.

kukuni. Type of black magic where a sorcerer dies because an object he took from his victim's corpse was burned.

kumakalehua. To hang, as a bunch of bananas, a hog, or a man (a transgressor) for sacrifice upon the tree which was to be used in building a *heiau.* The tree was generally the *lehua.*

kuoha. Prayer used to bring a wife to love her husband and the husband to love his wife.

kuwā. Prayer made when a new house was finished and grass over the door was trimmed. Such a prayer was used in the completion of a canoe.

lamumaomao. Word used in the ancient prayers bespeaking the building of a *heiau* and an offering of a sacrifice. (A.)

lana. Lowest floor of the oracle tower where offerings were placed. (MALO 176.)

lana nu'u mamao. Oracle tower, framed with strong, sacred wood, no walls, but containing three levels: *lana,* the lowest floor, was reserved for offerings; idols were placed on the *nu'u,* the second level, also the site of ceremonies conducted by the priest and his attendants; the *mamao,* at the top, was the most sacred of all the platforms, where only the king and high priest were permitted. (MALO 176.)

laukana. Applied to someone who seldom prays in secret; uninterested in religion.

lawa. White cock offered in worship. *Lawaa'ea'e* or *lawakea,* a white fowl mixed with red feathers.

lehua. *Ku ma ka lehua,* ceremonial hanging of offering, as of banana, pig or man; to impart *mana,* divine power, to an *'ōhi'a lehua* tree, especially one to be used in making an idol or image for the temple. (PE.)

lele. Altar for sacrifice.

lelea. *Kapu* imposed by the priest on the *'awa* while the chief was drinking it. (A.) Prayer uttered by the priest as the chief drinks *kava* so that the essence of the *'awa* will fly *(lele)* to the gods. (PE.)

lele wai. To purge, cleanse, purify.

li'ili. Place where sacrifices were laid before the altar. (A.)

limalima. Prayer in which the priest made many gestures with his hands. The ceremony was called *ho'opi'i na 'aha limalima,* the *limalima* assembly rises.

lolo. Name of the hog sacrificed on the finishing of a canoe, start of a journey, or completion of instruction.

lopu. *Ko'i* (hatchet) offered in sacrifice; consecrated adze, as used in carving.

luakini. Place in a *heiau* where sacrifices were offered. The highest such house of worship or temple in the *heiau*.

luanu'u. Dressed out with a large *kuina* (sheet) of *kapa,* as temple gods on important occasions.

lūkā. Group of women assembled for prayer.

lukamaea. Prayer used in ceremonies by women, said to date from the time of Papa.

lupalupa. Purifying ceremonies of various sorts, to insure growth or to cleanse contaminated persons. Prayer for the soul of someone just deceased. (PE.)

mahulu. Name common to three gods in the house of Lono.

makaīwa. Mother-of-pearl eyes, as in an image, especially of the god Lono. *Lit.,* mysterious eye. (PE.)

makanau. *Heiau* of this name—now the site of a sugar plantation —on the brow of a hill named *Kohā-i-ka-lani* (resound in the sky) above Hilea, Ka'ū, Hawai'i.

mākūkoa'e. Tropic bird phantom, a poetic name for death and the spirit of death. *Ua mākūkoa'e 'oia,* the tropic bird phantom is hovering over him [he is dying]. (PE.)

mali'u. Chief deified and become an *'aumakua*.

maluhia. To be under a *kapu;* to be subject to a solemn silence or stillness, as at some parts of the ancient worship.

malu ko'i. Services attending the cutting of the *'ōhi'a* tree for a *heiau* and the carving of images to be placed in the *luakini*.

malu 'ōhi'a. Sacrifice of a person at the cutting of a tree for a god; name of the *kapu* setting apart that tree.

mamao. Top platform of the oracle tower, most sacred level of this three-level structure. Only the king and high priest stood on that platform to conduct services. (MALO 176.)

mana. Name of the place of worship in a *heiau;* a house in the *luakini;* supernatural or divine power; to reverence or worship, as a superior power.

ma'o. Name of a great *heiau.* No data. (A.)

māpele. Tree used in building a *heiau* for the worship of Lono. (A.) Thatched *heiau* for the worship of Lono and the increase of food. (PE.)

mauha'alelea. Man sacrificed at the cutting of the *'ohi'a* tree, before the image was shaped.

maukoli. To make an offering stingily or on a small scale to the gods.

moa 'ula. Name of a *heiau* where human sacrifices were offered in time of war.

mōhai. Expiatory sacrifice; general word for offerings to the gods.

mōhai pāna'i. Offering of a hog to a god by a mother on weaning an infant.

mōlia. To bless, curse, according to some following word or phrase; to set apart for the gods.

mōliaola. Form of worship in which the priest offered a sacrifice and prayed for the life and safety of the people.

mo'o Kū. Priest of the lineage of Kū and devoted to his service.

mo'o Lono. Priest of the lineage of Lono and devoted to his service.

mū. Public executioner; person employed to procure human victims when a *heiau* was to be built. His duties included carrying out the execution.

naenae. Offering to the gods to appease their anger; sacrifice. See **kānaenae.**

nu'u. Middle level of the oracle town. It was the platform where the images were placed or where the gods stood.

'olē'olē. To have a wide grin, as an idol.

'oloa. Small white *kapa* put over the god or image during the intoning of the prayer. Also called *kōpili.* The *kapa* was also used to cover the oracle tower or *anu'u* in the *heiau.*

'ōlū'au, 'ao lū'au. Name of a ceremony in the worship of Kanaloa.

'ōlulo. Statue; idol.

'oma. Space between two armies where sacrifices were offered.

ōpū. Name of a heap of stone or other materials on which the image or figure of a god stood.

'ōuli. Omen; sign in the heavens. *Cap.,* name of the god of those people who prayed others to death.

pai. To finish a prayer in preparation for war. (A.)

pale'ōpua. To pardon the offenses of transgressors, as the priest did in olden times by offering sacrifices.

palikū. Order of priests of Lono said to have come from Palikū, a foreign country.

papahola. Artificial, level space on which the *heiau* was built, but containing a greater surface area than the building; hence, a court or yard in front of a temple. (2 Nal. 1:2.)

pāpāi'awa. Clapping hands while singing and praising the gods.

papaiō. To set up the *akua makahiki,* the year god, and carry him off.

peleu. To break a *kapa;* to violate some article of the chief that was sacred; to hide one's sins or offenses from a chief. (A.)

pi'opi'o. To pray, as with the *pule 'anā'anā,* sorcery or black magic.

pōkinahua. Name of an *'aha* or assembly for honoring the chief.

pō kinikini. Word used by the priests in prayer. It is also called *pō manomano,* a place where the wicked dwell forever, filled with many dark nights.

pōlioia. Eternal darkness; place of torment for the wicked.

pō manomano. Place where the wicked dwell forever; eternal night.

pou nanahua. Name of a temporary post back of the *mana* house within the *heiau* enclosure. Later a *haku 'ōhi'a* image was installed in its place. (PE.)

poupouana. Service for the erection of the *haku 'ōhi'a,* an image used for a temple dedication. (MALO 169.)

pua'a he'a. Last hog eaten on the eighth day of dedication of the temple. No food could be left over without dreadful consequences.

puaki'i. Image for idol worship.

pukuawa. Fear of anger of the gods. (A.) Final offering of *'awa.*

pūlo'ulo'u. Ball or bundle of white or black *kapa* tied to a staff, erected or placed in front of the dwellings of high chiefs, priests, and a *heiau.* This custom was introduced by Pa'ao, the high priest of Hawai'i who came from Upolu, Tahiti. It is preserved on the Hawai'i coat of arms as the insignia of the ancient *kapu.*

puolani. To lay something upon a consecrated place, as an altar; to bind or tie up, as a sacrifice.

pu'uone. Name of a *heiau* for fortune telling; divination.

pu'upu'uone. Beach hut serving for the teaching and practicing of divination and fortune telling.

uhauhui. Religious ceremony in the *pule 'anā'anā* or *ho'opi'opi'o.*

The prayer was offered to the god Pua. Another name for this ceremony is *'auhau hui.*

'uhinipili, unihipili. Name of the class of gods called *akua noho.* They were the departed spirits of deceased persons. See **'aumakua.**

'ūlili. Religious ceremony in the *pule 'anā'anā.* Also called *'auhau hui.*

ulua. Sacrifice obtained by the *kāpopo.* The fish *ulua* was used instead of humans if the latter were unavailable.

'umihau. Last hog sacrificed at the moment the fighters went into battle.

unu. Place of worship, a small *heiau;* rude altar for fishermen or the god Lono, patron of agriculture.

waihā. To request from the gods in prayer. Similar to *waipā.*

waihau. Small *heiau* patronized by farmers.

walewaikapo. *Wale* (spittle) and *wai* (water), i.e., the water is spittle. Used in a prayer or blessing.

WORSHIP: Christian

In 1820 the arrival of the missionaries (Congregationalists from New England, under the direction of the American Board of Commissioners for Foreign Missions) answered the pleas of Henry Opukaha'ia, enunciated just before his death, for Christianization of his people in Hawai'i.

This category is a kind of glossary of Christian activities. The immediate goals of the missionaries were the preparation of a series of school texts and the translation of the Old and New Testaments into Hawaiian.

Because Christianity was an introduced religion, the majority of the words in this category are introduced words or ideas, or adaptations of them into Hawaiian pronunciations.

The names of the books of the Bible are listed on pages xxvii–xxviii.

'Ahahui Hoikaika Kalikiano. Christian Endeavor Society.

'Ahahuina. Congregational.

'aha mokupuni. Island conference of representatives of Congregational churches.

'aha pae'āina. Statewide annual conference of delegates of Congregational churches.

bapetiso. Baptismal.

'ekālekia, ekalesia. Members of the organized church; body of professing Christians. (Oih. 8:1.)

Epekopala. Episcopal, Episcopalian.

ha'i ola. Preacher of salvation or eternal life; declaration of such.

hale pule. Church, chapel. *Lit.,* house of prayer.

hīmeni. Hymn, anthem, sacred *mele.*

hō'ike. Gathering of various Sunday School classes for recitation and hymns of biblical lessons at Hawaiian churches.

ho'ohānau hou. To baptize.

ho'okupu. Church offering. (Ezera 6:8.)

Hō'olepope. Protestant.

Ho'omana Buda. Buddhism.

Ho'omana Kalīkiano. Christianity.

Ho'omana Na'auao. Christian Science.

Ho'omana o Iesu Kristo o na Po'e Ho'āno o na Lā Hope nei. Church of Jesus Christ of Latter-day Saints.

ho'omana Pope. Catholic religion.

Iehova, Ke Akua. Jehovah.

Iesu Kristo. Jesus Christ.

kahu. Preacher, minister.

kahu hipa. Shepherd.

kahuna pule. Preacher, priest, reverend, minister. Formerly name of a native priest, now applied in Christian churches.

kakekimo. Catechism.

Kakōlika. Catholic. *K. Loma,* Roman Catholic.

Ka lā i ala hou ai ka Haku. Easter, Protestant.

kalana pule. Prayer service.

Kalawina. Congregational; Calvinistic.

Kalīkiano, Kilīkiano, Kristiano. Christian.

Kalīki, Kalīkimaka, Kalīkamaka. Christmas.

kalokalo. Formerly an informal prayer to the gods. Now used in a Christian sense, it is an appeal to God, a plea for assistance.

kāula. Prophet. (Oih. 3:24.) See **makāula.**

kaumaha. Service rendered to God.

Ke akua, Iehova. Jehovah.

kehena. Hell.

ki'o ahi. Hell.

kopilimaki'o, kopirimatio. Confirmation.

Kristo makio, hopirimatio. Confirmation, a Catholic term.

kumu mana'oi'o. Creed.

lani. Heaven.

lapa'au. To heal.

Lāpule. Sunday. *Lit.*, day of prayer.

leo hoʻonani. Hymn.

lua ahi. Hell.

Lukelano, Luterano, Lukela, Lutera. Lutheran. *Eng.*

lūlū. Offering to the church.

meka. Mass.

makāula. Prophet. See **kāula.**

maleʻana. Marriage.

mauli ola. Power of healing.

Mekekiko, Mekokiko. Methodist.

mikanele, mikionele. Missionary.

mikiona. Mission.

moe. Marriage.

Molemona, Monemona. Mormon.

mōliaola. Prayer for life and health. *ʻAha ʻāina mōliaola,* Feast of the Passover.

ʻohana. Family; gather for family prayers.

ola. To heal; health, life.

Pakoa. Easter, a Catholic term.

papakema, bapatema. Baptism.

papekiko. Baptize; baptismal.

Papekike. Baptist.

pelika o ki manaʻoʻiʻo. Covenant of faith.

Pelekepulikano, Pereseburitano. Presbyterian.

pō. Hell.

pōmaikaʻi. Blessing.

pono. Heal.

pule. Prayer, blessing, grace; to pray.

Pule a ka Haku. *Lord's Prayer.*

pule hoʻokuʻu. Closing prayer in a Christian service.

pule hoʻolaʻa. Prayer of dedication.

pule hoʻomaikaʻi. Prayer of thanksgiving, benediction, grace.

pule hoʻomaka. Beginning of a prayer; opening prayer.

pule hoʻopōmaikaʻi. A blessing; to ask a blessing.

pule mehameha. Silent prayer.

pule meka. Mass.

pule ʻohana. Family prayer.

ui kula Sabati. Sunday School.

Unikalio. Unitarian.

YAMS

There are many similarities between the yam and the sweet potato, and therefore, in terms referring to them. It is easy to distinguish the sweet potato from the yam, which in a wild or semicultivated state is now called a Polynesian introduction to the Hawaiian Islands. It has been confused or linked with the sweet potato by English-speaking peoples. The three main varieties of yam are represented by the *hoi, pi'a,* and *uhi.* Captain Cook and his mariners bartered trade goods for generous supplies of the *uhi* because the crews ate it readily, and the tubers kept well at sea.

hoi. Wild, bitter yam *(Dioscorea bulbifera),* called *pi'oi* on Kaua'i. It is a vine with a round stem, heart-shaped leaves, and small tubers *(la'ala)* that develop on the aerial stems and produce plants when they fall off. It is prolific and an uncultivated plant. The aerial tubers are poisonous but in time of famine can be eaten if thoroughly washed and cooked. (HP 167–168.)

pi'a. Variety of yam *(Dioscorea pentaphylla)* with a vine that is angular in cross section, palmate leaves, and small tubers. It is pure white like the arrowroot. Less common than the *uhi,* it was probably never cultivated. Its small aerial tubers were cooked before eating. (HP 142.)

uhi. Yam *(Dioscorea alata)* commonly used throughout the Pacific islands. It was also used as a staple food by Captain Cook and his crews. It is considered the true yam. The vine is slightly angular in cross section with longitudinal wings, and it grows large tubers. The mealy tuber was not suitable for making *poi.* (HP 166.)

uhi 'ālela. Variety of yam with a tuber of white flesh and skin. Grown in Puna, Hawai'i. (HP 168.)

uhi kalakoa. Yam having a tuber with mottled red and white flesh, white skin, and a green vine with "red wings." (HP 168.)

uhi ke'oke'o. Variety having a tuber with white flesh and skin and green vine and foliage throughout. Used only for food, not medicinally. (HP 168.)

uhi laha. Yam having tubers of white flesh. A variety found in Kona. (HP 168.)

uhi lehua. Yam with tubers of light, pinkish flesh and a vine with "red wings." Presumably the same as *'ula'ula.* Found in Kona. (HP 168.)

uhi Niʻihau. Kona tuber with pink flesh and purple foliage. (HP 168.)

uhi poni. Variety of yam with a tuber of white flesh and purple foliage. Grown in Puna, Hawaiʻi. (HP 168–9.) *Poni* is also listed as a sweet potato. (HP 142.)

uhi ʻulaʻula. Yam, well known in the Hawaiian islands, with white flesh, red skin, and green vines. Used both for food and medicine. (HP 168.)

Bibliography

Abbott, Isabella Aiona, and Eleanor Horswill Williamson. *Limu, an Ethnobotanical Study of Some Edible Hawaiian Seaweeds.* Honolulu, 1974.

Alexander, W. D. "Introductory Remarks." In *A Dictionary of the Hawaiian Language* by Lorrin Andrews, pp. ix–xvi. Honolulu, 1865.

————. *Short Synopsis of the Most Essential Points in Hawaiian Grammar.* Rutland, Vt.: Charles E. Tuttle Co., 1968. First published in 1864.

Andrews, Lorrin. *A Vocabulary of Words in the Hawaiian Language.* Lahainaluna, 1836.

————. *Grammar of the Hawaiian Language.* Honolulu Mission Press, 1854.

————. *A Dictionary of the Hawaiian Language.* Honolulu: Henry M. Whitney, Printer, 1865. Revised by Henry H. Parker as the *Andrews-Parker Dictionary of the Hawaiian Language,* 1922. Reprinted by Charles E. Tuttle Co., Tokyo, Japan and Rutland, Vermont, 1974.

Apple, Russell A. *The Hawaiian Thatched House.* Hawai'i National History Association. San Francisco, 1971.

Ashdown, Inez. *Ke Alaloa o Maui, The Long Road Around Maui.* Honolulu, 1971.

Beckwith, Martha Warren. *Kepelino's Traditions of Hawai'i.* Honolulu: Bernice Pauahi Bishop Museum Bulletin 95, 1922.

————. *The Kumulipo, a Hawaiian Creation Chant.* Chicago: University of Chicago Press, 1951.

Berger, Andrew J. *Hawaiian Birdlife,* Second edition. Honolulu: University of Hawaii Press, 1981.

Bryan, E. H., Jr. "Checklist of Birds Reported from the Hawaiian Islands." Honolulu: *The Elepaio,* April 1941 (no. 12) to June 1942 (no. 12).

Bryan, William Alanson. *Natural History of Hawai'i.* Honolulu: Hawaiian Gazette Co., 1915.

Buck, Peter H. (Te Rangi Hiroa). *Arts and Crafts of Hawai'i.* Honolulu: Bernice Pauahi Bishop Museum Special Publication 45, 1957.

Bushnell, O. A. "Hygiene and Sanitation Among the Ancient Hawaiians." *Hawaiian Historical Review, Selected Readings,* Richard Greer, ed., pp. 3–36. Honolulu, 1969.

Chamisso, Adelbert V. "On the Hawaiian Language." Translated from the German by Paul G. Chapin, 1973. Unpublished. Original manuscript Leipzig, 1837. Copies, Samuel H. Elbert and Masonic Public Library, Honolulu.

Cumming, Constance Gordon. *Fire Fountains.* Edinburgh: W. Blackwood Sons, 1883.

Degener, Otto. *Plants of Hawai'i National Parks.* Ann Arbor, Michigan: Braun-Brumfield, 1973.

Edmondson, Charles Howard. *Reef and Shore Fauna of Hawai'i.* Honolulu: Bernice Pauahi Bishop Museum Special Publication 22, 1946.

Elbert, Samuel Hoyt. *The Hawaiian Dictionaries, Past and Future.* Hawaiian Historical Society, Sixty-second Annual Report, pp. 15–18. Honolulu, 1954.

———. *Spoken Hawaiian.* Honolulu: University of Hawaii Press, 1965.

———. "The First Hawaiian Grammarians." Social Science Association. Honolulu: Paper presented April 23, 1978.

———, and Samuel A. Keala. *Conversational Hawaiian.* Honolulu: University of Hawaii Press, 1965.

———, and Mary Kawena Pukui. *Hawaiian Grammar.* Honolulu: University of Hawaii Press, 1979.

Emerson, Nathaniel B. *Pele and Hi'iaka, a Myth of Hawai'i.* Honolulu: Honolulu Star-Bulletin, 1915.

———. *Unwritten Literature of Hawaii: The Sacred Songs of the Hula.* Collected and translated with notes and an account of the hula. Rutland, Vt.: Charles E. Tuttle Co., 1965. First published in 1909 as Bureau of American Ethnology Bulletin 38, Washington, D.C.

Feher, Joseph, Edward Joesting, and O. A. Bushnell. *Hawai'i: A Pictorial History.* Honolulu: Bishop Museum Press, 1969.

Fornander, Abraham. Fornander Collection of *Hawaiian Antiquities and Folklore,* vols. 4, 5. Honolulu: Bernice Pauahi Bishop Museum, 1917–1918.

Gosline, William A., and Vernon E. Brock. *Handbook of Hawaiian Fishes.* Honolulu: University of Hawaii Press, 1960.

Handy, E. S. Craighill. *Polynesian Religion.* Honolulu: Bernice Pauahi Bishop Museum Bulletin 34, 1927.

———. *The Hawaiian Planter, His Plants, Methods and Areas of Cultivation.* Honolulu: Bernice Pauahi Bishop Museum Bulletin 161, 1940.

———, Mary Kawena Pukui, and Katherine Livermore. *Outline of Hawaiian Physical Therapeutics.* Honolulu: Bernice Pauahi Bishop Museum Bulletin 126, 1934.

———, and Elizabeth Green Handy. *Native Planters in Old Hawaii: Their Life, Lore, and Environment.* Honolulu: Bishop Museum Press, 1972.

Hassinger, John A. "Catalog of the Hawaiian Exhibits at the Exposition Universele, Paris, 1887." *Hawaiian Almanac and Annual* (1865): 68.

He Buke no ke Ola Kino no na Kamalii, e Pili Ana i na Poino i Loaa i ke Kino o no Kanaka ma na Wai Ona a me na Laau Hoohiamoe [A book about the health of children, pertaining to harm done to man's body by intoxicating liquors and drugs]. New York, 1887.

He Kumu Paikau no na Koa Hele Wawae o ke Aupuni Hawaii [A manual of arms for the infantry soldiers of the Hawaiian Kingdom]. Honolulu, 1854.

Henshaw, H. W. *Birds of the Hawaiian Islands.* Honolulu, 1902.

Hillebrand, W. F. *Flora of the Hawaiian Islands.* Heidelberg, 1888.

Hitchcock, H. R. *An English-Hawaiian Dictionary; with Various Useful Tables: Prepared for the Use of Hawaiian-English Schools.* San Francisco, 1887.

Hyde, Dr. Charles M. "Some Hawaiian Proverbs." Thomas G. Thrum's *Hawaiian Almanac and Annual* (1883): 52–53.

———. "Some Hawaiian Sayings." *Hawaiian Almanac and Annual* (1883): 53–58.

———. "A Chronological Table of Noted Voyages, Travels, and Discoveries." *Hawaiian Almanac and Annual* (1884): 53–58.

———. "Some Hawaiian Conundrums." *Hawaiian Almanac and Annual* (1884): 68–69.

———. "Hawaiian Names for Relationships." *Hawaiian Almanac and Annual* (1884): 42–44.

———. "Hawaiian Poetical Names for Places." *Hawaiian Almanac and Annual* (1887): 79–82.

———. "Hawaiian Words for Sounds." *Hawaiian Almanac and Annual* (1888): 57–79.

———. "Pilio ʻōlelo Hawaii, Hawaiian Grammar." Honolulu: *Hawaiian Gazette,* 1896. In Hawaiian.

———. "Random Thoughts on the Hawaiian Language." *The Hawaiian Monthly* (1, no. 10): 209–211, 236–238.

Johnson, Rubellite Kawena, and John Kaipo Mahelona. *Na Inoa Hōkū, A Catalogue of Hawaiian and Pacific Island Star Names.* Honolulu: Topgallant Publishing Co., 1975.

Judd, Henry P. *Hawaiian Proverbs and Riddles.* Honolulu: Bernice Pauahi Bishop Museum Bulletin 77, 1930.

Ka Baibala Hemolele o ke Kauoha Kahiko a me ke Kauoha Hou [The Holy Bible, Old and New Testaments]. New York: American Bible Society, 1941.

Kamakau, Samuel M. *Ruling Chiefs of Hawaiʻi.* Honolulu: The Kamehameha Schools Press, 1961.

Kay, E. Alison. *Hawaiian Marine Shells, Reef and Shore Fauna of Hawai'i.* Honolulu: Bernice Pauahi Bishop Museum Press, Special Publication 64 (no. 4), 1979.

Kent, Harold W. *Dr. Hyde and Mr. Stevenson.* Rutland, Vt. and Tokyo, Japan: Charles E. Tuttle Co., 1973.

Krauss, Beatrice H. *Native Plants Used as Medicines in Hawai'i.* Honolulu, 1979.

Krohn, Val Frieling. *Hawai'i Dye Plants and Dye Recipes.* 1978.

Kuck, Loraine E., and Richard C. Tongg. *The Tropical Garden.* New York: The Macmillan Co., 1936.

Kuykendall, Ralph S. *The Hawaiian Kingdom. Vol. 1 1778–1854: Foundation and Transformation.* Honolulu: University of Hawaii Press, 1947.

Larsen, Nils P. *Medical Art in Ancient Hawai'i.* Hawaiian Historical Society Report. Honolulu, 1944.

MacCaughey, Vaughn. "The Algae of the Archipelago." *Hawaiian Almanac and Annual* (1918): 129–155.

Magruder, William H., and Jeffrey W. Hunt. *Seaweeds of Hawai'i.* Honolulu: Oriental Publishing Co., 1979.

Malo, David. *Hawaiian Antiquities, Mo'olelo Hawai'i.* Translated by Nathaniel B. Emerson, 1898. Bernice Pauahi Bishop Museum Special Publication No. 2, Second edition. Honolulu, 1951.

Mitchell, Donald Kilolani. *Hawaiian Games Today.* Honolulu: Kamehameha Schools Press, 1975.

Moir, William Whitmore Goodale. *The Native Hawaiian Canes.* Honolulu: Intern'l Society of Sugar Cane Technologists, Fourth Congress, Bulletin No. 7, March 1–16, 1932.

Munro, George C. *Birds of Hawai'i.* Honolulu: Tongg Publishing Co., 1944. Rutland, Vt.: Bridgeway Press, 1960.

Neal, Marie C. *In Gardens of Hawai'i.* Honolulu: Bernice Pauahi Bishop Museum Special Publication 40, 1948. Revised edition, 1965.

Pope, Willis T. *Manual of Wayside Plants of Hawai'i.* Honolulu: Advertiser Publishing Co., 1929.

Pukui, Mary Kawena, and Samuel Hoyt Elbert. *Hawaiian-English Dictionary.* Honolulu: University of Hawaii Press, 1957. Third edition, 1965.

———, Samuel Hoyt Elbert, and Esther T. Mookini. *Place Names of Hawaii.* Honolulu: University of Hawaii Press, 1966. Second edition, 1974.

———, E. W. Haertig, M. D. Catherine A. Lee, and John F. McDermott, Jr. *Nānā I Ke Kumu* (Look to the Source). Honolulu: Hui Hanai, Queen Liliuokalani Children's Center, 1972.

Randall, John E. *Underwater Guide to Hawaiian Reef Fishes.* Pennsylvania: Harrowood B. Newtown Square, 1981.

Roberts, Helen H. *Ancient Hawaiian Music.* Honolulu: Bernice Pauahi Bishop Museum Bulletin 29, 1926; N.Y. Dover Edition, 1967.

Rock, J. F. *The Indigenous Trees of the Hawaiian Islands.* Honolulu: 1913; reprinted Rutland, Vt.: Charles E. Tuttle Co., 1974.

Thomson, James B. *Ka Huinahele Hou: Oia Hoi ka Arimatika Kulanui; Malaila i Aoia ai ke Aio a me ka Hoopiliia ana o na Helu* [The new combined arithmetic; or an arithmetic for the high school, in which the kind and properties of the numbers are taught]. Translated by C. J. Lyons. Honolulu, 1870.

Titcomb, Margaret. *Native Use of Hawaiian Fish.* Wellington, NZ.: Polynesian Society (no. 29), 1952, Second edition. Honolulu: University of Hawaii Press, 1972.

Westervelt, W. D. *Hawaiian Legends of Volcanoes.* Collected and Translated from the Hawaiian. Rutland, Vt.: Charles E. Tuttle Co., 1963. First published in 1916.

————. *Hawaiian Legends of Ghosts and Ghost-gods.* Collected and Translated from the Hawaiian. Rutland, Vt.: Charles E. Tuttle Co., 1964. First published in 1915 as *Legends of Gods and Ghosts.*